A SUITCASE FULL OF DREAMS
EXPANDED & RE-PACKED
(Globe-trotting Through Life)

Da

The world is a book, and those who do not
travel read only the first page

St Augustine

Delta Tango Publications
York, North Yorkshire

For the Williams in my life: father & son; & Helen; a daughter lost.

First published in 1998
This edition 2015
by **Delta Tango Publications**
York, England, YO19 5RB

British Library Cataloguing in Publication Data.
A catalogue record of this book is available from the British Library, Wetherby, Yorkshire.

ISBN 978-0-9534082-3-8

A SUITCASE FULL OF DREAMS
Expanded & Re-packed
by

David Taylor

Pen and ink drawings by
the late **Arthur Whitlock GAvA**

Concorde Cover painting by
Norman Appleton GAvA
Reproduced with the kind permission of the Artist

Photograph on page 20 reproduced with the kind permission
of Anglia Television.

FOREWORD

David Taylor served with me when I was flying helicopters in Malaya during the early days of RAF rotary wing support operations. Exciting times, especially so in that the flying took place on the front line of a long-forgotten campaign - the Malayan Emergency, 1948-60. By today's standards, the tactics, the flying techniques, and the machines themselves were all rather primitive, so life was always interesting, frequently difficult, and occasionally alarming.

Nevertheless, the campaign was very successful, and in his book, Dave has allowed the reader a nostalgic insight to those times, with tales that are usually confined to the annual reunion or the bar at the local branch of the RAFA or ACA.

Air Commodore Tom Bennett CBE RAF (Retd.)

AUTHOR'S NOTE

Since the first edition was self-published - sixteen years ago - this tome has sold well, which must point to me getting something right. Despite my having no agent or publisher, along with their associated publicity and help in getting it into the bookshops, the book did end up paying for itself. Something of a rarity in self-publishing I am led to believe, even if achieving this did take a lot of hard graft, shoe leather, and occasional pushy sales technique on my part.

That original Suitcase has now been completely re-written, expanded and re-packed. Many more recollections from my early years have been summoned up and added, along with tales from the intervening years and on through to the present day.

For older readers, nostalgia abounds, of - to my mind - better days. Back when the world was a much safer, simpler, less devious, more pleasant and relaxed place in which to reside. For those who missed that, catch up on life as it used to be lived.

A SUITCASE FULL OF DREAMS

INDEX OF CHAPTERS

TRAVEL LOG

From Cosford, in the Midlands, to Dishforth, north of York
And the countryside of Wiltshire, of such places we will talk
All was peace and comfort, though something was amiss
Those foreign lands I'd need to see, 'fore settling down to this

My appetite was whetted at Her Majesty's expense
Three years in Malaya; for my service, fitting recompense
Next a clapped-out troopship; to England I'd go back
From Alor Star and Ipoh, to Bradenstoke-cum-clack

But life was just beginning, there being so much more to see
And with a job that paid my way, the world was mine, for free
So now began adventures in countries brought to me
By boats and planes, cars and trains; by air, by land, by sea
Ships, not tall, in fact quite small; miles of walking most of all

Fertile lands and desert sands, sunshine all the while
Caribbean islands, ruins on the Nile
Not just beaches, swaying palms, and placid waters, blue
Bugs and nasty beasties; those, and fever too
Lush green fields and wetlands. Mountains capped with snow
Painted deserts; strangely named. Valleys, and plateaux

From Yucatan to Cuzco, along the Gringo Trail
On down south to Chile, and back again, by rail
Walk the Via Dolorosa, relive the past thereby
Climb up to Massada, to learn the when, and why
Memories too - though precious few - of a country called Iran
The dust and heat, the sweat and sleet; Mullahs, mosques, and
Isfahan

Sunsets and silhouettes, the memories flash by
Of Springbok and Impala, and tables in the sky
In Aotearoa; Land of the Long White Cloud
Men and women, dressed for sport, roll balls along the ground
What are they doing - what deeds pursuing
All the way from Auckland, south to Milford Sound

I have been and I have seen the wonders of this world
As a veritable cocktail of sights and sounds unfurled
Here, a Siamese temple; the chateau of Loire
By the Harbour Bridge in Sydney, I knew I'd travelled far

So stranger, follow me, but discreetly tread my path
My! that sounds good, true as well; so let that be my epitaph

*   *

INTRODUCTION

1991

It wasn't that I was afraid of death, just didn't fancy being around when it happened; an apocalyptic thought that sprang to mind when an ominous shadow engulfed me as I stood there, out on the after-deck. It was not an immediate thought, of course, but it did instigate the actions which follow such a thought, for the shadow halted, sinister, threatening. I looked up, seeking the owner, for even a shadow has to belong to someone, or something. This particular shadow was cast by the boom of a dockside crane that reached up, high above. But it wasn't that which suddenly caused me to think about the dangers we sometimes face in life, it was the jib attached to the end of that boom which prompted such a thought. Well, to be truthful, that which hung from the jib itself. For directly over my head was a thirty-ton anchor - Admiralty Stockless type, if it's of any academic interest. Should that decide to fall, thought I - immediately engaging every instinct in the rush to relocate myself - it's not going to do a lot for me, cosmetically. Nor physically, come to that. Not that I was any great shakes in the tall, dark, and handsome department to begin with. No way. It wouldn't improve things, is what I'm saying, for despite strict adherence to present day safety standards - overalls, hard-hat, safety boots - I'd likely end up flatter than a jaywalking hedgehog. Nor was it merely the thought of my being squished into the deck-plates that hastened my rapid departure to a position of relative safety, but also - for at times I consider myself to be a thoughtful person - the mass of paperwork someone would be required to complete should the worst happen. That in itself didn't bear thinking about - *"He was there one second, then I heard this loud noise. I turned round, and there he was, gone! We found him beneath the anchor."* - but perhaps other things did bear thinking about.

When your very existence is threatened is the time you tend to think of all the things you were going to do, but hadn't, rather than those things you never intended doing, but had. Over the years I'd scratched a few notes about such thoughts. My intention, to someday work on them, so as to leave some kind of a record. Perhaps with a view to eventual publication, perhaps not. So maybe now was the time to call them up, put them to some use. I could write about the everyday dangers with which we are often faced, for there are apparently many more than we realise! In fact, when thought about, if one reads and believes the newspapers, or watches TV, we don't really stand much of a chance at all. Most of what we eat, so we are told, is bad for us. If not this month, it will likely be so next month. And if not bad, certainly not good. The same goes for smoking, drinking, sex, the "chemically polluted" water we drink instead of the wine we're advised not to. Even watching TV itself. Anything, it seems, that gives pleasure. Not only that, the essentials and the unavoidable too. The rain, so they say, is probably acid; thought to be lead-laden is the air we breathe; we shouldn't expose ourselves to the sun's rays for fear of contracting cancer, and like that. But these subjects are forever being discussed and rehashed. So why not go the whole hog, make it an autobiography, of sorts. Not of someone rich and famous, or even a sports "star", or television "personality", but an autobiography of an everyday life. Almost impossible for anyone to be more anonymous than myself in today's "celebrity" conscious world. No letters before or after my name, no awards either, apart from a General Service Medal, for which you basically just needed to turn up at the right place at the right time. Alternatively of course, that could also be the wrong place at the wrong time!

So, an autobiography. Even then certain names would probably need to be changed, thus dissuading people from issuing writs, or possibly seeking me out with the intention of doing even worse things to me than anything I ever inflicted upon an insect in my youth. Situations and occurrences would, at times, need to be watered down slightly, so as to render them more believable. In fact, it would probably have been more prudent, or - depending on viewpoint - spineless, of me to moderate my views on certain events, people, and places. But, being a forthright, honest Yorkshireman, there was little chance of that ever happening. Call a spade a spade, I say. Or should that be a shovel?

SCARBOROUGH REMEMBERED

We all seem to harbour, to some extent, a latent, nostalgic desire to one day return to our beginnings. The old home town and the family abode kind of thing. The older we get, the stronger the urge. This is not the way it should be of course. One should instead look ahead, hopefully towards how things may be in years to come. In fact, that's essential to future planning. But as this generates so many question marks and frustrations (even more as life progresses, it seems) I prefer the nostalgia of looking back over what has already gone. Let's face facts, fast approaching 80 there is, after all, much more behind me now that there is ahead! Although I do have a few exciting things still planned for the future, looking back tends to greatly reduce the number of conditional conjunctions with which looking ahead presents us. There are, after all, enough of those already.

*

Latitude and season were justifications for the sun to be found hanging low in a hazy sky. It would remain so. Attempting to be bold, it failed miserably, weakened by the time of year and its position in the heavens, for winter was almost upon us. There was a chill in the air, too, frost on the ground, which in itself could account for the lack of people. I seemed to be almost alone as I sought memories of my past.

At the moment, all I had was a name in my head: Whin Bank. A name for which I sought substance. Possibly the family home at the time of my birth, or the home of a relative. Possibly a street, or area.

From my present location, Scarborough, Yorkshire's premier seaside resort, lay before me, so I closed my eyes and created summer. Now the memories began to form. The start of it all. Sea, sand, gulls, entertainment, and a Knickerbocker Glory at the Harbour Bar, so good you know it's doing you bad. There were also fish and chip shops - real fish and chips, - kiss-me-quick hats, mussels, shrimps, winkles, and rock; followed by a short sea voyage on the SS Coronia. There again, with that slight chop on the sea, perhaps not!

Originally Skardborg, the town had been founded by a Viking chieftain named Thorgils Skardi. Way back in the fourteenth century he established a base here from which he hoped to attack Scotland. Whether or not he was successful in his venture remains in doubt. Regardless, Skardborg was now on the map; so the reference library told me. Naturally, with all this taking place well before I was thought of - in fact, even before my grandparents' grandparents' grandparents' time - I certainly have no personal recollection of it.

*

I reopened my eyes to the present. This I did remember. Of course I did: that curve of sandy beach which formed the South Bay. It began just past the rocks below the Spa ballroom, stretched away from where I stood, along to the fish docks and harbour; lighthouse standing sentinel on the headland which separated the South side from the North. All were well remembered, all still there. It was the times that were gone, almost beyond recall.

The sea was to the east. Landward, the road replicated that curve of sand, as did the buildings bordering the road: theatres, amusement arcades, restaurants, interspersed among the shops - almost all closed and shuttered at present. And there in the centre, looking very much miscast, stood what had once been St Thomas' hospital - originally the Royal Northern Sea Bathing Infirmary. And if that doesn't allow the imagination to run riot I can't think what will!

Behind me - and even were it still there I wouldn't have seen it - was where Galaland had once been sited. Built as an aquarium in the late eighteen hundreds, it reopened as a subterranean promenade and amusement centre in nineteen twenty-five, was thus well established by the time I came along. I recall rainy days spent down there beneath the roads, pavements & gardens, wandering among the stalls and cafes, along with all the other people seeking shelter from the weather. Indeed, Galaland became known as *The Umbrella* for that very reason. Down there, scattered amongst the Indian architectural pillars, had been Palmists and fortune-tellers, waxworks, peepshows - what the butler saw, kind of thing. (By today's standards, not a lot, believe me!) There were slot machines - one penny, old type, 240 of those to the pound sterling, before decimalization - and a slide down which you rode on coconut matting. And of course, down there, sheltered from the weather, one kept dry. (Today the site hosts an underground car park.)

Overlooking the bay, on the hill of the headland, stood the remains of a castle. Completed by the Normans in eleven fifty-eight, it was shelled by the Germans during the first World

13

War. Who knows, maybe they had something against the Normans. But they did also manage to hit the town, accounting for quite a few casualties.

All this then, plus Jaconelli. A good Yorkshire name, eh? Fact is, the Jaconelli family seem to have been part of Scarborough society since time immemorial. Probably hitched a lift over with the Skardi's. They ran an ice cream empire, and many of them served on the council, providing at least one Lord Mayor, if memory serves me.

Then I had a sudden memory surge: myself, with my brother and sister, and our mother, at the seaside. Couldn't say when it had been, just one of those mental pictures which are now and again filed away. But it was clear, and it was at this very beach, although it was then summer, therefore crowded. The West Yorkshire miners and mill workers flowed over in their droves during the summer, months. A day trip to the seaside, by coach. There were deck chairs galore, rolled up trousers, knotted handkerchief hats, and donkey rides. Seagulls wheeled about above the harbour, screeching noisily. One presumed they wanted fish, but they seemed equally prepared to accept chips - or to dive and snatch them from young hands if you weren't careful.

A far distant life. An entirely different season. But these were exactly the kind of mental images I sought.

In my mind I followed Marine Drive and Royal Albert Drive, ending up on the North Side. Peasholm Park. The miniature railway on which we used to ride out to Scalby Mills. And there was the swimming pool, along with the Open Air Theatre in Northstead Valley Gardens, where I recall watching a performance of Hiawatha. What I couldn't see, up the hill and around town, I knew to be there. The Mere, Odeon cinema, across from the end-of-line railway station. To the south was Oliver's Mount - highest point in the town, around which ran an International motor cycle racing circuit - and to the west, behind me, was the cricket ground. Here was where the great and the good of National, and sometimes, International, cricketers often turned out for the Annual cricket Festival, held in September. There was a lift to carry you up and down the cliff face, or a path winding through the picturesque Valley Gardens if you were reasonably young and fit.

But these were images formed during later visits, not those early days. Then it was the fish and chips, the ice-cream, and Scarborough Rock. These were the things we mostly remembered. You could watch them make the Rock in the front of the shop that sold it, down there on the seafront.

Leaving that seafront I now set off up the hill, southwest, navigation in the hands of my subconscious. Huntriss Row I had never forgotten, likewise Aberdeen Walk, as together with Westborough and Newborough they formed part of the town centre.

As I continued on my way, other vague recollections briefly stirred the memory, but nothing too familiar. St Mary's cemetery passed by on my right. Anne Bronte was buried there, I remembered. She'd often visited the town, and had died here.

Eventually, I found myself out by the hospital, an area in which the tourists and day trippers would hopefully have little interest. I didn't actually recall making a decision to head this way, it was as if my legs, in collusion with my brain and motor functions, had decided this was where I should be. So I wandered around, feet still seemingly taking me where they would. Stepney Drive, Stepney Rise, Stepney Road. The names meant something. Those streets certainly triggered another faint spark of remembrance, though not the houses thereabouts. These were archetypal upper-class homes: perfectly trimmed lawns, neat and colourful gardens. The kind of house I'd love to have been brought up in, but knew I hadn't been.

Then I came upon Whin Bank. A road, then! Yes. This was more like it; solid, semi-detached suburbia. Now the memories really began to surge forth.

'Can I help you?' a voice asked. 'Are you looking for someone?'

I turned, surprised to find my eyes moist. She was middle-aged. Obviously a friendly type, as had been the small-town way.

'Looking for lots of people, love' I replied, somewhat sadly. 'But they aren't here any longer.'

*   *

Chapter One
MY DADDY SHOOTS GERMANS

1982

'**A**viation?' It was the way she said it that momentarily stopped me in my tracks, though not for long, as by this time we were well into the drink and the getting-to-know-you stage of conversation. The matter of just *what* to drink had earlier created problems of its own.

'Fancy some wine?' I asked of the girl with whom I was dining. Elizabeth was her name, a true Yorkshire lass.

'Yes, please, David. That would be nice.'

'What do you fancy then?' I thought it a natural question to ask, and courtesy demanded I did so.

'Well...?' She shrugged and smiled. 'You're not one of those er.... connoisseurs are you?'

'Not a connoisseur, no.' More of a common sewer, I thought, though it was a thought I kept to myself.

'Does it matter then?'

'Of *course* it matters!'

'Sweet or dry, you mean?' she asked.

'Or red, white, French, German, New World, still, sparkling? Plenty of choice. What's your mood?'

'I hadn't really thought about...... What would be right for now?'

Allowing myself to be foolishly swayed by current popular choice I ordered a bottle of Mateus Rose, which we drank whilst we talked. Not a girl of the world then, I surmised. It was a thought that seemed to gain strength during a later stage of our discourse.

'Aviation?' She repeated, furrowing her brow and wrinkling her nose, giving the impression that the word was incomprehensible to her. I, not wishing to lose her apparent attraction to me, decided on a lighthearted explanation.

She'd been probing as to my interests. In life, that is. As far as my immediate interest in her went I felt sure she'd be able to hazard a wild guess.

Throughout life I had held similar conversations with lots of interesting girls, but this was one that had stuck in the memory, for this girl had been different. Very different, actually, though not quite exclusive, for she was eventually to become wife number two - therefore soon became conversant with the niceties of wine.

16

Along with the usual hobbies and pastimes - travel, photography, motor racing - I'd listed aviation. Probably because it *was* one of my interests. A major one at that. And it was this she had queried.

'Yeah, you know,' I'd replied. 'Fuselage, wings, some form of propulsion.' I'd flapped my arms and craned my neck, imitating a swan on take-off. She'd laughed. A pleasant, tinkling kind of sound, which told me I was doing all right.

'And what first kindled your interest in that?' she'd asked, which is where we got bogged down somewhat, for that was something I wasn't too sure about. Never had been. All I can say is that I don't recall ever giving serious consideration to the idea of settling down comfortably in suburbia, with a family, and a conventional job. Not once. Nor do I remember staring into the sky when I was young, watching the birds swoop and glide around, wishing I could do the same. Though I do recall occasionally wondering what kind of a view those birds had of the land below.

*

THE THIRTIES & FORTIES: Poverty, unrest, war. It was a period of rationing and hard times. It was also a period of national unity. The formative years of my life.

There were not, as far as can be ascertained, any connections throughout the generations. Pubs and publicans, yes. Aviators? Not a one as far as I was aware. The publicans were there by the barrel-load, it could be said, and they all appeared to reside in and around Scarborough, the place in which I'd popped into this world sometime during the twenty-four-hour period that was to become known as April 2nd, 1936. A vintage year for Kings, I was later to discover.

There was an advantage to being Scarborough born, so I was told. Grandad Sale, who had connections within the cricketing fraternity, made sure I was well aware of the fact almost as soon as it was possible for me to comprehend: 'Thar's lucky, tha knows, lad. Being Yorkshire born an' all.'

'Why's that, Grandad?'

'Makes thee eligible to play cricket for t'County is why, David. Should thee prove to possess t' talent and inclination, o'course. Long odds, like, even if tha does. But at least tha's eligible.' (Yes, back then Yorkshire was the only county that still insisted on it's players being Yorkshire born and bred; did all right by it too, over the years. But all that went out of the window with the introduction of "overseas" players.)

Alas, as was to become apparent early on, balls and I were somewhat incompatible. At least in a sporting sense that is. A school report relating to physical training states: "Tries hard but has no actual ball sense." Ah well, by the time I was old enough to understand what had been implied, Yorkshire didn't need help from the likes of me. They were way down the Championship table already, which didn't please the locals overmuch. As obvious as a neon sign at the North Pole, that. For another thing to be learnt early on was that Yorkshire folk are a proud lot. I was advised to remember that our county was the largest of them all. At least, I believe that was the implication.

"Rest o' t'country's just tacked onti Yorksher, lad," was how it was put to me by an uncle.

*

So, aunts, uncles, grandads and grandmas there were, publicans all, which would account for my father, in 1939, taking out a licence to run his own pub, in Norton, halfway down the road to York.

Along with Norton came Malton, the two towns effectively divided by a murky-looking waterway of unknown and terrifying depth, at least to a young lad: the river Derwent. Though when it came to declaring assets, Malton claimed not only the railway station, but also the racing stables, for which the area was justly famous. This, despite the fact that the majority, if not all, along with that railway station, were sited on the Norton bank of the river, which made that boundary seem rather discretionary. Particularly so, being as we weren't even served by the same council! Malton was in the North Riding of Yorkshire, Norton in the East.

Or could these injustices be related to age, Malton dating back to well before the Roman era - when it was thought to have been called Derventio. Doubt had crept in because the Romans recorded Eboracum (York) as being only seven miles distant, rather than the eighteen we know today. Malton, the first of the two settlements, was certainly well established by the eighteen forties, when Charles Dickens would occasionally visit. In fact, it is said the area provided inspiration for two of his novels: Martin Chuzzlewit, and A Christmas Carol. Or possibly Malton's fame was related to the fact of its boasting two breweries, and around thirty pubs, for a population of just over four thousand. Doubt over the actual pub count has to be blamed on the function of the pubs themselves; I always seemed to lose track after about the first half dozen.

The Griffin Hotel, Norton, was the place Dad took on, although Mum was actually the named licensee (seems they knew something I didn't), which is how I came to spend a goodly part of my early life in a pub. Not a propping-up-the-bar kind of life, not at four years of age, even fourteen, come to that. No, the drinking came later. So much later, I apparently felt I'd been left with quite a bit of catching up to do. At least, I imagine that's how it must have appeared to others.

So, publicans aplenty, but none that appeared to have been in any way connected with aviation. Strange, this, for one of my family heirlooms is a silver-topped, Royal Flying Corps cane. Such a link would have been well before my time, of course, for the RFC became the RAF way back in April 1918.

When I knew them, Grandad and Grandma Taylor ran the Nelson Inn, on Scarborough's Victoria Road. Here they remained until retirement, in the late 1940's, which at the time made that particular Grandad the oldest licence-holder in town. Grandad Taylor had also owned a motor coach business up to 1935, and had held the first contract, issued by the local education authority, to carry schoolchildren. My father had been one of his drivers.

There was also an Aunt Peggy and an Uncle Jim Clancy, who between them managed the Rosette, out Newby way. Then there was the aforementioned Grandad Sale. Yet in all the time spent in their company, no mention was ever made of the RFC, or RAF. But despite this, it was likely that one or other of them must have served in the armed forces at some point, for their lives encompassed the era of the "Great War." In fact, I believe it was Grandad Sale who told me he could never understand what people meant by the term Great War. 'Great for whom?' he'd questioned. He'd said he assumed it to have been so named by people who were never actually at the front! So maybe he had been? I do know my father met my mother at the Cayley Arms, Brompton, at a time when Grandad Sale was landlord of that establishment. This was prior to his moving to the Cliff Hotel, on Scarborough's Huntriss Row - just down from Laughtons - actor Charles' family home. So maybe Grandad Sale was the connection to aviation then, tenuous though it might be? For the Cayley Arms was named after Sir George Cayley (1773-1857): inventor of the first *real* aeroplane, which flew close by here.

Wilbur and Orville Wright?

Wrong!

Kitty Hawk, North Carolina? December 1903?

Nay, lad, forget all that.

The above claim, although true, rarely fails to raise the odd eyebrow, principally because the bulk of Sir George's notes were not rediscovered until 1927, by which time Wilbur and Orville had grabbed all the glory. But even they had been aware of George Cayley, for in 1909 Wilbur did in fact acknowledge his pioneering work. To quote: "About a hundred years ago an Englishman carried the science of flying to a point which it had never reached before and which it scarcely reached again during the last century."

Perhaps this gives Sir George a little more credit than he was due, for it was actually 1849 when he built and flew the first glider capable of carrying a person - a small boy making two flights down the slope of Brompton Dale.

Replica of a Cayley glider airborne at Brompton Dale. It was flown twice by test pilot, Derek Piggott. First, as here, during a re-enactment of the famous "Coachman" flight for an Anglia TV production, then, ten years later, for the IMAX film "On the Wing". It now resides in the Yorkshire Air Museum at Elvington.

Four years later came what Sir George described as "a

governable parachute", in effect, another glider. And this time it was to be the turn of a full-grown man, albeit not himself. Sir George, an astute and far-thinking eighty year old, decided to forgo the possible fame, volunteering his coachman for the task instead. But by day's end there was a vacancy for the role of coachman in the Cayley household, the incumbent having handed in his notice upon landing, if such an inglorious return to earth could be so described. A few bumps and bruises, we hear, but can you imagine the scene?

"Ey up, Sire. Sitha. Yon shilling a month gets thee a coachman, an' that's all. Nay mention was made about't role o'test pilot. Me terms of reference don't include t'likes o' yon."

"Now come on, John, old chap, you're only a passenger after all. Besides which, surely a few bumps and bruises are to be expected in the advancement of science?"

"Be that as it may, me lord, get someone else. I'm off."

And that - so we are told - was it, off he went. No sense of adventure it seems.

So, there you have it, Scarborough - or at least Brompton Hall, seven miles distant - Yorkshire, the eighteen hundreds, the very heart of aviation's early days. And if not the actual inventor of the aeroplane, Sir George can certainly lay claim to being "The Father of Aviation", and of the science of aerodynamics. His ideas were far in advance of those of the Wright Brothers, for what he envisaged was an aeroplane with true tri-axis control. Wing warping? Forget it, that was for the future! Indeed, it seems the only impediment to your actual powered flight back in the 1850's was lack of a suitable power plant, internal combustion not yet an option. Had it been so, Wilbur and Orville - yet to be born - would likely have missed out. Big time. Not many people know that, as Michael Caine might say. And, if it's of any academic interest, Sir George was also the inventor of both the linked-plank-belt - from which were eventually derived tank and caterpillar tracks - and the tension wheel: the spoked wheel used on the modern day cycle. Don't suppose many people know that, either.

I later discovered a photograph of Grandad Sale, at a dinner, seated alongside Sir Kenelm Cayley, the 10th Baronet - Sir George being the 6th. So, was there a tenuous link here? Maybe that cane originally belonged to a Cayley? Now there's a thought.

Apart from being an hotel landlord, Grandad Sale also held the catering contract for the Scarborough Cricket ground for a period, hence, I suspect, the reason for yet another family heirloom: two silver cigarette cases. Although they are today slightly battered, I suspect they may be fairly valuable, being as they are engraved with the autographs of around four dozen cricketers and other sportsmen. Many of them cricketing legends. How about Bradman and Hutton for starters. Then there are such as Wilf Rhodes, WR Hammond, H Sutcliffe, Jack Hobbs, Verity, and Bill Bowes.

*

Despite that RFC cane, it's more likely the aviation seed was subconsciously planted during those wartime years of my early life.

No evacuation for us. Indeed, ours was an area upon which the evacuees were to descend in their droves, a lot of them experiencing countryside for the first time. But this was a time when the Yorkshire countryside also became saturated with the airfields of Bomber Command. Norton *was* the countryside; we were therefore literally surrounded. Like mushrooms, these airfields seemed to spring up overnight, twenty-five in all. Amongst their number could be found the emergency landing ground at Carnaby, and Driffield - the very airfield from which, years later, I'd make my first flight. There were also the Halifax repair facility at Clifton, York, and the training base of Marston Moor - site of a decisive battle from another era: July 1644, the biggest battle ever fought on English soil when, during the Civil War, close on fifty thousand combatants faced each other across this piece of then barren ground.

*

Although most of these airfields are now defunct - abandoned to some unrelated activity, to become industrial parks, or returned to the plough - during the Second World War they were hives of activity. Whitley and Wellington, Halifax and Lancaster, would depart from those airfields' extensive runways, filling the night sky with a synchronised, cyclic throbbing as they formed up prior to departing *en-masse*; heading for the continent.

In my freezing cold bedroom I'd climb into bed, pull the covers up to my chin and lie there, snug and warm, thinking and listening. I didn't really consider the idea of there being brave young men up in those aircraft. But of course, there were, and, dressed in sheepskin-lined leather they were going to war on my behalf, just like Dad, who was away doing his bit on the Indian subcontinent. By now a warrant officer, he was serving in the Royal Electrical and Mechanical Engineers, sorting out the war, or my future. But that's not quite how I saw it then, according to an entry in what could possibly have been my very first schoolbook, dated 1941. There, amongst childish script of the not joined-up kind were to be found the declarations: "Mother likes my kitty"; "Rover can catch the ball"; "My daddy rides in a car", along with:

My Daddy shoots Germans

Ah well, don't suppose there was a notable difference between Germans and Japanese - at five years of age they were all classed as "baddies". And never mind that Dad was unlikely to find himself in a situation that actually required him to shoot at anyone, he was a soldier, wasn't he? Anyway, that book also made reference to a Ruth and John - whoever they might have been - and in it I also declared myself to have two more brothers, "one called George, the other, Maureen"! (Morreen, actually. Not too good on the spelling back then. Not too clever on the matter of genealogy, either, as there were only three of us children.) But the cover of that book does carry the subtitle, *A Free Expression Book*. It also has some recognisable aircraft drawn inside the front cover, so at five years of age there must have been at least an inkling of something deep down in the subconscious.

I don't recall the details of Dad's departure. There had been no tearful goodbyes, no signs of a uniform, that I remember. He suddenly seemed not to be around any more. And it was to be four years before he returned, invalided out, suffering from climate-induced bronchitis and emphysema even before it was all over. Pensioned off by the War Office, he was to suffer breathing difficulties for the rest of his long life. Then again, he *had* returned. A lot didn't, so at least I had that to be thankful for.

Some of those airmen overhead would likely not return on the morrow, either. Some would never return, for this was a period when "Goodnight" could very well turn out to be "Goodbye". Not stupid, the Germans, you see. Soon figured out that if bombs were being dropped, there had to be someone up there dropping them, so they retaliated. Didn't bear too much thought that, which is probably why I mainly listened; the night sky filled with the sound of wave after wave of aircraft. A reassuring sound to lull a young lad to sleep, those engines. Almost an aeronautical symphony: Merlin's Twelfth, by Rolls Royce.

Come dawn, they'd be back. Not all. Rarely in formation. And now the sound would be of an inferior quality: ragged. Engines would be running rough, out-of-sync, some not running at all, their propellers feathered. From what I'd heard, I knew some of those airframes would be in bad shape, too; punctured by flack and cannon shells, and occasionally our own bombs, if you were at the lower levels of the formation! But if they got that far they just about had it made. Just about. Though in war, of course, there were no actual guarantees of anything.

In the beginning, I'd abandon my bed to peek out of the window, which called for considerable fortitude on my part - a lack of heating had offered Jack Frost the opportunity of carving his intricate designs all over the glass. On the inside! That was the residue of my frozen breath there, which I now unfroze with a few early morning exhalations. It didn't take too long to clear a patch large enough to peer through, but by then there were no aircraft to be seen. Ah well, a minor discomfort for me, a few more lessons learned.

Other odd images of the period occasionally come to mind, rare though they were up our way: the muted stutter of machine-guns, the thump-thump of cannon-fire from somewhere distant, far above. Scratchy white contrails would be etched across the sky, and dark specks could sometimes be seen, writhing and twisting in some deadly game, often in silence, sun glinting off a canopy. A smoky trail or flicker of flame would signal the death of an aircraft, severed wing or tail fluttering down, slowly, seemingly gracefully. Perhaps a parachute, perhaps not.

On the ground, life went on as normally as was possible. Up there was another world, almost passing unnoticed by those not involved, especially us kids. For us, war was a word almost without meaning.

There were crashes during training as well. More aircraft than the Luftwaffe would account for in fact, for men barely out of school were being taught to fly. Not boys, you'll note, men. Deprivation and war causes people to grow up fast.

Sometimes, if the wreckage was close by, friends and I would visit the site. We'd search for pieces of plexiglass, fashion rings out of them, and model aircraft.

All around was open countryside. Elysian fields could become Agincourt or the OK Corral. Woods and copses, hills and valleys, became Sherwood Forest or Darkest Africa. We could be anywhere our imagination chose to place us, though it was hardly pirate territory. Pirates would have to await the end of the war and a trip back to Scarborough. For there, on a lake known as The Mere, was a replica of the *Hispaniola*. On this we would sail out to an island nearby (the lake was very small - at least from a grown-up point of view). Here we could really search for buried treasure, digging for the imitation doubloons with which the sand had been liberally seeded. Meanwhile, to get in the mood, I read the popular stories of the time: Peter Pan, Treasure Island, Lady Chat ... oops! (It was actually Hank Janson.) There was also Captain W E Johns with his Biggles adventures, which I found enthralling.

Despite frequent air-raid warnings - from the rise and fall wailing of the siren's "Alert", to the steady, calming tone of its "All Clear" - I don't recall ever hearing the sounds of bombing, just hearing *about* it. That on the RAF station at Driffield resulted in the first WAAF casualty of the war, along with a dozen or so airmen. Then came the attack on York: April 29th, 1942, one of the Baedeker raids. So called, I later learned, for targets selected by the Germans from the Baedeker Handbook for Travellers. Cities which featured buildings of historic and architectural interest were to be given priority. A response, we are told, to the allied fire-bomb attacks on Lubeck and Rostock. Over thirty percent of York suffered; the Guildhall destroyed, station and marshalling yards severely damaged. Let's face it, the German bombers had been allowed ninety unchallenged minutes over the city! Read into that what you will, for although the city was ringed mainly by bomber bases, there were fighters based not too far distant.

During these years the only contact with Dad was via the odd, mimeographed, censor-approved letter, and an occasional parcel of, among other things, sugared almonds, which I didn't particularly like. But in war-torn Britain they were the first sweets I remember seeing, or tasting.

There are clear images of the one mile hike to school, in all weathers. Accompanied to the Infants, for the first two or three years, up Wold Street, both boys and girls. Then it was on to Norton Boys County Primary, along Commercial Street, ominously next door to the Police station, or Cop shop as it was known to us. But this wasn't really so much a threat to us as were the Headmaster and his teachers. Any infringement of the rules was dealt with swiftly, and I suspect, joyfully, by some teachers. Hands or backside was our only choice. One reason I hardly ever walked to school with brother George was because he was always late. Worth six of the best, that. I must have been fairly compliant, for I only recall a couple of unscheduled visits to the headmaster's study, and that was enough. George never seemed to learn by it, carried this trend through to later life, rarely on time for anything. Probably figured he'd earned the right!

I was a tousle-haired child in mismatched clothes: short trousers, shirt and jacket. Not out of place though, for most children were dressed in similar fashion; whatever was available, mostly "hand-me-downs. And we all clutched an identical brown cardboard cube by a string handle. Not lunch, these contained a rubber and metal monstrosity; black, and ugly. The then ubiquitous gas mask. And of course, drills were frequently held during which we were compelled to wear the things, giving us the imagined look of wide-eyed beings from a distant planet. Still, as an effective means of reducing excited childhood chatter to a muted background of wheezing, hissing and grunting, the exercise could be deemed a success by the teachers. Even if, inevitably, someone would end up clamping a sticky hand over the air intake of someone else's mask, face positively aglow with the discovery that the unfortunate lad's eyes appeared to be almost sucked out of their sockets. And, in the way of all boys, others would eventually follow suit, the less intelligent sometimes ending with their hand over their own air filter!

Later images are of the Italian prisoners who were billeted in a large building across the river in Malton, originally someone's country house. I always assumed they must have been officers, for the main camp was out on the road to Pickering - today, an Award-Winning WWII museum known as Eden Camp. I recall one of the cooks stationed at that house in town, a jovial Welshman: Taffy, of course. Often to be found by the entrance gate, he used to give us various bits and pieces to take home; bits and pieces that could occasionally be substantially more than the ration book provided for in several months. Things I later learned none of our prisoners were afforded by the enemy: butter, sugar, maybe tea.

There was no barbed wire to be seen, just soldiers who

patrolled the area. Though why I have no idea, for the prisoners seemed to be allowed almost a free rein. We'd see them in town, and they worked quite happily on the surrounding farms. Seems they had no wish to escape. Shrewd thinkers, those Italians - soon had it figured: WWII wasn't going to be as spectacularly entertaining to them as had been those Lions v Christians Coliseum fund-raisers two thousand years back.

Then came the Americans; swarms of "Yanks", and I can tell you now, the old saying is true, they really did give us gum, chum. That was one of the complexities of the time, to us kids, there seemed to be lots of American soldiers, few British. It was only later that I learned those American "soldiers" had actually been airmen; Members of the US Army Air Force.

As well as that gum, and chocolate, they also brought with them Big Band music, especially in the form of Glen Miller. Though it was the English girls who were to benefit most, for they were wined and dined, and presented with such unavailable commodities as make-up, and nylon stockings.

Although money was never plentiful, we didn't exactly go hungry. We got our ration and, living in a farming district, possibly a little extra. More than the odd rabbit, for instance. The war didn't seem to have affected their prodigious rate of reproduction, and they too, like Bomber Command, were out there, all around us. So we didn't starve, but there was certainly no abundance as far as staples were concerned. We each had our own jam-jar - Maureen, George and I - which, once a week was filled with sugar - though not necessarily to the top! It was our very own ration, to do with as we pleased. When it was gone, that was it until the following week. Such things were good schooling in self-discipline and moderation. The same rules applied to what few farthings (a quarter of an old penny) halfpennies, or maybe even a penny we were occasionally given, or earned. Like most kids of that period, we learned the value of money the hard way, therefore we appreciated what little we had. Nor did we go out and spend it right away. We were savers. Lessons which were to stand us in good stead in future decades. If we got into financial difficulties it was our own fault, not someone else's - as seems to be the thinking amongst today's generations! If you can't pay for it, you can't have it. It was along these lines that we were brought up, and I've always lived that way.

*

My most lasting memory of the war years is that of Maureen,

shaking me awake one day. It was May 8th 1945. 'It's all over,' she told me. I was nine years old. Well, it was nearly all over, but it seemed no one had told the Japanese, for war still raged in the Far East. Until America dropped a couple of atomic bombs, that is. (When thought about in later years, I was in full agreement. It certainly saved thousands of lives, many of which would have been Allied lives. It also put the world on notice of the devastating power of these weapons, which only became more powerful with time, thus averting other possible wars, from which there would be no winners!)

Regardless of the celebrations - the bunting and the street parties - peace didn't seem to make a lot of difference for quite a while, the country taking time to recover. These were the years of austerity. But eventually, father returned from wherever it was they'd been treating him, and, during the fifties, food, sweets, petrol and clothing came off ration. I recall the name on the first bar of confectionery I was able to buy: Rowntrees Motoring Chocolate.

Food was the last thing to come off ration. That was in 1954, nine years after the war ended. (I heard on TV recently that school meals began in 1955. Strange that, for by then I was long gone from school, and I remember we had school meals. They cost a dozen or so pence a week, which was still quite a sum back then.)

There were comics, too: Beano, Dandy, Rover, Hotspur, Champion. I recall one of them featured a steely-eyed sergeant pilot that went by the name of Matt Braddock. Then came the Eagle: Dan Dare, spaceships, and technical cutaways. Wow! Goodbye, fairies.

But I seem to recall that Father Christmas had not yet been fully consigned to the myth and legends file, even if, privately, both George and I were by now actually aware that it was our father. But what of those war years when he had not been around? Santa had still paid his annual visit then, even if he didn't leave a lot in those pillowcases left hanging, hopefully, at the bottom of our bed. But during our youth it had always been that way, so disappointment was never evident. We were happy with whatever there was, even if only an orange. I say "even if only an orange", but in actual fact an orange was quite unusual. A big thing, really, for there weren't a lot around in those days.

So, Santa Claus and fairies. But there never had been fairies at the bottom of our garden, either. As for garden, my bedroom window afforded me an uninterrupted view of both the gasworks and the railway tracks, separated from each other by that river. Back then, pre-Dr Beeching, those tracks were the London North Eastern Railway; trains every half-hour or so in the summer. Noisy? Of course. But over time you became accustomed, barely noticed it.

Over the years, passengers on the York to Scarborough run, would have seen - had they cared to look - various changes at the back of the Griffin (even to *label* it "garden" would be taking flattery to the extreme, it looked about as dry and barren as I imagined the Sahara to be!). The tumbledown, brick garage was as permanent a fixture as vibration from trains passing by bare yards away allowed. The outside loos and the boundary fence were of slightly more stable construction, the fence fabricated from old railway sleepers. Which reminds me, I was in the wars from day one of our move to Norton, losing half a finger to that fence in a macho, climbing incident. (Can you imagine that in today's "where there's a blame there's a claim" society? It would probably have resulted in a lawsuit, and counselling to boot! *We* accepted the responsibility ourselves. It was our fence - even if the railway company did erect it - I had made the decision to challenge it. Lost out. OK, so I cried a bit, was taken to hospital, the damaged half finger removed, and that was it. Get on with life. Which, in my book, is as it should be.)

But fences and loos apart, things at the back of our house were subject to change from time to time. Sheds; cars; pigeon lofts - the siting of which was also prone to change - chicken runs, rabbit hutches, washing flapping in the breeze. There had even been a boat at one time. A sort of offshore cabin cruiser affair, propped up on poles. Handy, eh? Twenty miles inland!

*

Then came the winter of 1946/47, one of the worst on record. Even so, it was a great time for us kids. Lots of snow, which meant tobogganing, and snowball fights, plus the occasional, unscheduled school holiday - but only when the boiler for the heating failed, and the free milk froze - although these were few and far between. Most of the time we just trudged through the piled up snow to get to school, then carried on as best we could. (In those days, the country - especially the schools - didn't grind to a halt just because of a snowfall. It *was* winter after all!)

At home, up in the room where the bottled drinks were stored, there would be an occasional "pop" as yet another lemonade bottle exploded due to the extreme cold. And this was the house in which we lived!

But nature really is neutral, swings and roundabouts kind of thing. When the snow went, the river came. Weather forecast? Forget it. What we needed was a shipping report! Unfortunately, by this time that boat no longer resided in our back yard. The only time it could really have felt at home, when the Derwent, usually little more than an ambitious stream, took ambition beyond the limit that spring, overflowing into the pub. (It often burst its banks in winter, but it rarely reached those 1947 levels.)

For a period we were obliged to live upstairs, although the pub rarely failed to open. I recall wooden-planked walkways atop upturned beer crates, by which means the customers kept their wellington-booted feet dry whilst they lubricated their insides.

During normal winters the pub lounge was a place which attracted me, for it was the only warm room in the house. It was also where our first TV was located, and there was always a good fire for the customers - who came first. Sound thinking, really, when reappraised in later years. After all, was it not they who put bread on the table, milk in the fridge? Which reminds me. I always thought that fridge to be a waste of money, particularly during the winter months, for, lounge apart, the whole house was a bloody fridge! The upstairs loo in particular, which is why I used those outside, which were just as cold, but much closer. I favoured the Ladies, it being closest of all, and less draughty, although favoured may not be quite the correct word. Suffered, I suppose. But one has to look back at these things philosophically. It was part of growing up, and a few difficulties early on in life never hurt anyone. At the time though, I begrudged those customers their comfort, primarily because I was not allowed to share it. At least, not during opening hours; conflict between my age and the law, it seemed. Little things like that seemed to matter back then.

I even recall the time that TV received a sort of modification; an oil or water-filled plastic addition which clipped on in front of the screen. It was supposed to magnify the picture. Not one of the world's greatest inventions!

Mention of TV reminds me of the radio on which we used to listen to the BBC Children's Hour - the equivalent, I suppose, of today's Blue Peter, on TV. There was also Dick Barton, Special Agent, along with sidekicks, "Snowy" White, and Della Street. I recall standing by that radio one day, long before there was even mention of such a thing as TV, at least to our young ears. Sister Maureen and I were listening to something or other, and I clearly remember saying, "Wouldn't it be good if you could see pictures on there," pointing to the cloth mesh speaker grille. So it seems possible there had been mention of such a thing as TV, sometime or other, and my memory had retained some of the basic facts.

There was something else about that radio, too. Not learned of until many years after the war was over. As we listened to the news, introduced on the BBC by the first bars of Beethoven's Fifth Symphony - da, da, da, dah - we were also, unknowingly, party to coded messages which were being passed on air to Resistance groups on the Continent. Wonder what the Germans made of such lines as "The potatoes are ready for picking," or something similar.

*

There had been pets, too. Both before and after the war, but not during. Rabbits, for instance. A pair to begin with, but, rabbits being what they are, in due course a bunch of small ones magically appeared. Lovely little things, all ears and fluff, cuddly and furry. Then a dog got in. A Rottweiler, and.... Ah, well, no need to draw a picture. So much for the bunnies.

Dogs we'd always had. Small, friendly types. Terriers, mainly. They were replaced every few years, naturally, but the funny thing is, I don't recall ever being around when the end came. To my mind they suddenly seemed to change. One went away somewhere, another took its place. Nothing to do with a diet of leftovers, by the way, despite the fact that, after the briefest twitch of a canine nostril, those dogs would vacuum up almost anything within sight.

I recall a Patch - white socks on his pitter-patter front paws - and a Spot. There always seemed to be a Spot. Then there was Mickey, he who had the confrontation with an adder up on the Moors. No harm done, apart from a swollen nose and possible loss of face. Or was it Tessie who sniffed out the adder? No, come to think of it, Tessie was the one who savaged my school library book when I foolishly left it on the arm of the sofa. Took some explaining away, that.

Budgies had featured, too, at odd times. Not what one could term a successful line in pets, the budgies. They somehow never seemed happy with their lot, even though they were frequently given the opportunity to fly around the room, despite their tendency to crap all over the furnishings. A carelessly left-open window and they were off like a prisoner from Wormwood Scrubs; two at least, I recall. I suppose this must point to a certain degree of unhappiness, as it's a known fact budgies would rather perch than fly. One even contrived to hang itself from the cord supporting its mirror. Mum tried to hide the fact from us, replacing it with an imposter before we returned from school. Alas, the difference was soon spotted, so she was reduced to admitting to the truth. The replacement was the second of those that winged away, out the window like. Scratch the budgies.

There was an escapee among the rabbits as well, almost forgot about that. A female. Only this time we avoided the mistake of getting her a mate, something which she perhaps took as an affront. We made sure she was always fenced in, which didn't bother her in the least, for, being a very efficient tunneller, our garden soon had the look of a training ground for Stalag Luft III. She was forever digging her way out, only to be returned by an irate neighbour.

'Bloody rabbit's taken a fancy to my lettuce and carrots, again. It's into the pot next time.'

She'd apparently taken a fancy to something else, too, for a few days after her return came a period during which she showed a distinct lack of interest in escape; nothing whatever to do with the neighbour's threat. Obviously the magic wand had been waved, for the cage suddenly became home to considerably more than a single rabbit!

Then there was that other episode. Not pets exactly, but close enough.

'Ah could see t' point, Bill if tha'd done it durin't war. Could have been tha contribution to t' "Dig for Victory" campaign. But what's this, "A Chuck for Luck?"' I recall a customer, saying at the time.

I hadn't understood what he'd meant, until I discovered my play area - aka the back yard - was to be shared. Dad, ever the optimist, acquired some hens, along with a cockerel.

'We're about to go into t' chicken and egg production business, Olaf, ' Dad had replied. 'Not commercial like. T' help things along.'

'Cost summat will that.' He was a regular, Olaf Wilson, and I'd heard tell he knew about such things. 'Need to feed em corn, tha knows. They aren't like cats and dogs,' he advised Dad. By which I was beginning to understand. Cats and dogs *were* different, weren't they. No specialist foods to buy for them. Not back then. They ate what we did. Or, to be truthful, what we didn't; the leftovers. And believe me, there wasn't a lot. Not a lot to start with, so there was little waste; but the cats and dogs seemed healthy enough for all that.

As far as eggs went, I was all in favour. Anything would be better than the powdered variety we'd been used to eating. Spam I could take, actually liked it, still do to this day, but dried eggs? No thanks. Even the dogs and cats turned their noses up at those. So I welcomed the hens, and we got along fine. They just scratched about, pecked at this and that, kept out of my way; no problem. But that cockerel was another matter entirely. An evil bastard, if you'll excuse my French. (Yes, from the French, batard: child of the pack-saddle.) Anyway, that cockerel had mean-looking eyes and a vicious streak. Malevolent and hostile. He definitely ruled the roost, so to speak. A real bully, this, chasing small, frightened children. I mean, I had to be very young, didn't I? Otherwise I wouldn't have been afraid.

He'd lurk close to the back door, ready to pounce. I knew, because I'd sneak a look from behind the curtains first. He knew I knew, for there the old sod was, cocking his head and peering at me. He'd fix me with a baleful look. First one beady, red eye, then the other, jerking his head round officiously, comb flapping. Then he'd strut around, almost daring me to venture out.

What did I do? It was back to the upstairs loo, I'm afraid. I had to use it after dark anyway, for I knew the bogeyman would get me if I went outside then. Similar thoughts made me thankful to be sharing a big, old-fashioned double bed with brother, George, despite the constant bickering about who had all the blankets, or more than their fair share of mattress. The way I figured it, two in a bed meant the bogeyman wouldn't get me. Or him, come to that. Therefore an advantage to both of us. But at that age I tended to worry only about me.

Anyway, that cockerel was to get his, for one day he aspired to downright bravado, foolishly challenging a customer going about his natural business. Naturally, when drinking, you occasionally have business to attend which requires your presence outside; if that is where the loos happen to be.

'Hey, Bill, yer bloody cockbod's deed,' "Chick" Hopper - as this particular customer was known; an apt name given the circumstances - revealed upon his return. The cock bird had, it so transpired, caught a convincingly aimed workboot about the audio sensory canal, cocking its toes as a result, so to speak. Well, it would wouldn't it, the boot was size twelve!

I wasn't at all sad. After all, that's life. One minute, king of the castle, next, lunch for five. Don't suppose I thought that at the time, but no doubt would have had I been capable. Even so, I think I secretly declared Chick to be, "my best friend. Ever." One more thing, it was now so much quieter at daybreak. No, didn't miss that cockerel at all. Maybe the hens did, for there suddenly seemed to be few eggs; a temporary glut of roast chicken.

Now I could get back outside, Dad's heavy, leather-covered brass binoculars to hand. He was a racing man, Dad, only natural in Norton; jacket and tie, trilby on his head, enclosure ticket hanging from his lapel, those binoculars slung casually over a shoulder, (on occasion he even drove a horse-box for one of the stables). But between times those glasses were mine, for exciting things were to be seen up there in the skies. Aviation was finally making itself felt, drawing me in.

*

It was a time when springs seemed to drift easily into long, hot summers, and living in the countryside became a decided advantage. I remember them as lemonade and ice-cream summers (both of the home-made variety, and absolutely delicious. Just two of the many things of which modern youth are deprived, thanks to today's Health and Safety "Gestapo"). They were also swimming-in-the-pool, or river, type summers. The pool, or swimming baths, were a bare hundred yards up the road from the Griffin, on Church Street. There was no church evident, although there must have been at one time, for entry was by way of an ancient graveyard, its moss-encrusted headstones tilted this way and that, the site of the actual church now occupied by the pool, I suspect.

At the height of summer, that pool would echo to our excited yelps and chatter, the high-pitched voices of pre-pubertal youth. But whereas most dove in without so much as a ripple, I held my nose and jumped. For although I was an accomplished swimmer, I hadn't yet plucked up the courage to launch myself headfirst. From the edge of the pool, that is. Those other clever dicks, not satisfied with the height of the board, were, like lemmings on steroids, hurling themselves off the balcony, which ran across the top of the changing rooms. They would also use the boundary wall, separating the pool from the railway, with its steel-upon-gravel tracks.

I recall it as being a mainly happy childhood. We were rarely indoors, largely unsupervised, not thought to be at risk at all. Nor were we. Well, certainly not the kind of risks today's children face, imagined or otherwise. We wandered around fearlessly.

There was the odd mishap, of course, only to be expected amongst adventurous children. It was a feature of life, and of growing up. But for the most part we simply got back on our feet, dusted ourselves down, wiped away the tears and blood and generally got on with things. Sometimes a plaster or more may be needed, but that was it. There was never a thought of looking for someone else to blame (or sue!). Health and Safety be dammed, safety was our own responsibility. We knew and accepted that, as did our parents. Life was lived as it should be, not as dictated by some faceless, unelected Civil Servant, who had probably never faced real danger in their life.

Fields, which previously had been predominantly green, were suddenly interwoven with red and yellow, and they seemed to stretch away forever. Days were peacefully quiet, despite the sounds of aircraft, which were anyway music to my ears. There seemed to be little but the laughter of children and the sounds of nature: the cooing of a dove, the perpetually buzzing bees. Such days seem hard to find now. Possibly they were not common then, either. Rose-tinted, retrospective images, perhaps? I don't think so. For this was the tranquillity which followed the years of war. Heady days, when summers appeared to be just that, with sunshine in abundance. Only fly in the ointment was the insistence that we retire to bed early, especially during the school term. It was usually around seven or eight o'clock; would therefore remain light outside for hours yet, the world still fully functional.

*

I recall going to help the local butcher on his rounds some days. Not as a job, for payment, just for the fun of it. He was a friend of Dad's, as well as being a customer. There were actually two brothers (or was it three?). They ran the Butcher's shop. I do recall Don and Jack, and it was Jack I'd go off with on his rounds. He had a little Bedford van, two seats in front, meat, chopping board, scales and knives in the back, and we'd go visiting the outlying villages. The people were friendly, and lots of gossip ensued, usually over a cup of tea and some home baked produce. I enjoyed those trips on sunny, summer days.

But that day in September 1950 had not been such a day.

'Mum has gone away,' Dad told us one morning.

'For a long time?' I asked. It hadn't really sunk in what he was telling us.

'Forever, David. She's gone to Heaven.'

'Like Patch, you mean?'

'A bit like Patch, yes, although different as well. Dogs can be replaced, you see, Mums can't.'

Later that day I discovered there was another difference: Dogs didn't get wreaths, Mums did. "Always gentle, always kind, a wonderful memory left behind." I cried a little that night, for that had been the first really major event of my short life; the sad experience of losing someone close.

I later learned that Mum had been admitted to hospital with some fairly minor ailment, had developed pneumonia and failed to recover. It was only after she'd gone that I realized I had never really known her. But isn't that always the case? Sister Maureen, being female, had been closest, which is also normal. I suppose I'd have been closer to Dad, had he been around to get close to.

Now he was. Goodbye, Mum. Hello, Dad. My introduction to the realities of life. And death.

As if in compensation for my loss I now found girls starting to take me seriously. Well, as serious as it got at that age, in those times. I'm not suggesting they stepped out of their knickers and threw them in my direction. Wouldn't have known what to do about it if they had, apart from suspecting it would probably be fun finding out. Sex? As far as I was concerned it could well not yet have been conceived. (Poor choice of words!) That's not to say the attraction didn't exist. It was there all right, from my side; it just wasn't being reciprocated. But the girls did now speak to me, laughed at my jokes rather than my disasters, which unfortunately still occurred, albeit rather less frequently. It was a start, even if I was clumsy and ill-at-ease in their presence.

*

Maybe Mums could not be replaced, but I was soon to discover they could be substituted. Our substitute was a lady named

Mabel. She was to be live-in nanny, barmaid, cook, cleaner, and a shoulder to cry on. She was good at it too, had a wealth of experience. During the war, Mabel had served in the WAAF, a sergeant on the balloon sites. Previous to that she had been "In Service", and the tales she had to tell about that would make yet another novel or two for Barbara Taylor-Bradford.

Along with Mabel came her daughter, Pamela. Another female for me to tease. And whenever we had chips for dinner (or tea, as it was then known), Pamela, being female, always got served first. So I would "borrow" one or two of her chips until such time as mine appeared. Laughs and tears all round.

Mabel was eventually to be welcomed as our stepmother; remained so until the day she too went to heaven, many, many years later. Long after Dad.

*

In the true manner of all boys, I participated in the many youthful activities of the time: Cubs, Sunday-school, Church Choir at St Peter's (Honest! Cross my heart and hope to die). Well, they paid didn't they.

'As a choirboy, David, you'll be working for Jesus. You'll also earn threepence every Sunday,' the choirmaster explained, during his attempt to recruit me.

'He doesn't pay a lot, sir, does He? I mean, they pay a shilling for delivering the papers.'

'Ah, yes, the newspapers. Well, it's not actually Jesus who will be paying you, that's the church's job. And we too pay a shilling; for weddings.'

'Ah! that's OK then, I'll just do weddings.'

'No, David, it doesn't work like that. To be considered for a wedding one is required to be a regular Sunday performer.'

Talk about bribery and corruption, and this from the church. I didn't say that, although I may have thought it. But I joined anyway, for a while. It was the thing to do, and even threepence was a fair sum at the time.

As it happened, I didn't seem to get a lot of weddings. In fact, nary a one. Probably a result of too many Sundays spent on the riverbank, where I'd taken to fishing, in all weathers - one episode of such foolhardiness resulting in a bout of bronchitis. Ah, but on a summer's evening the riverbank could be glorious, fish or no fish, often the latter, except for the single occasion during which I was lucky enough to catch what turned out to be a prize Perch. Weighing in at two pounds fourteen ounces it was thought significant enough to inform the local paper of the catch. They did file a report on it, though I was later to learn that had I sent details of my coup to the *News of the World* angling correspondent, it would have won me a prize rod for the week's best catch. Ah well, another lesson learned. Explore the market before reaching a decision. So, overall, not too successful then, the fishing, except maybe from a fishy point of view. Luckily there was a chippy close by - Jackie Taylor's - where I could get my maggot-tainted hands on three-pennyworth in the evening's dying light. I was usually able to scrape together enough coppers for that; pennies and halfpennies saved from when people gave them to me. They meant a lot, those coppers, both to me and to those who gave them. But they gave them anyway, that was the way people were. As for the possible health hazard of maggot-tainted hands... well, there wasn't one, was there. I wiped them on my trousers first!

Living in the countryside meant we did quite well as far as local produce went. There were always ample fresh vegetables, a lot given us by our regular customers; though I don't for a minute believe Dad would have reciprocated by way of a free drink! This didn't seem to worry those customers at all. And there were still plenty of rabbits to be had. In fact rabbit stews, and pies, were a regular feature of our diet, until the government of the day introduced myxomatosis. Anyway, as well as food, those rabbits offered us kids another form of income, for we could sell the pelts for threepence apiece. Moleskins likewise added a few more coppers to the kitty.

Mention of coppers brings to mind thoughts of a different kind. We were mainly law-abiding, as were the majority back in the days when the police actually had some power. Believe me, when the local "Bobby" told you to do something, or perhaps *not* to, you did or didn't, as the case may be. This was for minor offences. Such things as murder were extremely rare, creating major headlines. But of course we still had capital and corporal punishment at that time, which must prove something! It certainly instilled discipline in the classroom, and on the streets, so we generally behaved ourselves. Human rights! Whoever came up with that? In my view, if you are found to have broken the law, until you have paid whatever penalty the courts deem necessary, you forfeit whatever rights you previously had. Rights need to be earned, just like anything else in life.

Then there were the mishaps. Like the time I was distracted by a girl whilst riding my bike along Commercial Street. Full exposure, too, for this was Norton's major thoroughfare. (In fact it was along Commercial Street that King George and his Queen drove by as we stood on the pavement outside our school and waved the patriotic, paper flags we'd been given. Who said Norton wasn't important. OK, so the Royal Family were touring their Kingdom. But they couldn't possibly be visiting every town of this size.)
'Hi, Jennifer.'

A beautiful name, Jennifer (also not this girl's real name). Nice ring to it. It certainly suited this girl. Matched her face, matched her budding young curves. Definitely a looker, I told myself. Like, *kaboom!*

So, in the act of trying to impress one of the graceful beauties who were constantly to reject my feeble advances, I took my eyes off the road, one hand off the handlebars, gave her a smile and a wave. It was an opportunity not to be missed, for, once you'd conquered the basics, a bicycle was a means of showing off. It seems I attempted it too close to the start of the learning curve, for it was at this point I became vaguely conscious of something being not quite right. Nor was it. Bang! Slap into the back of a parked car. I don't remember the make, but make wasn't important. What was important was the fact it had a sloping back, nay, a launching ramp. For a moment there I seemed well placed to beat Gagarin into orbit, possibly would have had not gravity finally claimed me. No wonder I was orever being rejected. She could set my heart aflutter from fifty feet, that Jennifer. I seemed to have no effect on her from as close as arm's length. Was never allowed closer!

I'd always assumed Jennifer's lack of interest to be related to my pre teen physique: skinny arms and legs, spotty face, unworried innocence. I once miscast myself for a local fancy dress parade, felt afterwards I must have looked pretty ridiculous dressed only in swimming togs, tan, courtesy of Rowntrees Cocoa. Probably the skinniest, meekest Tarzan the world had ever seen. Had it rained I'd no doubt have been the weirdest, too. I hadn't felt foolish. There again, at ten years of age I didn't exactly have a greatly developed sense of honour. I could have starred in those Charles Atlas adverts of the time, as the guy *not* kicking sand. Girls tended to agree, I hadn't been slow to notice. So I suppose it was only to be expected Jennifer wouldn't even crack a smile as I picked myself up and dusted myself down. In fact I swear she turned her back on me, stuck her pretty little nose up in the air. Ah, well, not the first or last time disaster had struck in the process of my trying to impress a girl. Life can be so cruel at times.

There were to be many similar incidents, a lot, admittedly, nothing to do with girls. The extremely macho, late-late braking technique, for instance. This involved building up a fair lick of speed as you approached the gang, straddling their stationary bikes and lost in some group discussion - probably by now relating to aviation. Anyway, the idea was to leave your braking to the last second, jam all on, skidding to an impressive halt only inches away. This, naturally, required precise judgement and timing, possibly also that missing ingredient, the consummate "ball sense". Not exactly my forte, I was to discover. And, to complicate matters further, if the road happened to be damp, or one brake block had fallen out, unobserved..... But planting both feet firmly on the road slowed you hardly at all, and served only to wear out the soles of your shoes that much quicker. And even if it did warn the gang that something untoward was about to befall them, it was far too late for them to take evasive action. Scree... 'Look out! Ahhh....' No, never did quite master that late-braking technique. What the hell. Some people have it, some don't. But that is not to say I *never* would. (Those bikes were heavy, too. No fancy alloys then. As for seats, they appeared to have been designed with no particular part of the anatomy in mind, least of all that which relates to sitting. Still, we rode them for miles - York,

Scarborough, Bridlington, over the Wolds and Dales.)

Then there was the time we were returning from a day of potato picking. Yes, they were actually picked by hand in the old days. It was an activity for which we were given two weeks' holiday from school so as to be able to help out. Great times. During morning and afternoon breaks we'd be fed fresh, home-baked pies, and the strong, milky tea would come in buckets. We brought our own packed lunch with us, but again the tea was provided by the farmhouse.

We weren't obliged to go and pick potatoes, of course, but as we could be paid up to ten shillings a day to do so - in days when a single shilling was a fortune - most certainly did. Let's face it, money only becomes unimportant to those that have it by the sackful (there again, the more some have, the more they seem to want!) Our sacks were filled only with potatoes, which was to lead to an incident on the ride home.

It was another case of "Hi ho Silver!" as I once more parted company from my bike, taking yet another header over the handlebars.

"Thick Mike" was deemed to be the cause this time, though the likely proximity of his own possible demise, through strangulation, could well have been a contributory factor. He was blue in the face, due to him carrying his knapsack - full of freebie potatoes - with the strap around his neck, across his Adam's Apple, rather than over one shoulder. With his already slow faculties apparently on the wane, he was all over the road.

'What are you doing, Mike? Move ov...er, ahhh...' Too late. The lamp-bracket protruding from the hub of his wayward front wheel, penetrated the spokes of my front wheel. That incident was to cost me half a front tooth. My fault again I suppose, should have remembered: Mike was one of the kids who used to stick his hand in front of his own gas mask. And to think, he was probably the first person to be declared, "my best friend. Ever." A status that had just been automatically cancelled. I probably even called him a pleb, for it was a word we frequently used back then as a form of mild rebuke. (The dictionary definition being "a person of unpolished manners", and we were very much so, I imagine, therefore nothing drastic. I would never have imagined its use, years later, being cause for taking someone to court. That Parliamentary Copper could have been called far worse had that upset MP resorted to current terms of name-calling, none so mild as pleb. And would not a simple matter of cracking open a gate demonstrated more "polished manners", apart from saving thousands of pounds in public cash, and two careers!)

Just remembered. I wasn't even wearing a crash helmet! But of course, we didn't back then, not on a pushbike. They were even a rarity amongst motorcyclists.

There was one time when a crash helmet may have been of use to my father, though. As a result of Grandad's motor coach business, father had been a driver from an early age, and I don't recall us ever being without a car, even if it got little use. Running a pub was a full time business, especially as a landlord. You were tied to a particular brewery, opening hours more or less as dictated by them, so there was little free time. I remember our Sunday lunch was usually taken around two thirty pm, shortly after closing. And as the doors had to opened again at seven pm, this left little time. Still, I do recall the odd Sunday afternoon trip up on to the Wolds, or to visit the relatives in Scarborough. But dad would sometimes get up very early in the morning, to go mushrooming, or shooting rabbits, occasionally taking me along, if he could coax me out of bed at around five o'clock! But he usually took along his mates. A mate, actually, for at the time under discussion the car was a Standard Flying Nine soft-top. Room for a couple of small children in the back maybe, but not an adult. Anyway, one morning, due to ice on the road, they ended up inverted in a potato field! Luckily, no one was hurt, nor was the car too badly damaged - they built them well in those days. I still recall the registration of that car: DAJ 616. Now isn't that something worth remembering. Strange, the things you do remember, as opposed to those you don't, the latter probably the more important!

It must have been around this time when the gang, wandering around in the country, as we did, came across some secure, windowless Nissen huts lining the side of one remote road. There was no one anywhere around; in fact the huts appeared to have been abandoned. So curiosity got the better of us, and we decided to see what they contained, if anything. We somehow effected an entry - so the doors couldn't have been that secure - only to discover box upon box of cloth covered packages of something that looked like spaghetti. It was in fact cordite. Maybe they were labelled or something. Anyway, knowing what cordite was used for, we assumed possession of a few packages. They were probably two feet long by eight inches in diameter, maybe a couple of pounds in weight. It must have been November time, as I recall throwing one complete package on a bonfire! Lots of fierce flames but little else, being as it was in the open. Later, we took to filling empty rocket cases with the stuff, a little at a time, sticking them in a bottle and applying a lighted match. The results varied upwards on a scale from, "a short hop", "over the rooftops", to, "bloody hell!" It was just as well our experimenting ceased at this point, though that was mainly on account of the rocket cases not being able to contain a greater amount of the propellent. When we next checked, the Nissen huts had disappeared, along with their contents. I often wonder how some unfortunate storeman explained away his discrepancies.

Thinking about this, years later, that eight inch diameter estimate would have to have been about right; eight inch shell - take quite a charge to propel one of those a few miles.

Life was interesting, for sure, but we were young children, had never known anything different, so the war had little impact on us. A majority of people lived as we did, that was life back then. You made do with what was available. What you weren't aware of, you didn't miss.

*

The late forties, early fifties, were times when every schoolboy showed some interest in what was happening, aeronautically. More than a few no doubt harboured ideas way beyond their potential. Me? Apart from wanting to wear my underpants outside my trousers, and possess x-ray vision that was about it. I had absolutely no aspirations towards becoming a pilot. In fact, with a parcel of fish and chips in my hand I was already in a world of my own, a Yorkshireman through and through. After all, let's face it, Yorkshire fish and chips are the best in the country, therefore, by connotation, the world. You see, up there we cook 'em in beef dripping, not your airy fairy vegetable oil. Well, we used to, before the kill-joys which masquerade under the collective health authorities, and European Union, started to frown upon anything that gave pleasure. Even so, the best places still use dripping. There's twenty centuries of history, heritage, and development gone into developing the world's most perfect after-pub meal, and along come the do-gooders trying to take it all away. Not only do-gooders, but the Chinese and Indians as well, with their take-aways.

Once I'd left school and was earning my crust rarely did a night pass when I didn't have "one of each" for supper, sometimes twice a night. I loved the fish and chips they served in those days. They were grand.

But yes, aviation, and the aircraft themselves, were definitely starting to attract my attention.

As well as finding a use for the wrapping of fish and chips, newspapers also covered all the aviation stories. After all, it was such stories that created probably the most spectacular news available back in those more tranquil, law-abiding days, for, apart from travelling at unbelievable speeds, those early jets appeared to fall out of the sky at a phenomenal rate. At times, it seemed as if even the immutable laws of flight had suffered a temporary setback. And those airfields were still all around us.

I read about trial flights of the prototype aircraft of that period. Such classics as the Hawker P1067 - eventually to become the Hunter - Vickers Supermarine Swift, and the butterfly-tailed 535, plus all the prototypes which led up to them. Strange new shapes were to be seen, too. Aircraft which carried nomenclature such as DH108 (Swallow), Avro 698 (Vulcan), and AW52 Flying Wing. There were also the Javelin, Valiant, and Victor. AV Roe had a model 707 - in this case, a delta - long before William Boeing brought out his airliner. Peter Twiss captured the world airspeed record for Great Britain in another delta-winged model (Fairey's FD2), at well over a eleven hundred miles per hour, if headlines were to be believed. And in those days they usually could be. (Anyway, Peter told me all about it himself, albeit not until 1998.)

Given the preponderance of bases still active in the area, Yorkshire skies were never quiet; our particular area a designated low-flying zone. Despite this, most of the interesting stuff flew way up yonder, which resulted in Dad's binoculars working overtime, tracking twinkling silver specks at around thirty thousand feet. Those planes trailed vapour across the stratosphere, thin white scars defacing the canvas of ice-blue. But the sky is self-cleansing; we may tarnish it, blemish it, stain it, but not for long. That first breeze, the falling rain, the passing storm, all play their part.

Yes, to an impressionable young lad, the sky up there was a constant source of wonder. And one aircraft that didn't require the use of optical aids was the giant, ten engined, B36D; Strategic Air Command's big stick, known as the "Peacemaker". Recognisable by sound alone - the distinctive harmony of six piston engines and four jets - they droned over in the upper reaches, sounding like they were powered by high-revving, multi-cylinder two-strokes. Then there was Bristol's mighty Brabazon, flown by Bill Pegg, which put in an appearance prior to its demise through being cancelled; an around-the-island demonstration flight.

Nostalgia? Of course. As Grandad Sale once said, 'Nay, lad, there's nowt wrong wi' nostalgia'. So here, to me, are some more nostalgia generating moments. *My* boyhood heroes bore names such as Mike Lithgow (who was to lose his life to that T-tail deep stall phenomena when testing the BAC1-11), Neville Duke, Falk (who rolled the mighty Vulcan, thus earning himself the nickname, Roly). And there was John Derry (tragically killed in the DH110 at Farnborough), and John "Cat's Eyes" Cunningham, (WWII night-fighter ace, and of Comet fame). Others, too: Dave Morgan, Jock Bryce, Geoffrey Tyson, Weldon, and Zurakowski, test pilots, all, and superstars of the day, for it was *their* names which were to feature regularly within the pages of the press. Quite often on the front page.

*

Meantime, from across "The Pond", tales filtered through of strange happenings at Muroc Army Air Base, on America's West Coast. This was the place that would eventually become known as Edwards Air Force Base, after Captain Glen Edwards - a pilot who lost his life testing the Northrop YB49 flying wing from there. That aircraft - competing for a bomber contract at the time - was thought to have exceeded its structural limits whilst in a dive. Whatever the cause, that crash was to result in Muroc becoming Edwards - indeed, most of Edwards' streets are named in honour of pilots who lost their lives when test flying from the base - and the bomber contract going to Convair. I, via Dad's binoculars, now spotted B36's rather than B49's.

There were no computer predictions then to give a clue as to how an aircraft was expected to handle or perform, no supersonic wind tunnels to aid design. So, as if in a bizarre effort to prove Murphy correct, the designers occasionally got it wrong, as did the odd pilot. (It is said that Captain Edward Murphy, an engineer at Edwards, gave cause for the age old, previously unnamed law, "If anything can go wrong, it will" to become eponymous, because of his frequent use of the phrase.)

The Edwards base was "way out yonder" in the shimmering heat of California's Mojave Desert, and, from runways built upon its dusty, dry lake-beds, flew the X-planes.

These were piloted by such as Crossfield, Bridgeman, Walker, Hoover and White. But the one who was to become most famous of all was Charles "Chuck" Yeager. As far as aeronautics went, he became my boyhood hero. This was to last for a long, long time. Until I learned about Bob Hoover. (It is said you should never meet your heroes. This I found to be true when I got to meet both Yeager and Hoover much later in life, was confirmed when talking to them face to face when, Hoover immediately assumed the position. But he became my hero only *after* I had met them both.) In actual fact, Hoover was the pilot originally selected for the sound barrier flight, only he blotted his copybook by foolishly beating up an airfield during an unconnected flight - in response to a request from a friend. Unfortunately, someone reported the infringement and, being an honest, nice guy, Bob admitted to the misdemeanour when questioned by his CO. Which was as well for, in the early days of jet flight, his CO told Hoover that he was already aware, being as Hoover was the only guy in America flying a jet fighter that day! The result being that "Chuck" Yeager became the man who finally destroyed the myth of a barrier by exceeding the speed of sound - and him with a broken collarbone at that! Which only went to prove it was a job that called for courage, skill, and, by all accounts, copious amounts of alcohol, a handy little watering hole known as Pancho's dispensing the latter. Named after the young aviatrix - Florence Lowe (Pancho) Barnes - who founded and ran it, Pancho's was part of the Rancho Oro Verde Fly-Inn Dude Ranch, but it was nicknamed by the WW2 pilots who trained nearby, "The Happy Bottom Riding Club Ranch."

(Not well known at this time was the fact that Miles Aircraft, a British company, were developing an aircraft known as the M52, and this was thought to stand a better than average chance of beating the Americans in the race to break the sound barrier. Then, inexplicably, the project was cancelled by the British Government; all technology - including the crucial all-flying tailplane - ending up in American hands, and being incorporated in the Bell X-1, the aircraft flown by Yeager. Shades of the TSR2 debacle, two decades later.)

*

If not a direct result of the war, this then was perhaps when the avian bug was contracted, for it was certainly a stimulating period. The Great Adventure. Dawn of the jet age. The sound barrier, fast jets and record breaking. A new era entirely.

But no matter how or when the seed was sown, this was the time propagation occurred. I became mad keen on aircraft. That I was hooked became clear the very first time I walked into a lamppost, my attention being directed towards the sky rather than on where I was going. Much the same as had happened that time with Jennifer. The main difference between riding my bike into a parked car, and walking into a lamppost, was that the distraction now went under another name: aviation. My next love affair had well and truly begun. I had become what would today be known as an "aviation anorak", thus beginning a long affinity with aircraft, and aviation in general. I found myself writing letters to aircraft manufacturers on both sides of the Atlantic; the British Isles and America. I requested brochures and data on their products, the Americans being particularly responsive; at least on the civil side. Glossy brochures were frequently dropping through our letterbox, and I just wish I still had them. Can't think where they went, but the only one remaining in my possession today is one from Westland Helicopters.

But there was a problem. The aircraft were too distant. They were minute, inaccessible; optically-enlarged specks in the sky, or illustrations and photographs in a book. I had to find a way to get closer, actually to touch them.

The answer came in a flash of inspiration. I'd already gone the Cubs/Scouts route, was not yet into girls, as it were. Therefore my sole preoccupation became aviation, rather than procreation. So, immediately exchanging neckerchief and woggle for blue serge and beret, I joined my local branch of the Air Training Corps - 1323 Middleton Squadron (now 1323 Ryedale Squadron) - and from that day on, the obsession really took off, it could be said. Aviation was to become the major attraction in life, to which even girls took a back seat, although not literally. Room could be made available for a passenger on a bike, as some of the lads proved, but as I appeared not yet to have fully mastered the art of remaining on board alone, any thoughts of carrying girls were to be dismissed. At least until the old biological urge asserted itself more fully. After all, I was only thirteen, going on fourteen. The Sixties were yet a distant decade ahead.

*

In a building containing a series of semi-dilapidated rooms, down a passage beside the Buckrose Hotel, adjacent to that swimming pool, therefore close to home, they taught us the

47

rudiments of military life, particularly as it applied to the Royal Air Force. The basement entry contained a discarded RR Derwent jet engine on a stand, along with a decommissioned Link Trainer. Climb the stairs and there were lecture rooms, the CO's office and if I recall correctly, a small bore (.22) rifle range, though that was up one more storey. The end wall was the butts, and it overlooked the river and gas works, just as my bedroom window did. We were taught the basics of the theory of flight, aircraft recognition - at which I proved to be very good - and basic drill.

It was the ATC that eventually led to that first cryptic entry in my logbook: 4-5-50; Oxford X7279; air experience; Driffield - not too far away. A mind-boggling flight, that, and one of some significance, the entry, naturally, featuring at the top of page one in my logbook. It was the high point of my life so far, a real charge to the system. I *had* already touched the sky, of course I had, as has everyone, for the air we breathe is also the sky, it begins at ground level. What I hadn't yet experienced was the kind of levitation that denotes flight.

It is sometimes difficult to recapture certain memories and feelings from a distance of fifty-five years, but ones that do stick in my mind are those of that first flight. Even today I only need experience that sudden surge of power and adrenalin which signals the start of a takeoff, and there I am, back at Driffield, up into the clouds and down memory lane. Been that way forever, it seems.

It was a glorious day, I recall. The sky was clear blue. Not the deep blue of summer, but a sort of cornflower colour. The sun was high, the clouds small, white and puffy, the air still. Birds and bees twittered and hummed above the green grass of the airfield.

'God couldn't have arranged things better,' my friend, Peter Williams suggested. 'A perfect setting to put us at our ease.'

'Yeah,' I agreed. Yet, despite the glow of excitement which coursed through my body, it was with some trepidation that I stepped from the mundane into the first machine that would lift me off the face of this earth. It carried the yellow bands of Flying Training Command, I noted, and as we climbed aboard I looked across at Pete, gave him what I assumed to be a macho smile. 'Hope the pilot is an instructor, and not a recently-converted pupil,' I whispered. I expect I also secretly prayed.

The aircraft had been built by Airspeed, a company born nearby, in the city of York, author, Neville Shute, one of its founders. Not that it's of any significance, for all aircraft seem to possess that same, familiar, difficult-to-describe smell. Particularly military aircraft; a world apart, those. There is a mishmash of hydraulic fluid, rubber, leather, high-octane fuel, and sweat. Possibly a touch of wood, glue, fabric, and dope, back then, too. The combined odours of machinery and man. That was the first lesson to be learned when, on that sunny spring day, I traded fresh country air for that which now assailed the senses.

The interior had a used look about it; a thousand scuffs and scratches, chipped paint, crazed perspex, leather seats shiny with wear. I, along with Pete and the others, lowered my bum into one, and secured myself with a canvas lapstrap. Not a lot of help in the matter of gaining my confidence, that.

Especially once the door was slammed closed, sealing us in. Still, I had my faithful parachute to hand - the harness I wore, clip-on chest pack by my side. (As had everyone, despite the fact that one lad - totally disregarding the canvas handle - elected to pick his up by that nice, shiny, D-ring. This of course released the silken contents to fall about his feet like an impatient bride discarding her wedding gown. Not the first time that had happened - the parachute, I mean - but being a cadet rather than a fully-fledged airman, he was excused the normal re-packing fine of two shillings and sixpence.)

The pilot looked back, checking that everyone was as ready as he was. He then reached forward and began the process of start-up.

A propeller turned jerkily a couple of times, cylinders coughed and died intermittently, belching blue-grey smoke rings, until the engine finally caught, sending a shudder through the airframe. To begin with, that engine ran as raggedly as my heartbeat, but as it warmed so it roared into healthy life, exhaust gasses now a rich blue. The act was repeated, engine number two, which is when the previously inert machine suddenly became alive with noise and vibration. We then began to taxi across the grass, hollow-sounding thuds echoing throughout the cabin. Tailwheel, bumping over uneven ground? Or my still-ragged heartbeat?

At the end of the active runway, with the tarmac stretching ahead in diminishing perspective, each engine was systematically checked: magnetos, temperatures, pressures. All must have shown the right kind of readings , for the throttles were pushed fully open, machine active, eager, straining against brakes which were suddenly released....

Up to this point it had been little different from riding a farm tractor, but now my heart was really pounding. Excitement, or fear? I attempted a little self-assurance. Nothing to be fearful of. People fly all the time. Nothing magical about it. Nothing new.

To me there was.

We moved. Disappointingly slowly at first, with some reluctance, it seemed. Then we were pounding along, gathering pace rapidly. On and on. An apparently ineffectual attempt. We were bumping, bouncing, the tailwheel lifting, but we weren't flying. Until, parting company with our shadow - as Peter Pan had once feared - we were. On the way to Never-Never-Land? It felt that way, to me, for we were floating, the only vibration an out-of-sync rumble, which ceased as the pilot juggled the throttles.

Airborne at last, the machine seemed really to come alive. It hadn't, of course, it couldn't, it just felt that way, climbing, banking, turning this way and that. The fields and villages of my native county slid past below, filling my mind with cascading thoughts... The earth was down there, I was up here - up where the clouds formed, where the birds flew. At last I was seeing what they saw, and it was a wonderful sight.

Not only was the aircraft in its element, so, I was soon to realize, was I. That familiar Yorkshire landscape dropped away, below and behind, along with any misgivings I may have harboured. I then realized it had also taken with it any imagined problems I may have had, too (a feeling that was often to be repeated in later life, although problems then usually had more to do with reality than imagination). It was velvet smooth, almost dreamily peaceful. Reassuring to discover that the theory of flight was in fact reality. A fact, in fact! The Air Training Corps had taught me about such laws: basic aerodynamics - lift versus drag, power over weight, and so forth. I imagined air flowing above the wings speeding up relative to that which passed beneath, creating low pressure and suction on the upper surfaces, a prerequisite to the defiance of gravity.

The country that now passed below seemed foreign to me, for I could no longer recognise anything. What I had always imagined to be fields of enormous dimension were now being revealed as small green patches divided by hedges of a darker green. Cows and sheep had become unrecognisable brown and white dots. Woods and copses were transposed into mysterious dark patches, rivers and streams became threads of silver. Significantly, birds flew by *below* me! In one field a tractor, drawing a flock of seagulls along behind, silently ploughed furrows which, from up here at least, appeared perfectly straight.

But it wasn't to last, for all too soon we were slowing and descending. We banked into a final turn, horizon tilting in the windscreen, that distant crescent of hangars drifting past, nose coming round until we were lined up with the runway ahead. The pilot, leather helmet on his head, held the oxygen mask to his mouth and spoke briefly into it. Oxygen had not been required at the altitudes at which we had flown, therefore the mask was left hanging until such time as the pilot needed to talk on the radio. Now he reached over to fiddle with something else, the aircraft slowing even more as flaps and gear sighed into place ready for the landing. (In earlier marks of aircraft the landing gear needed to wound down manually, though in that case the pilot would seat a cadet alongside him; a front seat view in exchange for some hard graft.) We were on finals, engines throttled back, nose high, floating, floating, until, with a barely perceptible bump, we were down. That was it. Flight over. We were taxying in, earthbound once more. I was back on that farm tractor, and the hollow-sounding thuds echoed as before, but everything else was different. The sounds and the smells were now familiar rather than new, apprehension had given way to wonder. But, most significant of all, I realized bonds had been severed.

Often, it seems, we don't recognize the good times in life until they are well past, but for me there were to be two exceptions, of which this was the first. It was absolutely fantastic (as would be the second!). I experienced a sensation I was unlikely ever to forget. I had become intoxicated by the science of flight, had broken the bonds which shackled lesser mortals to earth. My growing love of aeroplanes became even deeper.

*

Within the month, myself, along with other members of our ATC squadron, travelled north for the annual summer camp, and I do mean up north. All the way to Leuchars, Scotland. A foreign shore at last? Had to be, didn't it, for they spoke kind of funny up there: och, aye, dinna ken, and stuff like that. They also played something called golf, drank a lot of something called whisky and, on occasion, some of the men even took to wearing skirts!
Something *we* could well have taken to wearing would have been a wet-suit, especially the day we walked back to camp, after hacking divots out of St Andrews' hallowed fairways. We'd decided that rather than follow the road round to the bridge, we would take a shortcut across those mud flats!

We did make it halfway, only to discover what any map, or commonsense, should have told us; a river flowed through it. Ah well, win some, lose some. Back to square one!

On the RAF base at Leuchars, a venerable old Avro Anson was to provide the means of defying gravity. It was an aircraft type with which I would soon become rather familiar. But not this particular week. For also in the offing was a flight in another type. Something rather special, even back when there were more than one or two around. This flight, we were informed, was to be awarded to the cadet who had already logged the highest number of hours. Unfortunately, that information proved to be false. I say unfortunately, and such was to be the case for that high flying cadet, for, with but a piddling thirty minutes in *my* log, and some quirk of fate, I found myself en-route to RAF Waddington, down amongst the Lincolnshire potato fields. I'd apparently traded a flight in an Anson for one in a Lancaster, not that I was complaining. Four plus hours as against thirty minutes. Was this some kind of omen, I wondered?

To my everlasting shame, I have to admit the only moments I am able to recall of what should have been a memorable flight were - somewhat hampered by my parachute harness - clambering over the main spar on my way forward. Then, at the end of it all, of standing by the aircraft on the ground.

Surely, at that age, whilst avoiding flak, I would have kept a wary eye peeled for an imagined attack from "the Hun in the sun"? Or did I crouch in the nose, watching Holland slide past below as we headed for the dams of the Ruhr? And what about the sound of those famous Merlins, that aeronautical symphony of the war years? Not a bit of it.

I do remember the touchdown though - difficult not to - although I won't dwell on it, apart from saying we thumped down in a landing the pilot certainly shouldn't have been proud of. In fact, had he been honest with himself he'd have logged at least two landings.

Whatever the reason, for 1950, that was it. A particularly barren year of but two powered flights, not counting gliding training at nearby Rufforth of course. Those flights were in the Slingsby T21 Sedburgh, also built locally, in Kirkbymoorside.

Seated alongside the instructor I watched, waited, and listened as he nodded to a cadet, who then lifted a wingtip. Wings level, the instructor now ran through his pre flight checks. "Controls." He seemed to whang the stick from side to side, back and forth, kicking the rudder pedals. "Full and free travel," he confirmed. Next he checked the instruments, not a great task, this - just an airspeed indicator, and the red and green balls of the variometer, neither of which required setting up in any way! - checked the spoilers, trim, and release mechanism. Satisfied, he called to another cadet, standing off to one side. "Take up slack." At which the cadet signalled underhand with a bat to the man on the distant winch. The cable, snaking through the grass, began to straighten. "All out," he called, as the cable tightened. The bat was now waved overhead, giving us full power on the winch, cable creaking as it took up the strain and we began to move, faster and faster. The lad on the wingtip charged along with us, but only for a short distance, until the controls became effective. Then we were up and away, cable singing in the air below. 200 feet, ... 400, 600. Then the pilot jerked a knob to release us, the cable, with its small stabilising parachute falling earthwards. A slight moment of apprehension; we were 800ft above the ground! in an aircraft without power! Then I settled. We were airborne in silent flight, the view magnificent, sensation, terrific.

A few more flights in the Sedburgh and then it was on to the T31 Cadet, in which the instructor sat behind the pupil, out of sight. He was a passenger now, may as well not have been there, for you had control. And, sometime in the near future, he *wouldn't* be there!

So much for the gliding, but those two powered flights did account for five and a quarter hours, an annual total not bettered for the next five years, although, to me hours had become less important than types. There was the Wellington, in 1951 - another coup, that. ATC summer camp again, RAF Finningley this time, down by Doncaster, with day and night flying on the agenda. Next was the Anson, at Dishforth - another place that, two years hence, was to play a significant role in my aeronautical life. The Anson, too, was to perform a important function, for, apart from fifteen minutes aerobatics in a Tiger Moth, the Anson was to be the only type on offer over the next two years.

*

And so to that Tiger Moth (N5130). Although fifteen minutes may seem rather short in the matter of flight time, these were to be action-packed minutes for a lad, for during this flight it seemed the intention was that the wheels should point anywhere but at the ground.

I waddled out to the aircraft at Doncaster airport - a grass strip within the confines of the racecourse. My parachute - which doubled as a seat cushion - was already strapped to my behind, making walking a difficult and ungainly performance, even for a grown man. I recalled seeing a lad at school walk like this after he'd been caught short and suffered the indignity of an embarrassing accident. I felt it to be entirely possible I may well duplicate his act at any moment. As for climbing aboard, that was doubly difficult. But in this I was helped by the pilot, who then fastened the Sutton Harness, strapping me as tightly as possible into the biplane's open cockpit. He also fitted my helmet and goggles.

'You all right?' he asked.

'Of course,' I told him. What did he expect me to say? Even if my mouth was as dry as a Muslim's wine cellar.

I could see little ahead but the instruments, and there are not too many of those in a Tiger Moth. Then came the start-up - the prop swung by hand - and take off from the grass; exhilarating stuff. Biggles. The wind in my face. I imagined the only things to be missing were a silk scarf and a moustache. And possibly a touch of panache?

Too late now to change your mind, I told myself. Anyway, I was all right. Wasn't I?

In perfect conditions we climbed to fifteen hundred, apprehensive, heart-thumping feet, high above Doncaster, my degree of anticipation climbing to match the altitude. Then we levelled out, and I noticed the pilot's grinning image in the rear-view mirror. He raised a thumb, I responded likewise. But I was too enthusiastic, raised my arm too high. The slipstream caught my hand and shook it around so much I felt I must look like a hitchhiker with diarrhoea. Well, the next few seconds will reveal all, I thought, dragging my arm back in to safety. And so they did, for this is when it happened.

The nose dropped and we were going down, absolutely vertical, speed increasing as green fields filled the windscreen, expanding rather rapidly as we hurtled towards them, it seemed. Then back came the stick, G force pushing me down in the seat as we recovered, and we were on the way up again, into a loop. Green fields to brown earth to blue sky to brown earth to green fields. Wow, what had I been worried about? Fantastic.

It was when we went over the second time, to remain inverted, that I said my prayers, and my goodbyes. With the engine popping and banging away, my goggles, not fitting too well anyway, disappeared off my head. So what? Didn't really need them seated as low as I was, thought I. Which is when *was* suddenly became the operative word. Being of relatively small stature meant there was a fair bit of slack in the Sutton Harness, I therefore found myself to be sliding up in my seat, which of course meant *down,* towards Donny racecourse. Oh, no!

For a heart-stopping second or two I thought I was a goner, about to be involuntarily ejected. One hand - the one that didn't have a white-knuckled grip on whatever piece of airframe happened to be convenient - shot towards the ripcord release. It would have been embarrassing if I'd popped the 'chute, but I didn't. I couldn't. Don't know what it was I had hold of, but it certainly wasn't the D-ring. No matter, my departure was firmly halted when the shoulder harness finally did its job, preventing me from emulating Icarus, albeit with myself starting at a much lower altitude.

Then we were right side up again, the sky in its rightful place, wings level, engine running sweetly, my heartbeat decreasing. A further bonus was that my bum was back where it belonged, firmly on that parachute pack. The grandstand at Donny racecourse seemed destined to remain deserted after all.

A quick check of the rearview mirror assured me of the

fact that the pilot had also retained his seat, and after that nothing mattered, which was as well, for we went through the repertoire: loops, rolls, stalls, even a spin. OK, the spin had me worried, but only a little, and not for long, for recovery from it saw us on a sideslipping approach to that grassy runway. The only remaining worry was whether or not I would be charged for what had amounted to a rather tatty old pair of goggles. But even that turned out to be a negative problem. I discovered them hanging off the back of my leather helmet once we'd landed and I was taking a stomach-settling walk back to join the rest of the group. Naturally, they were there, well secured, just as I had been.

'How was it?' my mates asked.

'Fantastic,' I replied. Well, what else would they expect me to say?

*

1951. The Festival of Britain, war in Korea, unrest in Iran and Egypt, the first hydrogen bomb test, the Goon Show; that kind of year. It was also the year I decided to quit school, this being the earliest age at which you could chose to opt out. At that age, the way I had it figured, neither Shakespeare, Wordsworth, nor Algebra were going to be of much help to me picking potatoes! I didn't have any great ambitions, you see. So opt out I did, not realizing at that age just how important education was.

It was goodbye to the exams, those sighs of relief, or groans of despair as we opened test papers and scanned the contents. (Back then, exam results didn't warrant mention in newspapers or on TV. No A, B, C, and on down through the alphabet "passes", either. You achieved the required 60% or above for a pass, or you failed. Nothing in between.) Goodbye also to the smell of chalk dust, to school meals, and free milk. An undistinguished schooling from an undistinguished State school, then, though I don't suppose I fared too badly, according to a report dated 1950. Third in class? Not too shabby, I suppose, out of a class of around thirty, though I must have had some pretty dumb schoolmates, given my results in certain subjects. Take art, for instance: "Has done better". And art was one of my favourites, even if I wasn't much good at it. The trouble was, I could visualize things perfectly. It was when those images were transferred to paper that discrepancies were to be found. Like giving a Rubik Cube to a chimpanzee, I'd occasionally produce something recognizable - aeroplanes dropping bombs; square cars; rectangular buses - but even those were more by luck than talent. (Although over the years I did improve, especially on the aeronautical side. Lockheed's beautifully curvaceous Constellation and the Handley Page Victor, with its smooth flowing lines. Both were to become positive favourites. But by then I suppose I was at last becoming aware of just how beautiful and attractive curves could be, especially when applied to the right type of body.)

Perhaps I'd been elevated up the order because my failures were in relatively minor subjects. Things like gardening, religious instruction, and woodwork. But science? Can't understand that. Possibly my very favourite subject. Must have been an off day when I sat the science exam. As for biology, well... a little practical during the birds and bees phase could have proved useful in later years. For me, at least. Some of the lads seemed to have done all right. Getting a little private tuition on the side, as it were. I recall one lad who became known as "Shaggy" McDonald. No need for details on how one acquired such a nickname; suffice it to say, it had less to do with his appearance than it did with the fact that he reputedly "got plenty". Can't keep away from it, they said. And there was I - no doubt along with scores of others - the enigmatic "they" - couldn't get near it. Whatever "It" was supposed to be!

'It's not just for peeing through, tha knows.' That's all Shaggy was prepared to say, when broached on the subject.

OK, so the biology would come naturally, but upon leaving school I didn't exactly feel truly conversant with the mechanics of the three Rs. In fact they were so far removed from my frame of reference I wasn't even sure if three was the number of R's there were supposed to be - and if so, what about the matter of spelling!

But I *was* conversant with the basics: I could read, write and spell, add and subtract figures well enough, without the aid of a calculator if I may say, which were yet years away. (Much later in life, computerized cash registers having become the norm - if not essential - I recall asking the price of something, somewhere. I think it may have been a sightseeing boat trip along the Thames. Anyway, when advised of the price, I asked for three - because there were three of us! - and as the girl started tapping away on the keys of her machine, I told her the price. She continued tapping until the answer came up, then looked at me, astounded. "How did you know that?" she asked.

An even better example was a time I was shopping in a

supermarket. The lad on the checkout was a trainee - so a sign advised us, and it showed - for after scanning only three low cost items the price indicated was around £30! I pointed this out to him, and after a bit of head scratching he began again. I watched even more closely than normal, and things were still not right, but so as not to hold things up I let him carry on, and paid. I then went straight to Customer Services and pointed out a glaring error on my receipt to the supervisor. The lady reached beneath her desk and came up with a calculator. I said, 'You don't need a calculator to see that.' She retorted, 'I do,' and continued punching buttons. The she looked at me and said, 'You are right. We owe you £70', and handed me the cash. My total bill was only around £90! So she was right, she did need a calculator. But most of all she needed to learn how to use one!)

I was also aware of other things that mattered in life: minding your manners, saying please and thank you, showing respect for your elders (most of the time), and self discipline. Little courtesies that seem long since to have disappeared from everyday life.

There was to be no further formal education in civilian life, but the lack of a piece of paper didn't seem to hinder me, apart from the fact that I couldn't decide what it was I wanted to do. I therefore took a job as a relatively low-paid, trainee motor engineer - perhaps mechanic. I joined a local company, Park Engineering. Small and specialist, with only around half a dozen employees, it was owned and operated by a church minister, who was also an astute engineer and businessman. Definitely not a garage, for the core business was refurbishing engines for local garages. We re-bored cylinders, or fitted new liners; ground crankshafts; re-metalled bearings, or fitted shells; even repaired cracked blocks. Today, they throw the old engine away and fit a complete new unit. It's the cheaper option, we're led to believe!

This work was carried out in a long wooden shed on stilts, which meant it was freezing cold in winter. So, being the junior employee, one of my tasks was to light the stove first thing in the morning. This took time to heat the place up, but it was assisted in this by the very large bath of hot paraffin, used to clean engine parts etc before they were worked upon. This bath also needed to be heated, although I don't recall how this was actually achieved. But can you imagine the fire hazzard: a wooden hut, oil, petrol, hot paraffin, welding torches, and a glowing, potbellied stove! Health and Safety really would have had a fit. Such things would never be allowed in this day and age. The business would have been another of those to be shut down. I can see their line of reasoning. But accidents only occur if one is aware of the risks, and still fails to take care. We never encountered any such problems.

I learnt a lot of engineering practice during my short time in the business. I also managed to remain reasonably happy, for between bouts of stripping and cleaning engines, re-metalling bearings, making tea, sweeping up, and liberally coating myself with oil and grime, I continued to pursue my new-found love.

*

Along with around twenty thousand others, my eyes were directed heavenwards. We awaited a sign of some kind. This had nothing to do with the Almighty, although we were a kind of cult. Why else would ten thousand presumably sane people gather at an almost deserted airfield?

'See anything?' I asked my friend and fellow ATC cadet, Ivan, who lay nearby on the grass.

'A seagull just flew over, but apart from that, nothing but sky and clouds,' he replied, but he kept looking. 'How about you?'

'I'm looking.'

What we sought was the aircraft the commentator advised was now beginning its dive, aiming itself directly towards us. But as Ivan had said, there was nothing to be seen, apart from a few puffy white clouds set against a familiar background of blue. I'd even missed the seagull.

My day had already been fulfilling, for earlier I had been close enough to Neville Duke to be able to take his photograph, along with that of the Hawker Tomtit he was later to fly, but the real excitement was here and now, building all the time.

It was yet another of those almost-perfect sunny days, peaceful and comforting. The air felt so dry it almost seemed to hum with stillness, yet there must have been a modicum of humidity present. Not exactly conditions that were likely to generate excitement, but it was there all right, I felt it, as did everyone. You could sense that.

Neither of us quite knew what to expect, but my adrenalin was certainly flowing, and I was carried away by it. Up on that plateau I felt less exposed, less vulnerable, lying on the ground, on my back. Watching. Waiting.

Still nothing, and now the place was almost silent. Apart from a few muted words it was as if the rest of the crowd, too, was holding its collective breath.

Suddenly, a voice broke the silence. 'There!' A finger pointed. Another voice, another finger, this to be followed by a plethora of fingers.

I sat up, turned my eyes in the direction indicated, caught a minute, brief flash of silver, then it was gone; if it had even been there. Was my imagination running wild?

'You see it, Ivan? I did.'

'You sure?'

'I think I did.'

No. It was there all right. The excited babbling of the crowd told me so. The tension rose. 'How loud d' you think it'll be?' I asked.

'Dunno,' Ivan replied. 'D' you think it'll harm our ears?'

'Dunno,' I said. 'Ask that fella next to you. Surely someone's heard it before?'

Then, before Ivan could ask anyone, so had I. Not once, but twice. Boom-boom! In rapid succession. The characteristic double report of an aircraft breaking the sound barrier. Not ear-shattering at all. Nor was it faint. A sound you could actually feel, especially when it is aimed right at you; the supersonic shockwave. Another truly magical moment in life.

It was to be many long seconds before the actual aircraft put in an appearance, a low whine announcing the arrival of an F86 Sabre. It continued its dive, headed our way, wings swept back rakishly. As yet distant and small, it looked incapable of generating any great degree of sound.

That was Yeadon, on the site of the old Avro factory in West Yorkshire (now Leeds/Bradford International Airport) on a warm spring day in 1952, one of the first of my many visits to air shows.

In those far-off, gung-ho days of public entertainment, the rules for display pilots were apparently few and far between. No Health and Safety Executive (for Executive, read Gestapo) back then, so they flew fast and low, almost skimming the ground. Towards the crowd if that was deemed most effective. And it often was, for there is little to match the effect of a fast jet travelling directly towards you, as had that Sabre towards us.

Even the faint whine diminished to almost zero as the aircraft grew larger and larger, wide-open mouth gulping air.

'Looks like one of those desk-top models, floating in the sky,' Ivan observed.'

'Yeah. But why no noise?' No matter what else I had learned, I was obviously as yet unaware of the difference in speed between sound and light. But Ivan was. There again, I'd always assumed him to be smarter than me. Not that I'd ever have told him so.

'Science, remember? Sound and light? Only a difference of one hundred and eighty-five thousand, nine hundred and ninety-eight miles per second,' he quoted.

'Huh! Must have been asleep when that came up. Or at home, ill. Had to be. Let's face it, a difference of that magnitude I wouldn't have missed.'

'Tell you what, he's shifting all right,' Ivan said. 'Full chat, I reckon.' (It was the phrase we used; these days it would probably be "megga".)

He was, too. Unburnt Avtur was being chucked out the back at a ferocious rate, vortices shimmering above and below the wings as he finally levelled out. And, even if it did still the crowd, that silence was deceptive, nor was it destined to last. A fraction of a second after the machine flashed past it became a silence torn asunder, a thunderous blast leaving the air crackling in its wake.

'Bloody hell!' my friend exclaimed. But by then the aircraft was gone, a rapidly decreasing speck travelling in the vertical plane, the visual thrill heightened by the aural effect. Truly spectacular, even if those were pre afterburner days. (Things were to become appreciably more spectacular over the years - Vulcan, Lightning, Phantom, Tornado, Eurofighter - know known in the RAF as the Typhoon.)

It still wasn't enough for me. I had actually touched an aircraft, yes. I'd even flown in one or two, and almost fallen out of one, I often kidded myself. But the opportunities for flight were too few. I decided I'd become a collector of types rather than a mere spotter - a collector of registrations that is. And for a type to qualify on my list, I had to have flown in it. So far I'd bagged the Oxford, that Lancaster, plus Wellington, Anson, and Tiger Moth. Not bad for a start. But I needed more. Lots more. And I thought I had discovered just where to get them. Hands-on, as it were.

*

1953. Frankie Lane was telling us, *I Believe*, Guy Mitchell was raving on about a girl who, *Wears Red Feathers*, and David

Whitfield was appealing for yet another girl to, *Answer Me*. All these, the popular music of the time, along with Crosby, Sinatra, etc, were brought to us courtesy of Radio Luxembourg's Top Twenty. BBC was the domain of Big Band music: Ted Heath, Stan Kenton, Benny Goodman et al. But for me the year was a turning point. Unable to accept my station in life as an eight-to-five nonentity, I decided to make a break for freedom, to seek excitement, stretch my wings.

For eighteen months I had been a trainee mechanic. What I learnt during that period was to serve me well in future years, but right now, I decided it wasn't what I wanted. Nor, it seemed, was I what the girls wanted, for regardless of the fact that incident-filled outings on *terra firma* were becoming more of a rarity, I was still having little luck in the biology department. This despite the fact I regularly attended the local dances; the drapes, the blue suede shoes, quiff in my hair, condom tucked away in my wallet. (But beware the telltale outline. Could be embarrassing when pulling out your wallet to buy a girl a drink?) I'd obtained a pack of three from the hairdresser, the least humiliating place from which to buy them, as, when paying for my haircut, the standard question had been asked: "And would there be anything for the weekend, sir?" A mumbled reply had them palmed across, along with my change. One lived in hope.

Three of us split them among us, for there was little chance of getting to use even one. Still, if I learned nothing else in the scouts, I knew what it meant to "Be Prepared".

Come to think of it, I believe I may still have mine!

*

About the time the posher and tub were replaced by a rudimentary washing machine, and a modern refrigerator at last graced our kitchen, I was to leave home for the first period exceeding two weeks.

I'd been presented with a travel warrant, the first of many. I suppose it was really a one-way ticket to the future, for this was no mere journey I was about to undertake. It had to be an adventure, in that I wasn't sure where it would end, what I would be doing, or what I was about to become. It could turn out to be a road to nowhere, but I had to find out. One thing was for sure, I had but two choices: slide further down the social scale, or climb up it. I figured I'd try for the latter. Back them, most did. In this I was helped by a quote from Dad: "It's not the start you have in life that matters, David, it's how you conduct yourself from that point on. And the finish. That's how you'll be judged."

I would return to Norton. Eventually. But by then things would have changed. Childhood was behind me, part of the past. Life would never be the same again.

*   *

THE WAY WE WERE
1998

*W*here have all the years gone? It seemed like only yesterday when horse-drawn ploughs tilled these Yorkshire fields, rich, dark earth curling over like heavy surf, gulls following close behind looking for all the world like they too were being towed along. And what of those rainy Sundays when I would sit with friends in Malton's only fifties-style coffee bar - up Saville Street - they too seemed eons in the past; both coffee bar and friends. They are, of course, for it *had* been the fifties. Even so, the recollections were clear: Interior windows steam-dampened by the Gaggia - a glass and chrome monster with a vast array of knobs, levers, gauges, pipes and tubes, like something out of science fiction. It sat on the counter, hissing and gurgling as if in accompaniment to the juke box which pounded out the latest hits, but it did produce what we saw as a good cup of coffee, known to us back then as Expresso. Which in fact it still is, prior to steam-heated milk being added.

In recollection, they were gentler, more tranquil times that now, viewed over the decades, seem to have passed far too swiftly. But isn't that always the way with time; some hours pass far too quickly - especially if you are pressed, and there is a girl involved - others can seem like a lifetime. Years are obviously subject to a similar analogy. Did the sun really shine more in the days of our youth, I often wonder? Did we really enjoy the card-like qualities of snow and frost at Christmas? Or are these just memories, viewed through those rose-tinted glasses of retrospect?

But life in general *had* been different back then, just as we had been different. Not only in the obvious ways of having less money, no television, and no luxuries. (It seems there are few luxuries today, either. But for a far different reason. Things that would once have been classed as luxuries are now taken for granted; demanded almost, preferably for free.)

These thoughts came to me as I took a nostalgic walk along the banks of the Derwent, each thought providing the inspiration for another.

When we were young this river had appeared to be grand. A wide, silvery waterway of unknown and terrifying depth, which effectively divided one town into two. Today I saw it for what it was: an unimpressive brown smear, a river of laughable minuteness, across which, in places, I imagined I could probably wade. I also saw its use as a boundary as being a political ruse. After all, don't two towns require two sets of bureaucrats, as opposed to one!

There again, as previously mentioned, Malton did have those two breweries, and around thirty pubs. Got to know some of those pubs quite well eventually: The Gate, Green Man, Ginger Dyson's, a couple more in the market, maybe the Blue Ball. But I'd invariably end up at Paddy's; the Cross Keys, on Wheelgate. Still, no matter, a lot of them are now history, as are the breweries which had owned and supplied them.

Whatever, Norton was where I grew up, so it is Norton that affords memories aplenty, for they *are* now only memories. There was the glow of the forge at that blacksmiths shop which I passed on my way to and from infants school, off Wood Street. Embers were fanned to a white heat by means of a long wooden pole which operated the bellows. I hear the "ring, ring" of the hammer as the smithy bounced it off the anvil between blows, the dull thud as it struck white-hot metal, smoke rising as a glowing shoe seared a hoof, myself flinching as it did so, expecting the animal to lash out with its foot. It didn't, even as the nails went in.

I went through the usual gamut of boyish things. Collections of this and that: birds' eggs, cigarette cards, the odd Dinky toy. (Today the bird's eggs would be illegal, those cards and Dinky toys probably worth a fortune.) There had also been the Meccano phase, and the American comics - Captain Marvel, Superman and such. I recall dad coming home with a cardboard box full one time. Goodness knows how he came by those, but what a treat. They lasted me for weeks.

Ingrained memories of Norton, North Yorkshire, then. This, after all, was where I had spent my boyhood, in a pub; the Griffin Hotel.

Almost directly opposite the Griffin had been the local cinema, the Majestic, handy for freebie viewing, that. And it had been rather majestic, certainly the most imposing building in town. Impressive steps led to small-paned glass doors which, bracketing the "stills" display, gave access to the foyer. Another pair of doors bracketed the box office, but were set back, out of its line of sight. Ease one of these open a crack, lo and behold, there was the screen. It was a vantage point from which I viewed the clips of many a movie; occasionally warranting the odd clip round the ear from an unusually alert commissionaire. But the Majestic is no more, for the record reads: Built 1923, closed 1953, demolished 1966. In fact the whole block had gone: Elliott's corner shop, the chemist, next door - Timothy White's - and Nestfield's forge. All demolished long before the days when people began to appreciate old buildings. The cinema not even given over to bingo. A garage and filling station now occupy the site.

Actually, the Majestic was not the cinema of choice for us youngsters, that was the Palace, up in Malton, for it was here that the Saturday morning shows were screened: Buck Rogers, Tom and Gerry etc. Nor did we go to the cinema, or the movies; to us it was the pictures.

*

The old home town I found to be somewhat depressing. It wasn't that the memories of childhood had been swept away. Not at all. Most of it was still there, but not necessarily in the form I remembered. Nor had it changed for the better like a lot of places had, for it wasn't a tourist town. More degeneration than modernization here.

The atmosphere was shabbily authentic, but it was no longer complete. Gone was the family grocer up Castlegate, the site now hosting a hardware outlet. I recall the way that store used to look once rationing had been lifted. The window, the legend it bore; raised gold lettering on a dark green background: Thos Taylor & Son (no relation, unfortuneately!), Purveyors Of Fine Foods. Walk inside and a blend of sights and aromas would assail the senses. Coffee beans, the large silver and red contraption which ground them, taking pride of place on the long, wide, oak counter. From the ceiling hung cured York hams, ready for slicing, or to be sold whole. On the polished hardwood floor were sacks of this and that: tea, sugar, flour, rice. There were tubs of butter. Little was pre-packed, apart from the crisps - packets of which contained a blue paper wrap of salt, to do with as you pleased (it would appear that, back then, salt *wasn't* all that bad for us!). Service was as the word implies, a pleasure, and personal.

Gone too was the little house up Wold Street from which, over the top half of a stable door, we used to buy that home-made ice-cream. More like iced custard really. Delicious for all that; in the memory.

Even had the house remained, I knew production of that ice-cream would now be banned by modern hygiene laws. Ostensibly introduced to protect us from ourselves, but which

67

more and more appear to be a ban on anything that offers satisfaction. It's as if Brussels, finding something that gives pleasure or enjoyment, immediately felt the need to dream up masses of legislation, effectively to ban it. Same thing applies to the few "chippies" that remain. So as to compete with the Chinese and Indian take-aways, pizza parlours and the like, the "chippies" had been driven to offering battered sausages and hamburgers. Fish and chips *are* still available, though it's doubtful they'll be cooked in anything other than some refined, homogenized, low-cholesterol, vegetable concoction; with a full complement of those mysterious E-number additives, of course. Mustn't forget those. And just what are *they* doing to our bodies over the years? Only God, and time, has the answer to that. Then there are the chips themselves: frozen, and crinkle-cut. Signs of the times; maximum profit for minimum effort. As for service, forget about that altogether. It now seems to be a case of shops selling what *they* want to sell (whatever offers the best return), rather than what the customer would actually like to buy.

As there were no such things as computers, and televisions were few and far between, we kept ourselves entertained in other ways. Healthy, outdoor entertainment - most those activities now frowned upon, if not banned outright. There was no Health and Safety Executive to mollycoddle us, thank God. Basic health and safety was the prerogative of the individual, as it should be. Even so, we rarely washed our hands after visiting the toilet, rarely suffered for it. Our immune systems were obviously well up to scratch. We climbed trees, and fell out of them. We played conkers without injuring ourselves, rode our bikes without any head protection! There were no fast food chains and no mobile phones! God! How did we ever survive!

*

I turned into a road I'd once known so well yet now hardly recognised. I was a stranger to this street.

But no. Some of the older buildings looked vaguely familiar when studied up close. For instance: replace the double-glazing in number ten with a small-paned bay, imagine that fancy PVC door to be paint-flaked wood, remove the pseudo-concrete finish from the brickwork, and presto! That was where my friend Mike, aka, "Taggo", had lived. And back then, especially in the summer, that door would have been wide open most of the time, an invitation for friends to call in for a cup of tea and a chat - another thing that is no longer possible in our modern, crime-ridden, but supposedly better society.

Not a stranger after all, then; the street was a stranger to me. I'd expected it, though. They said it happened to people returning to a childhood haunt. But even if some of the originality did remain, the magic had definitely gone.

Gone too was the corner shop where I'd once squandered my pennies on the few sweets that were available. Gone was that forge next door. There used to be two forges, I remembered. Absolutely necessary, what with two breweries, whose drays were horse-drawn, and a farming community in which tractors were a rarity, to say nothing of the racing stables. Not now. No breweries, no blacksmiths. A sad loss all round.

That town held the history of my childhood, the Griffin, particularly so, and now it too was no more. The building was intact, externally, only its days as a pub were history, my father seeing it through to the end. I remembered the day they removed the sign from outside. With the removal of that sign the life went out of the house; for me it died. My father missed it too, even though he moved just across the road, from number seven to number ten. He had the sight of it to stir the memories, if that was what he wished, and the knowledge that he had been the last landlord of that particular Griffin. It was something he'd vowed, ever since the brewery first talked of closing it down: that they would close it around him.

But I realized I couldn't expect the town not to have changed, for it to remain my own private museum of nostalgia, on the off-chance I may one day return.

Mabel and Dad lived at number ten for quite a number of years, but now both are gone, even if they remain in spirit.

But it was outside town where the memories really came flooding back. Yes, you need to travel further these days to find yourself out of town, but once there, you could almost be back in the past. If it wasn't for the school.

Norton Boys Secondary was the last school I'd attended. What today would be termed Comprehensive, were it still in existence, right there on Commercial Street, next to the "Cop shop". That it is not, accounted for this more modern, less aesthetic structure out here in the country. At least, what *had* been country; now the outer fringes of town.

Gone too were the bike sheds. Pity that. Handy, those bike sheds. Chiefly for what purportedly went on behind them.

That thought produced a smile. Rumours and stories, most of which I dismissed as untrue. After all, it had never happened to me. Difficult really, in a boys-only school.

Of such are boyhood memories made. Or shattered!

And so, back to York, where I now live.

As it looked like being a nice day I had travelled over by train, for old times sake. I find myself using the trains much more these days, quite enjoy the experience. The run down station is still credited to Malton, still sited in Norton. Boarding the train from Scarborough I found it too to be very different now: open carriages, no slamming of doors, for they are mostly electronically controlled by the driver or guard. This prevents people from doing stupid things, then suing the railway for allowing them the freedom to think for themselves.

On our way. The River Derwent looks smaller than ever. A high sun beamed down upon empty fields which looked as if they shouldn't be empty. They looked like they should have children chasing across them, waving butterfly nets or clutching jars of sticklebacks.

Through the valley and past Kirkham Abbey. The ground here, too steep for farming, was given over to forestry. Trees and ferns, native wildflowers; weeds to city folk. Cows went about their lazy existence, head down to the grass. The hillside revealed a warren of rabbits, not so lazy, these! There was a group of pigeons, now a crow, a pair of pheasants, unworried as they pecked around, seemingly aware the guns were legally silenced. Until the Glorious Twelfth that is. Glorious for some. But the pheasants couldn't really know that, could they?

Other fields were planted with crops: turnips, potatoes, wheat, barley. Old stations flashed by, most now converted into country cottages, some tidy and pretty, some best described as rustic.

Eventually, the number of buildings multiplied. Houses first, then industry. Now schools and playing fields, now car parks. Rowntrees chocolate factory. We were back in the City of York, final confirmation as we crossed the Ouse and drew into the station. It too seemed hardly to have changed since that far off day in February 1953.

*   *

PHOTOPAGE-1:

Page 72 Top: Aged 4, with George, 5, & Maureen, 7. 1940. **Centre:** A few years later, jungle-bashing in Malaya 1958. **Bottom:** Slim & trendy in the Swinging Sixties.

Page 73 Top left: Aged about seven. School photo. **Top right:** In the ATC, ready to climb aboard a Tiger Moth. **Bottom:** Ex-ATC friends pose for a group photograph with our ex-CO Eric Cryer. L to R: Norman Wilson, Michael Headley, W Stevenson, Malcolm Wilson, the CO, Ivan Halstead, Bob Gerard, Terry Hornby, Graham Tinsley, David Taylor.

Page 74: Father in floods. The cellar was always first in line.

Page 75 Top: The big one, 1947. Taken from an upstairs window, naturally. **Bottom:** Granddad Taylor's Garage, Scarborough, along with two of his charabancs.

Page 76 Top L: Aged two, contemplating a shoe perhaps? **Top R:** Dad and his pigeon loft. **Bottom:** Sunday on the Moors. Maureen, George, ?, myself, Mum & Tessie.

Page 77 Top: The Griffin Hotel, home for around twenty of my formative years. **Centre:** Mother: Doris Lucy Sale. **Bottom:** Stepmother Mabel & Dad's wedding.

Page 78 Top L: Niece Anne & sister Maureen. **R:** George, whilst at Scarborough Boys High School. **Centre L:** Grandma & Grandad Taylor. **R:** More like "The Godfather" than Grandfather: George Sale (right) and companion. **Bottom:** The cabin cruiser. Only it was long gone by the time the floods came!

Page 79 Top: A Lancia coach. Scarborough, 1930s. **Centre:** Packed in and ready for an all male day out. **Bottom L:** When I had enough hair to perm. The girls appeared to like it. **Bottom R:** Dad in the army. WO1, probably 1942.

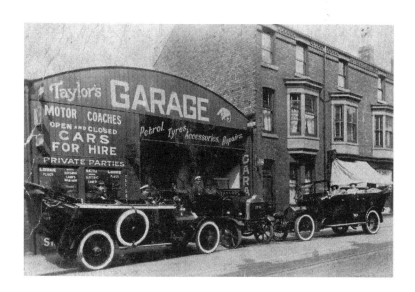

Chapter Two
TAKEOFF

All railway stations have a fascination of their own. In the 1950's they could be cold, depressing places at any time of day, but at seven o'clock on a February morning, York was particularly so. Yet here was I, at this unearthly hour, already on my second station of the day. The first had been Malton, from where my parents had seen me safely on my way for what I saw as a the first short leg of a very long journey.

A new week had already begun. Not just a new week, possibly a new start in life. For here in the gloomy cavern of concrete, steel, and glass that was York, things did seem entirely different. This was the real beginning, for I was now alone, mentally at least. And even though a number of other people did await trains, they were silent and moody-looking, despite the fact it was already Tuesday. No fractious children charged around, no dogs barked, there were no loud goodbyes, no station announcements, few trains. There was, in fact, nothing but a distinct chill in the air, and a lonely silence. This was to be disturbed only by the arrival of a train. Thankfully, mine.

It was the 17th of the month. The year was 1953. My only luggage consisted of a small, cheap, compressed-cardboard suitcase. My first suitcase. The first of many. Though I wasn't yet to know that. This one held little apart from my hopes and dreams. Where I was going I wouldn't need much more. But dreams, once validated, become memories

My boarding was to be followed by a slamming of doors, the last minute rush of late-comers, the search for seats, the stowing of luggage, the shedding of gloves, of hats, and coats. Then, with a blast on his whistle and the wave of a flag - answered in turn by the engine's whistle, shrill and echoing - the guard boarded the train just as it gave a jerk and prepared to move off. The wheels of adventure had begun to turn, though we were not yet underway, steel wheels on steel tracks momentarily slipping and spinning. Then they found traction, and we did move. Forward. On into the unknown. But there was sure to be more than adventure ahead, for wasn't this a new life I sought? And me without qualifications of any kind, apart from my secondary education, the will to learn, and a modicum of military knowledge, courtesy of the Air Training Corps.

Though my face remained stoically calm, internally I was in turmoil. Being a shy lad that was something I'd already learned; to put a brave face on things, no matter what. When challenged by Norton's dreaded "Beverley Road Gang" it was either that or the shame of bursting into tears, for the chances were you'd likely get a beating, anyway. (This is called bullying. It has, and always will be, part of life. One needs to learn to deal with it oneself. These days, when children no longer seem prepared, or able, to fend for themselves, such incidents would likely end up in court, part of that seemingly never-ending quest for compensation. Or they would at least make the newspapers.)

The engine hissed steam and chuff-chuffed clouds of sulphurous grey coal-smoke. This broiled upwards, collecting beneath the already soot-encrusted roof which arched high over the platform. The drive wheels again spun briefly, smoke following the curvature of the blackened, rivet-studded girders, and the glass roof. It dissipated as it rolled down the sides, depositing grime upon grime. Pigeons cooed and fluttered about as they were engulfed, not seeming too perturbed at all. "Should have been here when the bombs came down," you could almost imagine them saying.

I was travelling on my own for the first time in my life. Leaving home. And - although I didn't realize it then - apart from short visits, I had left for good. It was the start of a journey which, I fervently hoped, would surely bring me fame and fortune. OK then.... But at the very least it might satisfy a craving.

I settled myself in the Third Class compartment. Bit degrading, that, to my mind, but back then the railways only offered a choice of First or Third (no idea what became of Second!), my military travel warrant assigning me to the latter.

Out of the eight seats on offer, four faced the future, the rest looked back to where I'd been. No matter which I chose, it was an arrangement that left me the option of either staring my fellow passengers in the eye, looking beyond them, out of the window, or of inspecting their luggage - located in the mesh racks overhead. Pictures, mounted mid-way between face and luggage, did offer an alternative, but even the most avid art critic would be hard pushed to find more than a few minutes interest in those. Gaze at them for any length of time and they started to affect your mind. Colours mutated, lines became blurred. Let's face it, how long could a print of Filey Beach or

Scarborough Castle command the attention? I chose to look towards the future.

The carriage smelled of smoke and soot. It seemed to be ingrained in everything connected with the railways. They too had their own special smell then. Just like my aircraft.

Slowly gathering speed we passed the backs of houses, not noted as being their best profile: sorry little gardens filled with ramshackle sheds and greenhouses, just as ours had been. But once we got up speed the city soon fell behind, taking with it my past. Norton/Malton left behind. York left behind. The world I had known, had seemed condemned to forever, all left behind. Urban gave way to suburban, then once more to rural, and though the lines were now national, the scenery still belonged to Yorkshire. Ploughed, deckle-edged fields, trees and meadows, rivers and streams, hills and valleys - the playgrounds of youth. Despite a lust for change, I'd miss all that. I'd miss home, too, and the rolling moors. I already did. The hollow cry of the curlews, the bleating of the moorjocks, the bees in the heather, the wind, telephone lines that at year's end would resemble sheet music - swifts and swallows the crochets and quavers, travellers about to seek the winter sun. Up there on the high ground it could be a lonely place at any time, deadly in winter. But most of my images had been formed during the summer months.

Forget it. All behind you now.

I switched focus to the telephone lines beside the track. They, it seemed, wished to droop towards the ground, but were not allowed to do so. It was like watching a piece of elastic being jerked this way and that: down, down, down, up, down, up, up, down, then zooming skywards as the train approached a tunnel. Quite fascinating... for a while. I turned my attention instead to those steel wheels; listened. Just like when we used to travel by train to the seaside, they were talking to me. Same familiar chant, but now the message was interpreted differently. Instead of "soon be there, soon be there, soon be there", it was now "leaving home, leaving home, leaving home." Then, as we crossed a junction: "never again to return." But I didn't believe that. Truth be told, they say whatever you wish them to say. So I let my mind wander instead, piecing together events that had led me this far. I looked upon this journey as turning a corner on the past, what little past there was at the ripe old age of sixteen and a half.

To me, it seemed endless.

I took the other alternative to Filey Beach and Scarborough Castle, lay my head back and closed my eyes. The idea was to concentrate on what may greet me upon arrival at my destination. But as I relaxed, I again found the images to be those floating back from over the years.

*

It was a sunny September and the school was on holiday. I was in a field which, to young eyes, seemed to stretch away to eternity. Row upon row of potatoes. Armed with a bucket, I, and a dozen others, trudged along behind a tractor, picking the "spuds" by hand, the earthy smell of freshly turned soil heavy on the air. It was back-breaking work for ten to twelve hours a day, but we were well-paid, and well fed: fresh, home-made apple pies, and buckets of strong, milky tea. And to think they actually gave us time off school to partake of this, which made it a double bonus: no school dinners, and lots of aeroplanes zooming around. I could stare to my heart's content without the threat of being thrown out of the classroom window. Oh yes, they didn't mess about, our teachers. There again, neither did some of the pupils. I recall a rather meek English master whose mild manner was exploited by the tough kids. They knew, of course. Tough kids always know, in school or in life. Clem could never throw anyone out of the window, would likely have gone out himself had he tried. I remember one lad being pulled out for punishment, but it ended up with Clem in a headlock, being punched in the face. His glasses fell to the floor, were immediately stamped on by someone else.

One isolated incident, but at least, back then, a teacher could retaliate. Or, if necessary, have the headmaster retaliate for him. Old Frankish didn't mess about either, it was six of the best, minimum. Only choice we had was hands or backside. Some choice. Yes, it hurt; it was meant to! No harm in that. But it did have the effect of making one think; instilling a modicum of discipline.

*

I awoke to the clamour of movement, people standing, preparing to disembark. We had arrived. Wolverhampton. Almost the end of the beginning of my new life, to paraphrase Winston Churchill. Just the branch line to negotiate now. Albrighton, Shifnal, Cosford Halt, and that would be it.

As I wasn't in farming, or any other "reserved occupation", nor poised to enter university (what, me, a lad from the sticks, in 1952?), Her Majesty would shortly have

83

made demands upon my person. This would have been in letter form. But, rather than an invite to a Royal Garden Party, it would have requested my presence for two years in the service of my country. National Service, it was called. Nor would there have been any chance of escape on medical grounds, for I had already been passed A1: fit to serve.

So here was I, not yet of an age at which I could hold a driving licence, unable to vote for my Parliamentary representation, yet about to join the fighting forces. I had decided not to let conscription claim me for the Army, so to pre-empt the call-up I had volunteered instead to serve twelve years in the Air Force - on completion of Boy Entrant training. OK, twelve years as opposed to two. Surely a much better option than the lottery of serving those two years in some branch of the Army? Had to be, didn't it? After all, I'd be around my beloved aircraft, and I would have a trade at my fingertips. And, should I be successful in my eighteen months training, there was another advantage to be gained: I would pass out as a senior aircraftsman, effectively bypassing the first three rungs of the promotional ladder.

That was the way my thinking went, though my arrival at RAF Cosford left me to conclude that perhaps I had slightly misjudged the situation - not an unusual position for me to find myself in, given my age, and lack of worldly experience.

Upon reporting in I had requested the use of a toilet, somehow became detached from the rest of my group. On enquiry I'd been told to remove myself to some other location, an Induction Centre, or some such. 'You'll find it over there,' said a bored looking airman, waving a hand vaguely in the general direction of the rest of the world.

OK. Nothing for it but to show some initiative. I headed off towards the area indicated, in a general sort of way. Well, let's face it, it had been a general sort of indication.

I set off along what I hoped was the right road; no doubt would have been had I chosen to travel in the opposite direction. A couple more roads - backtracking as it were - brought me to an open area. Which is when I saw them, away in the distance, a group of civilians. Could only be the rest of my intake, I decided, setting off in their direction like a bowling ball towards the pins. Which was about the time I discovered that open area to be "the hated parade ground" - that large expanse of tarmac which forms the central point of almost all military establishments, especially training camps - and to be regarded as sacred. To walk across the hallowed surface, using it as a shortcut, is a definite no-no. (I later remembered someone telling me we'd been taught that in the ATC, as surely we must have been. Anyway, by now the data was irrelevant.) It seemed I had barely set off when I was suddenly overcome by the feeling that there was somewhere else I would rather be. Anywhere but where I was, halfway to my destination, via the shortest route.

Too late. Didn't require a master's degree in sociology to spot that. My secondary education served well enough.

'You, lad! Come here!' About six thousand decibels!

That was something I did remember hearing about parade grounds, they were reputed to be places where loud voices shouted orders and hurled abuse about. No abuse as yet, but the voice - even if not six thousand, was definitely on up there at the top end of the decibel scale - *was* issuing an order. And although I knew the command to be directed at myself, I imagined at least fifty other lads within hearing range automatically looking round, wondering what in hell it was they'd done wrong this time.

Considering this could be the end of the world as I knew it, I thought I coped quite well. I ran smartly to where he stood, coming to attention before him.

'Yes, sir?' Oops! That was something else I remembered, albeit again far too late: never address a senior NCO as sir. That, to them, is as good as an insult. Seems they felt it degraded them, for many considered themselves to be better than officers, especially the drill instructors. This was one of the unwritten rules of service life, of which there appeared to be many. The written rules - in which few but the Service Police and lawyers seemed to have an interest - were contained in a rather unnerving tome known as Queen's Regulations, abbreviated to QR's. Which at present was of academic interest only. The sole exception to the rule I had just transgressed was the Warrant Officer, who was definitely a "sir."

'Not sir! Sergeant! You'll address me as such. What am I?'

I could have told him. 'A Sergeant, Sergeant.' So am I, I felt like adding. Would have, had not the thought occurred that there are times when it pays to be frank and times when it doesn't, even if I was a Sergeant in the ATC. In fact, just as well I hadn't turned up in uniform, for, as a yet to be initiated civilian I was let off with a stern warning. Maybe the fact we were both named Taylor had a bearing, though I seriously doubted it. A tolerant and understanding admin sergeant, then? I doubted that, also.

As it turned out, there was such a thing as a tolerant and understanding admin sergeant, a positive pussy-cat, relatively speaking. He was also later revealed to be our flight commander, after the initial training period. His drill instructor, yet another Taylor - corporal this time - nowhere near as forgiving a creature, I was to find. I took to him much as would an arachnophobe to a tarantula in the bed. There were others, too. Some who appeared to have been recruited on decibel count alone. Certainly nothing that in any way related to IQ, so we told ourselves.

(The drill instructors may have thought themselves better than officers, but they were nowhere near as intelligent, it seems. There are many stories going the rounds, but one of my favourites concerned the drill sergeant who was instructing a group of trainees on the parade ground at an Officer Training School. Most officer trainees would be in their late teens or early twenties, and would likely possess a university education. Despite this, they too faced the rigours of the parade ground, and the wrath of the drill NCOs, and they too were verbally abused, although they were usually addressed as Mr.

So, when one errant young man was prodded in the chest with the sergeant's pace stick, and advisedly told, "There is a piece of sh.. on the end of this stick, Mr Peters. Do you understand?" The young man, very quick on the uptake, replied. "Yes, Sergeant. Which end, Sergeant?"

We are told the parade immediately erupted into laughter, disregarding the sergeant, of course. And I doubt the miscreant laughed for long, either.)

So, I was off to a grand start. Within a couple of minutes I had succeeded in transgressing two of the sacred rules of military life, rules of the unwritten variety. The good news was I'd done it before taking the oath of allegiance - attestation, as the process was called. As I hadn't yet signed on the dotted line, I was still a civilian, therefore, relatively immune to service discipline at present. In theory I could have walked out of the gate. Felt like doing so for a second or two back there. Others would not be so fortunate, for once we had been inducted, issued a service number and kitted out, that would change with a vengeance. Walking out at that point would constitute being

AWOL (absent without leave), a rather serious offence, to say the least.

It took no longer than a couple of days for us to be accommodated, documented, indoctrinated, and medically inspected, en-masse; the works. Even at school all they ever did was check my head for nits, this guy poked and peered everywhere, even going so far as to put his hands where previously only I put them, to relieve myself, in one way or another. This inspection was known as an FFI: free from infection.

We were supplied with brown paper and string, with which to wrap up our civilian clothes for posting home. An indication we wouldn't be needing those for quite some time; another physiological link to civilian life was being severed.

They were gruelling days, the evenings of which were spent relaxing on our beds, which made them seem not so bad (the days, that is). This, I suspect, was a deliberate ploy, for as soon as we did sign on, laying on a bed became a thing of the past, along with any freedom we might previously have enjoyed. The drill instructors would see to that, making frequent, unexpected, and decidedly unwelcome visits, suddenly flinging open the door.

"On your feet you 'orrible lot. What do you think this is, Billy-bloody-Butlins?" They never actually said "bloody", you understand, something a little livelier. Type of word you may use to express displeasure when hitting your thumb with a hammer! (And us just innocent young lads!) Then, after a few beds had been routinely overturned, kit scattered, they'd deliver their verdict. "This place is a pigsty. Get it cleaned up." An extremely rude awakening, that.

What we had previously thought of as gruelling days were now seen to have been nothing like. We could well *have* been at Butlins before induction, as the drill corporal suggested. Not any longer. We had now entered a regime of tight Service discipline. "Lights out" was sounded at twenty-two hundred, "Reveille" at zero six hundred, a bugle player from our recently-formed marching-band allotted the honours. Served him right for volunteering. Seemed I was to be the only one who could manage such foolishness with impunity, and even that was for the future.

Nor did lights out mean only that. It also meant "get to sleep", we soon found. Not advisory either, it was as good as an order. But after a long day of being harassed, not to difficult to comply with.

We were marched everywhere; workshops, church, even to the Mess, for meals. In between times we were on the parade ground, being taught how to march.

Once again my ATC experience came into play, for at summer camp, or when visiting RAF Stations, I had already experienced the initial trauma of sleeping away from home, sharing a room with others, some of them strangers. Many hadn't, and it took them time to adjust to the situation.

'Did you hear the one about the old guy who was being questioned with regard to his sex life?' The words drifted across in the darkness.

'Go on, I'll buy it,' another voice replied.

'He was asked how often he "did it"?'

'And?'

'"Infrequently", was his reply.'

"That one word, or two?" the questioner asked.'

It raised a chuckle from some, a comment from one lad who had obviously already enjoyed the experience.

'God, don't mention sex. I could use some of that right now.'

'You've done it then have you, Jonesy?' I asked.

'Definitely be two words in my case,' Jonesy replied, which caused me to wonder if I was I the only one that was sexually inexperienced?

'What the hell am I doing here?' someone else asked of the room in general. 'I want to go home. Wish I hadn't signed on.' Seemed like he was missing something, too. Probably his mother by the sound of things, but all his remark did was to evoke some unsympathetic advice.

'Too late now to change your mind, boyo.' This from our tame Welshman, named Farmer, whom naturally we called Taff! Which is when the lights flashed on again.

'Quiet in here,' bellowed a voice from the end of the room. Big Brother, in the form of the Leading Boy in charge. He lived in a one-man alcove; a separate room incorporated in the end of ours.

A loud fart rent the air. I knew who that would be; he of the blue-flame trick. No matter, next time the lights went out, so did we, for even Boy NCO's had the full weight of the service behind them. In fact the room became so quiet it would have been possible to hear a *goldfish* fart, never mind old Tillson.

Next morning came the production-line haircut, the old

short back and sides trick. Naturally, this had been expected, though probably not the extent of it! I saw lads almost burst into tears as well tended locks dropped around their feet like underwear at a medical inspection. Out went the DA and the Tony Curtis, not enough left to warrant the use of Brylcream. Me? I didn't care. My hair was nothing to begin with; styled by Multimix, kind of thing. What I now sported could only be termed an improvement.

Clothing fit where it touched, although our dress uniforms were "tailored". Even so, this appeared to be the work of tailors who had probably been butchers in civvy street. Nor did they bother asking on which side you dressed. There again they did have quite a task on their hands, almost every derivative of the humanoid form being on display before them. If a uniform did appear to fit particularly well, it was probably an indication that you were somewhat deformed!

'Are we actually supposed to wear these?' one lad asked, referring to underwear and socks that were almost certainly a hangover from the recently concluded days of the clothing coupon. I knew just what he meant. They did feel uncomfortably rough and itchy. There was also more than enough room in there for what little I possessed!

'These shirts don't have collars,' complained someone else.

'They do now,' replied the storeman, passing over collars of the detachable type, along with studs to hold them in place. 'They'll need starching,' he advised. 'No problem, though, the laundry will attend to such matters. With a vengeance,' he added.

Too true, I later found. Almost required the use of a metal press to bend them into shape. Even then, I, with the physique of a matchstick, could probably have got my chin inside.

One other small matter: little was of any use in the form in which it was issued. The dull, pimply surface of our boots needed to be smoothed and shined to the mirror-like finish of patent leather, as did tarnished, dimpled brass badges and buttons. There were various tricks which went towards achieving this of course, passed down from more experienced boys of the senior entries. (One of my ex-school, ex-ATC friends was in the Entry preceding ours, the 17th. That was Ivan Halstead - my companion during that sound barrier experience at Yeadon - two others were to follow on behind me, in the 19th;

89

Jimmy Jackson, and Graham Tinsley.)

But those senior entries did not pass on these tricks of the trade for free. We had been made to realise almost from the start that we, at least in RAF terms, were the lowest of life forms. Even Boys of the senior entries were to be treated as minor Gods compared to us. They needed to be obeyed, too, else swift retribution would ensue, including occasional physical violence. Therefore, if one of them decided you should clean his boots or brasses, you did so. It was a well-established ethic. Part of the strong, unwritten etiquette that existed between the various entries. This would, in time, infuse a superb esprit de corps into us. Our opportunity would come in four months time.

For the brasses, fine emery-paper was helpful, although our blankets would probably have made a good substitute, which is why we were thankful of the cotton pyjamas with which we were also issued. The emery was followed by cardboard, liberally doused in Brasso. Last of all came the lifesaving, Duraglit. Boot-leather, primarily the toe-caps, was painstakingly smoothed by a mind-boggling combination of Cherry Blossom and a heated spoon. I often wondered who first thought that one up, for it worked a treat - as long as you were careful with the heated spoon. The final polish was down to old-fashioned elbow grease - spit and polish, literally.

Naturally, cap badges were subject to similar treatment as other bits of brass, and behind them we wore a coloured disc - green in our case - as we did behind the Boy Entrant "wheel", worn on the left sleeve. The colour an indication as to which Wing and Squadron you belonged. For similar reasons the SD cap sported a chequered band, blue and green for us.

The B/E "wheel" was meant to be sewn onto the sleeve, but as this created problems when cleaning, most boys drilled and tapped the wheel in workshops, allowing it to be screwed on and off - initiative to the fore - thus avoiding the chance of a stray element of dried Brasso being lodged behind. Probably undetectable to us, but, unless you were very skilled, you could be sure an eagle-eyed drill NCO would spot it. They knew all the tricks of the trade, so it was these they looked for. After all, they used them too. But they were God!

Most important of the items issued to us, in our view at least, were the knife, fork, spoon - known throughout the service as eating irons - and mug. 'Essential items, those,' the storeman advised. 'Guard them with your life. No irons, no food. No mug, no tea. Naturally, there *were* losses, which meant keeping your own under close scrutiny, or under lock and key when not in use, for once again, replacements needed to be paid for.

Using your initiative once again, along with workshop tools, you could, if you were in the right trade, stamp said irons with your service number.

I suppose in these days of high ideals, with hardly anything remaining in the luxury category, the food we received would be classed as rubbish. But to us ration-book, and school meals kids it was OK - at least for a time - and we certainly started to fill out on it. Three regular meals a day, guaranteed. Even so, at the rate we burned off the calories we always seemed to be hungry.

Although medical facilities were first-class, the procedure for attending sick parade, then facing the MO (Medical Officer), were both complex and labourious.

'Six o'clock, Sarge!' one lad exclaimed, when we were advised of the time needed to report. 'That would mean getting up before Reveille!'

'If you're ill enough, lad, you'll make the effort.'

'If I'm that ill, Sarge, I'll be dead.'

'Just don't die while I'm in charge, or you'll be bloody sorry you were even born.' We had a laugh at that, but only after the sergeant had departed.

I suppose this did tend to weed out the malingerers, as it was no doubt designed to do. May as well get on the parade ground with the rest of the lads, unless you *were* seriously ill. Same thing went for church parades - fall out the Roman Catholics and Jews (they went elsewhere) - pointless declaring yourself to be an atheist, that only ensured you'd be peeling potatoes until long after the church service was over. Best just to fall in with the rest of the "captive" congregation.

All this the price of becoming an airman, should I be so lucky as to survive the next eighteen months. Even then it was no guarantee I would get to fly any more often than I had in the ATC. But that wasn't all. We were shouted at and subjected to base humiliation, expected to take it. Get it wrong on the parade ground and we were threatened with all kinds of dire consequences, many of them no doubt illegal, some impossibilities! But even though the rank of corporal was usually only acting (to give them authority), to us they were God, needed to be obeyed. No choice. Discipline was tight, blind obedience expected, though not always forthcoming. With lads of our age the natural temptation was to flaunt the regulations, even though lapses rarely went unforgiven. A minor infringement - brasses or boots not shining to a standard deemed acceptable to the drill corporal, hair a touch too long for his liking, or maybe just because your face didn't fit today - could see your name featuring on a Form 252. Not exactly one of life's more pleasing experiences, for sure.

The Air Force, I discovered, (probably the Army and Navy, too) was run on forms, some of which you needed, others you certainly didn't. F1250 was your identity card - very important, that - one you definitely needed; its loss or destruction would be but the start of many problems for the person it used to identify! F700 was pretty important, too, once you arrived on a squadron. This was the aircraft log book, in which every detail of a machine's life needed to be recorded and signed for. And in the event of a crash, the F700 would immediately be impounded, its data minutely scrutinised. The very reason for the rule which stated that the Form 700 must never take to the air in the aircraft to which it relates.

There was the F1443: railway warrant; F1771: travel claim - extreme care required here, no cheating allowed, less the wrath of authority descend upon you with a vengeance. Then there was the F295: leave pass, a much-prized and highly sought after item.

RAF Form252 was the exact opposite, this was a charge sheet. Definitely one to steer clear of. Your name on one of those would, in a jiffy, earn you as many days jankers as your Flight Commander thought appropriate for the misdemeanour committed. This requiring your presence on the (at least) twice a day defaulters parade, in full webbing, all its attached thirty-odd pieces of brass to be highly polished, to be inspected by the Orderly Officer. And if you believed discipline to be already tight, here it was extreme. A wayward piece of fluff, an unavoidably rain-spotted button, piece of brass or badge; such carelessness could earn you another seven days in an instant. Nor did it do any good to sulk, or refuse to answer a leading question. Such was construed as dumb insolence, a catch-all offence, that. If you weren't careful you could find yourself reporting for weeks on end. But camaraderie was such, even at this early stage, that help was often on offer from other boys in the billet; all would usually muck in to help with the polishing of brasses etc. (This camaraderie is what binds servicemen together, not just throughout their period of service, but long after, too. It is what they most miss when returning to civilian life.)

There were numbers for us, too. Very important. For that is what we were reduced to; a number. There could, after all, be any number of Taylors', as I had already discovered. Possibly more than a few *David* Taylors'. But I was the only one with that unique seven-digit sequence which identified me: 400, my "last three", the most important part. The whole sequence needed to be indelibly committed to memory, for it was required on every form you signed, and every officer or NCO who addressed you seemed to want to know at least your "last three". Who knows, maybe they collected them, like train or aircraft spotters, compared results in the mess, over a beer: "Got a four hundred today, and a two nine seven."

So important was your number deemed to be you'd probably have had need to cite it before being allowed to die, should such a misfortune befall you while still in the service. (Even now, sixty-three years later, I have no trouble reciting my full number, nor do I know of any other ex-service person that has.)

*

Slowly, we were gelling as a group. Friendships began to form from day one, total strangers in a strange environment ensured that would happen. Even so, as is normal with such a cross-section of society, there would be the occasional serious disagreement among our ranks (minor, really, but not seen as such to macho youth). And although we were not yet men, we *were* grown up boys, therefore disagreements needed to be settled. Away from the eyes of authority. In one of the storage or laundry rooms. Toe to toe, a group of blood-thirsty onlookers seated on the racks of shelves which lined the walls, for blood was sure to be evident.

It was like a scene from a Western: "I'll meet you in the laundry room at nineteen hundred. Be there."
(Yet another discovery, that, as the sharp eyed reader may already have noticed: the military worked on the twenty-four hour clock. Nineteen hundred (hours) relating to seven pm. That was more or less the way our day went: oh six hundred, wakey wakey; oh seven hundred, breakfast; ten-thirty hours, NAAFI break; twelve hundred, lunch, and as trainees, twenty-two hundred was lights out; so on and so forth. Although for some reason there was no twenty-four hundred, or midnight. It was either twenty-three fifty-nine, or zero zero zero one.

Twenty-three fifty-nine was also our private designation for, how shall we put it? Anyone of less-than-white pigmentation shall we say? Yeah, should be able to sneak that past the race relations board. (Much as with your personal service number, most ex servicemen still relate to the twenty-four hour clock long after leaving the service.)

Fighting, of course, was a chargeable offence, but walking into a door, or falling downstairs was just plain carelessness. It was all a far cry from the childish performances I recalled taking place in the school playground.

"Fight! Fight!" The cry echoed across the schoolyard of Norton Boys County Secondary, an indication that yet another minor dispute, having failed on the diplomatic front, was about to degenerate to the amateurish inept fisticuffs stage. Well, sort of.

Two lads grappled with each other, and after swinging a few inept blows one now had the other in a secure grip. Both were head down, face to bum, one with his arms pinned, the other apparently wondering what to do next. They staggered this way and that inside the circle of onlookers. The kind of movement one would expect of an elephant turning around: done without regard as to who, or what may be nearby, the onus being on those within range to remove themselves, or face the consequences. We duly did, giving them the room in which to do absolutely nothing.

Then, disaster struck the lad doing the holding. His nose started to run, and not a spare sleeve within reach, not without releasing his grip. Ah, but - and here you could almost see his mind at work, cogs rapidly resolving the situation - there, right in front of him, a cotton-coated back. Without a moments hesitation, nor a thought as to the consequences, nose dragged its way across shirt, a snail-like trail marking its passage. Everyone saw it, of course, and we all broke up. Nobody let on what the laughter was about, but within seconds the fight was over, unresolved, anger dissipated. Who knows, his mother probably thought it had been a snail.

That had been my friend, Brian - although I don't believe he'd been awarded that highest of accolades, "My best friend. Ever." I'd meet up with him again, thirty years hence, in New Zealand.

*

So, what of those aeroplanes that had been the catalyst to my joining up in the first place; the hands on experience I was seeking? Well, here at Cosford, two weeks passed during which I hadn't so much as been within sight of one, although I had learned the rudiments of close order drill. Naturally, once again us ex-ATC cadets were a jump ahead of the rest, we'd done it all before: shoulders back, chin in, arms straight, thumbs uppermost, wrist cocked towards the ground. Only here it was slightly more serious, in that if you didn't like being shouted at, or verbally abused, you could hardly pack up and bugger off to the chip shop.

'Squad..... Wait for it! Squad.... att..en..tion,' barked the drill instructor, in answer to which a hundred polished boots recorded ten point five on the Richter scale as they simultaneously crashed to the tarmac, rifle by your side. In open order we were commanded to, "From the right... Dress." "Close order... march," came next, after which it was, "Right... turn. By the left... quick...march." We'd be wheeled right and left, about-turned, marched some more, halted. We'd be commanded to "Slope arms, Present arms, Order arms," then, after an hour or so, we'd be marched off to wherever it was we were due next. And so it went, day in, day out. Physical fitness featured prominently in our training, too, with many an hour being spent in the gymnasium.

Our total drill instructor contingent consisted of two corporals and a peppery little sergeant with WWII ribbons. (After the war, lots of aircrew lost their flying status, and with it, in many cases, their rank. One option to retaining your rank was to become a drill instructor, of which, due to the introduction of National Service, there was a great need.) If we were terrified by the corporals, we were in mortal fear of the sergeant; as, apparently, were the corporals, also!

Early one winter morning - after we had just about managed to keep in step as a squad in our new hob-nailed boots - the sergeant decided to personally teach us the art of changing directions whilst on the march.

We set off in column of route, though matters were made next to impossible by the very severe frost which had turned the parade ground into a skating rink. We skidded, slid, slithered and grabbed at each other for support as we vainly attempted to remain upright and keep in step.

The sergeant swept up alongside, arms wind-milling, eyes bulging, purple of face, bellowing expletives.

"Left-Right. Left-Right. Dig your frigging heels in! If you stupid beggars digs your frigging heels in, youse'll find you won't frigging fall over," he bellowed. At which point both feet went from under him and he went down with a thump.

Give him his due, with hardly a pause, he continued his verbal tirade, "But if you does frigging fall over, this is the way to frigging land! Heels together, feet at an angle of 45 degrees, arms forced down by your side, thumbs in line with the seams of your trousers! Stomach in, chest out, wid your frigging eyes looking straight ahead!"

But long before he got to the thumbs bit, we, and I suspect, the corporals, were all laughing fit to burst.

Come Sunday we'd be marched to church, in Number One Blues; our best uniform. I hadn't been in a church since I left the choir and took to delivering newspapers; more money the incentive there. The Air Force also paid me, even more than I'd received for a wedding, although nothing like an average week's wage for the time - far from it: two shillings and sixpence (12.5P). But that wasn't so much for going to church, it was my weekly stipend. And I had to go on parade and salute for it, a measly half-crown. Which got one lad to wondering: "Once I'm in the Air Force proper, receiving paper money, what will be the requirement then? A full bloody march past?"
(Even this weekly pay was not all ours to spend as we wished, for their were enforced expenses to be covered: haircut, soap, razor blades, blanco, Duraglit and suchlike, all to be purchased from the NAAFI with our own money, to keep us and our kit looking smart. I suppose official thinking must have been along the lines of, "They are only schoolboys. We feed, clothe and house them. They are too young to drink, not allowed to marry, fornicate or smoke without permission, so all they need is a bit of pocket money!" But what little we did retain would barely buy us a cup of tea. We never had any money, so even when we were eventually allowed off camp we could hardly go farther than we could walk, and couldn't do a lot once we got there!)

Pay Parade was held in one of the large hangars, with a lovely smooth concrete floor. All the squadrons lined up, and when an NCO called out your name you responded as per the requirement. All very proper and formal. But there were laughs to be had here, too, as in the instance of a boy we'll call Smith. When the NCO called out B\E Smith's name, he came smartly to attention, marched the ten or so feet to the pay table and came to a crashing halt in his studded boots; well, almost. He then either attempted a salute, as required, or to regain his balance as his boots sought grip, and promptly disappeared under the table, feet first. Much to his credit, the Paying Officer - usually very junior, therefore more likely to be overly officious, so as to exercise their limited authority - simply leant over the table, looked at the lad laying flat underneath and said: "It's only what you've earned. No need to grovel for it, Boy!"

I soon had gleaming buttons and brasses, had learned to spoon, spit and polish my boots to that mirror-like shine, wash and iron my clothes, press my uniform - pleats and creases razor sharp. (A little soap helped keep them so.) I'd also learned to make my own bed. No, not really. Make it in the Air Force approved manner is what I mean. This called for it to be unmade: one blanket was stretched across the mattress, drum-skin tight, the rest of the sheets and blankets folded in a precise shape and form - rather like a large rectangular Swiss Roll, pillows on top (from here on, to be known as a bedpack) - the whole kit and caboodle was then placed at the head of the mattress. How you arranged the sheets and blankets at night was left to your own creativity. Or, as in the case of the "apple pie" bed, occasionally someone else's. An apple-pie bed - in which the bottom sheet was doubled back on itself, so when the unfortunate Boy tried to get into bed, he couldn't. Not before sorting out the problem - was probably bottom of the pile when it came to misdemeanours, for, being young and wild, some incidents were absolutely unbelievable. How about a little friendly arson, for starters. We weren't all blue-eyed boys, you see. In fact, rumour had it that quite a few young offenders were offered the option of joining the Boy Entrant's scheme rather than being sent to borstal; whether this was actually true or not I have no idea. I never met anyone who admitted to being in that category. But even if true, they would have no doubt become better citizens as a result.

After the first month we were reassessed, which was when - personal reservations notwithstanding - I found I had done rather well. Almost too well, it seemed. I was recommended for transfer to the Aircraft Apprentice Scheme, at RAF Halton. But as this was also to entail a change of trade, to Air Wireless/Radar, the decision was left to me. So it was I escaped that fate. I didn't fancy the trade at all, turned it down, this despite the fact that Halton was No 1 School of Technical Training, Cosford being No 2. Ex Halton Apprentices could also expect to be looked upon very favourably by the Air Force after pass-out, many attaining aircrew status, and of reaching "Air" Rank; the very top of the pile. But that wasn't all. The

Apprentice course was a full three years, as opposed to our eighteen months. Forget it. I'd stick with what I'd got. Besides, I was by then beginning to settle down at Cosford, had established friendships. Anyway, I hated sudden change.

Thinking about it, years later, I feel this was probably an opportunity missed; but I never really had cause to regret it.

*   *

Chapter Three
THE CLIMB-OUT

Shotguns apart - and that fired from the hip (of which, more later) - I *had* used a rifle before, both in the ATC, and when out shooting rabbits with my father. But they had only been .22 calibre. Here at Cosford we were taught to shoot the venerable Lee Enfield .303. This was a much more serious piece of kit, even from my position, one hundred and eighty degrees from the business end. And, as opposed to the ATC's twenty-five feet indoor range, here the target was four times that distance away.

`On my command. Squaa..ud, load.'

I quickly worked the action, loaded the five-round clip with what I felt was some expertise, snapped the bolt closed, loading a round into the breech. Easy, peasy, this. The weapon was ready, so was I. Ready to take on the world at large. John Wayne at Guadalcanal.

'Squaa..ud... Five rounds grouping... In your own time... Fire!'

This I did. Albeit with some trepidation, squeezing the trigger slowly, as one should. That this was more through not knowing what to expect than teaching, I don't mind admitting to. It's the next bit I'm not too proud of. The effect wasn't quite as anticipated. Nothing happened. Not a thing! World War Two was being re-enacted all around, yet the weapon in my hands remained stubbornly silent. Not even the dull click of the firing pin descending on a dud round. I assumed the gun to be jammed. Which, in a way, it was.

'Let's try again, shall we, dumb-cluck?' the instructor said, reaching down to release the safety-catch. (At least I think that's what he said.) John Wayne's image retreated in disgust as I once more squeezed the trigger.

BANG! Bloody hell! Much louder than I imagined. Well it would be wouldn't it, this explosion was taking place an inch from my right ear, stock kicking me in the shoulder like an agitated mule. It left my head ringing, my arm numb. If I wasn't careful this thing would do me more damage than it would the enemy.

As if to confirm its continued presence, the gun exploded again. I wasn't at all happy, but carried on until the magazine was empty.

'How's that for grouping, sarge?'

He gave me a look of utter contempt. 'Possibly very good,' he replied. 'Who the hell knows? One thing's for sure, we aren't about to find out, are we. I don't know where you were aiming, lad, but that target is in pristine condition. Just have to wait and see if we receive any complaints about deceased animals from the farm.'

OK, but I did have an excuse, I'd been distracted, hadn't I? I just couldn't believe what was happening on the next mat to me. Had to be on my right, for my left eye was closed in that squinting-down-the-barrel pose. One minute he was there, then he was gone. So small and light, I swear he had to wriggle forward a couple of feet to regain position every time he pulled the trigger. A lot of good he'd be in the field of action. Me too, come to that, and I had previous experience. I'd been quite good with that .22, at short range.

So much for my first visit to the butts. Next time will be better, I promised myself.

They even taught us the rudiments of throwing a hand grenade. Dummies, of course, but they did toss the odd thunderflash around, just for effect. Big Boy's fireworks, those.

'The reason we use dummies,' the sergeant explained, 'is that, although the grenade is somewhat more lethal than a bow and arrow, in your bloody hands it would probably be nowhere near as accurate. Anyway, it's what you do after the throwing that's important: get the hell out of it. Lie down behind something solid.'

Next came the Bren.

'More like it, this, sarge,' I said. 'Hardly any kick at all.'

'No, lad. That's because the recoil is used to stuff the next round up the spout. But it's no second division piece of tackle when it comes to dealing with the enemy,' he assured me. That was something else I'd discovered: these RAF Regiment types could become almost human if you showed the slightest bit of enthusiasm. Still, I couldn't think why it might be possible I needed to become familiar with any of these weapons. I was in the Air Force wasn't I? not the bleeding army. Wasn't that the main function of the RAF Regiment, to protect us? Anyway, I would have thought one of the first rules of combat should be to put your opponent on inferior terms. Not a lot for the enemy to worry about with us then. Not in those days there wasn't. Although it was always possible they could have died laughing. One could only hope.

Naturally, above all else we received training in our selected (in some cases, allocated) trade. Mine, given its full title: Instrument Mechanic (Navigation), under training, or, I. Mech (Nav) u/t, in Air Force parlance.

It was like the first day at school all over again, and in a way I suppose that is just what it was. Different only in that our classrooms were now located in cold, hangar-like buildings, known as workshops. Wood and sackcloth dividers formed separate cubicles, each dedicated to a different subject within the same trade group. We would make the rounds eventually. But there were blackboards and chalk dust, notebooks to scribble in, lessons on this and that, and, of course, more of those dreaded exams. No free milk.

They taught us state-of-the-art electronics. Although back then, in the dark ages, this probably bore closer relevance to fish and chips than it did to microchips. As transistor technology had not yet fully asserted itself, fifties state-of-the-art came mainly in the form of vacuum tubes, heavy gauge wire, large and small resistors, capacitors and the like, along with seriously high voltages which, when diverted to some unsuspecting lad's metal chair..... Well, no need to go into detail is there, save to say the results were usually effective enough to engender many a curt, crude, and often colourful, remark. We were slowly getting the hang of things.

We also wallowed in the principles of navigation, pondered over the intricacies of the equipment necessary to put those principles into effect. These were the data providers: compasses, sextants, altimeters, airspeed indicators, sextants, drift recorders and the like. We weren't specifically required to know how to operate them - that was the job of the aircrew navigators - but we did need to know what they should be capable of achieving, and be able to ensure that they were. There were mirrors, lenses, prisms, collimators, and other such optical devices used to reflect, refract, or focus, beams of light. These could also, with a little ingenuity and guile - we weren't slow to discover - redirect and focus a ray of sunlight onto a specific target, say an unsuspecting earlobe, often with exceedingly spectacular results. They could also be quite effective when used to burn holes in sackcloth.

We had Pitot heads and static vents, upon which those altimeters and airspeed indicators relied for their readings. And airspeed indicators could be made to record spectacularly high speeds by the simple expedient of placing ones mouth over the end of a pitot tube and blowing into it. But be wary; that tube had a built-in de-icer - which got extremely hot extremely quickly when not subjected to a three hundred knot, high-altitude airflow - and there was always one joker who would just have to switch it on. Gave a whole new meaning to the phrase, Hot Lips, that. (Although now in the Armed Services we were still boys at heart, would remain so for some time yet. In fact, as one ex-Boy so succinctly put it at a reunion many years later - for we were still prone to the pulling of various pranks even then - "Growing old is obligatory, growing up is not.")

We then got the standard lecture on airspeed: why it is of critical importance to a pilot. Why - because it is measured in knots, and one knot equates to one nautical mile per hour - there is no such thing as knots per hour. The difference between airspeed and ground-speed was revealed to those of us who hadn't served in the ATC: 'Ground-speed matters only in so far as establishing an ETA (estimated time of arrival), has little bearing on flight. It's quite feasible for an aircraft to have a negative ground-speed when faced with a strong headwind. It *will* remain airborne, but it could be travelling backwards over the ground. Airspeed is the important element in that it relates to the speed of the airflow over the wings, and that's what keeps us airborne, creating lift.'

So much for the theory of flight then. Pretty ancient stuff really, for old George Caley had that sussed back way in the eighteen hundreds, remember?

As expected, and no doubt intended, there was much hilarity and ribald comment when the instructor produced an instrument whose dial was graded in something listed as FART. This, he revealed, was the German measurement for airflow. I, and apparently everyone else in the class, always assumed it meant the same thing in English!

Then there was George of another kind: the SEP2 autopilot - developed by Smiths Industries (hence the nomenclature: Smiths Electric Pilot, version 2) - so advanced it smacked of science fiction. (Although when compared alongside today's programable marvels of technology and miniaturization it did next to nothing, apart from fly the aeroplane. It would now be considered positively Jurassic.)

Bombsights also came under our jurisdiction, whereas gunsights bore the classification, Instruments - General, a separate trade as far as training went. Oxygen systems, engine instrumentation, fuel gauges and the like, fell under the same category. In the Air Force proper, we were to find, there was no such demarcation. You normally covered the lot.

On top of all this trade training came our further education. We were reacquainted with maths and geometry, introduced to algebra, calculus, and trigonometry; mysteries and miseries I seemed to have escaped at secondary school. No chance of that at Cosford.

*

Although I slept on a mattress that bore closer resemblance to a cement waffle than to a feather bed, it didn't matter. I was usually too tired to care. There were even times I slept on the floor, after prematurely preparing my bed for next day's inspection, or when one or other of the senior entries had made the traditional, early-hours bed-tipping sweep through our room. Though these were not as frequent as they would have been were it not for our accommodation advantage.

Whereas the odd numbered entries found themselves billeted in POW style wooden huts - through which a raiding party could enter at one end and depart by the other, wreaking havoc along the way - even number entries (ours being the 18th) had the luxury of a modern, centrally-heated, multi-storey fortress that went by the name of Fulton Block. Single entry/exit rooms, stairs and corridors offering us a kind of minimal security.

I also learned new songs during my time at Cosford, the words of which they seemed to have forgotten to teach us at school. These were picked up during the occasional cultural evening, when a group of us would gather together in harmonious accord around the NAAFI piano, words and arrangement attributable to servicemen over the generations. Let's see: *There Was A Monk Of Great Renown...*, *Ring The Bell, Verger...*, *The Ball At Kerrimuir*, and, *Little Angeline*. A favourite, that last, though at a family gathering all would probably be about as welcome as a french kiss.

They were a mixed bag, the eighteenth entry, as are bound to be any group of individuals, male or female. There were a number of oddities among us, too. The guy on the parade ground who got it all wrong when marching, left arm with left leg, right to right. The harder he tried the worse it got. I bet he felt a right prat. Then there was an armourer who looked like a boxer, or maybe he'd just been released from prison. Well, why not. Robert Mitchum made it from prison to the silver screen, and Jack Palance looked like he could have, even if he hadn't. Come to think of it, that's who he reminded me of, this armourer, Jack Palance. Though it wouldn't have been in my interests to voice that opinion. At least not in his presence. Or out of it, come to that; too many individuals around who might see dropping you in it as a way of gaining his friendship. And that was one thing I wouldn't have wanted: him as an enemy. Especially as he seemed to be a regular participant in the laundry room punch-ups. (I can still see that face today, can't put a name to it.)

Then we come to someone I can definitely put a name to: Titch Nelson. No, definitely not related to the Admiral so named. Titch was the dwarf-like creature who had experienced problems with that nasty Lee Enfield. Alternate nickname: short-arse. Oops! No, of course he wasn't dwarf-like, or short-arsed. Well... what I mean is, he was then, but in this crazy era of political correctness the term would probably be, vertically disadvantaged, or some such. Silly bloody description, really. I mean if you're down there where you can look up a girl's mini-skirt you're hardly at a disadvantage, are you? Be that as it may, having never been an avid subscriber to the concept of PC, to me he would forever be a short-arse. But whatever he was, he shared our room. And in common with most small folk, especially one as meek as Titch, he was the one to be picked on. (Today it would be classed as bullying. Suppose that's really what it was then, only in those days it wasn't termed such; was looked upon, and accepted, as part of growing up.)

Also sharing our room - along with about twenty others - was a lad who proclaimed himself to be an accomplished hypnotist. And if he wasn't, there were certainly some among us who should have been up there with Mitchum and Palance, or even Gielgud and Olivier, he was that good. Certainly had me convinced. This despite the fact he was never successful with me. I, apparently, was not an ideal subject. Titch, it seemed, was. It took about a minute to put him under, a couple of seconds to bring him back. No problem. Unbeknown to Titch, in between, his subconscious had been primed. He'd been told to collapse every time he looked in a mirror. And so it came to be. Even a brief glance as he walked past was enough. Nor was there any way for him to be faking it, not the way he hit the floor. It was instantaneous, as if his bones had suddenly become non-existent, or a puppet which had its strings cut! And he didn't so much as move a muscle until brought round by a click of the fingers, for which he'd also been primed.

But there were some sad types among us, too. The Leading Boy in charge of the room, for instance (yes, he who lived in the one-man alcove). It happened to be Friday, Bull Night, when the room had to be prepared for that rigorous, Saturday morning inspection. This guy allotted Titch the job of polishing the mirror. Well, sad or not, it was so unbelievable I had to laugh. It was like watching a reverse jack-in-a-box, the subconscious in serious need of a de-prime were our mirror ever to pass inspection.

In time these weekly inspections became fairly routine. Not only the room and ablutions, our kit was also on display, a rigorously enforced arrangement, each item allotted its own place on that drum-tight blanket which covered the mattress - a strictly defined pattern. The perfect layout took quite a time to achieve, hence the need to occasionally sleep on the floor. It was clean anyway, that floor never lost its shine, everyone skidding about the room on felt pads, and woe betide those that forgot.

'Pads!' The call would echo down the room the moment anyone so much as thought about stepping in through the door minus the required foot protection. In this, we became our own strict masters, especially if it involved that sacred patch of floor known as your "bed-space". My bed, and the floor surrounding it was my own private little island. This was where I lived, where my kit was kept - either in the tin locker beside the bed, or beneath the bed itself, along with my little cardboard suitcase full of dreams - and no one but no one set foot in that space without my express permission. Well, senior entries apart, that is. And NCO's and officers. And those tougher than myself. All right, probably everyone except Titch. But they shouldn't have, is what I'm saying.

The initial polishing of the floor was achieved by use of a device known as a bumper. Basically a felt pad attached to a cast iron base, hinged to a long handle. Swing the handle and the base did the lion's share of the work, for it was heavy. So heavy, that if released mid-swing, taking into account the shiny, non-stick surface of the lino, it would charge off down the room like a herd of elephants run amok. It was another mindless game we occasionally played, though not too often, for any irreparable barrack room damage was our responsibility, had to be paid for. Awful trouble, too, should it slam into the door the moment the duty sergeant chose to enter the room! Not me, sarge. Honest.

Didn't matter who had been responsible. Certain in the knowledge he would never find out, we all paid the price. Took ages to sort our kit, set it out again.

The rest of the bull eventually became monotonous rote, even the monthly ritual of the Commanding Officer's parade. The only fly in the ointment was if we required a new pair of boots, or a new uniform. We then had to start again, from scratch. But the most likely item for replacement was the SD - for Service Dress - cap. As these looked rather silly in their official form, most were heavily doctored, turning them from duckbill, to something more akin to those worn by the Gestapo. Mild doctoring you could get away with, cut, slash and prop to excess and you were ordered to replace the item. Most, therefore, had two caps; one for use on camp, a heavily doctored version for use when on leave.

The annual ritual known as AOC's inspection (Air Officer Commanding) was something else again. Paint was applied anywhere paint would stick. You know the old service adage re the annual inspection: If it moves, salute it, if it doesn't, paint it.

*

A total of eighteen months were spent at Cosford. Little flying, lots of learning. Had to make up for the loss of that advanced education somehow. Even this early I'd begun to realize adulthood was not something conferred upon one by time, by reaching some magical age. It, like most things in life, had to be earned. And earn it we did. Life was one long learning curve, the end of which, at times, we seemed destined never to reach. There *were* aircraft around for us to get our grubby hands on, training airframes, long since retired from flying. But better than nothing. I recall Spitfires and suchlike in Cosford's airfield hangars. In fact they had a whole plethora of aircraft stored there, but only a few were allocated to us for training purposes - Mosquitos, Tiger Moths, even a Lancaster.

One thing I still wasn't able to get my hands on were girls. As far as I was concerned, there weren't any. At least none that fancied the likes of me. Not much chance, really. We weren't allowed off camp for the first month, after that, only in uniform. (As previously noted, all civilian clothes were required to be posted home almost as soon as we signed on the dotted line.) The only time we did get to wear civvies was when home on leave, although uniform was occasionally preferred at these times, so as to prove you had made a break to the wider world out there.

But, back in Wolverhampton, uniform wasn't really the problem, for the girls seemed quite attracted to them. No, it was the other three to four hundred like-minded, lusty lads, that were the problem. Some, by their own account, no longer virgins. I was inclined to believe them, too, for I recalled "Shaggy" McDonald, at school. He'd apparently been into it before he was fifteen.

I, being inexperienced and shy could never have expected to compete with any degree of success against the likes of these guys, especially if the rumours were true.

'You know what?' Mike said one day. And it was obvious we didn't, because he hadn't yet told us. But we knew he was about to.

'Those sneaky bastards are resorting to the use of bromide in the tea.'

'Who, Mike?'

'The authorities, of course.'

'What the hell's bromide?'

'Don't you know anything, Taylor? Chemical that's supposed to curb our natural tendencies, ain't it.'

'Ah, I see,' I said, though I didn't really.

'Just a rumour then,' replied Jim, who we knew to have a girlfriend in town. 'I seem to manage all right.'

And suddenly I did see. Well, good for Jim, but never having had a girlfriend to call my own, I didn't really miss them. Not yet. But the old biological clock was certainly ticking away. And I had to agree with Jim. At that tender age, the bromide, if used, seemed to have little effect, if the state of the sheets was any indication. There again, maybe it was delayed action stuff? Is there a possibility it actually takes fifty to sixty years to penetrate the system? Now there's a thought. I'll bet even "Shaggy" McDonald is facing hard times these days. No, poor choice of words. If you get my drift, he won't be, will he?

*

In amongst all this came Christmas, when we were given leave to travel home. We had to depart and arrive back in at camp uniform, but at home we could wear what we liked. And I'll bet a lot of Boys occasionally wore uniform, just as I did, to go out and parade around the streets, showing that we were moving on in life.

Then it was the end of our first year at Cosford. In fact, at times it felt more like day four hundred and fifty at the end of a very long year!

*

The only real disadvantage of having to wear uniform, then, was that it precluded any thoughts of a visit to the pub, everyone being only too aware that, as Boy Entrants, our age was well below the legal minimum. Which only made a drink all the more desirable.

There was nothing to stop someone else procuring a bottle or two from the off-licence on our behalf, of course. Which is exactly what a group of us did. One time. Alas, I may have assumed myself adult enough to handle it, but my metabolism thought otherwise, leaving me nursing a brain-to-eyeballs headache next morning. Didn't enjoy my breakfast second time around either. Put me off Port for years, that.

Apart from the novelty of being able to wear civvies, there was another facet to going on leave. From the very first it felt strange, for despite the hard times, the inspections, the shouting, the bullying by NCO's, I found I missed the life at Cosford almost as soon as I stepped out through the gates. The camaraderie, and the friendships, that was what would be missing.

Another thing missing was my flying. Eighteen months, two flights. Both extremely welcome, for sure, though it was the first of them that affords the most detailed memories. It was taken during annual summer camp, at Millom, Cumbria. It was also the first time I had flown without the back-up security of a parachute. We were almost in the Air Force now, no longer pampered-to ATC cadets.

I have a vivid recollection of lying in a glassed-in nose, watching the ground float serenely past. I was in my element once more, the earthly shackles broken. But I had cause to worry. Nothing to do with the lack of a parachute, for in this situation a parachute would have been as useful as a chocolate fireguard. We appeared to be on course for a collision with the mountain Black Coombe, the crest of which lay dead ahead. With the accent on dead, of that I was sure.

The ground rose gently, seeming about to bisect our course about a hundred feet below the peak. And remember, by this time I had been afforded some little insight into basic trigonometry, and navigational procedures. The closer we got, so the impression of speed gathered pace. Grass and rocks blurred past at a fantastic rate - everything being relative, of course - until, flash, we cleared the summit by inches. Well, it seemed so. OK, so maybe my little insight fell short of the required experience, or maybe my eyesight was faulty. Would you believe two hundred feet? Whatever, I was immediately imbued with a tremendous feeling of elation. Only natural when finding you are still alive, after expecting to be dead. And not only did the peak disappear, so to did the earth beyond. The reverse slope fell away, a thousand feet or so, almost sheer. Quite dramatic, that. As was no doubt the intent.

This was also the flight during which, still prone in the nose, I found myself to be floating around, weightless, when some wag, commenting on the machine's inability to perform aerobatics, invoked the pilot to put it into a stall. About as aerobatic as an Anson got to be. Not that exciting an aircraft, you see, but at least I was flying again. For that I was thankful.

Smoking was something else that was prohibited until you attained a certain age - seventeen, I believe - and even then you had to apply for permission, be issued with a pass. This wasn't much of a deterrent though, for I'd estimate possibly as many as forty or fifty per cent were smokers. And on our salary that proved to be a problem to those that were, and a good source of income to those enterprising types who weren't. Buy a packet of ten "ciggies" for a shilling and they could be sold towards the end of the pay period for at least sixpence apiece; a handy little profit to be made good on payday. Believe me, there were never any dog-ends left laying around. All would be gathered up and their contents combined to make another cigarette. In any case, most of the time nothing remained that *was* useable, a pin being inserted close to the end of the cigarette and it smoked until it almost burnt your lips. In desperate times the pinned butt was shared around, passed from hand to hand. For a smoker, this could easily result in such as the following:

One evening, the day before pay-day, one Boy found himself to be rich beyond his wildest dreams; he had exactly tuppence in his pocket - the price of a cup of tea in the NAAFI - and one complete cigarette! With about a dozen lads in the room, he knew if he lit up there he wouldn't get his fag back until it was on the end of a pin. So, he decided to sneak off to the NAAFI, get a cuppa, and smoke his last fag in hiding. Off he went, finding the NAAFI to be empty, as expected; nobody had any money left. He got his tea, found the darkest corner, sat down at a table and lit his cigarette, furtively looking around.

He took one long, glorious drag and made to remove the cigarette, but it had stuck to his lips. His fingers slid to the end, got burnt and released their grip on the fag, which immediately dropped into his tea, where it spread out. Had anyone entered the NAAFI right then, they would have found a very sad young lad sat in the corner, feeling very sorry for himself, quietly sobbing.

I was always glad I hadn't then started to smoke, but I think that period probably laid the foundations for me doing so. Let's face it, almost everyone did at the time.

*

The gathering at Farnborough, Hampshire, was always an event anticipated with pleasure. In those days the display was staged annually, but due to service commitments, and lack of resources, I was lucky if I was able to attend every second or third year. But as a member of the Boy Entrants' Aircraft Recognition Society, my 1953 visit was courtesy of the Royal Air Force.

Recognition had always been my thing, even before my ATC days. Hazy shots of aircraft in cloud; small sections - a wing, nose, or tail - long distance shots; esoteric shadows or fuzzy silhouettes, it made no difference, I could name them all, type and mark. I didn't need to think, they registered themselves immediately. It was automatic. Not just aircraft, either. I was very good at cars, too. And birds, of the feathered variety; though country living was a likely influential factor here. Being an avid collector of their eggs probably also had a role to play, too.

After the John Derry disaster of the previous year, new rules were in force at Farnborough. There were restrictions on height, speed, and direction of flight for the demonstrations, though the show was nevertheless still full of spectacle. We were still to be allowed our sonic booms, courtesy of the Hunter, and Swift. And this was the year the Handley Page Victor, and Short Seamew both made their debuts.

Digging out my programmes I see that year it cost one shilling and sixpence (7.5p), although we were given ours. The following year it was down to one shilling (5p). Not a trend that was to continue!

Life was made orderly by discipline, ritual, and routine, therefore too demanding ever to qualify as boring! So the months came and went, as did members of our group. We lost a couple at the three month crunch-time, more over the

110

duration: those unable or unwilling to cope with the rigours of the discipline-for-disciplines-sake, or score well enough in exams. Most were given the opportunity of dropping back an entry, to start again with the Nineteenth, four months behind. Ernie Cornish was one who joined us due to a period of illness, stepping back two entries from the Sixteenth. Those deemed unsuitable for service life were said to be released. A phrase more suited to the end of a term in prison, I would have thought. There again...

I guess I was lucky, or had underrated myself, for I made it all the way. We were the Senior Entry. Those blue and green checkered hatbands, three inverted stipes on the bottom of our sleeve an indication that we were top dogs. The stripes, worn on the left sleeve, were awarded both as a symbol of progression from junior to senior entry, and the passing of exams. I also had a single stripe on each upper sleeve, denoting my promotion to Leading Boy.

It was probably around this stage of one lad's career that the following was said to have taken place.

A young Pilot Officer (lowest of the commissioned ranks) stood with his lady-friend on the steps of the Astra (camp cinema) when a Boy Entrant walked past, entering the cinema without saluting. The P/O felt rather indignant about this - as Pilot Officers tended to do, especially if newly commissioned - and no doubt in order to impress his lady friend he called the Boy back. "Don't you usually salute an officer when you see one, Boy?" he demanded. "Didn't you notice my rank?" he said, pointing to his sleeve. The Boy leaned closer in the dull conditions, looked at the thin blue ring encircling the cuff and said, "Well it is a very small one, Sir!" With which he smartly saluted and dashed into the cinema, leaving a somewhat embarrassed junior officer speechless; his lady friend with a grin on her face.

*

It was September, 1954. Summer was coming to an end. A good time for it. Not September, that always falls in September, as does the end of summer - officially - although summer itself appears to fall in July; usually around the twentieth! But forget all that, when I say a good time for it, what I mean is the one parade we'd all been eagerly awaiting: Pass Out. Not physically, mind - well, maybe one or two - but this was the parade which was also to signal the end for the Eighteenth Entry. Tomorrow, the Nineteenth would be top dogs, but this

111

was to be the Eighteenth's very own, special day. And so it had been. Top brass gathered, parents and guardians were in attendance, the sun even shone, and the parade was in the hands of Boy Entrant NCO's. Cue in the music. Not orchestral, for we had our very own band, remember: bugles and drums. And while probably not quite up there with the likes of Cleckheaton and District Brass Band, it was certainly good enough to march behind. And our drum major was in a class of his own. (Often fancied the job myself, but too many accidents with a broom told me I wasn't to be the one. Should have practised outside the room, I suppose. Well clear of light fittings, mirrors, and windows.) The guy who did have the job could twirl that mace over the water pipes which crossed twenty feet above the road, then catch it, no problem whatsoever. Though I doubted he'd be foolish enough to attempt anything so pretentious on this day. Even if it was more spectacular than a mere twirl round the neck. It was sort of frowned upon by people in authority, of which there were a considerable number present. Nay, there were even people in authority of authority in attendance. Way up there in the lofty realms of Air Rank. Even my parents attended after driving down from Yorkshire.

And so, with bugle and drum packed away for the last time, the sound of marching feet gradually fading, the shadows lengthened as the sun slid down the sky. Another hour and those shadows would have spread like a damp stain, the entire camp becoming wrapped in the cloak of dusk. Thirty minutes after that, it would be dark. Which didn't matter to us, for by then, we'd be gone.

School was out again. More like college this time, but I was the better for it. Transformation from apprentice motor mechanic to fully fledged, Senior Aircraftsman, Inst Mech (nav), was complete. I was fit, well, and full of a confidence I'd never felt before, even if I was still a virgin. Excitement was high. I was about to be let loose on an Air Force that had bases in all kinds of interesting places, for we then still had a reasonably sized Empire to protect.

I had, in fact, already completed six months full-time service, for, being a late starter I'd reached the qualifying age of seventeen and a half before completion of training. This meant I had been earning substantially more than the seven shillings and sixpence I was by then being paid, the balance deposited in a bank account on my behalf.

'Been that way from day one,' the accounts sergeant

revealed. 'That half-crown was an allowance, not your full worth, lad. You now have a substantial sum in the "Posbee" (from the initials POSB, for Post Office Savings Bank, a government institution, therefore favoured by HM's Armed Forces. We'd all had an account opened for us). The residue of eighteen months pay, plus interest,' he told me. Welcome news indeed. And as I was now of an age where I could legally take a drink, I'd feel more at home back home, in the Griffin. I was legally entitled to those home comforts which the law had previously denied me. I was also of an age at which I could fight for my country, even though I wouldn't be entitled to vote for another three years or so. (You needed to be twenty-one back in those days.)

My departure from Cosford was unique as far as my future service career went in that I was not given chance to volunteer for my next assignment. I was detailed where to go.

No matter. Had I realized I was not yet qualified to serve overseas, it was probably one of the places *I'd* have chosen, given the chance.

We were now fully-fledged airmen, except those still under age, that is, and there were a few of those. As a job it was certainly different to civvy street. Different situations, different rules, still very regulated. We'd received the training, now needed to go out and do what needed doing. It was unlikely we would ever meet up again.

(Given the fact we had been a close knit group every day for the past eighteen months - we ate together, marched together, lived together, even spent what spare time we had together - I was to remain in close touch with only one of my trade entry over the years. Brinley Richards and I had clicked from day one, remained friends from the day we signed on, to the end. (I even recall being invited to go home with him from Cosford for one break. But if I remember correctly, a wave of flu swept the camp, and the break was cancelled.) On departure from Cosford, we wrote to each other regularly from wherever in the world it was we happened to be. We even ran into each other on a couple of camps - one in the Far East, when Brin came out on detachment - yet in my whole twelve years I never met another member of our entry. We occasionally visited each other, especially so during retirement. In May 2011, I attended Brin's funeral. A very sad occasion. Friendships as strong as that happen only rarely.)

So it was, blue kitbag now supplementing my cardboard

suitcase - its complement of dreams as yet unfulfilled; ie, converted into memories - I was off into the wide blue yonder of the outside world. Hopefully to begin yet another adventure.

Years later I recall Ronnie Barker, as Fletcher, in the TV series, Porridge - or in the words of his script writer - saying, "dreams is freedom". I was now about to discover that dreams were indeed freedom, and many were the times I looked forward to entering that dark world where truths so often dissolved into myth.

*   *

Page 116 Top L & R: From Boy Entrant to lifelong friend, Brin Richards.
Centre L: A 1953 Selfie. **R:** Brin, and "Ginger" Dalton.
Bottom: RAF Cosford billet, ready for inspection.

Page 117 Top: Aerial View of RAF Cosford. Fulton Block to the fore. **Bottom:** 18th Entry Passing Out Parade.

Page 118 Top L: Caley Arms, Brompton Dale. Grandad Sale was once landlord.
R: Scarborough Bay from Valley Gardens.
Centre L: Malton, across the river Derwent from Norton.
R: Thornton le Dale. Well within reach on our cycling forays into the countryside... As were **Bottom L:** ... The Yorkshire Dales, seen here in Winter, and **R:** Whitby. The harbour from halfway up the steps to East Cliff.

Page 119 Top: GAL 60; General Aircraft design, on display at Brough. As ATC Cadets we were invited to act as programme sellers at their 1950 Open Day.
Bottom: GAL were taken over by Blackburn, who developed the aircraft which became the Beverley on entry into RAF Service.

Page 120 Top: My "Hot" Ford 105E Anglia.
Centre L: Jim Clark stand-in! **R:** Schooldays. My cycling proficiency now improved, Jimmy Jackson cadges a lift outside his home. **Bottom:** By Scarborough Castle whilst on leave from Boy Entrant training.

Page 121: Farnborough 1953. My visit was courtesy of RAF Cosford. **Top:** HP115, testbed for Concorde-style wing.
Centre: Avro Vulcan, testbed for Concorde engine - underslung, centre.
Bottom: The Fleet Air Arm's DH Vixen formation display team.

Chapter Four
A PASSION FOR FLIGHT

1955

*T*he dying hours of night brought with them an aura of stillness which settled itself over the surrounding countryside, along with the early morning dew. In breaking daylight, through the remnants of a hazy mist could be seen strange, spectral-like, almost arcane shapes. These too were silent and still. Taken as a whole the scene looked as tranquil and undisturbed as a Constable landscape. Those somewhat abstract qualities weren't destined to survive though, were in fact already being breeched by nature itself as the birds began tuning up. To the slightly fuzzy mind, the dawn chorus seems overly enthusiastic. Is it possible the birds are already aware it is to be yet another fine day?

Out here on the dispersals the air was about as fresh as one was ever likely to experience in this environment. Chill and crisp. Early morning freshness. The combined aromas of moist grass and earth, even if they were slightly tainted with overtones of Avgas, Avtur, oil. All of which went some way towards clearing my mild hangover.

Out here, too, where work was just beginning, even the sounds are of a different calibre. Gentle sounds on the brittle air: the swish of canvas as covers are removed; voices, muffled, indistinct. Early morning voices. There were also the odd, harsh, metallic sounds of equipment on the move, of preparations being made, but even these seemed to be slightly muted. All in all, the sounds of a new day coming to life out on the airfield.

Of course, this didn't necessarily apply to all areas of the camp; the various messes had been serving breakfast for some time; Air Traffic, Flight Planning and the Met Office would all by now be up to speed.

Given time, the first gold rays of an early sun poked their way through, and as it did so, even the voices seemed to gain strength and vitality, became terse, authoritative.

'Switches off?'

'Switches off.' Confirmation that the ignition was inert, this from the fitter seated in the cockpit, high above the oil-stained tarmac of the dispersal. (From up close that Hastings was large, in comparison to any other aircraft I'd been near. The cabin looked huge, and, being a tail-dragger, the walk up to the cockpit was therefore steep. More of a climb than a walk.)

So, with no chance of an engine inadvertently bursting into life, the huge, four-bladed propellers were turned by hand, one man per blade, two complete rotations of each propeller, a check against hydraulic lock; oil collecting in the lower cylinders of a radial engine could wreak havoc on start-up. Four engines, four props.

As we got on with our work, so the aircrew put in an appearance. They too had checks to perform, both inside and outside of the aircraft; the necessary preparations for flight - covers and any external locks removed.

Different sounds now: electric motors, pumps for fuel and hydraulics. Hatches, doors and panels are secured, controls checked. Externally, all non essential equipment was packed up and moved from the immediate area, particularly clear of those propellers.

Any one of the ground-crew could be called upon to take charge of start-up procedures. A lot had no wish to, so, once I had the experience, I usually volunteered myself for the post. It was a responsibility, sure, for that aircraft was basically yours for a time, but it wasn't exactly an onerous task.

'All clear?' The voice from the cockpit; aircrew this time, the captain, his face framed by the clear vision panel surrounds, and the blue, cloth helmet he wore - back then, bone domes were the sole preserve of jet jockeys.

A final check of the surrounding area to ensure start-up procedures were being observed, chocks and fire extinguisher in place, superfluous ground equipment removed. 'Clear one,' I answered, raising the forefinger of my left hand. My free hand pointed to the engine in question - number one, port outer - right forefinger describing a circle in the air, a signal the area was free from obstruction, that the propeller wasn't about to transform an errant airman into Pedigree Chum.

'Starting one,' came the reply. It was to be the last verbal response between us.

A starter whined. The propeller turned, labouriously it seemed, as if reluctant to pick up speed, or unable to. A half-hearted cough appeared to test the quiet as a single cylinder fired, then died. A blue smoke-ring spun through the still air, drifting gently away. One more cough - full-throated this time - then another, until the comparative silence was finally shattered into a million pieces, Bristol Hercules bursting into angry life.

The torque, as it attempted to tear the engine from its mountings, pointed to the vast amount of power available, propeller eventually disappearing in a whirling black, yellow-tipped disc, the wash behind it putting paid to that smoke-ring once and for all.

With the pilot now also reduced to using hand signals, the three remaining engines were started in sequence: port inner, starboard inner, starboard outer, each initially belching out fearsome clouds of blue/grey smoke. This too was flung away by the swirling propwash, to disappear over and beneath the wing, over elevators which were held in the full up position - to prevent the tail lifting - then away behind to flatten the grass back there where it was untrimmed. Barely visible tongues of flame erupted from exhaust stacks which would soon glow a healthy red. Cowl gills are set, brake pressure checked, flying controls - full and free movement. With engines now warm, settled into a steady rhythm, and running off the aircraft generators, the pilot signals for the trolley-acc (a mobile battery-accumulator used during start-up) to be unplugged. An airman does so and pulls it clear to where it is in the pilot's sight. Now the chocks are waved away. I relay the signal to the airmen who stand waiting, bare inches behind those whirling, lethal steel discs. Then I hold up both hands ready to marshal him off. With a harsh, throat-clearing burst of power, the machine was taxying off in response to my signals until, with a snappy salute, I hand over control to the pilot. The aircraft was now his responsibility. Up to that moment it had been mine.

A quick dab on the brakes to verify their operation, and the aircraft is out onto the perimeter track. They'd be running checks all the way to the end of the runway: temperatures, pressures, magnetos, fuel-cocks, flaps. The list was endless. In God we trust, everything else we check and double-check. That could well have been the pilots' motto, and a good one, too. More than one aircraft has been lost by taking off with the flying controls still locked. Even Test Pilots are not immune. The Boeing 299 - later developed into the B17 - suffered just such a fate. Hard to imagine, yet it happens. (Even today, to the older type of aircraft.)

As control surfaces - mainly elevators and rudder - could be damaged by being blown around in the wind, aircraft on dispersal have these controls locked. This sometimes took the form of an external lock, a red-flagged contraption attached to the control surface itself - as on the Hastings - or, like the

Valetta, a control lock located in the cockpit, on the throttle quadrant. Sometimes the ground crew would release them, sometimes not. But no matter what the aircraft, ultimate responsibility to ensure they were removed, or disengaged before flight, rested with the aircraft captain. Which, when it came to the Valetta, was often cause for an entry to appear in the F700: "Port oil-temp gauge inoperative". The reason? As in its earlier days it had been known for the Valetta's locks to be engaged during flight (rather embarrassing) the release spring on this type had been subjected to a manufacturer's modification; the spring was re-tensioned. One slight problem: it was now so strong that extreme care needed to be exercised when disengaging the locks. The lever needed to be eased off and held firmly, if not it shot forward with such force it would hit this gauge dead-centre. Many a time I've stepped into the cockpit only to find the shattered remnants hanging down behind the panel on the end of their cable.

'Yeah, well, it would be bloody inoperative, wouldn't it, sir. Stands to reason, what with its face stove in and all.' Still, better the loss of a gauge than an aircraft. No problem with the Hastings, though, and I knew all was well with the controls here, I'd checked them myself, kept an eye open as the pilots did the same as part of their pre start-up checks.

So began another day out on the flight-line. Which, by this time, with over twelve months on the camp, was well and truly where my heart was.

It was lovely at this time of year, the summer, but it could be a very different matter in the winter months, when the frost was down, snow on the ground, and on the aircraft. This work still had to be done then, and more. The wings and flying surfaces would require deicing. Airmen would be less mobile, wrapped up in heavy protective clothing; gloved and booted. Far better to be working in the hangars then; but not for me. No matter what the weather, I was a flight-line man through and through.

*

My full-time service began with a posting to Transport Command, at RAF Dishforth, North Yorkshire. Probably one of those very airfields that had taken root during the war years, fashioned out of the surrounding farmland. It's possible some of those wartime bombers that lulled me to sleep at night had departed from these very runways. Likely, in fact, for here had been based Whitley, Wellington, and Halifax. Not exactly one

125

of the more exotically-interesting type places to which I'd hoped to be posted. Places that were talked about way back when, as they say. Names I'd heard bandied about when old timers got to waxing nostalgically, as old timers tend to do. Far away places, with strange sounding names, to quote the words of a one-time popular song. Only these were different. Far away, yes, but not places referred to in the song. These mysterious and strange sounding places were dotted along the routes to our colonies: El Adem, Mersa Matruh, Fayid, Wadi Halfa, Habbaniya, Drigh Road, Akyab, et al. (Not an airfield, that last, just a bit of Latin I threw in. Evidence that my *de facto* education was proceeding apace, for I certainly didn't learn that at Norton School for Boys. This was straight from the University of Life.)

Anyway, at the time I imagined I'd need to gain some experience before I could expect a posting to somewhere so exotic-sounding, and Dishforth didn't seem like a bad place to get it. Dreams of travel would at present have to remain just that, but at last I had my aeroplanes. No more fixing imaginary problems on imaginary aircraft with imaginary tools, this was for real. A mistake now could lead to far more serious consequences than a poor result, or a failed exam. Aircrew relied a great deal upon the ground personnel, for, to a certain extent, their lives lay in our hands. *We* needed to get things right, too.

Dishforth was literally a stone's throw from my home in Norton, and most week-ends were free, as was any off-duty time. I could wander off camp whenever I liked, wear whatever I liked. My free time was my own, to do with as I pleased. Quite a pleasant change from having no free time at all. But, what with the timing of buses, and the number of changes required, the quickest way to get home called for hitching a lift. Not too difficult back then, that post-war/National Service period when more than a certain amount of goodwill was extended by the public towards members of the Armed Forces. To the wearers of uniform, hitch-hiking was a simple matter. Almost anyone would stop, which is how I came by my first ride in a Rolls Royce. Of course, there was also the fact that, back then, one didn't need to be so mindful of picking up a "wrong 'un," as they say. More likely to be the other way round, in fact. Plain-clothed service police, posing as civilians, would occasionally pick up a hitch-hiking airman. They'd readily proceed to chat them up, posing leading questions on station layout, aircraft types and numbers, personnel strength, etc. Any information that may be deemed to be of use to an enemy. This was particularly common practice around the fighter and V-bomber stations, but I did hear tell of cases in our area too. It made us wary, as was no doubt the intent.

Had I so chosen, I could have gone home quite often, but found I rarely did. By this time I had come to realize that home was wherever I wanted it to be, and the bonds of camaraderie were such that the preference was often with new found friends. The RAF, you see, had already made me more discerning, independent, self-reliant, aware of my capabilities and limitations. I could now have aircraft and girls. Still in that order, but girls were certainly making headway up the list of priorities. Obviously so, for I seemed to devote a considerable amount of time to the act of trying to lose my virginity. I was also of age as far as drinking went. A popular drink at the time was Black Velvet, a mixture of cider and stout for us (the cider in lieu of champagne for those who could afford it - certainly not service personnel of the lower ranks). Also popular was Chicken-in-a-Basket, the then current fad in bar meals. Basically chicken breast and chips, served in a wicker basket, over the counter, of course, for few pubs had restaurants. The deadly combination of a few pints of that Black Velvet, followed by greasy chicken and chips, rarely made for a pleasant end to the evening. Especially so on the bus ride back to camp.

I read the New Musical Express, and Melody Maker, tuned in to Radio Luxembourg late on a Sunday evening, keen to hear what record had made number one this week. I smoked, too, as did almost everyone, the atmosphere in our crewroom often rivalling that of a misty autumn day. Senior Service and Players were the popular brands, but the multi-coloured Sobranie Cocktail or the strange, oval, Passing Cloud were ones with which to impress the girls. Life was almost as good as it got to be. We were paid a great deal more than at Cosford, so had cash to spend. Another thing, and a big bonus. Whereas at Cosford we'd had to pay for replacement items of uniform out of our wage, small though it was - and were told when something needed to be replaced - in the Air Force proper we were allocated an Annual Clothing Allowance, with which to buy new items of irreparably damaged uniform. Another bonus, and one which ensured you looked after that with which you were issued, was that at year's end, any unused allowance was paid to us as a credit!

So, with money in our pockets, our stamping grounds were the surrounding villages: Dishforth itself, nearby Norton-le-Clay, Marton-le-Moor, Boroughbridge. Or the more distant towns: Thirsk, York, Ripon, Knaresborough, and their wealth of pubs and good ale (all Real, back then). There was also the odd bird of the female type along to feather my nest, and we rocked around the clock to Bill Haley and the Comets. The girls usually drank orange juice or, occasionally, Babycham, certainly not wine, for pubs did not serve such a thing. That came probably ten or more years later for the pubs; not for me!

Dishforth was proving to be a revelation after the seemingly hostile environment of Cosford. Yes, we still had the odd inspection and parade, a regular part of service life, those. Here, though, they were nowhere near as frequent, nor as demanding. And, given a little ingenuity, it was possible to avoid a lot of them. Well, ingenuity was something with which I was familiar, mine having been developed and tuned to a fine art over the past eighteen months. But at Cosford it had been almost impossible to implement, other than on the Wednesday sports afternoon. Cross country running had been the standard option. A gentle trot along the road, out of sight, only to return via a hole in the fence round the back. There you go, a quiet afternoon on your pit. No falling asleep though. There were spot checks, so one needed to remain alert at all times.

Dishforth required nothing so devious. Now designated a recreation period, Wednesday afternoons no longer posed a problem. We could do as we pleased: York races, Thirsk races, Ripon races, Wetherby races, and like that. Sport, you see. Known as the Sport of Kings. After all, I had been raised among the stables of Norton (known to the racing fraternity as Malton, you may recall).

As far as parades went, well, an air test, shift work, or some carefully arranged leave would take care of most. Even missed one during a visit to London on RAF business. I'd been selected to represent Transport Command in the annual All England Aircraft Recognition Competition. I was proud to be so honoured, but was soon to be put in my place. Show some of those guys a rivet and they would relate not only the aircraft type and mark, probably give you the serial number, too. Still, I didn't fare too badly; and perhaps *they* hadn't missed a parade!

One parade it would have been foolish to miss was the weekly pay parade. Not the full march-past that lad at Cosford had so foolishly envisaged. In this respect, Dishforth didn't differ a lot from Cosford at all. Well, not often. But one week it did, for the paying officer happened to be a friend from my schooldays. Only he was now a Pilot Officer, and trainee transport jockey, which ruled out my calling him Trev, or even Trevor. Nor would it have been prudent to suggest he slip me an extra quid or two, for old-times' sake. (He had, after all, at one time also been proclaimed, my best friend. Ever.) All he got now was a snappy salute, and my last three. I got what I was due, along with the hint of a smile.

On the subject of pay, one rather outspoken National Service airman friend once related to me how upset he became when the amount he received seemed to vary week by week, with no explanation forthcoming. Well, it wouldn't would it, on pay parade? You saluted, quoted your last three, signed, took what was offered then moved off. This went on over the weeks until eventually, deciding to take matters in hand, he phoned accounts, expecting some lowly clerk to answer. All he heard was the background noise of typewriters click-clacking their messages of bureaucracy.

'What's wrong with you lot?' he demanded, after detailing the reason for the call. 'If you don't have anyone that can count I'll come and do it for you.'

'Just a minute. Do you know who you're talking to?' came the startled reply. 'This is Flight Lieutenant Wilson, accounting officer.'

'Oh, is it? Well do you know who you're talking to, Flt Lt Wilson?'

'No,' the officer replied, suddenly not sounding at all confident.

'That's all right then.' My friend wisely hung up.
*

Dishforth was the home of 242 OCU (Operational Conversion Unit), its job, to train fresh-faced young pilots - wings on their left breast still white and sparkling - the rudiments of handling multi-engined transport aircraft: Handley Page Hastings, and the stubby, cigar-shaped Valetta, by Vickers, the last piston-engined transport to be built by them. The Valetta was also operated by the resident, and fully operational, No.30 Squadron.

At last I was among machines that actually took to the air rather than simple training airframes. The servicing was for real now, all our training coming to the fore. But I was soon to realize that training was only a small part of it, experience counted for a lot, too. Take for instance the F700 entry for a Valetta: "Autopilot will not engage." It wasn't long before I too was able to proclaim, "Not again", without even setting foot in the cockpit. The autopilot featured an emergency cut-out button on the control wheel, within range of the pilot's thumb. Trouble was, the wires for this switch were routed down inside the control column, and given time they would chafe, thus shorting out, disengaging old George just as effectively as it would had the pilot punched the button. A quick rewire saw the problem cured, aircraft again ready to take to the air, George back in control. Not only that, I found I was able take to the air with them, just to check things out. As a result, many hours were logged on these two types during the next three years. Odd trips were also occasionally available in the aircraft assigned to the Station Flight; an Anson and a Chipmunk.

Air tests apart - for which I usually volunteered - all my trips were scrounged. Flights were there for the begging anyway. Plenty of room in a transport aircraft. I didn't care what kind of sortie they were on, nav-ex, night flying, even pounding round on circuits and landings. Monotonous, people said, but heavy-handed trainee pilots almost guaranteed life would never be monotonous, which is why such an exercise was known as circuits and bumps. These guys had been trained to fly on Percival's Prentice and Provost, and the twin engined Avro Anson, toys to what they now had in their hands. Believe me, the Hastings, with its huge, ultra high profile doughnut-like tyres, really could be made to bounce if not handled correctly. I was to find they could also be - often were - bounced off the surface of the nearby road, too.

The main runway on any station is naturally aligned so as to take advantage of the prevailing wind. At Dishforth, ours ran north/south, parallel to, but at a slightly lower level than the A1, or the Great North Road as it then was. But adverse winds would occasionally force a switch to the shorter east/west runway, the threshold of which was extremely close to the boundary fence, which almost guaranteed an undershoot would take in the aforementioned road. ATC controlled traffic lights, and the rubber streaked surface of the A1 served as confirmation of this, those lights protecting civilian road users from unnecessary collateral damage.

Engines were shut down during take-off, and in the air. There were flapless landings, and overshoots galore. How could it ever be boring?

Then we came to the good part. I was soon to discover that, upon completion of their course, each crew was required to make what was termed a route trip; an overseas flight down a specific route - Air Force supply lines to the Middle and Far East. To add authenticity, some freight and a few passengers were taken along, a list of volunteers' names kept for this very purpose. Add your name, and as soon as it reached the head of the list you were contacted. The only problem then lay in persuading your section commander he could afford to release you for the required period: two or three days, a week, whatever. Well, volunteering was my forte, so in went my name, quick as a flash. This, despite the fact that the first rule for survival in the forces appeared to be, never ever volunteer - for anything. Forget all that, I saw here the chance of fulfilling some of those dreams. My meagre collection was about to be expanded.

Maybe I had an understanding section commander, or maybe my presence was not as important as I figured! but my absence was to become a regular occurrence. As soon as I returned from one trip, my name was back on that list. And I don't recall ever having to turn one down. Or perhaps my section commander happened to be looking out of the window the day I almost trashed a Hastings. My fault, I'm afraid. Certainly would have been in the eyes of the Air Force, simply because I was in charge of moving the aircraft, even if I did need to rely on other people knowing what they were about.

We were set to tow the aircraft from in front of the hangars out to a dispersal, a job I'd done many times. None of your fancy towing gear in those days, mind. There was a simple arm which hooked onto the tail wheel, allowing a modicum of directional control (providing the guy manning the arm had devoured the appropriate number of Weatabix for breakfast, that is!). David Brown was to provide the pulling power, via what appeared to be a modified farm tractor. This was attached to the aircraft's main wheels by a wire towing bridle. It could move the aircraft ahead, therefore, but being flexible, a steel cable naturally contributed zero in the realms of retardation.

So here we go. The guy on the tail wheel was ready, the tractor driver was ready, I was ready, as were the guys beneath each wingtip, ready to check clearances between other aircraft, and buildings. The sort of immovable objects it was felt desirable not to approach too closely.

'All ready?' I enquired of the guys in the cockpit. 'Brakes on?'

'All ready,' came the reply.

'Chocks away,' I called, signalling to the airmen beneath the wings. 'Brakes off' - this to the cockpit crew. 'Take it away.' I signalled to the tractor driver.

With a sharp, angry hiss, the brakes were released, and as the tractor took up slack on the bridle, so the aircraft began to move. Didn't take much, for it was on a slight downhill slope. In fact it gathered momentum rather quickly. A little too quickly, thought I.

'Brakes on,' I called as the bridle resumed its slack state, aircraft moving faster than the tractor was pulling, which was not a good moment to discover that the guy in the cockpit had either misread the gauge, or failed to check the pneumatic pressure before giving me the go-ahead. Naturally, according to sod's law (or was it Murphy, up to his old tricks?) the pressure was far too low, even if existent. This became apparent quicker than almost immediately, for not a lot happened. Not a lot in the way of retardation, that is! Emotionally, all hell let loose. And, as such circumstances do tend to make one sit up and take notice, it felt like my bowels were about to do likewise.

'Brakes on,' I called again, desperation beginning to show through when nothing happened. Not even the courtesy of a reply.

'Cockpit,' I called, loudly, was rewarded as a head briefly poked its way out, only to tell me to, 'Stand by.' The head then made a rapid withdrawal.

'What do you mean, standby?' I called, hoping someone was listening. 'We're rolling here, get those bloody brakes on.'

'We're working on it,' said a seemingly disembodied voice.

Working on it? Bloody hell. Ahead I could see nothing but gloom and doom; the squadron's crewroom looming large in our path; a very bleak outlook as far as myself and the Royal Air Force were concerned. With a future that looked about as stable as a ten-storey tower of playing cards, my brain was rapidly evaluating the options, striving to arrive at some magical solution.

I looked across at the guys on the wingtips, perhaps for inspiration, but they seemed to have lost interest, or hope, not a sign of help forthcoming from that direction, forget it. Nor did there seem to be a glimmer of hope from the tractor driver, in fact he looked about ready to abandon ship. Couldn't really blame him, what with that lot bearing down on him. But when I waved, rather frantically I suppose, he remained aboard, actually followed my instructions to the letter, attempting to turn the wayward beast, albeit without success. I could well imagine his thoughts: bail out and the blame could fall on me. Stay with it and... "I was just obeying orders, sir." Covering his ass, was what. Something I had obviously failed to do.

I looked aft for salvation. No way. The aircraftsman supposedly controlling the tail wheel struggled to turn it, failed miserably. One more hope shot to hell. Obviously *hadn't* had his bloody Weatabix.

I noticed the lads upstairs in the cockpit had now applied full corrective rudder, seemed to me we were rapidly approaching the speed at which it would become effective. Yet despite all these efforts it still appeared the aircraft was about to make an interesting addition to the fixtures and fittings in the pilots' crewroom, a generally inadvisable practice, I would imagine. After all, it's usually the other way round, aircrew going out to join their aircraft. And how would that look on my CV? Experienced at towing aircraft into hangars, via the fire door! Forget the crewroom, that was a mess anyway. Luckily, it didn't happen, for the Lord dealt bountifully with me that day, or with those guys in the cockpit; they, after all, were closer to

Him than I was.

"Never before had I seen the hand-pump operated with such frenzy (so that's where all the Weatabix went), so many eyes willing the pointer of the pressure gauge to rise," I was later told by one of the observers from upstairs. But rise it did, along with my hopes and, one presumes, theirs also. Seems they'd started on the pumping bit the second they released the brakes, realizing their error immediately; mistaking brake pressure for system pressure.

Not sure if the tailwheel actually left the ground once pressure was restored, I doubt it. Seemed the guy at least had the sense to apply the brakes progressively, as soon as that once more became an option. In fact, it obviously didn't appear at all dramatic to anyone not in the know, for there were no repercussions, no startled personnel rushing out to lend a hand, or offer advice. Nor was there a scattering of tables, chairs, and newspapers, in the crewroom, white faces pressed against windows, bodies flying out the door. Not a bit of it. No, repercussions are probably for the future, when I pass away a year or two earlier than I otherwise might have done. Grey haired and withered, at forty-two. Tell you one thing, I checked the system pressure personally before moving another aircraft. Nor did I take any chances either; that pointer almost needed to be wrapped around the top end stop before I'd even have the brakes released!

But I wasn't the first or last person to overlook things.

'How are we doing, Dave?' the engine mechanic asked, poking his head through the over-wing escape hatch.

'Hardly seems to have moved,' I replied.

'Um, OK, keep an eye on it, please', he said, sounding a bit worried.

He was out on the port wing, refuelling the Hastings on which I was carrying out my preflight checks in the cockpit. In those days you refuelled an aircraft similar to refuelling a car, stuck the fuel nozzle in the over-wing tank and held it there whilst the bowser driver controlled the flow.

It was night, and to save himself repeatedly having to stop the fuelling process, trudge back and forth across the wing, through the escape hatch and into the aircraft he'd asked me to keep an eye on the relevant gauge.

'Still no change,' I informed him a little later. I'd finished my work, was ready to go and sign off in the F700. 'I've checked the gauge, that seems OK,' I told him.

'Strange.' Then, after a pause for thought, 'Hey! anyone there?' he called down to the ground.

'Yeah, mate, you finished?' the bowser operator replied.

'No. Something appears to be wrong. We don't seem to be getting any fuel.'

'Getting fuel all right,' the operator replied. 'It's pissing out all over the tarmac on the other side. Seems it has been for a while, but I just noticed it.'

'Well why the hell didn't you say so?' the mechanic shouted.

'Just, bloody did, didn't I.'

It turned out to be a fuel management problem. Someone had left a crossfeed pump switched on, a result of which the fuel was being transferred into already full tanks in the starboard wing, thence out of the overflow!

Knowing how keen the Air Force were on details, I often wondered how that fitter explained away all those extra gallons of Avgas.

*

The call came. I took the phone and listened, learned that my name had topped the magic list, and was I ever excited. I was going abroad. Abroad! The very word was exciting. Those far away places at last. Dreams about to be fulfilled. Where would it be? Mersa Matruh, in Egypt? Wadi Halfa, Sudan? Maybe as far as Habbanniya, Iraq; Hyderabad, India; or on east, to Singapore itself, all names that rolled of the tongue of many a long-serving airman. Some I'd even been made aware of as far back in my Air Training Corps days. The excitement soared as the seconds ticked away, person at the other end of the telephone revealing the facts. I listened, but excitement dwindled rapidly, to be replaced by disappointment when I learned what was to be my destination.

RAF Valley is in Anglesey, North Wales. OK, a different country, but still part of the British Isles last time I heard. Bleak and miserable; I'd heard that, too. On top of which, the bloody aircraft, a Valetta, went unserviceable, big time - requiring an engine ignition harness change. They had to send an engine fitter, along with the parts to fix it, plus another aircraft to carry the passengers back home. I'd certainly been hoping for better. Ah well, one has to begin somewhere, and after that it did get interesting. UK, Europe, the Mediterranean, Middle East, I visited them all. Even dropped in at some of those exotic-sounding places to which I'd at one time hoped to be posted,

135

was immediately pleased I hadn't been. Fayid was one, in the Canal Zone (Suez, of course), and Castel Benito (later renamed Idris, after their last King), in Libya. I can still remember the smell of the place, sort of peculiar to the Middle East. Don't know what though: Dates? Camels? The dry air of the desert? Who knows, probably a combination of all those things.

During this early, educational, phase of travel I was learning too - about not allowing myself to be ripped off; a painful process. I recall one instance in particular, probably the first. It involved, a country where spirits of the earthly kind were at a premium, a number of duty free bottles, and someone who knew someone else with an interest in acquiring same. (himself, as it happened!)

Servicemen weren't paid a lot back then, and the price offered would probably have sounded good even to such as John D Rockefeller. Of course, this should have alerted us to begin with. Anyway, a deal was struck. This man would introduce a buyer, would even drive us to his house, which he proceeded to do. There were numerous delays en-route, of course. He had to see this man and that, make arrangements. "Much lire, my friends. Have patience." But we eventually arrived, somewhere. Then it was time to walk, down a side street off a side street in what must have been the least populated area in town, perhaps even in the world. A respectable-looking area though, reassuring, that. A maze of streets and alleys - well lit - an open door, long, marbled corridor, sparkling clean. Now the crunch. We must wait. He'd take the bottles, see which were acceptable. We demurred, vociferously. Not that bloody stupid, even if we may look it.

"Okay, no deal." Just like that, not willing to compromise.

We demurred less, needed the money, could pick up more duty free on the way home.

"Trust me. Haven't I gone out of my way for you?"

Smooth talking bastard. Capitulation. He slipped away.

Had we awaited his return, with piles of loot, we'd be at that door still. How could anyone be so gullible? But that's how one learns about life. So obvious. Isn't it always, after the event. Like they say, hindsight is twenty-twenty vision. We laughed about it among ourselves, what else was there to do? But inside I was fuming, determined it would never happen again. Ha!

So much for Europe and the Middle East. Yet for some reason the Far East seemed to evade me. Maybe someone knew something I didn't?

My next trip took me to Malta, via Istres, in southern France. Istres is the French equivalent of Boscombe Down or Farnborough, and many experimental aircraft were to be seen scattered around the base. Types such as the Leduc O.21 ramjet aircraft were observed, plus the Sud Ouest Trident, and the Hurel-Dubois HD31 high aspect ratio research aircraft. (I was to meet up with the HD31 again, more than twenty-five years later. Long since decommissioned from test flying, it had been put to work in Gabon. What a coup for the logbook that would have been. Unfortunately, it never happened.)

What passed for countryside in Malta, ie the area between the airfield at Luqa and the capital of Valetta, appeared to be a succession of small stony fields surrounded by tumbledown stone walls, small villages and numerous churches. Twisty, narrow roads wound their way between them. The church theme continued in Valetta, only here they were more cathedral like. The town itself began on the high ground, occupied by the Phoenicia Hotel and the bus terminus, then flowing down to the sea via steep narrow streets, with numerous steps for the pedestrians.

We stayed overnight, which gave us a chance to visit some of the sights and bars, including those on Straight Street, otherwise known as "The Gut". Interesting place, Malta!

At present, life, as the saying went, was "swinging". This, the current euphemism that defined anything that was OK, good, or excellent, was the catch-phrase of Norman Vaughan, of "Sunday Night At The London Palladium" fame. The word became vogue during the fifties, as these things occasionally tend to do. Today's equivalent would probably be "Didn't they do well?" or "To see you, nice," as used by Bruce Forsyth. But then it was "Swinging". Which brings to mind a particular evening at the Astra, the camp cinema at Dishforth - and almost every other RAF base, for Astra was the RAF cinema chain.

The incident happened during a particularly dramatic sequence: no music, no dialogue, no sound effects, not even the cracking of a branch or a whisper of wind, on screen or in the theatre. The cowboy hero, prowling the woods in this stillborn silence is seeking someone or other, finds him; a pair of boots at face level, the attached body out of scene, above, obviously strung

137

up. Suddenly, from out of the hushed auditorium and threatening gloom came a solitary voice; loud, clear, quick as a flash. 'Swinging,' it said, drawing the word out to its full extent. And did that ever wreck the suspense.

Back on the flying front I was to discover that relatively few people seemed to bother volunteering for the route trips, for which I was eternally grateful. But I never ceased to be amazed by the number of airmen who showed no interest in aviation whatsoever. How could anyone join the Air Force and not want to fly, or at least fail to be excited by the presence of aircraft? Even National Servicemen? Was it possible to spend two years of your life surrounded by the elements of aviation, yet remain untouched by them? The answer seemed to be an emphatic `yes'. I loved this environment, surrounded by all the things that went to create it. Not just the aircraft, but also the hangars in which they lived, the specialist equipment required to service and operate those aircraft, the taxiways, the runways from which they flew, even the grass which makes up the bulk of a military airfield. I could accept that others wouldn't find it so enthralling, just found it hard to understand why. There again there's no accounting for taste. Let's face it, I've heard tell some people are actually turned on by columns of figures, a visit to the ballet, railway engines. "One man's meat...," as the saying goes.

Still, this was the age of National Service. And if one were being offered a choice: Army or Air Force? I suppose.... Well, not really much of a choice at all, is it? I'd come to that very same decision over two years ago. To me, being around aircraft, working on them, touching them, was my nirvana. First line servicing gave me even more scope than ever, for *all* arrivals were within my domain. In this there was another bonus to my being at RAF Dishforth. This station, due to its position, and usually clement weather, was classed a Master Diversion airfield. Meaning it's services were available twenty-four hours a day, almost three hundred and sixty five days a year, and as such, I was also treated to a wide variety of visiting aircraft. I recall Hunters, Swifts - remember those? - Meteors, from Mk4 through to NF14, and Ansons. The Navy occasionally dropped by also, bringing with them such aircraft as the Avenger, Gannet, Skyraider, Seahawk and Attacker. There was that Lancaster conversion, the Avro York, too - Dan Air calling in nightly for a time, delivering the newspapers during a national rail strike. Which was how we got to read the Daily Mirror at three in the morning. Yes, I know, but I was a Yorkshireman after all, and it was free! Sophistication would come with time.

There was the Lockheed Neptune, too, from nearby Topcliffe - at times a little *too* nearby, it seemed. Close enough for the heading of their main runway to be on a par with our cross runway. We actually had a Hastings land there thinking he was at home base. His error only became apparent when Dishforth tower questioned his request for taxying instructions once he'd reported being on the ground; no aircraft to be seen by Dishforth Air Traffic Control. I believe I did mention these pilots were trainees, didn't I?

We had visits from F-86 Sabres - my introduction to the sonic boom, back there at Yeadon. Even the incredibly ungainly-looking Blackburn Beverley, just entering service, put in the odd appearance. In fact I well recall the first visit of this lumbering giant; it's departure in particular.

The aircraft began its take-off roll, pace unhurried, engines roaring, seemingly in frustration, for it rolled, and it rolled, and it rolled. It appeared to have as much enthusiasm for flight as would a block of flats, which is exactly what it reminded me of (I even recall hearing of a pilot who compared it to flying a block of flats from the top floor). But it was eventually successful, clawing its way into the sky just as quickly as multi-thousand horsepower and somewhat parochial aerodynamics allowed. Well, the aerodynamics were fine as far as the coefficient of lift went, but I could imagine form drag as being a bit of a problem. Not exactly stealth technology, this! Such a performance, that once it was safely airborne I felt as if I should applaud. Others were less gracious.

'Well, even a chock would become airborne if you whirled it round on the end of its rope,' one of my mates remarked.

This was one of the less disparaging remarks overheard at the time. And I did hear tell of one bemused American who - upon first setting eyes on Blackburn's "biggie" - was heard to comment, "Sure as Hell won't replace the airplane." Nor did it, but over the years it did do an excellent job in the role for which it had been designed, that of short/medium range transport and general load carrier. The big failing of the Beverley turned out to be the engines' seemingly voracious appetite for oil. It was said that if the aircraft wasn't dripping oil, or burning it, it didn't have any! It even had a top-up tank in the wing, from which, on the longer flights, oil could be pumped into the engine reservoir whilst airborne. This of course meant some unfortunate needed to crawl into the wing, right behind those roaring engines, to do the pumping.

Me? Amongst all this I was the proverbial dog in the sausage factory. My only regret is that I have no photographs of this era, security being so tight at the time. Cold War and all that. Photography on or near the base was not just frowned upon, it was a definite no-no. Although I do have a photograph of the Beverley, in its prototype form, then known as the Universal Freighter, or GAL60 (for General Aircraft Limited). It was taken at Brough, near Hull, where it was built. Another Yorkshire success. The photo was taken back when, as ATC cadets, we'd been invited to act as programme sellers during an open day at the airfield, which was Blackburn's base.

Another frustration of this period was that I never did get to fly in the trainer version of a single-engined fighter, piston or jet. But although it was something I longed and hoped for, I didn't really need to. Servicing visiting aircraft meant I had sat in plenty, and given my imagination, that almost amounted to the same thing.

My first priority was to check that the safety pins were fitted to the ejection seat. Then, after recharging the oxygen system, carrying out my cockpit checks, servicing the flight instruments, I'd remain awhile. Right hand on the stick, left on the throttle, my eyes would traverse the multitude of dials, switches and buttons, left hand now fancifully flicking, tapping, and pushing.

My salute, as I prepared to taxi out, was in return for the one given me by the imaginary ground-crew.

I could smell the oil and exhaust in the imagined slipstream outside the open cockpit of a biplane, feel the sun streaming through the pressurized canopy of a modern jet. I'd speak into the dead radio, requesting clearances and landing instructions, performing a zero-zero high-speed pass before zooming round to join the circuit, managing a quick burst with the Aden cannon at the station commander's car on the way. The lighter side of life. These harmless imaginings in no way satisfied the urge to fly in such types, but they perhaps helped ease acceptance of the fact that the chances had anyway been minute, especially on a transport base.

Dishforth was to introduce me to the darker side of aviation, too. The realities and dangers brought home one night as I wandered along the dispersal to work on an aircraft. Flying was in progress, a chubby Valetta - nicknamed "pig" because of its appearance - charging urgently down the runway on its take-off run. Even though it was dark, the red and green navigation lights defined the dim silhouette as it roared away from me, exhausts glowing red as they spouted blue flame. A take-off, or landing, being something I was never able to pass up on, I watched until darkness enveloped the aircraft, then turned away.

Suddenly, a deathly silence replaced the healthy-sounding roar of its twin engines, as if my turning had switched them off. Then the silence was gone, to be replaced by a fearful noise which chilled me to the core; the heart-rending whumph of a fuel-heavy explosion. In a field over on the far side of the A1, the resultant holocaust lit the night sky.

Overcome by a feeling of helplessness I gazed at it briefly before turning away once more. I couldn't watch the fiery demise of one of our aircraft and its crew. With heavy heart I trudged back to my work. Nothing I could do to help. Nothing anyone could do. No possible way for anyone to escape from such an inferno, I imagined. Wrong again. I subsequently learned that all on board escaped with only minor injuries, even though the aircraft was a total loss. Amazing.

We later had a Hastings go down over Ripon golf course, and that crew were not so fortunate. All perished in a crash which was to feature in the national press, front page. Must have been a slow news day, though I do recall there was something strange about the photographs. None of the propeller blades were bent back. The lower ones stuck straight in the ground, as though the aircraft had hit with no forward speed whatever. A flat spin maybe? The date: September 13th 1955 - but not a Friday.

I was airborne again that evening, the aircrew questioning my sanity. They were flying because they'd been detailed to, and it was what they were paid to do, they said. They didn't want to. Why was I volunteering to accompany them? To me it was a question that didn't really need answering.

That crash had an even more profound effect on me, for I seem to recall being forcibly volunteered to join the funeral party - rest on arms reversed, the final salute, and such.

But these were unobserved crashes, events disguised by darkness, or hidden behind a newspaper headline. Next time was to be different, for it's a sickening sight to watch helpless as an aircraft falls out of the sky.

*

A DC3 of 1325 flight - on detachment at Dishforth before heading out to Christmas Island and the British Nuclear Test Program - overflew the airfield, an ominous trail of smoke evident, belching from the starboard engine. Smoke became visible flame, fierce, obviously well established. At the controls was Master Pilot George Radcliffe, up around three thousand feet. People down below willed him to bring it in. Surely he had the room to manoeuver, if only he had the time. The nose went down, a steep dive. An attempt to douse the flames by forcing the airflow to snuff them out. It seemed to work. But as the pilot recovered from the dive, height now around fifteen hundred feet, so the burning engine detached itself from the wing and fell away, leaving open oil and fuel lines to feed the flames. Which is when reality struck home. The cold and terrible certainty of how things were going to end. Time, space to manoeuvre, options, had all run out at once. That aircraft was doomed.

Now clear of the station, and nearby village, but totally out of control, KN129 seemed determined to follow the path of its missing engine. A wing dropped lazily and you could imagine the pilot fighting to regain control of a totally uncontrollable

machine. He had no option, for, naturally, Transport Command crews do not carry parachutes - bad for passenger morale. Those watching, probably everyone on camp by this time, seemed dumbstruck, and if willpower alone could have changed things there would have been no problem. But there was little chance that willpower could achieve that, nor did it. The aircraft spiralled down, seemingly in slow motion, looking as though it was about to begin a display routine. Then, in the final seconds of its avian life it rolled onto its back before vanishing behind distant buildings. A muffled explosion and the tell-tale column of oily-black smoke mushroomed up to signal the inevitable outcome. Other aircraft circled overhead a field in the Minskip area like vultures over carrion.

We later learned the chances of a landing had apparently been fifty-fifty, but the pilot had seen his priority as clearing the married quarters and nearby village, before turning to making the attempt.

Three lives lost. How many saved?

*

Two years and I was on the move again. Melksham this time, in the rolling Wiltshire countryside. After the modern barracks of Dishforth it was back to the wooden hut regime. Ten beds a side, a pot-bellied stove in the centre. I recall many an hour seated by that, soaking up the heat. The beds closest to it were too warm, the rest of us freezing.

It reminded me of home, the Griffin in the early days:

Our fire was an old cast-iron grate affair with back boiler, an oven built in to one side. It supplied the taps with hot water, a kettle held water for tea, and from the oven came most of our bread. Apart from being the sole source of heat it also provided us with toast, my bread - spiked on a brass fork - vying with sister, Maureen's bread for sight of the glowing coals. I spent many an hour standing in front of that fire, too, back to the coals, legs astride. It was the only warm place in the room. Which is why damp washing hung above my head, suspended from one of those ceiling rack things. But, (as with the Melksham stove) there was heat only if you stood close.

So the huts were cold, but at least they were weatherproof. No leaking roof, no rebellious winds whistling in through badly fitting doors and windows. And cold I was by now well used to.

Melksham was yet another training establishment. Technical. Another six months of schooling, both trade and academic. Another bout of square bashing and the bull; part and parcel of any training camp. But the regime was nowhere near as tough and restrictive as had been Cosford, and successful completion of this course did offer another step up through the ranks. Shortly after my return to Dishforth, I found it effectively to be two steps up the promotional ladder.

A service requirement was to be *au fait* with Station Routine Orders. Issued and displayed regularly, these detailed everything that was happening, or about to happen on the station as a whole, and to various individuals. Duties were allocated, postings in and out, requests made known. When I noticed a request for an Instrument Fitter to exchange postings with a person of like trade in Singapore, I immediately volunteered. Found myself promoted to corporal in a vain effort to keep me where I was - the overseas post calling for a junior technician, my present rank. Too bad, Dishforth, seems they required corporals as well, for I soon found my name to be featuring on SROs, listed under what were termed PWRs (Provisional Warning Report, for overseas service) on Draft 1511B.

This phase of my service career saw me through to August 1957. I'd very much enjoyed it, was in a way sad to be leaving.

Looking back there was the camaraderie, and places remembered. Knaresborough, particularly the bus station on a Saturday night, awaiting the last bus. We'd always finish up in the Board Inn, next door. Wouldn't particularly miss that though. The memory of being legless, and feeling unwell, I mean. The old carrot and peas all over the pavement trick! Then there was the Black-a-Moor, a pub name that springs to mind, though for the life of me I can't recall the location. Must have had some good times there, one imagines. (Around forty years later, driving back from Harrogate to York, I missed a turn. After driving along in the country for a while I passed through a village, and there it was, the Black-a-Moor. Must have been a good watering hole for us to travel that far from camp. Would have to have been on the bus route, too, for no one I knew in the service owned a car in those early days. But I also have recollections of many a special night spent there, too - demob parties and the like - so maybe that pub itself *had* been special.)

As I tramped around the station collecting signatures on my clearance chit, I recalled how that camp had looked three years ago, when going through the reverse procedure upon arrival; my first operational posting. The contemporary accommodation, matching blocks (an improvement, even on Cosford's Fulton block). Then there was that crescent of hangars which overlooked the airfield proper, Hastings and Valetta, crouching there, almost looking as if they were awaiting my presence, possibly even wondering where I'd got to. Real aeroplanes at last. And I recalled how big an aircraft the Hastings had at first seemed; that long, steep trek from entrance to cockpit. It *had* been big, until the Beverley came on the scene. A Hastings stood there now, fresh from yet another sortie. I could visualize the atmosphere up in that recently vacated cockpit: the whine of gyros running down, instruments dead or dying, switches off. Outside it would be the metallic ticking as the engines cooled and metal contracted. Everything was now awaiting the attentions of the fitters and riggers who would shortly arrive to rectify any faults noted by the crew, and entered in the F700. Then, providing no night flying was scheduled, they would put the machine to bed. I also recalled working out there in the depths of winter, in the ice and snow, how I'd discovered, almost by accident, that working at night in such conditions entitled us to a tot of rum. Only problem was, the rations were dispensed by the medical staff, in sick quarters, rather a long trek in the middle of the night. I made the journey only one time. Too far. I had never been keen on rum anyway.

I'd arrived here fresh-faced, technically knowledgeable, but operationally inexperienced. Not so now. After three years on the line I not only had the knowledge, I also possessed the experience to back it up.

The memories seemed fresh, yet so much had happened since that first day. Anyway, time now to move on. New, exciting experiences to record, I hoped. So I forgot about the past, filed the memories, packed my suitcase with my newly acquired tropical kit - issued during a trip to RAF Innsworth, in far away Gloucestershire - along with my dreams and aspirations, looked ahead to my new posting, in a new land.

Apart from being kitted out for the tropics, there was also a required visit to the medical centre, where my arms appeared to have been used as dartboards, each receiving several inoculations and vaccinations. Not taking too many chances, the Air Force. Still, I *was* going overseas. Aviation in imagined paradise. What more could one ask of life? Well, a little more cash, for starters. That wouldn't have brought with it too many objections. Be that as it may, I was ready. All I needed now was an aeroplane.

The thought of a troopship never even entered my head. Although perhaps it should have.

*   *

146

Chapter Five
EN ROUTE TO THE WORLD

*T*he garden, with its hibiscus and travellers palms, was enclosed, nicely shaded, quiet and peaceful. The hotel buildings served to screen it from the traffic noise and chaos just a short distance away, out there on the streets. Attending to one's every wish in this sheltered environment, uniformed waiters flitted silently amongst rattan furnishings set out on the grass beneath tropical skies. It was in this tranquil setting - ensconced in luxury, surrounded by the gifts of nature - that such as Maugham, Coward, and Mitchener took tea and wrote. For although humidity in the Lion City is generally high, out here in the garden the climate always seemed more endurable.

Lion City? A direct translation from the Sanskrit: Singa, meaning lion, Pura, city; the island state of Singapore.

This oasis for novelists, the Palm Court - to be found within the encircling arms of Raffles Hotel - is probably one of the few places in the area which remained basically unchanged since the heady days of Empire. But in 1957, Raffles was definitely a no go area for the likes of myself - Out of Bounds to BOR's (British Other Ranks), ie, this was Officer territory, just as it had been under Japanese occupation, and, although ostensibly, during the days of Empire.

Indeed, Singapore itself was one of the last remaining bastions of those days of Empire, for at that time the whole island sat there, redolent of another age. I know this, for it was the place to which I was posted. RAF Seletar to be precise.

No quirk of fate, this. I'd volunteered again. In fact, opening my mouth was probably the most dangerous thing I did during my military career. I always seemed to be volunteering for one thing or another. Singapore, though, was certainly acceptable. No, better than that, it was absolutely wonderful. The exotic location I had long craved was finally mine, come what may. What else could I wish for?

Well, an aircraft or two would have gone some way towards making things perfect. Aircraft on which to practise my trade, not the one I'd flown out in - a Hermes - basically, a civilian version of the Hastings. Both built by Handley Page, though the Hermes slightly larger, and with a tricycle undercarriage.

At Innsworth I'd been issued with my first passport (that

impressive blue and gold version back then of course, courtesy of the Home Office and Air Ministry, long before we became "Europeans", and the Air Ministry became part of the MOD), it accorded me the status of "Government Official" as my occupation, and we wore civilian clothes during the flight; a precaution. I assumed it had something to do with the need to overfly unfriendly territories, and that, should an emergency occur in such airspace, forcing us to land.... Well, it was a civilian aircraft full of civilians, wasn't it? At least as far as the niceties of diplomacy allowed.

*

Images of my immediate arrival on the island are still perfectly clear, for it had been a totally new experience to that which I had so recently left behind: green fields, English beer, Elvis getting "All Shook Up", fish and chips and the like. Out here there was a soft, tropical night to greet me as the aircraft's door opened on my new environment: a velvet sky, the sweet, scented air, the incessant clicking of the cicadas. As I stepped out a warm blustery breeze flicked at me like a feather duster. It was the kind of night most people back home could only dream about. For a minute I thought I'd died and gone to Heaven.

But that warm tropical evening also temporarily served well to embellish the truth - a white lie that embroidered the ordinary with a colourful and imaginative border - for what didn't greet me out there at the airport was the fetid smell of open storm-drains, and the rancid pools of stagnant water. Even the river was filthy. There were mosquitoes, and cockroaches. Oh, and also the durian; a popular, and apparently very tasty tropical fruit. But the durian had its downside insomuch as it was banned from being consumed in most public places. The reason for this became obvious once you got a whiff of the interior; a smell akin to the winner of a vile nappy contest, so I am led to believe! Never did drum up the courage to try it.

But none of this was I to discover, or notice, until later, for they were the kind of things that seemed to have been kept secret from the writers of the guidebooks.

Then there were the people, Chinese-looking and all. I somehow hadn't expected that. Don't exactly know what I had expected, hadn't really thought about it to tell the truth, too wrapped up in excitement. (I have since. After Singapore every new location was researched thoroughly, well before I set foot in the place. Even the two weeks holiday was subject to the same scrutiny. With so short a time on offer no point squandering a couple of days finding out about something you could already be doing. The obvious exception to this self-imposed rule was to be Nigeria. Reason: the market is not exactly awash with guidebooks on Nigeria. Well, it wouldn't be, would it? Not exactly a popular tourist destination! In fact, not a popular destination at all I would have thought, Nigerians excepting.)

Apart from all the above, I immediately fell in love with Singapore. The atmosphere was magical. Though this was the first, there would, over the years, be innumerable such arrivals, such nights.

Of course, it wasn't all sun and powder-puff clouds. The occasional storm would sweep through. Once in a while, especially during the monsoon season, would come a storm of truly frightening proportions.

The sky would growl to the slow rumble of distant thunder, drawing one's attention to the north-west and the turmoil which was building over mainland Malaya. Large, puffy, cumulus clouds, far away up country developed steadily during the day, their billowing tops eventually thrusting up into the troposphere. Solid looking, and glaringly white, they would boil and continued to grow, climbing higher and higher as the afternoon wore on, until they formed massed ranks. Soon the tops were flattening out, transformed by high altitude jetstreams into the familiar anvil shapes of Cumuli-nimbus - the thunder head - serving notice of the forthcoming depression.

Another steady drum-roll would draw the attention, still distant, but patently moving our way.

Within maybe twenty minutes, the sun, flashing briefly around the remaining high, domed peaks, trimmed them with a lining of silver. Magnificent and majestic, but possibly deadly too. Now the sun would slide from view, swallowed up by the gathering storm.

The temperature would drop as if in sympathy.

The air would now be heavy with humidity, sky and sea becoming inseparable as clouds dragged their skirts of rain across the surface.

The Malayan mainland, barely a couple of miles distant over the Straits, would disappear without trace behind the black wall which swept inexorably towards Singapore, the sea ahead of it streaked with whiteness as the wind lashed the surface.

Then the clouds would cast off their leaden grey

appearance in exchange for an ugly, purplish look, quickly dissolving into a thick blackness amongst which lightning flashed and streaked, zig-zagging down in long filigreed forks.

Palm trees, which moments ago stood serene against the darkening backdrop, would stir, faintly at first, barely disturbed. Then the movement would become pronounced as the breeze intensified, now a wind, escalating and strengthening until it whistled and howled.

It would become very dark and threatening as the first heavy drops of wind driven rain splattered, hissing, onto concrete which still retained much of the heat stored during the day. Black spots suddenly appeared, then, just as quickly, evaporated. But these were just the preliminaries, the ground soon becoming overwhelmed as the rain swept on, engulfing all before it, slanting closer to the horizontal than the vertical, carried on the strength of the wind.

Palms, now barely visible through deluge and darkness, would bow over before the onslaught, old and infirm fronds being plucked out and borne away, twisting and tumbling on the savage wind. Lightning would be intense, like a gigantic photoflash, jagged forks illuminating the sky and throwing the scene into sharp relief, whilst also casting eerie shadows. Each flash would be followed by the sharp crack and boom of thunder, rattling the glass in doors and windows, flash and thunder being instantaneous.

The ferocity of the storm would be both frightening and awesome. A vivid display of the raw and violent forces of nature at work.

Rain would beat a harsh and unrelenting tattoo, cascading down at such a rate as to overwhelm everything. Grassy lawns succumbed as huge lakes formed in the depressions. The reason for those huge storm drains becoming immediately apparent, for they'd be filled to the brim with a raging torrent of swirling, muddy water; a danger to the unwary.

Truly a thunderstorm of frightening intensity. But such storms rarely lasted, sun eventually breaking through, temperature climbing again, steam rising from concrete and bush alike. OK, not quite paradise, yet, for humidity almost constantly hovered around the eighty per cent mark, temperature recording a similar figure. But I could imagine paradise as being only a few short steps away.

Then there were the Chinese girls, slim and graceful, their cheongsams split right up to the thigh.

I had been overseas before: Malta, France, Libya, Egypt; those training flights from Dishforth. But those visits had been fleeting. They'd served to stimulate the wanderlust in me, but that was about all. Besides, this was the first of the truly exotic locations. Here I wore khaki cotton rather than blue serge - shorts by day, longs at night - the standard issue fitting about as well as a three-fingered glove. Lily-white skin apart, I soon discovered it was my ill-fitting uniform with knee-length shorts which made me as conspicuous as a tarantula on an iced cake. Everyone else seemed smartly dressed, and I was astute enough to ascertain the reason why. So it was quickly down to a local tailor, whom I had outfit me from scratch. As this area was to be my theatre of operations for the next two and a half years, I decided I may as well look the part, especially as it cost so little (just as well, for we were paid so little!). Out went the shiny black shoes, to be replaced by the soon-to-be-scruffy, fawn, suede desert boots, whose wear seemed almost universal, officers and airmen alike. (Unofficially, it seemed shoes were for parades only.) Then there was the matter of arms and legs. Compared to those who had been here for some time I was ghostly white, a result of which was that I - along with all the other new arrivals - became known as a "Moony" - for moon man. Just had to grin and bear being addressed as such by the well established inhabitants, along with the cries of: "Get yer knees brown," and "Get some in." Meaning, time in the area. And time is what it took to gain a tan; no rushing. This we were to discover during the embarrassment of being lectured by the medical officer on the dangers of sunburn and venereal disease, both apparently rife in the area. Both therefore a threat, if one did not take adequate precautions. Both were chargeable offences, carrying the designation, "self-inflicted injury," along with the annotation, WOAS (whilst on active service), a charge like that could be serious enough to warrant a Court Martial, for this *was* an "active service" posting.

The VD threat was serious enough for them to make us watch a film showing its possible damaging effects on certain parts of our anatomy. Which is where the embarrassment came in, for the audience also featured "Moonies" from the Women's Royal Air Force; all lily-white and blushing pink.

The obvious answer would have been for us lads and lasses to get together, as it were, thus reducing the possibility of picking up anything untoward. But life is never quite so

151

simple!

Care needed to be taken all round, then. For as well as nut rot, foot rot and gut rot were also prevalent, not to mention the dreaded malaria-carrying mosquito. Hence the insistence on our having to wear trousers and a long-sleeved shirt after dark. It was therefore an order we tolerated - a majority of the time.

When first volunteering for overseas service I'd actually opted for Hong Kong. There again so, it seemed, had everyone else! This being the case, I wasn't surprised or dismayed to find I didn't get it. Singapore *had* been my second choice, and I look back on my time there as a series of images; half-remembered dreams.

Fortune smiled upon me from the start for, with trooping by sea the norm, I was flown out - probably a legacy of the recent Suez crisis - the canal still blocked by sunken wrecks.

That flight was an adventure in itself. At a time when Singapore direct was still little more than a dream, G-ALDV, a Handley Page Hermes of Skyways carried me from Stanstead to Paya Lebar in all of three days. A total of thirty-seven flying hours - for a trip which is now but a reasonably comfortable twelve hours non-stop by Boeing 747-400.

No in-flight drinks, and no movies back then, either. And interior noise levels from four roaring piston engines was quite wearing. Meals were in sandwich form, came in cardboard boxes, often tasted like they were made out of them, too. Nor could we always climb above the worst of the weather, despite the aircraft being fully pressurised. The choice lay between, through, or around - and around cost the airline money! The aircraft also required refuelling down-route, which meant sectors of around four to six hours duration. A leisurely trip for us then, but if dwelled upon, one had to wonder about crew fatigue, for they didn't 'slip' en-route as is now the norm. Of course, dwell on it was what I did not do. Not back then. And by now it no longer matters. (G-ALDV did crash six months later, but this was when on a test flight from Gatwick. Apparently the elevators locked whilst in flight, the aircraft spiralling down out of control.)

Brindisi was our first stop, down on the heel of Italy. From there it was across the Middle East to Baghdad. Next came Delhi, Calcutta, and Bangkok, with a couple of hours on the ground at each location, to refuel the aircraft and stretch the legs. Then came that spectacular arrival in Singapore.

Just one night-stop was made en-route. That at an establishment with which service personnel travelling this route became familiar: Minwaller's Grand, in Karachi. Ey up! as they say back int' West Riding. Not one of life's more exhilarating experiences, that. Karachi, I mean. The rest of the flight was great. And at the kind of heights we achieved, around seven thousand feet, the sightseeing was pretty good, too. I felt pity for those unfortunates who were down there bobbing about on the oceans. They had left long before us, would arrive long after, which would make them our "Moonies", provided, of course, they didn't take steps to circumvent that minor embarrassment by generating a suntan during the voyage out. Which, of course, is exactly what they did do! Even so, as with us, it was the KD that gave the game away.

I don't have any vivid memories of the trip from the airport, just vague recollections of an RAF coach, lots of kampongs, palm trees and rubber plantations, then passing through the rows of shops, restaurants and bars that made up what I later discovered to be Jalan Kayu (known to us as Seletar village), and on through the impressive entrance gates and guardroom of the camp itself. The next few days were taken up by the now familiar ritual of being posted to a new unit - the arrival. This entailed visiting all the usual sections so as to register your physical presence. Important this, for not only did it give you an insight as to the layout of the camp - workplace, NAAFI, Malcolm Club, Astra cinema etc - it also ensured you would get fed and paid. And with Seletar covering such a vast area - it was effectively split in two by the runway, the two halves being known as West Camp and East Camp - the arrival procedure could take some time. In fact the camp was so big it boasted an internal bus service, but as my presence was not required over on West Camp at this time, it was of little use to me in the arrival procedure.

It was during this period I was to discover that not only was the island recalling days past, but that the RAF was caught up in it also. To me, Seletar resembled a museum, in that its aircraft, too, were reminiscent of a bygone era. A museum, maybe, but at least it was a living museum, and one dedicated to aviation. Spitfires, Mosquitos and Beaufighters still graced the sky - aircraft types which had long since been retired from front-line service in the UK Commands, as was the equipment with which they were fitted. From the electronic marvels of instrumentation on which I'd been so painstakingly trained, I was now faced with the wonders of an ancient science; air and oil driven contraptions as fitted to the remnants of a World War Two air-force. My first thought was along the lines of, "Boy, talk about crude!" But of course they weren't, were they, not back when they'd been designed. Interesting enough now, for sure, but even these aircraft, it seemed, were not to be honoured by my presence.

I'll admit that I did briefly think of the possible opportunities now open to me, new types available to feature in my log book. (Later on in my tour, people close to me - those aware of my predilection of flying in anything at any time - briefly assumed I had bagged the Beaufighter, when one crashed! On a single engine approach to Seletar the aircraft had dived into the sea. The pilot was killed, but his target tug operator, a Cpl Taylor, survived. Obviously a different Cpl Taylor.)

Despite my elation at finding myself in Singapore, that elation also took a nose dive. It seemed my luck had at last run dry. No first-line servicing for me. No second-line, either. Worse. Much worse. Not even any aircraft!

Assigned to 390 Maintenance Unit (a supply and repair base that served not only the whole of the Far East Air Force - from India to Australasia - but also Army and Naval aviation, too), I immediately became bored with the testing of instruments in a climate-controlled environment. It was like working in a refrigerator, then walking into an oven. An insight as to what frozen fish might feel when transferred to the microwave, were it possible for fish to feel anything, that is. Particularly in the frozen stage.

The civilian staff were multi-lingual - meaning we either conversed in a recognizable version of the English language, or waved our arms and pointed. And believe me I can wave my arms and point with the best of them.

I didn't care for this place at all, nor did I possess the enthusiasm needed to repair instruments, rather than the aircraft they came from. Besides, it was like working to union rules. We were required to clock in! Not only, but also, our daily routine was logged and recorded: time in and out, equipment checked, hours logged, which was to create something of a problem in itself. I discussed the situation with my compatriot, John "Smudge" Smith, who, apart from the Warrant Officer in charge, appeared to be the only other Englishman around. There *were* Scotsmen, but at times they didn't seem to speak

154

our language any better than the balance of the workforce: Sikhs and Malays.

'I see there's a set schedule for the testing of each item, "Smudge". A time specified for each test, right?'

'Yes. Well, a theoretical time. One that could well have been set by a militant, union boss. Take this altimeter, for instance.' He held it up. 'That is allotted ninety minutes, which means you can manage five in an eight hour day.'

'So, what's the problem?'

'The problem is, these times are nowhere near realistic. Give me fifteen minutes and this altimeter will be finished. Five times fifteen?'

'Ah, yes. I see.' Even my secondary education could figure that out.

'The problem therefore...' "Smudge" was intent on spelling it out, '...what to do for the next six hours?'

He was right, too, I was to find. Every day felt like it was Monday. So boring, the visit of the NAAFI van became the big event of the day. But you can only stuff a limited amount of sticky buns and "sarnies" down your neck in a given time. As for NAAFI tea, well, there must be an absolute limit on how much of that one could safely sup in a day, leaving room for the odd pint of *Tiger Tops*, in the evening, naturally. (*Tiger Tops*: a pint of the local larger-type brew with a touch of lemonade, although most eventually dispensed with the lemonade.)

Even School Bus Detail became a boredom-breaking change. Did it ever. This entailed escorting the children of RAF families to & fro between their accommodation outside the camp, and Infants school inside, or the Secondary school over at RAF Changi, utilizing RAF transport. This was usually a three ton truck, or gharry, wooden seats down either side in the back. And I use the term "children" in the loosest sense possible. These kids, in their minds, seemed automatically to assume the rank and station of their service parent, be that AC1 or Group Captain, but although I was only a corporal I could be seen to have the advantage, for I was armed. (An "active service" environment, remember?) Which got me to thinking: was this ancient Lee Enfield meant to offer those kids some protection from the communists - who were at present waging war, over there in Malaya, as well as attempting to stir up trouble in Singapore itself - or was it meant to protect *me* from kids who often attempted to wage war in the back of the truck or bus?

Still, to me it was a welcome break from being stuck in that MU - so much did I dislike the place.

The barrack blocks at Seletar were huge - in fact, "G" block, across the runway in West Camp, was supposedly the largest accommodation block in the Royal Air Force. (Just as Seletar Officers' Mess was reputedly the largest Mess.) Each of the three floors of the airmen's accommodation was comprised of two long rooms, with, at the end of each floor, two small, two-man rooms. These were for the use of corporals, and I shared one on the second floor of "B" block with work-mate, John "Smudge" Smith. Which brings to mind a story.

Prior to my arrival, John's room mate was Cpl Tom Brown, who, as John put it, claimed to be Anglo-Indian. But John told me that the only thing Anglo about him had been his name. Anyway, Tom, preparing to depart Singapore, had received the finances for his end of tour leave, and had secured the cash somewhere in the room for safety. You know the kind of thing, so safe that when you needed it you couldn't remember where it was you'd put it! He couldn't ask for guidance from his room-mate, as John had been away at the time - either on leave or detachment. Tom apparently searched everywhere, to no avail, and reaching the conclusion it had been stolen, called upon the services of the "Snowdrops" - (the RAF arm of the Military Police, so-called because of their white cap covers, and the pristine white webbing they wore). Not entirely unexpected, they didn't find it either, so Tom was S$180 poorer; a fair amount of cash in 1957.

John returned from leave to find Tom gone, as had one of John's prized possessions: a Malayan Railways sign - "Do not use toilets whilst train...." etc, in four languages. This proved to be irreplaceable, for shortly after it had "just fallen off the loo wall and into John's hands" the railway decided to fix them securely, sealed behind plastic.

Sometime after my arrival, John was clearing his UK uniform package off the top of his locker when out fell a bundle of money - S$180 to be exact! Too late for Tom by far, but, being of equitable moral standards, we decided the best thing for it would be to share it between ourselves, even though I hadn't been around during the period of loss. In fact, talking to him some years later, John seems to think it was my idea we share it, says he suggested we hand it in, whereas I had replied, "I make that ninety dollars each. Which is when we became aware that Cpl Len Wildish was "at home" in the adjoining room, separated from us by a wall that, for reasons of ventilation, didn't quite reach the ceiling. Len, it seemed, also had an opinion, for drifting over that wall came the words, "I make it sixty each."

Of course, we handed it in, didn't we? No we didn't! For "Smudge" valued his Malayan Railways sign at S$180!

"Smudge" and I were into model aircraft - those highly detailed plastic-moulded things. (Shows how boring working in that MU had become!) We were, in fact, rather enthusiastic builders, which was to eventually pose a problem: where to hang them all in the limited space allotted us in which to live? Answer: Impossible. So it was that we dreamed up yet another mindless pastime. One in which the older models found themselves loaded with Chinese firecrackers - small, but loud and powerful - suspended from a fan blade, set in motion, fuse lit. Wow! Quite spectacular, and we did have a bearer to clean up the room. But as we'd inevitably end up picking pieces of plastic out of our clothes for days on end, we eventually devised an alternate method of destruction. A length of cord was run from our second floor balcony, to the trunk of a distant palm tree. The aircraft would now slide gracefully into oblivion, wreckage scattered over a wide area of grass, once again leaving the clearing up to the native bearers.

Bearers were another feature new to me, proving once again that RAF service overseas was on an entirely different plane to that in the UK; much more relaxed. Out here, as long as we did our job, and conducted ourselves in a not too inappropriate manner, we were basically left to enjoy life to the full. No unnecessary bull, few parades, hardly any restrictions, guard duties apart - of which there were many. The bearers were just another facet of this easy life. For a couple of dollars a month these guys - mainly from the Indian subcontinent - would clean the rooms, make our beds, change the sheets, see to the laundry, clean our shoes and generally clean up after us. And, being as they were earning much more than any of us ($2 multiplied by around eighty, at least) they were also quite happy to loan us the odd dollar or two when we ran short; at a rate of interest that would make even a loan-shark blush! No wonder that every so often one bearer would suddenly disappear, only to be replaced by another, usually a relative. The original would have flown (or more likely sailed) off, back home to India for a couple of months break with his family.

As well as bearers there were also the "sew-sews",

Chinese ladies who would wander round the blocks - embarrassingly for us, on occasion, even though they did continuously call out, "sew-sew", to warn of their presence - offering, for a small payment, to darn our socks, adjust and make running repairs to our uniforms etc.

Smithy and I also acquired a stuffed toy in the form of a panda, whom we promptly named Fred. It was Fred therefore who volunteered to test our state-of-the-art parachutes from that same second-floor balcony. A much better option than the childhood kitten which "volunteered" to serve in a similar role at the Griffin, (much like George Cayley's coachman, I suppose). In fact, I rather suspect that was the point at which my subliminal interest in aviation first began to assert itself. Just an inkling, mind, but it was enough. Which was to be unfortunate for the kitten. For although I eventually reached the stage where the parachutes worked quite well, as with most experimental projects the early models left a lot to be desired, especially for that kitten. Came down rather rapid-like, at times. Yes, you get the idea; roughly the same velocity it would without a parachute, should it foolishly choose to launch itself from such a height. No problem though. They do always land on their feet. Well, almost always. If not, it would look a bit bemused for a second or two, but as long as all four legs worked it would flick its tail and ears - as if also checking their operation - then off it would charge. Anyway, if all else failed there was always that old "nine lives" backup.

But as that was now all of ten years in the past, you can bet even the kitten would have used up its tally of nine in that time. No such problems with Fred then, which was just as well. Especially as the state of our particular art left a lot to be desired. Seemed I'd forgotten the lessons learned during my earlier erudition.

Each of the upper two floors of our barrack blocks had one of these balconies, as did the ground floor, but, due to location, and the fact that it wasn't enclosed, obviously theirs could in no way be classed as a balcony! They encircled the whole block, and being about four feet in width were quite handy for other than exploding models and parachuting pandas. You could sit out there and read, or write. And often, during the day, mattresses would line the surrounding balustrade, enabling the sun to evacuate unwanted lodgers from within their creases and crevasses: bed-bugs, which couldn't stand bright light. Maybe the birds got them, maybe the floor beneath, but they certainly disappeared in a hurry. The metal bed-frame, especially the springs, you just doused lightly with petrol or some such, and briefly set alight. Of course, heat didn't do a lot for the tempering of the springs, which is probably why our matresses often sagged so much!

The rooms were well aired, louvered shutters replacing glass in doors and windows, and these were normally thrown wide open, apart from when the wind and rain came. Electric fans gently stirred the air within. Projecting out at one side from the centre of each floor were the ablution and toilet blocks.

*

'Fancy a trip down the village?' Smithy enquired of me one evening (meaning Jalan Kayu, a short stroll outside the camp gates). And as I was doing nothing in particular I readily agreed to join him for a beer or two.

'How about a curry?' he suggested, once we were settled in air-conditioned comfort, a glass of *Tiger* to hand.

'What! That foreign muck? Come on, "Smudge", you know me, your typical Brit abroad. I'll eat anything, so long as it features sausage, egg, and chips.'

'Right, you get what you like, I'll order curry, you can have a taste of mine.'

'I won't like it, I can tell you now.'

Can't say, until you've tried it.'

'I just did say.'

But he ordered anyway, and he watched me as I took a small amount on my spoon, tasted it. He'd known I would, for I hadn't exactly rejected his offer out of hand.

'There you are,' he said, 'told you you'd like it.'

'Who said I liked it? I replied, reaching across for more, a spoonful this time. 'Need to try a bit more, that's all.'

'Good, eh?' he persisted, as I shovelled it down.

'Well, yeah. Not good, but maybe not so bad,' I admitted, somewhat reluctantly.

'Okay, I'll order another, and we'll share it,' he said, which he promptly did. And that was my introduction to the world of the curried egg, from where, I at first imagined, it was but a short hop, skip, and jump to unrefined napalm. Which it almost was, literally, for across the road was a pukka Indian place, complete with dirt floor. I believe it was known as "Pops Curry House," at least to the airmen, and it was to here we went from that day on. Although I did at first demur.

'No bloody air-con, "Smudge"!'

'What do you need air-con for, hardly any walls.'

'Yeah, and the place is full of cockroaches.'

'Ah, but wait 'till you try their curry. Get that beer down your neck and shut up.'

As usual, when it came to curries and such, Smithy was right. Should have been, for this Halton trained ex-Aircraft Apprentice had spent much of his early life in India, his father, I believe, in the Diplomatic Service. But that curry was to change my outlook on foreign foods for evermore. And given the circumstances, it was probably as well "Smudge" did introduce me to the dish, being as we shared a room.

As opposed to Jalan Kayu, we were occasionally to be found in the George Club, very close to our block. It was here that "Smudge" would order, "Soossee Nooee Yang Bay-dow" regularly. Said he had no idea of the actual translation, but that sausage, egg, chips and double baked beans arrived every time.

So, curried eggs, beer, barbecues at the Malcolm Club, the George Club, exploding plastic models, visits to the Astra cinema, and unsuccessful parachutes; what an interesting social life we led. There again, we did occasionally venture into town, when funds permitted. I even managed to put aside enough to enable me to replace my plastic Kodak Box with a new type of camera: the revolutionary, Japanese, Asahi Pentax single lens reflex, with instant return mirror. That camera, and it's successors, lasted me right through to the digital age

A fact of life for personnel stationed in the Far East was that they probably owned more quality cameras than the whole of the Royal Photographic Society back home. Cameras were cheap, so everyone went for the best: Twin-lens reflex Rolleiflex or Rolleicord, the Leica, or Contax. All made in Europe you'll notice. The same went for watches, mainly Swiss: Rolex, Patek Phillipe, Omega and suchlike. Seiko were still but a thought in some Japanese head, though not for too much longer! Just as the photographic world was about to be turned on *its* head with the introduction of that Pentax - the world's first single lens reflex to feature an instant return mirror - the Japanese were also about to stake a claim in the chronology market. Big time, it could be said!

There was a thriving photo club on the base, of which I became a member, and there was, of course, a magnificent swimming pool. Along the Embankment, over the creek bridge and down by the wireless transmitting station. The pool was sited in well kept, grassy grounds, on which concrete tables and seats were set out. There was a NAAFI-run restaurant on site from which to purchase meals and drinks. A very popular place was the swimming pool area, especially amongst families and schoolchildren, who had plenty of time to indulge. Sports of course were a big thing at Seletar, and any RAF camp come to that. You could indudge in almost any sport that took your fancy. The camp even boasted its own nine hole golf course. But, pool apart, none of this was for me; that lack of ball sense maybe. It all helped keep madness at bay, but I did pine for my aircraft. I could photograph them, get close, but that wasn't the same as giving them my loving attention, or procuring the occasional flight in one.

As the days dragged inexorably by, it seemed there was to be nothing. Then, just when I was of the opinion that - so far as my welfare was concerned, God had taken early retirement - along He comes and hands me a bonus.

I'd been keeping my eyes peeled, an ear to the ground, looking and listening, hoping something interesting would turn up for which I could volunteer my services; aircraft-wise, that is. From my point of view, anything had to be better than the present situation.

After barely a month with the MU - though probably the longest month of my entire life, at least thus far - the section commander, a rather personable and astute Warrant Officer, called me into his office one morning.

'Corporal Taylor', he began, 'How's it going?'

'Okay, sir, I suppose.'

'Not happy here, are you?' he suggested, demonstrating to me the fact that he had his finger on the pulse.

'No, sir, not really. I'm a first line man at heart.'

'Good. Just the man then. There's a requirement for an instrument fitter on the one of the station's other units. Would you be interested in a one month detachment?'

The fact that I was being asked, not forcibly volunteered, made me suspicious right away. This, after all, as I believe I have mentioned, was an "active service" posting. People were being shot at in the jungles to the north. But my suspicions were soon to be dispelled. Anyway, what the hell, I was dying of boredom where I was. Would prefer to go out with a bang.

*

Singapore is separated from those Malayan jungles by a body

161

of water known as the Straits of Johore, across which lies the only physical link between the two countries: a one kilometre causeway. This carried not only road and rail traffic, but also the pipelines which do likewise for Singapore's water supply, bringing it over from Johore Bahru. (One reason the Japanese were able to take the Island so easily was that, once in Johore, they controlled Singapore's water supply.) But apart from forming the border, the Straits had another function: those waters served as runways for Seletar's flying boat squadrons. They had done so ever since the base first opened, in 1928. In fact, the station had been built primarily with flying boats in mind; the Supermarine Southampton equipped Far East Flight (soon to become 205 Squadron) being the first unit to occupy the base. Now - in the dying days of RAF flying boat operations - it was the joint 205/209 Squadron, a Sunderland equipped unit, previously known as the Far East Flying Boat Wing - 205 and 209 in conjunction with the remnants of Hong Kong based, 88 Squadron, until 88 was disbanded at Seletar. This was what I was being offered. I just couldn't believe my luck.

Last of the services' flying boats, the Sunderland first flew in 1937, had given sterling service during World War Two, the Berlin Airlift, the Communist takeover of China - remember the Yangtze Incident? An 88 Squadron Sunderland had been involved there, managing to transfer medical supplies and a doctor behind enemy lines to HMS Amethyst - and on through the Korean conflict.

These aircraft, the last of the almost seven hundred and fifty produced, were now approaching the end of their time gracefully, serving in one final conflict.

More like it, this. A situation made tailor-made for the likes of myself it could be said.

'I realize you aren't familiar with the aircraft, or their equipment,' the WO continued, 'but instruments are more or less the same no matter which type of aircraft they are fitted to, so that won't pose a problem, will it?'

'No, sir. I've never yet trained on any specific aircraft on which I've worked. Pick it up as I go along: the quirks of each particular type.'

This was true, as he was no doubt well aware. On arrival at Dishforth I'd never before set eyes on either the Valetta or Hastings. And, needless to say, each of the visiting types was also new to me, especially single seat fighters, so this was no different. What's more, the position was on offer. A few steps closer to paradise.

I said yes ever so indecently quickly, never for a moment regretted doing so. In fact, I enjoyed it so much I eventually contrived to turn what was to have been a detachment of a month, into a posting lasting a year. Just as well, for I'd dreaded the thought of ever returning to that MU.

I'd traded the air-conditioned freezer that was the MU for a small hut - our crewroom on the beach - not even a fan to stir the air. But we *were* sited in the relatively small gap that separated our slipway from the Seletar Yacht Club.

As on any operational flying squadron there was considerable rapport between the aircrew and their technicians on the ground. Team spirit, the essential bond that is plainly evident, for let's face it, this was the front end of the Air Force, what it was all about, the very reason for its being: getting those aircraft into the air and keeping them there. (The unity and loyalty of squadron personnel, once forged, lasts a lifetime - evidenced by the number of annual reunions, the majority, these days, relating to squadrons, units, even stations which no longer exist.)

It was during my time with 205/209 that I finally made my first trip to the Crown Colony of Hong Kong. One of the Squadron's duties, for a period, was to have an aircraft continually based at Kai Tak on Search & Rescue (SAR) standby - Lindholme gear (inflatable dinghy and emergency stores) attached to the bomb racks which slid out beneath the wings. The aircraft usually sat at anchor in the bay formed by the main runway, onshore, and the new runway, still under construction, which extended out into the harbour. I was lucky enough to find myself detached to Hong Kong for a six week period. With but a couple of training flights - and thankfully no emergencies - there was not a lot for us to do on base.

Downtown was an altogether different kettle of fish. Ah! the memories: Chanticleir - a restaurant bar on main street, Kowloon. Honolulu Bar: "enchanting music for dancing, genuine drinks(?), delicious food", so stated their gaily-coloured business card. It was something all bars gave out, possibly so you could later remember where the hell it was you'd been the previous night. They still adorn the inside covers of my photo albums. Lucky Star Bar & Nightclub was another, in the Wanchai district - oh, oh, Suzie Wong territory, that. Think maybe I met her sister. Said she wanted to improve her English, didn't she? And here's me, assuming she meant the

language!
*

But Hong Kong was more than just bars and nightclubs. A myriad of aromas permeated the atmosphere, so many they intermingled into a deliciously confusing amalgam, the nose often requiring help from the other senses to be able to identify them: petrol fumes, coffee, wood shavings and dried fish. Incense and sandalwood, too. Joss-sticks burned in a temple across the way, smoke rising vertically in the still air. The temple was small, but magnificent in red, gold, and green - significant colours here in the east. Carved and gilded dragons wound themselves everywhere, green-glazed terra-cotta examples forming the upturned corners of the green tiled roof.

I wandered on, fascinated, past open-fronted shops and stores. From within one came the click clack of Mah-jong pieces being rapped on a marble-topped table, and the unintelligible, sing-song voices of the players. Another doorway, and a happy, grinning face looked out to wish me "Goodbye", which I assumed was meant to be "Hello". On second thoughts, depending what went on in that dark and mysterious interior, it could well *have* been goodbye!

I came across a market in which bowls and tins were piled high; spices of every type and colour. There were mountains of chili powder of varying ferocity, weird and wonderful mushrooms, root ginger and ginseng, and garlic by the ton. Then there was an "exotic" section: dried bugs, beetles, and centipedes, the latter fully six inches long, bundled and boxed, ready for .... whatever! Long ribbon-fish were displayed, flat and glistening, like strips of beaten silver. There were squid also, and cuttlefish, abalone, crabs, all fresh and moist. Live eels swam in tanks, and dead flatfish were cleaned and laid out to dry wherever awnings allowed the sun's rays to penetrate. And the dried shark fins, of course.

Other flesh was offered for sale also; quality cuts of beef, pork and lamb, along with the lesser cuts, at least in my opinion; trotters, heads, tails and offal. Other pieces defied description, the origins of such I would hesitate to hazard a guess at, let alone eat!

In the evening there was noise. The noise of the traffic and the sing-song voices of the locals, plus the music which seemed to blast out of every bar and club. Neon bottles poured neon champagne into neon glasses as neon can-can girls kicked their neon legs. "Kit Kat Klub" read a sign around which endless red neon arrows chased each other, before diving down towards an otherwise anonymous doorway. To one side a svelte Chinese girl with long, glossy hair, balanced on high heels. Her form-fitting cheongsam provided an ostentatious display of tight buttocks and slim thighs. The cheap scent she wore mingled with a hundred other assorted aromas; food, carbon-monoxide, garbage, and sweat. Those, and more, ebbed and flowed in the night air.

The girl made a pretence of looking in the window of a nearby shop, but her actions made it plainly obvious she was selling, not buying. And I had to admit, the goods appeared to be quite stunning. Maybe she too just wanted to improve her English!

High overhead, against the black roof of the night, a star streaked across in its death arc.

This whole area was a wonderful, colourful kaleidoscope of shops, bars, restaurants, clubs, and hotels. All were dimly lit, airconditioned, and comfortable. Homely type places with cheap drinks and obliging hostesses. And this, being well before the days of the long-haul package tour, or the American Rest & Recreation invasion (from the war in Vietnam), meant I, and the thousands of commonwealth troops stationed here, had the field almost to ourselves.

Luckyman Hall, The Sportsman's Arms, they sound ominous, too. Must have been, for their cards are also still lodged in my albums, as is the one they gave you to hang on the rim of your glass if you found a need to leave the bar for a while: "Do not touch, gone to wee wee," it stated. The Waltzing Matilda gave us a scroll.

Hate to think how much I spent in these places, time, or money. But, unless my memory is playing tricks, it was well worth it. It beat Norton and Malton into a cocked hat, that was for sure; to say nothing of Cosford. A lifetime of learning.

I found Hong Kong to be exactly as Ian Fleming had portrayed it in his travel book, *Thrilling Cities*. I thought about this as I sat in one of the bars featured in that book, and immediately realised why he had favoured this place. Enough characters - bearded work-worn sea captains and the like - scattered around in here to feature in any of his James Bond novels. And had I decided to strike up a conversation with any one of them I felt sure some very interesting stories would have been the result.

It took a Sunderland just five minutes short of twelve

hours to haul itself up the coast from Singapore to Hong Kong. It was a time I was to see progressively reduced over the years: seven hours forty-five by Hastings, three hours fifty-five by Comet 2, three and a quarter hours by Boeing 707. By boat, the time was measured in days!

*

Those Sunderlands may have been vintage but the facilities at Seletar were probably a hundred percent improvement on what had been available during World War Two, especially at the remote outstations. I'd heard tell of bush huts for the crews, and refuelling by hand-pump from makeshift jetties. We refuelled by barge, and our jetty was substantive. A long concrete affair with a control station at the seaward end, and a roving crane for lifting heavy loads. Next to this was a magnificent slipway - along with that jetty, built in 1928. Here the aircraft could be winched ashore, once the beaching gear had been fitted. Major servicing could thus be carried out in the comfort of a hangar, hulls kept reasonably clean. Though one prankster pilot would probably disagree with the latter, especially after the take-off run that took him down the Straits, well out of our operating area. Almost as far down as Sembawang Naval Base, aircraft still firmly attached to the water. What the hell, maybe he was seeking some assistance from the earth's curvature to get him airborne. No matter, the exercise was a failure in more ways than one. Apparently not too chuffed about having a Sunderland tearing about in what they saw as their territory, the Navy types. Neither was our Wing Commander too chuffed about receiving a call from the Admiral, or whatever. Shouldn't have joined if they couldn't take a joke. I thought it hilarious, can still see that plume of spray disappearing from view, well past the area cleared for take-off, aircraft inside it rocking back and forth as the pilot attempted to unstick it. Took him quite some time to taxy back, too.

As far as routine servicing of flying boats went, this was anything but routine. There was a Marine Craft section for a start, the Royal Air Force's own sailors, with their floating fuel bowsers, ammunition scows, lighters, pinnaces, fire tenders, high speed launches, and crew transport. Hence that jetty and its control tower.

I'd ride a launch out to the aircraft, bobbing at its mooring buoy out there in the Straits of Johore, climb aboard and complete my task. One thing to remember - when working outside the aircraft - tools needed to be secured to ones person via a length of string, were they not to be lost forever. Oops!.. Clink.. Plop.. Damn and blast! Look out, fish, here she comes: 5/16 x 3/8 Whitworth o/e.

With my servicing complete I'd use the Aldis lamp to signal the pier-master in that control tower, requesting the launch's return. This I knew could take some time, for it wasn't likely to come out just for me. They'd await more calls, combine them efficiently. So, imagine if you will, the intrepid fitter, task complete, ninety plus in the shade, palm trees on the nearby beach barely stirring in a lazy breeze, sea as flat and smooth as unrolled silk, a wing that made a perfect diving platform (I had eventually mastered the art of entering the water head first). But, as usual, paradise did have the odd flaw. For instance, I lacked of a glass of something long, cool, and wicked, close to hand, and I knew my swimming hole was domicile to venomous sea snakes. (Come to think of it, they probably fit the "long, cool, wicked" description to a tee, albeit minus the glass.) Like most snakes, though, they offered little harm unless threatened. But try telling that to a naive airman! Still, I never heard tell of any of our personnel being attacked, either when swimming, or fitting the beaching gear to the aircraft. Though over the water in Malaya they apparently lost more lives per year to snakes than they did on the roads, the majority of the victims being fishermen. Snakes would get caught up in their nets, and the fisherman would grab them bare handed, so as to free them, often misjudging things.

What with poisonous snakes, and some kind of conflict going on, didn't sound like too healthy a place, this Malaya.

The hardest part of these impromptu swimming sessions, unless you had help, was the difficulty in getting back on board the aircraft. The base of the entry door naturally being well above the water line, with a step down once inside. Oh-oh! Watch out for the family jewels.

*

So excited was I at the time that only brief fragments of my first waterborne take-off are lodged in memory. The safety launch had first made a sweep down the watery runway, checking for debris - any flotsam and jetsam that could wreck an aircraft travelling at speed - our engines were running, we'd cast-off from the mooring buoy, all checks were complete, and we were now lined up and ready.

With throttles pushed open and the roar of four engines at full power, the spray flew back, obscuring the view downstairs in the wardroom, where I was located. There was a reluctant build-up of speed - degree of reluctance dependant upon hull cleanliness (barnacles the problem here) - as hull and wing-tip floats cut creamy furrows in turquoise water. Then we were "on the step" and the foam subsided as we charged across the surface. A lunge, a couple of bounces, and we were airborne, water-streaked perspex clearing as we clawed our way into the tropical sky. A boat had become an aeroplane. Fleeting but emotional recollections.

My services were requested one morning to make adjustments to an autopilot, a task which was completed whilst airborne. This usually took well under an hour, but I found dusk to be settling as we floated back down to the Straits again, Pratt & Whitney Twin-Wasps roaring healthily, just as they had for the past twelve hours and twenty minutes.

As we slowed, the bow wave shortened to a feather of creamy ripples, wings creaking and groaning as weight was transferred from them to hull and floats. It was as though the machine itself were sighing with relief, secure in the knowledge it was all over for yet another day. The aeroplane had once again returned to the maritime environment, engineer forward of the retracted front turret ready to hook the buoy, pilot controlling speed and direction. And even though they were offered a little assistance from drogues which could be deployed from the galley ports, one either side, it was no easy task. There was no way of braking on water. You can't throw an aircraft in reverse like you can a boat - at least you couldn't in a Sunderland. A miss and it was round again, plus a round of drinks on the luckless engineer, or whoever had not deployed his drogue as per instructions! The pilot would find himself facing the same forfeit should he forget to dress the propellers upon shut-down: ie one blade up, two down. This allowed maximum clearance for the crew launch on its approach. This launch would have been standing off to one side until the aircraft was moored, and engines shut down, before approaching from the rear, beneath the wing and propellers, to slide alongside at the entry door, exhaust burbling away. But care was still required, for the tips and leading edges of those propeller blades could be deadly on flesh and bones. The spray attacked them relentlessly, eventually creating very effective saw-like edges. An additional job for the riggers was to file the roughness out every so often. (Not too healthy in the interests of blade balance, I wouldn't have thought!)

It had taken me all of twenty minutes to declare the autopilot fully operational. After which we had then proceeded on a routine sortie: Borneo and back. At Labuan we actually made an approach to the runway. Not exactly a touchdown, of course not, but extremely low. Some would have said cutting the margins a little fine. Maybe, maybe not, depends on the pilot. But this was so low he must have been very good, or very lucky. In fact, had the beaching gear been fitted I swear we'd have laid rubber down the centre of the runway. Probably effective relief from any boredom that may have accumulated in the interim, but it didn't affect me that way. I wasn't bored to begin with. Here I was, aviation enthusiast par excellence, actually being paid to fly around all day.

I later heard tell of a Royal New Zealand Air Force Sunderland pilot who cut the margins even finer. Too fine, in fact, actually managing to scrape his keel along the hard stuff. Not recommended, that, as he was soon to discover, assuming he wasn't already aware of the fact. And all he had to fall back on was the excuse of a sudden downdraft or possible wind-shear. The kind of thing margins are meant to cover. This incident took place during a public flying display at the opening of Wellington's new airport, and apparently it somehow caused fire to break out in the aircraft's bilges. (Yes, they were flying boats, remember. They had bilges, bulkheads, and ports. Stuff like that.) Anyway, fire wasn't the real problem. That was successfully extinguished on the flight back to base at Hobsonville, north of Auckland, where the aircraft was safely set down, although it then began taking on water rather rapidly. Unfortunately, despite the pilot's attempt to make the slipway or beach, the RNZAF found itself with one less Sunderland on inventory, the aircraft foundering well before it reached the shoreline.

They were comfortable old aircraft, those Sunderlands, had been designed with long flights in mind; hour upon lonely hour of sub-hunting, far out over the Atlantic. The "lounge" or wardroom, as it was correctly known - on the lower deck - featured leather-upholstered banquettes. These were arranged fore and aft, either side of a folding table, ideal for dining, or a game of poker. Meals were prepared on board, over an open flame stove. And, if memory serves correctly, this just happened to be located beneath the wing centre section, in which was carried the hundreds of gallons of fuel required for such lengthy flights! Can't be right, can it? OK, there was an upper deck above the galley - radio, engineer, and navigator's stations.

I do recall one autopilot adjustment flight that didn't go quite as planned, though. Probably my first, shortly after joining the squadron.

As I've explained, the equipment fitted to these aircraft was far removed from that upon which my training was based, so I was obliged to learn as I went along, with whatever input I could glean from those with more experience.

In this instance, along with an instrument mechanic, we had changed the main unit, containing the gyros. It was connected to the aircraft controls via a light steel cable, which in turn was wound round a scroll gear on the rear of the gyro unit. The actual adjustment in the air merely called for some minor tweaking of this unit, down by the pilot's feet. So once up to a safe height, I positioned myself down behind the instrument panel, close to the object of the exercise - plenty of room in a Sunderland. A tap on the pilot's foot had him engaging the autopilot, and as he did so, the aircraft's nose went up, rather sharply. Immediate disengagement followed, further adjustment, the tap on the foot - and now the aircraft wanted to dive. A couple more attempts with similar results told me the story: the cable on that scroll gear was reversed. Therefore, instead of correcting for a nose up or nose down influence, the autopilot was actually compounding the problem. Oops! Back to the drawing board. Like I say, you learn as you go along. Today it would have been designed so that cable could only be fitted the right way. (No, today it is all electronic!) Still, the crew weren't too perturbed. They got to fly for a couple of hours instead of sitting around in the crew room.

I was once more happy with my lot. After dark I would occasionally take a relaxing walk along the jetty, as though not wishing to release the aircraft from my sight. The sky would be clear after the rain, night air washed fresh, scented with the blossoms of frangipani, Jasmine, Magnolia. In the background, nature's symphony would be tuning-up: frogs and cicadas providing the percussion, mosquitoes, the strings. At my side, a pale, liquid moon would match my pace, reflected off the waters of the Straits, which gently lapped around the jetty's supports. In such conditions a witch on a broomstick would not have been misplaced.

That was all it took for me to become melancholy, despite that fact that out there on the water, aircraft bobbed at their moorings, each with an armed guard aboard, for let us not forget, this was an "active service" posting. It was one of the more pleasant guard duties, though. A good chance to get in some fishing. In comparison, guard duty at Seletar's huge explosives and ammunition compound, known as 9X Site - which served not just Seletar, but the whole of the Far East Air Force - was a job the rest of the camp's personnel despised, it being an area favoured by the snakes and mosquitoes, as well, it is said, by the ghost of a long departed Japanese Colonel, riding a white horse. Stories of other ghostly sightings did the rounds, too, some attested to by shots being fired, or airmen ending up in a state of shock. Flying Boat Wing staff were excused this duty, they being required to guard their charges out there on the water instead.

*

It was during the hours of darkness that the interior of the barrack blocks echoed to a sound of a different kind: lizard-like geckoes clung to ceilings and walls by means of their suction-cup feet, tiny heart pulsating visibly behind their transparent epidermal layer. Every now and again they would issue forth with the call by which they were more commonly known: chit chat. They provided a service, too; lapping up mosquitoes and other small pests. But every so often one of these harmless little creatures would miscalculate it's fancy footwork - rather like the younger version of me on my bike. Down it would plop, possibly onto a bed, charging off immediately, but not before startling the occupant more than it had itself. This was especially true if that occupant happened to be a Moony, who had been primed by the old hands to watch out for these "deadly poisonous creepy crawlies that are apt to launch themselves upon you." I've seen guys almost mesmerized, laying there staring at them, afraid to close their eyes, until some kind soul let them in on the ruse.

Aerial invaders of the larger kind were usually accounted for by the ceiling fans. I'd lay there in the dark, beneath my mosquito net but above the sheets, a towel providing a modicum of cover. (Too hot for pyjamas, and after three years Far East service I have never worn them since!) The louvred windows were thrown wide open, for even with the fan at a fair lick it would be hot in our two-man room. Heat was another disadvantage conferred upon us by the room being so small, apart from the lack of space to hang models.

Of course, an open window was an invitation to all and

171

sundry, and I'd often hear the familiar whine of a Rhinoceros beetle. They'd whistle and whang their way around the room, ricocheting about like a bat with faulty radar. It was as if involved in some clumsy suicide bid. Until they'd inevitably meet up with a fan blade travelling in opposition to the direction of flight. Whack! Straight back over the bowler's head for six. Splat! against the wall. End of story. Very yucky. Quite something, that. Especially when a flip-flop shod foot would merely pin the tough little sods to the ground. As soon as you lifted clear, they'd be up and away.

Given the chance, so would I. And here the opportunities for flight were endless, and encouraged. There were air-tests - after major maintenance it was seen as an act of faith by the aircrew if a number of ground tradesmen volunteered to join the flight. I was there in a flash, every time. As frequently demonstrated, I didn't need any encouragement when it came to volunteering. There again, I suspect my IQ may begin with a decimal point.

Air-tests apart, there were mail-drops to Royal Navy vessels - buoyant waterproof container being tossed out of the open galley hatch, aimed to land as close as possible to the waiting launch. Though I don't suppose a direct hit would have been at all appreciated! There were anti-piracy patrols, routine flights, and saturation bombing missions over Malaya. Hard work, the latter, for the bombs - up to twenty pounds - were primed on board, then, unofficially, dispatched by hand, no precision required. The bomb racks were reserved for the heavy stuff. This never met with the Armament Officer's approval, but it was the only practical way.

*

Although, in the realms of climate, Christmas out here was just another date on the calendar, it was certainly well celebrated. Usually a fairly boisterous affair in one way or another, the camp seeming to almost shut down completely for a couple of days; with the exception of the various clubs and messes, of course!

There are reports of bicycles being ridden off the five metre board at the Swimming pool, although this seems to have been fairly normal during the Christmas break. A large degree of licence seemed to be the order of the day, even the Station Warrant Officer (ultimately responsible for all discipline, and normally the most feared man on any station) making himself scarce. Most of the barrack blocks featured elaborate bars on one floor or another (there was actually a competition for the best themed bar, usually judged by the CO), and, as is traditional, the Station Commander, Officers and Senior NCOs, took time out from their celebrations to serve Christmas dinner in the Airmen's Mess. Then it was off to the various bars for a spell, a good percentage eventually succumbing to the demon drink, which is when any outrageous acts were performed. The more spectacular usually reserved for after dark.

One Seletar classic, still talked about to this day, was the 1955 heist of Spitfire SM997. Of this I have photographic proof.

Somehow undetected, a group of junior officers and airmen (with at least one member of the RAF Police said to have been involved!) pushed and towed (with the help of a Standard Vanguard) a complete, but non-airworthy Spitfire, all the way from the West Camp airfield, to the East Camp parade ground. A distance of well over a mile along fairly narrow, sometimes twisty roads, via station Married Quarters, and passing close by either the CO's house, or the Guardroom. Of course, next day, questions were asked, but, naturally, and probably as expected, no one had seen or heard a thing. Even with the proper equipment, it apparently proved to be quite a difficult task to return the aircraft to its original location.

As well as the best Block bar competition there was also one with a fancy dress theme.

As Don Gent puts it: "In 1955 `"B" Block, ground floor (MTRS) won this with their Buffalo Bar. They also cleaned up in the Base Fancy Dress Competition, with their cowboy theme outfits, cobbled together by Doug Sargeant, whose trade was fabricator. The whole thing was pulled together by a concerted effort, taking several weeks and considerable "Government Expense!" This proved worthwhile when MTRS were presented with the First Prize: a vast quantity of Tiger & Anchor beer. So much booze we threw the bar open to anyone on camp."

Peter Cox recalls his arrival on the camp that year, just prior to Christmas. `I was doing the normal arrival rounds, checking in with various departments and sections, as we all did. When I entered the Padre's office I was greeted with the words, "Welcome to the four day drunk."

So much for my Seletar Christmas, for in 1957 - as far as I was aware - nothing really spectacular took place at all.

All too soon my time with the squadron was up, my first year in the Far East drawing to a close, but by then the

Sunderland's days were numbered, too. It was obvious the end was approaching the day the whole squadron was ordered to pose for a group photograph in front of one of the aircraft. Beached, of course. A bit difficult lining everyone up otherwise. Bags I the top row!

Then we became 205 Squadron (Sunderland detachment), the squadron itself reforming at Changi with the Shackleton Mk1, just entering service in the Far East Air Force. 209 would also reform and re-equip, this time with the Scottish Aviation Pioneer - ex 267 Squadron - moving up country, closer to the front line. So the 205 Sqn numberplate at least retained a link with the camp. A good move really, for 205 had been the very first flying boat squadron at Seletar, forty years previous, hence the Latin inscription on the squadron crest - Pertama Di-Malaya, first in Malaya. Now they would be the last. And not just at Seletar, but in the Royal Air Force as a whole. The end of an yet another era.

Singapore was still officially in the war zone, even though it had long since been declared "white" (as opposed to "black" for the operational areas in Malaya). Testimony of this was in the almost indestructible dog tags with which we were issued, and required to wear at all times: name, rank, serial number. Further evidence was provided by the exercises which were occasionally foisted upon us. I recall one such where an SAS troop were the attacking force, the idea being for them to enter the hangar and symbolically blow up our aircraft. We, of course, would prevent just such a thing happening, so we were told. A game, really, to check on security. But it was a game which kept us up all night.

I was patrolling an area close by squadron headquarters when I detected movement out of the corner of my eye. A shadowy figure was attempting to sneak past along the storm drain. Almost dry, of course, but none too pleasant for all that, enough slime and gunge to keep game show host Noel Edmonds happy. Still, from stories I'd heard, I doubted that would worry the SAS a great deal.

Gotcha, you bugger, thinks I. 'Halt! Who goes there?' I challenged, as required. Yes, still the same old procedure. I made a production of cocking the weapon I held; an ominous sound that echoed in the night. It was almost guaranteed to stop anyone in their tracks, as it did this joker.

Back through the darkness came the authorized reply: some password or other, just like this fictional fellow, James

Bond, who was becoming popular at the time.

'Advance and be recognized,' I called, sticking to the script, even though I wasn't too sure about the scenario. It might be a game to us, but from tales doing the rounds those SAS guys played rough. To them, the game was always deadly serious. Fine, so far as my country's enemies were concerned, not too pleasant a thought for such as me, in this kind of situation. For although, in reality, we were on the same side, tonight we were technically not. We were enemies.

I wasn't going to him, for sure. If he was who I thought he was, nasty things could await me. He'd likely floor me and head for the hills, disappearing into the darkness. I could end up with anything from a sore head, to a bayonet up the rear! No thanks, he could come to me, out here in the light, where I could see. And where I had a mate to back me up.

Advance someone, or thing, did, emerging from out of the murk and gloom, heading in the general direction of the business end of my rifle. Gradually, almost as if by parthenogenesis, a figure took shape. A figure dressed as an RAF officer, Flight Lieutenant no less. Yes, well... Maybe. Maybe not.

'Could I see some identity, sir, if you don't mind.' No please, for I didn't ask so much as ordered, enjoyed doing so. I felt I was quite within my rights in such a situation. Especially as I was at the advantageous end of a weapon, which was still pointed threateningly. It was the usual, ancient Lee Enfield. Unloaded, of course, they weren't taking too many chances. But would he know that?

When he handed me his ID, I realized he would. It was a card: photo, name, rank. Official observer. OK, due etiquette. He now received a salute, for he had his rights, too. Silly sod had been testing me, which made me feel quite chuffed, even though he had been easy to spot. Should have known the SAS wouldn't have been so careless, or compliant. Still, it was enough to keep me on my toes. No one else tried it on that night, I can almost guarantee.

Almost? Well, yes. You see, when we opened the locked hangar next morning we found it to be a bit of a mess. A bit good these lads. (There again, don't suppose we were the fiercest opposition they had ever faced.) Paint was everywhere. "SAS were here", and other such messages, plastered across walls and floor. Take some cleaning off, that. But they were welcome to it, this "gweilo" (literally, white ghost, even if I was by now well bronzed) was off "up country", as they say. Goodbye SAS. Goodbye Sunderlands. Goodbye the "all services" Britannia Club, downtown Singapore, directly opposite the luxurious splendour that was Raffles Hotel. The Brit Club, with its home-from-home food, good social atmosphere, and its swimming pool, was usually the first stop on any visit to town. After some time here our behaviour would usually degenerate to a level not acceptable in the area of the Raffles, so we'd be off to various local bars and clubs, often travelling by trishaw (bicycle powered rickshaw). If the requirement was for more than one machine - as was often the case - we would coax the drivers into a race.

"Come on Johnnie, you number one. You beat him. No winee, no payee."

That's all it took, and off they'd charge, like Ben Hur on steroids. They'd cut corners, rush willy-nilly down unlit streets, spindly legs going like pistons. It was a game they joined in, well knowing that not only *would* they be paid, but could expect a handsome tip. It wasn't in our interest not to pay. Too much hassle. For although, to us, they did all look alike, the reverse didn't necessarily apply. They seemed to have a good memory for faces, and the RAF Police tended to get slightly upset should we in any way distress the locals.

Occasionally, if we'd drunk enough (OK, somewhat more than occasionally) we'd sit them in the seat and have a go ourselves, for a couple of yards or so! Nowhere near as easy as it looked, which made me realize just how fit those scrawny-looking Chinese must be.

Well, it was goodbye to all that. Goodbye too, that Indian curry shop, outside the camp gates, Pops, where my room mate had converted me to the curry platter. Here the air was spiced with a combination of coriander, turmeric, cumin, chilies, garlic. Not an English smell. A different form of cooking from a different land.

A rickety, open-fronted affair, that shop, its hard-packed dirt floor patrolled by cockroaches the size of... well, bloody big cockroaches is what they were. But even those were not enough to deter Smithy and I from frequently partaking. Washed down with ice-cold *Tiger* it had to be one of the great curries of our time. A real sinus clearer. There again, maybe not. But ah, the memories. I now have only to pass within sniffing distance of an Indian restaurant for the images to flow. Palmed paradises of the Asian continent: Hong Kong, Malaya,

Singapore, Thailand.

It was goodbye also to the joss-scented Chinese restaurants that formed the bulk of Albert Street. The real thing, these. Forget your fancy high class places, with high class prices. Good as they might be, we couldn't afford them, so we took to the street.

The Albert Street kitchens were located on Tilly-lamp lighted barrows, positioned at the roadside. Marble-topped tables were sited in the mysterious-looking depths of the buildings behind, up rickety wooden stairs. Fatty's, which is usually where we'd end up, seemed to be the favourite. Up there the floors were polished wood - a step or two up from packed dirt - solid, yet uneven. The lighting was dim, but the inescapable cockroaches didn't seem to mind. Forget the decor, the food was great, the aromas, out of this world. Real flip-flop food. (Fatty's was still in evidence in 2014, albeit now in a fancy modern building, nicely glassed-in, and airconditioned.)

In matters of hygiene, of course, eating in this fashion did have its drawbacks. It could mean an extraordinary amount of time needed to be spent in the toilet, and third-world toilets are not exactly places where one would wish to spend an extraordinary amount of time. (I expect this, and later years in Africa etc, did fine tune my immune system over time. Now, very little seems to bother me, unlike today's "Elf an' Safety protected kids; their immune systems rarely put to use. And if you don't use it, you lose it. To my way of thinking!)

One place we did seem to spend an extraordinary amount of time was in the bars of Bugis Street. (Pronounced boogie.) It was fun to sit at tables set out on the street, drinking beer and watching life pass by. Especially the girls who flaunted about, attempting to sell themselves to us. The best looking girls in town worked the bars of Bugis Street. Only they weren't! This was a street of transvestites. We were well aware of the fact, but many strangers were not. They were that convincing, and it was interesting to watch the wheeling and dealing going on. Were some of those strangers to be in for a shock and a load of disappointment if it eventually progressed as far as the sliding a hand up a shapely leg stage! Imagine the scene as he reaches what he imagined to be his objective. The "girl" turns on all her charm. 'You like?' she asks.

'I regret, sir,' replies the stooge. 'I am not cognisant of the body in question'. At least he'd probably use a group of words which more or less amounted to such a reply, though perhaps not so elegantly put. This would occasionally be followed by a fist to the face.

Close by was Thieves Market, alongside the Rochor Canal. You could buy almost anything there, real or fake. Buy your own watch if you weren't careful. Same thing went for Change Alley, in Raffles Place. I'd forever remember the times spent haggling down there: the cheongsams that no one at home would be able to get into, or want! Those garish velvet cushion covers, decorated with tigers and dragons, likewise.

Yes, I'd miss all that. What I wouldn't miss were the storm drains. What was normally a mere trickle of water four feet down could quickly become a raging torrent during the tropical downpours that occasionally occurred. Nor would I miss the colourful but hideous Haw Par Villa, otherwise known as Tiger Balm Gardens. Their graphically explicit sculptures, depicting various acts of barbarism, enough to give anyone nightmares. If that's an example of Chinese mythology - to which they are supposedly related - you can keep it. No, I certainly wouldn't miss that.

Sunderlands apart, what I would probably miss most of all were the Swimming pool, and, particularly, the Seletar Yacht Club, located on the seafront, next to our crewroom. In fact, that Yacht Club as good as *was* our crewroom, during the day, especially towards that day's closing. Many an evening had been spent sitting out on the veranda of this simple, single story, attap roofed, wooden structure. Seems the Sunderland personnel had been awarded a kind of honorary membership, for we always seemed to be extended a welcome - at least during weekdays - whereas they were usually quite strict re non-members using the place.

I'd often sit there, taking in the sultry night air, *Tiger* to hand, watching the effects of the sun's setting over the Straits of Johore, Malaya less than a mile distant. Out at anchorage, aircraft bobbed on the water, mooring lights aglow, for when afloat these leviathans of the air needed to comply with maritime law, even so far as being required to carry a handbell - for use in foggy conditions - and an anchor. This was a piddling little thing that would have found difficulty holding a rowing boat in position, but it did adhere to the letter of the regulations.

Yes, it was to be goodbye to all that, good and bad. This was how it was then, and I could well imagine how it had been in the very early days of Sir Stamford Raffles. A time when tigers roamed the island. No lions though. Never had been. The place got its name after a Sumatran Prince encountered what he *thought* was a lion. At the time he was probably leaving the pub after a heavy night. Lucky him. I saw much stranger things than lions when in that state. You see, the way I had it figured, the bedtime drink was absolutely essential in the tropics. Yes, we often started very early, I realize, but by the time we'd finished it would be bedtime, wouldn't it? Anyway, my point is, the drink helped us sleep. At least it did me.

So, goodbye Singapore, hello Malaya, a place I'd longed to visit ever since I'd been based in the area and looked across at it every day. I had travelled the length of the peninsular by train - on my way to Penang, for a break at Tanjong Bungar, where the RAF maintained a leave centre - but that was different. Apart from jungle, and the occasional kampong, all I managed a glimpse of were the domes and minarets of Kuala Lumpur, of which - being a predominantly Muslim city - there appeared to be an abundance. In fact the most spectacular were those of the city's Moorish-style railway station, at which we made a brief halt, en-route to the north.

Our train wasn't even ambushed or shot at, as they occasionally were, the very reason we were obliged to travel fully armed, weapons actually loaded this time. It was the first time in my service career that I was issued a rifle where the intent was that I use it to shoot someone, should that become necessary.

Trains were an easy target, for a single line ran all the way up the west coast, passing through the fringes of the jungle. Little did I suspect that one day soon I would be able to study that jungle in extremely close detail. Just as well it didn't happen on that journey (even if I did secretly wish for it to). I could well imagine the confusion and chaos that would have reigned had it done so.

England it certainly wasn't. In fact, out here, England was best forgotten. I didn't like to think about it. Cold and snowy, rather than hot and humid; roast beef and Yorkshire pudding, as opposed to those curried eggs and chapattis. No, it didn't pay to think of England. That was some place far away across the sea. A place from which you occasionally received a letter. Or, to which you sent one.

So, it was to be goodbye Singapore, hello Malaya.

Hey! Hang on a minute! Didn't I just get through saying

people were being shot at up there?

*   *

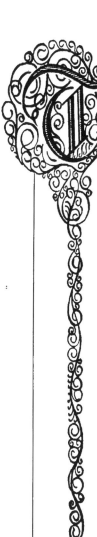

THE PRESERVATION OF MAN

THE horse and mule live thirty years,
And nothing know of wines and beers.
The goat and sheep at twenty die
With never a taste of scotch or rye.
The cow drinks water by the ton
And at 18 is mostly done.
The dog at 16 cashes in
Without the aid of rum or gin.
The cat in milk and water soaks
And then in 12 short years it croaks.
The modest, sober, bone dry hen
Lays eggs for nogs, then dies at 10.
All animals are strictly dry
They sinless live and swiftly die.
But sinful, ginful, rum-soaked men
Survive for three score years and ten
And some of us, the mighty few,
Stay pickled till we're 92.

PHOTOPAGE-3

Page 184 Top L: Hastings TG609, aircraft that took me on my first long range visit. **Top R:** Malta, my first short range overseas visit. **Centre L:** Singapore at last. Raffles Hotel 1957. **R:** Entrance to the Great World; one of three major recreational areas of this type in the fifties.
Bottom: Sunderland 2ⁿᵈ line servicing hangar.

Page 185 Top L: Aircraft on mooring, crew launch alongside. **R:** The all analogue Sunderland instrument panel. **Centre L:** Engine runs on the compass base. **R:** Low flyby at Labuan - Note clearance between wing tip float & ground, then compare with "engine runs" photo - that is what I call low! **Bottom:** Home again.

Page 186 Top L: Cuisine Sunderland style. **R: 390MU** multi-lingual advice. **Centre:** Seletar Yacht Club, our crew-room, slipway, with Sunderland servicing hangar behind. **Bottom L:** Fitting tail trolley before beaching. **R:**Oops! ML745 suffered this fate due to tail trolley failure. Nearing the end of its life anyway, the aircraft was written off.

Page 187: 205/209 Squadron ground crew alongside RN270, 1958. Open panel beneath the wing is the port bomb door. Bombs/depth charges were carried internally, fitted to racks which tracked out beneath the wing.

Page 188 Top L: Fred, ready for a practice jump. **R:** Fully armed rear turret. **Centre:** ML797 over Seletar, the RAF's last flying boat. A painting by Douglas Swallow GAvA, commissioned by the author.
Bottom L: In action with my Ashai Pentax, 1957. **R;** Fooling around with the ice cream seller.

Page 189Top: Aerial of waterfront & Flying Boat base. **Centre:** "On the step - Sunderland on the take-off run. **Bottom L:** HMT Oxfordshire, my transport from Hong Kong back to Singapore. **R:** Hong Kong approach from a Sunderland cockpit.

Page 190 top: Sad times. Sunderland scrapyard at Seletar 1959.
Bottom: Flying boat jetty & control in the good old days. (Much

more atmospheric in colour)

Page 191 Top: Singapore River; 1957 & 2009. **Centre:** This crash on the old runway at Kai Tak, Hong Kong, was cause for the new runway, **Bottom:** (barely discernable, top right) to be opened early.

187

Chapter Six
UP COUNTRY WITH ONE FIVE FIVE

Aquick glance at a map of the area served as confirmation that mainland Malaya was the dragon's-head-like peninsula that appears about to devour the island of Singapore. (Once it became Malaysia, it apparently attempted to do so, literally.) Not that I was unfamiliar with the geography of the area, just felt I should refresh my mind. Malaya is, in fact, that area referred to by service personnel in Singapore as "Up Country".

In my case, "up country" bore reference to the RAF airfield associated with the capital city, Kuala Lumpur; commonly referred to as KL. City and airfield alike were located on the western side of the peninsular, as were the majority of towns and cities in Malaya. There were one or two in the east, but these were accessible only from down south, or by air. There were few cross country roads, and, having ridden it, I was already aware that the railway traversed only the west coast. Almost the entire central region, from the Thai border down to the south of KL, was covered by a vast, mountainous green jungle, known colloquially as "The Ulu." My first impression was that Malaya looked like the ideal spot for a vacation, but I was soon to learn otherwise.

'Be advised, lad,' a grizzled RAF Regiment sergeant told me, 'this is the front line. The terrorists infest that jungle, not to mention snakes and wild animals. On top of which you've got aborigines, armed with blowpipes from which they fire poison-tipped darts. Very accurately', he added, with some emphasis.

As far as the terrorist threat went, the proof was all around. Just eight miles due north of the city, in the hills, are located Batu Caves; a Hindu shrine that was especially relevant during the festival known as Thaipusam. But at the time even this area was still declared to be "Black"; evidence that Chin Peng and his boys were that close to the capital city.

As often seemed the case in Southeast Asia, come the end of the Second World War, the communist-inspired guerilla bands who had fought against the Japanese - with weapons supplied by their allies (in this case, the British) - did not always have the allies interests at heart. Their idea was that, with the cessation of hostilities, they would take over the country for themselves, even though few of the leaders were Malay nationals. With this in mind, here in Malaya, Chin Peng, and his Malay People's Anti-Japanese Army, had secreted away countless stores of weapons. He'd also had his followers indoctrinate the local populace in the ways of communism. And now, after living in, and off it, for over two years, the MPAJA were now well acquainted with that jungle.

Interspersed between town and jungle were the rubber plantations, vital to the economy in the days before synthetics. Just such a place was that in which the trouble began: Sungai Siput. Barely warranting a name on the map, this innocent isolated outpost was deemed ideal for a communist incursion, with three expatriate plantation managers being slaughtered. This all happened long before I arrived in the area, the conflict by then in it's eighth year.

I was flown up to KL from Changi, courtesy of the Royal New Zealand Air Force, in one of 41 Squadron's boxy-looking Bristol Freighters (described by an American in Vietnam as "looking like the packing case the aircraft came in"). OK, not exactly first class, but what military aircraft is? (The answer to that would become evident a couple of years hence. One of which was also built by Bristol; a sort of scaled down Brabazon.) That the Freighter was known to crews and passengers alike as the "Vibrator", or "Frightener", says it all. But at least it got me safely to my destination.

The RAF base at KL was also the civil airport, or vice versa, the single runway shared with the airlines: BOAC - Comet 4; Malayan Airways - DC3 and Viscount; Cathay Pacific - Douglas's varied piston-engined range, and the Lockheed Electra, vying for space with Air Forces of the UK, New Zealand, Australia, and the fledgling air arm of the host country. It was also where I saw my first Boeing 707, Qantas (VH-EBA) making a low pass down the runway on a delivery flight to Australia. It was the airline's first jet.

With such an amount of activity taking place it would be embarrassing should the runway be rendered *hors de combat*, even for a short time: which is where Murphy once more came into play.

*

The noise carried clearly to the squadron crewroom. It sounded like someone had loaded cutlery into the spin-dryer in mistake for the dish-washer. Rushing outside I saw an RAF DC3 "voice" aircraft sliding ignominiously along the runway on its belly, sparks flying. At least what, until a few moments ago, had *been*

193

a voice aircraft. The speakers beneath its wings were now mashed into the tarmac. ("Voice", or "Skyshout" aircraft were used in the psychological warfare role. Fitted out with play-back equipment which, via high-powered amplifiers and equally high-powered speakers, their job had been to fly over the jungle, broadcasting messages to the terrorists, and dropping leaflets advising them as to the benefits on offer should they surrender.)

Emergency crews arrived on scene almost as soon as the Dak ground to a fiery halt - even so, they were far too late, the aircrew having already abandoned ship; they'd appeared to be in rather a hurry, too!

Yet another case of taking-off-without-first-removing-the-control-locks syndrome, I was later to discover. Remember that? *Someone* obviously hadn't. Rather embarrassing, really; the RAF *had* just rendered Kuala Lumpur International Airport *hors de combat,* that runway being closed for a time, although they didn't stand on ceremony. Using steel hawsers the aircraft was literally dragged clear, and not all in one piece. That DC3 was definitely *hors de combat.* In RAF terms, from cat 3 to cat 5 in a flash!

There had been an earlier incident involving this, or a similar aircraft, when it was found the recording had inadvertently been erased. This time, it was the flights themselves that had been erased, permanently, that aircraft having been the last one of its kind, although the Valetta and Twin Pioneer did later step in to fill the void.

So this was KL, the place at which I joined number 155 squadron.

Quite a change from the Spitfires the squadron had flown during World War Two, Westland's Pratt and Whitney powered Whirlwind HAR4 was the aircraft which would provide me with a new and vastly different experience of flight; rotary, as opposed to fixed wing. A quantum leap, one might say. Vertical take off, hover, sideways and rearward flight. There was a new language to be learned, too: Casevac - for casualty evacuation, and Fort Express, with which I was later to become familiar. And how about Lima Zulu - landing zone: a temporary clearing hacked out of the jungle at a convenient location, for as well as suiting the enemy, this place was ideally suited to helicopter operations, the type making an immeasurable contribution to the communists' eventual defeat.

Other talk related to pull-off checks (not what you might

at first think!), the ground cushion, translational lift effect, and blade tracking. There were droop stops, a collective control (the up and down stick), and a cyclic control (the back, forwards, and sideways thingy), and the tail end was fitted with an anti-torque device: something that resembled whirly hair trimmer.

Change was what my Seletar room-mate "Smudge" Smith would now be experiencing, too. For in their implausible ways, the RAF had seen fit to have "Smudge" take my place on the Sunderlands, for the final months of their existence. There again, maybe "Smudge" only had months remaining on his tour, whereas I was barely halfway through mine.

My first experience of helicopter flight was definitely a bit of an eye opener. The cockpit itself was probably eight feet off the ground, with good all round vision, and this is where I was seated, alongside the pilot. I watched as he went through the start-up procedure. The engine fired up, then the rotor was engaged, and we welcomed the cooling draught. The pilot completed his checks, then we lifted off, vertically. Not that high, for being under air traffic control we were obliged to track over to the end of the runway as if we were a fixed wing, taxying. Then the nose dipped and we were away, gathering speed and height before we turned and headed off to wherever.

I'd expected this posting to be different, and it certainly was. This was military helicopter flying in its infancy, at least as far as the British forces were concerned. The Whirlwind then was a far cry from the relatively safe, computer-assisted, turbine-powered, clutch-less machines of later years, and the potential for an incident was never too far distant. But we didn't allow such thoughts free rein at the time, couldn't afford to. Besides, comparisons between era are only possible with hindsight, the dangers only then becoming obvious. Anyway, we were full of ourselves, had very good pilots who practised incessantly. Sometimes, on the way back from a day's operations I would be asked to switch off the hydraulics to the flying controls, so my pilot could get used to the feel of it, in case of a failure. Looked like hard work to me, and it apparently was.

'Much like losing the power steering on a car,' Taff, my pilot, told me. But a necessity here, rather than an added luxury. Five minutes is about my limit,' he said.

There would be practice autorotations, too: power off, collective to zero; the procedure to be followed in the event of an engine failure, or should the tail rotor drive shear. (That anti-torque device: no power, no torque to correct for.) Autorotation allowed the rotor to freewheel, which - much like the fruit of the Sycamore tree - provided for a reasonably gentle, fairly controllable descent. Just like riding a big, Big Dipper. Close to the ground, without actually touching down, power was reapplied and away we went. I got used to those, quite enjoyed them in fact, which was to stand me in good stead later on in life.

Maybe ours were a special breed of pilot, for they certainly instilled confidence, and I never once felt anything but at ease when flying with any of them.

But incidents there were, aplenty. In fact I recall Pete, a rather egotistic crewman if ever there was one, becoming disgruntled by the fact that he was one of the few who hadn't yet been involved in anything untoward! Well, neither had I. Nor did I wish to be. I was sane and selfish enough to wish my share upon someone else. He was welcome to them. Still, takes all types, as they say. And, merry gathering that we were, we were certainly no different when it came to the matter of varying personalities.

Pete (or Lofty, as he was known. Not so much for his ego as his size), must have been away the day the RAF Recruitment Branch came to take publicity photographs, for he, no doubt, would have leapt at this chance of fame and glory.

What was called for was a shot that could have been entitled "inspecting the tail-rotor gearbox", though for some reason there seemed to be a distinct shortage of volunteers to fill the role of inspector. Then Fred had a bright idea.

'What about whatisname?' he suggested, miming drinking from a glass. "Whatisname", an airman - who shall remain nameless - had taken to drink; a result of the "Dear John" he'd recently received. Unfortunate, that, for he was one of that rare breed who were unable to take more than about half a pint before reaching the "absolutely legless" stage.

'Brilliant,' replied Chiefy Henderson, our boss, and an ex Dambusters flight engineer. 'Go get him. And make sure he's in a fit state to do the job,' he added, a twinkle in his eye.

Problem solved. "Whatisname" was so plastered they just draped him over the tailboom and took their pictures, confident in the knowledge he wouldn't be going anywhere in a hurry.

This guy's drunken escapades also bought him into

constant conflict with the "Snowdrops". So, to prevent him going downtown and getting into trouble, his friends would buy him a pint in the NAAFI, then put him to bed. Even so, he escaped often enough to become well known amongst the local community. So well known, local taxi drivers took to carrying him back to camp in the boot of the car, so as to keep him from being apprehended at the gate.

*

Our work was on the front line in the 'Emergency' - Malaya 1948-60 - and aircraft operating away from base required the services of a crewman - ordinarily the domain of fitter (engines), or rigger (airframes), at least as far as official policy was concerned. But I was determined not to be excluded. I learned quickly in those days, soon acquired sufficient knowledge to enable me to carry out the necessary duties: ie, I could refuel and inspect the aircraft, knew basically where to kick and tap when a problem occurred. (Throw away the manual, old chap, use your initiative. Especially out in the bush.) For instance, the starter motor had developed a habit of not always engaging when the starter button was pressed. The cure for which required the clamshell doors - which formed the aircraft's nose - to be opened, allowing access to a little toggle on the starter itself. A tweak on this usually cleared the problem, but in certain cases it could create another. As happened the time a Flying Officer, transit pilot, was ferrying an aircraft down to Singapore, with an officer of Air rank as his co-pilot passenger (The Air Officer Commanding Far East Air Force, in fact). They'd stopped off en-route, to refuel on the village green - aka football pitch - at some out of the way place. An ideal time for our old enemy, Murphy, to strike. He always seemed to be hanging around backstage, awaiting just such an opportunity.

'Not again,' wailed to FO, as the starter failed to engage. 'A common occurrence, sir, unfortunately,' he explained.

'So what is the procedure now? asked the Air Vice Marshall.

'Well, sir, being as we don't have a crewman on board, one of us needs to tweak the thing whilst the other initiates the start up. I wonder if you'd mind doing the tweaking, sir?'

'Point me in the right direction,' says the senior officer.

This was done. But with the result being a marked lack of success, they decided to trade places. The AVM would climb back into the cockpit, the F/O would do the tweaking.

Success. But it was a success that was to swiftly degenerate into failure. The starter engaged, the engine fired, but unfortunately, "Sir" had the throttle almost wide open. Engine revs rose in rapid response, the clutch made a snatch engagement, the rotor suddenly turned. In this situation, the weights in the sagging blade tips tend initially to droop even further, rather than lifting the blades, which can result in damage to the tail-boom, across the top of which runs the tail rotor driveshaft. Which, as dictated by Murphy, is exactly what did happen. Oops! Chop, chop, no drive to the tail rotor, a damaged boom. And guess who took the blame for that little lot? A clue: it wasn't anyone of Air rank. (Years later, at a reunion, a friend, Jim, who at the time of the above incident was a Flight Sergeant, and for some reason on quite friendly terms with the AOC, told me that next time he and the AOC met up, he asked what had happened. "Never you mind", or similar, was the reply. Jim replied, "It's OK, sir, I'll read about it in Flight Safety" - the monthly accident report. The AOC, who was in charge of most of what went on in the Far East Air Force, simply replied, "No you won't". The privilege of rank!)

But I had learnt to handle that start-up problem. More importantly, I could safely climb into the cockpit once the rotor was turning; an essential attribute. Use your head, don't loose it, could get messy! Yet that too did happen.

It was November 1958, and somewhere west of Tanah Rata, in the Cameron Highlands, the jungle was about to be filled with drama of a different kind.

A Sycamore (XL822) of 194 squadron was on detachment at Ipoh, when a casevac flight was called for. The incident took place on the return trip. Flying the aircraft was Master Pilot "Nobby" Clarke - an aviator renowned for his nicotine intake. In fact, in those pre-GPS (or any other form of navigational aid) days, Nobby's navigation was said to be related to the number of cigarettes it took for any leg of a particular trip (he'd use the Verey pistol outlet as an ashtray/extractor). The flight sectors would be designated by Nobby as 3, 4, 5 etc cigarette sectors. Along with him on this flight were his crewman - fairly new to the job - with a mental patient in a straight-jacket cast in the role of casualty.

'I experienced sudden engine failure,' Nobby later told me, 'so I set it up to autorotate, selecting a nearby river as my target, the only clear area to be seen. But it turned out to be a white-water rapid, filled with huge boulders. This called for a last minute change of plan. No option of overshooting and going round again, in autorotate you pick your spot and aim for it, and here was I, collective in the fully up "help me Jesus" position. Nothing for it but a quick jink on the cyclic, which had us ending up in a nearby bamboo thicket, scything down a hundred Sunday Times' editions worth of unprocessed newsprint. The blades shattered, naturally, being made of wood, but before the remnants had ceased rotating, myself busy shutting down, the crewman was halfway out of the door, being struck on the head in the process. Despite wearing a helmet, that was him unconscious. There was mention of the helmet not being a good fit, or of it not being fastened correctly, though that was probably irrelevant. Let's face it, Dave, a bone-dome is scant protection against a blade hitting it at any kind of speed.

'I had managed to get off a distress call, but with darkness encroaching I found myself to be deep in the sh... er... bandit country, with only a nutter and an unresponsive crewman for company. Tell you what, though, that patient made an amazingly swift return to the realms of the sane, upon being offered his release.

'This is conditional upon you helping me tend the crewman,' I told him.

'OK,' the guy replied. 'But first you must give me back my gun. It's packed away with the rest of my kit.'

'Well, I balked at that idea, didn't I, but then I thought about it. I definitely needed help, so went ahead anyway.'

(No wonder Nobby was a fully paid up member of cancer incorporated. This incident apart, he was also one of the few pilots to have survived the runaway-tailplane-actuator-syndrome; a problem endemic to the early mark of Canberra bomber.)

Unbeknown to Nobby the eighth cavalry were already on the way (the seventh were wiped out at Little Bighorn, if memory serves me), and another Sycamore was already airborne, in search of them. This second aircraft was eventually forced to depart the area before locating the wreck, due to the same darkness which was encroaching upon Nobby and Co. The rescue aircraft diverted to Fort Brooke, spending the night there. The third and final Sycamore of their detachment did manage to land a medical team - doctor plus one - in a nearby clearing (nearby as the crow - or helicopter - flies, that is). But as this coincided with the very moment darkness finally did descend, the arrangement was that the pilot would allow them fifteen minutes, after which, if no word was received, he also would retire to Fort Brooke, returning at first light.

Retire he did. Very daring too, it seemed.

'I was new to the Sycamore,' the pilot later said. 'In fact I had never flown any helicopter in the dark, so most of my time seemed to be spent hunting down the switches for the cockpit lighting. And when I found them, the lights were so dazzling I felt I'd be better off without. Only I realized I needed to keep an eye on the rotor rpm! But it did ensure my eyes were well tuned for the landing at Brooke. They'd positioned a bloody Land-Rover so that the headlights shone straight into my eyes, rather than away from the direction of approach!'

Meanwhile, back on centre stage, the doctor had managed to break an ankle - his own. A bit careless to say the least, but it was that kind of country. Still, he didn't have far to travel for medical advice, didn't need worry about bedside manner, and there were no prescriptions to scribble out.

They were all found the next day, brought out, including, after a time, the aircraft, which was eventually repaired and returned to squadron service.

'No such luck for the poor old crewman,' Nobby told me. 'He succumbed overnight.'

So, could I handle that kind of emergency, if necessary? Well, who knows for sure until it happens? But I was confident I could. On top of which, I could rough it with the best of them during night-stops in the field.

All it required now was a course in jungle survival at the school located part way up Fraser's Hill, on the peak of which was yet another leave centre. The fresh, cool air up there called for a log fire in the evening, but it was hot and sweaty enough during the day's activities. They possessed all the key ingredients to make it so: heat and humidity, secondary jungle, mud and slime, poisonous snakes and such.

'A supply-drop parachute makes a fine bed, and forget about trying to swat the mosquitoes, next morning they're so bloated they're grounded.' That was the kind of advice we were given. I found it to be true enough.

Splat! Yet another mossie spreadeagled itself on the wall, joining the dried-up versions which already reposed there, legs akimbo, protruding from within a rustily recognisable brown blob.

'Hey! Check the size of him. That red blotch on the wall used to be my blood.'

'Look, don't worry, Dave, we have ten to twelve pints of the stuff. Enough to provide Dracula with a three course lunch, never mind the odd mossie.'

'What about Malaria?'

'Never heard tell of anyone being so afflicted. Cast it from mind as long as you take the tablets (we were supposed to take quinine tablets every day). Enough to worry about already without piling on the agony.'

I must have performed well enough, for I was issued a set of jungle green: shirt, trousers, boots, and the vital floppy hat, the means by which those in ambush situations differentiated between the good guys and the bad. Along with the kit came a commando-type dagger, handy when refuelling in the field from five gallon cans (known as flimsies). A quick stab and a deft flick of the wrist had the seal removed, another stab in the opposing corner so as to allow a steady flow. Refuel through a chamois filter, fling the empty well clear, providing the rotor wasn't already turning. Notorious for sucking loose debris into the disc, a helicopter. The downwash would blow loose items out and up, where they'd be drawn in from above.

I was also issued with RAF form 1767 - Aircrew Flying Log-book. Bureaucratic English, that. I flew of course, the log-book remained safely back at base. The only thing I missed out on (at least to begin with) was the meagre flying pay awarded to official crewmen, but that didn't bother me at all. A minor sacrifice for the honour of occupying the left-hand seat: in fixed wing terms, the captain's position.

For some reason - the true facts about which, appear to have disappeared in the mists of time - the captain of a helicopter sits on the right. Something to do with airfields usually having left-hand circuits, so one story goes. The apparent thinking behind this was that it would separate the helicopter circuit (slow) from the fixed wing circuit (fast) thus avoiding confusion between conflicting traffic. But there are other versions as to the reason, one of which is said to originate in the States. This has the very first rotary wing instructor (Les Morris, of Sikorsky) taking the left-hand seat, as on a fixed wing type, thus putting the pupil on the right, where, upon qualifying - having become used to the position and not now wishing to reverse his control orientation - he remained. Sounds feasible. Especially if you consider the cabin door -

thus winch - were usually to starboard, therefore a pilot seated on the right would be better positioned to keep an eye on things. Then there's the idea it was purely to facilitate exit in the event of an emergency, it being easier to exit from the right due to the positioning of the collective control. Myself, I favour the American version, as vacating the cockpit with the collective raised - when it would impede exit - hints of abandoning ship with the rotor still turning! Ask any helicopter pilot the reason and you'll get any amount of conflicting ideas, though most never seem to have spared it a thought; have no idea whatsoever.

Anyway, the left was where I now sat, making me feel even more like someone out of a Biggles novel. An up to date version this time, what with my bone-dome and throat-mike, plus newly-cultivated moustache (which wasn't destined to survive for long; made me look old when I was still very young. Anyway, Biggles didn't have a moustache). One more thing, the cockpit - no matter on which side one was seated - was a far better option than the cabin, for believe me, nobody flew first class in an S55, either, Royals apart. The interior wasn't just spartan, it was bare. Anti-corrosion coated aluminium skin and stringers, ribbed and skeletal; none of your fancy airliner panelling here. Even the seats, when fitted, were basically... er... well, basic. Sound proofing? Forget it. Those overhead quilted covers appeared to be more decorative rather than of any practical value; though they did prevent *some* of the gearbox oil from dripping onto the passengers. The floor consisted of plywood panels, known as load spreaders - to help spread the load, naturally - and to prevent wayward bayonets and suchlike from penetrating the aluminium skin, beneath which were located the fuel tanks.

Because of the hostile environment in which our helicopters operated, we carried a wealth of firepower: one pistol - pilot, for the use of - one M1 carbine, crewman, ditto. Possibly a little short of what would be required to start World War Three, but that was never the intention. All that was needed was for us to protect the aircraft, and ourselves. Not exactly *creme de la creme* in the hardware stakes, neither were they the best weapons for the job. But all that was to change. After assessment of our ability on the firing range - the crewmen, that is - the rifle was replaced by a lightweight "chatter-gun". These were furnished with two magazines, which we taped together, back to back, just like in the movies. The assumption, one supposes, that so armed we may stand a chance of hitting something. At least we could look and sound the part.

Although by now quite adept with a rifle, at a target - that ATC and Boy Entrant training finally paying off - it would probably be a far different matter when faced with the reality of another human being. Someone who meant business, was prepared to return fire. Well, I now had a serious weapon in my hands. One that could possibly reassign the odds in my favour. It was a thought that only needed a hook on which to hang it. A hook readily supplied by a subconscious which seemed continually to seek adventure. Imagination ran riot, and I lapsed into brief introspection of the way it could happen.

In my mind I saw a couple of guys charging out of the jungle, myself engaged with the refuelling, George - the human pilot - still strapped in the cockpit, controlling things from on high, finding himself not to be in a position that enabled him to make a fast draw. Restrictions of harness and space resulting in his pistol being pointed at a vulnerable part of his anatomy, its removal dictating a need for much care, therefore time. Sid James rather than Jesse James.

No matter, help was at hand.

Now I don't go around advocating violence and such, but that wasn't the Salvation Army out there, not dressed the way they were; clothing that gave the appearance of having been designed in such centres of haute couture as Moscow or

Peking. No, it was fairly obvious these buggers weren't here to carry out a sociological study on the travelling public. With this in mind - plus the thought that, as crewman, protection of the aircraft was one of my functions - I'd immediately hurl the fuel can aside and, aided by the reflexes of youth - instinctive, faster than thought itself - I'd swiftly snatch up the Sten. In a twinkling, with all the dexterity of a yet to be discovered Schwarzenegger, I'd quickly cock the weapon, flick off the safety, hose the area down, and, if necessary, eject the magazine, turn the taped package around, click home the charged unit and carry on hosing. (I saw myself as having come a long way since those early days at Cosford.)

'It's OK, sir,' I imagined myself shouting above the racket. 'All under control.' And so it would be, at least in my head. Chackka... chackka... chackka - though faster than you could say the words - flora, fauna, and terrorists, disintegrated in a hail of lead as the air was filled with the sharp tang of cordite.

'Take that you commie bastards. Teach you to mess with One Five Five.' Blowing smoke from the barrel I'd then calmly make the weapon safe, placing it within easy reach. After which I imagined myself carrying on with the task of refuelling, whistling away merrily, with not a care in the world. An extraordinary act of heroism against an insidious and determined foe. That, I imagined, would surely earn me a medal. At least a Mention in Dispatches. Well, are we not all allowed our one moment of glory?

In my mind's eye, that was how I saw myself. I could well imagine it happening, but, of course, it never did. Luckily, I suppose, for - recalling my schooldays, my bicycle, my pitiful efforts at the late-late braking technique, the ensuing pile-up - I suspect no one would have had much to fear, with the possible exception of the flora and fauna. Hell! Maybe even, George. Not good for pilot-crewman relations, that. And how would it look on my resume? Doubt it would qualify me for a lawful job. That apart, how then would I get home? Occupation of the left-hand seat did not magically engender one with the necessary skills required to take off and land the thing, though we were allowed plenty of practice in flying it. I harboured few doubts about my ability to keep the thing in the air, once it was up there, chugging along merrily. Not too difficult a task that, just as long as nothing untoward went wrong in the meantime. *Getting* it up, then putting it down again was where problems were likely to occur. Well, maybe not so much the putting down bit, provided Her Majesty was prepared to strike thousands of pounds worth of aircraft off charge.

An MiD (Mentioned in Dispatches) was "allocated" to the squadron during this period. Not that any of us had done anything say, "above and beyond the call of duty", as it were. There again, maybe we all had. Well, most of us. Anyway, as I recall, the decision was made to put the names of all squadron personnel into a hat, shuffle then up, and hope for the best. Then, by some quirk of service life, the "draw" was won by the admin clerk. Still, he was a good friend of mine, so maybe I qualified by association.

Pete, MiD, was also the person responsible for my future addiction to the sport of motor racing. His enthusiasm, augmented by the discovery that these machines also operated close to, and occasionally beyond, the limits, ensured my immediate interest. Besides, as he pointed out, those fellows, Moss and Hawthorn, did seem to be doing quite well. Apart from which, they were Brits, in there amongst the foreigners, showing them how it should be done. At least Moss was. Until recently, Hawthorn *had* been.

*

A trip to the Cameron Highlands showed me another face of this diverse country. Were it not for tea plantations and the sun I could have been back home in England. Cottages, and village green type places. This hill resort was located one hundred and forty miles to the north of KL, at an altitude of six thousand five hundred feet, where the air was cool. It was also an area of dense trees, a profusion of wildflowers and waterfalls, and hills that were alive with beautiful butterflies. Yet another resort area which didn't seem at all hostile. Especially when, in the evening's dying light, plantation managers could be seen relaxing on their verandas, gin and tonic to hand. But the bandits were out there all right, not too far away. Waiting, no doubt with malice aforethought.

Mention of hostile environment brings to mind our odd forays into the city of Kuala Lumpur itself, for as far as I was concerned, this was where the real danger lay. For a start the monsoon drains here were no less fearsome than those in Singapore, nor were the cockroaches any less prevalent. But those weren't perceived threats.

The capital played host to diverse regiments of not only the British Armed Forces, but those of other members of the

Commonwealth too. Many of them seemingly expert in the field of unarmed combat. And like all experts, it appeared one needed to continually practise the art so as to remain on top of things. This they certainly did. All too often. Usually in the various bars and clubs dotted around the area. Juke boxes etc were firmly secured and caged, so as to prevent improper use. The troops were just honing their skills, as it were, upon one another. Indeed, one was left with the impression their skills were in dire need of a honing, so enthusiastically did they become embroiled. Only natural really. These guys had been trained this way, aggression was now part of their make up, although the fact didn't seem to be taken into account by the authorities when arrests were made. I witnessed action aplenty on that front, but during my twenty-one month spell with the squadron the only terrorists to cross my path were either as dead as a Monty Python parrot, or prisoners. I did see a lot of jungle though.

We flew into small strips and clearings hacked out of the wilderness. Many of these were located in mountainous regions, accessible only to the Scottish Aviation Pioneer, and its larger, twin-engined brother, or by helicopter, with a limited load, as I was to find.

I figured we were well short of our destination to one of the forts - way up in the mountains - yet here we were, descending already. I looked across at George, the question clearly etched upon my face.

'Can't make it, Dave. Not with a full load. At this altitude the engine can't handle it, doesn't have the power. Going to have to dump you, make a couple trips.'

So, down we went, out I got, taking part of the freight with me. It looked a decidedly lonely spot. A small clearing. With only the jungle for company, I hoped.

'Forty minutes,' George assured me, before departing. 'Then I'll be back.'

'OK. I'll marshal you down when you return. If you don't see me, don't land,' I told him. Precautionary measures.

I waved him off, then watched as my lifeline climbed away, to disappear in the distance. A dot that became gradually smaller and quieter, until it finally vanished altogether. Then the silence closed in. It seemed like a total silence, at first. Almost eerily quiet now that helicopter was gone. I was on my own, twiddling my thumbs, out in the middle of hostile territory. At least I hoped I was alone. Or was my earlier vision about to become reality? And if so? Well, due to military training instilling in me instincts I hadn't realised I possessed, I realised I had the trusty Sten in my hand, even though I couldn't recall snatching it up during my exit. Not only that, the magazine was in place, the weapon now cocked and ready, safety on. Automatic reactions. I also had death on my mind. The only question to be answered: whose? Still, nowhere is it written that if you play safe and hide you will live to be a hundred and die happy.

I was as prepared as I could be.

Gradually, as I sat there - though never in full view - the sounds of nature returned. The atmosphere was again filled with a buzzing, chirping, and clicking. Reassuring sounds, for they were an almost certain indication that, nature apart, I *was* alone. And then came another reassuring sound, one that told me I was shortly to be no longer alone.

George had his ETA figured pretty close, I knew because I'd been checking my watch. Rather frequently as it happens. Thirty-five minutes and forty-two seconds had ticked away before I picked up the familiar sound of a Pratt and Whitney Wasp, of blades slapping the air; the signal that my whirlybird was returning. Then there it was, a fairy godmother, curving in over the trees, preparing to land. Relief. For I knew then I would soon be on my way. And so I was, after I'd stepped out of hiding and marshalled him down, as promised. All good experience, for it was at times like that I realized just how much our aircraft meant to the Army in the field.

In actual fact, when thought about later, it is unlikely CT's would have put in an appearance out in the open, during daylight. Unless of course they had already been ensconced in the tree line, and had observed the drop off. In which case they would probably have waited for the aircraft to return, as they would know it must.

There was one time I did get rather concerned though, the day my machine curved in over the trees, trailing smoke. Had me worried for a while there, until it landed, and the rotor brake was found to be not fully released! Didn't really need to look, the air reeked of overheated brake lining. Not a big problem, all had cooled down by the time I'd finished refuelling; but it would require a thorough check back at base. Then we were ready to depart once more, my thoughts now on bath, beer and bed.

*   *

Chapter Seven
A RABBLE OF BUTTERFLIES

Some of the jungle strips we flew in to were attached to forward bases of the Malayan Police Field Force. Known as forts, these bases - a dozen or so in all - were in reality little more than an armed enclosure set in an isolated jungle clearing. Reminiscent of something out in the Wild West, with but a simple barbed wire fence replacing encircling log walls. Ineffective at stopping bullets, though it would give flesh and blood pause for thought. And there were armed watch towers. From these forts, patrols would head off into the jungle for weeks at a time, carrying with them most of what they needed to survive, though being occasionally re-supplied from the air.

The forts, too, relied on the Air Force for their supplies. Brooke, Betis, Keemar, Shean, and Legap, for starters. Evocative names to those who were there. These names, and others, such as Grik, BMH (British Military Hospital) Kinrarha, and the eponymous, Paddy's Ladang, were to feature regularly on our operations board, especially those (two) without the luxury of a grass strip attached. Often we would visit two or three on an operation spread over two days, spending the night at one or another of them; as in the aforementioned "Fort Express". I've often thought it would be nice to know how those forts came to be so-named, what stories lay behind their choice. Where in fact did the names originate? Who were, or had been, these people, or places after which they had been named, what had they done, or been? Particularly, Paddy, for instance. Fort Brooke apart - named after the Lt Colonel Brooke, then CO of the SAS - I never did find out, just assumed them to have been other high ranking officers, government officials, or perhaps local Malay names.

They were interesting places to visit, too, for, upon invitation, a short walk from most forts would take you to a clearing (or ladang) in which would be situated one or two of the native longhouses - one of the reasons for the forts' being.

'A prime reason for the existence of these forts,' I'd been told upon joining our squadron, 'is to protect the aborigines who live nearby. Actually to prevent the communists from subverting them, and from living off their crops and livestock.' To which one of the squadron pilots had later added a chilling postscript. 'Not for philanthropic reasons is the odd sack of cooked rice left laying around for the terrorists to "discover". Those bags are rumoured to have been liberally seeded with bamboo slivers. A particularly nasty way to die, so I've heard,' he'd said.

'A bit dirty, isn't it?'

'As they say, fight fire with fire. The terrorists play far dirtier tricks on the Security Forces.' (The name given to the Combined Services operation.)

The longhouse visit was a trip I made whenever possible, Pentax in hand.

Built on stilts, one of these bamboo, rattan, and thatch dwellings would be home to a multitude of families, often with no form of interior division. Not that it mattered, bamboo floors are extremely springy; one couple humping and everyone would be bouncing up and down in unison. The floor space would also be shared with the dogs. Pigs and chickens rooted and scratched around in the dirt, ten feet below where I stood. Dust motes and smoke drifted in the air, accented by the shafts of light which poured through gaps in the barely adequate exterior walls, and the floor.

Such a visit - encompassing as it did, a different culture - was like stepping back in time, to visit an ancient world. A blend of remote primate in an exotic though basic environment. It was a world of wood fires, and of cooking beneath the sun, and stars. Women would sit around weaving, making things from whatever grew, roamed, or lived close-by. Men fashioned darts for their elaborately-decorated blowpipes, coated them with poison. A poison it was said for which there was no cure - would kill a man in one painful hour. With these they'd hunt monkey, and deer, which the women would cook in their cast iron pots. They also concocted a fearsome grog, for which, after one sip, I dreamed up all kinds of excuses as to why I had to refuse more. Yeah, that bad! But they seemed to enjoy it. Truth be told, had I been living out here, rather than just visiting, I'd no doubt have become rather partial to it myself.

Basic living, basic comfort, basic dress; it was all they wished for.

Then there was Fort Chabai - remotely located in a valley deep in the jungle - where I, along with my mate, Sam Saunders, once elected to spend a week's leave. Could have gone to Singapore, Hong Kong, Bangkok, almost anywhere in the Far East really, but we chose Chabai. Today it would be no contest. There again, today I'm no longer in jungle-bashing shape. Back then I was, or so I thought. And had I not taken advantage of the opportunity, I could well imagine the result: a nagging thought, forever wondering what I'd missed out on. No problems now; been there, done that, as they say. All those other places as well.

But that Chabai break really was an eye-opener. It seemed like a different country out there, away from the cities and towns: KL, Ipoh, Penang. It *was* different, of course. This was the "Ulu". Nature in the raw. Mountainous, primary and secondary jungle. Absolute peace on earth, so long as you omit the occasional mindless forays during which we discharged a multitude of weaponry on the make-shift range.

'Got something here for you to try, Dave,' "Butch" Walker, the Malay Police Commander said one morning. 'Anti-personnel, semi-automatic shotgun. A fearsome tool.'

True enough I found. It really could devastate the greenery - and, one imagines, anyone or thing lurking within - with impunity. All it required was to be pointed in the general direction of a threat and fired. Not that different from my first encounter with a really serious weapon, in point of fact. A sparrow decimation exercise, if I recall the facts correctly.

It was one day after school, long before I joined the ATC. I went home with a friend who lived on a farm. Not the first time I'd been, for he too had also once been declared, my best friend. Ever.

'Ever fired a shotgun?' Mark asked me.

'Never fired a gun of any kind,' I told him.

'Fancy a go?'

'If it's OK. I mean, is it allowed?'

'Dad won't mind,' he said, which didn't actually answer the question. But, let's face it, at that age you tend not to question morality too closely, never mind the safety aspect of such a move. So, as there was no one around, borrow it we did.

'Better borrow a few of these,' Mark suggested, grabbing a handful of cartridges. 'Well, not exactly borrowing. They're unlikely to be returned.' He laughed at that. We then set off across the fields.

'Keep your eyes open, Dave. What we need is something upon which to inflict untold damage, preferably something that moves.'

'Loads of cows and sheep,' I pointed out.

'Come on, you silly sod. The demise of one of them is unlikely to pass unnoticed.'

'Guess not,' I giggled. 'Especially if it happens to have a bloody great hole in its flanks.'

'Yeah, right. What we need is vermin of some kind. Something too stupid or trusting to realize the nature of the threat, thus less prone to dash off.'

'Like a hedge filled with twittering sparrows, you mean?' I indicated to just such a target, right there in front of us.

'Get em,' he said. And as it just so happened to be my turn to carry the weapon, I aimed in the general direction and let fly, if you'll forgive the pun.

'Bloody hell! I didn't expect anything like that,' I told him.

'What, the noise and recoil? Yeah, I suppose I should have warned you. Anyway, your aim was good.'

'Didn't aim,' I told him. 'It just happened to be pointing in the right direction when I pulled a trigger.'

'No matter, you actually hit the hedge.'

And so I had, but whether or not I hit anything else was open to question. Certainly, feathers and leaves flew in abundance, as did a quarrel of sparrows, heading for pastures anew, as sparrows will, given the slightest encouragement. Never did find anything they'd left behind. Not so much as a scrap of wing, or any other limb or organ. Not even a trace of blood and gore.

'Yeah, but look, a twelve gauge from five feet? Well, I mean, what else could you expect?' That was Mark's reasoning. And after much discussion it was agreed I could chalk up at least five probables. It was a phrase I recalled being used by the RAF, during the Battle of Britain.

Similar then, though this shotgun at Chabai was intended to deal with somewhat larger prey, therefore the size of the shot was somewhat larger, maybe a dozen balls as opposed to a few hundred! I discharged it at a thick plank of wood. It made fairly neat holes in the face, but looking at the rear, it was absolutely shredded. Ideal, should a wandering patrol inadvertently stumble into an ambush situation - though stumbling into an ambush in the first place would hardly constitute an ideal situation. Could spoil your day, that kind of thing.

*

Outside the area cleared for the camp and its barbed wire perimeter was the oh-so-short airstrip - carved out of a nearby hillside - its length effectively further reduced by lack of a straight-in approach, or exit. One way in and out; no choice being the choice. No undershoot or overshoot area either, should the pilot get it wrong. But at least he'd be going out lighter than when he came in. This was where the Pioneer came into its own, with its low-speed manoeuvrability and STOL characteristics - short-take-off-and-landing, that is - employing as it did such high-lift devices as leading edge slats and Fowler flaps. Quite something to stand and watch, that steep, twisty, terrain avoidance approach, flaps and slats at full stretch, Alvis Leonides snarling defiance. Even more thrilling was the view from inside the cabin, directly behind the pilot, whose eyes were the only form of ground proximity radar fitted to this machine. I'd be perched atop sacks of rice and suchlike, attempting to wedge myself in place, hands grasping whatever there was to grasp. Always bearing in mind the pilot required full and free use of his arms, and the controls. It was another very basic aeroplane that did exactly what it had been designed for, and did it extremely well.

Beyond the strip lay an all-encircling wilderness of untamed jungle. A verdant barrier of flora, limestone cliffs and mountains, along with their associated silence. I say silence, because that's the way it often appears; sounds so natural, serene and comforting, they could usually be disregarded. A background of echoey, tropical-rainforest type music. Nature's nonstop symphony: a cawing, croaking, creaking, buzzing, and whining, with the possibility of an occasional thought-provoking roar thrown in for good measure.

Meandering around two sides of the camp - and twenty feet below our level - ran nature's contribution to our comfort and well-being: a small river, or large stream. Fast-flowing, self-cleansing, ice-cold. And there is a pureness to be found in the waters of a mountain stream which is apparent nowhere else. This was our bathroom, ideal for washing, drinking, and, when the sun was at its height, a cooling dip.

'An important point,' I'd been told, upon arrival. 'Make sure you drink and swim upstream of the camp. Downstream is the place to take a leak, or a crap.'

Days began early out here. Not with the crowing of your common-place cockerel, but to the chattering chorus of gibbons and monkeys, located high in the treetops. Dawn itself was six-thirtyish and, being up in the hills, surrounded by mountains, as we were, it was sure to be cold, damp, and often misty - which was in fact the cloud base. So, whilst the morning shave may not have been one of mankind's more enjoyable experiences, washing in those waters was certainly guaranteed to either kick-start your heart into life, or to end it prematurely. But the first sight of that river in the early morning was something else again, for the surface could be mirror-like. So calm it appeared to be still rather than flowing, thus further enhancing the tranquillity of the place.

I say the days began early, not sunrise, you'll note. It would be three or four hours past dawn before the sun was high enough to smile down and chase the shadows and mist out of our valley. I'd realized it would be something like this, for I'd seen it many times on the way to early morning operations, a helicopter being a much better option from which to view this event.

A sea of wispy cloud-like mist would slide down the tree-covered slopes, to collect in the enclosed valleys below. Lakes of cloud which obscured everything but the mauve, tree-layered peaks which poked their way well clear. Nothing else to be seen from up there, apart from the occasional, colourful, yellow-beaked Hornbill, gliding from one area of high ground to the next.

Here at Chabai the air was so fresh it was almost pure oxygen. Tasted like it too; sweet, untainted, regenerative. And there was something else I'd noticed about the place that made it rather unusual, a total absence of that uniquely-shaped soft drink bottle with which America appeared to have swamped the face of the earth.

Just as the days began early, they ended early too, for in the tropics darkness descends rapidly - around seven in the evening - which is when the jungle bursts into life. Patrols apart, that is. They need to be settled well before then, for out here the sun plummets from view rather than sliding below the horizon, giving you bare minutes to prepare yourself.

With darkness came the incandescent, pulsing glow of the fireflies. The only light being in the form of candles, or flickering oil lamps. The only electricity was a small generator used to power the radio when needed.

It was a vacation you couldn't possibly buy, although maybe most wouldn't wish to. After all, paradise is a personal thing. In fact, it has been said that paradise is often close by where you live, that we don't recognise it as such until we are no longer there. If for me that meant Yorkshire, with its Dales, Moors and Wolds, then I'd possibly agree, but right now I was happy where I was. If not paradise, this was close to perfect tranquillity. Until I once more lost my mind, that is, jumping in with both feet this time. Not the river, you understand.

Infallibility not being within man's scope, I actually volunteered to go on a two day jungle patrol, a situation that could well have been positively unhealthy. Talk about crazy. I mean there were people, and things, out there, intent on doing us harm. I just felt it would be something different, something new. There again, let's face it, so is death; new to everyone, that. A first time, once in a lifetime kind of thing!

It hadn't yet filtered through to my subconscious: the fact I wouldn't have been cleared to take leave in Chabai were it not considered to be reasonably safe. Had I requested a fort that had recently been subjected to an attack, as some of them occasionally were, my extended visit quite possibly wouldn't have been allowed. The thing was, all intended destinations in this theatre had to be officially approved before leave was granted. Getting killed on duty, in the service of your country was one thing. Getting killed whilst on leave, apparently a different matter altogether. To start with, given such an eventuality I'd immediately become AWOL, on top of which the amount of paperwork would be horrendous. Not that any of this would be my worry, but it would have been my squadron commander's. There again, he hadn't appeared too worried when I'd approached him about it. He'd merely waved a finger around his temple and grinned at me. I'd wondered what he'd meant by that?

But volunteer to go on a short patrol I had (Sam, too. Or maybe it was him that instigated it), and now we were on the way, I wished I hadn't. Okay, we were armed, but so were the terrorists. And this was their kind of terrain. They'd had years of experience, knew how to make best use of it. There was something else to consider, too: Death wasn't the be all and end all, there were degrees of discomfort to be endured in the interim. That verdant barrier for starters. It now turned out to be more than just that, it was a barrier in all three dimensions, each apparently filled with malign intent. We soon found ourselves surrounded by a dense wall of foliage, through which we had to hack our way. By we, I mean of course the Malay police and their Iban trackers who plunged ahead, machetes flashing and slashing. I tagged along behind. It was OK for the first hour or so, as we followed a well defined track. But then we veered off, into the unknown, it seemed.

'Naturally, we choose path of least resistance,' Mustafa,

the leader, and my self-appointed guide, told me. 'This a kind of track.'

'Could have fooled me,' I said. 'Well disguised and protected, eh?'

'No, Dave. It just not used much. Well-used tracks are the very places ambushes are likely to be set.'

Track or not, that jungle was a green hell that fought back. It whipped, slashed, and tore, seemingly totally intent on preventing any forward progress whatsoever. Branches and barbed vines plucked at my clothes like malevolent hands, flicked dangerously near my eyes. My feet churned up the spongy carpet of the forest floor, releasing its musty fungal smell. Rivulets of sweat trickled down my back. Or were they the feet of insects on the prowl? Difficult to tell, really. But for the circumstances they could well have been a lover's fingers working their magic, the feeling was similar, the reaction entirely the opposite. Nor was there any chance of disregarding the sounds when you were in there among them. Sounds which now took on a more eerie quality rather than serene and comforting. Not just the cicadas and bullfrogs, or the whine of a mosquito, for they were always around, even back in the city. Out here there were new sounds to consider: the screech of a monkey, the shrill cry of a bird - echoing - even the roar of a tiger - distant and receding. Mustafa identified them all for me as we moved on. Occasionally he'd suddenly stop, hold up a hand, motioning me to freeze. Pointing to a bush, he'd whisper a name, "Lesser-spotted gol-gol", or whatever. I'd look, see nothing but still leaves, the bird splendidly camouflaged by splotches of shadow. Then, movement would catch my eye and it was gone. I was lucky if I managed to snatch a brief glimpse. Ah, well, so much for the gol-gol. By now I was almost ready to give up, too tired to talk.

'Nothing to fear here,' Mustafa said, 'normal sounds. Those we welcome. It's a silent jungle that spells danger. Nature quietened by human presence,' he continued. 'Then is the time to stop and exercise care. Create a matching silence, listen for that tell-tale crack of a branch being stepped on by a carelessly placed foot, the muffled curse, or a negligent cough. They're the kind of sounds that indicate the presence of unwelcome attention.'

He seemed to possess surplus energy, Mustafa; I could have used some of it. Real jungle-bashing, this, to me. Cue in the haunting refrain and subtitles if you like, but beware of airborne teeth. The fauna had come out to play.

*

The sun's light didn't penetrate too well down here - trees well over one to two hundred feet tall (that third dimension), and the almost impenetrable canopy they formed, saw to that - but its effects did, ie the heat, as did the frequently heavy rain.

'Probably the reason it is known as rain forest, eh?' Mustafa quipped, in reply to my muttered curse as I almost went down.

The ground was wet and slippery, the air as still as a dead man's breath. It was hot and humid. Rather like being fully dressed, trapped in a sauna; a thought that had me longing for a dip in that ice-cold stream back at the fort. Wouldn't even bother to undress first. Wouldn't have mattered anyway, I was already wet through, would remain so until it was time for bed.

'You must always keep your dry set of clothing to sleep in,' I'd been told at the pre departure briefing. 'Next morning it's back to the damp, stinky set.'

'Be a bit chilly, won't it?'

'At first, but they'll soon warm up. But if you keep the dry set on, they won't remain that way for long, then you'll have nothing to sleep in. That could be the death of you out here.'

Dark thoughts flooded my mind as I tramped along mechanically beneath the shrouding green canopy. Things occasionally squished and crunched beneath my feet. I didn't look, didn't wish to know. We'd only been underway three or four hours, even if it did feel more like a month. Out here, time, days of the week, they were irrelevant.

I was sweat-stained and weary already, facing the stigma of looking defeat in the eye. A situation that was unlikely to improve in the near future. Possibly the distant future, as well, for we appeared to be advancing with all the speed of a badly crippled snail. The men at point, machetes flashing, were by now having to hack a path through almost virgin bush. Sweat trickled down my cheeks. Or were they tears?

But I couldn't quit now, be worse off if I did: no one to take me back, sure to get lost on my own. I thought briefly about how that would sound back at the camp. 'Took this Air Force type out on patrol with us, but he couldn't hack it, decided to return to base on his own. Never saw him again.'

Oh that one of our helicopters would make an unexpected appearance; a quick, passing thought. But even had that happened I knew it would depart without me, for there was also ego at stake here. Some of these guys were smaller than me, much older, yet they were carrying twice the gear I was - mine as well as their own - making out quite nicely, thank you. Or so they made it seem. No, I was strong willed, so best to face facts: the aching tiredness, the sweat, the pain, all had to be endured, they would last but days. Failure to carry this through would haunt me for the rest of my life.

So I pushed the dark thoughts to the back of my mind, silently cursed to myself - along with the rest of them, I was sure - and carried on. It did seem to get easier with time, though time itself was definitely dragging. And despite the fact my pack only weighed a meagre twenty pounds, compared to the fifty or sixty the rest carried, it definitely contained enough momentum to bring me crashing down more than once.

By the use of hand signals, a halt was called every hour or so. A welcome break, I'd at first thought. Not so.

'Leeches,' Mustafa explained, peering down the inside of my collar. He had me pull my trouser legs out of my socks, and there they were, sucking away. He used the glowing end of his cigarette to burn them off, the rest of the patrol assisting each other.

'There'll be more,' he told me. 'Buggers get everywhere. Well... almost. We'll have a full clean-up tonight.'

I didn't like the sound of that, but there was no time to think about it, for in came the next assault: mosquitoes in combat formation, peeling off like fighters diving to the attack.

'Big buggers, eh?' Mustafa was grinning. Not a lot seemed to worry him.

'Big? Could have been designed by de Havilland, at Salisbury Hall,' I said. But the humour was lost on him when I had to explain it.

'What about nets?' I asked, for I knew I didn't have one. And now it was Mustafa's turn with the humour.

'Nets!' he exclaimed, somewhat dramatically. 'Forget 'em. These guys work in pairs. One lifts a corner, the other drags you clear.'

I could almost believe it. Come out to play? Wouldn't have surprised me to find this lot had been lined up in columns of three, smacking their lips and presenting arms at the first sound of our approach. (But why did they all seem to target me?) And let us not forget the snakes, elephants, and tigers that lived hereabouts, they could do you a lot of no good, too.

*

My heart skipped a beat. I felt fear steal through me; an icy coldness that raised the hairs on the back of my neck. There was something up ahead, I just knew it. An ambush maybe...? Or was it a tiger on the prowl? Watching? Crouching? Awaiting the moment?

Whatever, I prepared myself for the expected rattle and crash of automatic fire, or of teeth and claws launching into an attack, rancid hot breath on my neck.... No. It couldn't be either. Too much noise from the area's full time residents. Not the aborigines, these were nature's tenants. The odd monkey which gave advance warning of our approach, and the brightly-coloured birds which chattered and screeched, complaining of our intrusion into their territory. But by the same token I realized they were also sounding the all clear, for it is a lack of noise that normally presages danger, as Mustafa had explained. Even so, I sensed there was something. The feeling was too strong to disregard.

I wasn't wrong. But it turned out to be a threat of another kind.

I don't know what made me look up, other than intuition, but it was as well I did. A black and yellow banded krait was coiled round an overhanging branch. In my mind, poised to drop. To wrap itself around me, sink its lethal yellow fangs into my throat.

Discretion at such a moment seemed infinitely the better part of valour, so, moving quickly enough to secure myself a place on the Olympic squad for whatever, I stepped aside, foiling the imagined assault. I now felt a new sense of awareness, exhilaration almost. Life would go on, of course, I realized that. It's just that, fifteen seconds ago I was certain it would be going on without me. Even so, I envisaged the agony as the poison attacked my nervous system: spasm, paralysis, death. That's the sequence, so I'm told. Hell! What next?

Breakfast was what. Dawn found me jerking awake in my makeshift bed, beneath a makeshift shelter, both thrown together for me by someone more experienced in these matters. The idea was to get your arse clear of the ground, and to keep as dry as possible. (That it hadn't rained during the night was a bonus.) The bed was constructed from two poles and a canvas sheet, the shelter - or basha - fabricated from more poles, ponchos, a plastic sheet and palm frond roof. But it had served me well. I had enjoyed a good six hours beneath my mossie-net (Mustafa had been having me on). Despite that, after yesterday's slog I felt like I could use another six. Not that I wasn't fit. There were no undue aches or pains, just a lingering tiredness, a boot-full of blisters, and the marks where those leeches had latched on.

As I struggled to confront the present, so the danger slipped away. The imagined ambush, the snake; mere figments of a departing dream. My foolhardy subconscious up to its usual tricks. But the threats were real enough, as was the pounding in my chest, dreams proving to be as powerful as reality so far as my heart was concerned.

Fortunately, we were due for a supply drop that day as not all the patrol would be returning to the fort with us. The majority would move even deeper into the jungle, where, close to a trail known to be used by the guerillas, they would lay in ambush. Whatever the outcome, it was unlikely they would return to Chabai within the week.

So, as preparations were made, I relaxed as best I could, used the time to overcome my nightmare, cast aside the images. Plenty of time as it turned out, for we first had to await clearance of the usual early morning mist. It hung from the trees in wispy threads, had about it the look of rotting lace. At least the associated moisture served to curb the activities of tiresome flying pests.

The rising sun completed its task on schedule, almost as if programmed to do so, for even as it cleared we picked up the distant sound of an aircraft approaching; talked to the crew on the patrol's transceiver - no hand-held, lightweight, microchip-controlled piece of kit, this either. It must have weighed twenty or thirty pounds, probably the same again for the hand-cranked generator. Despite this, it did have its plus points: it worked well, we had contact, and I wasn't required to carry it. The aircrew had spotted the smoke from our signal fire, had the general area located. Easy to see when flying over the jungle, smoke; a certain give-away. It was what we kept an eye open for when flying towards an operational area. Forewarned is forearmed.

Now, homing in on the carbide-gas-filled balloon which had been raised above the surrounding treetops to mark our exact position, a Valetta of 52 Squadron dropped fresh supplies and other incidentals. The aircraft crew had to be very precise with the drop as they clearing was small. Miss it by 20-30 yards and the chute would never make it to the ground, end up hanging too high in the trees to be recovered. This time it didn't do that.

It was an operation which allowed even more time for me to effect a recovery, although I suspected I wouldn't find it so difficult from now on. It was also an operation which left these guys with even more baggage to lug around for, groceries apart, parachutes had normally to be recovered back to base. Well, on a big drop, a token number. Most would likely be reported as being "inadvertently damaged", or "deemed beyond salvage", as this one probably would, well away from the fort. Soldiers, it seemed, became quite attached to the material from which they were fashioned. The canopy made decent bedding, or was useful for keeping things dry, but the soft nylon cord was especially treasured. Handy for lashing things together, that. Such things as the bed I'd used last night. And it was highly unlikely a team of accountants would be sent in to investigate the loss of a couple of 'chutes.

At times like this, what with excess baggage and all, I was thankful I'd joined the Air Force, and that these guys held us in some regard. Now I could see why. They occasionally had reason to rely on us. A five minute flight could save them a day's walk, less than an hour in the air was equivalent to a week on the ground. So a chopper was appreciated at any time, in an emergency it could mean difference between living and dying.

Then there was the patrol itself. No bloody stroll in the woods, that, bluebells and butterflies kind of thing. Butterflies, yes. Rabbles of them - which, I believe, is the collective noun for butterflies. They were exotic, both large and small. So colourful that, if there was such a thing as a deadly butterfly, these - given nature's propensity to use bright colours as a warning - were clearly prime contenders. As for the blood, of that there was an abundance. An abundant loss, that is. What with mossies and leeches I was surprised to find I didn't need a transfusion upon my return to the outside world. Who needed the threat of terrorists on top of that lot?

Anyway, at the time I suppose I was still young enough to think myself invincible. And even if the patrol did turn out to be uneventful on the action front, it certainly wasn't boring. Hard graft is what it had been. Absolutely unbelievable, my volunteering for something like that, was the way I saw it. Though to these guys, or members of the SAS, yesterday probably *would* have been deemed a stroll. But I was nowhere near SAS class, I was an instrument fitter in the Royal Air

Force.

But later, back in the relative safety of civilization, I regarded it all as a satisfying, character-building achievement, during which I discovered the limits of my fortitude to be much higher than I'd dared hope. Still, as the saying goes, when the going gets tough, the tough get going. From here on I resolved that I would; get going, that is - in the opposite direction. Not tough, me.

Even though we were engaged in a war zone we rarely saw it as such, were reminded of it only by the fact that when flying we were armed, albeit lightly. The enemy had no anti aircraft weapons, and rifle fire was only a worry when flying low. No, any danger to us came mainly from our aircraft, for these were the very early days of helicopter warfare, and it was a learning period for both air and ground crews.

Seemed that Chabai vacation had been about as close as you could get to serious combat without an actual exchange of fire. Combat conditions in which the action never materialized, apart from in my head. So, there you have it. I never, knowingly, had a shot fired at me, nor did I kill, or even shoot, at anyone. On top of which, I hadn't *been* killed. Which is not too a bad way to end the day, for getting yourself killed happens only once.

The above also holds true with regard to fully developed tigers. I never did see one in the wild. Which is not to say one didn't see me.

I did see a cub, though. It was a guest at Chabai for a time, awaiting transport out. Seems the mother had been shot by an army patrol when they inadvertently stumbled across one another. Both parties possibly a little careless, though the army better equipped to deal with that kind of confrontation. And if they used that anti-ambush shotgun? Well... don't imagine the remains would have made for a decent rug. Regardless, from that point on there had really been little choice, not if the outcome was to be in the army's favour. Naturally, with a cub in tow she'd been overly protective. Anyway, it all went to prove the threat was ever present; as was the threat of terrorist attack.

*   *

Page 224: Top left: Oops! 1. Remains of a DC3 after a take-off with the controls still locked. Aircraft was cut up to clear the single runway; a commercial flight waiting to land.
Top right: S55 down after engine failure - No choice, you pick your spot and go for it. Aircraft was stripped of major components , then left to rot. **Centre L:** Abbo guard. **R:** S55, heavy landing after failure of hydraulics to the controls. **Centre Lower:** On Ops.
Bottom: Aborigine Longhouses.

Page 225: Oops! 2 **Top:** Eagle apparently objected to sharing its airspace with a 267Sqn Pioneer; the attack appeared deliberate. **Centre L:** Aborigine group. **R:** Not quite Biggles. Author in the LH seat. **Bottom:** S55 down in a rice paddy (another engine failure). Crewman, Len Raven.

Page 226: Malayan forts. **Top left:** Chabai, general view, **right:** Officer's Mess. CO, Butch Walker, shirtless, facing camera. **Centre:** Aerial view. A small clearing in dense jungle, and its oh so short airstrip, carved out of the hillside.
Bottom: Fort Shean & its unique signboard. Pioneering, even?

Page 227: Whirlwind (now painted rescue yellow) off Penang Island. Similar photo was used for 110Sqn Christmas card, 1959.

Page 228 Top: Health and Safety eat your heart out. Brian Purvis makes an unconventional wheel-change on a Sycamore, whilst the pilot holds it in the hover. **Centre:** Three astern, on ops. **Bottom:** Landing in an enclosed LZ.

Page 229 Top: Tiger cub at Chabai (destined for Bell Vue Zoo - Manchester, UK). **Bottom:** Master Pilot Taff Walker (left) gets down to some last minute route planning in the field.

Page 230 Top L: Lightly-loaded Gurkhas, disembarking after an op. Sam Saunders, crewman. **Centre:** Gurkhas, lend a hand with the refuelling, whilst I take photographs. **Bottom L:** Abbo with blowpipe. **R:** Cooling off in a jungle stream.

Page 231 Top L: Pete Dace boarding. In the field we needed to do this with the rotor turning! **R:** Flt Lt Burke is presented with Champagne after completing 1000 helicopter hours. Centre: S55 clutch adjustment on the strip at KL. Pete "Lofty" Dace (shirtless, back to camera). **Bottom:** Bristol Sycamores en route.

225

Chapter Eight
ROTARY WINGS, SHIPS, & OTHER THINGS

*T*hey did give me a medal, after all: the General Service Medal - issued for active service postings - on its mauve and green ribbon, with clasp: Malaya. It was engraved around the edge; name, rank, serial number. That unique sequence of digits confirmation that this GSM was meant for me alone. Pretty insignificant when compared to some of those passing by the Cenotaph during the Remembrance Day parade in London, admitted, but we all had to start somewhere. (In 2004 mine did pass by that Cenotaph, along with those earned by my father, worn on my right breast. This is the one parade that every ex-serviceman should experience at least once.)

I am not suggesting my GSM was exclusive, or that I received an invitation to attend the Palace. Everyone serving in Malaya during the period of the Emergency received it, right down to cooks and admin wallahs safely back in Singapore. No fancy parade even, you more or less drew it from stores, much as you would a new beret or a pair of boots. It just took a little longer, was all. Fill in a form, wait a couple of months for it to be engraved, and there it was.

To be doubly sure, I did check with the stores sergeant when I went to pick mine up.

'Is there any kind of presentation ceremony, Sarge?'

'Sure there is,' he replied, sliding a little white cardboard box across the counter towards me. 'Sign here.' The box was followed by the inevitable form. 'No need to trouble Her Majesty,' he said. And that was it. As stated, even those back on the island got one. There was no basic requirement actually to set foot in the combat zone, it was enough to survive a specified period in the general theatre of operations. OK, so Singapore had its dangers, too: Happy World, Old World, New World - dance hall, amusement park, sports stadium type places, the accent seemingly being on bedroom-type sport, naturally. At least, so I'd been led to believe, would you believe? Hazardous enough in itself, that kind of thing, I allowed, recalling the medical briefing we'd been given upon arrival in the area. That aside, even though I saw my part in this limited war as being no more than a grand adventure, for which I was being paid, I always felt I was more deserving of mine. Medal, that is. (The official title for the Malayan conflict was "The Emergency", for there had been no actual declaration of war. The reason for this was purely business, and the effect such an official declaration would have had on insurance rates!)

Pity the rudimentary stores procedure regarding replacement of boots and beret - or the issuing of medals, come to that - didn't also apply to the issue of aircraft spares. There again, beret and boots had to be paid for, personally, even if they did give us an allowance for such purchases.

With regard to procedure for the issuance of aircraft spares, there was one incident which caused me to question the commitment of personnel stationed in Singapore. It concerned one of our Whirlwinds, at the end of a visit to my old base at Seletar. The aircraft was urgently needed back at KL, but the pre-flight inspection revealed a blade to have been damaged, requiring replacement. Well, that shouldn't pose a problem, should it? After all, the MU (Maintenance Unit) for the whole of the Far East Air Force was at Seletar, East camp, so they were contacted.

'Yes,' the NCO in charge of aircraft stores confirmed. 'We do have a blade in stock.' And 'Yes,' he would dispatch it to Seletar, West camp - where the aircraft was located. 'Just a moment, though. Isn't 155 Squadron based at KL?' he questioned.

'Well, they are, but this aircraft is on detachment. Here at Seletar.'

'Ah, but any replacement parts must go via the squadron, otherwise it will take forever to sort out the paperwork. I'll have it dispatched immediately, shouldn't take more than three days.'

'Three days! But this is an AOG situation' (Aircraft On Ground - at that time, the highest priority for spares requirement. This was to be superceded with the introduction into service of our nuclear fleet, when it became VOG: "V" Bomber on ground).

'Which is why I'm dispatching it forthwith.'

The stores phone was to ring again, less than ten minutes later. This time the call was from the Officer Commanding 155 Squadron, in KL, via the Station CO at Seletar. He was said to have issued a curt reminder that this was actually a combat environment (attested to by the award of that medal), and that as, presumably, we were all working for the same Queen, they had better get that aircraft back up to the front line, immediately.

Within thirty minutes the replacement blade had been

transported from one side of the camp to the other, direct. A ten minute drive. The aircraft was back at KL, and in squadron service the following day.

*

During a typical day's operations we'd depart base early in the morning, one, two, sometimes even three aircraft; a positioning flight whilst the sun was still low, the air reasonably cool. But by the time we were ready to begin operations, cool air would be a thing of the past, the sun now well into its daily arc, and we soon worked up a sweat. We would prepare the aircraft - refuel, yet another pre-flight check, a quick visual this time - whilst the pilots briefed the Army commanders in the field. Troops would lay around in the heat of the day in full combat dress, trying to snatch a little rest while the chance was available. If it was some place not too remote, the Salvation Army would often be on hand with tea and wads. It never ceased to amaze me, the strange places at which the Sally Ann would turn up, and I would forever be thankful to them for that. Even so, the forts were the best places from which to operate. The hospitality of the Malay commanders was legendary in our circles.

Then came time to begin ferrying. Troops and gear aboard, start up, aircraft away. Depending on altitude and conditions, fuel load, etc, we were capable of carrying between two and six men a trip, though if six, they would need to be lightly loaded Gurkhas. (The goats and hens could follow later.) Oh, and about those SAS guys I thought I'd said goodbye to in Singapore. Wrong. They were here, too. Seems they were to be found anywhere there was a hint of trouble. Those guys - plus all the gear they somehow managed to lug around - we could only manage two to three a trip.

The aircraft would return every ten to twenty minutes, ready for another load. (Couldn't drop them too close to their intended destination - especially if it was to be an ambush situation - helicopters are noisy, could be heard from a long way off.) No shutting down on the return, either. (Baring problems, the engine was unlikely to be shut down until completion of the lift.) Troops aboard, refuelling, another quick visual, all done with the rotors whirling. Even though the blades were well clear, the troops would duck their heads, as they had been taught. Standard practice when working around helicopters. It's always advisable. Some helicopters are a lot closer to the ground, apart from the fact that it only takes a freak gust of wind to bring a blade down to decapitation levels.

234

No point bucking the odds when the end result could be far worse than a Court Martial.

On and on it went, all day long, with only the odd break to give the aircraft another quick once over. A gulp of warm water, then it started again. Hard work beneath a pitiless sun. And the sun's rays not only beat down from above, they also rebounded off the parched earth, augmenting the effect.

Swirling clouds of dust blown up during lift-off and landing would cake our sweat-damped bodies, for we often worked naked to the waist. And no matter that we turned to face away and protected ourselves, it would still penetrate our eyes, fill our noses and mouths. Not only was it difficult for us, so it was for the pilots. With such short sector times there was not much chance for them to relax, either. Take-off, a short hop, descent into a jungle clearing - hopefully secure - away for another quick turn-around. And so it went, always with the chance of a mechanical problem, or of being shot at, to keep them on their toes.

It was a relief for us all when the aircraft settled for the last time at the day's end. Only then would it be shut down. One more service check, refuel, tidy up, load our kit into the cabin, then climb up into the cockpit, eight feet off the ground. It would still be hot, sun glaring in through the perspex above and to the sides, and I'd be sweating profusely. But I was always aware of that giant fan above my head. Once that began to turn I knew relief could not be far away. Nor was it. Ten minutes and we were a thousand feet up, and cool. Down below was spread that verdant carpet of jungle, looking peaceful and calm from our viewpoint.

And the troops we had spent all day flying into the interior, into that seemingly peaceful calm, what of them? Ah, yes. What indeed? They'd be tired, dirty, and hungry, as was I. I would be so again, tomorrow, and probably the next day, too. But in between I could look forward to a shower, clean clothes, a decent meal, a beer or two - possibly more - and a relatively soft bed. I also had the advantage of having had a brief insight as to what those soldiers could expect; not a lot in the way of creature comforts, that was for sure. But the majority of them were National Servicemen, had no choice. Should have signed on for ten, lads; joined the RAF.

*

Many hours were logged on the Whirlwind during my time on the squadron, plus - continuing my resolve to fly in whatever to wherever, whenever - odd hours in numerous other types, including Cathay Pacific's, Lockheed Electra. Yes indeed, that one! I was on my way up to Japan, on leave. An interesting trip all round. Malayan Airways DC3 from the island of Penang, to Kuala Lumpur, via Ipoh. The Electra to Saigon and Hong Kong, where I switched to a DC6B for the Taipei, Osaka, Tokyo, legs. On the return trip the Electra transported me between Bangkok and KL. In fact the aircraft in which I flew, carried, among the in-flight reading material, the current edition of *Life* magazine, one article of which concerned itself with the way this very type had, until recently, been divesting itself of its wings, thereafter, proving Newton correct.

Renowned for the quality of its photography, the magazine featured shots of some very spectacular holes which had been bored into the US landscape when gravity triumphed over aeronautics.

Considering one actually had to purchase airline drinks in those days, I imagine profits on that flight were what could be termed "adequate". Especially as the problem was still to be resolved, the aircraft meanwhile being operated under a speed restriction.

But to me it was just one more diverse entry in the logbook. If they hadn't already had an inkling as to the cause, the aircraft would have been grounded. It's a bit like flying on Friday the 13th. Best day to fly, really, you can usually take your choice of seat. Not that I'm superstitious, but I am from Yorkshire, where superstitions and old wives tales do abound.

*

Recalling times past: 205/209, the nightlife on offer sixteen hundred miles to the north, the good times we'd had up there, I (once again along with Sam Saunders) decided my next leave should be taken in Hong Kong. It was an easy decision to make, once we'd discovered we could fly there, courtesy of the Royal Air Force rather than commercially. It was to be my first flight in an aircraft whose airspeed was measured in mach numbers rather than knots, and the only service flight for which I was ever required to pay: Two dollars and fifty cents for a trip in a Comet 2 (around twenty-five pence, in 1959 Straits Dollars). We were what was termed "indulgence passengers": a phrase used by the Air Force to define service personnel travelling on one of Her Majesty's aircraft by courtesy rather than by right. Space available, as it was more correctly defined by the Americans. On RAF aircraft, seats were theoretically allocated in reverse order of rank, at least that was the official line, though I couldn't imagine any movements officer being brave enough to bump, say a Group Captain, in favour of a mere Corporal. Whatever the case, Sam and I were offered seats for the flight up. Luxury, although that couldn't be said of the in-flight catering: the unique RAF box-lunch - a piece of fruit, a sandwich of indeterminate vintage, and possibly a boiled egg. Even so, the outward journey was the good news. The return was another matter altogether. There being no flight available to get us back before our leave passes expired, we were required to make alternative arrangements, which meant returning earlier than originally planned. No mach numbers this time, and I doubt the rate of knots achieved would serve to get even a bee airborne. (Which, incidently - according to one aerodynamicist - is an impossibility. Seems he'd figured the power, plus the lift to drag/weight ratio of a bumblebee was not conducive to flight. Be that as it may, they *do* fly. So much for experts.) So, back to our mode of transport, which didn't.

Although this was my first view of a large passenger liner, its size didn't overawe me. Not at all. At least, not at first sight. But the troopship *HMT Oxfordshire*, grew and grew with my every approaching step until, at the dockside, it literally towered above me, held there by ropes thicker than my arms. I cast a glance at the steel sides, followed them up to the superstructure, way above, was still unimpressed. Until I was up there on deck, looking down, that is. I was in aviation, and when not airborne, a total land-lubber. So, understanding none of the complexities of displacement, draught, and ballast, and choosing to disregard the fact that it *had* sailed in here, I felt sure that as soon as it cast off those heavy lines, and parted from the safety of the pier, the whole thing would simply turn turtle. But of course, it didn't. Twenty thousand tons moved away gracefully, an ever widening chasm developing between concrete and steel. People on the concrete waved up at the people on steel, who waved back at them, and I, caught up in the euphoria of saying goodbye, joined in. I didn't actually know anyone down there, of course, and no one down there knew me. But they weren't to know I knew they didn't know, so they wouldn't care. Come to think of it, half of those people down there probably didn't know anyone up here, either. It reminded me of one of those film epics which feature the departure of a Transatlantic liner; albeit without the bunting and streamers. Then we were too far away for it to matter. Tugs fussed around like terriers, clearing us from the pier before casting us loose in the shipping lanes of busy Victoria harbour. Soon we were out there among the junks and sampans, the freighters and liners, warships of the American Sixth Fleet, the Royal Navy, the wallah-wallah boats, and the non-stop to and fro of the efficient, old (circa 1898), Star Ferry; the best means of viewing the city from seaward.

Then Hong Kong was but another memory, and we were cutting a path through the green waters of the South China Sea, its surface inviolate until our arrival. Flying fish skimmed the waves and sped down the valleys, porpoises played "chicken" across our bows, and during the night the phosphorescence in the wake left us spellbound.

It wasn't a long trip. Four or five days after the ship's horn sounded its own farewell to the Crown Colony, I was back with my unit, in the action zone.

*

As the front line moved north, so did our area of operations, over the border into Thailand, although we still made the odd trip down the peninsula. One such was an operation around Kuantan, located over on the east coast. And it was here that I scrounged a flight in an Auster AOP9 of 656 Squadron, Army Air Corps.

The mission called for the dropping of delayed-action grenade simulators over a known guerilla area, just to keep them on their toes, so to speak. Hopefully to drive them into the waiting arms of the troops which were patrolling the area. The grenades were on a static line release, attached internally to the airframe. Once thrown out, this line pulled the pin, thus activating the delayed action mechanism. My duty, as sole passenger, was to toss them out as directed by the pilot. Must have been two or three dozen in all, and once dispersion was complete, the pilot called for recovery of the trailing static lines. When I attempted to do so, this became a mission impossible, for the turbulent air of the slipstream had managed to wrap them around the tailwheel. Still, that was preferable to them flapping around in the breeze. Could have done a lot of damage to the fabric covered fuselage and control surfaces had that been the case. As it was they didn't seem to affect our landing back at base.

Ah, well. Perhaps not the spectacular success the Army would have wished for, but at least the grenades were on target. As for the representative from the Royal Air Force, well... much like Greece voting for Turkey in the Eurovision Song Contest, or vice versa, no points were to be awarded. Full points though for the eagle which mistook one of 209 Squadron's Pioneers to be a tasty morsel: it attacked the aircraft at around two thousand feet, scoring a direct hit on the cockpit area, ending up half in, half out of the side screen. Max points for aim, though they couldn't be awarded, the bird perishing in the process.

*

So it was, in August 1959, that 155 Squadron combined with 194 to become110 Squadron - an ex Vultee Vengeance and Mosquito unit during WWII. We then found ourselves regrouping at RAAF Butterworth, North Malaya, a base of the Royal Australian Air Force, with their F86 Sabres and Canberras. We moved from KL lock, stock, and barrel - including the Squadron dog which went by the name of Kitchy (Malayan for small, which I assumed he had been when a pup). Not so small now, and I recall he wore his ears like a matador's headgear.

We followed the front as it progressed northwards. No period of consolidation though, operations continuing throughout.

Butterworth was purely a military base, with no civilian traffic vying for use of its single runway. But the implications of having a single runway, on a fighter base, were not lost on the Aussies, for shortly after our arrival, a monstrous, runway clearance vehicle was also to appear on the scene. This was a specialist multi ton piece of equipment whose doughnut-tyred wheels were fully twelve feet in diameter. So large in fact that steering was by way of an electric motor mounted on each wheel. The whole thing could be operated by remote control, the driver punching buttons at the end of a long armoured cable, well clear of any wreckage, or fire.

For a couple of days, this brand new, very expensive toy, resplendent in its bright yellow paintwork, could be seen tracking up and down the seaward end of the concrete pan, the opposite end to where our aircraft were dispersed. It was obvious the Aussies were familiarizing themselves with the operation and controls, checking out the machine's capabilities. But it seems the smooth concrete was not enough of a challenge for them, for they next took it onto the beach, and into the sea! Oh, oh!

It promptly got bogged down, slowly sinking into the

sand. As with my teen-age condom, I believe it may still be there.

*

There may not have been any civil traffic around to distract me, but across the dispersal from where our helicopters were based was where most visiting aircraft were parked. V-bombers would stage through here - Valiant and Vulcan - plus the odd fighter type. Then there were the Gannets, on delivery flights to the Indonesian Navy. It all helped break any between-operations monotonous spells.

Butterworth was on the mainland, directly across from the holiday island of Penang - duty free, and but a short ferry trip away. So this was a place with which squadron personnel were to become quite familiar, if they weren't already. Many of us had previously visited the island to stay at the RAF leave centre at Tanjong Bungar. We'd travelled up by train from KL, or, in earlier days, Singapore. That train journey could also be an adventure in itself for, as the CT's would occasionally set an ambush along the rail line, military personnel travelling on the service were called upon to act as a deterrent. Issued with a rifle and ammunition. The idea was that, should it become necessary, we would lay down our lives in defence of the train and its civilian passengers. I don't even recall there being any restrictions as to rules of engagement. If the train was attacked we went into action (or out of it, whatever the case may be). The thing to remember was that should an engagement take place from which you were to survive, not only would you be held responsible for the return of the weapon, but also be required to account for every shot fired, by way of producing the empty cartridge cases! Naturally, they didn't hold you to this were you not to survive. (Not too clever an option, that). That was what we were told, though being as I was never involved in any such engagement, I cannot confirm it as being fact.

With Penang bearing obvious similarities to Singapore, our visits to the city were rather like something out of Leslie Thomas' *Virgin Soldiers*. Well, they would be, wouldn't they? We were role models, in a different colour uniform. Needless to say, I won't go into details. Suffice to suggest: them that's been will know, them that hasn't, wouldn't wish to. The undecided should perhaps read the book.

There were other places on the island worth a visit, too, on the cultural side that is. Up on the hill known as Ayer Itam was a magnificent seven tiered pagoda, reputed to contain a

240

thousand Buddha. (Buddhas, maybe? Or how about Buddhi?) And what of that one thousand? Figure of speech, or fact? Never did count them, personally, but I must have taken a thousand photographs of the place. (OK, twenty or thirty.) And guess what, not one of them was smiling. There again, they generally don't, do they, Buddha?

A short distance away was a Snake Temple - once only for me, I hate snakes, even if they were drugged. There was a Waterfall Temple, too, all red and gold; lucky colours as far as the Chinese are concerned. Should one wish to soak up the sun, fine and dandy, the island was ringed with glorious, palm-fringed, sandy beaches. If not the beaches then how about a trip up Penang Hill on the funicular: magnificent views, cool air, so the guide book told me. There was a tea room up there as well. A pleasant interlude until the pubs opened, though in reality they were open all day.

Now don't get me wrong. Nothing wrong with culture, in limited doses, and during the hours of daylight. But of more interest to us at the time were the bars, clubs, and restaurants, which is where we would spend our nights on the island.

I recall some of the aircrew spending a night or two on the island, too. Literally. They'd been detailed for a survival course, set in the surrounding hills. Or maybe it was an initiative test. Survival, initiative, what does it matter, they were dropped off, without food, needed to fend for themselves for a couple of days. Which they successfully did; apparently well before the exercise had even begun!

Naturally, so as to avoid any chance of the whole process becoming overly burdensome, you understand, they had taken precautions, made previous arrangements. By a strange coincidence, a Whirlwind just happened to fly over a certain area at a certain time, and as it did so, certain items "accidentally" fell out of it. Strange how the toilet rolls - which formed part of the cargo - happened to partially unroll themselves on the way down. This, of course, should have made recovery relatively easy, had it not been primary jungle, the clearing into which the items fell much too small even for a helicopter to touch down. Ah well, someone would no doubt find a use for them.

So, survival? Initiative? To pre-empt is to prevent; is that not how the saying goes?

*

Far different from both the rigours and pleasures of Penang,

Grik (pronounced Gree), a frontline operations base almost on the Thai Border, was another place with which we were to become quite familiar. This was where that Chabai tiger cub ended up, eventually becoming quite tame. It was looked after by an officer of the Manchester Regiment, under whose bed it slept. Probably did other nasty things under there as well. Apparently this officer used to walk it around on a lead, until - so the story goes - it one day went missing. This caused a bit of a stir amongst army brass as it had been promised to Manchester's Belle Vue Zoo. Iban trackers were engaged in the search for it, all to no avail, so it was assumed to have returned to the wild, or possibly to have been cubnapped.

But no. Two weeks later, tired, filthy, and hungry, it returned to it's place beneath the officer's bed, apparently looking for all the world like it'd had enough of life in the wild.

Hard to believe, maybe, true nevertheless. And it did eventually end up in Manchester. (Had it been aware of that it probably wouldn't have returned. Just imagine, having to look forward to the rest of your life in Manchester. I mean it's not even in Yorkshire, is it?)

Grik was the place from which we performed troop-lifts into the interior, and carried medevacs out, especially if the Kiwis had a rugby fixture that weekend!

Taff Walker, a Master Pilot colleague from the time tells of one such operation in which he was involved. The op order apparently called for the evacuation of two "casualties", but when he arrived at the LZ there turned out to be eight, not one appearing to be in desperate need of medical attention, or assistance. And as they were all strapping lads, carrying loads of kit, it required four sorties to bring them out.

At least they did win their game, eventually going on to lift the end of season trophy. Win, that is, not steal. (At our 2004 reunion, I heard Taff Walker referred to - by someone who would know - as probably the best helicopter pilot the Air Force ever had.)

*

It was about this time the roads round squadron headquarters began to echo to a rather different sound than the clattering rumble of Pratt & Whitney's Wasp. This was the Honda 50, a rather neat little moped with a clutchless gearchange. Not loud in the singular, but a bit wearing when all the aircrew seemed suddenly to get the urge to own one, notable exceptions apart. One expatriate patriot pilot named Paul (Gray, that is) opted instead for the BSA Bantam.

'Absolute crap,' was the opinion of Tom Browning, a Honda owner.

Paul, who loved it, replied to the effect that at least it was, "British crap".

Nobby Clarke's selection was a very posh Vespa, which he almost immediately fell off (probably trying to light yet another cigarette), rendering himself *hors de combat* for quite some time. Then there was Tom Bennett. Tall, young, ginger hair, with matching moustache, good-looking (Ah, but weren't we all? OK, maybe not Nobby). Tom was different again, being the proud owner of a "stinkwheel" (a bicycle contraption with a French built motor driving the rear wheel). He had a large wooden box made, which was then fitted to the rear. This was, he explained, "for putting things in". Of course it was. So one day some of the other pilots did. They filled it with the lizards which were a common feature around the area. That other Tom, the debonair, Tom Browning (whom I suspect to be the instigator, for this was his kind of thing), says he was quite surprised when, during the round-up, capture, and box-filling phase of the operation, one of the little sods had the audacity to bite him when he grabbed it from behind.

Three rebels then, which left at least half a dozen Hondas; apparently available in any combination of colours, so long as they were cream and blue. And of course the noise became a little more than wearing when they took to riding in formation, round and round the single-storey block which formed our Squadron HQ. Who knows, maybe they were working off the frustration of never having enough choppers serviceable at one time, or at base, for them to be able to achieve a decent formation in the air (and if the moped formation was anything to go by, the airborne version would have been a sight to behold). Or maybe the idea originated with the monsoon fly, with which we were occasionally inundated. Like large flying ants they would magically appear in their thousands, nay, millions, shortly after a heavy downpour. On arrival they would immediately shed their wings, join up in long trains and wander around like strings of circus elephants playing follow my leader. (Imagine that. Unless you *are* in the lead, the view ahead never changes.) They'd then disappear, just as suddenly and mysteriously as they had at first arrived, leaving us almost ankle-deep in obviously no-longer-needed wings. Where they came from, or went too, who knows, or cares? OK, so maybe David Attenborough would.

As with all new toys, though, there was a slight problem with the scooters. Easy to handle, yet, unlike a car, with a moped one needed to place ones feet on the road when stopping at traffic lights. It was something to remember. Not too difficult a thing, I would have thought, especially for a pilot. And it probably wasn't, at least when sober. You out there, Deke Bradley?

His antics, I heard tell, mirrored those of the German motorcyclist in that popular TV programme, Rowan and Martin's Laugh In. (In fact Deke, being Canadian, reminded me of someone about whom I had once read: a member of Alexander Graham Bell's "Aerial Experiment Association" of 1907. Apart from Bell, Glen Curtiss, "Casey" Baldwin, and Tom Selfridge - the first man to die in an aircraft accident - the group had included a Canadian engineer who, although reportedly could not be trusted to sit astride a motorcycle without falling off, was acknowledged to be one of the finest flyers of his time.)

That seemed to be the way of things in the Far East Air Force. Every squadron I served on, people got up to some outrageous deeds at times - stunts that would never be contemplated back home (at least outside of the Officer's Mess) - but when it came to aircraft, flying them, or servicing them, everyone reverted to being very professional, very serious, very quickly. We wouldn't have had it any other way.

Until amalgamating with 155 in 1959, No.194 squadron - Bristol Sycamore equipped - also operated out of KL, but a couple of disastrous accidents - the cause of which was determined to be break-up of their wooden rotor blades (possibly due to the harsh operational environment) - led to their being grounded.

The intention had been for the Sycamore to eventually replace the Whirlwind HAR4, which was rather underpowered - or overweight. (The Royal Navy's 848 Sqn - first to operate Whirlwinds in Malaya - faired better. Their aircraft were built and supplied by Sikorsky, in the USA. The RAF version, built under licence by Westland, were constructed from a heavier gauge metal, hence extra weight - which of course relates to less payload for the same engine power.) As a result of those Sycamore crashes, that changeover was put on hold. The RAE, (the Royal Aircraft Establishment), at Farnborough, later came up with a solution (Araldite rather than UHU was one rather

244

tongue-in-cheek suggestion), so by mid-1960 we were being re-equipped with a modified version of the type, these working alongside - for a time - the ubiquitous Whirlwind.

Another slight hiccup in the phasing out of the Whirlwind was experienced when two RAAF Sabres, disputing the same piece of sky, managed to collide in mid-air, over dense jungle. The last Whirlwind was retained for a couple of days as it was equipped to receive signals from SARAH - for Search And Rescue And Homing - whereas the Sycamores were not. (The almost appropriately acronymic, SARBE - Search And Rescue BEacon - would have been more fitting to this story, but these were as yet in the future.)

With this operation successfully concluded it was goodbye Whirly 2. And it was to be not too long before the Sycamore was also replaced by an updated version of the Whirlwind. This was the much safer, turbine-powered, Mk10; many of our Mk2's being converted. Although by the time that event took place I'd become nothing more than a mere statistic in the squadron's past history. A very minor player at that, even if I had done my bit.

But before we leave it, a couple more Taff Walker stories, if only because Taff has a sackful of them. The first concerns another operation in which he was involved, over the Thai border at a place called Betong, yet another location with which we were becoming quite familiar as the front moved ever northward.

Taff was scheduled to fly some Thai police into a place known by them, somewhat tongue-in-cheek, as Fort Ha Ha, an area of really deep jungle. These guys were carrying kit-bags, and as they placed them aboard the aircraft so the crewman, ensuring they were positioned with regard to the centre of gravity - rather important in a helicopter - thought he saw one of them move. Being a conscientious type, or maybe just plain nosey, he opened it up, and out popped a young Thai girl. Talk about home comforts out on patrol! We were used to the Gurkhas carrying edible livestock in with them - chickens and things - but this was ridiculous. Curried girl? I hardly think that was what they had in mind!

Then we come to a character known as "Whacker" Cox; presumably due to his tendency of addressing all and sundry as "Whack". An old Malaya hand, Master Pilot "Whacker" was awarded a DFC whilst flying the Westland Dragonfly on ops there, but this incident took place after his return to Blighty,

245

where he had since been commissioned. Thorney Island was the venue.

Whacker had apparently been detailed for a late afternoon wet winching exercise in a Mk2 Whirlwind, and, regardless of the limited power of the engine, and prevailing conditions, he asked a pilot friend, Fred, if he'd like to go along for the ride. Fred, having never flown in a chopper before, but about to convert onto the type, said he would be happy to, duly hopped into the left-hand seat.

Fred now takes up the story.

"It was a hot, windless day, the sea like glass as we arrived over Chichester harbour and came to the hover - not exactly ideal conditions, I thought, given our all-up weight and lack of power. The heat and humidity only made matters worse, and still air meant an almost total absence of that rotary-craft phenomenon known as translational lift effect. This became self-evident when I looked out, surprised to see the port wheel in the water. As it was still attached to the aircraft, I pointed the fact out to Whacker, who said it was OK, he was working on it. And it certainly looked like he was, juggling control column, collective, and throttle.

"I looked out again, just checking on progress, but by this time the wheel had disappeared completely, water now lapping at the underside of the fuselage. Not good, eh?

"Although I hadn't flown *in* a helicopter before, I *was* aware of the pertinent facts: we were overpitching, ie rotor rpm too low; as was, therefore, airspeed over the blades. Now the only way to recover from such a situation is to decrease blade pitch, or gain translational effect by picking up forward speed, both of which called for the sacrifice of a little height; somewhat difficult when part of the aircraft is already below sea level. To put it mildly, lacking any kind of floatation gear, it was obvious we were in deep trouble. Or should that be deep water?

"Don't you think it's time to get out, Whacker?' I asked.

"'You're right, Fred,' Whacker replied, calmly shutting down the engine, as if at the end of a day's flying. Which, in a way, I suppose it was.

"Don't recall the details but I was in the water in record time, heading for the beach at a fair rate of knots. No problem at all exiting from the left-hand seat, though I was a bit concerned about Whacker. Well, maybe not Whacker so much as the NCO winchman who was down in the cabin. Wasn't it, after all - as captain - Whacker's duty to remain to the bitter end? Nevertheless, I was about to turn back when I saw this guy waving at me from the shore. He was shouting, too, obviously keen to attract my attention, so I continued swimming towards him. I presumed he would have news of the others. Didn't cross my mind, the thought that, had they already been ashore they'd have to have been really motoring.

"I eventually reached the beach and dragged myself out, knackered. 'What is it, mate?' I asked, somewhat breathless.

"'Oh, nothing, really. I was just trying to point out, you could have walked from where you were,' came the answer.

"He was right, too, the sea was barely three feet deep.

"We all survived of course, and the aircraft was eventually recovered, albeit, not exactly in pristine condition. In fact it was later struck off charge. Apparently, due to the advanced state of corrosion, odd pieces kept falling off. Not really fundamental to the safe operation of an aircraft, that.

"Whacker eventually left the chopper world, ending up on the Blackburn Beverley. Bit of a change, for sure. I was going to say bit of a come down, but, given the circumstances, that would be cruel."

*

So it was that the carefree fifties drifted into the Swinging Sixties. I became aware of this when one fixed wing pilot with whom I was acquainted, insisted on replacing the formal, "Gear down, please" with the more trendy, "Dangle the Dunlops, daddio."

Having completed two and a half years of Far East service, it should have been time for me to go home, for by then I was tour ex (for expired). But I wasn't yet ready, didn't even keep a "peachy" calendar (on which you crossed off the days to go before your return to the UK). I was enjoying myself so much I let the RAF know; actually volunteered for, and was granted, an extension of six months, making a total of three years in the Far East. In fact - as the astute reader may already have gathered - I found myself volunteering a lot during my service career. Normally acknowledged to be a foolhardy practice, in my case it generally seemed to bring about the desired result. Complete fluke, of course. It wasn't a matter of what suited me, it was what suited whoever was in charge. If our wishes happened to coincide - as it seemed they often did - then so be it. (I did actually volunteer again during my extended tour. The RAF, looking to boost the number of Flight Engineers, called for suitable volunteers, so, rather fancying the job - and being of the required trade group - I applied. Then, within a couple of weeks, realising I was still enjoying myself where I was, I foolishly cancelled the application. In retrospect, one of the major regrets in my life.) In fact, what I should have been volunteering for at this time was to sit a trade test for promotion to senior NCO rank - qualifying as Flight Engineer would have conferred this upon me automatically! - but the enjoyment bit intruded here as well.

Eventually, the time did come for me to depart the Far East for home - my name once again putting in an appearance on SROs, where POR's (Personnel Occurrence Reports) told me so and, once again, with trooping by air now becoming the norm, I never even spared a thought to travelling by sea. Alas, in September 1960 I found myself allocated a berth on the troopship *Nevasa* for a rather lengthy cruise. It seemed my luck had finally run its course.

Not exactly cruise liner conditions though. There again, as we were being paid, not paying for the pleasure, maybe it was not so bad after all. More experiences to add to the growing catalogue of experiences, for any long sea voyage is naturally accompanied by a sense of adventure. Our first port of call was Colombo, Ceylon, as it then still was. A bit of a disappointment really - the port call, not the country - but that was my fault entirely.

What happened? Oh, a silly thing really. Hardly worth mentioning, but... Well, all right then....

The hassling and bartering started even before we'd dropped anchor. Just as we would later experience in the Canal, bum-boats drew alongside, trading taking place over the rails. Voices called down, mainly unintelligible replies drifted back up. Baskets filled with dubious offerings were then raised to the deck. Some of the offerings were then removed, to be replaced with cash, the baskets being lowered back down.

I watched with interest, but wanted for nothing, couldn't wait to get ashore, which we eventually did.

The visit went quite well, actually. Another day in another land, both new to me. New friends, too. A wander round - the sights, a meal (rather a good curry - well, in a place like Ceylon what would one expect), a few drinks - and it was over. We then gathered on the quayside, awaiting the launch that would return us to our vessel, riding serenely at anchor out there in the bay. And from that viewpoint I thought it looked rather glamorous. White, with a thick blue line around the side, radiant, glowing in the dying embers of a setting sun.

As usual, everyone was bragging and showing off their purchases, each boasting about how little they had paid.

'Got this carpet for the equivalent of a fiver. Not bad, eh?

'Yuh was ripped off, I only paid three quid.'

'Obviously not as good quality, yours, is it?' So on and so forth.

Again I'd bought nothing, seen nothing that attracted my attention, despite the fact I had been almost dragged away at one point. It was some fellow who apparently had the most fantastic deal to offer me. He didn't speak English too well - in fact, hardly any at all - but if I understood the terms correctly, it seemed to involve me giving him a rather large amount of cash, for which he, in return, would give me some entirely worthless item. Definitely a breach of the trade descriptions act, were such a thing possible in this place.

'No thanks. Been that route before.' That was my Yorkshire upbringing coming into play. We can be rather frugal when the mood takes us, I'll admit to that. Instead, I joined the rest of the lads for a drink. Even then we weren't left alone. Local traders kept hassling us, trying to sell us gifts to take home. Their wares were pressed upon us, quickly passed around for close inspection: necklaces, watches, "old" coins, carvings "precious stones". At times it seemed we were awash with offerings. Almost as quickly they were passed back, usually to the accompaniment of detailed instructions on what they should do with them, and themselves. The first almost a physical impossibility, the second more like wishful thinking.

It was here on the quay where I was to temporarily upstage everyone, producing a sparkling necklace which I swung around on a finger.

'Hey, look at that. Cost me nowt,' I declared. With which, the necklace flew off the erect digit, described a glittering arc against the dying sun, and plopped into the bay. Judging by the speed with which it plunged beneath the waves, certainly not plastic.

'Ah well,' I said, a touch of resignation on my voice. 'So much for my souvenir of Colombo. Could have been worth a fortune, that.'

Next came Suez, but not before the inevitable hold up in the Bitter Lakes, off Ismailia; assembly point for the

249

northbound convoy up the single lane Canal. Hardly had we anchored, taking our place in the queue of ships waiting to go through, than we were surrounded by the customary bum-boats. These small boats contain an oarsman, usually a boy, along the owner of the merchandise, the standard variety of tourist offerings: attractive leather pouffes, very gaudy carpets, leather camels, horse-hair fly-whisks, the inevitable tarboosh, or fez, most of it very cheap, unsuitable for European homes, or utterly useless.

But the real entertainment is to be found in the method of doing business, rather than the acquisition of goods. To start, a coiled rope is hurled up to the promenade deck, where the nearest person is urged to make it fast to the rail. This is the umbilical cord of all future developments. At the trader's end, where the middle section of the rope lies, a basket is tied on. Negotiations can now proceed. 'Me Me Ismail - 'ullo, ullo. You buy pouffe?'

Eventually a bored onlooker agrees to inspect some article. The next stage is the battle of wills, for It is soon made plain that neither side trusts the other. The 'gentleman' in the bum-boat wants the money sent down in the basket first. Naturally, the itinerant buyer wants to inspect the goods before any money changes hands. There is no rule of procedure. Sometimes one gains the moral ascendancy, sometimes the other.

Our vessel is now festooned with ropes, some locals even having somehow managed to establish themselves on the promenade deck, selling dirty post-cards, amongst other things. The gully-gully man has penetrated one of the anterooms. Here he produces chickens out of eggs, eggs from mouths, baby chicks from ears, and all manner of feats of sleight of hand.

So passed the few hours until the one-way traffic is clear. Time for us to enter the Canal proper, in the evening. In the meantime we watch the southbound ships emerge and sail past.

As the hour approaches for us to weigh anchor, so the bum-boat operators ask for their ropes to be cast of from the ship's rails. An altercation is in progress. An Army gent claims he has been gypped, has sent down the money and now the merchant refuses to send up the goods. Losing patience, another passenger grabs a fire-bucket full of sand, drops it over the side. Direct hit! It goes straight through the bottom of the bum-boat, which slowly sinks, a garden of pouffes, tablecloths and runners blossoming out around it, slowly drifting away on the current. As the ship gets underway another irate boatman finds himself surfing along behind, having failed to secure the release of his rope.

We started off up the Canal, but although night was approaching the temperature appeared to be rising rather than falling. The swan-like grace of the feluccas, ghostly against the palm-flecked horizon, a silhouetted line of camels plodding along on the west bank, and the stars, hanging like chandeliers, painted a complete picture of 'the mysterious East'.

Then, sometime later, came Port Said, northern end of the Canal, gateway to the Mediterranean, and on to Gibraltar. All stepping stones along the route back to Blighty, all negotiated successfully.

*

So ended another phase of service life, the most interesting of all up to that point in my existence. More goodbyes, more memories to be filed away like snapshots in an album. More experiences, more friendships developed, before being left behind. Hopefully, more to be made in the future.

Were there though? For a fleeting moment I was suffused with the feeling that, during the last three years I'd seen it all and done it all. Left nothing for the future. Then, somewhat relieved, I realized that couldn't be possible. There remained lots of exotic places I felt would be worthy of a visit. I had yet to set foot in the USA, Central and South America, Canada. And the whole of the African Continent had yet to feel my presence, and vice versa.

But they *were* for the future. All too soon, bright blue skies and high digit temperatures would be replaced by the predominantly grey overcast, and the cold. The exotic by the mundane. Sun, sea, and flying fish, would be replaced by gulls, white cliffs, and the changing seasons. No bad thing, this last, for the mysteries and splendour of seasonal change - the colours and moods that change inspires, along with the fluidity of light and landscape - are denied to people in the tropics. Three years I'd been away. Three Springs, three Summers, three Autumns, three Winters, yet I hadn't really noticed. The missing seasons had been just that; apparent only by their absence. Our years had been split basically by two seasons, a dry one and a wet one. Everything else remained basically the same: colours, temperature, the mood of the landscape. Even sun and sand can become boring after a time. Yes, I'd look forward to seasonal change. Just as long as that change wasn't too drastic.

I also considered the certainties left behind, the uncertainties that lay ahead. Not sure if I was ready for all that. I missed the Far East already, but my only link with it now was this stretch of ocean upon which we cruised, and the sky above.

Then there were the memories. Of course there were.

I vowed to return, one day.

*   *

The Ballad of One Five Five

Come one, come all, where'er you may be
Sit down a while and listen to me
The truth I will tell of the world's greatest skive
On a Whirlybird squadron numbered One Five Five

There was Clayton and Geddes, and a boss they called Ron,
And Browning and Puddy, but now Puddy has gone.
Best bunch of guys you ever could meet
We sweated together in tropical heat.

Old Wal' you know was in charge of the store.
Finding spares for our choppers, his biggest chore
For the kites they were ragged, all tattered and torn
And we worked like the devil to keep them airborne.

The aircraft themselves once totalled fourteen
The pilots and crewmen wore jungle green.
As they flew overhead, our hats we would doff
Thinking, there goes another, to be written off.

The first we lost went into a stream
Some parts of that one have yet to be seen.
From then on we lost them, 'bout every two weeks
On beaches, in clearings, even the creeks.

The end of the story is sad to relate,
They gave us Sycamore's "'fore it's too late."
And once these aircraft began to arrive
It was the end of our squadron, the bold One Five Five.

*   *

Thanks to squadron members "R.A.B." and "Terry",
who penned the original words, of which I have
taken the liberty of amending slightly.

NOTEBOOK THREE
SINGAPORE REVISITED

2006

I had once again left my beloved Yorkshire far behind, departing on a journey which would carry me halfway round the globe. To be truthful, I should say "all the way round," for I would continue flying east on my return home, rather than backtracking to the west.

As the landscape of early morning fell away below, we sliced our way through the grey opacity, up into the blueness of a seemingly empty sky; a scene of transcendent beauty. Our shadow - an almost perfect outline of the aircraft - chased across the cloud-bank below, the silhouette encircled by a mini rainbow.

Yeadon - now Leeds Bradford International or, in airline parlance, LBA - was three hundred miles astern. Heathrow, from whose runways we had just departed, was barely ten, though it was already two thousand feet below where I sat, comfortably ensconced in my economy-class seat. The machine, although heavy with fuel, freight, and around three hundred passengers, climbed steeply, such was the performance of the four Rolls-Royce turbofans slung beneath the wings. Engines like this are capable of converting aviation fuel into lots of noise, heat and, especially, power, which is exactly what they were doing. Air was being devoured by the ton, compressed and superheated, to be blasted out at a far greater velocity to that at which it had entered. From there it was a simple matter of physics: equal and opposite reactions, thrust versus drag, lift, and suchlike; the immutable laws of science and aerodynamics. No problem. Twelve hours and I was back from whence I had departed, all those years ago.

*

It wasn't quite as I remembered, this place. None of the familiar smells greeted me as the aircraft opened its doors once again on Singapore. We now exited the aircraft directly into the terminal building. No aroma of jet fuel pervaded the senses, nor those of mimosa and frangipani. And I'd arrived in the harsh light of day rather than the softness of a tropical night. But these, I was soon to discover, weren't the only changes.

Was this really the place where it all began, forty nine years back? My RAF overseas tour, that is. It certainly wasn't the same any more. OK, few places are untouched by the passing of time, and even though this was not my first return trip, this island seemed to have changed more than most. For a start, it was now a Republic.

The airport at Paya Lebar was a thing of the past, too. Opened only a couple of years prior to my arrival in 1957, it had replaced the old Kalang airport, out on the waterfront. (Or what used to be the waterfront!) Changi had likewise replaced Paya Lebar, switching from military status to become one of the most modern airports in the world. It was now a huge complex, much larger than when it had been an RAF base, as was the island itself. Land reclamation had imposed vast changes to both the north and south coasts, completely redefining the waterfront area, along with that invisible boundary which separates Singapore from Malaya. This had been defined as the centre line of the Straits, but with the Singapore coastline gradually creeping north, so did that boundary; a source of growing concern to the now renamed, Malaysia. As for Singapore, the road we had so often followed along the south coast of the island, out to Bedok Corner, was now well inland.

The road we took into town was a very modern, tree and flower lined, multi-lane dual carriageway. There were bougainvillea covered flyovers, and it was all so peaceful and relaxing.

When we reached the city I noted that had changed, too. As well as growing out, it had grown up. Cloud-piercing up. Raffles Hotel lay in the shadow of what had at one time been the world's tallest hotel: the seventy-three storey Westin Stamford and Plaza. Orchard Road, once on the outer fringes of almost everything, was now the hub; a shopping Mecca for tourists. The Cathay Cinema remains, at the city end. This, previously one of the two most prominent buildings in the city, has also been dwarfed into insignificance.

But the traffic did not seem to have changed much, the roads still crowded. This despite the fact that entry to the city was restricted, achieved by limiting entry to even numbered registration plates to certain days, odd numbers the others. And there was also an additional tax payable for entry to the heart of the city, this collected electronically from a card displayed in your windscreen.

There was now an underground railway system, known as the MRT (Mass Rapid Transit. And is it ever! Covering most of the island, this is complemented by an above-ground extension known as LRT (Light Rail Transit) - computer-controlled trains which will take you right to Seletar's doorstep. If you prefer road travel, the trip to and from Changi is via either the Pan Island Expressway (PIE), or the East Coast Parkway (ECP), magnificent, tree-shaded, flower and bush-lined multi-lane super-highways, which again become choked with traffic as you approach the city. Tampines has since become a third expressway.

The MRT/LRT is very clean and efficient. You purchase a plastic card, much like a credit card, and as you enter an MRT station you merely swipe your card. Repeat the process as you exit the system and the fare is deducted. All is airconditioned comfort, as are the busses, which accept the same card, so all the driver does is open and close the doors, and drive. No hold ups with people sorting out cash, or asking 'How much?' The card does it all for you, logging where you got on, and where you got off, then deducting the appropriate amount. No cheating, either. The driver listens for you logging on, and if you fail to log off the system knows. Try and cheat by not swiping as you disembark and the system will exact revenge next time you use it, deducting the maximum fare for the route you are on, no matter how short a distance you travel!

Water is still imported across the causeway from Malaya, only now, after being purified, the majority is re-exported, back from whence it came, at a considerable mark up in price!

Bedok is alive and well, though now a picnic area, with ten-pin bowling, MacDonalds, good restaurants, and play areas. The original Cricket Club still exists, and they do still play their matches on the Padang, against the backdrop of City Hall and St Andrew's Cathedral - it too almost lost amongst the mega-storied architecture. Entry to that Cricket Club still remains very restricted.

Occasionally, amid all the modern buildings, I'd stumble across one of the old, colonial-era houses: a merchant, or senior expatriates' traditional style home. Concrete and wood structures, raised above the ground on cement piles so as to allow cooling air to pass beneath, and with an encircling veranda. Due to high humidity, the burnt-orange tiled roof would be darkened in places by patches of moss and fungus, and walls would be blackened with mould. They would be set amid a garden of cool greenness; coarse grass and Traveller's Palms, with Flame-of-the-forest, Hibiscus, Bougainvillea and Magnolia adding colour to the oasis, the most famous of which is still to be found within the grounds of the Raffles Hotel. But even Raffles hasn't escaped the changes. Expensively refurbished, I was saddened to find *their* oasis, the Palm Court - where, not too many years ago, I had sat with my first wife and sipped a Singapore Sling - was now out of bounds to all but registered guests; though none sat out there, for even the tables and chairs had been removed. Oh, and no photography inside the lobby, if you please; photographs are available from the many retail outlets which now form the exterior surrounds. But by the time I'd been informed of this my video was already in the can. The laid-back era of Coward and Maughan, it seemed, was no more.

What the hell, now I could afford it I entered the Tiffin Room: light and airy rather than the staid, dark-panelled, clubby-type atmosphere recalled from a previous visit. All I'd managed then was a drink, could barely afford that. But what I'd really been paying for was the privilege of looking round. I'd even had a pee in one of their loos. Not that I needed to, but I'd heard how luxurious and lavish their loos were, wanted to see for myself. Not outstanding that had been my verdict. Thinking back, I know which version of the Tiffin Room I preferred.

Now, amid the glitter and gloss, the damask and silverware, and the sunlit tables, I partook of their curry. Hygienic, tasty, impeccable service. But it was a white-man's curry. No sweat, no runny nose, which immediately had me pining for "Pops," the old Seletar curry shop.

The Singapore River has probably seen the biggest changes of all. One-time hive of activity with the coming and going of the lighters, carrying cargo to and from the ships lying at anchor offshore - in what were known as the Inner and Outer Roads - its waters were now deserted. Back then those lighters would discharge their freight into the heaving clutter of godowns (warehouses) which lined the banks. Interspersed amongst the godowns were dozens of rickety, open-fronted shops, packed with everything from spices to incense, clothing, raw cotton, silks, electrical and electronic goods, along with the latest offerings from the world of photography. There were fruits galore, and dried fish - very important, that, especially the sharks' fins.

An aromatic clutter of herbs and pungent spices would be piled all around, open sacks and tins, in bowls, and on trays. A dazzlement of colour. Greens and browns, saffron, white and orange. The red of the hot chili peppers, the green, red, and yellow of the capsicums.

All had been swept aside, replaced by touristy restaurants and bars. One compensation: the river was cleaner. Much cleaner, sweeter smelling by far. Of the lighters - still with eye painted on the bow, so they could see where they were going - the few that remained had been modified to run tourists up and down the river. For what? So they could see what was no longer there? Perhaps not, for most would never know what *had* been there.

Neither were the Inner and Outer Roads any longer extant. Where ships once lay at anchor was now a freshwater lagoon, bounded by reclaimed land, home to hotels, gardens, and a barrage. Maritime anchorage was now further offshore.

Change Alley? Would you believe Paris chic? High class art, Havana cigars, designer clothing; the real thing these days. There is a touch of the old place, if only in name: Change Alley Aerial Arcade. It spans the highway, but bears only a passing resemblance to the original.

The only thing to remind me of earlier times were the barrows which served fresh drinks, a hand-turned mill squeezing the juice from sugar-cane, or tropical fruits.

Not bad then, the changes, though not all good. For although it is probably one of the safest, cleanest, and greenest, cities to be found anywhere, it seemed to me that a lot of the character had been swept away. Not all. Hence Tanjong Pagar Conservation area. The original buildings remain, brightly painted and tidied up, yet even here the spirit seems to have departed.

After being shut down for a time - ostensibly to clean up *its* image - Bugis Street is again open, now renamed New Bugis Street. Correctly so, for it too retains little of the original character; just another tourist area. The boy-girls who used to entertain us with their antics have been moved to another area. Out of sight, out of mind.

Albert Street is another to have suffered. Its roadside kitchens, its rickety stairs, its balconied parlours, all gone. Replaced by something called the Albert Street Mall. Fatty's still remains, albeit now housed in airconditioned comfort. Very few trishaws remain. Just as well, really. Wouldn't catch me in one now, not in today's traffic. Lost my sense of adventure, you think? Not really. But I do now tend to think more about survival. These days the traffic is so horrendous that entry into the town centre, by car, is, as already mentioned, strictly controlled, during the day. The congestion charge was here long before Ken Livingstone came up with the idea. It is electronic, and really works. At night, it seems anything goes. Hence my reluctance to venture out in a trishaw.

Gone too are the open storm drains, the stench of rotting vegetation, and most of the cockroaches. Not really gone, I doubt. More like, rarely seen. The majority of mosquitoes also seem to have packed their bags and headed for pastures anew. Probably "Up Country."

*

The entrance struck a chord. A familiar place in a once familiar area: Stamford Road. (One thing that had not changed, I noticed, the street names remained the same: Selegie Road, Bras Basah, River Valley, Tampines, Rochor Canal, etc, which made navigation much easier for us old hands). I peered through the window. Yes, of course. The basic layout appeared to have changed hardly at all, though back in my RAF days it hadn't been known as Harry Keely's Pub and Lounge, just a plain old bar. I even recalled one of the girls who had worked there, answered to the name of Dumb-Dumb. Not because she didn't know what was what, because she was. Couldn't speak a word. Didn't need to; not exactly a barmaid, you see! One other change: the place was now airconditioned. It reminded me of how that MU had been, at Seletar; bloody freezing if you were dressed in anything less than a suit. Main problem with that: to wear a suit out on the street was to be slightly overdressed. Now, as then, I wore short-sleeved shirt and shorts. We used to sit in the heat to drink cold beer, an electric ceiling-fan stirring up the air enough to keep us comfortable, and to deter the mossies.

Another big change. As well as growing up, the city has also grown down! There are underground shopping Malls, both these and their connecting walkways, airconditioned. One can walk great distances with rarely the need to venture above ground.

So, better, or not? I wasn't really sure. Cleaner, certainly, but perhaps a little too clinical. And at a price, for it isn't cheap these days, not with beer averaging six quid a pint.

Funny, that. How with such as myself beer always seems to be the yardstick. All right then: cameras, computers, and such? Forget it. You can buy them far cheaper in the UK. Happy now? All I bought was an illegal piece of ivory, which I picked up along Bras Basah Road. It depicts the four wise monkeys. Yes, I know the originals only featured three, so I leave it to your imagination to figure out as to what it was the fourth monkey felt his hands should protect! Which reminds me: what of the Worlds; Happy, Old, and New? Yes, you've guessed. They also failed survive the cleansing in their original form. Wouldn't be surprised if my ivory turned out to be plastic.

But for all that, Singapore remains one of my favourite cities. I'll go back, anytime.

And as for that public transport system, the MRT, LRT, and the busses, well someone from the UK should go over and take a look. Everything is computer controlled, and it works perfectly. By the way, don't bother looking for the driver on the LRT; there isn't one. Once again it is computer controlled. The MRT is heading the same way, but I doubt the busses ever will!

Of course, by the time you read this it will probably be out of date. Changes are being continually introduced as technology advances, making the system ever more efficient.

*

And what of Malaysia, just across the Straits from Seletar? Big changes there, too, apart from the title. Whereas all you'd see of Malaya from our flying boat base had been mangrove and jungle, the whole area is now a huge industrial complex. Offshore oil had a lot to do with this, automatically bringing changes in the wake of the wealth it creates. These days the helicopter is associated with the oil industry rather than the military, although the military do have lots of them. And you no longer require one to fly into the "Ulu", you can drive there. Drive across country as well. In fact there is an East-West highway that cuts straight through our old, isolated base of Grik, now renamed Gerik. That is the northern East-West highway. There is another to the south, across from KL. You can even drive close by where some of those forts used to be located, then deep in the jungle.

Only one fly in the ointment: as with most Third World nations that find themselves to be suddenly oil rich, they've overspent on such prestigious and useful items as the worlds tallest building - the Petronas Towers in KL. (But not for very long!) Now it all seems to be collapsing around them; the economy, not the building.

Time will tell. In the meantime, I'm off back to my favourite place of all: New Zealand.

*   *

260

Page 262: Top L: Ayer Itam Temple 1959 - now known as Kek Lok Si. **R:** Flt Lt (later Air Commodore)Tom Bennett with pet. It is actually a cardboard cutout!
Centre: Butterworth. Victor V bombers on exercise from the UK.
Bottom L: Butterworth barrack block. **R:** Kuala Lumpur Gov. Buildings.

Page 263: Top: Blade tracking the old (potentially dangerous) way. Once false move... **Bottom:** Fort Brooke.

Page 264: Georgetown from Penang Hill. Butterworth would be in the haze, off top left. **Bottom:** Refuelling stop at Malacca.

Page 265: Top: Roping exercise practise, and for real. **Centre:** Tail rotor adjustment on the strip at Butterworth. **Bottom:** Casevac with the Royal Australian Air force.

Page 266 Top: Courtesy of a Royal Australian Army photographer. Four crews pose on completion of an Op. Pilots: Flt Lts Tom Browning & George Puddy; Sqn Ldr Frank Barnes (our CO); Flt Lt Deke Bradley. Crewmen: Sam Saunders, Merv Stokes; the author; Fred Macdonald.
Bottom:

Page 267 Top: Overnight accommodation in the Jungle. **Centre L:** Resupply by Vickers Valetta C1. **R:** Locator balloon. **Bottom:** Malayan Open-cast tin mine.

Page 268: Top: No.1 Royal Australian Regiment awaiting helicopters to fly them into action.

Page 269 Top: Belvedere twin Rotor helicopters arrived after I had departed.
Bottom: Statue of Sir Stamford Raffles on the Singapore riverside.

Chapter Nine
TOP OF DESCENT

*T*HE SIXTIES: Sex, drugs, and the Beatles.

The saying goes that if you remember the sixties you weren't really there. Strange, for I was certainly there, and I remember them well. The Mini: car and skirts. Woodstock and Vietnam. There were maiden flights for both the 747 and Concorde. And in 1969, a year when the minimum wage for farm workers was set at a mere thirteen guineas (£13.55), Prince Philip declared the Royal Allowance of £475,000 to be not enough. "We may have to move out of Buckingham Palace. We've already sold off a small yacht, and I may have to give up polo," he was alleged to have stated on American TV.

Then there was the event of the decade.

*

I first learned of the Kennedy assassination when I walked into the junior NCO's club at RAF Lyneham on that fateful Friday in November 1963.

'What's going on?' I asked of the room in general. I was curious as to the story behind the scenes of mass confusion which were being played out on the television.

'They've shot their President,' a stunned mate informed me.

No need to ask who had shot who's president, that was immediately apparent from the screen; crowds of politicians, and heavily armed police. And despite all the good things that had happened since my return from the Far East, three years previous, I remember that moment clearly. It was to be one of those time and place things that forever stick in the mind.

Another of those stick-in-the-mind experiences also took place during the Kennedy era. I recall standing at the Sergeants' Mess bar at RAAF Butterworth, Malaya, in October 1962, during the missile crisis in Cuba, smugly thinking this was probably as safe a place as any to be whilst the world stood seemingly on the brink of nuclear annihilation. (Despite being in the RAF at the time, it was to be years later before I discovered there had been nothing "seemingly" about it. We actually *had* been right on the very brink, even in the UK. V-Bombers fully crewed and bombed up (nuclear weapons!), sitting on the QRA (Quick Reaction Alert) pan at the end of the runway. From here, without help from the ground-crew, a Victor or Vulcan could start all four engines simultaneously, automatically disconnecting itself from the ground power as it taxied straight onto the runway and took off on its one-way flight. (All crews would know where they were going, but there were no details of any return flight. There would likely be nowhere to come back to!)

Basically, all it took was one finger on one button! The whole world was aware the situation was fairly serious, though only those closely involved knew just *how* serious, how close we actually came to that button being pressed. Two weeks during which it could have gone either way. Luckily, JFK persevered, ensuring it went the right way. That was the way back then, security was total. Even the press were effectively gagged by what was known as a "D" Notice. I still shudder today when I watch television documentaries relating to that time.)

But the assassination I remembered far better than I was to recollect my demob. Far better even than the final stages of my homeward voyage from the Far East, in 1960.

*

'Bloody weather,' Phil complained as we leant on the rail, waiting to weigh anchor for the final leg. 'Looks like summer's long gone already.' Phil was one of the guys I'd hung around with during the journey home. A shipboard friend, nothing more.

'Yeah,' I agreed, for it *was* cold, considering the time of year. It was wet, too.

'Typical Europe, ain't it. Here we are, in the Bay of Gibraltar, and already the bloody weather is declaring its hand.'

'But the forecast did say it was expected to clear,' I reminded him.

'Never happen, mate. We aren't in Singapore now.'

'Seems those years in the tropics have reprogrammed your brain, Phil, effectively erasing all memories of a European sun,' I said. Mine too, I thought, although I realized the conditions hadn't exactly depressed me. It was what I'd expected September at this latitude to be all about.

Weighing anchor off Colombo signalled the start of what I assumed would be the most adventurous leg of the voyage; burning sun, calm seas, tropical islands. Not so. There had been a bit of a blow during our crossing of the Indian Ocean, which didn't seem to effect me at all. I recall the thrill of leaping up just as the vessel topped the crest of a wave; time it right and you could clear the deck by six to ten feet as the vessel

271

dropped into the next trough. Get it wrong and I suppose it would have been easy to break a leg! One more thing: no queues for the mess, even the thought of food having apparently lost its appeal to the majority. They seemed to have consigned themselves to a slow death below decks, heading above only to occasionally puke over the side. But most recovered quickly once we entered the Canal, at Suez. From that point on, the decks had resembled those of a cruise liner as almost naked bodies stretched out wherever it was possible for a body to stretch. We all soaked up the last of the sun as the vessel slipped into the Mediterranean for the run to the Rock, and another brief run ashore. After Gib the only remaining obstacle on my epic three-year journey was the Bay of Biscay, which, thankfully, we caught in a rare, benign mood, although the sky was grey and threatening.

Then came Southampton. More of the same grey overcast, tugs pulling and nudging, gulls screeching, saline-laden air, docks and cranes, warehouses. Not much of a welcome then. There again, the major difference between my arrival here, and the departure from Singapore, was a weather-induced mood. I'd boarded under the sweltering heat of a tropical sun, full of joyful anticipation at what lay ahead. Even as I disembarked, anticipation remained intact, only now it was tinged with apprehension. My arrival back home in Yorkshire served only to reinforce this feeling, at least initially, for after the greetings, one of the first questions put to me, after three years away, was, 'When do you go back?' Confirmation perhaps, if it was needed, that I was now "grown up". A man of the world.

Following disembarkation leave - where Dad's binoculars had once more been pressed into action (Canberra, Vulcan, Jet Provost, etc) - I found myself in the depths of the beautiful West Country. Wiltshire. Perched atop Dauntsey Bank, to be precise, with Bradenstoke-cum-Clack close by. Who could ever forget a name like that? But there were many such names in this area. Upper and Lower Slaughter, for instance - so named, as when William the Conqueror granted the Saxon landholding to one of his knights, a Phillipe de Sloitre, the name proved such a tongue-twister the locals corrupted it to Slaughter. Just thought you should know that.

Although I wasn't to know then, RAF Lyneham was where I would be based for the final four years of my service career. I say based, for that was the reality of it. I probably spent more time *away* from the camp than I did *at* it, which made them the most prolific years of my life to date. As far as travel and experiences went they were certainly that.

If people thought we spoke strange up in Yorkshire, down here was different, for sure. This became obvious almost as soon as I attempted to engage in conversation on my first visit to a local pub. A man stood next to me at the bar, and I asked him a question. He looked quite bewildered at first, and the time he took to reply made me feel that this was perhaps the most awesomely complex question he had ever been called upon to answer. Or maybe he was just winding himself up, for once he started, there was no stopping him. It sounded like he could have been relating Cook's first voyage of discovery, so long did he take. And, to confuse things yet further, his hands flew this way and that, like he was warming up for a bout of martial arts. Then he suddenly stopped. I think he may actually have just paused for breath, but I got in quick and thanked him. Hadn't the heart to tell him I barely understood a word - lots of arr's and ee's, but little else it seemed. Not that it mattered a great deal, for by then I'd forgotten what it was I'd asked him. But I did manage to translate most of what it was he said as I downed my pint and prepared to leave.

'Tell ee what, young fella. Ee don't say a lot, but ee's awfy hard to understand.'

So, come October 14th 1960 I was back, in my element, with Transport Command, though by choice this time, for I was a man with a mission. I had a cunning plan in mind, and although it was already in operation, I realized I was as good as aiming for the moon this time, and even the Americans had not yet landed there. Live and learn, as they say. Well, after three years in the Far East I was still alive, and during that time I had certainly learned something. Quite what, I wasn't sure, for it hadn't dissuaded me from volunteering. Maybe three years in the tropics *had* effected my brain.

This was really the time I should have been volunteering for something more positive in nature. With six years experience in my trade-group, I should now have been applying to take promotional trade tests for my advancement through the ranks. But what I had in mind was something that promised much more excitement, even if was not exactly the most intelligent thing to do. It was therefore a toss up between promotion, and the fulfilment of dreams. So I'm afraid the dreams won.

The Lyneham posting was phase one of my plan, the easy part, preference of choice being one of the perks offered on completion of an overseas tour. Not that your preference was automatically granted, for, naturally, service requirements took precedence. But, without Lyneham, phase two was doomed to failure. In fact there would have been no phase two, for this base was my launch pad; the launch therefore, a success.

I was assigned to first-line servicing - out among the operational aircraft, second-line being AES (Aircraft Engineering Squadron), where major maintenance and servicing took place; not my kind of thing at all. I'd always found first-line to be much more interesting, and this was, to be sure. Exactly what I would have wished for, had I not had something else in mind. Something I suspected to be an even better option; provided it was an option!

I allowed a couple of months to pass, giving myself time to size up the situation, gain experience, slot myself into the system as it were.

Although three squadrons were based at Lyneham, 99, 511, and 216, ground-crew were pooled rather than being allocated to a particular unit. Same thing applied to the Britannia aircraft. Whilst 216 Squadron had exclusive use of the Comet, C2 & 4C, neither 99 nor 511 had any specific aircraft assigned to them. Both flew the Britannia, each drawing their aircraft from a pool, as and when required.

With the two months up, I played my hand. I was volunteering again, this time for an internal posting: to join Transport Command Mobile Servicing Flight, a select group that had come to my notice as far away as Malaya.

We'd had a flight of Vulcan's stage through Butterworth, en-route to an exercise in New Zealand. They'd been accompanied by a Britannia, carrying the servicing personnel and, as was my wont, I'd wandered over to have a look round, both types being new to me, and of far greater interest than the by now familiar Whirlwind. The Vulcan was huge aircraft, the view from the cockpit very restricted. As a result, the start-up procedure was far different to my Hastings days. Here the crew chief would be connected by headset to the aircraft, listening to the pilot run through his checks, walking round the aircraft so as to confirm control movement, air brake extension etc. This was explained to me by one of the ground-crew who had approached me, for you didn't get near a V-Bomber without question. After the Vulcan came the Britannia, and although few restrictions applied here, I was approached.

'Hello, Dave Taylor, isn't it?'

I looked round, recognised a face I hadn't seen since Cosford, six years ago. Same entry, similar trade - he was Inst Gen, whereas I was Inst Nav - yet I couldn't recall his name. But I think he realized that.

'Rex Chapman,' he said, offering his hand. 'Instruments, general,' he stated, as if offering an excuse for my forgetfulness.

'Yes, of course. What are you doing out here, Rex?' Which is all it took. He showed me round and explained about what it was he did, which is when I became aware of the opportunities available with Mobile Servicing Flight. That was for me, I decided, and determined there and then that it should happen. And so it was that chance meeting had sown the seeds, the inkling of yet another plan.

Now, here I was, nine months on, at Lyneham, successful once again. And it had all seemed so easy. Luck,? Fate? Destiny? Who cared. It was what I'd set out to achieve, so I wasn't about to instigate a sociological study into the hows, whys, and wherefores. They'd accepted me, I accepted them. Common courtesy, isn't it? OK, I was rejecting the higher rank option, along with a better pension. But unless I was to sign on, I wasn't in line for a service pension anyway, not in the nineteen sixties. You needed to serve 22 years then to qualify for that.

So it was I joined the chosen few. A couple of dozen at most, Rex no longer among them. We, also, were pooled, flew with any squadron, any type of aircraft.

'Not just the Brit and Comet,' Willie Wilson - another instrument fitter with MSF - told me. 'Any of 38 Group aircraft, when they're operating away from base, especially in places where there's no RAF presence. Which, of course, means travelling with them to... Well... wherever.'

'Such as? I asked.

'Wait for the Monthly Planning Requirement,' he suggested. 'It's due out tomorrow, then you'll see.'

I found the Monthly Planning Requirement to be an event that generated quite an air of excitement and anticipation in our crewroom, for those who happened to be there at the time, that is. It detailed the expected requirement in aircraft and crews needed for the following month. Lots of exercises with the Army, continuation training for aircrew in countries which offered more favourable weather conditions in the winter months, and such like. Then there were the specials, flights to the Far East, USA, Australasia, along with VIP flights to wherever. Everyone selected their preferences. Those who were already away in some foreign land were likely to miss out, but it was a swings and roundabouts kind of thing. Next month we could be away somewhere when the MPR was issued.

The atmosphere was just as smoky as any other crewroom I'd been in, our fifteen by ten base at Lyneham - feet that is, not metres. Enough seats for half a dozen, then came the wooden toolbox; pretty bum-numbing after a while.

'Help yourself to tea or coffee,' Willie said, pointing to a Burco boiler which bubbled away, steaming up the windows.'

'An advance on the communal bucket we used to brew up in back at Dishforth,' I remarked.

'Bucket?' Willie questioned, wrinkling his nose.

'Yeah, but shiny, new. Used only for tea. Strong, sweet, and milky, stirred up with a broom handle. This is bit more civilized, even fresh milk. We used condensed cow.'

In the Far East, the Coke machine had replaced the tea-urn.

*

Even our MSF training was different. As there were no RAF courses covering the civilian equipment fitted to the Britannia 312 and Comet C2 and C4 - which had, after all, been designed with the world's airlines in mind - I was to find myself dispatched afar, even deeper into the West Country. This time to Smiths Industries, in the heart of the beautiful Cotswold countryside. A timeless area in a region of rural calm. Thatched roofs and cottage gardens; butterflies and bumblebees kind of places. There were ancient churches, and the country pub; the very essence of all that is best in the English countryside. After that it was off to Hertfordshire, and the de Havilland factory, at Hatfield.

After the Comet 1 disasters of 1954 it was almost inevitable de Havilland would find themselves up against it. From being five years ahead of the field, with airlines knocking at their door, they paid a heavy price for stepping into the unknown. (A chance that had to be taken were we to compete in the field of air transport. A wartime agreement that had Britain concentrating solely on the design and production of fighters and bombers put the Americans way ahead, as had no doubt been their long-term plan.) And no matter how good later versions of the Comet might be, orders would now be hard to come by, for tough competition was on the horizon - the 707. Boeing, after all, had the advantage of a military test programme, and all that that entailed; the 707 being originally designed for the Department of Defence. In contrast, de Havilland had been left to fund their own research, a lot of which was presented to the Americans on a silver platter. Especially the results of the Comet 1 investigations: damning evidence of the dreaded, but as yet largely unfamiliar, metal fatigue.

Still, orders were forthcoming. The remaining Mk1's were rebuilt as C2's, originally to fulfil an order by BOAC, but all were eventually modified and sold to the RAF. The airline opted instead for the longer range Mk4, various models of which also went to such as British European Airways, and to a certain Middle Eastern airline. 'Which appeared to flight-test every safety device built-in to the seven they acquired,' one of the instructors told us. 'Almost every "test" attributable to "finger trouble."' (I was to remember that in later years, making a mental note to steer clear of that particular airline.) The Mk4C - last of the line - apart from attracting airline orders, was also supplied to Transport Command, becoming the C4.

Training complete, I was now about to begin a life living out of a suitcase. Not as bad as it sounds, for after the Sunderland, Valetta, Hastings, and other diverse types, the Britannia and Comet were magnificent aeroplanes. The Comet in particular was a slender, sleek, beautiful looking aeroplane - certainly the most graceful aeroplane in the sky until the arrival of Concorde - and I couldn't wait to fly in one. Nor was the Britannia too shabby. These were the service aircraft in which we did travel first class, relatively speaking. I hadn't been expecting anything as perfect as a Rolls-Royce, but these were probably the nearest avian equivalent as far as Service aircraft were concerned at the time. They were certainly technically far in advance of the Sunderland and Whirlwind. For instance, on the Britannia, there was no direct connection between control column, rudder pedals and control surfaces. Ailerons, elevators, and rudder were free-floating, controlled by trim tabs, and it was these that were connected to the control column. As for engine controls, the throttles were all electric - an Electrical Fitter and Flight Engineer's nightmare. Yet when it came to the navigation department, we were a generation behind the V-Bombers and high-tech fighters; albeit light years ahead of the

Sunderland's "wind, piss, and scroll gear" machinery.

This apart, living out of a suitcase was to prepare me well for future years. My suitcase was now of better quality, and much bigger, room for many more dreams; the formidable-seeming layer with which I'd returned from the Far East would barely line the bottom of this case. Just as well, really, I was to need the space.

The advantages of joining MSF were twofold - the varied nature of our work, and the amount of travel involved. The travel came in various guises: rapid response alerts; ferrying troops to the world's trouble spots; liaison exercises with the army - ie training for the above - introductory trials with new aircraft types away from their home base; route proving flights down possible diversions, for future use, or to bypass likely unfriendly territories. Such flights usually involved the use of Commonwealth and US Air Force bases.

We also participated in Royal flights and VIP tours, for which the aircraft were specially fitted out. For these, the Comet 4's shiny silver exterior was highly polished; a labourious and thankless task for those whose job it was to prepare the aircraft to this standard - spit and polish, all arms and elbows. I knew that, for I'd sometimes take a peek when they were in action. If there is anything more satisfying than looking at a nice shiny aeroplane in which you are about to depart for warmer climes, it has to be watching someone else making it shine. (A careful check needed to be kept on the polishing practice once it was realised the aircraft skin was suffering, becoming that much thinner!) There was an exclusive interior fit, too, especially for the Royals.

Next in order of preference were much-prized flights with Paris based NATO Defence College personnel. A choice here, were you lucky enough to be selected: Southern Capitals, or Northern Capitals, (Europe, that is) where NATO staff officers familiarized themselves with their area of influence, and we familiarized ourselves with the women and bars, with lots of sightseeing thrown in. We alternated in these duties with the United States Air Force, year and year about. (Flying the tours, that is, not the women and bars. The Americans proved themselves quite capable on that front.)

NATO apart, there were trooplifts - both on exercise, and for real during the occasional emergency in a British or ex-British colony - and, during England's cold winter-months, when the snow lay heavy across the Wiltshire countryside, and the wind howled mournfully around and between the hangars, there was the welcome advent of continuation training for the crews in the much more agreeable climatic conditions which prevailed in Cyprus. Also to Cyprus (and Australia) were the so-called "Hot Load" flights. 'Don't ask!' I'd been advised. So I didn't. I never knew for sure, didn't particularly wish to, but it was fairly obvious that these were radioactive cargoes, involving nuclear devices of one kind or another, otherwise, why would our unfamiliar passengers be carrying Geiger-counters! Anyway, much better that than a snow clearance party back at Lyneham. In fact, so frequent were our visits to places such as El Adem, Nicosia, Aden, Gan, and Singapore that they were to become almost second homes to us. And, due to our year-round tan and apparently easy-going lifestyle, we became known as "The Sunshine Boys" to certain elements of the Lyneham community. I suppose they saw us as the Air Force equivalent of the Jet Set. Something with which I'd at times have found it difficult to disagree, I'm happy to say.

There were also occasions - luckily infrequent - when we were required to visit a Royal Naval Air Station. Although land based, the Navy treated all their establishments as if they were ships at sea, even going so far as to name them HMS something or other. Therefore, when going off base, out into town, you were actually "going ashore", so were obliged to wait at the main gate for a "Liberty Boat". That didn't go down too well with a group of our guys, used to walking in and out as they pleased. But when it was explained to them they seemed to accept it, turned round and walked back a way. They then formed a line and walked backwards to the gate, arms pumping, looking like something out of Monty Python. When challenged they simply stated they were rowing ashore!

Another guy was puzzled the time he was walking across the grass, and some irate Petty Officer shouted at him "Man Overboard!" In RAF terms it is simply, "Get off the grass!"

*

Gan - then an RAF staging post in the Indian Ocean (now popular with holiday-makers, who pay a fortune to go there) is one of the Maldive group of Islands, and a refuelling stop on the Far East route. And it was during a departure from there that I was to face my only real emergency in a Britannia. Not a lot to worry about, in retrospect. But isn't that the case with any emergency that is brought to a successful conclusion?

Take off, along with the landing, are the moments of

greatest danger on any flight, combat missions excepted, of course, which I imagine to be dangerous in the extreme!

One evening we were pounding down the runway of this palm-fringed semi-paradise, outbound to Australia. Full fuel load, maximum all up weight, ambient temperature on the high side. This was partially compensated for by a runway which was at sea level. (The lower the altitude, the higher the density of the air; the higher the density the greater the lift.)

In keeping with Murphy's law, V1 (not enough runway remaining in which to make a safe stop) came and went before we lost power on an engine, were therefore committed to take off. Not really a problem, so long as the three remaining engines behaved themselves for the next, crucial couple of minutes. VR (rotation - ie take-off speed), and the aircraft lifted off as the engine was shut down, propeller feathered, corrections applied. Even on three engines V2 (minimum safe flying speed) came up fairly quickly, aircraft climbing away. At least, back where we were seated that seemed to be the way of things. Procedures had been adhered to, the moment of risk vanquished. The only danger now lay in discharging tons of fuel into the atmosphere before we could make a safe return to the runway, the aircraft at present well over the weight limit for a landing. There was no question of continuing the flight, for to set off across more than three thousand miles of ocean on three engines was a definite no-go situation. Almost an invitation to disaster, that. Let's face it, is not gravity far stronger over water? Either that, or golf balls have a fatal fascination for ponds and the like!

The next hour was spent circling, dumping fuel, fingers crossed. Out there were two sides of the fire triangle: fuel and air, conceivably in an explosive mix. Thankfully it wasn't put to the test, for the third component - sufficient heat to cause ignition - remained absent throughout, even if, to my mind, the possibility did maintain a slight presence: a wayward spark, a perverse burst of flame from an engine, a bolt of lightning. Yes, I know the chances are minute in the extreme (the RAF used JP1 fuel in preference to the more volatile JP4), but it only needs lady luck to turn her back one time.... In this case she didn't. We landed safely, overnighted at Gan whilst the problem was fixed, then continued on our way.

Two other incidents were to occur over time. Not exactly emergencies, but could easily have become so.

Northern Canada. Goose Bay was well astern, our

Britannia now lined up for a landing at the Canadian Air Force base of Churchill, Manitoba, when a situation occurred.

It was foggy and cold outside. Very foggy, extremely cold. Minus twenty-two degrees centigrade, to be precise; cold enough to spread major concern amongst the male brass monkey population. Difficult conditions, then. Instrument Flight Rules prevailed, naturally. And although approach aids had now advanced to the basic Instrument Landing System stage, radar and a talk-down (GCA approach) still played a part. In other words, it could be hazardous. Though in this respect service flights were generally much safer than their civilian counterparts. Service pilots took less chances, for the cost of diverting a service aircraft was borne by the taxpayer, didn't detract from the profits, as it were.

In this instance our first approach was a miss. Overshoot procedure: full power, flaps one third, gear up.

Oh, oh, small problem: still three greens. The landing gear stubbornly refused to retract. Much better than the reverse, of course, but still a problem. Now what? Divert, with the gear down, or go round again? Much better to try again, it seemed, for round we went. A wide circuit, long, straight approach, concentration intense, one imagines. With nothing to be seen outside, attention would be focussed on the instruments and, in the headset; the disembodied voice of a distant controller.

But not for us, back in the cabin. That our rearward facing seats gave us a view of where we had been rather than where we were headed mattered not one iota at present, fog looks the same when viewed from any direction. We had only what our imagination allowed us, and faith in the crew. Just as the crew needed to have faith in that controller, their training, and in what the instruments were telling them.

Down and down we went, as if gingerly feeling the way, which, in effect, we were. It was always reassuring to catch a glimpse of any odd light that came into view, more so if they happened to be the approach lights, as on this occasion.

We floated above the glistening surface, then, a slight bump, the rumble of rotating wheels, and we were down, worry replaced by relief. Suddenly the air smelt sweeter, the cabin felt warmer, more familiar. And once we were out on the tarmac, nostril hairs frozen solid, we discovered the answer to the problem. Particles of freezing fog formed a solid sheet of ice on the forward surfaces of the undercarriage struts. It was inches thick, smooth and translucent, effectively welding the gear in place. Strong stuff, this ice.

A difficult place in which to work then, Churchill, due to the extreme cold. In fact, once the wind speed reached a certain level, all external doors on the camp were automatically locked. Taking into account the wind chill factor, it was deemed far too dangerous for anyone to venture out, and as all buildings were interconnected, via heated walkways, there was really no need.

The next incident involved one of those shiny, sleek Comet C4s, probably my favourite aeroplane at the time; although, for me, nothing really replaced the Sunderland.

En-route from Gan to Aden with the Secretary of State for Air and his entourage, we were approaching the island of Socotra, in the Arabian Sea. With Aden due to be closed come the kind of independence that faced them once they kicked us out, interest had been shown towards the possibility of establishing a base on this island. So, as Socotra just happened to be reasonably close to the descent path into Aden, we were going down for a fly-by assessment of the situation.

The sky was devoid of cloud, the air clear, the island well visible. To me it looked like a sandy, brown-coloured Table Mountain, rising from the sea. Calm and tranquil as we approached from the north, but once we crossed that ridge the aircraft suddenly dropped. In no more than a second or two we lost around five hundred feet. The cause? I suppose something similar to what today is known as wind shear. Luckily it didn't extend down to the white-capped sea, but it was bad enough. Scared the crap out of me, I'll tell thee that for nowt. Don't know what it did to the S of S's secretary, for he was seated in the cabin at the time, typing up some report or other. We were strapped in, he, apparently, too busy to do so. And of course, when an aircraft goes down, anything not secured goes up, in effect: secretary, papers, typewriter, the lot. I can still see that guy floating around in the cabin. He looked like an astronaut in training. Luckily, his typewriter landed clear of everyone, though not so lucky for the typewriter. That, you may say, was a write-up write-off. More tax-payers' money down the drain, though at present that civil servant appeared to have more pressing things on his mind. He was back in his seat the second equilibrium was restored, tightening his seatbelt fit to cut himself in half.

Once on the ground at RAF Khormaksar, on the Aden peninsular, a check of the gravity-meter revealed readings which were way over the limits. We had recorded G-readings more familiar to a fighter aircraft. A major airframe check would be on the cards back at Lyneham, and care would be the watchword on the way there.

I believe the Russians eventually established a naval base at Socotra, the British, either not interested, or not allowed to be.

*

Only slightly less familiar than the pseudo second homes mentioned previously, were points of call such as Thule, in Greenland - a stopover on the Polar route to the Far East - Christmas Island (the British administered Pacific Ocean version, as opposed to the Australian territory located in the Indian Ocean - although this did occasionally also feature), Ascension Island, and various bases in Australia, New Zealand, and the United States.

Not only did I travel worldwide, I began to cover a lot more of the UK, too. With money saved during my three years overseas I was now able to purchase my first car, a maroon Ford Anglia 105E. And why not? Willie had recently got himself a Mini, was having great fun with it.

What I'd have really liked was one of the recently-introduced Jaguar revelations: the E-type, but that was way outside my budget. Just about triple, in fact. Neither was it exactly a learner's car. (Although Flight Sergeant Henderson had taught me the basics, allowing me to drive 110 Squadron's standard issue Standard Vanguard pick-up, up and down Butterworth's uncrowded roads, I had yet to attempt the Department of Transport - now DVLA - test.) My pride and joy cost six hundred and forty pounds, brand new. A good price I thought, though probably not too well received down at the Woolwich, where my account recorded a temporary zero. But this acquisition gave me the independence to follow my growing passion for motor racing. And, after a suitable period, driving test now passed, along with a course in race driving at Brand's Hatch (Tony Lanfranchi my instructor) it wasn't long before the Anglia's engine had been lightly breathed upon at Rob Walker's Wiltshire premises: uprated valve springs, twin choke Weber carburettors, etc. The suspension was beefed up too, brake efficiency increased, and the car now boasted a wood-rimmed steering wheel, along with full harness seat belts

- long before even basic restraint became a legislative requirement. With these mods, my Westover driving boots, the Jim Clark driving gloves, and the shades, I was ready. Oh, one other thing: the copper pipe extension on the end of the exhaust; to make it sound like the racer it almost was. After all, the 105E was the engine that really started Cosworth Engineering on the road to success.

The boots, gloves, etc weren't just for show either, for I was a technical driver, now conversant with understeer, oversteer, weight transfer and suchlike. I drove for pleasure, rather than a means of getting around. I mean, had I got the breaks, perhaps the world might never have heard of Nigel Mansell!

I recall having a dice with a bog standard Anglia one day. That racing course at Brands had really set me up, taught me the basics towards becoming an above average driver. I was aware of mine, and the car's, capabilities. I therefore out-braked him by a mile going into a corner, pulling away easily - you could safely do that on the relatively uncrowded, non-restricted roads back then, so long as you knew what you were about, and were familiar with that particular stretch of highway. Not really a dice therefore, but when I stopped further up the road to check on the radiator water level or some such, this guy pulls up alongside.

'Jeez, what have you done to that thing?' he asks.

'Oh, it felt a bit sluggish, so I've just stopped to put the other plug lead back on,' I ad-libbed. He left in rather a hurry. Muttered something about heading for his local "go faster" shop.

Often was the time a group of us left Lyneham at three in the morning, arriving at Silverstone well before the gates opened for F1 practice. It could be the British GP, or any one of the other F1 "Trophy" races that were regularly staged in the UK at the time. (The British Grand Prix at Silverstone is where the faithful would gather in their thousands, for this is the motoring event which signals the arrival of the English summer, even if not necessarily the sun! The equestrian counterpart is The Derby, or Royal Ascot, Cricket's contribution being the Test Match at Lords. Tennis? The hallowed courts of Wimbledon, with strawberries and cream. Whilst on water, the action is at Henley. But in motor racing, the honour lies with the garden party that is the British Grand Prix at Silverstone.) Breakfast would be taken at a local transport "caff"; what today would be

284

termed a "greasy spoon." Not a bit of it; good, cheap food was what. So maybe the decor was a little sad: greasy walls, Formica tables, their red tops marked by brown snail-trails - kind of thing unattended lit cigarettes are prone to leave - but what could you expect at those prices. After a feed we'd often nap in the car, waiting for the circuit to open. Then, at day's end, we'd call in for a drink at such a place as the Green Man, on the road to Brackley. This is were we discovered Team Lotus to be staying: Jim Clark and Trevor Taylor, along with C A B Chapman himself. They were all sitting there in the very room in which we were drinking. One time we arrived just as Innes Ireland was about to depart, in a white E-type. Made me envious, that: the contoured, hip-hugging leather seats, the short, snappy, gear-lever, woodrim steering wheel, high-profile tyres on shiny wire wheels, and, most of all, the speedo, boastfully calibrated all the way up to 160 mph. Not a true indication of top speed, I know, so I thought about going over and asking him the age old question: 'What'll it do mister?' Trouble was, I thought about it too long. He leapt in and was gone, blasting off down the road in a screech of rubber.

We'd drink the night away and be back at the circuit entrance by 2am on race day. There would probably be a dozen cars queuing at that time, but when we awoke the line would extend for miles back down the road behind us.

Once admitted, we'd go charging off across the grass, all heading for that particular place at which each seeks to be first to arrive. Then out would come the scaffolding, the wooden planks, and the plastic seats; the impedimenta of a personal grandstand.

This was pre-chicane, super-fast Silverstone, when, in the wet, cars would howl down the straights, the treads of their fat tyres throwing great rooster-tails of water into the air. Then they'd be snaking and twitching under braking, to go slithering round the corners in heart-stopping, opposite lock slides, barely under control.

I look back on them now as being the golden days of racing, at least as far as I was concerned. You could actually get close to your heros, take photographs, talk to them, ask them to sign autographs - rarely refused. We'd travel far and wide to the various international meetings, of which there were many: Thruxton, Snetterton, Aintree, Brands, Oulton Park; all corners of the Kingdom held Formula One meetings back then, even, occasionally, the smaller circuits such as Mallory Park and Castle Coombe.

Having seat belts fitted in the Anglia proved to be a wise move, too. Came in handy, those. Especially the time I contrived to turn the thing over.

'Bit of a misjudgment there, Dave', Ginger, my mate suggested.

'Come on, the other guy was mainly to blame, him being on my side of the road and all,' I replied.

'Should have made allowance for just such a possibility. One of the basic rules of the high-speed driving,' he advised. Ginger was another speed enthusiast. Older than myself, and possibly a slightly better driver, though I wasn't about to admit as much, naturally. Especially now, whilst we were both hanging upside down! I was, after all, an egotistic male.

'Hey, I don't care who the hell was to blame, let me out of here,' another voice cried.

Ah, yes. The three passengers in the rear of the two door car. They'd ended up in a heap on the roof, which was now the floor. You see, my thoughts about safety belts hadn't included the rear seats.

We all clambered out and heaved the car back onto its wheels. No damage to personnel - ego apart - little to the car, really. Although one headlight was now focussed on the treetops, as if searching out roosting birds, and if I used the wipers they tended to slap me about the face, the windscreen having scattered itself across the tarmac.

It was down to my friendly local garage early next day. First job, so as to reduce the chance of any get-out clause from the insurance company, I removed the Webers, etc, before the assessor arrived to look the thing over. Not too bad, fifty quid and it was back on the road in a day or two. Taught me a lesson, that. There were to be no more such incidents. Well, apart from... No, it's not worth mentioning, really. But I must say, the lady was rather understanding about her poodle.

I got her a replacement, though, of course I did. Second-hand, like!

All this interest in the art of driving; the technicalities, skid pan training, and putting everything I'd learned into practice, paid off a few times over the years. A couple of times recalled in particular, when I'd pushed my luck a little. In the wet, pulling out to overtake a truck I thought was a little too slow for me. (I hated driving behind anything that restricted my forward vision, still do, as it means you are governed by driving to their standards rather than your own.) But on this occasion, once I'd snicked it down a gear and pulled out, I realised why he was slowing. There was a roundabout some way ahead, and a line of traffic queuing to enter it. Now my training came into play. Jumping on the brakes would have spelt disaster; locked wheels, no way could I have stopped in the distance available. So I reverted to cadence braking; on the brakes until you feel the wheels locking, off the brakes, and so on. I was able to slip in front of the truck and slow enough so as to not hit anything or endanger anyone else. It was all more or less automatic, and boy, did it make me feel good. I imagine that truck driver would be pretty impressed also, seeing my brake lights flash on and off.

Driving into Swindon one day I went round a bend at my normal pace, only to find the road had been recently resurfaced on the exit from the corner. The back end slid out, I flicked on opposite lock, perfect. I held it without any drama. A little lucky possibly, but again it was automatic, thanks to that skid-pan training. The average motorist would likely have been in trouble on both these occasions, I suspect. But driving the way I did takes one hundred percent concentration, so I'd been ready.

I'll let you into a secret, too. Such incidents don't half make your heart beat faster!

*

Meantime, back at Lyneham, my first overseas trip was a trooplift out to the Middle East, where Iraq was threatening Kuwait. That was in 1961, so it would seem things don't change a lot over the years. Another trip during my first year with MSF saw us dispatched from RAF Benson to RAF Wildenrath, West Germany, to take part in the Argosy proving trials. The flight out was courtesy of the aircraft itself - Argosy - that four-engined, twin-boomed turboprop, which left itself wide open to the nickname "Whistling Wheelbarrow. It had been designed by Armstrong Whitworth (later to become part of the Hawker Siddeley group, which in itself eventually became British Aerospace. God, seems like another lifetime). A Hastings flew us back across the Channel for the Easter break.

*

We were to return to Germany courtesy of that lumbering giant, the Blackburn Beverley, a 47 Squadron aircraft allotted the honours. Different again, especially when compared to the sleek grace of the Comet. A real workhorse, this. Descend into the empty cabin and it was like flying in a barn!

287

All in all, it was an interesting trip during which personnel stationed at Wildenrath introduced us to some very agreeable pubs round about. Over the Dutch border, for instance, a place named Sittard. I remember the name of the town, you see, not too much about the pub, *that* agreeable.

What I do remember was the particular night we were invited to a house for supper, after the pub closed, which in fact made it early morning. There was a girl involved - of course there was - the fiancee of a friend of a friend; honest! She had invited us all back home along with her fiancee, to her parents house, where we were made welcome. Very much so, for the table was soon awash with plate after plate of cold cuts and salads. An early breakfast, or late supper. There was bread and beer too, enough to feed an army, and there were only six of us, plus the girl and her parents. But nine became ten when the girl's brother returned from *his* soiree to *his* pub, slightly the worse for wear. Not that we were entirely of sober mind ourselves, but we were all still capable, he proved not to be.

We were merrily tucking in to the food and drink, the brother by this stage well into a physical re-enactment of his escapades whilst serving with the Dutch paratroops in Indonesia.

'Ambush,' he suddenly yelled, grabbing a convenient umbrella, which magically transformed itself into an imaginary Sten gun, chattering away in his hands. Then, in an excess of enthusiasm, he flung himself to the floor, rolling for the nearest cover, which happened to be the table. Unfortunate, that, for his judgement was as poor as his reactions, his momentum such that he took the lot with him. Meat, salad, bread, butter, beer flew every which way, scattering themselves over the furnishings, and everything in the vicinity thereof, which meant us. This made things rather difficult when attempting to put together anything like a decent sandwich.

'Hey, Pete. Toss me some beetroot, will you? It's over there on the wall, just below the Rembrandt.'

'Chackka-chackka-chackka.' The brother, unperturbed by the chaos he'd created, was busily mowing down the communist hordes he imagined to be secreted away around the room.

'Yeah, right, Dave. Meantime, would you mind scraping some butter off the curtains for me?'

'Look out! Grenade!' A shell-less boiled egg flashed past my left ear, on its way to oblivion. That kind of thing. So much for the room, not to say the Dutch obsession with cleanliness and order. Take some cleaning up, that lot. As well he was family rather than one of us, we had enough of a reputation to live down as it was.

We also had the avenue of "Amstel" trees with which to contend on the drive home. These were actually very solid Poplar trees which lined the road on either side. They had been so named by us because, after a night on the Amstel, it wasn't unknown for one of them to apparently leap out in front of the car on the drive back to camp, over the border in Germany. There were so many they almost always got you. Couldn't miss really. Dodge the trees and you'd likely end up in the canal.

*

An opinion readily endorsed by some visitors to the flight deck of an airliner, and observing the apparent lack of activity by the crew, is that aircrew, pilots in particular, have a very easy life. But, being aware of just a little of what it took to get there in the first place, and the amount of training it takes to remain there, I was never of this opinion. It is the same where most professionals are concerned; they manage to make it look easy.

When travelling around the globe by Britannia or Comet, as MSF personnel, we were usually regarded as part of the crew, which gave us access to the cockpit at almost any time.

I took full advantage, for I liked to keep an eye on things up front. Got some good movie footage from up there: the snowy crater of Kilimanjaro; the approach to Gan, though that certainly wasn't taken on one particular approach to the island. I remember that well.

During the monsoon season the weather could be downright belligerent over the Indian Ocean (on it, too, recalling that troopship on the way back from Singapore). So when I noticed the navigator strapping himself in, full harness, I knew it was a signal for me to return to my seat in the passenger compartment, to do likewise. For, take-off and landing apart, the crew, with the exception of the pilot in control, rarely used seat restraints. A quick glance at the weather radar before departing told the story: dense cloud formations on display, extreme brightness in the centre; warning of heavy precipitation and turbulence, a sure sign that things could get rough. Not nice at all. Kind of information that makes the rectum twitch.

From the safety of earth, clouds appear as those fluffy, rose-edged or silver-lined picturesque additions to nature's canvas. But when viewed as the backdrop to the speck of an aircraft, even one the size of a 747 - so large that some of the passengers are actually seated ahead of the crew - can their true enormity be gauged, the forces within be possibly imagined: high velocity air currents, rain, ice crystals, lightning. A turbulent, seething, mass that, in an extreme case, could pluck an aircraft out of the sky and tear it apart as effectively as did those Chinese crackers to our plastic models, back there at Seletar. It is a big sky, and no matter how large an aircraft looks on the ground, up there it is very tiny indeed. This was precisely the situation in which we now found ourselves.

The pilots would be relying solely on instruments and electronic aids, blind to anything outside the cockpit. Dexterously, by use of their weather radar (cloud and clonk, as it is facetiously known in the RAF), they would guide us around the most vicious of the storm cells. Even so, we seemed to hit every pothole in the sky, wings flapping and flexing, as they are designed to do, for they are an aircraft's shock absorbers; if they didn't flap they'd break. It's at times like that you really value your basic lapstrap. And this is when the pilots really get to work!

I was certainly happy to touch down on a rain-soaked Gan that night. Happier still next morning to find we had a free day in this place where the sun once again blazed down, nature's tantrum of the previous night long forgotten, and forgiven.

Gan is one of a group of coral islands which form a rough circle around the still, blue waters of a deep lagoon. Addu Atoll is the name given to this particular group. It is surrounded by the vast expanse of the Indian Ocean; tranquil-looking blue-green waters which hosted most of what is dangerous around here: Sea snakes, Lion fish, Stone fish, and sharks. Lots of sharks. Big healthy brutes too, so it is said.

'Don't worry, Dave, they know and abide by the rules. You won't find them inside the reef,' Jim - my snorkelling companion and fellow MSF crew-member (Radio and Radar) - advised.

'Fair enough,' I replied. For, having recently been stationed here for a year, I assumed he'd be one to know.

Between the beach and the drop off, which forms the inner wall of the lagoon, is the stretch of coral-strewn shallow water in which I now lay, motionless. Through the faceplate of my diving mask I looked out upon the technicolour world which existed there. A magical world, in water barely two feet deep. Fish darted about at the least movement, wary, until eventually curiosity overcame caution and they moved closer. One or two braver individuals at first, but then, as if fearful they were about to miss out on something, they all edged in. Many shapes and sizes were observed, in colours only a rock star would dream of putting together. Reds, blues, greens, yellows, in any and all combinations. There were stripes and spots, wispy fins, transparent bodies, flat, round, long and slim, short and fat, the whole collection, though none appeared to be more than an inch or two in length. I assumed it was nature's training area for young fish learning the ropes. I was spellbound, but Jim indicated for me to follow him out to the edge of the drop off, where we could expect much bigger fish. So follow him I did.

As the jagged coral sloped gently upwards we had to rely on the swell to lift us over the lip, a matter of precise timing. But once over the drop-off, the wall was sheer. The coral on the face was abundant, and multi-coloured. Wispy tropical plants waved at us, goggle-eyed fish investigated, the vertical wall disappeared into the darkness far below. Down there the world looked as mysterious and threatening as a gangster's sunglasses. Exhilarating? Would have been, but for the bloody great shark that cruised the depths. It appeared to be waiting just for us, or someone of matching stupidity. "Munchies", I imagined it thinking; Fooled you.

Tell you what, I don't know how I made it back over the lip, but I was on the beach in no time flat. Sod the swell, colour me gone. Getting older, I suppose. Or maybe it was self-preservation coming into play; thoughts of living long enough to reach a ripe old age.

As postings went, Gan was good with respect to environment, but in terms of just about everything else, it was poor. The expression "piss poor" didn't exactly fit the bill, for competitive drinking appeared to be a fact of life on the island. Apart from a Changi-based Air Sea Rescue Shackleton, out here on periodic detachment, no aircraft were based there permanently. The airfield's prime function was merely as a staging post and refuelling stop on the route to points east and west. Fine for a day or two, but a Posting here lasted a whole year. Singles only. Families could not be catered for being as there were no facilities. Problems enough if a flight carrying families became unserviceable on the island. In fact, the only permanent white female presence was a welfare lady - not that kind of welfare either!). No thanks, deal me out. Given the situation, it was no wonder such inane diversions as the jetty cycle race were devised.

The jetty was five feet wide, fifty yards long, so, with two riders side by side, they would race to the end. Stopping - apart from being impossible - was apparently much less important than it had been to me during my youthful pile-ups. Winning was the prime aim here, ie, crossing the line first, which meant committing oneself, totally for the line was at the lip of the jetty. Though, "the sensation of becoming airborne, to splash down in the warm waters of the Indian Ocean, is not too bad at all," so I was informed. The bicycles were of course tethered with a fine line, as resupply out here would have been difficult. Ah, well, whatever turns you on. We'd had our day, now had other places to visit: Singapore, Hong Kong, Australia, New Zealand, and like that. The schedule was hectic, so we loaded our aircraft up with beer etc, and departed. In the freight bay they would be nicely chilled by the time we arrived at .... wherever!

We'd also be sure to call in for some more duty free on the way back to Lyneham.

*   *

Chapter Ten

FINALS

*O*n VIP flights, and specials, we were often afforded a temporary promotion to acting sergeant; unpaid, of course. It helped bridge the social gap between aircrew and ground-crew, did absolutely nothing for a bank balance that seemed continually to be in a state of shock. But there were occasions when even rank appeared to have been consigned to the scrapheap. One such was at RAF Changi, where we were due to stop overnight, at the start of an Australian tour. The aircraft captain was a Wing Commander, the Squadron CO, in fact; a true "officer and gentleman" type.

'Everything is arranged, sir,' the young officer at the desk of the RAF Changi Transit Hotel informed the Wingco. 'Flight-crew to the Officer's Mess, ancillary personnel, the Sergeant's Mess.'

'Pilot Officer er.. Smith, is it?' the Wingco asked.

'Yes, sir.'

'Well, Mr Smith. As we are scheduled for an early morning departure, it would be rather helpful if we could remain together as a crew, be accommodated in the Transit Hotel.' Very pleasant, no hint of intimidation, though naturally, being at least a quartet of ranks down the ladder, the transit officer complied, magically finding rooms in a facility he'd recently alluded to as being fully occupied.

Things like that were what bound the crews together. We relied on them, they relied on us. It worked well, just as long as protocol was observed when necessary. Of course, all crews were different, and I heard tell of the occasional captain being considerably less accommodating. But they were either in the minority, or I struck lucky more often than not.

Apart from sharing the same hotels - quite often at the luxury end of the market in places where no service accommodation was available - we'd also socialize together. At Gan we'd load case after case of duty free beer into the aircraft hold, by the time we reached wherever, they'd be well chilled. We'd then all gather in one room or another, and start on the pre-dinner drinking.

Crew Chief apart, as we only carried one rigger (Airframes) and one fitter (engines) - both of whose turnarounds were much more involved than ours, especially so if a fault had been reported - once we ancillary tradesmen had completed our servicing, we helped out with refuelling and cleaning the aircraft. In fact cabin cleaning became quite popular. After off-loading our consignment of bodies, we'd often discover unbelievable amounts of cash when clearing up the debris. This would have slipped beneath the seat cushions, and on to the floor; live rounds too, if the army had been involved. Although we didn't want the live rounds - they were of no use to us - neither did we want them floating around our aircraft, so they were turned in to the powers that be.

We also lent a helping hand with any faults that required rectification, for we were a team, too. Team spirit got the aircraft turned round much quicker, which left more time for the essentials, such as demolishing the remains of the liquor cabinet at the end a VIP flight.

There were stopovers in places such as Fiji, and Bangkok, where I at last got to see most of its three hundred temples, visit the floating market on the Chao Phraya river, view the Emerald Buddha and the Royal Chapel. I even visited Choi Cowboy, with it's wall-to-wall girlie bars, and rode in a three-wheeler Tak-Tak, a kind of two-stroke taxi that goes nowhere fast, although, because of its size, slightly faster than a regular taxi. Such is Bangkok traffic.

Other glossy-brochure type locations featured hotels in places as diverse as Wellington; Ottawa - where it was the Chateau Frontenac; Istanbul; Nairobi - the New Stanley, on Kimathi Street, with its Thorn Tree bar; Rome; the Excelsior, on the seafront in Nice. Nowhere in Khartoum could ever in a million years be classed luxurious. The Caravelle Hotel, Saigon, missed out as it was filled to capacity with "American Advisors". (Seemed a minor skirmish was brewing hereabouts.) Instead, on this VIP tour with the Secretary of State for Air, the RH Julian Amery, we found ourselves to be guests of British Embassy staff for a couple of nights, their families having been repatriated due to the aforementioned skirmish (a hint, perhaps, that a Vietnamese-style skirmish was not to be so minor after all). And what a thirsty bunch those members of the Diplomatic Staff turned out to be, not that we were exactly paid-up members of Alcoholics Anonymous ourselves, officers included. Definitely no difference between ranks in that respect. In fact it would probably be true to say the officers came out ahead; on the wrong side of the line. The stories I could tell, but won't. Needless to say, had they been flying for the airlines, they probably wouldn't have been! If you get my drift. Not on the days in question.

Myself and the radio tech, Jim - yes, the very same guy who had taken me snorkelling at Gan - found ourselves "billeted" with a Second Secretary, in rather palatial quarters. It happened to be this chap's birthday, and he had arranged to go out to celebrate with friends. So, after ensuring we were well settled, and advised on where and where not to go in town, he invited us to help ourselves to his rather prodigious stock of duty-free liquor, then left us to it. Oh, no! Not again.

Jim, I now found, was apparently a cognac fanatic - though on this occasion I'd have said more "common sewer" than connoisseur. With our host barely out of the door, Jim immediately latched on to a bottle of Remy Martin. And so persuasive was his invitation, I found myself imbibing along with him; try anything once, me. But not right away. Seemed I first needed a little gentle coaxing before adding to my assorted intake of liquid refreshment.

'Try this,' Jim suggested, pouring a decent shot into a large snifter and handing it to me. 'You'll like it.' It reminded me of time at Seletar when "Smudge" Smith was introducing me to curried eggs.

'Don't like whisky, why would I like that?'

'Nothing like whisky. Much better, believe me, I know about such things.'

'Like you know all about shark etiquette at Gan, for instance?' I felt the need to remind him.

'Ah yes, sorry about that. Seems I was misinformed there. But no harm done, you're alive aren't you? All the necessary pieces still attached? Anyway this is first-hand knowledge.' He stuck his nose in his glass, closed his eyes, and inhaled the fumes. 'Ahhh,' he sighed, ecstatically. He looked like Bisto Boy.

It was enough. So, despite his *faux pas* with the shark, all was soon forgiven. I followed his example. Found I rather enjoyed the ritual, the taste, the sensation, tried a second glass just to be sure. As with that first curry, six years previous, found I rather liked it. Either that, or, after all these years, I'm still trying to make up my mind about both. Now there's a thought, or an excuse.

'Never imagined I'd like brandy,' I told him. Wrong thing to say; my *faux pas*. He was on it in a flash, like a Scotsman onto a bargain. Or a Yorkshireman, come to that.

'Cognac,' he corrected, 'not brandy. A vast difference.

All cognacs may be brandies but all brandies are certainly not cognacs,' he explained. 'This,' he stated, holding up his glass like a trophy with which he'd just been presented, 'comes only from the very heart of the Cognac region, in France. Brandy can come from anywhere. Often tastes like it has.'

I did mention he was a bit fanatical about the stuff, didn't I? Yes, thought so. And this was when the night was still young. I learned a lot more about Cognac before he was through. For instance, did you know that... ? No, maybe not.

That evening we merely finished off the half-empty bottle, before heading downtown to seek out the rest of our crew.

Large, heavy, green-glazed planters edged the pavements. They sprouted what appeared to be a cross between an oversized yucca and a small, tufted palm. There were sidewalk cafes set out under pull-down awnings in true French-colonial style. But there was little in the way of entertainment in this city (a result of 'First Lady', Madame Nhu's so called "Morality Laws"), so the night turned out to be a fairly quiet affair, for a change. No one outrageously incapable, no undue problems. Oh, we did happen across one totally legless example of expatriate humanity. But, after all, it was his birthday.

It was later on this same tour we went sightseeing. On the leg from Bangkok to Saigon we called in at Angkor - a series of temples, each of which had served as capital of the Khmer Empire (1113-50). Phnom Bak Kheng, known as Angkor Wat, the first capital, through to Angkor Tham, the last. These vine-covered ruins lay deep inside the Cambodian jungle, all but lost to the world at large, for they were located in an area which would, in later years, become the infamous Killing Fields of the Khmer Rouge.

With entry to the area being already self-restricting, with regard to the travel safety angle, this was to be sightseeing with a difference; from the air. Which was just as well, for the site covers over forty square miles.

Our Comet C4 descended and slowed, to pass just a few hundred feet overhead. It was probably the closest you could safely get at that time, and I'm not too sure about that being entirely within the bounds of safety. You know, like I had a sneaking feeling we'd probably have gone even lower had the trees not prevented it. As it was I prayed the pilot would not sneeze, causing the aircraft to suddenly charge off in an entirely inappropriate direction!

Later on in this tour came the time I finally got to land at Labuan, where five years ago I'd experienced that low pass in a Sunderland. Rather marginal as far as the Comet was concerned too, it seemed.

Landing wasn't a problem, the aircraft being light. But a rather tall, solitary palm was located at the far end of the shortish runway, and as this was seen to pose a potential problem during take-off, the captain arranged to have it "disappeared" during our stopover. Pity, that, for come take-off the wind had shifted 180 degrees! Still, after taxying out to begin our departure, the aircraft was pushed back to the very limits of the runway threshold - our tail occupying the piece of sky close by where that tree had once been. This ensured that every inch of the runway's length would be available for take-off. A precaution, you understand. It was a VIP flight.

A contrast to this was the runway at Easter Island, where I was to visit some years in the future. So long, it doubles as an emergency landing ground for the space shuttle. Not much more to Easter Island, apart from that runway, and a scattering of unexplained statues.

From Labuan we were originally scheduled to continue on to Australia and New Zealand; places I had yet to visit. So it was a bit disappointing to find our VIP recalled to London due to some political crisis or other, the rest of the tour cancelled. It seems Prime Minister, Harold MacMillan, was about to axe seven of his Cabinet Ministers, and although "ours" was not one of them, his presence was required back in parliament, thus putting paid to my first visit to Australasia.

Still, lose some, win some, as the saying goes. Shortly after arriving back at Lyneham we were off again. Same ground crew, same aircraft, different aircrew for yet another VIP tour, concentrating solely on Australia and New Zealand this time. Three more weeks of luxury as we toured Australasia with the AOC Transport Command, Air Chief Marshall Sir Edmund Huddleston.

Naturally, there was another side to the accommodation coin. Hong Kong, for instance: a corrugated-iron Nissen hut on the RAF Base. The same old huts we'd used when based there with 205/209. Comfortable enough - considering the few hours we seemed to require their use - but very noisy when it rained. They were firmly anchored, too, steel cables ensuring they stayed put during the typhoons the colony now and again experienced - as luck would have it, not whilst we were in attendance. Which leads nicely to a NATO exercise in which we participated.

*

Larissa, Greece. Exercise Falltrap, one and two. (Part one embraced flying the troops and their equipment out from the UK on some NATO exercise, part two being the return leg, a month or so later).

Thirty-five years ago. My... that long! We were accommodated in what were termed "field conditions," aka, tent city. Row upon row of what amounted to canvas billets, with few facilities. Luxury for the likes of the SAS, maybe; not at all what the Air Force was used to, never mind "The Sunshine Boys" - even if the tents *were* already in situ upon our arrival.

But that first night it rained heavily. So heavily it was soon rushing through our tents. It was one of those freak, continuous downpours which happen but rarely in this area. I asked one of the locals about it. "Seen nothing on this scale for at least twenty years," he insisted. "Well..., apart from the one two years ago. And the one a year after that."

First priority then was to get out of the tents. But, as luck would have it, two things were seen to be in our favour. The first was that close-by stood what appeared to be a derelict building - a kind of barn really, on a concrete base - along with it's adjacent scrapheap of discarded material. The second, we just happened to have amongst our number the one person who was the true master of resourcefulness. Well, we all were really, needed to be at times, but Mike Ortega was a real expert, especially in situations like this. Kind of person who could make things appear magically, as if from thin air.

So, rather than squelch around in a sea of mud, we decided to move into the derelict barn, for it looked dry and secure. It was. So secure we were obliged to force an entry. Though it was not a padlock that required a great deal of ingenuity or resourcefulness. It offered little resistance to the attentions of Mike. Not only was the barn not as secure as it at first appeared, neither was it derelict. We discovered it to be filled with sacks of something or other, probably grain. But it was dry, the sacks soft enough to sleep on. It offered a much better option than the quagmire outside, though there was one negative factor; a profusion of bloody great, poisonous centipedes, each fully six inches long - which probably made them millipedes! (One of our guys who was bitten by one had to be repatriated to the UK for treatment.)

Next on the agenda was to turn our attention to the lack of facilities. But we did have that scrapheap and we did have Mike. So it was not to be very long before, thanks to a discarded water tank, some rusting brackets and sections of pipe, we boasted the only shower in the area. Add to the recipe some petrol burners beneath the tank - someone's kitchen facilities must have suffered a loss there - and voila! A *hot* shower. Luxury! Even the aircrew were attracted our way by this piece of kit, in which the cold water was siphoned across from a 44 gallon drum, up to the Coke tin shower head, where it mixed with the very hot water. But the aircrew, being mainly officer class, didn't just wander over and step in, all were polite enough to ask first. One Master Flight Engineer, after seeking Mike's permission, stripped off down to nothing but his Royal Warrant badge - which he wore on his wrist on a canvas strap - and stepped in. Unfortunately, part way through his shower the cold tank inadvertently ran dry, resulting in a shower that suddenly became very hot indeed. We were first made aware of this by the very loud bellow which emanated from within. It sounded rather like, "Bastard."

We couldn't help laughing as the guy quickly emerged, still starkers but for his badge of rank. This seemed to enrage him even more, and he was last seen charging off through the mud, chasing after Mike who, naturally, had already departed the scene, stage left.

"You did that on purpose, Ortega", he yelled. But Mike, despite the glutinous mud sucking a wellington boot off one foot, was well away. And of course, dressed the way he was, our Master Engineer wasn't about to pursue him over any great distance. As the saying goes, Clothes maketh man. Naked people have little or no influence on the normal run of events. Especially so when one hand is occupied in trying to protect and hide one's vulnerable parts!

So, we had a shower.

Now we were dry and clean, what next? Not a lot to be done about the "long drop" toilet facilities, which proved to be an ideal breeding ground for microbes and flies. It was the usual open pit, a long wooden seat with holes in the required places. Some poles and sacking gave a modicum of privacy by creating individual stalls, though the whole thing was open to the elements. Very basic therefore, as was our preferred method of debugging the place: a light dose of 100 octane

Avgas, followed by a match and a hasty retreat. Effective enough, provided one took care. But, as usual, there was always the odd idiot who decided they needed a really good dousing. "Fred" was just such a person. Not one of ours, I hasten to add.

'A touch more for luck,' quoth he, upending the can he carried. As it was rather a large can I decided the time had come to relocate myself, immediately engaged every instinct in the rush to do so, as did everyone else, with the exception of Fred. Oh, and there was....

'Hey! What the ....?' cried a voice from one of the stalls. A futile and irrelevant question, even had it been completed. From that point on, exactly what became obvious!

It wasn't a huge explosion, at least, not relative to nuclear standards. There was a kind of rumbling noise, which added a touch of reality to the name, *Thunderbox.* And it did clear the toilet block, literally. Crap and sackcloth everywhere. A couple of singed rear-ends, too, I assume. Bits and pieces of whatever, rained down on those passing by. Unfortunate timing, that. Especially for those who had chosen that particular moment to go about their business, as it were. The shower was a popular place that day. We felt we should have been charging for the privilege.

Yes, I was happy to see the back end of that operation, if you'll excuse the pun. Not all gaiety and laughter, you see. We did struggle a little, now and again, even if the aircrew wives, back in the UK, took to sending out apple pies etc on incoming flights.

Rumours did circulate to the effect that, come the end of the exercise, a certain farmer, whose barn had evidently been broken into, put in a claim for some outrageous sum to the powers that be.

*

There is a well known Catch 22 type adage in the RAF that states, 'You can't do it unless you have done it before.' Meaning you needed to serve some time on a unit before you stood any chance of being selected for a plum job. On Mobile Servicing Flight this seemed to apply to VIP flights, or other "Jollies". But not in my case it seemed!

1962 was the RAF's year for ferrying NATO Defence College graduates around, and I had apparently bagged one of these much sought after trips - Flt No.1532, Exercise Southern Express. Lucky, eh? Well, in a way. But I had recently presented Flight Sergeant Holt - the very person whose job it was to allocate our schedules, amongst other things - with a bottle of his favourite whisky (any whisky in a bottle, probably), which I miraculously just happened to have left over from a previous jaunt. Miraculous indeed, given I didn't even drink the stuff! It was what I termed forward planning. Others referred to it as bribery! Yet I noticed that didn't deter them from also indulging in the practice. Not Pete though (another survivor of that Dutch ambush, you'll recall). There again, Pete didn't always get the prime trips. As I mentioned, a lot depended on if you happened to be around at the right time. Must have done all right on the whisky and cigar front, Chiefy Holt. But I was happy, too. Especially so when this turned out to be the trip during which I made the most memorable flight of this whole period of memorable flights.

The chance presented itself on the penultimate stop of the tour. Paris had come and gone, as had Valletta - Malta, Ankara and Istanbul - Turkey, and Athens, the Greek capital. We'd been shown the sights, we'd been wined and dined royally. Now it was the turn of Napoli - Italy. See Naples and die, so the saying goes. Easy enough to imagine it happening, too, should you wander into the wrong area of this city.

Our hotel - The very suave Excelsior - happened to be in the right area, on the seafront, across the bay from the Isle of Capri - magnificent in the sunset. Mention of which reminds me that the hotel had a magnificent, glass, double door frontage. The reason this sticks in my mind is that on the prime day of our tour, it was blowing a gale outside; gale of the century kind of thing. I was standing in the lobby, for some reason feeling a little hung-over, when suddenly there was a resounding crash. Someone had left an inner door propped open, and when the outer door was opened, the wind took control. The inner door slammed shut with a vengeance. On reaching the stops, the bronze frame ceased all forward motion but the glass didn't. The approximately eight by three foot engraved pane, retaining its outline shape mometarily, but now composed of thousands of tiny pieces, seemed to take a couple of paces forward before scattering itself across the marble floor. Hope they had good insurance.

But I'm getting ahead of myself.

We'd had one free day, another was on the schedule for tomorrow, so a trip to Pompeii had been organised. It sounded interesting enough, but I'd been listening in to the whisperings, decided I would much prefer to join the Admirals and the Generals on their day out, if it was at all possible. Well, nothing ventured, nothing gained, so I made discreet enquiries. The Americans promised to follow it up, check on the level of our security clearance - which was high - and let us know. This they did, in the bar, later that night. Those who wished to avail themselves of the offer should be outside the hotel at some ungodly hour the following day. As it was a day whose start was bare minutes away, we had a couple more drinks to see it in, a couple more to discuss the matter - although my mind was already made up. We then retired for a couple of hours sleep.

Thoughts of what lay ahead ensured I was up and about in good time, even if I wasn't feeling exactly on top of the world. OK, an Alka Seltzer will fix me up, says I, popping one into a glass of water. Time was short, couldn't wait for it to dissolve. The hell with it, I thought, I'll drink the pieces. I could vaguely recall times when I *had* felt better.

As the astute reader will by now have gathered, drinking was more or less a prerequisite on such tours; the price to be paid, a cross to be borne as it were. And there was everyone thinking we were having a good time. But should you perchance feel sorry for me, don't. You see, the big disadvantage to waking up bright-eyed and bushy-tailed is that you immediately know that is as good as you're going to feel all day. I, on the other hand, often had something to look forward to, and on this particular day that something happened to be much more than the simple process of recovery from another hard night.

A story told me by a 99 Sqn signaller gives some idea of what we occasionally had to endure as word spread.

"Landing at Offut AFB, Nebraska, on a flight from Lyneham, via a refuelling stop at Gander, we were shown into a crew room where beer abounded. One of the Americans, obviously a Texan, wore the inevitable cowboy boots - although at present he didn't. His boots had been removed and put to a better use. They had been filled with beer, just as another Britannia crew were shown in, tired and parched.

"Ah, here come some more Brits. Boy, can they ever drink beer" said one of the Americans, offering a full boot.

One eager crew member stepped forward, took the proffered footwear and proceeded to empty it in one go. Then, wiping his lips, he says, 'Pity it wasn't a size twelve.'"

It was at times like that one felt proud to be British.

Anyway, back to Nice, and the forthcoming tour.

Aircrew apart, only myself and one other made it from our group. Just! Nothing to do with oversleeping, the time of day, or too fierce a hangover. Problem was, Capri had vanished overnight, swallowed up in a bank swirling cloud. So it was to be the weather that almost jinxed it for us - just as it had that hotel door! But it actually ended up doing us a favour. A rather large one, as it happened; much appreciated.

The trip out was scheduled to be by launch, but because of this inclement weather, and the very heavy seas brought about by that gale, travel by air became a necessity. Well, no problem as far as the Americans were concerned. If there was room we could still be included, if not, it looked likely to be the lava-encrusted offerings of Pompeii.

It took half a dozen flights all told, and we had to wait until the end, naturally. Don't know how many times I counted bodies, divided by the number of passengers per flight, checked my watch, crossed my fingers, promised God I'd be forever good, maybe even threatened to stop drinking, but it worked. A Grumman TF-1 Trader eventually carried me across the Bay of Naples, for a deck landing on the then mighty, *USS Forrestal*. Pretty small by modern standards, I understand, but it seemed huge to me - it carried ninety to one hundred aircraft, and the flight deck was over one thousand feet long! Let's face it, the largest ship I'd ever seen had carried me back from Singapore, and let me tell you now, twenty thousand tons was a lightweight by comparison to this leviathan.

Given the time allotted, the pre-flight briefing was to the point and necessarily... well, brief. Despite this, I felt a little more consideration could have been given to the choice of words selected, for, after hurriedly pointing out the escape hatches the crewman began.... 'The moment we hit the water.....'

Not the water in our case, but a deck landing didn't appear to be that much different, to a first timer. Seated down the back in that windowless fuselage we were therefore blind to the approach, but despite this there was no mistaking our arrival, for the punctuation of that flight bore all the hallmarks of a car wreck. There was a thump, quickly followed deceleration in the one-twenty to zero knots in two seconds kind of range. You see, carrier-based aircraft aren't landed so much as thrown onto the deck. A rather violent means of arrival, but one which supposedly permits a fairly accurate prediction of the touch-down point: ideally, apparently the third of four arresting wires. I believe we hooked the second. Whatever, I'd just added yet another milestone to my catalogue of aeronautical adventures.

The NATO staff officers were escorted away by the welcoming committee: lunch, political briefing and Yankee hype, followed by a whirlwind tour, one suspects. The Britannia boys - flight-crew and ourselves - having been assigned a guide of our very own, were conducted through areas of particular interest to us: lunch, below-deck hangars, tech workshops, launch control. No rush, no bull. Hype aplenty, but that was only to be expected. No booze either, not on an American flag vessel. No way.

Then came the highlight of the trip. An exclusive air show during which the carrier launched, displayed, and retrieved its complement of aircraft - well, at least thirty of them.

Guard helicopter apart, the piston-engined Skyraiders were first. Then came the jets: Phantom, Skyhawk, Skywarrior. These were followed by their "eye in the sky", the Grumman Tracker; as opposed to the Trader in which we had arrived onboard.

It was an awesome display. Even more so when they each demonstrated their available firepower: bombs; heat-seeking missiles - fired at flares; cannon - fired at the ocean. Spectacular but harmless explosions in and above an empty sea. Modern high-tech entertainment. And of course, an empty sea placed no restrictions on the speeds attained by those Phantoms, which is when high-tech became high velocity. Talk about fast and furious. It was a matter of afterburners, compression vortices, and breaking the sound barrier. God, what I would have given for a trip in one of those beasts.

The display was concluded by a thirty aircraft formation flypast - usually known as a Balbo - before they were all retrieved back on deck.

And with the NATO complement comfortably seated on deck - once it was clear of aircraft - we found ourselves sited on "Vulture's Row," halfway up the island, overlooking the whole operation. Down below, multi-coloured groups of men scuttled hither and zither about their tasks in that crowded and dangerous environment.

Ours was a spectacular viewpoint, and from it I watched with growing interest, paying particular attention to the launch procedure, excitement building as I anticipated it happening to

304

us. But unfortunately, come day's end, the sea was deemed calm enough for us to be safely transferred ashore by boat. Pity, that. I was quite looking forward to being catapulted into the sky from the end of some British-invented steam contraption, from a British-contrived angled deck. Still, certainly not "just another day at the office." This had been the stuff of which dreams were made.

After that outing, the remainder of the tour seemed rather anti-climactic. Even three days in sunny Rome failed to capture my complete attention - Trevi Fountain, Spanish Steps, Via Veneto, Coliseum; places to which all first time visitors tend to gravitate. Then there were the restaurants and bars: the pasta, pomodori and formaggio, the Barolo and the Asti Spumante. That was Rome. From there it was back over the Alps for another short stop in Paris - one of the world's really great cities - where we deposited our guests before returning to Lyneham. Anti-climatic? Not really; a gem of a tour.

This was followed by two more exercises - Cross Channel - to Toulouse, France, and Brightwater, to Shepard AFB, Texas. This saw me through to Christmas, 1962.

*

The next tour on my schedule was to be another gem. At least it sounded like it *could* have been. A Royal Tour of Nepal, with HM The Queen, and Prince Phillip. Hadn't a clue as to how I even came to be selected for this - the ultimate of all tours, I would have thought - the requirement being for DC3 (Dakota) experienced personnel. Well, I had *seen* a few in my time. Even flown in one or two. Watched one crash, too. I suppose that constitutes a certain amount of experience, albeit not quite the kind one would wish for. So maybe it was to do with mild personality, smartness of dress, amiability? No, not me then. In any event, after a return visit to RAF Innsworth, in the heart of the Gloucestershire countryside, to be kitted-out with de-luxe, tropical uniforms, plus making various other preparations, my participation in the tour was suddenly cancelled, as was Her Majesty's. Coincidence, eh? Well I hardly think HM The Queen cancelled in sympathy for my exclusion. Fact was, the whole tour was cancelled. For what reason, I don't recall hearing, for no one ever seemed to confide in me on such matters. Something diplomatic or political, I suspect. Pity, that.

Probably as a result of all this touring and rich living, it was during this period that I turned my attention to the pleasures of gourmet cooking, and fine wines; although there was no way I was about to abandon the Indians. In fact, we discovered a place in Swindon that served a real mean vindaloo. But the days when I might have walked into a restaurant and ordered an egg omelette or a red *vin rouge* were long gone.

1963. The year began with a detachment to Bahrain, where I was to spend three weeks more or less seconded to 54 Squadron and their Hunters. (This squadron were also part of 38 Group, which encompassed Transport Command.) Different indeed, for a transport type. But I quite enjoyed the experience. Pity they didn't take along a two-seat T7. Could have volunteered to go along on an air test. I would have loved that.

Two exercises to Cyprus followed the Bahrain trip, New Venture and Sunspot. (I often wondered who dreamt up the names for these exercises! Surely they didn't have a dedicated team in Command HQ, whose job this was.) Then came a Polar trainer to Thule, Greenland, returning via the North Pole, we were told. What I never thought to ask was, which North Pole, for there are three: True North, at ninety degrees North, zero degrees EW; Magnetic North, at around seventy-seven degrees north, one hundred degrees west; and Geomagnetic North, at sixty-nine degrees north, seventy-nine degrees west. I suspect Magnetic, navigation being the point of the exercise.

This was followed by a quickie to Nairobi, before being rushed up to Dishforth to retrieve a grounded Comet 2. No seats fitted, so it was a "park yourselves on the floor and hang on" type return trip.

The following month I was to be found on the VIP trail once again. A World Tour, Chief of Air Staff Designate along for the ride. Or maybe I've got that the wrong way round?

This saw us heading for Thule once more, over the North Pole to Elmendorf AFB, near Anchorage, Alaska. From here it was Hickam AFB, Honolulu; RAF Christmas Island, then across the Date Line to RNZAF Ohakea, New Zealand. Next stops were in Australia: RAAF Fairbain, Canberra; RAAF Edinburgh Field, outside Adelaide; then Darwin, en route to Singapore, where our passenger was apparently required to attend a conference or some such. From Singapore it was back to Australia: Darwin; RAAF Richmond, Sydney; back across the Tasman Sea to New Zealand for a week at the RNZAF base Whenuapai, Auckland; then Wellington. Following this came Canberra again, where, shunning RAAF Fairbain (it was a VIP flight, after all!) a week at the rather plush Rex Hotel became one continuous party. And what a party.

This was long before the Aussies and Kiwis liberalized their drinking laws. The days of the notorious "six o'clock swill", after which hour most Australian cities exuded the kind of gaiety one would hardly expect; more akin to that of a Welsh temperance society on the Sabbath. This was to confer upon us a distinct advantage. Being resident, we were able to circumvent this archaic state of affairs by the simple expedient of propping open the hotel's cocktail bar. Which, naturally, we did. The barman at the Rex, an amiable, Australian-Scot, seemed happy to have us, plus the large circle of Australian friends we suddenly accrued. Another thing in our favour was the fact that whereas pubs were men-only institutions, in hotel bars, women were made welcome also - especially by the likes of us.

What a week that turned out to be. So good, the recollections are only fleeting. A bunch of Aussies invited us to a party, then issued a challenge to drink Crew Chief, Ron King, under the table. Oh no! Ron was about six feet tall, and big with it. And boy, could he throw it back.

I recall the last of the Aussies handing Ron the front door key before sloping off to bed, asking him to please lock up as we left.

Then there was an aircrew versus ground-crew tenpin bowling challenge. For a cask of beer, what else? Honours to the ground-crew this time. Difficult for it to be otherwise, most of the aircrew appeared to be pretty well legless even before the contest began. Can't imagine how that came about!

During all this the Chief of Air Staff designate and his party were away doing whatever it was the CAS does. Probably similar to what we were doing, truth be told.

After a couple more stops in Australia - RAAF Richmond, and Darwin - it was back to Lyneham via the usual Singapore / Middle East route, after almost a month away. Tough, but someone had to do it!

So that was my introduction to Australia and New Zealand, but not the true picture. As I was to discover many years later, we had barely scratched the surface, had really seen nothing of these countries.

Trips to Cyprus, via Sardinia - with 111Sqn's Lightnings - and Bardufoss, Norway, for Exercise Barfrost II, allowed us to catch our collective breath before departing for Canada and the United States with Lord Louis Mountbatten, in his role as Chief of Defence Staff. A real privilege.

After the usual positioning flight to London Heathrow, with the night spent in a nearby hotel, it was over the pond to Gander, Toronto, Ottawa and Montreal, before crossing the border to Washington, and Andrews AFB. Next ports of call were at the US Naval bases of Norfolk, Virginia, and Jacksonville, Florida, before departing to cross the Atlantic back to LHR, thence Lyneham.

We would occasionally be required to line up in front of the aircraft at the end of a tour, to be thanked by the VIP, often to be presented with a gift on his behalf, on completion of such a tour: cufflinks, a bottle of whisky maybe, or something equally useful. (I was usually able to trade whisky for cognac. If not I could always give it to Chiefy Holt) But I do recall one Tory politician who seemed to think an autographed photo was something we might well treasure! No names, no packdrill. It was a long time ago, and believe it or not, I never once wondered what happened to that photograph. Well, you wouldn't, would you!

The Mountbatten tour was followed by an exercise to RAAF Pearce, located just north of Perth, Australia, with the Royal Ulster Rifles - Exercise New Pastures - after which we ferried 45 Commando to Southern Rhodesia, for some threatened crisis in Swaziland. Then it was back to Australia, to return with the recently dispatched RUR.

Another exercise to Niarobi followed - Sandbird - with 41 Commando, then the Cyprus crisis began and we were busily engaged in ferrying service families back to the UK. This was early 1964. Shortly after this, I was demobbed.

Varied and decidedly interesting work, compared to the regular schedules of other service personnel. Another big plus factor was that rarely were we around at Lyneham for parades and inspections.

With many departures taking place late at night, this usually meant a dawn arrival somewhere or other. Many a touchdown was therefore greeted by a warming sunrise - summer in the Arctic Circle apart, for there, at that time of year, the sun never sets.

Like seamen, whenever we MSF types got together we recalled trips, crews, countries, and, of course, girls. With more landfalls, in more cities, we probably knew more bars than did the sailors. And believe me, there are lots out there well worth remembering. Both bars and girls.

But it was the VIP trips that were always most interesting, for on those we would often spend days on the ground between sectors. Whilst our VIP passengers did their thing, we found ample of time to survey and experience the local sights. The Parthenon and ancient Greece in Athens; the Blue Mosque, Topkapi Palace, and the Golden Horn in Istanbul, along the Bosporus; brief glances of Canada and the East Coast of America, Australia, New Zealand, and like that. And never once did I feel the least bit guilty knowing the taxpayer was funding my travel, along with those expensive hotels. After all, I was a taxpayer, too.

Outstanding times. Events that would be unbelievable to people in civvy street, and to some in the service. Mike Ortega again. A crew was sent from Lyneham to RAF Scampton, Lincolnshire, to clear a problem on a Britannia that was about to depart with V Bomber ground crews and their aircraft on an overseas detachment. By the time repairs were complete, the aircraft which had brought Mike and crew to Scampton had long since departed for elsewhere, so they had no means of retuning to base. On explaining this to a Wing Commander who was travelling with the Britannia, he simply suggested they travel with them to Changi, Singapore, from where aircraft regularly departed for Lyneham. It was only a twenty thousand mile trip! But that is what they did. They then spent four days in the Changi Transit Hotel before anyone enquired as to who they were and what they were doing. From that point on it did not take long for them to be found seats on the next flight down the route to Lyneham. Once back at base a few questions were asked as to where they had been. But this was Mobile Servicing Flight, their people were away most of the time. So that was it.

Of course it couldn't last, nor did it. The 1974 Defence Review decreed that cuts be made somewhere and, with the Comets already gone, the Britannia was next in line. But by then, of course, I was history as far as the RAF were concerned. My name had featured on POR's for the last time early in 1964, and I'd long since found someone else willing to pay my way to travel around the world.

*

I even got to fly a Britannia one time. Beautiful take off, even if I say so myself. The chance to experience this was courtesy of a friend (maybe ex-friend), Tony; technician in charge of Lyneham's Britannia simulator, a magnificent piece of kit.

'Quite a time consuming job to get this lot back on line after it has been crashed on the approach,' he informed me, though possibly not quite in those words. Still, I suspect it was never intended to be flown solo. Flying controls, gear, flaps, throttles, the lot. Rather a handful for a qualified pilot, never mind your wayward instrument fitter cum frustrated fighter pilot.

That then was Lyneham. Another sackful of memories to be filed away. Well over three years worth. Probably the best years of all, up to that point. Or was that a thought generated by the fact that these happened to be the most recent. Whatever, now came decision time. To sign on and complete twenty-two years in the service, thus qualifying for a pension, or to depart for civilian life. As signing on would more or less commit me to climbing on the promotional ladder - foolish not to - something I had always been reluctant to do, I decided to sever my ties. So, doubt and anxiety partly alleviated by yet another fiendish plan, I went for it.

This resulted in many more goodbyes to convey to friends and colleagues, Comet and Britannia, part-time lovers and romantic places. It was also goodbye to the Royal Air Force itself, although their goodbye to me, after twelve years service, was a mere ninety pounds cash. Not exactly a golden handshake. There again, I could have taken a suit in lieu, but .... well, yes, exactly. Still, the Air Force had taught me a lot over the years, had afforded me more good experiences, and thus education, than any amount of cash could possibly buy. Valuable experiences. But the big advantage of leaving home was that I gained a sense of independence. I was also able to stand on my own two feet, knew I wouldn't go far wrong in not relying on others to help me out of situations I was perfectly capable of getting myself into without the help of anyone. On top of which, I had seen the world. So I thought! But the RAF had at least introduced me to that world. Anyway it was a shrinking world, militarily, a shrinking Air Force, a shrinking Empire. El Adem, Bahrain, Aden, all gone. Given a few more years and Gan would also disappear, as would Changi itself, along with Seletar, at least as far as the RAF were concerned. I decided it was also time for me to go. Move on in life.

So it was that my military service came to an end. I felt a wistful sadness in a way. Twelve years out of my life, then. Good years, too, despite the occasional hardship, real or imagined. Anyway hardships are part and parcel of life, and overall, I think luck ran with me more than the reverse. Or maybe the volunteering had worked in my favour. Was it possible I'd manoeuvred myself into positions where luck played right into my hands? Wasn't it Louis Pasteur (possibly, Dr Johnson - maybe even someone else entirely!) who suggested, *Chance favours only the prepared mind.*

Whatever, I had no regrets about those years. None at all. So, even though I was a little misty-eyed, I was now ready for a new challenge. But what kind? Of that I wasn't sure. All I knew for certain was that it had to be this way, despite thoughts that life on the outside would surely be anti-climatic when compared to life in the Royal Air Force.

For a time I felt like I was walking away from something that had given so much, following a trail that led who knew where. But when doubt caused me to stop and look back over my shoulder, the path back there seemed to have disappeared completely. Which left me with no alternative but to forge ahead, get on with the rest of my life. I didn't even contemplate how long the road ahead might be, where it may take me, or how far I would travel before I reached the end - either of the road, or my life. Out there were new experiences to be encountered, new places to be discovered, old favourites to be revisited. Australia and New Zealand had wet my appetite for more of the same, as had America, despite my first visit replaying like a scene from a bad movie. Ah, yes. I almost forgot about that.

It happened during our visit to Shepard Air Force Base, Wichita Falls, Texas. Yet another exercise - Brightwater, you may recall. This involved elements of the British and American armies, at nearby Fort Bragg. Some new type of cannon, I seem to remember. Something that was supposedly much more efficient in the art of wiping out human beings. We'd carried it out in the Britannia, along with the troops who would operate it.

We offloaded the whole caboodle at Shepard, consigning it into the capable hands of the respective military establishment, getting on with our own work, preparing the aircraft for its onward flight.

Upon completion of servicing and securing our aircraft for the night, we were invited out by the American crew who'd helped refuel our Britannia. An invitation we gladly accepted. Only natural, that, bad manners not to. They took us by car to Oklahoma city - over the Red River and across the State line - where, for a change, we visited the odd bar or two.

We'd left *The Piano Lounge,* or some such, after a bit of a scuffle, one of our hosts having been threatened by a Latin type. Apparently the girl he'd been attempting to chat up was this guy's sister, and he had taken umbrage to the fact that our host had possessed the audacity to approach her. The two of them got into it, the Latin was floored, we felt it prudent to leave.

We were now cruising round, looking for somewhere interesting, when a police car passed us at speed, red lights flashing, siren howling. Real Hollywood stuff. But there was a problem, for it suddenly chopped across our bows and screeched to a halt. So did we, little choice in the matter. We'd have come to a stop for sure if we hadn't. A very sudden, and embarrassing stop.

`Out the car!' a voice commanded. We obeyed. Let's face it, they were actually pointing guns at us, just like on TV. For what, a minor traffic violation? I was aghast.

There were two of them. Not a tall thin one and a short fat one, but they wouldn't have looked out of place if they had been.

`Keep your hands in sight, and *don't* move,' ordered one.

`Up against the car and spread those legs,' demanded the other.

They looked at one another, as did we. It was like something out of Police Academy whatever. But they still had guns. And those guns were still pointed in our direction.

`Yeah, up against the car,' agreed the first.

Had the second also reversed his opinion I think I'd have cracked up, despite the threat to life and limb. As he didn't, I decided to try the "confused-English-gentleman-abroad" trick.

`Excuse me, officer. Could you please explain what is going on?' Alec Guinness at his talented best. And it worked!

`From outa town, huh?' He seemed rather more amiable, and I thought I detected a slight hesitancy in his manner.

`From England, actually,' I replied, proudly. I gave him a smile, to show I was friendly.

`That so? Well, up against the goddamn car, limey, before I bust yur mouth.'

Ah well. It almost worked.

Never did discover the ins and outs of what it was all about, for we left early next day, after we'd checked out the inside of the Precinct House, making a statement on events as we saw them in that bar. Could only assume the Latin had a relative on the local police force. Maybe the chief, who knows.

Not a very auspicious introduction to a country. But that wasn't typical America, was it? I mean, we'd just been unfortunate. Wrong place at the wrong time, kind of thing. Right?

Well, we had, hadn't we?

*   *

Page 315: Top: Comet C2 XK261 was the only C2 I never flew in.
Bottom: The airfield at Gan, Maldive islands in the Indian Ocean. Staging post on the Far East run for the RAF, now a holiday Isle.

Page 316: Top: Relaxing, afloat in the Dead Sea.
Bottom L: Mozambique `85, back in the LH seat. Jetranger ZS-HJY. **R:** Forrestal Balbo.

Page 317: Britannia XN636 "Argo". Both the Comet and Britannia were named after heavenly bodies of the cosmological kind.

Page 318: Top: Naples, Italy. Grumman TF1Trader, flew the author out to the USS Forrestal in 1962.
Bottom: USS Forrestal - full Deck

Page 319: Top: Skyraider hooks the No.1 wire. USS Forrestal, Bay of Naples, Nov.1962.
Bottom: The mighty USS Forrestal, awaiting our arrival.

Page 320: Top: Almost like an exercise: engine failure offshore Nigeria. Help is nigh for G-AOCZ of Bristow Helicopters. I wondered if this would qualify me for membership of the Goldfish Club? (It did.) Cenre: In the dinghy. Self, facing.
Bottom: Rescue at last. We had been in the water for around three hours, now they all arrive at once.

Page 321: Top: Antonio Gordhino maintains station whilst I latch an antenna onto the hook in preparation for my balancing act one hundred & fifty feet up. Definitely against today's health and safety rules, but it got the job done.
Bottom: Ocean Master II drilling for Mobil Oil offshore Nigeria. A Hiller E2 departs for Port Harcourt.

Page 322: Graham Hill winning at Monaco 1968. Graham signed a copy of this shot for me and it hangs in my office.

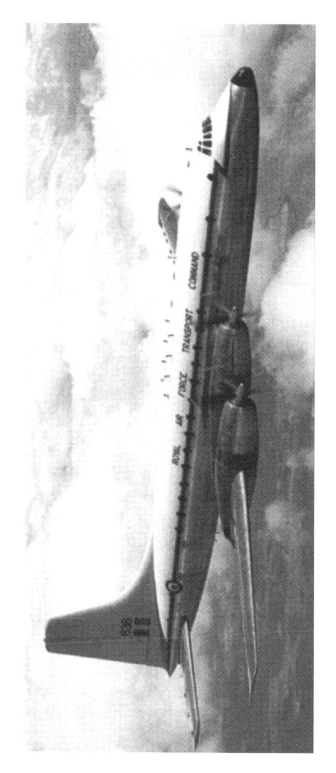

317

A RACE OF MEN

There's a race of men that don't fit in,
A race that can't stay still;
So they break the hearts of kith and kin,
And they roam the world at will.
They range the field and they rove the flood,
And they climb the mountain's crest;
Theirs is the curse of the gypsy blood,
And they don't know how to rest.

If they just went straight they might go far
They are strong and brave and true;
But they're always tired of the things that are,
And they want the strange and new.
They say: "Could I find my proper groove,
What a deep mark I would make!"
So they chop and change, and each fresh move
Is only a fresh mistake.

And each forgets, as he strips and runs
With a brilliant, fitful pace,
It's the steady, quiet, plodding ones
Who win in the lifelong race.
And each forgets that his youth has fled,
Forgets that his prime is past,
Till he stands one day, with a hope that's dead,
In the glare of the truth at last.
He's a rolling stone, and it's bred in the bone;
He's a man who won't fit in.

From a poem by **Robert Service**

Chapter Eleven
JOURNEY INTO THE FUTURE
1964

One would think a twelve year stint in HM Armed Forces, with their associated training and discipline, would be excellent preparation for release into civilian life, and on the whole this was probably true. But what to do with my new found freedom?

A large part of my service life had been spent touring the world, at the taxpayers' expense. It had been an occupation in which even flying was classed as work, whereas to someone like myself, every flight was an experience not to be missed. Let's face it, where else could one encounter such a magic sensation on a grey, dull, damp November morning than by punching a hole in the murk (or whatever it is aircraft do), to break out into clear blue skies and bright sunshine, those clouds now billowing, glaringly white when seen from above?

Take-off, and the all-encompassing dismal greyness would gradually clear until the cloud itself became thin and wispy. Unless flying unadvisedly close to the ground, this is actually one of the few times during flight that speed becomes readily apparent; those final moments of breakout, or vice versa. In next to no time the overcast would be left far below, spread out like an untidy carpet, or the cloud tops would look fresh and washed, brilliantly white, as opposed to used and dirty. Above the clouds is a special world. A world of dazzling, mountainous peaks, dream castles, chasms, and canyons, or of nothing more than a blue emptiness. Peaceful is what it can be; a sky that at times seems surreal, full of possibilities, and of mystery. It is a world to be shared only with God, the birds, and other aviators. The sun, moon, and stars are likely to be your sole companions. Then there are the sunsets and dawns. Both can be magnificent when viewed from such a superior location. Sunrise spectacularly so, especially when it occurs at the end of a long night sector, sky a kind of translucent green, high ground silhouetted against the growing light in the east.

At present these were all just memories, to be extracted from my suitcase of dreams as and when required. But that suitcase was as yet only partially full; room for many more in the years to come, I hoped.

Could have gone in for anything, I suppose. A fresh start. Police, accounting, mechanic, garbage collection, all no doubt honest enough occupations, which someone has to do. All would pay enough to live on, just about, but with little left over. So count me out. Not for me the nine to five of an office, nor a life in which left wing unions would dictate the conditions of my working life. I was too independent for that, needed something different. Apart from which I was by now fully aware of the alternatives, prepared to go and seek them out. After all, I was only 28years old.

For twelve years I had been living a kind of gypsy existence. Home was wherever I ended up. So I couldn't suddenly settle down, just like that. Besides, leaving the service had done nothing to diminish my interest in aviation, the passion was still evident, though perhaps not so strong for me to commit myself to a controlled working environment. At least, not here in England. The quest for adventure had not yet been satiated either, nowhere near. There still remained far horizons beyond which I felt the need to travel, so travel was the option I felt the need to pursue. The airlines I'd already rejected, mainly because of the union factor. I wasn't one who could be dictated to as to when I worked, and for how long, for how much. Same rules applied to the aircraft manufacturers. Anyway, I no longer felt the need to actually touch aircraft. To observe, and occasionally fly in one would probably suffice. So scratch the aviation angle.

I didn't have the means to go motor racing, which probably meant I also lacked commitment, thus I was again left with the travel. This, therefore, seemed like the best path to tread. So onward then, best foot forward, into the unknown. Besides, I wasn't exactly short of ideas, already had the inkling of yet another cunning plan.

Back in the old home town, a long-time friend and I had already discussed the possibility of emigrating to the United States. Ron had left the RAF three months prior to me, and as he held a First Mate's ticket in the Merchant Marine, he'd taken an oil industry related job in the North Sea, awaiting my demob. During this period Ron heard mention of a company in America with whom it might be possible for us to get a job. This was all the encouragement we needed; decision made. With any luck, working in America had to be better than working in England, and I figured it may just see me on my way to the kind of financial freedom I sought. Not the kind that gives one the power to trash hotel rooms, or to drive the Rolls into the swimming pool. Such behaviour I was quite willing to leave to the upcoming generations of pop stars. All I required were funds enough to ensure my future comfort.

*

First task was to contact the Ministry Of Defence; Air Ministry as it was then. For my service contract specified two years reserve on completion of my term - ie, I was still officially in Her Majesty's employment for that period. And even though I was unpaid, I did need to seek approval for permission to emigrate. As it happened, this was granted swiftly enough to make me feel almost unwanted!

So it was - less than three months after hanging up my Blues - I found myself airborne once more, winging my way across the Atlantic. Manchester Ringway to Idlewild (now Kennedy), via Prestwick, courtesy of BOAC and Boeing. Yet another new type for the logbook: the 707; and a degree of comfort previously unimaginable. Yes, I realized, I could easily tolerate a life of not working on aeroplanes, as long as I occasionally got to fly in something like this. The difference being, this time I paid my own fare. An occurrence which, up to then, was even rarer than the "Loaves and Fishes" episode, recalled from way back in my Sunday School days. Fortunately, this was one of the few and far between occasions in which it did happen. Paying my own fare, that is.

Ron and I had planned on a few relaxing days first, in New York City. It was a place with which Ron had become quite familiar during his previous maritime life, prior to RAF service. It was an area of this vast country to which I had never previously visited; city or State. But relaxation wasn't quite what we got, the way things turned out, for, as was seemingly becoming the norm, our plans ended up in tatters.

Rather than the respite we sought, there was to be another confrontation with cops. Not our fault, honest. It just so happened that the room we had rented was also being claimed by the landlady's ex-husband. They were apparently still in dispute over ownership of the property. No, change all that. Nothing *apparent* about it!

On only the second night, Ron and I, in our beds at the time, were awakened when this guy burst into the room, closely pursued by his irate better-half. Didn't seem like he was here to discuss the legal implications of our tenancy, either, for he was obviously drunk, seemingly with malice in mind. Just as well his ex-wife was present too, for she took the brunt of his ire. A shouting and slanging match ensued between him and his ex, during which I learned lots of new and interesting words. This tempestuous two-way invective was eventually to follow the protagonists back downstairs, out of the house, and on up the road, into the depths of Queens.

Half an hour later we had another caller. He seemed equally insistent on being allowed entry, so I got up to check on things, our door now locked and barred, from the inside.

This time, as he'd previously stated - 'Open up. Police.' - it was one New York's finest, fully tooled up as usual, requesting our version of events. He wasn't at all belligerent, just stood there, idly tapping one palm with his nightstick. But I knew his mate would be out there somewhere, probably lurking in the shadows, ready to lay down a hail of lead if called upon to do so. I'd seen the movies, watched TV, knew what it was all about. Didn't make a scrap of difference, even at three in the morning you don't contest such a request. Unless of course you maybe do have something to hide! We didn't. So we let him in.

All this severely disrupted our sleep, to say nothing of our visit to the Big Apple.

Two trips to the States, two confrontations with the cops. Neither of which should have involved me, both of which had. America was not coming out of this too well. What next, I wondered. Well, as there was a requirement for us to head south, down to New Orleans, with a chance to fly in Boeing's new 727 tri-jet, we decided to do so. In fact, later that same day seemed to be an ideal time; the first available flight, in fact. This decision was made easier given the fact that the company concerned had offered to pay our expenses, once we arrived in their fair city, even though they did decline on the air fare. Goodbye Times Square, hello Jackson Square.

A couple of memories come to mind of my early days in the city of New Orleans. The first was that The Beatles were due to perform somewhere close by, and I had been offered a ticket. I declined. So there went another of life's golden opportunities. (They had actually performed in York during their very early days, but as they were at the time almost unheard of, and I had never been one for pop concerts, I had declined to attend then, too. The theatre where they performed was owned by the father of a certain John Barry, who was also on the bill with his John Barry Seven. Hollywood, and fame, came many years later.) The second New Orleans memory was that of reading in the local paper of the death of Ian Fleming. Goodbye James Bond, I'd thought.

The original intent had been for me to take up residence in the United States, but the job I duly applied for, and accepted, when it was offered, was to take me - after four months in the Pacific Northwest, California and New Orleans - back across the Atlantic. Forget the immigration bit, for although a Social Security number *had* been assigned to me, and I *was* in possession of the all-important "Green Card", there was a requirement for me to remain in the States for some time yet before that card became fully effective. Not the Social Security number, mind. As that required me to pay US tax, it became effective immediately! Anyway, I still wasn't sure about the cops. Those fictional movies and TV shows were now looking decidedly less so. At this point I don't think I'd have been surprised had I come across Bugs Bunny wandering down the street!

Just as well I didn't become a citizen as it turned out. With the way things were, my service background would almost certainly have guaranteed my being drafted into the US Air Force, and a second spell in Vietnam was unlikely to replicate that first brief visit.

So began a period of intense travel. Anywhere, everywhere, anytime; all expenses paid. This, at a time when international travel was a rarity for the general population, especially in England, where even Spain was quite a number of years shy of overtaking Scarborough or Blackpool as a holiday destination. This more or less elevated my status to that of a rather elite group of people.

During the fifties and sixties, overseas travel was the sole preserve of the rich and famous, or of those whose companies were paying for them to travel! I was fortunate enough to be included in the latter group. Thus it was that my future travel cost a lot of someone else's money! Way to go.

Airline tickets were different back then, too. Apart from being an actual paper item - as opposed to today's electronic version, which you hardly ever see! - they displayed lots of useful data, and probably became collector's pieces (I have a box full, many issued by airlines that are no longer in existence). They were also of the "full fare, one class" variety. No economy, no Easyjet. Even Freddie Laker's Skytrain was still ten years in the future. The upside of this being tickets were valid for a full twelve months, and were open ended, ie, valid for a given number of air miles, rather than to a stated a destination. As such, using the same ticket, you had the option of switching flights, or airlines, at will, even part-way through a journey. Very convenient, though necessary for such as us, for at times we had no idea as to where it was we would be travelling next, or even when! The downside of course was that there was little prospect of the general public flying off on holiday, they just couldn't afford it. IATA, the airline cartel, had things nicely sewn up. At least from their point of view. (This contrasts hugely with an economy ticket today - 2015 - which is barely worth the paper it is not even written on! It affords you a seat - rarely of your choice - to a specified destination, on a specified date, and that is about it! Even on major airlines everything else can be a chargeable extra: baggage other than cabin, meals, drinks, seating preference. It seems all airlines are now budget!)

I couldn't believe my luck. I'd be in, say, South America, possibly Brazil, and I'd think, wow, here I am on the beach at Copacabana, and someone's paying me to be here. Who'd have thought it possible. Certainly not the teacher who long ago forecast that, unless I changed my ways, I was destined not to go far. That seemed an odd prognosis when sitting on a beach somewhere distant, sipping something cool. There again, I suppose I *had* changed my ways somewhat.

I made sure family and friends were kept abreast of my movements. Postcard from wherever, kind of thing: "Wish you were here", and suchlike. Pictures featuring palm tree lined golden beaches, and tropical rainforests. New Zealand was one such: "... the weather has been magnificent. Leaving tomorrow for Tahiti." And from that Pacific paradise, in which I arrived during a tropical downpour: "Yesterday I thought I'd forgotten to pack the sun, but it's out now in all its glory, so all is well. Then, from California: "Just happened to arrive in the middle of a heatwave. I hear you're having snow."

But wait. I'm jumping the gun a bit. We haven't even left America yet. Barely arrived, in fact.

*

Offshore Navigation Inc was an electronic survey company working mainly with the oil industry, mostly in the offshore environment, naturally. (Although Headquartered in New Orleans, for advantageous tax purposes the company was actually registered in Delaware, as are many American companies for the same reason.)

The job involved the positioning of seismic vessels, drillships, rigs, platforms, pipelines, whatever, with a relative degree of accuracy. Nothing that would be acceptable today, but standards, and the equipment, change. That was then. (The company did in fact secure a long term contract to conduct speed and manoeuvring trials of the US Navy's Polaris Nuclear Submarine fleet. But that was the sole domain of especially security cleared personnel. Not the likes of such as myself, a foreigner!)

Radiolocation, was the name of the game. The desired qualifications for which appeared to be an electronics background (an emphatic "yes"), plus some knowledge of navigational and survey procedures ("yes," though maybe not so emphatic). I also presumed, judging by the medical I was required to undergo, there was a requirement to be reasonably fit. Serious stuff this. There again, being the good old US of A, no doubt the charge for that medical would be equally serious. All was well though, those dollars were to be billed to the company's account.

Returning from this medical was to introduce me to another facet of American life, at least as far as the Southern States went. I flagged down a passing taxi, and it pulled up. But as I was about to climb in, I found myself being assaulted by a feisty old white woman with an umbrella. "You don't want that taxi" she screamed, whacking my arm. With which, said taxi immediately drove off, almost burning rubber in its haste to do so. It appeared that in 1964, the colour bar was still very much being forcibly enacted, especially in the Deep South. Apparently, white folk did not take a taxi driven by a black driver!

It seemed too, that in ONI's line of work it also helped if you were slightly crazy (oh, oh). Although a few months were to pass before that observation had become fully apparent. Not that I *was* crazy. That it may have helped if I *had* been, is what I'm saying. The scent of adventure was in the air. And if adventure was what I craved, it was certainly what I was about to get. Served up in man-sized chunks. The stuff that civvy street dreams were made of.

The idea was that a vessel could be positioned utilizing signals transmitted from two or three accurately located shore stations: similar to what Bomber Command achieved during the war with their Oboe (or was it H2S?). In fact the equipment we used (Shoran - SHort RAnge Navigation) *had* once been the property of the USAF - snapped up at a giveaway price by a far-sighted ex USAF senior officer - now modified and pressed into civilian use. The boats needed bodies to install, operate, and repair this equipment, as did the shore stations. Lots of people, lots of logistics, lots of problems in lots of countries.

For a start the equipment was not exactly state-of-the-art. It may well have been so in 1942, when it was used for aerial navigation and bombing - last used in this role during the Korean conflict of 1950. But this was 1964. Still, they did pay well - at least well for a Brit - and as the work was worldwide I would still manage more than the occasional flight, to many a country. Just what I wanted, wasn't it?

Well, possibly. Although the first job I went on had me wondering if I had made a wise choice.

After a very short training period in the New Orleans office - located in the beautiful Garden District - I was handed a ticket and instructed to fly up to Astoria, Oregon, wherever that might be, thought I. Upon arrival, I was to report to a certain hotel, to a certain person. OK. No problem there; this, after all, was America. Now on full expenses, I took a taxi to New Orleans International airport, Delta Airlines DC8, via Memphis, St Louis, and on to Chicago - Midway. Change flights: United Airlines DC8 to Seattle, then on to Portland, Oregon, before changing again. Bit of a comedown, this: West Coast Airlines DC3 for the final, turbulent leg through down-on-the-deck cloud and rain. Ten hours total, and there I was, in the top left-hand corner of US - Astoria, Oregon, on the Pacific Northwest Coast. It had been sunny and warm in New Orleans, here it hosed it down, almost continually. Which no doubt accounted for the lush greenery. It could also be slightly chilly.

Feeling quite pleased with progress so far, I took a taxi (although by this stage I, "grabbed a cab") and we splashed our way to the designated hotel - the John Jacob Astor - where I registered, and dumped my bags. I next checked with reception as to the precise location of the person I sought. 'You'll find him in the office,' was the reply. So I took myself off in the direction indicated, right there on the premises would you believe. The "office" was where I'd been told I'd find the area supervisor; apparently a well-known character around these here parts, as they say around these here parts.

Discovery number one: this "office" went under the name of The Fur Trader. (And why not? German born John Jacob Astor, after whom the hotel was named - as was the town, come to that - had developed a virtual monopoly on the fur trade back in the eighteen hundreds.) Discovery number two: the person whom I suspected to be my contact appeared to be well advanced in the act of trading - dollar bills, for booze. He had a glass in his hand even as I walked in, but from the look of things he was just topping up the beers he'd already had.

And just why did I suspect him to be my contact?

Had to be, didn't he? He was the only person in the place other than the barman, who was, nevertheless, being kept fairly busy.

The interior decor matched the name: log-cabin type walls and bar, beamed ceiling, real furs hanging around, minus their original occupants, of course. Above and behind the bar were pinned US currency notes of various denomination, each bearing someone's name. Emergency funds, I assumed. What a quaint idea.

The place was air-conditioned; cool and comfortable-looking. Rather inviting, one might say, so I wandered over to where my leader-to-be propped up the bar. His features matched the name I'd been given, for he had that Latin look about him: slicked-back dark hair, matching pencil-thin moustache, devious-looking eyes, aquiline nose.

'Excuse me. Are you Jose Shattles?' I sincerely hoped he was, for he looked like someone you needed on your side rather than against you.

Must have been the politeness that got him, for he spun round so fast he almost fell off his stool. But he recovered quickly enough, as a good supervisor should.

'Yeah. And you're?'

'Dave Taylor. Just hired on with ONI.'

'Hey, don't bug me with your problems, Dave. Pull up a stool and have a drink.' He reached out and slid a bottle across to me.

It was beginning to sound all too familiar. So, in order that the interests of world peace, international friendship and understanding should prevail, I sacrificed myself once again, even going so far as to drink from the bottle neck; something I wouldn't normally do. Big mistake. In this job, it seemed, to be caught without a glass close to hand was tantamount to being unqualified. I felt trapped, unable to make my escape. Good excuse, eh?

By the time midnight arrived there were five of us; not including midnight, which was the time. (Had it related to a person it would have been twenty-three fifty-nine, you may recall. Chapter Two. Remember?) The whole bunch of us were either employees of ONI, or about to become so, all in more or less the same shape. Well, maybe not Jose. He'd had a head start, after all. There again he was supposed to be our leader.

Jose didn't merely drink, he threw it back like he'd heard they were going to re-introduce prohibition real soon. Like maybe tomorrow. It showed; he picked up the tab. (Notice how quickly I was picking up the language.)

When we eventually departed we left midnight way behind, but like I said, time wasn't with us. Anyway, we only made it as far as the nearest pizza parlour, to which Jose insisted on driving us. (This was America remember, almost 24hour service, even out in the sticks.) He wasn't in too bad a shape, really. He could drive, even if he could barely stand. Couldn't change gear, either. Never got out of first, although he refused to give up trying, much to the detriment of the gearbox by the sound of things.

Jose also bought dinner - or was it breakfast? - no doubt on his expense account, along with those drinks. I didn't care, I was famished, hadn't eaten for ages. I had drunk rather a lot, but that wasn't quite the same; very little protein.

Then, almost as a prelude to the new day, Jose finally managed to get us thrown out. Luckily, after we had eaten. Actually, what really happened was that we were asked to leave, which, in a place such as Shakeys, more or less amounted to the being thrown out. Seems Jose had been getting rather vociferous over the Goldwater vs Johnson for President issue. Don't even remember who it was he supported, but it doesn't really matter does it. He stood on the table, addressing all who cared to listen, along with those who didn't! Ah well, I'd been thrown out of worse places. And at least they hadn't called the cops. Couldn't have stood that. Could barely stand as it was. Needless to say, Jose was not yet finished, he found us another bar. Or maybe that was as far as the vehicle was prepared to take us, for it ground to an ignominious halt, right outside the place. Convenient, eh?

Naturally, at the time I was still under the influence of twelve years RAF discipline, morality and brainwashing. Which is to say, any expenses incurred should be absolutely justifiable, otherwise the Air Ministry were liable to get... well, not just upset, they went straight for the jugular. In this industry, I soon learned, "tampering" with the expense account was a battle of wits. Could prove quite lucrative, provided you came up with a scam which would not stretch credibility beyond very elastic bounds. Why do you think oil costs what it does!

*

The moment I awoke next morning - out at sea, on a boat - was when I started to have second thoughts about what I might have let myself in for with this Offshore Navigation outfit.

No, I told myself, surely the second thoughts began yesterday? When I first set eyes on Jose.

Yes, of course. But things haven't improved, have they? At which point I gave up on the internal discussion. In fact, enthusiasm for my new job didn't just dive, it crashed straight through zero, well into the negative sector.

A boat? I couldn't even remember how I'd got there, didn't know what I was supposed to be doing there. OK, I suppose inclusion of the word "Offshore" as part of the company title should have provided me with a teeny weeny clue!

Anyway, here I was. And I wasn't at all well.

I figured we were at sea already. I also figured it had to be a big sea out there. So it was. The Pacific Ocean to be precise, they don't come any bigger. But when I say "big," I really meant in terms of wave height. To someone like myself, a self-confessed landlubber, it felt like they were enormous. Gigantic, even. Easy to deduce from the way the room was moving around me. Only the room was now a cabin; another deduction - and as such, not bad for a man in my state of health, even if decidedly less than helpful in terms of practical assistance.

I got up to have a look. Should have stayed where I was. The boat - very small in these seas - pitched and rolled alarmingly as it rode tumultuous, storm-whipped, white-capped waves. It rose and plunged, crashed and shuddered over the peaks from one trough to the next. It sounded very much like it was about revert to its component parts at any moment. Anything not secured was on the move. I couldn't have cared less, even though my stomach certainly wasn't secure.

It was to be two days before I again ventured out of my bunk, not that anyone seemed unduly worried. Apparently it was far too rough for us to attempt to start work anyway. And so it remained, for most of the time I was on board.

All I seemed to be learning were new ways in which to throw up, along with a new language: topside, below, and other nautical-type terms, some of which were familiar, from my days on the flying boats. The bow was still the pointy end, stern, the

335

rear. And those little round windows weren't, they were ports. The head was something new though, and this was the place I was most frequently to be found. Whenever I was upright.

It was two weeks before I saw dry land again - possibly the longest two weeks of my life. I couldn't wait to step ashore. And guess what? Jose was there to greet us. Well, not exactly greet. His mind was filled with other thoughts.

Evidently my brief spell seated in front of the equipment - less than an hour - constituted something of an apprenticeship. It had taken eighteen months to reach a similar status in the RAF. I'd seen Shoran in operation, had a brief go myself, was now apparently fully qualified, albeit a little inexperienced. No matter, Jose was ready to offer me another assignment, along with a drink, of course. Despite the fact recollection of those two weeks started to recede into the background the moment I set foot on *terra firma,* there wasn't the slightest chance of me accepting either. And Jose, much to his credit, was intuitive enough to spot that. Which is when he started putting on the pressure. This, I recognised and understood.

It was a pleasant day out there on the dock; hot sun, blue sky swept clear of clouds, insects buzzing around. A beautiful, nay, magnificent, part of the country to be in on such a day: mountains, trees, crystal waters. And not just any old mountains and trees, this was the Olympia National Park.

We stood and talked as the minutes passed us by, and, as if there were a statute of limitations on bad memories, I slowly began to see things in a different light. Well, I was rather thirsty, and the sun was way over the yardarm, so I yielded a degree or two. I accepted his renewed offer of a drink, agreed to discuss things further, in more familiar surroundings.

He next offered a rather substantial pay-raise, which I turned down. Reluctantly, I'll admit, bad memories now fading significantly. Besides, where else could I go, what could I do? I had thought of trying for a job with Boeing, just down the road, so to speak, in Seattle. But that had been when things were at their worst, out there on that boat. I now realized I had no idea how to go about such a move, had no contacts. Anyway, Jose had by now attracted my interest. I decided to see how far he was prepared to go.

He bought another round, offered an even more substantial hike in salary. The bad memories were definitely dimming, hardly any recollection at all now, plus I figured ONI must be desperate for personnel. (They were. For, unbeknown to me, Jose had just had two guys quit on him, and he'd had to fire a third. No choice there, the guy in question having phoned the company president, in New Orleans, at three o' clock in the morning. He'd then proceeded to tell said president that he thought Jose to be quite useless, and that he should be promoted to replace him. Not a good idea even at three in the afternoon. There again, he probably hadn't been drunk enough at three in the afternoon.)

It was about this time I accepted a third drink, then suffered an attack of the second thoughts. Well, let's face it, oldest excuse in the world: it seemed like a good idea at the time. Especially as I wasn't to be at sea. Nor did it require the services of a chartered accountant to discern that this was a very reasonable offer. But it was the attraction of a land job that really decided me. I was to operate a navigation site high up in the hills of this beautiful Olympia National Park.

'Just yourself and one other guy, a camper-van, and a trailer, acre upon acre of green trees, snow on the high ground, the blue sky up above,' Jose assured me, sounding more like a travel agent. Although, as I was later to discover, one minor point seemed to have slipped his mind. He'd made no mention of the fact that there were bears out there, too! Well, I'd faced the dual threats of snakes and tigers during my spell in the jungles of Malaya, and as with those, the bears never seemed to bother us either, so we tried not to bother them. The Pacific Ocean was also out there. Somewhere. Way beyond my field of view. As far as I was concerned it could stay that way. It was going to be all right. I was happy again.

Had Jose known, he could have got me for a lot less. My needs were few, and I wasn't even contemplating a donation to Oxfam. A bit devious perhaps, but what the hell. (Actually, thinking about it now, well after the event, it strikes me as being a lot devious. But, as I was to find, Jose wasn't exactly being straightforward, either. This was a high turnover industry, and in the early days, when jobs were plentiful, people switched around as the mood took them.)

It's possible sterling was a little below par at the time, but what I was to be paid was a fortune compared to what I could expect to earn back home. Even Arthur Scargill's lads weren't raking it in anything like on this scale. (In fact, joining ONI was a significant turning point in my life, for after receiving my first paycheck - as it was known in the US - I was never again to be without cash in my pocket, or in the bank. I even tended to feel naked if I inadvertently left my wallet behind. From that point on I never had a need to borrow cash, even to buy my first house. From then on, I lived by the doctrine that if I couldn't pay for it I couldn't have it.)

I only recall one small problem we encountered when operating from that specific, pre-surveyed point on that Washington mountain top. Well, not us in particular, the operator on the boat in actual fact. Seems he experienced some difficulty with his navigation the day my colleague drove the truck - inside of which was located the active transmitter - off that pre-surveyed point and down the hill to the local supermarket. The boat crew reported the fact that they felt our signal was not too reliable, the transmitted position apparently somewhat unstable! Oops!

*

Overall, I quite got to like the job, despite the fact it was male dominated. But my world had been that way ever since leaving school and joining the Air Force. Even prior to that, really, for the last school I attended had been boys only.

It wasn't that I could do without women in my life, no way. I needed them, but I also needed my independence. Too-close friends had always seemed to let me down in one way or another, at one time or another. I'd never found that to be the case with friends separated by distance. Maybe that's why I was a bit of a loner. Anyway, some of the female friends I met weren't exactly of the long term type. Take for instance the pretty young thing I met up with in a New Orleans bar.

After the basic introductions, she enquired, in her own

338

inimitable way, as to, 'Where y'all from?'

I glanced round, found myself to be alone, despite her use of the plural.

'York,' I told her. Even though I still lived in Norton, with my parents, I always told them York, especially overseas. After all, I doubt even Malton would admit to the presence of Norton. So York is what I told her. 'Know where that is?' I asked.

'Sure do,' she replied. 'Up north, ain't it?' You see, although a majority of Americans are friendly and knowledgeable - about America, American events and history - at times, it seems the rest of the world may well not exist.

'In a way. Up north and across the Atlantic. The United Kingdom,' I corrected.'

That stumped her, though she wasn't about to admit defeat, even if a reply did require the application of serious thought. I could almost see her mind in action. Maybe if I'd said England, or even Great Britain, the result might have been different. But I hadn't, so it wasn't.

'Well I'll tell y'all one thing,' she eventually said. 'Fer a foreigner yuh sure speak good English.'

OK, so she'd skimped on her geography in this instance. Anyway, it wasn't her mind I was interested in, and as far as biology went she hadn't missed out on a thing.

That was something else I needed to get used to: American English. For instance, the slogan "Nothing sucks like Electrolux" I once saw attached to a British made vacuum cleaner, would be unlikely to endear the product to a public whose understanding of the word "sucks", is for any item so described to be of extremely poor quality. Or, as Gerald Rattner was later to put it - in what eventually turned out to be the closing down speech of his jewellery empire - "crap."

I picked it up eventually. Soon learned it was impolite to ask a girl if she required "knocking up" in the morning. At least until we were on more intimate terms.

After a month or so in the forests of Washington State - as opposed to Washington DC (for District of Columbia), the nation's capital, two thousand three hundred miles away on the east coast - I found myself en-route to Long Beach, California, the company's West Coast office. Here I discovered I was scheduled to pick up another camper-van, drive it the better part of two thousand miles, to New Orleans, Louisiana - La, in postal terminology (hence the acronym, NOLA) - after first picking up a co-driver at the International airport in Los

Angeles. Another employee, back from another assignment in another place.

'No problem, Dave,' Al (Leffler), the supervisor for this particular area, told me, immediately issuing forth with a stream of directions on how to reach the airport by road, which, to my mind, sounded extremely complicated. I, meantime, was busy dreaming up some excuse as to why I would be unable to fulfil the role of driver.

'I'd much rather fly,' I told him.

'Me too, replied Al - whom I knew flew gliders for fun on a weekend. In fact, much more than that, I was later to discover. He was to become one of America's foremost soaring pilots - 'But we have all this equipment to be transferred back to NOLA, and two people heading that way. And when you arrive there is the chance of using that equipment on a job in Florida.'

So it was that Al won the day. Of course he did. Thankfully without the need of recourse to the nearest bar. Which is how I came to end up behind the wheel of an overloaded camper-van, which steered exactly like one would expect an overloaded camper-van *to* steer. That is to say, with all the finesse of a drunken hippopotamus.

It was rush hour on a Friday evening, I'd never before driven a left-hand drive vehicle on the right-hand side of the road, yet this was precisely what was required of me. Not only that, I was heading for the notorious Los Angeles freeway system, with little idea of where I was going, or what I was about to do. The very arguments I'd been dreaming up to present to Al as reasons as to why I should fly. But I'd discounted the fact that, this early in life, occasionally my mind literally soaked up information, and retained it. Mostly, it appeared, irrelevant, seemingly useless trivia. (Using up brain cells which could probably have been put to good use in later life?) But I now found a lot of the recent input was suddenly becoming very relevant indeed.

A bend in the road ahead, traffic lights. "Take a left there," I remembered. Or possibly, "hang a left". Same difference, I assumed, so I hung a left, remembering to head for the right-hand side of the central reservation on the dual carriageway. More lights, more bends, other significant points. "Right at MacDonalds, follow the signs, take the up ramp". And before I knew it, there I was, on the freeway, heading in the right direction. Not one false turn to my credit. The right stuff, or what?

This was California all right. The sun shone, Peter, Paul and Mary were "Blowin' in the Wind" on the radio, life felt good. As if to confirm the fact, a message board loomed large over the centre of the freeway. An electronic sign which, with an obvious lack of anything important on which to offer advice, proudly announced: THE WEATHER'S GREAT TO BIKE OR SKATE. It was, too. A sky swept clear of clouds, a cooling breeze, that pleasant sun.

All it required now was to continue on this course and follow the signs to the airport, which I did. But, not sure which lane out of five I was supposed to be in, I picked the centre one. It seemed as good a choice as any, for here the traffic appeared to be maintaining the kind of pace I favoured - not particularly slow, for they also posted *minimum* speed limits on this side of the Atlantic.

I sat there for what seemed like a long time, getting the feel of things, taming the hippopotamus, becoming complacent maybe. Traffic flashed past on both sides in those pre-restriction, pre-OPEC days; above and below also at the multi-layered junctions.

A juggernaut semi-trailer thundered by on my right, towering above me, cars swept past on the left. Camper-vans on the left too, much bigger and more luxurious than mine, flashing past nevertheless. It was like being trapped betwixt and between the Trucker's Grand Prix and the Los Angeles 500. Then something else flashed past on my right, a brief glimpse only: Los Angeles International; the airport turnoff. Sod it! I'd seen it far too late to attempt taking a chance on slotting myself into the gap one truck had so carelessly left between itself and the one in front. Could have made it easily had I been ready. There would have been at least a foot to spare. Nothing to do now but take the next turnoff, so I carefully prepared myself. I indicated a right turn and waited for someone to let me in. And I waited. Just as well the next turnoff was a few miles ahead, it took that long to switch lanes. Or possibly I wasn't yet aggressive enough in my tactics. But I was learning rapidly, out of necessity. Which, if you think about it, sounds like the bloodline of a racehorse.

A gap appeared. Closing fast, but still room. Preparing to tuck myself in close behind another semi-trailer, I edged over cautiously, until a demented blast on a horn forced an immediate rethink. The guy coming up alongside, ignoring my indicator, glared at me, held up his middle finger. An indication, I assumed, that I was still a mile from the next turnoff. There again, from the look on his face, maybe not.

Definitely not, it was here already. So, throwing caution to the wind, I slipped in behind him and quickly took the down-ramp. I then followed the freeway signs and rejoined, literally. So much for the navigation! I'd done a three-sixty instead of a one-eighty. I was in the same race, heading in the same direction. Sod it, again. Though I didn't exactly think along the lines of "sod it", you understand.

It took awhile, but I eventually made it off, and back on again, heading in the correct direction this time. Now it was simply a matter of finding that airport exit. Probably by now ten miles back.

Not only did I find the exit, and the airport - couldn't really miss that - I also found my way in, *and* somewhere to park. I also met up with the person I'd come to meet, at the place I'd been told we'd meet. So I was feeling pretty pleased about all that, until he revealed his plan of attack.

'Need to call at the house first, pick up a few things. It's downtown,' Bill Gleeson told me, handing me a piece of paper on which was scrawled an address. Just like Al, he reeled off a detailed list of directions on how to go about getting there.

'Fine,' I replied, once he'd finished. 'Lets go.' I handed him the keys. 'You drive, I'll navigate. It's what I do for a living.'

Which is how I came to be, well, not really a tourist, but a kind of working tourist. The main difference being that I saw a lot that the tourists never did. Although I did miss out on one place.

'How about a night in Vegas?' Bill suggested.

We'd been to "his place," sorted out his things, and were now underway east, well clear of Los Angeles. Bill was driving, I had the navigation in hand, so I made a quick geographical assessment from the map I held.

'Las Vegas is a hundred and sixty miles off course. Across the desert and into Nevada,' I told him, my tone slightly downbeat. Las Vegas to me meant such as Frank Sinatra, and Sammy Davis Jr, my favourites. I'd have given a lot to listen and see either of them in action.

'I know where it is,' Bill replied. 'And the diversion is zilch in terms of American distances.'

I was almost swayed, but hadn't really been with the company long enough to realise how much you could get away with. 'If we do, can we still make New Orleans by Monday?'

'Hell, no,' he replied. 'Even without Vegas we'll have to drive overnight to reach NOLA by Monday.'

'So it's a choice of Vegas, or that job in Florida?'

'Yeah, but don't forget, Al said Florida was only a possibility.'

'Which would you prefer, Bill, Las Vegas, or the chance of Florida?'

'Florida, I guess,' he replied.'

'Me too,' I said, making the decision for us. Sinatra would save for a more convenient time.

We agreed on driving through the night. We drove through the next day, too, until the heat of the Arizona desert got the better of us.

Lonely billboards at random intervals along the roadside petitioned us to eat this, drink that, drive Ford, or fly Pan Am. They also counselled us to buy, save, invest, spend, or visit. So we did, calling in at the next motel we saw. We had a couple of beers and a meal, then slept through the heat of the afternoon before setting off once more, in the relative cool of the evening.

Somewhere, far away, lightning flashed on and off, giving the impression that some unheard about war was being staged over the horizon.

*

Australia apart, America is one of the few countries that has stretches of highway so long and straight you can't actually see the end, it just runs on into an ever-receding vanishing-point. A bend becomes something of an event, for you actually have to exert yourself to turn the wheel. But if in the meantime you've fallen asleep, it doesn't really matter, it's so flat you just bounce around a little more, waking up in time steer back onto the blacktop. It counts as your excitement for the day.

Zip! There it was, gone. Bar, diner, filling station, house or two, motel. What used to be known as a one-horse town, though maybe one-dog town would be nearer the truth, for, according to author Bill Bryson - and, being American, he should know - there's almost always a dog, sitting there scratching, or maybe sleeping and dreaming, though he probably doesn't feature in the bullet-holed sign I noticed as we approached: Hickville, or some such: Pop 72. I wondered if they renewed the sign every time there was a birth or death. The question didn't occupy my mind for long, as it all flashed past in the blink of an eye. Now we could settle down to some

343

serious snoozing, for in this barren landscape those signs of habitation happened only rarely.

On and on we drove, Saturday and through Sunday. Sunlight, ferocious in its intensity, blazed down from an azure sky, therefore it was hot and tiring. We sweated and baked, stopped for a drink frequently, non-alcoholic, that is.

Sage bush flats stretched away seemingly to infinity, presenting us with a countryside that was to all appearances featureless, although through the haze, far away in the distance, mountains were vaguely discernable; probably the McDowell range, or the White Tank or Superstition Mountains, according to the guidebook I'd picked up. This state was also home to the Grand Canyon and the OK Corral, but neither were within our radius of operation. We did pass by places advertising "Genuine Indian artifacts." Navajo, Hopi, or even Apache, for these were their lands, and in all likelihood, past battlegrounds. There seemed little to have been worth fighting over, apart from mesquite and cacti.

We drove on. Following Route 10 we passed through Phoenix, Tucson, to cross the Rio Grande at El Paso. Then along came Austin, Houston, and finally - seventeen hundred miles and two days later - New Orleans. We were back in Louisiana, it was late Sunday night, maybe early Monday morning. Both too late and too early to do other than find a motel, and catch up on some sleep.

Checking in at the office later that day, feeling rather proud of what we had achieved, we discovered that, while we'd been achieving it, Florida had been cancelled. The job that is, not the State. Should have taken that detour to Vegas, maybe caught Sinatra and pals.

'Hi Bill. How y'all doing? Good to see you back, Dave.' was how we were greeted by Ray Landry. Ray was Operations Manager in New Orleans, the guy responsible for despatching us hither and thither about the globe. I'd get to know Ray quite well over the years, and a phone call from him would usually end up with myself reciting what became known as the four W's down the phone lines: 'What? Where? When? What the hell!'

'A bit knackered, Ray, but ready for Florida,' Bill replied.

'Florida? Is that what Al promised? Aw, hell Bill, that went down the tubes long ago. Got something else though. Probably suit you, Dave.'

Something I'd come to realize in the short time I'd been employed by ONI, was that, although the pace of life could at

344

times be described as slow, it was certainly never boring. Couldn't see anyone suffering a coronary. Cirrhosis, maybe, but that was for the future. The camaraderie was visible almost all the time, although we were, I suspect, generally lonely and depressed people. And, since alcohol is a known and accepted antidote for these conditions, we partook regularly, frequently, copiously, and often! At least I assume those were the reasons we did so. Sometimes it went on all day, other times we got down to some serious drinking. And as I was to discover over the years, there were also days when we'd get up for lunch, lay down again until late afternoon, then we'd get up and go to bed! We did though, on the whole, usually retain some kind of decorum, in that we rarely started before ten a.m. That's not to say we were never to be *found* with a drink in hand before such a time. But on the odd occasion this did happen, it was likely to be the finale of the previous day's piss-up rather than the prelude to the current day's. And for this I was being paid, quite handsomely in fact, in comparison to UK salaries of the time. So there and then I made the decision to stick with it for a couple of years. See more of the world, gather together a bit of a nest egg, then make a switch to something else. Get a *real* job. A *real* life.

It never worked out that way though. Of course not. Should have realized by then how true was that old maxim: Few plans survive being put into action.

*   *

NEW ORLEANS & OTHER STORIES
1978

*T*he headphones clamped to my ears crackled into life; '814 is clear to take-off,' the controller in the tower at New Orleans' Lakefront Airport advised.

Terry - another ONI employee - looked across at me and frowned. I frowned back, looked down and behind, for that's where the tower was located. Behind, and a thousand feet below Cessna Skyhawk N75814, the aircraft in which we were seated.

Terry keyed his microphone button. 'Lakefront tower. 814 is already airborne, passing through one thousand,' he answered, nonchalantly.

A pregnant pause, then came the reply. '814, Lakefront. Roger.' That was all. What more could he add, he'd cleared us for take-off not five minutes ago, as his records would show if he cared to look! Didn't exactly fill me with confidence, that, a controller not necessarily in control. So for the rest of the flight I kept an extra sharp lookout, listened intently to the radio traffic, just to be sure we knew who was where, and who else was around, even if that controller didn't appear to be too sure.

Terry Aylor and I were becoming slightly bored with New Orleans, the world capital of jazz, but not that bloody bored! Terry was much younger than myself - which may make me sound old, but I was still only 42 - he'd been with the company less time, too, but he was bit of a whiz-kid on the new systems: Transit satellite, Loran C, Argo, all of which were starting to replace Shoran.

This city was still home to our head office - though long since relocated from the Garden District, out to a specially commissioned new building in the suburb of Harahan, with the International airport close by. We were in town for a few days, between jobs, so to speak. Terry, who possessed the relevant private pilot's licence had suggested chartering an aircraft from the local flying club for a couple of hours. I didn't need a second invitation. It's that easy in the States, just like hiring a car. All you need is a licence, and a means of paying. Although, naturally, you are first taken on a check ride. Take-off, climb to altitude, stall recovery, land, upon which Terry had been handed the keys - in exchange for a signed, open-value credit card slip.

We flew around for an hour or so, viewing sights from the air that we'd seen many times from the ground: Canal Street - widest street in America, and the setting for the annual Mardi Gras parade; the Superdome indoor stadium, its simulated football field surfaced with that great American invention, Astroturf. Only here, in typical American fashion, it was called Mardi Grass. Then came the waterfront; a bend in the mighty Mississippi, complete with paddle-steamers. Up the road was the French Quarter - bars, restaurants, jazz, and fine old buildings, with their filigreed balconies. It all looked a little different from the air, naturally, for it was different, especially Bourbon Street; up here you were unlikely to get mugged. May get mislaid by air traffic control, although that was another matter entirely!

We broke minimum altitude regulations, zoomed down over Lake Ponchatrain, to beat up the company vessel, which was out training newly hired navigators (a big advancement on the days when I joined and was as good as press ganged, then left to find my own way around, up there off Oregon, and Washington State).

Later that same day, after returning our aircraft to its owners, we decided to visit the local racetrack. No horses to attract us though for an annual event was being staged; the New Orleans Jazz and Heritage Fair. It was summer and the conditions were near perfect: clear blue skies, a blazing sun, Cajun cooking (Cajuns are descendants of the French-speaking Arcadians, deported to Louisiana in 1755), and a raging thirst. Which brings to mind the local roller coaster, just down the road, in Ponchatrain Park. They called it, The Ragin' Cajun, and it was a cracker: old wooden trestle kind of thing. No Red Arrows type loops and rolls, but it did give a longer, far better ride than it's most of its modern counterparts of the time. (These days there are some really serious rides to be had, especially in such as the theme parks in Texas and Florida.)

Back at the racetrack grounds were limitless amounts of Gumbo, burgers, prawns, and ice-cold beer, along with sizeable crowds. Oh, and there was jazz aplenty.

As we stood there taking things in, including the ice cold beer I clutched in my hand, I spotted a likely subject for a photographic study: battered straw Stetson worn low on a head which featured a fine aquiline nose, gaunt, featured face, stubbled chin, long, straggly hair, glazed-looking eyes. Very glazed-looking, in fact. Suspiciously so. Best to check first, thought I, allocating the task to Terry whilst I prepared the settings. After all, this was America. Wouldn't do for the guy to take offence and pull a gun on me. No, much better that Terry ask. Anyway, he spoke the language.

'No problem,' he reported, upon his return, though he didn't really seem sure. 'Stoned out of his tree,' he told me. 'Thought I was bumming a toke, gave me a whole joint. Fancy smoking it?'

'Why not?' I replied. 'Try anything once, me. Incest and lion-taming apart.'

'Ah! You've probably heard the one about the trainee lion-tamer then?' Terry asked.

'Go on, I'll buy it.'

'Young lad. Asked what he should do if the lion approached him. "Look him in the eye and back up slowly towards the gate," the instructor says. "Always maintain a safe distance between yourself and the animal."

"And if he keeps coming?"

"Don't panic. Keep backing up, but never take your eyes off him."

"Say I'm up against the bars. What then?"

"In that case, just grab a handful of crap and throw it in his face, that'll stop him."

"What if there's no crap available?"

"Don't worry, lad, by then there will be," Terry finished. He then lit up, took a long drag, then passed the joint across for me to do likewise.

It was as well I'd taken my photographs first.

Maybe it was the alcohol we'd consumed, maybe the weather. Or could it be that we weren't used to smoking this stuff? There was also the possibility of it being "good shit", as they say. *Santa Marta Gold*, from Colombia, or *Punto Rojo*? Maybe even the legendary *Panama Red*? I'd heard tell by connoisseurs that these were the tops.

That was when it happened!

After a drag or two I found myself studiously trying to ignore Terry, and he me, it appeared, for we looked in separate directions as if by rote. A couple of seconds and I was unable to avoid a sideways peek out of the corner of my eyes. It was as if telepathy were at work, for my eyes met Terry's, doing the same to me, and that was it.

Humans start to laugh for all sorts of reasons at all sorts of times in all sorts of moods, and I had no idea of the reason on this occasion, but that was the moment Terry and I cracked up. Laughter became endemic if we so much as glanced at one another. And it was genuine. We giggled, spluttered, broke into uncontrollable, almost hysterical, laughter. It must have continued for a full ten minutes, and the only possible way to control it was not to look at each other, which proved nigh on impossible. The slightest pretext and off we went. I'd regain control temporarily before sneaking another glance at Terry and, as if programmed, there he was, doing the same to me. Off we went again. It brought tears to our eyes. We were airborne once more. Back up there in the clouds, no aircraft required, no flight plan to file, no clearance needed. It hit us that quickly. Talk about spaced out. Which leads to a graffiti I saw later that day: yellow spray-paint on a dark wall. "Why drink and drive when you can smoke and fly?"

We eventually found ourselves watching a frisbee throwing contest, concentrating as best we could, until the effects finally wore off enough so we were back amongst the sane. 'Those dogs weren't really throwing the frisbees, were they?' I asked Terry, later on. 'Please tell me they weren't.'

*

Early morning is not the best time to visit the French Quarter, all you're likely to see then are hungover tourists on the way home after a wild night on the town. In the mornings is when the authorities collect the garbage and hose down the streets. Every day. They need to! The bars and jazz clubs on Bourbon Street are shut tight, as is Preservation Hall, round the corner at 726 St Peter. Even the eponymous Jackson Square is as quiet as the statue of the horse-back mounted General after whom it is named. Well, almost that quiet. There was a rumour doing the rounds which had Jackson Square as being one place ONI recruited their personnel. It was said they hauled the drunks out of the gutter and signed them on! Not true of course. We weren't quite that bad. OK, maybe some of the guys looked and acted as if they could well have been recruited from such a location. Some probably had, on occasion, lain in a gutter or two, Jackson Square included. But they'd need to have sobered up before being considered as employees. As for Terry and I, one reefer was it, and that by default. Anyway, to some of the company's recruits, being signed on in Jackson Square would be seen as child's play. Like the guy I was later to meet in Singapore, where he now resided. An American who seemed rather reluctant to return to the States. One day I asked him about it.

'Can't,' he told me. 'Not since Uncle Sam and I had a little disagreement over the validity of the Vietnam conflict.'

'So? What happened?'

'I left the army, rather hurriedly.'

'They kicked you out?'

'Not exactly. Let's just say the impetus for departure didn't come from the army's side.'

Anyway, forget Jackson Square. The early morning place to be in New Orleans, if you have a valid reason for being anywhere but in bed, is the French Market, north of the river - still the Mississippi. Here they serve strong chicory coffee and fresh beignets - pronounced baan-yaa - a type of French doughnut, sprinkled with sugar. (Would be French wouldn't they, with a name like that?) Delicious all the same. A little later and you can breakfast at Brennans - 417 Royale - providing you meet the requirements.

Although breakfast is not usually considered to be a memorable occasion, there have, for me, been one or two exceptions over the years. Brennans was just such an occasion.

Located in the French Quarter, this restaurant is more tradition than anything. It's the place at which plantation owners of old would take breakfast. Which is where tradition comes in, requiring one to dress for the occasion - jacket and tie essential. It is also advisable to make reservations, well in advance.

My turn came one November morning in 1976, along with Catherine, my first wife. A champagne cocktail to kick things off. Eggs Hollandaise, with a Piesporter Riesling to wash them down, strawberries to follow. You also need lots of time. Ron Hewson - a New Zealand friend with whom we were staying - and myself, along with our respective wives, found need to take the rest of the day off. At the time Ron just happened to be Deputy Operations manager for ONI, so no problem there.

Providing you haven't breakfasted at Brennans - in which case you won't require any - The Court of the Two Sisters is as good a place as any to take lunch. Here you can sit out beneath a shady canopy of flowering Mimosa, surrounded by banana trees, have meal and a drink, relax to Dixieland and the warming sun.

*

In New Orleans the real musicians come out at night. The aforementioned Preservation Hall is a good place to start, if you must be in the French Quarter. Not much of a hall, just a very small room. Dingy, crowded, sit-on-the-floor kind of place. Ideal atmosphere for the old, and maybe not so famous, to jam it up. Good music though. But for real jazz, leave the French Quarter to the tourists. Find someone who really knows the neighbourhood and head for the outlying areas. If jazz is not so much your thing, then try Pat O'Brian's, also in the Quarter, for a lively night out. That's a fun place to be, if you can find room to squeeze yourself in. Or you can sit outside in the garden, the area warmed by large gas heaters in the cool of the evening.

New Orleans in a nutshell? Not really. For that, as the cliché-mongers would have it, barely scratches the surface.

I recall my first visit there, when joining the company in 1964. ONI were then located in the up market, aptly named Garden District, off St Charles, with its streetcars; one of which really was named *Desire*.

The tree-shaded avenues of the Garden District may have been a desirable area in which to reside, but the company were soon to outgrow their modest premises in this non-industrial area of the city.

But in '64 there was a Hungarian working with us, Paul, I believe - or whatever was the equivalent in Hungarian. He'd been lucky enough to escape from Budapest during the '56 uprising, made it safely as far as America. Then he'd gone and joined ONI! Even after eight years he was finding it difficult to adjust to life outside the Soviet Block. I discovered this when a group of us went out to lunch, Paul amongst them.

As usual, but especially so given as there was a Presidential election pending, talk eventually embraced politics. But, not used to the idea of people running down the government, Paul would lean close to me when he talked, conspiratorial like. And he'd forever be looking round, as if half expecting the door to burst open, and people with guns to come charging in. Well, being America, I suppose that was always a possibility, though if they did, they sure as hell wouldn't be the secret police.

*   *

Chapter Twelve
I'M GOING WHERE?

1964

*F*our months of North American hospitality and I was on the move again, this time to a country of which I had never previously heard. Yes, I had heard brief mention of a Dr Albert Schweitzer, and of a place called Lambaréné, but not the country in which they were both located. Never mind heard of, I wasn't even aware of the existence of a country called Gabon.

'What or where is that?' It was the first question I posed when informed that was to be my destination.

"An ex French colony on the West Coast of Africa," so Ray Landry informed me. "South from Nigeria, second on the left."

So, shortly after entering America as an intending immigrant - a whirlwind tour of New York, the West Coast, and the Southern States - I found myself in Africa, fighting the elements, up to my knees in mud and slime of the *Estuaire du Gabon*, outside the capital, Libreville.

Apart from very brief forays to Kenya and Rhodesia with the RAF, during which we saw little outside of an airport, this was to be my introduction to the real Africa, a Continent I was to become very familiar with over the next seven years.

Different? Compared to my air force days, certainly, for mainly this was post colonial Africa, a Continent in decline. But the flying hours were sure piling up, especially as a lot of these flights were in piston-engined aircraft: DC3, DC4, DC6B, DC7C. Douglas, it appeared, almost had a monopoly, particularly on the Africa run. With such types plying the routes, flights, it could be said, were conducted at a somewhat leisurely pace, for by necessity stage lengths would be relatively short. Five hours was about average, but with four eighteen-cylinder Wright Cyclones, or Pratt and Whitney radials continually pounding the eardrums, it was enough. We also used a lot of ad hoc charters, especially around Africa, and they were something else again. Real seat of the pants stuff, this.

'What about weight and balance?' I recall asking one helicopter pilot.

"Oh, just throw it aboard. If we can get off the ground, OK, if we can't we'll have to off-load something." That kind of thing.

After United Airlines had jetted me to New York, via

Atlanta, it was across the Atlantic by a 707 of British Overseas Airways Corporation. (In their advertising of the time the airline used the jingle, It's Quicker by BOAC, which, these being the dark days of vindictive unions and instant strikes, almost inevitably became corrupted to, It's Quicker by BOAT).

During our west to east progress we crossed paths with a sun that soon set behind us, creating darkness out there. It was a molten blackness that, although sprinkled with stars, remained deep and mysterious. A thick night through which the aircraft bored a steady passage, heading for its rendezvous with the runways of Heathrow.

Paris came next - a British European Airways Vanguard - and a five day all expenses paid layover, awaiting a visa and work permit for Gabon? This, we eventually discovered, could readily be obtained in two days, were one prepared to bow and scrape to some third world civil servant, or speak French. Both reasonable requests, considering the situation. But we can't all be perfect can we? Not all the time. Got to know Paris quite well over the years.

But from there on it was all downhill, starting with a DC6B of Air Afrique, ending up with me wading in the mud of that Gabonese river. And just what was I doing? Exactly what I was being paid to do, set up a navigation beacon on an almost inaccessible survey point.

This was a different Africa entirely, far removed from the places, usually capital cities, to which I'd previously made brief visits during my service career. I could well have been on a different continent. Different planet, even, for here there was an overwhelming atmosphere of things falling apart: dilapidated streets, crumbling buildings. Then there were the kids - citizens of these embryonic nations - hair matted and dust coated, as is everything. Flies crawling over snotty noses. Shirts torn and dirty, buttons missing. Shorts, equally dirty. But they were alive. Always a bonus, that. Laugh and the kids would join in. Not necessarily knowing what they were laughing at didn't matter at all, they just wanted to be part of the merriment. They were happy with their lot, didn't know of anything else. It was the way of the majority here in Africa.

Buildings were ramshackle, do-it-yourself affairs, formed out of wood, flattened biscuit tins and forty-four gallon drums. Their red corrugated-iron sheet roofs were rusted through in places, paint long since a forgotten memory. All pervading was the fetid heat, high humidity, and the mouldy, damp smell of disuse. Decay and corruption were widespread.

Unspoilt, they called it in the guide books. I would have said un-cared for, were I being polite. Even decrepit. Certainly not tourist Africa. This was the real thing, warts and all. More real even than the Africa of Hemingway and Conrad, which tended to have been slightly brushed and polished.

The first hotel I stayed at slotted right in to that decrepit category, for it looked as if it should have fallen down years ago. Willie, one of my travelling companions summed it up rather well. 'Jesus, what a dump! Wouldn't be surprised to find Livingstone was the last person to check in here.'

I had to agree. But it seems I hadn't taken into account the evening when I stood out on the balcony, drink in hand, at peace with the world. Now, darkness cloaking the seediness, it seemed quiet and tranquil. A time to reflect. Sun, having completed its arc across the heavens, was now well into its descent. Exotic reds, oranges, and pinks coloured the sky.

Then the frogs started up.

Things are a little different outside the cities. The further into the countryside you penetrate, the less imposing the conditions. This is the real face of Africa. Breeze-block walls and tin roofs give way to mud, timber, and thatch. Concrete floors regress to hard-packed earth. But the people don't appear to be unhappy with their lot; they fend for themselves, just as they've always done.

So, Africa was proving itself to be quite a change from the forests and mountains of Washington State. But, as I was about to discover, America had been a holiday. This was to be the true beginning of my life as a doodlebugger.

A what, do I hear? Well, let me explain. Doodlebug, given its American definition: any device, scientific or otherwise, used to determine the possible presence of underground minerals. Hence doodlebugging. The loose definition of which refers to the search for oil. It's also the common name for the larval stage of a certain species of the ant lion, a somewhat predacious bug, I gather. All true, I swear. I was passing a dictionary one day and took the trouble to look it up.

After Gabon, I doodlebugged all over the continent. All over the globe in fact. And should your thoughts immediately turn to travel, adventure, excitement, think again. Such experiences did feature, of course, but not all of the time. Nowhere near. Each and every job was different. Each a new event. Different country, new dramas, different grounds for laughter, or tears. Varied, and occasionally rather unconventional means of transport. Helicopter; light plane of one kind or another, wheels, skis, or floats; boat; four-wheel drive; mule; dug-out canoe; piggy-back, or on foot.

In Africa, many of the "Mammy" wagons - a sort of local bus - and fishing boats, are gaily painted, names and/or proclamations for the busses, eyes for the boats - same as in many places in the Third World, so they can see where they are going. When I say fishing boats, I refer to the up to thirty foot long canoes which are manned by up to a dozen people, powered by a lone outboard, and often to be found, unexpected, many miles offshore.

The busses in particular carry gaudy coloured fairground-type lettering along the sides, or on the front. One I recall in Nigeria, proclaimed, God is Coming, above the windscreen, whilst on the rear, God is still coming. Very religious, most Africans. In God we Trust, often featured, or God is in Charge. OK, just as long as someone is!

Whatever form my transport took, it dropped me - along with that which I deemed necessary for a stay of a month or more, plus the equipment I was to operate - somewhere way out in the back of beyond, usually miles from anywhere. Was going to say "civilization," but that word would have been genuinely superfluous. This, after all, was an Africa emerging from beneath the cloak of colonialism.

There were times (quite a few, as a matter of fact) when I wondered just what the hell I was doing in a place like this; wherever *this* currently happened to be. But that was early on, before I learned to accept any situation for what it was, ignored the things that didn't directly affect me.

The site could be high up a mountain, or on the seashore. It could be in the Arctic, or the tropics. Mainland, or some remote island. Wherever. But once there, I was on my own, needed to be self-sufficient, able to take care of myself, which, of course, included cooking. I soon learned how to knock up a meal out of whatever was available: a handful of rice and beans, to a tin of corned beef - luxury, that. Talking of which, a bottle or two of cognac never went amiss, either. Not that I was still in the process of evaluating the stuff, I'd long since given it the thumbs up.

OK, so the cooking was basic, but let's face it, the rudiments of the gourmet chef would have been slightly misplaced out in the bush. Even so, there was always a choice.

You know; Spam and beans, beans and Spam! It was often a case of eating whatever came to hand, no matter what state your hands might be in, or the hands that may offer you that unknown something.

"Ugh! I couldn't do that, I wouldn't." I've heard these words many a time. Said with conviction, too. Usually by a person in a state of post-prandial euphoria. Well let me tell you here and now, with absolute certainty, you would if you had to.

"But that's unhealthy," they'd say. To which I have a stock answer. 'Well, yes, I suppose it could be. There again, so could dying of starvation. Not only unhealthy, bloody stupid!' Anyway, as I think I mentioned earlier, your immune system is there to protect you. Use it or lose it. Which, in today's mollycoddled society, seems to be exactly what is happening!

Four months in Gabon and I was off again. Recently independent Nigeria this time, for a short spell. Barely long enough to form an opinion, really. Regardless of which, I made one: was favourably impressed. Which only goes to show how horrendously wrong a fleeting impression can be!

The Port Harcourt Club must surely take most of blame for that, a gastronomic oasis in the midst of a culinary desert. Jacket and tie were requirements in the airconditioned restaurant, trousers and long-sleeved shirt recommended elsewhere after dark. In theory, membership was open to all. In practice, few Nigerians could afford the annual fees, and those that could took out membership purely for reasons of prestige. They rarely used the facilities: multiple bars, golf course, swimming pool, rugby club, movies, or purely for plain socializing. To all intents it was still really an expatriates-only club, the bars of which proved to be extremely popular. The perfect place to unwind after the trials and tribulations of yet another day in perdition.

At the other end of the social scale came the Bradford Arms, a pub run by a fiery Yorkshire-woman. Its reputation was such that it became commonly referred to as the Broken Arms. There was also the Kingsway department store. A home from home in which expats could meet up for morning coffee, or afternoon tea.

But this was pre-Biafra, pre-coup Nigeria. Post de-colonization the country was still in a reasonably stable state. Once that first coup was successfully enacted, things were to change dramatically. But that is for later.

*

356

On the morning of March 3rd 1965, Burutu, on Nigeria's Forcados river, was its usual, laid-back, unexciting self: hot and sticky, despite a cooling breeze. In fact it was so laid back it was soporific. Talk about quiet. Open a bottle of wine with any amount of enthusiasm they'd think the revolution had started.

There was little on this river island apart from offices, the workers' accommodation, warehouse facilities, and a dock. Oh, there was also a club. Meaning, a bar - of course there was. The whole complex was owned by the United Africa Corporation - part of mighty Unilever - as were the surrounding plantations, sizeable acreage given over to the growing of a particular type of palm, from the fruit of which is extracted an oil used in the production of soap, as well as for cooking. Downstream, a few miles offshore from Nigeria's River Delta State, a slightly more valuable type of oil was being extracted from beneath the seabed.

Out on the grassed area cleared for it sat a Hiller 12E4, three passenger helicopter. It was awaiting its complement of three before flying out to Gulf Oil's Rig 49, located out to sea off the river mouth. The pilot - a practical joker of the old school - having completed his pre-flight, was already on board when the passengers arrived, though few would have guessed as much. Dressed in sixties hippy regimentals - light anorak, jeans, sweatshirt - he sat in the rear, reading a week-old *Telegraph.* Out here, week-old news from back home was about as good as it got. Or bad, depending on what was in the news.

Even as his passengers arrived he carried on reading, making a show of checking the time now and again, feigning impatience.

'Where the hell's the pilot?' he asked of no one in particular, sometime later. Then, 'Oh, well, if he's not coming I'll have a go. Get in. Can't be much to flying one of these things.'

The passengers' nervousness showed as he clambered rather inelegantly into the front seat and prepared to fire up. But, amazingly, like overwrought sheep, they did as he suggested, no thought spared as to how four people could have occupied the three rear seats. They even showed some reluctance to believe him once he revealed he really was the pilot. I believed, because I knew him. And by the time he had fired up the engine, lifted the collective and angled the stick forward, dipping the nose, machine curtsying before moving off, they believed him, too. They plainly didn't approve, but they believed. Or made out they did. Pity one of those other passengers happened to be a high echelon executive from Gulf Oil, lacking a sense of humour to boot! They shortly had a new pilot.

Two months and twenty-three adventurous helicopter hours later I was on the move again. This time, after a brief stopover in Rome, to our Middle East area office, in Khorramshahr, Northern Iran. As the saying goes, you can't win them all!

At the time, Iran was *the* hot-spot of the Gulf, as far as exploration went, but it wasn't to be long before the office moved on, to Beirut. A much better option in those long-forgotten days before that city's architecture was seriously restructured; the changes wrought by civil war. Any war, come to that.

The Lebanon of 1965 - Beirut, the capital, in particular - was a far different place back then. It was considered to be the Riviera of the Middle East. On the waterfront perched the five star St. George's Hotel, Ferrari, Rolls Royce, and other luxury cars parked willy-nilly along its frontage, whilst bikini-clad lovelies decorated the pool area. Exotic bars and clubs were strewn along fashionable Rue Hamra, the city itself being the financial centre for this part of the world. And, up in the hills beyond was the Casino Liban - its show a match for anything Las Vegas had to offer, so I was informed. Having missed out on Vegas I couldn't say for sure, but here I didn't miss out.

Later, once trouble began brewing in earnest, our office moved once again, relocating to much more fashionable, and stable, Geneva, where it remained for years. Well, the European manager, Fred Muller, was Swiss, even if he did reside over the border in France, where he found personal taxes to be of a more favourable nature!

So, back to Khorramshahr. Even Iran was relatively peaceful back then. Far more peaceful than anywhere in the Middle East is ever likely to be these days. Unbelievably so, especially when clear of the towns and cities. Although there were still certain negative elements to be overcome.

My assigned station was two days distant. We travelled by Jeep that first day, over unmade roads and tracks, to sleep under the stars on the flat roof of my guide's house. It was like stepping back into the pages of the Bible. Next day was spent on the back of a donkey (or ass), uphill mostly, to fetch up at the base of an almost vertical track. Too steep even for an ass.

It was hot, the climb slow and long, and by the time it was completed I was ready to quit. Probably would have had I thought it possible to retrace my steps. But despite being young and fit, there was no way I could have made it. Apart from which, the guy I was here to relieve was already up and running! That didn't fill me with a sense of well being about this site. Nor did the fact that the station was off the air, when it was supposed to have been operational. And he'd been in such a rush to depart, he even left two bottles of whisky behind. The remnants of what had been two cases!

My first task was to fire up the radio and check with the vessel on the current situation. Sure enough, they required the station to be on air, so, in a matter of minutes it was. I was quite surprised when the operator told me he was receiving signals at over 90 miles distant; an abnormal situation brought about by the station's height above sea level and the extremely clear, dry air, combining to create ideal conditions for the propagation of radio waves. We were in business. I found this to be a fairly regular situation in the Middle East, whereas in most of Africa, with sites usually at sea level, the air often moist, we had trouble exceeding a 35 mile range.

Along with personal belongings and supplies, I had brought two new tents, the originals being in shreds. I wondered about this, until the following morning, when all became clear. The wind up here blew almost continuously, yesterday being an off day. There were plenty of rocks around to hold down the spare aluminium mast sections to which the tents were secured, but these rocks were jagged and sharp, the tie-down ropes lasting almost no time at all. But before *my* tents were completely destroyed I'd had my helpers build a kind of drystone wall behind which to shelter. Something to afford me some respite from the wind. If there's a problem, solve it.

I recall many a night spent thousands of feet up in the mountains on my lonely outpost, ostensibly alone, but for the stars and peaks - although my second tent - what was left of it - housed two Iranian helpers.

Back then we rarely worked after dark, so no generator to run, which meant no lights, apart from a hissing lantern - and at this height, no bugs to attract. After my evening meal I'd kill the lantern, lay on my back in silence and stare into space. Not unseeing, just not sure of what I *was* seeing. And believe me there is plenty *to* see up there where the atmosphere was so thin, pure and crystal clear. Canopus, maybe, Polaris, Pegasus,

Cepheus, or whatever was in view in my particular sector of the night sky. Stars, twinkling and glistening far above, completely disguising the fact that most were actually dusty, waterless, lifeless planets. Dull and uninteresting to the majority here on earth. But not to me, for they shone with an unusual, extravagant brightness. It was as though each had been individually washed and polished, then, like precious stones, replaced on their backcloth of black velvet. Blue-white diamonds which twinkled and wheeled about in the heavens. So many stars their residual light lit the ground without aid from the moon. Starlight. And if man ever feels the need to determine the true measure of his size and importance in the way of things, he should do as I did: lay back and concentrate on that black void. And remember, it goes on for ever and ever. Certainly further than the mind can comprehend. I felt as if I was completely alone. Just myself, a few billion stars, and the blackness in which they were set. The deep, mysterious blackness of that infinite expanse of space. Impossible to believe ours is the only planet that was inhabited.

As I lay there, watching constellations swim slowly through the cosmos, it made me realize just how small, insignificant, and vulnerable we humans are.

There was movement in the firmament, too: shooting stars, comets, and the flashing strobes of unseen, unheard aircraft. I didn't need to see or hear to be able to deduce what they were: Jets, because of the flight level at which they were operating; civil, because of their direction and the steady course they held; DC8's, 707's, maybe the odd Convair 880 of Swissair, because those were the only civil jets plying the routes at the time. At lower altitudes were the Viscounts of Iran Air, the sound of their engines clearly discernable. What were also obvious were the man made stars; the satellites which drifted across. Easy to spot, those. They wheeled past a mere two hundred miles above where I lay. Whether travelling West to East, or Pole to Pole, they orbited the globe at regular intervals, every ninety minutes or so. You could almost set your watch by them. All these things happened up there, all this I saw, even though most of those stars were light-years distant. This just meant I was seeing them as they were, light-years ago! Come to think of it, perhaps some of them were no longer there! Think about that.

Up on my mountain I was as about as far from civilization as it was possible to get in that day and age, but I didn't miss it. For limited periods, that is. After all, this *was* supposed to be the Swinging Sixties. Didn't miss things as they were away from here, is what I'm saying. Didn't miss the cities, the crowds, the traffic; especially the fumes they created; Teheran in particular, where the traffic was chaotic. Two lanes at a red, traffic light quickly became four or five, even the pavement brought into use as drivers fought to be first away. No, this was perfect. Myself, two Iranians and a dozen chickens. At least, I started with a dozen.

I'd had this wild idea of a fresh egg supply, no doubt subconsciously linked to my father's post-war effort. Well, here on my Iranian mountain-top, the results were definitely similar; few omelettes, lots of chicken curry. Seems they never learn, these chickens. There again, there was not a lot for them to eat up there.

One morning I awoke to peace and quiet. After two continuous weeks the wind had ceased. I could have been in Heaven. So when the radio asked if I wanted to come down for a break, I foolishly replied in the negative. My thinking was that if I stayed for a month, it was possible I'd never need to return. Next morning the wind was back, never eased off again until the day I left!

At least when I did get down, after a month on that mountain top, I was offered, and took, a week in Beirut as my reward.

Despite the climate - hot and dry - the welcome change of environment, the excitement of seeing somewhere new - to me, that is, for the place itself is older than the bible - the Middle East didn't at all suit me for some reason. Just a few short visits to the area in the early seventies were enough for me to establish an intense dislike of the region, and its people. I quickly developed an urge to return to Africa, that continent already exerting its seemingly inexorable grip on me - as it was proclaimed to do by long time African West Coast expatriate residents, known as "Coasties." So that was where I ended up next. And it was to be along the West African coastline that - brief excursions to Europe apart - I was to roam forever. Well, on and off for the next seven years. It's just that, at times, it seemed like forever.

*

Up to this point I'd felt myself lucky, found it difficult to accept the fact that someone was actually prepared to pay me to travel the world, even though it wasn't quite like working for the

"Holiday" programme on BBC. I'd visit all kinds of exotic places, yes, eventually. But in between there were others, and all foreign lands are not necessarily exotic. This day and age (2015) I wouldn't venture near most of them, no matter what someone was prepared to pay. But that is probably more of an age related, comfortable in my own house kind of thing.

From Angola, north and west to Morocco and the Canary Islands, we searched for traces of those elusive hydrocarbon deposits known as oil and gas. At least we did the exploration and collected the data. The geophysicists and engineers did the evaluating. Not always with the degree of efficiency demanded of them either.

A field engineer is highly qualified; probably carrying degrees in such as mathematics as well as engineering. He needs to, for his job is to ensure that everything fits; jacket legs into underwater piles, flange to flange on underwater pipelines etc. No easy task. He measures up, applies his sines, cosines, takes account of water depth, tides, and whatever other magic it takes to arrive at the correct answer, giving us surveyors a final position on which to base our magic. Occasionally, they do get it wrong, although not in their opinion.

We were installing a 12 inch riser: the vertical pipe which runs down from the platform to connect with the pipeline on the seabed. It had taken the best part of a week to construct, then came the moment of truth. After a day of juggling with cranes, tugger winches, guide lines and physical labour, this 170 foot monster was finally manoeuvred over the side of the barge and eased into position alongside the platform. Down below, a diver was already in position, awaiting the arrival, ready to report when the base touched down on the seabed. But he never got to report, for the top had already disappeared beneath the surface before touchdown occurred.

`Seems you got your measurements wrong,' suggests client rep to field engineer (though probably in more forceful, colourful terms as far as language went).

`Measurements were spot on,' insists field engineer. `Problem is, there's just too much water.'

But the oil was there all right, richness of deposit seemingly in inverse proportion to the amicability of the country involved. Yes, Africa was to prove a different style of life altogether. Very little of that Iranian solitude to be found in Africa, Nigeria in particular. Should you so much as even think of stopping to enjoy a little peace and solitude, forget it. The moment you do, there will be fifty Nigerians around before you know it. And that's a conservative estimate! They metamorphose as if from nowhere the minute you think you're alone, then they will hang around like a consortium of voyeurs. And no matter what your business, they'll stay to watch!

Outside my single-storey, army surplus tent, hissed my Coleman lantern. Inside, and it would bring with it the heat, and its plethora of whirling bugs and moths. We also used Coleman stoves, designed specifically to use white gas. As this was unavailable almost anywhere outside the USA, we took to using regular gasoline instead. Nowhere near as efficient for cooking purposes, but very effective at burning down your tent if you got it wrong. Not a brilliant idea, that. Could be days before a replacement arrived.

It was relatively peaceful, and I was happy enough. The job wasn't difficult, strenuous only occasionally. But not for nothing did they pay well. I was away from home for long periods, cut off from life some of the time, often in places I would rather not be. Still, when thought about, lots of people out there in the big wide world weren't having it so good either. They were fighting to catch up with one another, breathing exhaust fumes as they did so. They were being injured, mugged, robbed, raped, and murdered. No, life wasn't too bad when viewed in perspective.

So, in the evening I'd sit outside, reading. Here I'd remain until the insects arrived in squadron strength. Then it was out with the light, and into bed. I'd lay beneath my mosquito net, dialling in the world on my personal, shortwave radio. It was my first action in the morning, too. I'd reach out for my radio and tune in to the BBC World Service, just to check the world was still there. Essential if you wish to keep abreast of things. Not just the rest of the world, current location also. The Beeb always seemed to be first to know.

I was working on the island of Fernando Po (Now known as Equatorial Guinea, or Bioko.) - a place of which most people have probably never heard mention - off the coast of West Africa, tucked into the corner between Nigeria and Cameroon. It is an extinct volcano, reaching up over nine thousand feet. But such is the air quality around that area, the peak is visible no more than two or three days a year from the Nigerian coast, usually just after a heavy rainstorm has washed the air.

The move there from Nigeria had been enforced upon us by the Biafran situation. I'd left my car behind, all my household possessions, escaped with my briefcase, some clothes, and my life. Not so bad then. But even when based on the island, at no time during my four months there did I see the peak of that mountain.

At the time of my sojourn, Fernando Po was a Spanish colony, and we'd receive company cheques from the States; operational expenses which, naturally, we cashed locally. We're talking here of cheques to the value of dollars by the thousand, one of which I was about to cash the morning I heard on the Beeb that Spain had devalued the Peseta. As a result, on arrival at the Bank I requested to see the manager, the only person available who spoke English. I asked him by how much the currency had been devalued, and you know what, he hadn't heard a thing about it. He had to check with head office, in Madrid. I found that absolutely amazing. Not a quick phone-call or fax, either. It was two days before he received a reply. As a result I received considerably more Peseta's in my account than did the company in theirs. Good to keep abreast of events, then.

One day - Nigeria, of course, for most bad experiences seemed to happen in Nigeria - I reached out from my bed and touched.... not the radio, but water! That jerked me awake in a hurry, for it suddenly seemed possible the world *was* no longer there. It was, but quite a way inland from where I now reposed, for I discovered my bed to be an island. During the night the tide had risen to unprecedented levels, flooding my camp to a depth of twelve inches or so. Things floated and bobbed around, including my radio. Electronics were submerged, lunch swam past even as I lay there. A problem, then? Well, if it wasn't, "problem" was a concept without meaning!

Luckily, the things remaining untouched, above water level, were the most important. At least to me they were: bed, generator, transceiver. I could at least call for help.

'Help!' I called. Well, let's face it, hardly a Mayday situation.

'What do you need?' asked Bill, back at base, once I'd passed on my report.

OK. This was no time for an exercise in logic. 'A boat or a pair of waders would be a good start,' I suggested.

'I mean, to make the station operational?' came the reply. Had his priorities, Bill. I could be drowning, needed to get things up and running before I took my last breath. In the event we merely raised the camp, set it atop an oil-drum and plank base. Nowhere near as comfortable as that time the river forced us upstairs in the Griffin, twenty years before.

I was later to discover I'd also contracted malaria, had to be airlifted out, after wading to dry land. A fortuitous piece of luck, really, for the water level never did go down. My malaria soon cleared, but, thankfully, before I was well enough to return, the site was finally abandoned, camp re-surveyed and moved inland. Or should I say, ashore?

Now, had I not known better, this would have been a time when I'd have thought Bill had it in for me, for I was sent elsewhere, further up the coast. Only to be held hostage, against payment to the local chief for use of a piece of land in which no one had previously shown one iota of interest. A maze of mangrove-swamped channels: more water, more mud, more mosquitoes.

Everything was supposed to have been prearranged, albeit minus the hostage-taking bit. Someone had negotiated an agreement, money had changed hands. Trouble was, there now seemed to be more than one claimant for this worthless piece of real estate. We'd apparently paid the wrong chief, or hadn't paid the right one enough. Now they had a pawn with which to bargain, and let's face it, if they were requesting my worth, it must have been rather a lot, mustn't it? I mean, had it been a couple of quid or so I'd have given it to them myself, then claimed it back on expenses. Or was I overvaluing myself?

Seemed maybe I was, reading the note I was handed: "Until you pay, you will not be allowed to live." The last word I took to be a spelling mistake. Hoped I was right. Sure, this was still pre Biafra - Kalashnikov not yet freely available to all and sundry - but they did possess wicked-looking machetes. One of which looked suspiciously like the one I'd recently "lost!"

We only required the use of this site for a few hours, and luckily a full moon allowed me to set everything up at night, when all but myself were asleep. Convenient, that. Though not necessarily from my point of view. I called the vessel, explained my predicament. Big mistake, telling them I was operational. They went to work. I waited; only now realizing the powers that be were unlikely to treat the threat as serious so long as the job was going ahead. But in those days we were young and impetuous; company orientated, I suppose. Meanwhile, the natives were getting restless. I may have been miserable, yet I had so much more than they did. And, providing I escaped in one piece, I also had the option of quitting. They were stuck with what they had, which, in their minds, also seemed to include what I had! So, in retrospect, maybe I was a bit hard on them when they attempted - often successfully - to steal anything they could carry off. I even hired guards from within the local community, but not only did the disappearances not stop, the guards themselves either stole, or directed operations. But that appeared to be the least of my problems. I was still waiting at noon. The boat, long since finished, had already left the area, and still no word on the arrival of the seventh cavalry. Good old Bill, company man to the last: as long as the job got done it seemed I was expendable.

I waited all day, finally receiving word that a helicopter would arrive the following morning, to bring money in, take me out. That evening, I was summoned to a meeting with the chief, asked to explain the situation, for want of a better term.

Lighting was courtesy of Coleman. A lantern which looked suspiciously familiar, though nowhere near as bright as when it had been mine, the glow now orange rather than white. Inferior kerosene and mantles, I presumed. Or maybe there wasn't enough pressure. It threw eerie, flickering shadows across the walls of the small room. Not very welcoming at all. The air was still and fetid; odour colonial rather than eau de Cologne. The smell was of packed earth and wood-smoke, and of unwashed bodies; their concern for personal hygiene being rather less obsessive than my own. Also, the roaches were back. Much smaller than the Singapore version, but just as proliferate. I didn't dare stamp on the little sods; it would probably up the cost of my release if I did.

Despite the locals now having been paid, the stealing continued, even as we were loading the helicopter. I made sure the electronics went on the first lift. No problems there, they were of little use to the villagers, but were our bread and butter. Tent and camping gear was a different matter altogether. I had the tent down and folded, ready to go; and go it did. Last I saw of it was as it vanished into the bush. It looked like a leaf being borne off by a bunch of giant ants. In fact things were disappearing so fast I had visions of the old Hiller 12E4 being next.

Not so. I wasn't about to take that chance. Old or not it was my only means of escape from this place. On its next approach I signalled my intentions to the pilot as I guided him in, leapt aboard as soon as he touched down, and away we went, leaving everything else behind. Nothing that couldn't easily be replaced. One more site we wouldn't be using again. So who were the real losers?

Thinking about it later, I realized how fortunate I had been to have a pilot who was quick on the uptake, shall we say. I recall one occasion when the locals grabbed hold of the skids as the helicopter took-off. They literally pulled it out of the sky. And as they had all grabbed the same side, the aircraft rolled over, crashed, and caught fire, with fatal results.

We had a Bell 47 touch-down on one of our stations, and as it did so, out of the bush swarmed a bunch of locals, ignoring the fences and signs we had been advised to erect. The inevitable happened, of course; one walked into the tail rotor. A glancing blow, but it was enough to wreck the helicopter's tail-boom. The guy lost one arm, one ear, one eye, and half a leg, and the ducks on site had a field day, gobbling up pieces of flesh. Naturally, the helicopter company ended up paying for the rest of that guy's worthless life. An arm and a leg, it could be said.

Mobil had one of their Nigerian trainee 'executives' try to walk though the propeller of their Twin Otter, whilst the engine was running! Instant Chum, chum.

It seemed then, there were to be nightmares as well as dreams, for we all experienced minor problems on our stations from time to time.

I was sunning myself on the beach one day, and, as became natural, had an ear tuned in to the high-speed radio, via which I would occasionally converse with my compatriots, and vice versa. It also issued instructions or relayed requests, but it helped break the monotony. This day, our tame Geordie, Bob, a dozen or so miles up the coast, was talking to Steve, the operator out on the boat. At least Steve was calling Bob, the conversation casual, to start with.

'Gamba, Geo Three. How are things in paradise, Bob?'

'I'm surviving,' Bob replied. 'But there's a cloud of dust just appeared out in the bush. Hang on while I climb the mast and have a look.' (The antennas on each station sat atop an aluminium mast, up to one hundred feet tall, depending on station height above sea level. Lightweight, so climbing them was officially banned, but we all did in times of need.)

With that, the radio went quiet for a time. I dosed briefly.

'You still there, Steve?' Bob called, a few minutes later. Not exactly orthodox radio procedure, but this was Africa.

'Gamba, Geo Three. Roger, Bob. What is it?'

'Bloody great herd of elephants. On the rampage by the looks of things.'

'Copy, Bob. Heading your way are they?'

'Tell you what, Steve. You lose my signal in the next half hour, don't bother calling. I'll be gone.'

The double click of a microphone button signalled that Steve had received the message.

Then there was the time in Spanish Sahara (now Western Sahara, the town names having also changed) when the Foreign Legion took me in for questioning. Not as a potential recruit either (although they did have me worried for a while). My fault, really. In the desert outside the town of Villa Cisneros was this Beau Geste-type fort, which I decided to film. Seems they didn't take too kindly to that, especially when I stuck my lens through the open gates. They demanded my film cartridge (Super 8mm), which, naturally, I gave them. Didn't fancy ten years involuntary service with that mob! Just hoped they didn't have the means of replaying the movie before I left the country, for - the minute I noticed their interest in me, and with sleight-of-hand of which Tommy Cooper would have been proud - I managed to switch cartridges, gave them an unexposed version. Small price to pay for my future freedom. I even thought about asking for a receipt, bu decided not to push my luck too far. Instead I quickly headed back up the coast to the capital, El Aaiun, and my Arabian-style hotel there, which brings to mind yet another story. This hotel, too, had the look of a fort, with pinkish exterior walls. The rooms were styled *a la* 1001 nights: tasselled wall hangings; silks, and cushions. There were arched doorways, low coffee tables fashioned from wood and brass, brass and ivory inlaid furnishings, whilst perfumes of the *Arabian Nights* drifted over intricately tiled floors.

I found conditions to be quite different when I reached what was to be my base of operations for this job, back in Villa Cisneros. Here I found myself staying in a catholic mission, there being no hotel in the town. No restaurants, either, but there *was* a good bar, and they also served snacks. Not one person in town spoke a word of English, so it was up to me to learn Spanish. *Cerveza* and *tortilla* I already knew, so I wasn't about to die of thirst or hunger. We were fifty-per cent there!

I had stations located up and down the coast, to which I could invite myself for the occasional meal, and I retained some camping gear to enable me to prepare things in my room, ignoring the "no cooking" signs on the wall. After all, *no habla español.*

So, not ideal conditions, even to such as me, someone quite used to less than ideal conditions, although my wife, Catherine, waiting over in Las Palmas, in the nearby Canaries, did fly across to join me for a while. She also soon learned to accept things as they were. But to someone not prepared to accept such... Well, hard luck, 'Doug'. What goes around comes around.

'Doug' was the oil company representative (known as the Client Rep) on board the vessel - supposedly overseeing the client's requirements, or his version of! - but he was not a very personable character at all. Another graduate from the John McEnroe school of grace and charm - the old time Johnny Mac, that is. Nothing suited 'Doug', and he wasn't shy in letting it be known. Didn't have a lot of choice in that as he was forced to rely on the goodwill of seismic company to relay his telexed reports to London, even though they contained nothing but harsh criticism of that seismic company's operations. So, when on completion of the job I was asked to organise airline seats for all out-going personnel, and discovering there was one less seat available than there were people wishing to travel, guess who got to stay behind? And the next flight not due for two days!

Whilst in the Spanish Sahara, at the time Catherine was with me, I recall a need to relieve one of the station operators for a few days. Due to poor planning, I needed to fly him back to Paris, Madrid, or somewhere, to renew a passport that was about to expire. Catherine and I were ensconced in a double sleeping bag - it got very cold out in the desert at night - doing what comes naturally, when the generator suddenly cut out. Boy, did that curtail things rather quickly! At least for as long as it took to get the station back on the air, and make some kind of repair to the zips.

And there you have it, you see. We *were* well paid, but, as I said, it wasn't for nothing. At times conditions could be extreme. Hazardous? Well, yes, that, too. Difficult for it not to be in countries where the roads themselves could be regarded a major hazard. As could the military dictatorsh... Excuse me. Government. But if it ever got too much, all I needed was to gaze into the empty sky. Up there was peace. An open, blue peace which stretched from horizon to horizon. God's playground. The sky was my escape route. I was free to take

369

it. And once up there, looking down, I could be anywhere, for all cities, towns, and villages become neat and tidy from the air. Height glosses over the slums, dumps, and inadequacies. Much as does a recent fall of snow back home. Such thoughts were calming. My worries became insignificant.

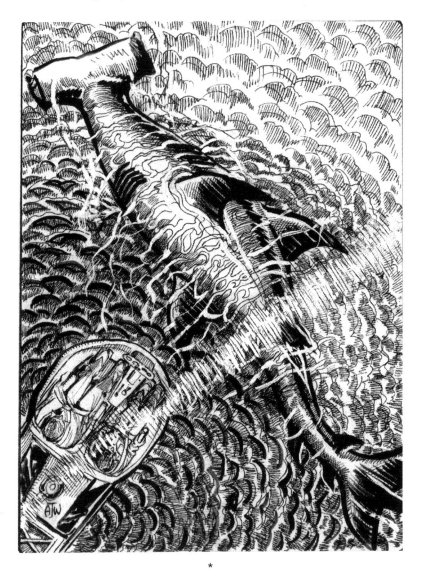

*

Then there was the flying. Take for instance the time I was en-route by helicopter over the Bight of Biafra, on my way to an oil rig, just myself and the pilot, Tom. There we were, tooling along

370

in a small, two-seat Hiller 12E, when we spotted a shark cruising along on the surface. A hammerhead. Easy to spot, even from fifteen hundred feet. Very easy, for it was actually a rather large hammerhead. In fact, truth be told, bloody huge!

'Will you look at that!' Tom said, as if I could have missed it. 'Shall we go down?'

Stupid question, I thought. But then I realized it wasn't really a question at all. He wasn't asking, he was telling me. Decision already made.

'Let's not,' I said, not at all curious as to the precise physical dimensions. But I was far too late. The power came off as the collective was lowered, and we were on the way.

Descend he did, to hover, barely above sea-level, directly over the creature, measuring his length against that of our suddenly frail-seeming, single-engined machine.

Did I say *his*? Hey, forget the Equal Opportunities Commission, or the concept of political correctness, he or she was academic, this sod was considerably longer than the Hiller's mere fifteen or so feet. Which immediately conjured up dire thoughts. As such things tend to do.

The engine did continue to run smoothly, but it didn't *sound* at all smooth. Not to my ears.

'Is that a slight misfire I detect, Tom?' I asked, only to receive a wry smile in return. 'Is the clutch slipping, causing us to sacrifice what precious little altitude we have?' A muttered reply this time, although in the negative. Are we over-pitching? I almost asked. I knew about such technicalities, had a wealth of experience. But it seemed we weren't, so I kept quiet, tuned my thoughts to other scenarios, imagination working overtime, as usual. So what about you, Tom? I wondered. Are you about to suffer a heart attack? Funny, the things that come to mind now and again. Not funny ha-ha, funny strange. But such sounds and disasters were only in my head. Normal things to imagine at a time like that, when the potential for trouble is high. Even so, despite the temperature being in the eighties, I found my arms to be covered in goose bumps.

'Is that overgrown fish just sunbathing, do you think, or is it hungry? I mean really hungry?'

'Come on Dave. Look, statistics prove....'

'Yes, I know what statistics prove,' I interjected, 'but as far as I'm concerned, when it comes to the matter of sharks, anything that moves is lunch. Didn't you read *Jaws?*'

That was the kind of flying to which I was to be

subjected, for the laws tended to be lax - what laws there were. Scheduled airlines attempted approaches that wouldn't have been contemplated by a military pilot faced by such conditions. The difference, you see, between revenue and non-revenue flying.

Not only the airlines, either. I recall an incident that would definitely have to be chalked up as a "near miss" situation the day I flew from Lagos to Calabar in the Mobil Oil Company's executive Cessna 411, call sign, "Red Horse".

The weather on the approach was bad, clouds almost down to the ground. The pilot was feeling his way through it, descending all the time. And I must say he was either rather good, or got lucky, for we suddenly broke cloud just above the trees, and there was the runway.

Only one problem. It was about one hundred feet off to the port side. I figured he was about to climb away and make another attempt, but no. He suddenly banked steeply one way then the other. The aircraft shuddered on the edge of a stall, horn bellowing its strident warning. And stall it did, but by then we were only a few feet up, and over the runway, so the pilot got away with a rather heavy, ungainly landing as he fought the aircraft from one side of the runway to the other. One landing I was very relieved to walk away from.

These were private, or non scheduled flights. When the time came to depart Nigeria it would be on a scheduled flight. But, to fly out of the country, you first had to board an aircraft.

In such as America you simply pick up the phone to make a reservation: 'Good day, Eastern Airlines. How can we be of service?' a cheerful voice would ask. Then, once I'd detailed my requirements, 'Fine, sir. That's New York, New Orleans, confirmed. Have a good day, and thank you for calling Eastern.'

Not so in Africa, where things were slightly different. For starters, forget the telephone. You almost needed a reservation to use that, if in fact it worked at all. Then, despite holding a "confirmed" reservation, made in person, you were still likely to find yourself resorting to the greasing of a palm or two, (known as "dash") in order to secure a seat. Still, with your confirmed reservation now officially confirmed, you could sit back and relax, couldn't you? Possibly. Just so long as the Head of State, or any of his minions, didn't choose that particular day to fly off somewhere or other. In the event of such a decision, he and his entourage would just commandeer the aircraft. I even experienced this phenomenon at a hotel in Gabon, the only hotel in town, as it happened. In that instance I was already occupying one of the rooms. *Was*, of course, being the operative word.

The Head of State apparently needed a room. Mine! No refund, no help in finding alternative accommodation, certainly no discussion about it. OK, so he needed a room or two, but so did I, therefore you'd have thought one would at least have chance to debate the situation. But debate it with whom? I never for a minute imagined those guys sporting camouflage drill and dark glasses to be his public relations advisors. Well, I suppose they could have been, but to my way of thinking an AK-47 seemed an unlikely item for a public relations advisor to be carrying.

So much for the "politicians". Now let's consider the matter of the transport itself. The flying during these formative years of Africa's oil exploration was, to say the least, varied. And, it seems, in retrospect, not entirely as safe as it might have been. Adventurous, shall we say. The average ground-check appeared to be of the "kick the tyres, light the fires" school of thought. At least in the charter sector, where most of the aircraft looked like cast-offs from some third-rate airline.

Thinking back (which in this case is the best time to think, for that implies survival), I often wonder how safe those flights had actually been. Not that it matters at all. Not now. All that matters is that I *did* survive, am still around to tell the tale.

During my early days in the area I particularly recall a flight on a Nigerian Airways DC3, the pilot a turbaned Sikh. We were en route from Lagos to...... Well, Lagos, actually, as things turned out. Focal point of the universe, as far as Nigerians were concerned.

Away in the distance were billowing, cathedral-like clouds. Here on the ground at Ikeja they appeared to be stately, white, and massive against the blue vault of the sky.

I boarded the aircraft to find the seats on the starboard side were what one might call... er... well, friendly is a word that springs to mind. You know, kind of thing you and your girl made a rush for in the back row of the cinema. Only in this case my seat was extra friendly, in that it was fitted with only one seat-belt. Oh, tra la la! My seat-mate happened to be of like sex, you see. Meaning he too was male. Upon complaining, a mechanic was dispatched to rectify the situation - seat-belt (or lack of) that is - whilst I stood in the aisle twiddling my thumbs and, no doubt the other passengers fumed. *Not content with securing a prized seat, he wants a bloody seat-belt as well.* Fair enough, I'd probably have thought the same had the positions been reversed. They weren't, so we waited until the job was done.

Shortly after take-off, at the top of the climb - on second thoughts, taking into account the rate of climb achieved by the DC3, maybe a little longer than "shortly after take-off" - the aircraft entered a dark canyon. Its walls were formed by sheer cliffs of the evil-looking Cumulonimbus which towered out of sight above us. It suddenly went black, as if a shadow had passed over us. At which point my earlier decision to complain about the lack of restraint became fully vindicated.

It started with a mild warning. A gentle shudder, as if the craft was limbering up, preparing for the worst. This came with frightening suddenness and violent buffeting. Turbulence picked us up and tossed us around like a child's toy, wings fluttering like those of a hummingbird. The darkness outside was occasionally lit by generous flashes of lightning - like maybe a trillion volts. An unseen fist punched us viciously upwards before we fell off the edge. Then the bottom just fell out of the sky, taking us with it. We were on our way down. Fast. Then it caught, held momentarily, before again surging upwards like an elevator that was rocket-propelled. A wing dropped, was corrected for, and we were yawing wildly, pilot always seeming to be a little behind nature. Then, just as suddenly as it started, it was over. The cabin brightened, and we were in smooth air. The horizon was back where God intended it to be, and we were right way up.

In conditions I was sure most aircraft would not have survived, our Sikh pilot had somehow managed to reverse course and make good his escape. So I thought. On reflection it was more likely the storm had spat us out like some unpalatable insect. It was one of those times when I wondered at the sanity of strapping myself inside a metal tube, surrounded by hundreds of gallons of highly inflammable fuel. Others probably wondered the same, although none were about to admit to it. Small, nervous smiles spread throughout the cabin like a friendly virus as white-knuckled hands relaxed their grip on the armrests. The way they'd been gripping them you'd have thought they believed they were keeping the aircraft in the air solely by way of that death grip.

The mood was now quite macho. "We have just courted death in the clouds, but it was nothing", type of thing.

374

But relief was to be short-lived, for again we turned, only to re-enter this monster on a different bearing. Trying to sneak up on it from behind maybe? He was a game one, this pilot. One of the more competitive types that hates to be beaten. Either that, or he had a madman's contempt for the weather. He was going for it again. Which was about the time I wished I'd never set eyes on him. Why couldn't he have been downed by a Sikh-eating missile in some minor skirmish in the Hindu Kush, or been taken out by turban guerrillas? To me, pilots were held in similar regard to doctors; I placed my faith in them. In this case, that faith was about to be tested to the full.

This time it was worse. Much worse. Weather radar would have told him that story, but lacking such modern facilities he had to find out the hard way. Violent currents punched us aloft one second, then, with contemptuous ease and a sickening lurch, threatened to drag us out of the sky the next. In reality, I suppose the longest period of free fall couldn't have exceeded two or three seconds, though you'd have had trouble convincing those aboard of the fact, myself especially. We were all over the sky, plunging one second, shooting up the next.

One person was past caring altogether, it seemed. A Texan. Well over six feet tall, he sported a straw Stetson which he wore the whole time, apart from during one particularly violent period when he snatched it off his head and waved it in the air. 'Yeeehaah!' he yelled, when what he should have been doing was praying. Everyone else seemed to be. Not me though, I was too absorbed in worrying about the possibility of my fiery demise.

'Yeeehaah!' he repeated. Back home I imagine he rode Brahman Bulls during his leisure hours.

A sudden, rending crash from somewhere aft signalled the end. It's literally all downhill from here, I thought. But no, it was just the end of the coffee. The small, meagrely equipped galley was suddenly larger, though now even less well equipped, cabin floor awash as the canister containing the beverage no longer did. It had been ripped off the bulkhead.

Whether (if you'll excuse the pun) at this point the pilot conceded defeat, or the elements decided to give us another chance, was difficult to determine, for the next thing we knew was that we had again been spat out. Safe. Albeit still on the Lagos side of the weather front. At which point the pilot did give up, although only temporarily. He returned to Ikeja, trading the whole lot in for a pressurised, turboprop F27 Friendship.

One hour later, Five November-Alpha Alpha Zulu climbed high enough to enable us to weave a stately slalom between those massed peaks, en route to Port Harcourt. Up here the sun shone brightly, as if nature were apologizing for her earlier tantrum. So eventually we did get to see our cloud castles. And we did enjoy our coffee.

*

The trip from Lagos city out to the International airport, at Ikeja, was another of life's less exhilarating experiences. A fact attested to, and exploited by, a particularly thoughtful piece of advertising. It concerned (at that time) one of the largest of international airlines, and it was sited beside the road leading out of the city.

I'll never forget that trip, the first time I made it. The taxi was a bone-shaking old wreck. Even to call it a car was an overstatement, although it had been, once. Most of the remaining trim was hanging off, as were some important-looking bits underneath. Odds on against even making it as far as the airport, I thought, as I sat on my wooden-box seat. And had I not paid in advance not making it would have been guaranteed, the driver didn't have enough petrol in the tank until I gave him the money for it.

That hurdle overcome, we were on our way. Not exactly at a spine-tingling rate of knots, nor sedately. On our way nonetheless. There seemed to be roadworks every hundred yards or so, holes in between. It was hot and humid, which ensured the many traffic jams would be ill-tempered affairs, making the journey seem that much longer. Everything appeared to be against us. Then, just as frustration and hostility reached their peak, we came across this advert. A huge billboard at the roadside, not at all discreet; to me, a welcome smile-generator. It simply read, PAN AM. LET US TAKE YOU AWAY FROM ALL THIS.

Amen to that, I thought.

Don't know how they got away with it, for Africans are not a race to take criticism lightly.

That smile lasted until I came upon the only redeeming feature the country had to offer, the airport departure lounge. Ikeja was not a typical Third World airport, something to patronize the area into believing they had entered the twentieth century. No way. Ramshackle rather than modern. Not cheery or welcoming at all, just the opposite. It looked like most other government buildings in Nigeria: run-down and filthy. And although civilian, given the number of Kalashnikovs on display - plus other assorted hardware - one could be forgiven for thinking it to be a military base.

Considering the degree of reluctance with which they allow you to enter their country in the first place, I never ceased to be amazed by the number of difficulties encountered when trying to leave. Therefore - once access had been granted, the hassle of check-in endured, I, and my wallet, suffering at the hands of immigration and customs - I relished the thought that I was but minutes away from boarding a flight to..... well, anywhere. Please. Just so long as it meant leaving the frustrations and tensions of West Africa far behind.

Provided you have booked with one of the major European airlines, preferably BOAC in my case, such frustrations you begin to jettison even as you climb aboard your aircraft, for, of course, once seated, you are as good as back in civilization. Cleanliness and compassion rule the day here, along with bright, friendly, cheerful cabin crew. Then, once seated, strapped in, and underway, there is the familiar soothing voice of your captain, a man who understands; he's seen it all before, many times.

From here on there was no holding me, the world my oyster. I actually made a personal promise I would never allow myself to set foot in Nigeria ever again. I seem to recall making similar resolutions re most of the Middle East also, once I had left there. Funny how things never seem to turn out according to plan!

One positive outcome of my time in Nigeria was that, despite the various pressure situations we occasionally faced, it was during this time that I actually quit smoking. Just woke up one morning, and as I reached for a cigarette, thought, I don't need this. And that, more or less, was it. An uncomfortable period at times, yes, but being alone helped. Even so, it took tremendous willpower, though I'd always known I had that.

*   *

377

Chapter Thirteen
GABON

*T*he billowing white clouds which had formed and developed during yesterday's humid heat - my cloud castles - had escalated to storm conditions, producing a spectacular show after dark. Lightning forked down, illuminating land and sea alike, but the storm had remained offshore, thus sparing me. Then it was over and peace returned, temporarily. The towering cumulonimbus, now much deflated and spent, moved on slowly, taking the lightning with them. The air was cool, moist, scented. And it was filled with a new sound. Outside my tent, in the darkness, frogs, cicadas, and other unseen creatures croaked, clicked and whirred. A tropical choral society whose performance would continue through until dawn. That was especially true of the amphibious creatures, for the frogs were all around. So many it was practically obscene.

With the onset of day in this Gabonese outpost, all was peace and serenity, apart from the continuous thudding of the roaring, crashing breakers. That sound was my constant and only companion, though I was now beginning to accept it as normal.

Five days ago two of us, plus the pilot, had left Port Gentil in a little Cessna 140, landed at some unpronounceable location. From there, travelling by Land Rover, we were deposited at a logging camp, deep in the tropical rainforest, where my equipment and supplies awaited our arrival. Here we'd spent the night. Luxury, that, for often there was no bed at all. A sleeping bag under the stars if I was lucky, if not, the mud floor of a bush hut, or the grimy deck of a small boat as it threaded its way up some remote African waterway. But whatever was on offer, it was usually more than welcome.

Wasting no time, we were on the road early next morning, Africa having unfolded slowly and dramatically with the dawn. Most of that day was spent in a canoe, being paddled along a narrow river. The banks crowded in on us, trees overhanging the water, soundtrack replete with noises of the jungle, yet with only the occasional monkey to be seen, or the iridescent flash of colourful plumage as a bird was startled into flight. Whatever else there may have been remained well concealed, though they no doubt kept a watchful eye on us.

A long walk followed, trek really, out of the trees then across sun-baked savanna. There was man-tall grass, which could well conceal anything from gorillas to elephants, for this was West Africa, not East. Over here a safari was a safari without tourists, and watch where you put your feet boyo. Which, apart from recalling my days in Malaya, brings to mind that legendary tribe, the Focawee.

Being pygmies (aka short-arsed, for non PC types such as myself) they were sure to be vertically disadvantaged in grass such as this. In fact, 'tis said this was where the tribal name had its origins, their unique method of navigation when faced by such an obstacle. The younger warriors were apparently to be seen bouncing up and down, as if on springs, spurred on by the cries of their less able elders; "Where the foc are we?"

No Focawee around here then, but with our accompanying bearers - whom we paid to do the work of absent machinery - we must have looked like we'd just walked out of a Daniel Defoe novel. Everything was carried on their heads, as was the African way.

Arrival at the designated site, late in the evening, saw our cast of thousands disappear. One minute there, next they were not. It was like the earth had opened up and swallowed them. Only three of us remained: myself, my supervisor, (or Party Chief, as they were known) and the guide who would eventually see him safely on his way back, once everything was installed and operational. Tonight we just concentrated on the tents and beds.

It was hot, sweaty work assembling the station through the heat of the day, and we didn't stop for anything, working through until the sun again went to bed. Up to that time I hadn't spared a thought for food, hadn't eaten a thing all day, though I had drunk plenty. Cases of bottled water were frequently attacked. That it soon became warm didn't matter, it was wet, and all I needed was liquid. Now it dawned on me how hungry I was, so I scratched around, grabbing whatever came to hand. A tin of beans, some rice, a bottle of Tabasco. Thirty minutes, and bingo! I could have been at the Ritz but the food wouldn't have tasted better. I then collapsed on my bed and fell into a sleep that was more like a short course in death.

It was left-over beans and rice for breakfast as well, though it didn't taste anything like as good first thing in the morning. But the water was once again cool.

Two days more and I was alone. Myself, the sea, sky, and the scenery. No, not just that, there were the smells as well. Rotting vegetation, the aroma of exotic blooms, my own sweat, all mingled to create an atmosphere I could feel and relate to. It was naturally peaceful. Far removed from the rush and clamour of civilization there were no deadlines to meet, no sense of urgency. Even the passage of time had little meaning. Night and day, darkness and light, yes, but not time itself. I was self-sufficient in essentials; food, water, medical supplies, electronic spares and fuel. That's right, I wasn't out here for the good of my health, I needed to keep a generator running, had a navigation beacon to maintain. It wasn't ideal, but it would do for now. Had to, no way for me to escape. But why would I want to. There were swaying palms, stretches of golden sand, and the ocean. OK, the water was brown rather than turquoise, the surf, curdled coffee as opposed to creamy-white, and beyond that surf were sharks. There were mosquitoes inland, but a predominately onshore breeze spared me those.

In either direction the beach ran straight on, until it vanished in a mist of spray. My immediate world consisted of sea, sand, trees and savanna. Nature in the raw. It was almost like being paid to go on a tropical holiday, even though we occasionally needed to work for a living. But once we were set up and operational, the work itself was rather minimal.

It could be a lonely life at times, yes, although loneliness, especially given the environment in which I currently lived, did have its compensations. I didn't need to suffer the pollution, crowding, and littering of the cities. Lack of mains electricity, water, and gas, meant I never got cut off, nor did I have bills to pay for these services. There were no taxes to pay. Neither were there any nagging worries. I experienced no problems, and the responsibilities were few. And as I didn't mind cooking for myself, I mostly enjoyed the isolation. Any local purchases - should I be fortunate enough to be offered any - were all "chargeable" for which I would be duly compensated. There were no schedules to keep, I was free to do more or less as I wished, eat and sleep whenever I felt like it, as long as my station was up and running when required. That kind of luxury you couldn't buy. And as I was being paid handsomely, it will come as no surprise when I say the days were many when I wouldn't have wished to be anywhere else.

Supposedly, according to the BBC World Service, it was all happening in the England of the 60's and 70's, but it was passing us by. It was at times like this I did occasionally feel cut off, there again, I could always silence the Beeb, my choice.

But maybe it was worth it for the solitude. I certainly attempted to justify it as being so. London, which at the time seemed to be the centre of the universe, was crowded and noisy, the roads jammed with traffic. Very unhealthy, I told myself. This didn't even take into account the various substances, intake of which was apparently required to maintain the enjoyment of life. Just about anything that could be swallowed, sniffed, smoked or injected, it seemed. Anything to remove the realities. All they were doing, it turns out, was living a dream.

But certain things *were* eventually missed. Aeroplanes, and the cocktail cabinet, perhaps? Ah yes, lack of a drink didn't pose any problems for me, but what of the aeroplanes. Maybe I was suffering withdrawal symptoms there. Or was I?

I did manage the odd flight now and again. And odd some of them proved to be, too, occasionally bringing to mind that hammerhead experience offshore Nigeria. One especially so, when yet another somewhat adventurous helicopter pilot was to place me in a comparable position.

It was a Bell 47 this time, as in the TV series, M*A*S*H, though just as flimsy and vulnerable as had been that Hiller - a perspex bubble, in which we sat, suspended at the end of a metal tubular structure. The pilot of this machine, spotting a family of gorillas trailing across the Gabonese countryside, felt the need to approach within feet of them. Close enough to allow a detailed inspection of their impressive dental structure, would you believe? Fair enough. Until the male - after first ensuring his family were safely ensconced within the surrounding bush - reared up to his full height and faced us. His fists beat on his leathery chest, his mouth was open in a defiant roar we could not hear, his teeth were bared in an anger we *could* see. Justifiable, admittedly. It brought to mind the scene from a film: King Kong snatching aeroplanes out of the sky.

'Hey, come on, Pete. There are limits to the conversation one can hold with a gorilla,' said I, 'Let's get out of here.' And Pete must have been in agreement, for take us out of there he did, rather swiftly.

But the scene was later to be repeated yet again. Different pilot, different helicopter - an Alouette two - a herd of elephants apparently deputizing for the gorillas. On that occasion we moved off and gained height once the leader started spraying sand at us. He, too, seemed slightly upset. As was I.

I have no objection to viewing the wildlife from a low pass, but there is low, and there is within touching distance! On these two occasions, plus possibly that with the hammerhead, I had felt endangered. There are limits as to how far you push the safety angle, and I felt that on all these occasions the margins had been exceeded. Not enough thought applied to the "what if" syndrome.

No wonder these pilots were threatened with instant dismissal if caught in any such act - like disturbing the animals. But to my mind it seemed the powers that be had the wording wrong. Bugger the animals, it should have been "disturbing the passengers".

So maybe not the flying so much, after all, but there were other things missing from my life. I'd only been on site a week, when, as occasionally happens, my mind conjured up visions of female company, soft beds, and cold beer. But - being a "Yorkie, therefore somewhat of an epicure when it came to the dish - oh for a newspaper-wrapped parcel of fish and chips. Cooked as they should be, used to be, before the authorities started to question anything that gave enjoyment. I had the potatoes, nothing with which to catch the fish. Ah well.

It was to be a couple of weeks before I had my first human visitors. Like a converse Livingstone, *they'd* come on safari to visit *me.* To them it was a day out. To me, knowing how close the nearest village was - or wasn't, actually - it was a safari. And the problems their visit posed were soon circumvented. Their version of French - which made me, with my fragmentary knowledge of the language sound like a linguist - was basically undecipherable, so we drew pictures in the sand, traded personal aromas, and shared a cognac. Well, base supplies did run to better things than bottled water, even if they didn't include a portable shower. The cocktail cabinet was alive and well after all.

*

Another week and it was visiting day again. Only this time my new-found friends asked, via a combination of mime, and more pictures in the sand, if I'd care to go fishing. I would. But, suspecting the favoured area was not the *pas loin* indicated, suggested *demain*, perhaps *apres-demain* would be better, as tomorrow, or the next day, the vessel, to which I was transmitting signals, would not be requiring any. So it was arranged.

When I eventually did get to go, I was pleased to have done so. Pleased also we'd made alternative arrangements as to the day of my going. It was down the coast a piece - as the Americans would say. The French? *Grande distance,* I'd imagine, or similar. Certainly not *pas loin*, for, to my way of thinking, "not far" meant less than the distance we covered. Substantially less! But it had been well worth the effort. A lagoon, estranged from the sea by a steep, sandy beach, but with a narrow channel that allowed stocks to be replenished at high tide. Patient, watchful wading birds also favoured these secluded waters. Out here the air was clear and fresh. The continual sound of the surf was muted by layers of low scrub and vegetation, which also formed a barrier against a spirited onshore breeze. So everything was far from perfect, for that breeze was what kept the mosquitoes and sandfleas in check. No matter, my prayers were answered. The fish were plentiful, obliging, and definitely *Grande,* so I did have my fish and chip supper, even if it didn't match that of my local chippie. My expectations had never been that high to begin with.

As I settled for the night, relaxed, at peace with myself and the world, all around was tranquillity. Well, almost. Nothing stirred in the landscape except the whispering grasses, but the surf still crashed and boomed along the beach, sounding like a battery of cannons.

There were days of sheer bliss. Days when the sun shone in clear blue skies, the temperature up in the nineties. Hot white sand washed by tropical waters and edged by leafy palms, their fronds barely shifting in the light, cooling breeze. And there were days of absolute hell. Days when heavy black clouds dragged their curtains of rain across the surface of the sea. Large, fat raindrops were driven horizontal on the strength of the wind, and there was thunder. Intense and fearsome. Nothing remained dry, little remained undamaged.

Even when visited by these horrendous storms and heavily rained upon, the water quickly drained away due to the sandy nature of the ground. As soon as the sun reappeared everything dried out rapidly. Unlike Nigeria, where, during the rainy season, under black and incessantly weeping skies, drains were soon filled to overflowing, roads were awash, everything soggy. The whole area became a quagmire, and it would remain miserably damp for weeks on end.

They came for me after a month. Not the men in white jackets, but it *was* time to go in for a break. Another tiny Cessna dropped by. My personal transport bouncing down on the grass of my back garden, as it were. I just closed up my tent and left. Something you could not do in many African countries. Well, you could, but the likelihood was, it wouldn't be there when you returned, belongings or tent!

That Cessna then carried me to town for a couple of days. And I was determined to find some fishing gear to take back with me.

*

My taxi pulled up in front of a concrete block; yet another third-rate hotel. Not concrete, glass and aluminium, they were for tourists. We didn't warrant being pampered to, wouldn't have wanted it anyway. There would be a bar of sorts - essential, that - what passed for a restaurant, a room - very basic - hot water if we were lucky. The electricity? Well, that could be off for longer than it was on. Plenty of candles though, standard issue around here. And that was it. The tourists would never put up with it. The difference, of course, was that we were here to work. The tourists brought money in, we took it out, or so the thinking went. In actual fact we probably spent far more than any tourist.

Port Gentil is a pleasant little coastal town. Trees line its streets, beaches line its shores, both sides of the peninsular on which it sits, and there are shaded sidewalk cafes and bars. One of these we favoured. It was on the seafront, relaxing, good for breakfast if we fancied it, excellent coffee if we didn't. We'd often begin the day there, and if we had nothing pressing, sometimes spend all day there. And we knew we'd be back early the next day, sitting beneath the trees anaesthetizing our hangovers with black coffee. Our agent's office was conveniently close by - our Telex contact with Geneva - so if anything urgent came up, that agent would know where to find us.

This town was the oil capital of an emerging African nation. French influence and language, French food and drink, for Gabon - along with other ex-French Colonial territories - although independent, was still heavily influenced by Paris.

December 31st found us at the most popular bar and restaurant in town. "Le Provencale" was knee-deep in Frenchmen, but that didn't sway us. Rather than the overpriced, celebratory, fixed menu, our group opted for chip butties. Not really *a point,* as they say, but to appease the owner somewhat, we also gulped champagne with considerably less restraint than the price demanded. In fact we continued to do so well into the new day, which was also the New Year. It couldn't really be termed the morning after the night before, as there had been no demarcation point, the session was still in full swing. We later transferred our allegiance to the nearby beach: a buffet lunch, along with a punch that was concocted from some imagined formula. This related basically to whatever was currently available in the local store: everything from Martini to Mou Tai - the latter a Chinese spirit that appeared to possess all the properties of liquid Semtex. It smelt bad, tasted even worse, but I can confirm it to be a drink of exceptional authority, not to say some belligerence!

*

A pleasant interlude, then it was time to return to work, thank goodness. By that time I felt like I was in need of a rest, or a kidney transplant.

The same old Cessna tail-dragger awaited me, although a different pilot this time; American. And was he ever different. As different as would the year eventually to prove to be.

'Hi, there. How we all doing today?'

I thought he was greeting me, until I turned to find him patting the metal of the engine cowling. He talked all the way through his walk round, addressing himself to the aircraft the whole time. Bloody silly, really, it was just a bunch of pieces screwed, bolted and rivetted together. A collection of parts: aluminium and steel, wood, leather, rubber and wire; an inanimate object. Yet I knew how he felt, just wished he'd speak to me. The odd word would have sufficed. No matter, the monologue continued throughout, even when my supplies had been loaded, we were strapped in, and engine started. I may as well not have been there, even though, in effect, I was paying him.

'How's your fuel then? Yeah! Fine. Oil pressure? Good girl. Mixture? Carb heat? Flaps?' The litany continued as his fingers rippled over switches, buttons and levers. Then, with a final check - to make sure I was aboard, maybe? - he finally acknowledged my presence with a smile and a raised thumb. I replied in kind.

'OK, we're ready...' I thought he really was addressing me this time. Wrong again. He hadn't yet finished. '....let's see what you can do today, old girl.'

It was a relatively long take-off run with the weight we had on board, and the heat, but the runway was built to take big jets, so no problem. Still, he coaxed her all the way. 'Come on old girl, you can do it. Yeah, there you go. What did I tell yer.'

It was the last kind word he said, for the air was turbulent and it seemed the aircraft was to take the blame for that. It was now 'Bitch. You old cow,' and, upon touchdown, 'Get your ass on the ground, goddammit.'

Even after off-loading he had no time for a coffee and a chat - not with me, at least - he was back on board immediately, apparently eager to be on his way. He fired up and, propeller disappearing in a shining arc, quickly taxied off.

The little plane turned, and with the application of power

386

trundled across the grass. The speed built up, agonizingly slowly it seemed to me. Even empty it appeared to struggle, engine straining at full power. I could imagine the pilot urging it on: "Come on you bastard. Son of a bitch, get up." Then, seemingly with some reluctance, it responded, barely clearing the trees on its way into the sky. I watched until it disappeared from sight.

'Goodbye, old girl,' I found myself whispering. Then I was alone once more. Alone with my thoughts in the now still emptiness of this place. The only sounds were those of nature in the raw: the calls of the birds, the clicking of insects, the occasional trumpeting of elephants, and that familiar - at present slightly muted - crashing surf.

*

A bar could be an airconditioned, glass and chrome decked room in an hotel, a packed-earth floored shack out in the bush, complete with home-made furnishings, or it could be anything in between. There were even subdivisions at the lower end of the scale: ie, a shack with a refrigerator, a shack without. The only common factor was the beer, though the cost varied considerably, price relating to degree of comfort. There again, comfort was self-determined.

Last night, my last in Libreville, we had opted for quality, deeming Antiones to be worthy of our presence. Pâté de Foie avec Truffe, followed by Coq au vin à la Bourguignon, with a Crème Brûlée to round everything off. Delightful. Naturally, bottle after bottle of wine had accompanied us on this journey of gastronomic enlightenment. At the moment life felt good. Of course it did, we'd eaten well, drank some good wine, downed a few *digestives*. That's what alcohol did, made you feel good, no matter how things were in reality. One reason drinking was so popular.

As he stood, Dennis *looked* as if he'd had one or two. The way he sauntered off to the toilet reminded me of the way they walked in those old westerns, the rolling gait: John Wayne, Kirk Douglas and the like. The real westerns. Dennis must have been having similar thoughts, for as he passed a full length mirror on one of the central pillars he paused, backed up a few paces, stood and faced himself, narrowing his eyes. Then, pow! pow! His hands came up, two fingers on each pointing as he attempted to out-draw himself. Pow! pow! Again, with just as much luck. So, oblivious of the attention he'd attracted, seemingly disappointed with himself, he holstered up and headed for the loo.

'Cowboy mad, Dennis,' Bob proclaimed to no one in particular. 'Says he has videos of all the John Wayne and Clint Eastwood westerns.'

'Ah,' said someone else, 'but we....' I dismissed thoughts of Dennis and looked round. It was Don, peering down into his glass as he spoke to Ted. Not about Dennis at all, but an entirely unrelated subject. I realized this as soon as Ted expressed profound disbelief at what was being discussed. At least I assume that's what was implied.

'Bollocks,' he said. Quite loud, too.

Jerry and Big Al shared a bottle of whisky. It stood on the table between them, contents well down, a fact that seemed to form the basis of *their* current debate: the philosophical implications of the bottle's condition. Lack of a degree in philosophy apparently didn't preclude either from forming an opinion. Big Al was first with his analysis. 'Bastard's half empty!' he exclaimed, as if wondering where the other half had gone. Jerry, having once admitted to a fleeting interest in existentialism - therefore probably the more qualified to address such a concept - seemed to disagree. 'Bullshit! It's still half full.'

Pow! Pow! From across the way. Dennis was back, still trying to out-draw himself as he passed by the mirror.

Luckily, I had packed the previous evening. No! No luck involved. Purposely. I had known what it would be like. Exactly how it was. The pain behind the eyes, the throbbing head, uncoordinated movements. I padded around without order, unsure of what it was I wanted to achieve. All I did know for sure, was that I needed to get to the airport by a certain time.

Never again, I thought, yet again. Must have been the wine in the Coq au Vin.

*

For most people travel is fine, if restricted to short bursts, but our digestive tracts were well able to cope with the local cuisine for a extended period. But should this period extend beyond the annual vacation, sometimes for months, especially if the locale happens to be in one of the more remote regions of the globe, you tend to miss life's little luxuries. (I don't mean the pate de foie, and champagne, they were available in abundance, especially on the occasion about which I am to relate. We're talking true luxuries here; real ale; fish and chips; and... well, like that. The things one was brought up to appreciate.) The Americans appear to be particularly affected by such

388

shortages. In fact they can be quite demanding. It's just that many Americans seem to feel their constitutional rights extend way beyond their country's borders. They usually end up finding out the hard way that this is just not true.

Take for instance a friend of mine, whom we'll call Larry, for no better reason than that being his actual name.

We'd been working in Gabon for some months, were missing some of the basics. Naturally, with its French influence and all, there were some very good restaurants around. Despite this, or maybe because of, Larry was one day stricken by a Mac Attack. That is to say, he felt the dire need of a hamburger. Ardently so. Which called for much serious thought, and a like amount of dexterous scheming. The serious thought came in bottles, usually labelled Chateau something or other, the scheming was entirely natural.

He's capitulated, I thought, sometime later, as Larry ordered a steak tartare. Probably overdone the serious thought bit, I allowed. There again, it was as close as you could come to a burger in this place, albeit raw, and in kit form at that. But my thinking was flawed, for I'd failed to consider the scheming element, so, once the kit was assembled to his satisfaction, Larry indicated to the maitre'd that he should take the result away, and grill it, *bien cuit.* And "toot bloody sweet, silver plate", if he knew what was good for him.

Which leads to another tale of the non-vernacular.

We were in Madrid this time, and Larry, being a bit of a linguist - at least, he fancied himself as such - had bought the relevant books and was immersing himself in the language. This he did no matter where we found ourselves. The will was there, the ability... well, that was something else. As will be seen.

We were in our usual restaurant, a popular and agreeable place. Probably the best steaks in Madrid, if not Spain. Expensive, yes, but we were "in oil and gas" as the saying goes. And as far as sayings went, it wasn't much, I'll agree, but it sufficed. I was, at the time - the early sixties - not short of a clod or two (another saying that has long since died, along with the old penny it pertained to). But I digress.

As I was entertaining a young lady, we, naturally, occupied a separate table, but Larry and gang were close-by. Close enough for me to observe what went on, and no doubt vice versa.

The house speciality was a tremendous steak dish,

which I ordered. This was achieved by the simple expedient of pointing to the relevant item on the menu. It was our preferred dish, so I knew I couldn't go far wrong. I also knew it was what everyone else would order.

Larry, meantime, wishing to demonstrate the fluency he intuitively assumed he possessed as far as language went, persuaded his companions to allow him to place their order. It took quite a while, I noticed - something similar to a Scotsman buying a round, or a Chinaman saying yes - but eventually it was done.

Our steaks came, and went, likewise dessert. In fact we were at the coffee and liqueurs stage by the time Larry's order appeared. His companions, by now on their Nth jug of sangria, were past caring.

At breakfast next morning, I asked Larry how he'd enjoyed his steak.

`Steak!' He looked me in the eye, and right away I knew that he knew that I knew.

`I just hate lamb,' he replied. Somewhat sheepishly, if you'll excuse the pun.

*   *

MORE TALES FROM DARKEST AFRICA

Friday night, and a poker game is underway at the house of an American oil executive, who happened to have a monkey as a pet. Fans and louvred doors keep night-time temperatures down to reasonable levels, fortunate that, for his mini anthropoid likes nothing better than to perch upon the blade of the old-fashioned ceiling fan, from where, providing the speed is set at its lowest - which it is - it's only too happy to observe the world drifting past below. Which, again, it is. Literally: flush, full house, ace high, whatever. The men down there also focussed on the cards, concentration absolute. This is serious stuff.

'Bet two,' a gravelled voice announced, dropping a couple of dollar notes onto the pile.

'Your two, raise you five.' Seven more notes joined the growing stack in the centre of the table.

'Call', said the next player, adding the appropriate amount.

'Fold, dammit. Cards ain't running for me tonight.' And so it went, one hand after another, one drink after another.

Then, players attention on the cards, another hand, this one unnoticed, reaches surreptitiously through the door, switching the fan to full chat. An appropriate phrase, that, for the monkey was soon to be doing so: chattering away excitedly, whilst hanging on for dear life. His arms and legs were wrapped around the blade, head towards centre. Such a position, of course, compelled the other end to be directed outwards. As it was. So, when the terrified beast eventually lost control of its bowels...

Needless to say, from that point on the shower suddenly proved to have far more attraction than a mere pack of cards, or a pile of money.

It was one of the things expats would get up to in an effort to relieve the tension of working in this unpredictable environment. How unpredictable? Read on.

*

Some countries have so few beggars that each of them is known by name. Nigeria is not such a country. It is, though, a country divided by tribal rivalries - bound to be, with around two hundred and fifty from which to choose. Another thing of which I soon became aware; each and every country always seemed to be in year eight of the latest five year plan!

When I first arrived, the government was fairly stable. (For an independent African nation, that is. Which says just about everything.) The Prime Minister, a Hausa, went by the name of Al Haji Sir Abubaka Tafawa Belewa. Exactly! In fact, I recall one BBC news reader admitting - once trouble was brewing and this name hit the headlines rather frequently - that it was quite some days before he felt comfortable with the pronunciation. He went on to say, "I'd just about mastered it, when they shot him!"

With a dead Prime Minister being of little use to the country, it was all-change time. Next in line - not as in accession, an election, or deputy leader of the ruling party, but as in leader of the coup, and head of the Army - was a Major General named J T U Aguiyi-Ironsi. Another mouthful, to be sure, even without regard to the initials; no idea what they stood for anyway. No matter. He hardly lasted long enough to trouble anyone.

Lieutenant Colonel Yakubu Gowan, a Yoruba, was next up. Once again voted in at the point of a gun. Meanwhile, away to the east, General Odumegwu Ojukwu, an Ibo, seemed to hold the opinion that it really should have been his turn. A minor disagreement ensued, the outcome of which resulted in the Eastern Region seceding from the Federation. They declared themselves to be independent: the Republic of Biafra. But as a large percentage of Nigeria's most prodigious oil-fields just happened to be located in this region, the outcome, inevitably, was civil war. Maybe not such a minor disagreement after all, then.

Some time after that tragedy was resolved, Gowan, paying a visit to Britain - silly man - decided that this was probably a nice country in which to retire. He was only in his mid-forties, but he had lasted eight years, so early retirement seemed like a good idea. Especially as he no longer had a job back home.

During his absence, someone else had availed themselves of the army's Kalashnikovs, voting themselves into power. And from here on it became a kind of "Who's turn is it this week" situation, dictators appearing to tumble faster than England wickets in an Ashes Test.

I believe there was one brief spell of civilian rule, but it wasn't to last. Neither, it seems, was it exactly democratic. Apparently - this having become yet another African country in which elections were a rarity - lots of people stood around with guns; to prevent confusion as to the mechanics of voting, you understand!

In most African countries, becoming an opposition politician is not looked upon as being a particularly wise career move. In Nigeria, the same could be said for the Head of State. Not exactly a pensionable position. There again, maybe it is, certain of them allegedly depositing indecent amounts of cash in Swiss banks over the years.

But as Nigeria doesn't exactly have a monopoly on Swiss Bank accounts, and Coups d'etat, the following stories may be of more interest. The salient points of each attributed to the Nigerian press.

*

As a former British colony, Nigeria observed the drive on the left rule. That was the law, though not one to which Nigerian drivers necessarily subscribed; seems they felt more comfortable in the centre. And should another vehicle have the effrontery to approach from the opposite direction, well... 'He'll give way, won't he? 'Specially if I delays veering off until de last minute?' It's a question that must pass through the mind - I won't say often, for that surmises survival - and one for which the answer often becomes all too obvious, all too late. A couple of problems arise, of course. A: The opposing driver's intentions are not taken into account - and, being another citizen of like mind..... B: Veering a largely unserviceable, severely overloaded vehicle, suddenly, tends to result in said vehicle charging off into the scenery with all the finesse of a rhinoceros running amok.

The twelve seat Volkswagen minibus - known as a Mammy Wagon - was quite popular on the long-distance taxi run, therefore it was not unusual to see newspaper reports along the lines: TWENTY-FOUR DEAD IN MINIBUS CRASH! Not the multiple pile-up one would imagine, as the sub-text often revealed: No other vehicle involved. Indeed, the road-sides were littered with twisted remains of the most horrendous wrecks. Difficult to see how they could ever have extracted the bodies. There again, it's possible they hadn't. Just as, on my return from the pub - particularly during coup season - I have to admit to seeing the odd corpse lying around. (They'd hardly stand, would they?) A passer-by may toss a banana leaf over it, maybe not. Most didn't seem to care. No wild, drink-induced dream, this, either, a figment of the imagination given

393

substance by the enveloping darkness. This was reality. Come morning those bodies would still be dead. And, in all likelihood, they'd still be there. The only mourners were likely to be the vultures.

As I was on leave when the next story broke. It was joyfully related to me upon my return by a colleague. Hearsay as it were, thus unsubstantiated. There again, Al being a conservative type, not prone to exaggeration, and this being Nigeria, neither can it be categorically rejected out of hand.

'A group of us sat in the hotel bar,' Al began. This I was quite prepared to believe. A not unlikely venue for such as us.

'In fact the place was crowded,' he continued. 'With good reason. For this night, as well as drinking and raising hell, we were there to watch the news on TV. And sure enough, on screen, as had been rumoured, the Minister of Transport put in an appearance. He was there to make a special announcement.'

'"The decision has been made," the Minister said, "to better tie in with the ex-French colonies, (which bracketed this most populous of West African countries) to switch to driving on the right." The Minister went on to announce that the change-over would be implemented in two phases, over a two-week period. "During the first week, taxis, buses, and commercial vehicles will make the change. Private vehicles will comply with the edict the during second week. This will, I feel, alleviate some of the confusion that would be bound to occur if everyone changed at the same time."

'Us expatriates thought this to be a splendid idea, and many glasses were raised to the minister's health and well-being.

'That we had not already been suffering from the effects of too much alcohol, or had miss-heard, was confirmed when the following morning's newspapers appeared. There it was in black and white; taxis, buses, and commercial vehicles one week, private cars the next. Amazing!

'Same bar, same hour, following evening. The news again. It was announced in Lagos that the Transport Minister, in a sudden fit of patriotism, had resigned his post, volunteering to drive a jeep on the Biafran front. A number of his staff - presumably feeling similarly patriotic - had volunteered along with him. The new Minister, by the way, felt that, after close study of the drive-on-the-right situation, the confusion would not be as great as at first anticipated, therefore everyone would change over on the same day.'

Everyone I talked to confirmed this story as being correct, and judging it alongside other stories I read in the local press, I could well believe it. One in particular comes to mind. Well, it would, wouldn't it, a story of true romance. There again, maybe not, for it concerned a man who was up in court for... well, not exactly indecent exposure, more like... er... Oh, what the hell, screwing in public is what it amounted to. Rape, in fact.

A woman was apparently bending over a well to fill her bucket, when along comes the accused and fills her, so to speak. Sounds like rape. There again, apparently no objections were raised until... well, later, when the woman faced the perpetrator of the dirty deed - or penetrator. Anyway, when the defence questioned as to why she didn't protest sooner, the woman replied to the effect that, until she faced him she'd thought it was someone she knew!

Can you imagine? "Oh! Hello there. Is that you, Sunday? Or is it Joshua?"

Then there was one about a girl who collapsed and died on a dance-floor. Not immediately, mind. She apparently convulsed a little first. Everyone else, it seemed, carried on dancing around her until the number finished. At which time it was discovered, so was she. When questioned as to the reason they hadn't offered help, other dancers replied that they were of the opinion she was demonstrating a new style!

One thing for sure, it would never catch on.

As in most ex British colonies, the language was somewhat different, too. In the Nigerian version of English, "food" becomes "chop". And there are expressions such as "How de body?" which translates to "How are you?" and they see things "Wid my very own eyes".

Enquiring as to how a local helper could manage to carry such a load as a sixty pound transmitter single handed, he explained in the inimitable fashion of the area; `She go for head, massa.'

Frustrations were part of the daily routine, if you didn't laugh you'd cry. Take the time Ian Easterbrook managed to get hold of a leg of New Zealand lamb. A real coup, that. Especially so, being as Ian was a Kiwi. Looking forward in anticipation, he instructed his house-boy to prepare it for that evening, when he would be bringing some friends home to dinner.

Just as well Ian had only revealed his fare as being "something special" rather than roast lamb, planning to surprise his guests. And surprised they were, for what they sat down to was lamb stew.

The replacement house-boy proved to be no better.

`What you want for dinna, massa?' he asked one morning as Ian left for work .

'Oh, I don't know what time I'll be in, Sunday, just get a chicken from the market and put it in the fridge.'

That evening, on arriving home, Ian went to get a beer. But as he opened the fridge door he found himself facing a live chicken. He said it stood there, centre stage, like an artist in the spotlight, head hunched, shivering on its feet.

So, as can be seen, in Nigeria, as in Africa itself, life was rarely boring. I recall going in the bank one day, asking to see the manager, who eventually appeared. It was someone I knew. Just like any banker in the UK he was dressed for the part; white shirt, tie, lightweight jacket. He had a bankers actions as well, only to be expected, for he *was* a banker; senior staff. Then I recalled how this man had looked last night when I ran across him entering a local dance hall. Anyone less like a banker I'd yet to meet - rumpled Hawaiian shirt, dirty jeans, and wrecked out of his mind. Nor did it seem like a banker's location, this drinking club cum dance-hall, open to the elements. Needless to say, all the girls were available, at a price.

*

Roadblocks became rife. Driving to work one day I was confronted by armed troops. Then one of them was inviting me to step out of the vehicle, to open the boot. This I saw as being a reasonable request. He was, after all, carrying a Kalashnikov, pointing it at my head. So out I got. They wouldn't be looking for anything in particular, I knew, just going through the motions, enjoying doing so. Though, if they saw anything they particularly fancied, they would no doubt help themselves. Power at the point of a gun. I knew the feeling, recalled that exercise at Seletar, the officer I'd challenged. Difference was, that had been a game, my gun not loaded. These would be, that was for sure.

Even safe in the knowledge that he didn't intend shooting me was no great comfort. Gun safety being as sloppy as it was this was no guarantee I wouldn't end up *getting* shot. I could imagine the scenario:

'What dat noise? Why you lay down, you tired? Hey, dis man leaking.'

It happens, but at the time the mind is occupied by other thoughts - the likelihood of my liberty being seriously curtailed, for instance - so it was only later, when I thought about the situation, that my heart fluttered for a second or two.

Another such situation occurred in South Africa, during the apartheid period. Getting lost whilst driving into Johannesburg from the south, my wife and I inadvertently ended up in the heavily protected township of Sowetto. No idea how we even got in, but the place was definitely out of bounds to white people! Especially so without the necessary permit, which, needless to say, we definitely didn't have! Entry had seemed strangely easy, especially as we weren't even attempting to enter. Getting out was another matter altogether. It was dusk and we certainly didn't wish to stop and ask directions. But maybe the dim light was to our advantage, for we were neither stopped nor, apparently, noticed for what we were. From all I'd read before, and heard since, that also had been a time of grave danger. Or had it?

*

It was another fine day over the Gulf of Guinea. The sun hung high in a sky dotted with fleecy white clouds. Nothing serious or threatening, yet. But they would build throughout the day to form billowing cumulus, possibly the towering cu-nim. A thousand feet below was the placid sea, its calmness disturbed only by a long, rolling swell.

There were six of us in the S55's cabin, on our way to Mobil Oil Company's Ocean Master Two offshore drilling rig. We were flying in a Mk.10 version of the S55 helicopter; turbine-powered, more reliable and muscular than the Mk.2 we'd used with the RAF in Malaya. We were fifteen minutes out from the island of Fernando Po, twenty from the rig, and I was well into the latest edition of *Playboy* when my attention was diverted.

Something serious, then! Had to be if it were to unglue my eyes from the centrefold.

It was.

There was a whoosh, a sheet of flame out of the exhaust, then the silence of a shut down engine. Oh oh! Thought I. Rather quickly, too, for when the engine stops on a single-engined helicopter, the only way to go is down. The direction in which we were now heading. But no problem, we had a well trained pilot who did all the right things. So smooth was the transition from forward flight to autorotation I immediately assumed it to be a practice, as in Malaya, all those years ago. Intuition told me otherwise, not with a load of passengers on board. It was an opinion that was confirmed when we actually set down on the ocean, the pilot calling for us to launch and board the life-raft, the aircraft's floats ensuring it did so. As we swiftly complied, he sat, half in, half out of the cockpit, transmitting a Mayday call. This was picked up by the captain of a overflying airliner, the call relayed to Santa Isabel tower. They, in turn, informed Mobil, which is when things really got moving. Just as well.

Within sight was a large freighter, heading our way but actually steaming towards Cameroon. So, to attract attention we set off distress signals.

Given the conditions, there was no way for him not to see those billowing clouds of flourescent orange smoke, but despite maritime laws that specify ships must offer assistance to anyone in distress, he steamed willy-nilly on his way. Maybe he also assumed it to be an exercise? It had been so perfectly executed it almost could have been so. No injuries, no panic. Little time for it really. It was over almost before we realized it had begun. Even if, once in the dinghy, with time to think, I realized the adrenalin had kicked in.

Apparently, the chief pilot also seemed to regard it as an exercise, for when later circling overhead - awaiting the arrival of the first of many vessels steaming towards us - he was to instruct our pilot not to let us touch the supplies.

'They're for emergencies,' he advised.

This from a man who was later to remark upon the size and number of sharks with which we were - unbeknown to us - encircled. They were probably gnashing their teeth just waiting for us to be served up.

All ended well though. After four hours bobbing around, sunbathing - not to be recommended, even on a day as calm as that - the rescue vessels arrived to pick us up. The helicopter remained afloat on its buoyancy cushions and was eventually towed back to the island.

Close offshore was a "stacked" rig - out of work between jobs. With their crane they picked the stricken aircraft up and placed it on the helideck. A quick engine change, a thorough check, and it was back in service in a couple of days.

During WWII, the Irving Parachute company awarded a pin - a small gold caterpillar with ruby eyes - to any aircrew whose life had been saved by use of a parachute; recipients could subsequently become members of the Caterpillar Club. A similar award - a Goldfish pin - was made to aviators who had ditched in the sea, and taken to their dinghy. In the ejection seat years there was also the Martin Baker Club, who awarded a special tie to those who had been forced to eject in one of their products. I was later to learn that the above escapade immediately qualified me for membership of the Goldfish Club - which I thought had ended with the cessation of WWII hostilities, as had the Caterpillar Club - should I wish to apply. Of course I did!

*

Customs officers, especially the Nigerian variety, were a continual bugbear, so, over the years I developed a few ideas for dealing with them upon arrival. (That I never had anything to hide didn't matter, they were just looking for a cash "donation", were prepared to hold you up as long as this took.) As most were only capable of concentrating on one thing at a time, I felt it a good idea to divert their attention. I'd pick the most senior officer, talk to him as if he were a long-lost friend, for they love their staff to see they have the respect of a European. I'd pull out a cheap calculator, pass it to him, show him what it could do, tell him to keep it. (We did a lot of work for Geophysical Services Inc, of which Texas Instruments was an offshoot - in fact, TI eventually grew so big it became the parent company - we therefore had access to bargain basement cost electronics.)

Then there was the toy dog ruse I once resorted to, purely as an experiment. I had back-up calculators in my briefcase, just in case; didn't need them. The dog was wound up and made to perform. It yelped, ran around, did somersaults, wagged its tail. The officer was delighted, grinning and clapping his hands like a child. 'Keep it,' I told him. He did, wished to see nothing more. Out came the magic chalk, on went the indecipherable squiggle. Alongside, those not so wise or experienced were having their souls bared to the world!

Departure was even more difficult. First came the queue for your tax exemption certificate to be stamped, which allowed you to queue up at the ticket desk only to learn that your ticket, which clearly indicates your reservation to be, OK - in airline parlance, confirmed - is not. Confirmation in most third world countries can only be taken for granted once you actually clear their airspace. Not merely when seated and airborne, mind, that's no guarantee you'll not be returning, aircraft required by

399

the President, say. One good reason for not utilising the local airline, providing there is an alternative. No, best not to relax until you are well clear of their airspace.

I recall the time Ron Hewson and his crew had just completed a job in Ghana, were about to depart to begin another, further down the coast. Different job, different country. Life was like that. We'd roam around for months on end without going home. Sometimes it was years. We got our breaks transferring from one place to the next, as in this instance.

As usual, it seemed pre-dinner drinking had got out of hand, and by the time dinner was over some of the crew decided to visit the Accra casino. Come midnight, Ron, and Lynne, his wife, decided it was time to round them up, remind them they had a plane to catch very early the next morning. Two of the party refused to leave, so, nothing else to be done, Ron left them to it.

When the rebels finally did depart they discovered there was no longer any transport running. So what did they do? Used their initiative, naturally. Talk about pushing your luck, these guys actually flagged down an army patrol, managed to commandeer a personnel carrier to take them to the airport, for a fee, of course. Too late, though. The flight had already left.

They eventually turned up in Gabon some days later, after an adventurous trip. But so had it been for the rest of the crew, it seems. Ron and Co. had boarded the Cameroon Airlines scheduled flight, as planned. The aircraft, a brand new Boeing 737, was routed from Accra direct to Libreville, Gabon. Only, this being Africa, that wasn't the way things went. It made an unscheduled stop en-route, in Douala, Cameroons.

The newly created airline had a fleet of just three Boeing 737's, and, it appears, that day was to be the official inauguration. Airline officials decided they wanted all their aircraft lined up for the ceremony, hence the diversion; or was it a skyjacking? Upon landing, the passengers were disembarked, bundled aboard an old, chartered, piston engined DC4, and sent on their way. Albeit quite a few hours late. And if you'd had a connection scheduled in Libreville? Tough luck. That's Africa for you.

*

During the early part of the year West Africa is affected by winds which blow down from across the Sahara. Known as Harmattan, after the name of the wind, it is a period when the air, so full of extremely fine grains of sand, becomes hazy, thus vision is very limited. The situation can last for up to a month, until the rains come and wash the air.

It was during Harmattan that one American captain was to find himself en-route from Port Harcourt, in Nigeria, to an offshore facility. This was early days in offshore exploration, long before safety "experts" appeared on the scene; in fact, possibly one of the reasons they eventually did! The vessels, to say nothing of the crews, were not necessarily ideal for the job, but as there were huge profits to be made, so safety often took a back seat. And why not, for to me safety has always been a personal thing; any job is as safe as the person doing it wants it to be. Anyway, a vessel in which the compass that was off by thirty degrees, dodgy radar, an unlicensed captain. So what, they had made the trip many times before. All the captain did was follow the river out to sea, turn right, run until he came upon a certain landmark on the beach, turn left, and in a couple of hours there was the rig. But what happens when you can't see the beach? Then the eight hour trip can take three days, and you will end up closer to Gabon than Nigeria! This guy would probably have made South Africa had the Harmattan not lifted!

*

In Douala, a major city in the ex-French colony, of Cameroun, West Africa, there is a road which descends a fairly steep hill to join the main road which runs along the bottom. A group of us were walking up this hill one day, probably heading for one of our usual haunts - Danny's Bar, the Akwa Palace Hotel, or La Fregrate - when sweeping past, heading down for the roundabout junction, going at a terrific pace, came a local on a bicycle. He wore national dress, a loose kaftan thing topped by a flowing cloak. Nothing unusual in this. Often they'd get caught up in the chain, or rear wheel, but his was streaming out behind, clear of the wheel, though all was not well. He was in big trouble, and he knew it.

"Accidente! Accidente!" he was shouting, hanging on with one hand, waving traffic aside with the other. Either that or he was waving goodbye. Seemed he had a problem with his brakes. Like a dire shortage of! From our viewpoint it looked hilarious, but apparently not from his. In fact he didn't seem at all amused. Not with that main road rushing towards him.

Give him his due, he was right about there being an accident. It happened when he arrived at that roundabout, where a gendarme was on traffic duty. Yeah, I know, a roundabout. But this is Africa. Anyway, this gendarme couldn't believe what he was seeing. He held up his hand, the universal sign for stop, but as that didn't seem to help any, he leapt out of the way. In the nick of time, too. But it was a close run thing, cloak catching his hat and flicking it off his head. As for the guy on the bike, or off it, as he now was, he arced upward at undiminished speed, giving a fair impersonation of superman. Arms ahead of him, cleaving a path through the air, cloak streaming. Quite graceful, for a while. Until he reached the top of the parabola, then gravity took charge. He plunged back to earth, an avalanche of arms, legs and clothing. I knew the feeling.

One thing never ceased to amaze me in Africa: the speed with which a crowd could gather, especially to watch someone else's misfortune. Didn't see the end result, for by that time the point of impact was hidden from view. But the bike was definitely a write off.

We continued on our way, intent on reaching one of those bars.

*

Life could actually be quite stressful at times, yet at other times it could be quite relaxed, especially when working for the French.

I recall the time we were required to set a location for a rig, offshore Gabon. So we flew down there. Shortly after our arrival we paid a visit to the client.... No! This is Gabon we are talking about, so I'll amend that to *shortly after arriving at our hotel*, ie the following day, for it usually took quite a time to clear immigration, catch a taxi into town, check in at the hotel and settle in. This in itself a tiresome procedure - "no, we didn't receive your telex", and all the other excuses as to why they didn't have a room. At least, not until money changed hands. After that for sure you needed a drink, or two - the relaxing part. So the checking of equipment was delayed, but we knew it would be in a terrible state. Anxious to get out of the place, those finishing a job don't always have at heart the best interests of those who will start the next one, even though it could be themselves. Let's face it, after a couple of months in West Africa, one is filled with this strange desire to step aboard an aeroplane as soon as possible. Going.... well, anywhere!

So, it was the next morning before we got to checking things out, reporting to the Elf offices, rigging the vessel, and then, advising when we were ready to depart to sea. The client, who was to ride the boat with us, suggested we set sail after we had lunch on board. So we sat down and he ordered up a meal from the galley. Well, fresh, crispy french bread, various cheeses and Hors d'oeuvres, and of course, a bottle of wine. We sat and ate, and talked, drank some wine, ate some more, drank more wine.... Then the client ordered more bread, once we had cleaned up the original, then more cheese, same for the wine. "That is the thing when eating like this," he said, in French English. "The bread runs out before ze cheese is finished, or the cheese runs out whilst there is still bread remaining, and you need to keep ordering more wine." But it was all going down extremely well. Finally, mid afternoon, topping up our wineglasses yet again, he said, "I sink we will go and set ze location tomorrow." Fair enough, he was the boss, and by this time we were happy enough to comply with his suggestion. Happy enough for anything. So we carried on eating and drinking. Why not. No point stopping now, it would soon be dinner time!

No, there is absolutely nothing wrong with the French way of eating.

*

It has been said that the best view of Africa is that seen through the bottom of a glass, preferably whilst seated on the after-deck of a liner, en route for England - or almost anywhere come to that.

My turn to depart the African continent came in March 1972, by air, and I made it relatively unscathed. The *quid pro quo* for this was... well, several quid, in actual fact. An amount that just so happened to coincide with the total contents of my wallet - in Nigerian Pounds, naturally, any "real" currency being well stashed! Nigerian currency was almost worthless outside the country anyway, but our company would reimburse us the the official rate. But at least I'd broken free of Nigeria. At last.

So there you have it. As can be seen, after living there for so long, anywhere else was bound to offer more than a passing attraction.

And so they did.

*

A Trip Around the Cape
South Africa, during the years of apartheid, was another matter entirely. We could have been another world.

If one could pick an ideal time to arrive over southern Africa it would have to be during the late afternoon.

403

As the Boeing 747, bearing the colours of South African Airways, broke through the light overcast on its final approach to Jan Smuts, so it afforded us our first view of the lush green Highveld of the Witwatersrand. Away in the distance we could make out the tall, concrete and glass structures which formed the central core of the city as Johannesburg sparkled brilliantly. A jewel set on a background of green baize. But it was an area beyond the office blocks to which the attention was drawn, for this was dominated by high, flat-topped mounds which, in the early evening light, glowed with such a strange yellowness they exuded an almost luminescent quality. These were man-made mountains. The tailings from mines located hundreds of feet below ground. A reminder, if such were needed, of the wealth upon which this city had been founded.

The aircraft touched down smoothly, its tyres caressing the runway as if grateful to be home again after the long non-stop flight from London. (As a form of protest against apartheid, SAA aircraft were refused landing rights in most African countries. Hence their use of the long range 747SP.)

I quickly realized that hostility was present only if it was apparent you had prejudged the country prior to arrival. Wife No.2 and I had no such preconceived ideas, and so, with a minimum of time spent on formalities we were admitted to the Republic.

I don't really know what it was I expected of South Africa, certainly nothing like what I saw; a country full of beauty, friendliness, and pleasant surprises. A normal country. No sign of the undercurrent of unrest brought about by apartheid. From reading the press back home one almost expected rioting in the streets, cities in flames. This was far from the truth. This could have been one of almost any of the so-called advanced nations; only the sparrows were multi-hued, the cats somewhat larger, not so cuddly.

Travel almost anywhere else in Africa, and, without going out of your way you can witness all of the things those countries say are happening here, where you don't see them! Possibly the only thing the South Africans have to answer for is being honest. Discrimination *was* practised, they admitted to that. But it's also rife in many black nations too, along with murder, oppression, corruption, and impoverishment, to name but a few. Only difference being, the governments of those countries would have you believe otherwise.

From a seventh storey hotel window I gazed out in

wonderment. Johannesburg was all I'd imagined it to be, and more. I saw before me a modern city, situated on a plateau which less than a century ago had been flat, green veld. It looked a dream from my privileged view.

Even as I watched, the sun dipped over the far horizon; slapdash, salmon-pink brushstrokes against a darkening, powder-blue background. Night falling with tropical haste. Almost as if someone had reached out and drawn the blinds.

That night we dined royally on succulent steak and lobster tails, which we washed down with superb Cape wines.

*

Rain had cleansed the city overnight and now the air tasted fresh and pure, an illusion, no doubt, but imagination can often be vivid enough to be believed.

Johannesburg was the gateway through which we arrived, and through which we would depart, but during the next four weeks we planned to see much more of the country, therefore the afternoon found us winging our way to Durban, in Natal. Here we stayed with one of Elizabeth's school friends, out at Gillits, up in the hills behind the city. Less humidity, far more tranquillity.

We spent that weekend in the beautiful Drakensbergs, where the grass was moss-like: green, soft and velvety, and beard letchin, or Spanish moss, was draped from the branches of the trees.

The days flew by, each bringing with it a new experience. There was the embarrassment of booking a trip to a game reserve, over the telephone.

`We have a tour scheduled for Shushuwe,' the girl at the other end replied in answer to my enquiry.

`Oh!' I answered, somewhat at a loss. `Where's that? I didn't see it in the brochure.'

A laugh tinkled down the line. `You did,' she said, `but you wouldn't know it.' Then she spelt it out: `H-l-u-h-l-u-w-e.'

In the event the tour was cancelled through lack of support, so we hired a car and went off on our own. But as insurance cover was non-existent if you took a hire car into a game reserve - for reasons which were soon to become apparent - we traded our hire car for that belonging to our host.

There were animals aplenty. So many it made me wonder what it must have been like years ago, when herds were thick on the ground. Before advancing civilization drove them deeper into the bush, and hunters depleted their ranks.

With the fist grey light of the African dawn we rose, before the sun had even cleared the horizon. On a far hillside woodsmoke drifted up from the beehive huts of a Zulu kraal, but in the stillness of the morning it layered and hung there, the smell of it permeating the air. But there were other smells also, intermingling. Smells unique to Africa: Animals, the open country, unwashed bodies and other, oddly familiar, yet unidentifiable, pungent odours.

This was the best time to view the game, before it became insufferably hot for both humans and animals alike, so with our guide we set off in an open-topped Land Rover.

Just like a gamekeeper, an experienced guide finds the animals by the simple expedient of knowing where to look, and of watching and listening. The calls and bellows each have a specific meaning and can be interpreted almost as easily by knowledgeable humans as by animals.

Graceful, long-necked giraffes towered above the thorny Acacia trees, and in the open areas Impala and Springbok bounded away, leaping high in the air, their dainty feet seeming to barely kiss the ground.

A clump of Camel-thorn trees were filled with nature's hanging baskets, home of the Golden Weaver Bird, their owners shrilling loudly as they fluttered about, some clinging upside-down by the entrance, trying to attract a mate.

The time flew, and almost before we realized it the tour was over and it was time to depart, for the gates closed at 1800hrs. Now back in our own car, we realized we had left ourselves just enough time to make it to the nearest exit, provided I drove like a Swedish rally driver. So I did. Until, rounding a bend I was forced to slither to a halt in a cloud of dust and curses. There in the middle of the narrow track was two tons of rhinoceros. (A "twenty tonnner", according to my wife's estimation!) Not dangerous, they said, as long as you were careful, and they didn't have young to protect. Needless to say, this one did. They both stood there doing nothing in particular, certainly not moving. I doubted they could even see us, for apparently they are very short sighted. But they knew we were around, having heard us arrive. Well, as long as they didn't start to amble our way - cognizant of the fact that rhino's amble at such a lick they couldn't even be considered to be running until in the 30 - 40 mph range - it went without saying that we too should remain motionless. This, I felt, ruled out articulating my right ankle and attempting to zoom past.

Anyway, the rules were firm: don't approach the animals, for fear of death - not that of the animals, I might add - and never leave your vehicle. There were, I noted, a notable lack of instructions on what course of action to pursue in the event of your being forcibly ejected from said vehicle, and I could just imagine returning the car to our hosts, along with an opinion: "These Japanese cars aren't really worth a shit. Look, a rhino did that just for practice!"

In the event they eventually wandered off into the bush, leaving me to break all records to make the gate in time.

Night was spent at the Zululand Safari Lodge, the bungalows we slept in being designed along the style of a Zulu hut. Circular, looking like white concrete barrels wearing a straw hat. But these were fitted with all mod-cons. Tourists, it appeared, wished to view the animals and observe the natives, but not to live in like fashion. Authentic safaris were available, but they required time, and, for the real thing - roughing it under canvas, albeit top quality - lots of money.

Wildlife roamed freely throughout the hotel grounds and we were surprised to find a rhinoceros grazing between the rondavels.

Later, unbeknown to us in the safety of our room, the hotel dog was foolishly terrorizing a zebra close-by. We became aware of this only as I opened the door to step out. As I did so, a dark streak flashed past and into the room, whilst outside I was faced with a snorting zebra which skidded to a dusty halt not yards away.

Putting events in order, I turned around to find a wet nose protruding from beneath the bed. It was accompanied by a mischievous yet doleful pair of eyes, watching me, pleading not to be surrendered to that big bully of a striped donkey which waited outside. The eyes won the day, of course, how could they not!

It rained that night. Heavily.

`Yeah,' said the barman, as I expressed amazement at the ferocity of the downpour, `When it rains here it really comes down. Dry one minute, then you're off looking for a boat!'

As we lay in bed we listened to the sounds of the night, a farrago of squeals, hums, whines, croaks, growls and roars. Some difficult to differentiate between bird and beast. The insect noises no puzzle at all as they whanged and whined around the room, sensing blood but peeved at their inability to penetrate the netting which screened us.

As we lay there in relative security we hazarded a guess as to the owner of a particular call, neither of us having much idea.

*

After a couple of weeks we flew to Port Elizabeth, on the south coast. Here we picked up a rental car for the drive - along what is known as "The Garden Route" - to Capetown, fifteen hundred kilometres to the west.

The road curved between spectacular mountain ranges and the sea, passing forests, lakes and wildlife reserves. There were resort towns which bore names such as Plettenberg Bay, Knysna, George, Wilderness, and Mossel Bay. And so on to the Cape, where the great, flat-topped mountain towered over the city, the boundaries of which began on the lower slopes, sweeping down and out, spreading themselves around the coast where the waters of Table Bay prevented further outward expansion. Here, to the west, it formed the suburbs of Sea Point and Green Point, and inland, to the east, Groote Schuur and Newlands, where I knew the Test cricket oval to be located.

Next we tracked off to the east, and the pretty Cape Dutch area around Stellenbosch, with its vineyards and large estates. This was real wine country. Vines stretched away towards the horizon, row upon row; an army on parade. The impression was of colourful regiments covering the rolling countryside. Vast areas from which, given time, would come gallons of delectable wines. The Cabernet Sauvignon, the Pinotage.

Then it was back to Cape Town, and from there, Johannesburg - London, SAA kindly upgrading us to their Diamond Class upstairs lounge for the long return flight. A totally pleasant, eye-opening trip to a magnificent country, during which I met very few people who were unhappy with their lot.

And what now, Post Apartheid? As in the rest of post colonial Africa things only seem to have changed only for the worse. The people have gained their freedom, yes, but freedom from what, and for what? The majority of everyday Africans I met in Africa, anywhere from Nigeria to South Africa, felt they were better off under colonial rule. At least under Apartheid they knew where they stood.

One difference for sure. At least the tourists and businessmen flew in now, in droves. The infection which had

408

kept them away, a disease of the moral kind, had been eradicated.

*　　*

Chapter Fourteen
DOODLEBUG DOODLES

'**W**hat is it you actually do?' The question was put to me repeatedly over the years, my answer usually being muttered and evasive. This I feel is due to one of the following: a/ to the layman, what I did was difficult to explain; b/ there were times when I wasn't entirely sure myself; or c/ I automatically assumed the person behind the question was merely socializing, therefore not particularly interested in a truthful answer anyway.

I could always have bluffed my way, I suppose, said I was a racing driver, for I had driven racing cars at Brands Hatch. But no, driving a racing car didn't make me a racing driver, just as flying an aircraft never made me a pilot. (By the same rules I was no gigolo!)

Unfortunately, one result of this almost silent, but unhelpful evasiveness - I have never generally been a prolific conversationalist anyway - was that people occasionally tended to grab the wrong end of the stick. Either that, or they had just finished reading the latest Le Carré novel. This in turn could lead to an even more oblique line of questioning, as I found happenening at one well remembered party.

An old school friend, whom I hadn't seen around for some years - therefore a mate rather than a friend - wandered across to where I stood. My only real recollection of him were his eyes; sad-looking, imploring almost, like those of an unsold puppy in a pet shop window.

Luckily he introduced himself, for I was completely at a loss as to his name. But I did notice he carried a bottle of what looked like very good wine, going by the label. As it was by now at the lower levels, I held out my glass whilst we talked, a gesture for him to fill it, which, to his credit, he did. He asked the usual questions, received the usual slightly evasive answers. Then, after making a show of looking round, as if to be sure no one else was taking an interest - or maybe to ensure I knew he knew what he was about - words were whispered, voice as hushed as that of an atheist in a cathedral. 'You're not.... involved with the Foreign Office, are you?' A reference, I assumed, to Queen Anne's Gate, or Vauxhall Cross, as it now is. You see, I read the spy novels too.

'What? You mean the Intelligence Services?' I replied, non too quietly. 'Not me. Pass on that.'

Despite such denials, I'm sure people still occasionally presumed I was. After all, it's not a thing someone of that ilk would be likely to admit to, is it? And my departures could, at times, be rather rapid and unexpected. Take for instance the evening I received a phone call advising me that I was urgently required in Norway, and no scheduled flight could guarantee my arrival in time, the vessel I was to join, due to sail shortly after dawn.

I was instructed to take a taxi to the military base at RAF Leeming - a full twenty miles north of home - from where, I'd been advised, onward transportation had been arranged. So, take a taxi I did.

Upon arrival at the guardroom I received a salute - well, it was rather grand for a taxi, I'll admit - along with a military escort out to the airfield where a light, twin-engined aircraft was scheduled to arrive. When it did, the door opened, a hand beckoned, and I, noting more than the odd person waiting around in the shadows, walked over and stepped aboard. Without shutting down, or a word being exchanged, the Bandeirante and myself, its lone passenger, disappeared into the darkness of the night. So what had been going through the minds of those officers and airmen standing around in the shadows, do you think? They too probably suspected me of being one of those "funny people"; the serviceman's euphemism for secret agents.

In actual fact I was whisked up to Glasgow, where I spent the night in a plush hotel. Next day it was off to Haugesund, Norway, in another chartered twin - one of Piper's American Indian tribe this time (Apache, as it happened) - once again, just myself and the pilot. It was a perfectly uneventful trip in the still, early morning air. Beautiful, too. And we landed at our destination long before the first scheduled flight was due to arrive. It was a flight I could well have been on, as it happened, for the ship's departure had been delayed due to reasons previously unforseen.

'You'd be embarrassed if I revealed how much it cost to get you here,' I was later told. Try me, thought I.

So, not one of those "funny people" at all. In reality, nothing more than a plain old doodlebugger, which, you'll recall, is a term pertaining to anyone engaged in the search for minerals, particularly so when it comes to oil and gas. Not the development and production side of the business, you understand, mainly exploration. A vast difference.

A prime requirement for any seismic exploration is an acoustic source. Offshore, this could range from the twenty to forty pounds of basic dynamite mix, as used back in the pioneering - non-environmental days - to the four thousand plus pounds per square inch compressed air of a contemporary, tuned airgun array.

Oh, oh. Here we go again. Mention of dynamite brings to mind a Norwegian guy I once found myself seated next to, on a flight to... well, Norway, would you believe. He introduced himself, then - usually a good move, to my way of thinking - bought me a drink. (Scandinavian, or SAS as it is known, must have been almost the last airline to get around to offering complimentary drinks.) Anyway, we got to discussing something or other when, after a couple more drinks the conversation drifted to a totally unrelated subject, as makeshift conversations generally tend to do. This time it was the merits, or otherwise, of building houses with the lower floor located below ground level. Interesting, eh?

'Difficult in Norway,' I prompted, knowing it was exactly what they did do over there. This despite the whole country appearing to be formed of solid granite.

'Ya, not so,' Olaf replied. A contradiction of terms for a start. 'I do it myself. A few sticks of dynamit' - that was how he pronounced it, dynamit - 'and whump.' His hands flew up. 'Ground or Germans,' he said. 'Same for both. Finish.' He then went on to explain how he'd gained his experience. 'During the war years, serving with the resistance.' Underground, I thought would have been a more appropriate term, given the subject under discussion.

Anyway, back to seismology. We have an acoustic source. Next requirement is a means of recording energy pulses reflected back from beneath the seabed, ie, hydrophones. These are towed behind the vessel, wired together in groups, the complete assembly - up to two miles in length - known as a seismic streamer.

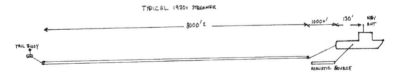

This acoustic source generates sound waves which penetrate

the ocean floor, and as depth of penetration is dependant upon strata and frequency, then a multi-frequency signal will give a variable return. These seismic data are recorded, and it is from such records a geophysicist, working his sorcery and b......t, will come up with an answer. This can range from, "No likelihood of oil here, old son," to the infrequently muttered, "Looks promising." In which case the area in question is subjected to further exploration magic, and or, the drilling of a very expensive hole which, in the end, is the only true test. And that, basically, is it. Except... It's not a lot of use someone discovering a possible source of barrels of the black stuff if they don't know where it was they were at to begin with. Which is where we came in.

Every shot, hole, platform, pipeline, or whatever, requires an accurate position fix, for which we supplied the coordinates. Simple, eh? Well, today, with the advent of GPS (for Global Positioning System - a series of satellites in fixed orbit around the globe) it is. Though not as simple as it could be. The reason? GPS - primarily a US military system - is strictly controlled by the Department of Defence, ie, the Pentagon, who trust hardly anyone. Even themselves, I suspect! So, to deny access to unauthorized users - in DoD speak, the Point Element (the enemy, or bad guys, to you and I) - data broadcast from the satellites is coded. Data available to the general public is transmitted on a separate code to that intended for military use, the quality of our data degraded by deliberately induced clock errors - termed, Selective Availability. Maybe thirty metre accuracy, as opposed to plus or minus one metre or less. OK for yachtsmen and the like, nowhere near good enough for the oil industry - or the airlines, come to that. We need the same kind of accuracy the military use for tossing their missiles around.

But a solution was soon devised.

With a receiver placed at a known location, it is a simple matter to calculate any data errors. You know where you are, you know where the GPS says you are. *Voilà!* as the French say. If these data - differential corrections - are then applied to any other receiver operating in the general area, almost all errors can be eliminated. In theory, error-free position data. And guess what? It works in reality too. Bingo! American prestige remains intact, we achieve the required accuracy. I still have a job. (That was back in the early nineties. Today, 2016,

Selective Availability is a thing of the past, hence the reason the GPS in your car is so accurate. Providing you bother to set it up correctly, that is! And keep your mapping data up to date)

A point of interest: During the original Gulf War - you remember, the world's first televised, as-it-happens, real-time war - SA was dispensed with, ie, switched off. This became necessary, as at the time there were not enough military-code receivers to go round, especially the hand held variety. The military therefore found a need to pop down to the local electronics store, there to purchase commercially available equipment. The SAS, for instance, were said to have used hand-held, yachting type receivers which, predictably, suddenly became extremely accurate. What chance now, those Scud missiles?

Another GPS story concerns itself with the very early days, when I was still unfamiliar with the system and all its nuances. An "expert" was dispatched to help with the installation, and to give me a few pointers as to its use. He was very helpful. Set everything up and checked it out before getting ready to leave.

'Great,' he says. 'Perfect.' He then handed me his card. 'If you experience any problems, give me a call. Any time, he stressed. Home number's on the back.' With which he disappeared, rather swiftly, as if he was late for something. The bar, for instance? Still, I was impressed. Until I *did* experience a problem. After hours, naturally; a weekend at that. So I called him at home, got his mother. Nice person by the sound of her. She talked about our Michael, how he wasn't in right now. She talked about the weather, the flowers she'd just planted, and wasn't it terrible how the government.... On and on it went. Trouble was, during all this she didn't once mention anything about what to do if the system hung up because your GPS receiver refused to accept the downloaded ephemeris data. Ah, well!

But that's GPS. Before the advent of such sophistication, back in the Stone Age, so to speak, at least as far as electronics were concerned, things were very different. Radio beacons, located at a number of onshore sites, transmitted a signal to a receiver on the vessel. This signal needed to be manually lined up on a marker pulse, the range read off a scale. Nothing automatic or fancy, navigation solely in the hands of the operator or, more often than not, fate.

What you had were two pre-computed ranges, fixing a

point at which you needed to position the vessel - although, before the advent of the portable computer (yes, there *was* such a time) even these needed to be computed by use of the human brain. You also had two indicated ranges, from which could be derived your present position. It was then down to the operator to instantly calculate range and bearing - you remember, Pythagoras, square roots etc - then position the vessel on the preplotted point. Not too difficult, for a single point. But for a preplotted sequence of any number of evenly spaced points, down which a seismic vessel was required to run in a straight line, not so easy. Difficult in fact, bearing in mind the streamer needed to be straight at the start of the line; ie, you were navigating two miles of ship, needed a long run in, needed to be accurate. When I say accurate, I mean relatively so. Back then? Plus or minus fifty metres, maybe. But even that required a well tuned installation; weather conditions which permitted the reliable propagation of radio waves; accurately located stations ashore, at least two of which were operational. It rarely happened. Therefore it has been known for an operator to run on time and bearing, an acceptable method for a very limited period, should you find yourself with but one, not altogether perfect, signal - again not entirely unheard off! Providing you started with two reasonable signals, ran long enough to establish the timing between shots, and course made good, it should, in theory, be possible to track the one station, maintain present heading, and call the shots off a stopwatch. Hopefully, once both signals returned, the line could be completed with but slight corrections to timing and heading. No one any the wiser, none of that dreaded "down-time" for either party. Alas, things don't always work out as planned.

'You can stop calling the shots now, Dave,' one not so gullible Party Manager called up to me. 'We've been aground five minutes.'

Oh, oh! *In flagrante delicto,* like.

Onshore meanwhile, many other problems were to be experienced, which is where ingenuity and adventure came to the fore. Stations needed to be set, on pre-surveyed sites. Then the equipment had to be imported, by fair means or foul. Yes, many's the time one of those large dugout canoes has rendezvoused with a seismic vessel offshore Africa, equipment hastily off-loaded, secreted ashore and assembled. Those smugglers of old had nothing on us.

Thus unhindered by stifling government regulations, the

survey could well be completed before the mountains of paperwork, bureaucratic dallying, size and number of kickbacks etc, had been negotiated and resolved. Sometimes they were never resolved, for communications out in the bush were often non-existent. As for your hypothetical bush telegraph, well..., even drums could be silenced for a few notes; provided such notes sported an image that bore a true likeness to the presidential incumbent!

Of course, the powers that be were often only too blissfully aware of our presence, happy to overlook such burdensome bureaucratic details, just so long as the relevant papers changed hands. Naturally, once again such paper featured a number, preferably followed by enough zeros to mount an attack on Pearl Harbour - as Clive James would have it. Free enterprise? Maybe. Though more than somewhat outside what is the conventional framework as regards such a system.

Apart from Africa, where corruption is anyway blatant, the financial handshake is also the natural way of doing business in South America, and elsewhere. Thus it was that - following in the wake of the Lockheed scandal (where large amounts of US dollars were handed out in order to secure military aircraft sales) - word came down from the parent company of a seismic operator to whom we were at the time contracted, that forthwith, everything was to be done by the book. Which is how we came to be standing by for two weeks in a Caribbean hotel. Whereas previously a day or two would suffice. Two weeks was the time it now took the relevant application to be officially processed and approved. Not that we were complaining. There *are* worse places to be stuck, on expenses!

As is the way with memories, it always seems to be the exotic which spring to mind. How easy it is to remember ten days in a luxury hotel in Rio, awaiting clearance of equipment that some aggrieved customs officer had deemed not to be accompanied by the correct documents. As previously mentioned, such documents - usually coloured - bore a portrait of the current dict... er, President, followed by a large denomination number. Or perhaps it was someone higher up the scale who decided the correct procedures had not been adhered to: ie, the above-mentioned documents fell somewhat short of expectations. It happened, and forgive me if I admit to not feeling entirely sympathetic towards my employers at these times.

Of course, that extended layover could happen in less welcoming circumstances. Most places in West Africa, or those of the Communist block, for instance. Much better there to get on with the job and get out, really, Although I must admit, we usually found something, or somewhere that offered acceptable entertainment of one form or another.

Columbia was another country in which I was to spend an enforced layover. The capital, Bogota, was a place that left me breathless. Not because of the sights - breathtaking enough, admitted - but the altitude. Over eight thousand feet above sea level takes some getting used to. One beer and you know you've had a drink. Bogota is also the kidnap capital of the world, so after a couple of days I left for Cartegena, on the Caribbean coast, a far more satisfactory option.

*

The limited range of our equipment required stations to be moved many times during the course of a survey, presenting us with many headaches and logistical problems, plus the means of generating a little extra revenue for that account in the Bahamas! (A bank that was later to crash, taking with it a considerable chunk of my savings. Actually, it didn't really crash so much as "move on"! The owner, a guy called Robert Vesco, just shut up shop and took off, mine and everyone else's savings taking off with him! Such is life. Easy come, easy go.)

There has been the odd bad investment, I'll admit. That bank apart, there was an Investment Fund - again, obviously investing in someone else's future as opposed to mine. There's been the odd gold mine, too, not to say gold itself (which dived in value the moment I became involved), and like that. (I never did get rid of that gold. Only a few ounces, admitted. But now it is worth around £1000 an ounce..... And had I not bought it, I would probably have squandered to money on something I no longer had.) Thing is, I never invested more than I could afford to loose - always a wise move - and, thankfully, the good investments more than covered the bad.

Back to the job. Shoran, (SHort RAnge Navigation) I used as late as 1984. Although by then in the last vestiges of retirement, enough was rescued from the ONI rubbish skip in NOLA, to enable us to conduct a survey in the Indian Ocean, off the Andaman Islands - definitely not on the tourist trail! It seemed the Indians were unwilling to pay for the greater accuracy of modern technology. Probably a good decision, for

417

that job ran a good few seasons, the monsoon weather often shutting us down until the following year.

Even by 1999 it was mainly computerized, digitized, automatic tracking GPS. All singing and dancing Pentium, Networks for Windows, and suchlike. The only physical input required was for someone to install and troubleshoot the systems, so as to ensure quality of output. Oh, and this paper-less office is also required to generate prodigious amounts of paperwork! Most of which will rarely be looked at by anyone ever again. Such is progress.

But all this gadding about meant I still got to fly. Quite a lot, in fact, in a variety of aircraft. I was to log many an hour on the scheduled airlines; piston engined aircraft in the early days, the DC's, by Douglas. They flew relatively slowly, through or around the weather rather than over. But from the comparatively low altitudes at which they flew, the sightseeing was good, even if the letdown could be quite scary in adverse conditions - wingtips lost in the fog. Bad enough in a Trident on the approach to Heathrow, and they were fully automated: auto approach, auto-throttle, Autoland. It was an extremely unnerving experience to sit there in the cabin on the let down into Heathrow, seeing nothing but dense fog outside. One could hear the engines adjusting the power so as to maintain the correct airspeed on the descent, knowing the pilots were sitting there doing nothing but trusting to luck, or the system. How did they feel about that one wonders?

In the third world there were no such facilities, it was a matter of trusting tired pilots. Then there were the semi-private, semi-personal flights; the charters. Nothing routine or scheduled about those, each an adventure in itself.

Undeterred by what they saw as petty rules and regulations, pilots often flew low, almost down on the deck at times. I appreciated these flights almost as much as the pilots obviously enjoyed them, although they were of course illegal. But with no radar control, little air traffic, few reporting points, what the hell. At times we could have been back in the barnstorming days.

Even the aircraft were different; whatever was available at the right price. Although we regularly used such as the DC3, Britten Norman Islander and Trislander, there were also many oddities: Beech 18, Westland Widgeon, Shorts Skyvan, Partenavia P68B, Max Holste Broussard; one I well remember, that. Gabon again, very low level. A bit lax on air traffic, so get it down on the beach, kind of thing.

Flying along the shoreline like that was exhilarating. The hot, oily smell of the big, noisy Pratt & Whitney radial throbbing away out front, leading the way as it were, high wing affording us a clear view. The creamy surf blurring past on the right, greenery leading to high ground on the left, golden yellow sand directly below. Real seat of the pants flying. Possibly, even a little risky at times. But what the hell, life is full of risk, isn't it? No risk, no adventure, which in itself equates to boredom - at least when one is young. The thing to remember, as ever, are the margins. On no account must you allow those to be cut too fine. And I have to admit, there were some pilots with whom I did not feel all that safe at times.

*   *

Chapter Fifteen

ROMANTIC INTERLUDES
1968

*T*he aircraft in which I departed Africa was a VC10; BOAC rather than Nigerian Airways, who also flew one of the type, until it crashed on the approach to Lagos, killing all on board. There were rumours of extra bodies being discovered in the cockpit, and of guns being found in the wreckage. But that is another story altogether.

Here I was, home again, along with all the feelings that are generated by the sight of that familiar landscape sliding past beneath the wings as the aircraft exits the cloud-base on its descent. The green fields of England; rolling countryside; a patchwork of fields and woodland; the occasional golf course; farms, pastures and open country; rivers, lakes, towns and villages, castles and cottages. Is there anywhere so green and peasant as England?

The romantically rural eventually gave way to suburban semis and urban terraces. Then along came London and its environs: the Isle of Dogs and the silver thread of the Thames; Westminster; Twickenham - stadium apart, row upon row of identical houses lining narrow streets along which were parked a rainbow necklace of toy-like cars - and the castle at Windsor, if approaching from the west. A football ground passed by, still way below; twenty-two colourfully striped insects moving purposefully about in pursuit of an invisible ball.

Up here the smooth, aeronautical lines were about to be broken, slats and flaps emerging from the leading and trailing edges of the wings, spoilers above; the geometry of low-speed flight. Beneath us, unseen, but felt and heard, the undercarriage would be sliding and locking into place, four-wheel bogies ready to support that which the wings would soon be incapable of supporting. Lower and lower we edged, as if feeling our way down, a perfectly controlled descent, vortices spiralling away behind in our turbulent wake.

Buildings: houses and shops; a school; commerce in its many guises; traffic-filled roads. All flashed past, for even low speed flight in a large jet is well on the way to one hundred and sixty knots.

Very low on the approach now, slower too - probably one-ten to one-twenty - almost at touchdown. Cars parked, people watching. White faces turned up towards the sky, towards us. Enthusiasts, like myself, unable to pass up on yet another wondrous and graceful approach. Over the boundary fence, shadow rushing up to meet us, to be reunited on the rubber-streaked runway. Away in the distance other aircraft depart their stands, fully refreshed, setting off to seek new adventures of their own.

To someone like myself, that is what flying is all about. It's not just a matter of getting from A to B. The travel is incidental, every flight is an adventure. The smaller the aircraft, the more personal the adventure. The mere act of settling myself into my seat fills me with excitement rather than apprehension, anticipation rather than trepidation. In airline parlance, A to B for this particular flight had originally been, LOS (Lagos Ikeja) to LHR (London Heathrow), although, for personal reasons, I had made a diversion.

So much for the arrival. I now felt slightly deflated as I joined the throngs rushing to clear immigration, to collect and manipulate a maverick baggage trolley, to clear customs, then transfer myself to Terminal One. I found the Domestic terminal to be slightly less chaotic. Now was the time to relax, even though there was yet one more leg to complete, LHR to Leeds/Bradford (LBA).

There would be other such arrivals over the months to come, therefore just as many departures, for I had time on my hands, money in my pocket and in the bank, plans to be fulfilled.

Having spent a few months on the job, I had accumulated quite a bit of what the Americans called "Off Time" (days off, or leave.). This could be taken between jobs, as and when one felt like it. Stop off somewhere new and exciting on the way, or at home itself. Wherever you fancied, and for as long as you wanted, for "Offtime" could be extended for as long as one wanted, unpaid, of course, after you had used up your accumulated days.

In Nigeria, or wherever it was I happened to be, I listened to the news from home, read the week-old papers, and the magazines, so I was well aware of what was going on. I felt the Swinging sixties were passing me by, longed to be part of it. So here I was, ready and waiting.

Now I had some cash in the bank I had decided to take some of that accumulated off time. Quite a bit of time, actually, for as well as catching up with those Swinging Sixties, the intent was to fulfil a dream and follow the Formula One Grand

Prix Circus around Europe.

I had put the plan into action immediately, diverting myself through Spain on the way home from Fernando Po, off the coast of West Africa. I did this so as to catch the Spanish Formula Two race at Barcelona's Montjuich Park circuit. Just as well, for that was the last time I saw Jim Clark drive. Six days later he met his death driving in a lower category German F2 race at Hockenhiem. The master was no more. This formed another of those time and place memories that stick forever in the mind.

Like every other enthusiast of the time (and over the years) I saw Clark as being the best ever. I had watched him many a time at races in England. Recalled the day in 1964 I'd witnessed him hop into three different cars and drive in three classes of race at Oulton Park: Lotus Cortina saloon; Lotus 19 sports car; and Lotus Elan GT; He won every race. He went over to America and eventually won their home-grown Indianapolis 500 mile race. That really got him noticed, and the Indy 500 was never the same again.

On Sunday April 7th 1968, I was at Brands Hatch with a friend to watch the BOAC 500km race, in which Jim had hoped to drive the Ford F3L - a new model Sports Car. Instead, Lotus, to whom he was contracted, had entered him in a minor Formula Two race at Hockenhiem, Germany. As we were on the way home from Brands, my friend asked me to stop briefly at a relative's house, as he needed to pick something up. I'd waited outside in the car, and as my friend got back in he said, "Jim Clark was killed at Hockenhiem." I just looked at him and replied, "If you had picked any other driver I might have believed you." But then I looked at him again, and his face revealed the truth. You see I, like most, believed Jim Clark was too good. It could never happen to him. I think it was Chris Amon, New Zealand F1 driver, who commented, "If it can happen to Jim, what chance do we have!"

Everyone has a hero, someone to look up to in life. As far as motor sport went, mine had been Jim Clark; farmer, gentleman, racing driver.

*

It was my brother, George, who first afforded me a glimpse of Sixties lifestyle. A brief glimpse it was, too. Nor was it happening up in Yorkshire, I'll tell thee that for nowt. So, after a quick trip up to the family home, or pub as it still was, I was soon to be retracing my steps. This time by rail, and is not looking out of train windows a good way to conjure up the memories. In days past I recall seeing advertising hoardings located in the fields alongside the track, now there were none. I wondered if this was evidence that trains now travelled too fast for anyone to be able to read the adverts, or had attention spans contracted. No matter, they'd been eyesores more than anything. Industrial adverts. Not the kind of thing that invited one to do anything interesting, or seductive. Now, I noticed, any industry sited close to the tracks advertised themselves, gratis; large letters painted on walls or roofs. But the telephone lines were as remembered, up to their old tricks: the seeming wish to droop towards the ground, only to be jerked back into place every few seconds.

*

London is big. Over nine million souls huddling together for shelter. To me, caught up in the mass of humanity funnelling into the underground, en-route to the centre, it seemed they had all come out at once. It would be the same all over the city at this hour: commuters flowing in at one point, being whisked through a dark tube to various destinations around the metropolis, where they would again spew out onto the streets. Be the same above ground, too, on the buses. Only the buses travelled at a more leisurely pace, caught up in the traffic snarl that was London. Too many cars, too much noise, too many people in too much of a hurry; too much humidity, too much hustle and bustle. I loved it all the same, it was another of my favourite cities. Not only that, it also contrasted sharply with the life I had been living.

On the underground I saw a man with a bicycle. Imagine that if you will, in the rush hour at Piccadilly Circus! "No smoking" signs were everywhere. No signs against graffiti though, which also was everywhere. Baker Street station seemed out of line with the rest; dim and aged, as if still awaiting the arrival of Sherlock Holmes.

Brother George had taken a job in London, set up home here, a small flat which he shared with old school friend, Martin - my class, not George's. We'd never been really close, George and I. He did his thing, I did mine. We rarely went out together, never played together, never even walked to school together - my choice, the latter, for more often than not he'd be late. I'd had no wish to be, knowing the consequences such rashness could bring in those days of corporal punishment. Got my share as it was. But that was all in the past. The older we got the closer we became. Anyway, this was different, George now had something which could be of use to me. His flat became a base to any friends or relatives visiting the capital. I recall times when, incumbents apart, there would be two or three of us staying there together, one on the sofa, two on the floor. A bit of a crush in the morning, for bathroom and toilet - two floors down - were shared with the occupants of the other flats.

I recall my visits mainly as a series of cameos. Not all that distinct, either, though not because of the usual Sixties reasons. I do remember Lyons Corner House, located somewhere near Hyde Park. Breakfast there, lunch probably at the Ace Cafe, out in North West London, its pinball machines and jukebox well secured. The Ace was a classic example of The Great British Transport "Caff," as they were known to the majority - especially those who inhabited the Ace, for this was a favourite hang out for motor cycling fraternity; the legendary "Rockers", or Ton-up Boys, the nearby North Circular Road their racetrack. Cafe was far too pretentious a word for them. Foreign too. Such as the Ace are almost a lost institution in these days of health food mania, not to say the Department of Health and Safety - who have managed to put lots of similar institutions out of business! Health foods? To me, health foods were things my father suggested I should eat. Or else...!

In the evenings it was often Mac's, 100 Oxford Street. We'd go there for the Trad jazz: Lyttelton, Colyer, Lightfoot, Barber, Bilk, *et al.* A crowded atmosphere, where waves of sound washed over us. Smoky, too, very much so. For back then almost everyone smoked, even though I no longer did. I breathed the atmosphere though, but even that doesn't appear to have affected my long-term health. There was also Ronnie Scott's; modern jazz here, and the place was a little more up market. Then there were the parties to which we were invited. At least George was, and no one seemed to complain if we tagged along. The absolute fringes of sixties parties, these. Must have been, for the recollections are clear. (That shared joint back in New Orleans was to be a one and only in my life. I was never bored nor stupid enough to be in need of drugs.) It was all there: The music; rock 'n roll - Trini Lopez, and of course, the Beatles - the long hair and short skirts. The clothes: colourful, outrageous, smart. The beautiful people, the good times; none of the drugs. Or if there were, most of these people were quite discreet about it.

I also recall Sunday lunches at the aforementioned Ace

Cafe. Ah yes, do I ever! One in particular. There were four of us, and we'd arrived late. Not unusual, that. Our day had been late in starting, due mainly to the late finish of the previous one, each overlapping the other. Life wasn't lived to some mystical twenty-four hour period, you see, so our days didn't necessarily end at midnight. They ended when you crashed, began again when you got up. Anyway, by the time we arrived at the "caff", all that remained on offer was minced beef, or Yorkshire Pudding - so the menu would have us believe.

'Bloody cook would get lynched if he served those up in Yorkshire,' Martin suggested, ordering both.

'Minced beef and Yorkshire pud! You'd likely get lynched, too.' I said. 'Still, there's nowt else, is there? I'll have the same, lass,' I told the serving wench.

We all had both, on the same plate - something we'd have been lynched for in Yorkshire. "Up There" - as opposed to "down south" (upper case for the former, you'll notice. Same rules that applied to "The Countryside"). Be that as it may, but "Up There" puddings are traditionally served first, with lashings of beef and onion gravy.

We favoured the Ace because, as well as the bikers, it also was an "in" place, for the likes of us. Plus it was cheap, which probably amounted to the same thing. Just how cheap I was to discover that night, or the following morning, take your pick. Zero three hundred hours to be precise, in military terms. Or three o'clock in the morning.

We must have retired early, for that was the time I awoke from a deep sleep, and I didn't feel at all well. In the inky blackness I groped my way two floors down to the toilet, confident in the knowledge that, at this ungodly hour, I'd at least be assured of a seat.

Wrong! In fact, there was a queue on the stairway. Only to be expected, I suppose. Could have been the original "greasy spoon", the "caff".

OK, so Health and Safety does occasionally have its uses. But hey! These days most would end up in hospital rather than just a visit to the toilet. The immune system no longer able to cope, because of it being pampered to and unused!

Whatever, that was to be my last visit to the Ace.

*

It was the change in environment that gave the game away. I was now back in Yorkshire, with its isolated farms and small-holdings, or as isolated as one can get on this crowded island.

There was a lone cow in a field. A skinny cow. A silly cow, in fact. A scarecrow cow, I realized. A tractor trailed a flock of seagulls along behind it, and away in the distance was the power station at Ferrybridge, its cooling towers creating an environment all of their own.

Not far now and I would be home again. Back from yet another Continental Grand Prix; Monaco this time, the most glamourous of them all. This is the one race on the calendar where you are still able to get close to the action, and mix in with the drivers and personalities. The town is small, and we all have to use the same streets, even if not the same hotels and retaurants! I was to make seven visits to the Monaco GP over the years, and I recall an incident that occurred on that first occasion, when I'd had the good fortune to team up with motor-racing photographer, Michael Hewett, with whom I remained friends over the years, even if we did only meet up at Monaco. (Although a professional, Mike - a greengrocer being his day job - only really concentrated on Monaco. I think he covered the race 20-30 times, and has produced two very popular photographic books on it.)

It was evening at the close of one of those perfect Mediterranean days. A day when the full heat of the sun had beamed down out of an endless azure sky, resulting in brilliant colours; stucco houses in glaring white, with contrasting, jet-black wrought ironwork, nothing in between, no shades of grey. There were dazzling reds and greens, the only hint of softness being in the terra-cotta slated roofs. The beaches had been crowded, an ogler's smorgasbord of beautiful women, and the day seemed to go on for so long that events of the morning felt like they had taken place a week ago. Now, with that tingling of the skin which told of a little too much of a sun which now sat on the horizon, we sat down to dinner.

I ordered a Salade Nicoise, pronouncing it Nick-oy-zee. Well, my French never had been that good. Not a subject they taught at Norton Boys School.

`Un Salade Nicoise,' the waiter intoned, laying particular emphasis on the pronunciation. As he wrote his eyes looked down his beaky nose, and he effected an air of studied superiority, flicking me a glance at the crucial moment, just to be sure I'd caught it.

I made no comment, allowing that if the height of his career offered nothing more demanding that the taking and conveying of orders, then there were few he was superior to anyway. I mean, who was sitting there ordering - especially at Monaco prices - and who was doing the fetching!

One thing about doing the Monaco race with Mike, he was the complete professional. This was still the pre digital age, and at the end of each day he would shut himself away in his hotel room, convert the bathroom into a darkroom, so as to develop his films. This way he could see what he had, or hadn't, covered to his satisfaction. This meant he never had time to attend many of the various functions to which he, as a member of the press, was invited, so he often passed the invitations on to me. Hence I had a foot in the door, met many people I would otherwise not have.

I grew to love the Riviera (and my French did improve slightly). It is a place where all the cliche's come true. Even the names evoke visions of sun, the beach, and the good life: St. Tropez, Antibes, Juan-les-Pins, Cannes, Nice, Monte Carlo, and Menton. Unfortunately, all are places where use of the credit card should be severely restricted if the resulting overdraft is not to make Greece seem like a good loan risk!

Here and now, back in Norton, I was in my element, though not yet quite in paradise. Although my idea of paradise was but a short drive away in the car I had bought - a Rover 2000, second hand, of course. Then, with added impetus, paradise became a step closer. In fact I was to visit the area quite often during this break, along with this girl I'd met on my way to the Belgian Grand Prix, at Spa. Not across a crowded room at a party kind of thing, more the gentle chaos of Southend airport's departure lounge, where she was a courier for a tour compny. I seem to recall a quotation from Tennyson - or someone of similar ilk - springing to mind, *In the spring a young man's fancy.......* something about thoughts of love. Nevertheless, it had been one of those rare occasions in which that penetrating first assessment - ranging far beyond the physical sight - was to colour the relationship for the future. A casual glance. A question. A coffee. And before I knew what was happening, it seemed I was in love. Not absolutely certain, but I suspected so, for it had never happened like this before. The moment she raised those sunglasses and wedged them in her hair, I was smitten. As was she, I suspect, for it was her that had initiated the approach. Nor was the physical sight of her at all lacking: Smiling, hazel eyes, pearl-white teeth, eyebrows - which could well have been purpose-built for seduction - gave her the look of a mischievous pixie. She wore tights rather than stockings - out of necessity I would have thought - and they were wrapped around legs that were... well, enough to say those legs were something else again. The mini had been designed with legs like that in mind. And the kind of minis she wore really showed them off to perfection. More than her legs at times, if she wasn't careful!

If anyone ever accused me of being a chauvinist I'd probably have agree with their assessment, but I found the type of girl I was attracted to usually preferred things to be that way. They liked men to do the things they expected men to do; opening doors, carrying the umbrella or the shopping, etc, common courtesies. Janette was just such a girl, an Essex girl who certainly did, though in no way did she fit the eighties stereotype "Essex Girl" image. Here was a girl who laughed with me, not at me. In fact, this auburn-haired beauty was to have such an effect on me I suddenly, inexplicably, became afraid of flying. Me! The person who thrived on aviation and flight. It now required the aid of a drink, or a Valium, to get me in the air. Strange, that. For, to someone of my ilk, romance was the sun rising over a remote airfield: the orange glow of the dawn, an ethereal mist, stark, immobile silhouettes, angular and noiseless. To me, that was tranquillity personified. Peaceful, still, silent, yet also alive, or at least ready to burst into life.

No longer, it seemed. The appearance of Janette on scene had put such thoughts on hold. And when I eventually had to leave and return to work, the current hit by Peter, Paul, and Mary, *Leaving, on a Jet Plane*, was to become our sad lament.

In the beginning, it was weekends down in Essex. The evenings ended in a Southend hotel for me, her parents house on a modern Rayleigh estate for Janette. During the day we would often walk the 3 miles of Southend Pier, dine out at the Pied Piper, Westcliff-on-Sea most evenings. It became our favourite restaurant.

The hotel arrangement only lasted for a weekend or two before I was invited to stay at her home. The Paddocks. Of course it was. All modern estates seemed to feature a Paddocks, a Pastures, a Meadows, or even a Cedars. Around the country estates like this were popping up almost overnight, like edible fungi. Comfortable-looking, snug, cheery.

Obviously, during my few brief visits there, I had been vetted and approved by her parents.

428

Janette had implied her father was "an executive with Ford." Upon meeting him, and being introduced - 'call me Keith', he said - I put it too him.

He laughed. 'In those words?'

'Well... not exactly. But she did say you were on the Board.'

'Just happened to mention it, I suppose? In passing?'

'Sort of.'

'That's Janette. Can be a bit of a snob, our Jan.'

'So you're not....?'

'Definitely not,' Keith replied with a smile, anticipating the question. 'It's just that, as was no doubt the intention, you assumed "board" to begin with a capital. Fact is, I work in the drawing office.'

'Ah! So she didn't actually lie then.'

'No. She wouldn't do that.'

Occasionally we would drive from Southend to London, spend a day in the capital looking round, a visit to a West End cinema, look at the sights; Not the Tower, Buck House, etc, but Kings Road and Carnaby Street, the sixties sights. Jan even had me dressing the part; the broad shouldered jacket, the flares, shirts and ties cut from the same material. The hair I managed myself.

*

I'd eventually coaxed Janette up to Yorkshire on her weekends off, and we'd drive around the countryside. Familiar places from times past, the long cycle rides of youth. I found I didn't need to check maps or look at signposts when driving, my brain having memorized the way with such precision. I also managed to divert us as far as Silverstone, for the British Grand Prix, and we visited a certain little airfield in Bedfordshire - Old Warden. Not so much memories and vivid flashbacks here. These were flashbacks in the flesh as it were, some of them original, some replicas. Flying machines I'd thought to be forever in the past, or at least long since grounded. Vintage aircraft of the Shuttleworth Collection. (Many years later, during retirement, I was to become a life member of the Shuttleworth Vintage Aviation Society, visiting the airfield for many of their summer weekend display days.)

Our time in Yorkshire was spent driving, then walking in the country, with only the odd day in town, buying whatever it was we needed, showing Janette whatever it was she wanted to see: Minster, Shambles, Clifford's Tower, a walk along the

City Walls - everything that was worth a visit, which took some time. But the moment our shopping and sightseeing was complete we'd return to the country. It really was paradise, this. A peaceful place. A place for lovers. Cloud shadows chased each other across the rolling countryside. Not a hurried chase. Slow and gentle, in keeping with the environment, and our actions. We breathed the scent of the heather, caught the bleating cry of sheep as we strolled along hand in hand, crossing babbling brooks via stepping stones or ancient bridges. The only intrusion as far as Janette was concerned, the occasional RAF fighter. Music to my ears, anathema to hers. Up there at least. Although she did attend the air shows with me. So maybe she saw it as an intrusion because of what we occasionally did up there amongst the heather. We were, you see, well past the teddy-bears and dolls stage by then.

'Listen,' I said one day, just after we'd made ourselves decent again. 'What do you hear?'

She tilted her head. 'Nothing.'

'Right. That's the countryside. Country silence, if you like. But if you concentrate the sounds gradually start to filter through.'

So she listened. Found they did. Common sounds that were all around, going unnoticed until you tuned yourself in to them. Birdsong, crickets, the buzzing of bees, bleating of sheep, and the mooing cows. There were smells too; the perfumed fragrance of the heather, the sweetness of the new mown grass, even the distant sea. The sights, sounds and aromas of a summer's day. Peaceful, relaxing. Nature in the raw.

Janette spun round suddenly, startled, eyes wide, ears filled with... not sound, noise; loud and shattering. The curtain of silence was ripped apart by the sudden blast of a jet aircraft. It passed low, directly overhead, banking sharply to disappear into the next valley, following the contours of the land, dragging its sound along behind.

'And *that* was the Royal Air Force. The Moors are a designated low flying area,' I explained. 'A Canberra PR9, by the way. Photo reconnaissance. Just as well it didn't appear sooner or they'd probably be displaying pictures of us in the mess this evening. Your posterior could have been recorded for posterity by a post-graduate pilot.'

'Your posterior, lover.'

'Ah, yes.'

430

Oh for the passion of youth. That which so often made us disregard the risk of discovery.

Perspectives changed continually. The turn of a path and one scene would vanish, to be replaced by something entirely different: moorland for a wooded copse; a sea of heather for fields of grass; and there, forming a glittering horizon, the waters of the North Sea, off Whitby. Another turn reveals a pretty little village previously hidden in the fold of a familiar view, country cottages huddled together, as if for warmth and protection. People pottered in their gardens, cutting lawns and tending plants. Dry-stone walls cris-crossed the countryside, walls which were totally innocent of cements and adhesives, yet which had remained intact for generations. We turned our backs on the giant "golf balls" of the Early Warning Radar station at Fylingdales, up on the high point.

Down in the valley we leaned over a hump-backed, stone bridge, watching children and dogs play in sun-depleted crystal waters. Sheep browsed on the verges as birds swooped and circled overhead. Whilst in the distance echoed a metallic ringing: the ancient game of quoits being played on the village green, horseshoes aimed at a metal spike. This was Beck Hole. Little more than a pub and a row of stone cottages which nestled in the folds of this great, green and purple, rumpled quilt. Here we stopped for a bite and a pint.

'It's lovely up here,' Janette said.

'Yes,' I agreed. 'But these are only the nursery slopes. Don't go away with the idea the Moors are all 'user friendly'. Up there, away over the hills, they can become remote and forbidding, especially so in winter. People have been known to get lost up there, to die in the snow.'

And when evening came - stealing in like a thief, with its gathering cloak of mist - we could be found in yet another York pub; oak beams and cosy surroundings. We'd settle comfortably by a flickering fire, supping and chatting, happy in each others company. This time it was the Cock and Bottle in Skeldergate, all ancient oak, white plaster, and atmosphere.

'You can almost imagine yourself being whisked back over the centuries,' Janette ventured.

'Funny tha should say that,' I replied, reverting to the vernacular. 'But in 'ere it's probably true.' I then told her of the presence that was supposed to roam hereabouts, and even as I recalled the story, I wondered if this, and other sightings, really were true. Does the ghost of a George Aislaby actually still haunt the Treasurer's House in Chapter House street? And what of the Roman legion which had been observed passing through that building's vaults? They were said to have been "cut off at the legs". Later, after some excavation had taken place, a Roman road had been discovered a few feet below where that ghostly column had walked. All had been attested to and recorded on more than one occasion, the belief that it may one day happen again even having created its own niche in the tourist schedule: York's famed "Ghost Walks."

Next day it was Whitby, on the coast, and it rained early on. Slab faced streets in dull shades of grey. The matt colours of despair.

But there were indoor pleasure palaces where people sat and played bingo, their faces masked in anything but pleasure. Then, after lunch the sun shone through, seemingly offering apologies for the earlier rain.

After dinner we strolled hand in hand along the cliff-top, pausing beneath the stony gaze of Captain James Cook, to watch the fog bank roll in from the North sea. It was below us, shrouding the port like a grey, fleecy blanket, though not thick enough to engulf the Abbey opposite - Dracula's haunt; for this is area is where the story was said to have first taken root - nor the top of the lighthouse, on the north arm of the pier.

We then drove home in reflective silence as another perfect day faded into history. Well, almost!

One memorable day we ventured out early. Daybreak was dull and overcast, the rain starting shortly after departing York.

Mostly I drive fast. Safely, but fast. (Too fast, Janette often thought, though she didn't say so - white-knuckled grip, foot repeatedly stabbing at imaginary brake pedal in a move which, had she been driving, would see us skittering off into the scenery - suffice to pass the message.) Anyway, you know how it is, a trip to the airport, schedules to keep, or just for the sheer exhilaration and plain enjoyment it brings. But not always, even in those days of no speed limits on the open road. Now and again I'm not in any particular hurry to get anywhere, so I ease off and enjoy the scenery.

This was the frame of mind I found myself in on this day, for this was to be a journey of memories. A journey I wished to savour. We were en route to a place I'd always promised myself a visit, never seemed to find time. Suddenly I had, and with a pleasant companion to accompany me.

We crossed into Scotland shortly after turning off the A1 and onto the A6105, passing through the little village of Foulden, still pretty, despite the weather. A junction branched off left, a track meandering down a narrow lane. In the corner of the field was a sign mounted on a wooden post. Swirls of blackened wrought iron surrounded a name, letters painted white. A silhouette of a sheep, also in white, perched on top. "Edington Mains," I read. The sign glistened with moisture, as did my eyes, for it was here the memories began.

The rain eased, then stopped, but the sky remained leaden and overcast when eventually we arrived in Duns, a small market town serving the needs of the sheep farmers of the surrounding Borders hills. Here I stopped to ask directions, and I'll tell you something, they still talk funny up here. They said, `Och aye,' and to `park doon the brae, the noo!' And, in contrast to the claims of Texans, everything hereabouts would appear to be "wee."

The tourist information office is located in a sandstone block set back from the street, and it was to here I was drawn. The glass panels of the inner door were plastered with notices describing various attractions in the area, but the one I wanted was inside this very building.

THE JIM CLARK TROPHY ROOM, a sign informed. A single chamber, but for motor racing's fans, the aficionados, this is as close to a religious experience as most of us will get.

The room is small, its walls lined with glass fronted cabinets which hold trophies and mementoes of the great driver's reign.

I slipped into another world as I studied the exhibits close to the entrance, the early wins during Clark's meteoric rise to fame. I was mesmerized. Others gazed reverently and spoke in whispers, but I was oblivious to them all. Cocooned in happy nostalgia, I lingered at each and every trophy, thoughts drifting back over the years, reliving the days.

Facing me was a gilt sculpture of the winged figure of Mercury. It bore an inscription; 20-July-1963 O'Gorman Trophy, RAC British Grand Prix, 1st. I lapsed into brief introspection, and in my mind's eye I could visualize a little green car on its yellow wheels. Lotus 25, chassis number R4. Effortlessly I recalled the details, I'd read them many times, and I'd watched it happen. I pictured it on narrow tyres - one set had lasted four races that season! - drifting round the curves, guided by the reclining figure in the cockpit. Light blue, cotton overalls, dark blue, open face helmet, and the single screen goggles. A spare pair hung round his neck. Arms straight, the left hand, encased in a brown leather, string-back glove, gripped the top of the red, leather bound wheel rim as he applied lock, head thrown back and inclined to the right, mouth open in exhilaration. Silverstone was the setting, but it could just as well have been Aintree, Brands Hatch, or any one of the many and diverse tracks at which the young Scot had raced. Some still active, others long since forgotten. Decaying now, or put to some other use. That same chassis, I recalled, had carried Clark to seven Grand Prix wins during the year - out of ten races! - giving him his first World Championship. The other three results? Second, third, and eighth, due to various problems.

I wandered slowly from exhibit to exhibit, each trophy recalling a different circuit, each evoking another memory. Spa; the pine forests of the Ardennes, and the long Masta straight. Clermont Ferrand; swooping and twisting round the Auvergne mountains of central France. The daunting 14 miles of the Nurburgring in Germany. Charterhall; at home in Scotland. Zandvoort, Monaco, and now the old airfield circuit at Full Sutton, in Yorkshire - long since closed - where he'd first been seen outside his native land. The Indianapolis 500, America's most famous race. That hallowed place had never been the same since Clark and Lotus put in an appearance.

One award was present only as a photographic print, the actual trophy, the Esso Golden Helmet - a gold, ruby encrusted affair - being locked away in a bank vault, far too valuable to be displayed here.

It took a long time to complete my tour, then I signed the current visitors book and wandered out. Those books must be worth a tidy sum, I mused, containing as they did, the signatures of many great names in racing, past and present. From all over the world they'd come, and thousands more from ordinary folk, just calling in to pay their respects.

The extraordinary thing about that, I thought, was that you *didn't* just call in as you were passing. It was miles off the major roads and tourist routes. These people, like myself, had gone out of their way to visit. It was a pilgrimage, really. And what a wonderful window into the past. What Janette thought of it all I had no idea, for she had lost me back there for a while!

*

These really were days of wine and roses, or close enough to appear so in retrospect. I even went so far as to buy myself a bungalow, in the country village of Dunnington, a couple of miles outside York. Yet another estate known as 'The Paddocks'. I now had the money, would need somewhere to live sometime in the future, when I felt it was time to settle down. But not quite yet, so the bungalow I chose would be the last to be built on the new estate, currently under development. At the time I had ample assets to be able to afford two or three, at then current prices. Should have bought them, for, as related previously, the bank I was currently using (in the Bahamas, where the interest rate was 10%) was later to disappear! But at a time for me when the damage was not fatal. All part of the learning process. The phrase, "never put all your eggs in one basket", had already come to mind, and been observed.

Somewhere to live would not be the only future requirement. I would also need something to keep me occupied once the travel was finished, possibly to create a little wealth! So whilst we were both still somewhat affluent, my mate Ron - with whom I'd first travelled to America - and I, decided to invest a little in the future. Laundrettes seemed to be the latest thing. They were becoming quite popular, so, whilst I was away on assignment, Ron sought out a likely location in York, just inside the City Walls, another area that was currently under development. And soon, so too was the Walmgate Bar Laundrette. We were in business. (It still is, 2016.)

Ron had recently got himself married, so the intent for him was to cut down on working overseas. He, therefore, did most of the organising; although I recall it as being myself who put up most of the funding, to be paid back, with interest, out of the profits. This seemed to work quite well, whilst I was home. Although for some reason, profits seemed to fall off quite dramatically during the periods I was away! I did get my money back, eventually, but to my mind all was not entirely well. So I later took the soft option and sold out my share to Ron.

It wasn't that I didn't trust him. There again..... Yes it was, I decided. For Ron was the kind person one should never trust. Especially so when it came to the matter of hard cash! I remember my father advising me, 'never go into business with a friend'. These were to prove wise words from someone I should have listened to more often. But all that was as yet in the future.

Generally these were halcyon days, and nights, when I found myself to be at peace with my very being. Satisfied, for a time. I now had something I'd always secretly desired. Yet other things were missing. To me, important things. Selfish, I realized. Far too late in the day, of course. There again, the one thing love never did have was logic.

*

It is not always necessary to see or hear it to know that a door has been closed to you. This particular door closed when it came time for me to return to work. Marriage? I wasn't yet ready for anything quite so drastic. At present, bungalow aside, thoughts of solitude took precedence over presumed domestic chaos. The Valium requirement no longer was, the wanderlust was still in my blood, raring to go. And as it would have been impossible for anyone to travel with me to my work, so it was that I lost Janette. *Leaving, on a Jet Plane* had played one time too many, it seemed. And although I thought of her often, my longing as acute as it was pointless, I knew it was over. Her place in my heart was now filled with emptiness. Right person, wrong time? Possibly.

But Janette was still around, especially in my dreams; those moments when you have no choice as to your thoughts. I just needed a few cubic feet of darkness and there she was, in my head, free to roam around at will.

Yes, we did meet up now and again, on the odd occasion over the next couple of years, but it was never to be the same. Although the flame was not yet fully extinguished, it had been significantly diminished - that special magic no longer evident.

Then, as eventually had to happen, my place in her heart was filled by a new love.

"Oh how bleak the Moors look now." It was a line I remembered from somewhere, either read or heard, didn't matter which, it fit the scenario well enough. It also matched my mood to perfection.

Good times then, while they lasted. And memories of those youthful days of naivety were to remain with me for some time, if not forever. There had been many delightful moments, each forming a magical memory: Whitby in the rain or sun; Robin Hood's Bay in the early morning mist; making love on the open expanse of moorland - a close call, that, our would-be voyeur approaching from an unexpected quadrant. And even though relegated to the far recesses, they were memories coated with sugar and spice. But, given time, even that coating began to dissolve, the memories along with it, which, of course, is not unusual.

Ah well. The next one would not escape me, I promised myself. After all, I now had my cosy little bungalow. And I'd met a girl whose favourite song became, the Roberta Flack hit, *The First Time Ever I saw Your Face.*

We didn't waste too much time before marching up the aisle. A joyous occasion which even had the manager of our Geneva Office donating a case of fine Champagne for the reception. He'd sent it via a postal service, so we never received it! The insurance made amends though and a second case arrived, too late for the reception, so not really too late at all!

The promise I'd made to myself proved me to be wrong again. After five good years of marriage, things started to go wrong between Catherine and I, once again my departures, and time away, the cause. But the end really began shortly after we lost our daughter to what was termed a "cot death". I had left home for Paris that morning to pick up a visa - en route for Congo, Brazzaville, far south along the West African coastline. But Paris was as far as I got. Before departure from there, in the late afternoon, I was advised to phone home. No details given, but the person passing on the message seemed decidedly taciturn.

I phoned and eventually got through to a tearful, distressed Catherine, only to be given the dreadful news. I took the first available flight back to London. An anxious wait, then on to Leeds, and a taxi home. It was gone midnight before I arrived.

Helen had been just short of two years old, even if, in that time she had seen and done a lot, including a long trip around America. I eventually came to terms with the disaster, but Catherine, as seems to be the way with mothers, did not. We remained together for another two years, seven eventful years in total. Unfortunately, during a lot of that time, Catherine's mother seemed to have moved in. Fine when I was away, which was often, but a lot of the time when I was home, also. Which did not sit well with me. And if I wasn't there, someone else too began to fill in for me, as it were.

Okay then, the one after the next, I thought as Elizabeth walked in to my life. Well, not exactly walked. It took quite a bit of persuasion, and time.

I was introduced by a friend, Sue - Ron's wife, now ex. It so happened I was having a party in the bungalow the following weekend. Sue, as usual, was invited, and so I invited

Elizabeth to accompany her. Somewhat reluctantly, it seemed, she accepted. I was later to discover that her hesitancy was related to her two daughters, the result of her first marriage. Katy and Victoria were a large part of her future, needed to be accepted along with Elizabeth. Naturally, they were.

I liked to surprise Elizabeth when her birthday came around, try to come up with something different. I often found it to be quite effective if I organised a dinner in some restaurant or other, only for her to find the place packed with friends and relatives upon our arrival - after we had stopped off at a local pub en-route. Even the children would be there, the ones who had been at home as we had left, the elder, strangely volunteering to baby-sit the younger. But Elizabeth turned up trumps on my 55th.

We had been invited to dinner with the next door neighbours, something which happened on a fairly regular basis, for we'd formed a clique of three family groups on the estate, each taking a turn as hosts. On this particular occasion, whilst awaiting the arrival of the third couple, we sat and had a drink or two, which was also normal. Then, after about twenty minutes, one of our girls called round to say there was a phone call for me. In my job, this was not unusual, anytime during the twenty-four hour day! So off I went, home, just ten metres away, where I was surprised to find the phone hung up, but even more surprised when people instantaneously appeared from every room in the house!

Thinking about it afterwards - the amount of traffic which must have been entering that cu-de-sac, and the number of people flitting about between the various houses, sheds, and garages - I realized it was maybe not so obscure after all. At least, to anyone but gullible old me. Another pointer should have been the amount of food step-daughter Victoria had supposedly prepared for the "few" friends she was having round - more than enough for the twenty or thirty that eventually showed up.

Good times, then. But even though we were to remain together an unprecedented - for me - twelve or so years, we too eventually drifted apart, even if amicably. Still not clear as to whether or not she ever did come to understand my interest in aviation, although I noticed she didn't take too long to get to grips with the wine.

William, our son, was born in January 1984, just six months after we were married. Oops!

So, after two unsuccessful attempts, I had to concede that marriage was not for me. Certainly not whilst I continued travelling the world, leaving my wife behind. Although both did occasionally get to travel the world with me at various times, on holiday and at work. In the days when most remained in the UK, Catherine and I had honeymooned in the Bahamas, which was when I discovered my bank to have "Shut down"! It had apparently ceased trading the moment the management had absconded with the cash! Well, it would, wouldn't it! Luckily, I always carried a bundle of Travellers Cheques and cash with me. Needed to, travelling the world as I did. US dollars, for in those days the US dollar was king, being accepted anywhere and everywhere.

(I soon learnt our Vice President didn't miss a lot when I later sounded him out on the opening of a new account in America. His reply was preceded by a wry smile. "They don't pay much interest, but your money is always there when you want it!)

No such problems during the second honeymoon as that was up the road in Whitby. We later travelled together to South Africa, Indonesia, and as far as New Zealand. Plus Elizabeth and William made a few trips out to Norway, to join me in the days when I was working up there.

'Both the girls I married had certainly been right for me - one I met through a dating agency, the other purely by a chance introduction - it was myself that had been the failure, I deduced; but only years later, of course. I was far too selfish; a difficult a person to live with; too much of a perfectionist - I even get upset with myself if the stamp I've just stuck on a letter is not symmetrically aligned! Apart from which, when I was at home I was by now writing, and writing itself is a very anti-social occupation. It draws you in. It is also a 24/7 thing, often demanding absolute concentration. And once so engrossed, little will divert your attention. It seemed to me the brain hardy ever shut down, many ideas being born during the hours of sleep - that essential few cubic feet of darkness. For instance, after much thought and deliberation, over a long period, the very apt title of this book just suddenly came to me during the early hours. I always had a pad and pen to hand on my bedside cabinet just for this purpose, for if not recorded immediately, many ideas can be lost. I only needed to jot down one or two prime words to be able to pick up on the thought next morning. All that remained then was to develop it.

As far as girls were concerned, outstanding memories of these three in particular still invade my mind at odd times, each recalled by many an inconsequential event: a certain piece of music - especially those two songs - a resemblance on the street, a particular perfume perhaps, for I never lost all of my affection for any of them. I assume a modicum of affection always remains where true love has been involved.

Janette, I never saw again, although we did once talk on the telephone many years later; a long distance call to Australia, where she was then living.

Catherine still lives close by my old home town of Norton, and we did once bump into each other. She frequently tends Helen's burial place, in Dunnington, where we had lived together.

Elizabeth lives within a couple of miles of me, as does William, so we get together for dinner now and again. In fact I was invited to her next wedding, as was her previous husband. Three husbands at one wedding! The children of course - both hers and mine - being the linking factor, although we do remain good friends to this day.

From a psychological point of view, it appeared I felt there to be a continual need to climb the next hill, just to find out where I was. And, having done so, where I was never seemed to be where I intended to be.

*   *

Page 443 Top: Long time girlfriend, Janette.
Bottom L: First wife, Catherine, on our Bahamian honeymoon.
Bottom R: Daughter Helen. A short though adventurous, life.

Page 444: For the second time of asking; wife, Elizabeth.
Top R: Son William at 21. **Bottom:** Good friend Ron Hewson, in the Antarctic. Must think he is Scott.

Page 445 Top: View from down the crevasse in which Ron almost lost his life. (Page **545**.) **Centre L:** In the hills above Ravenna, Italy. Checking out a new system. **R:** One of ONI's Arctic stations. Would you fancy a month out there? **Bottom L:** Not a great improvement, but at least warmer. A base station in Qatar, the Middle East. **R:** Drillship in the Canadian Arctic. Photo taken at midnight in summer. I simply stepped over the side and walked out across the ice.

Page 446 Top L: All mod cons - just about. Stokkoy station, Norway. Where I began writing during my final years with ONI. **Top R:** Equipment checks on board Chinese vessel Nan Hai 502, alongside at Zhanjiang, China. The only guy on board who spoke English - after a fashion - was the commissar, who knew nothing about seismic work! **Centre L:** Early days of seismic, dynamite rather than the compressed air of today. **Centre R:** The Drill floor on any rig could be a dangerous environment for the unwary...
Bottom: ...as could racing Karts. Preparing for the off. Shell's Kart track in Port Harcourt, Nigeria.

Page 447 Top L: Antonio & "our" Jetranger. **R:** Pat Carney & I in Nigeria, assessing the wine. About a year later Pat was murdered in his Geneva hotel room. **Centre:** Two views of the Flamingoes in flight, & two views of Xai Xai, on the river Limpopo, Mozambique.
Bottom: Two aging helicopter pilots at a 2011 reunion: John "Taff" Walker & Tom Browning.

Page 448 Top: Geneva 1969. Getting stuck into Fred Muller's Havana's and Quality Champagne: Dave Moore, Self, Bill Justice, Tony Hoggart.

Centre: Loading charges to blow off an unwanted well that could be a hazard to shipping... and the fish that could result from such action. **Bottom:** Being dined out at an Athenian restaurant during my RAF Lyneham days.

Page 449 Top L: Margaret Ashby, a long-time lady friend. **R:** Raising a 100ft antenna mast when working with ONI. **Centre:** Still with MSF at Lyneham. Being dined out again, this time in the Sergeant's Mess at RAAF Pearce, Perth, Western Australia. Author far right. **Bottom:** Heavy seas off Mozambique, with the helicopter tied down on the back deck.

Page 450 Top: With the Australian Branch of the Boy Entrants Association: A barbecue at Temora, NSW, and in Geelong, Victoria, after a visit to the Avalon Airshow. **Centre:** My bungalow in Dunnington, UK, owned since built in 1969. **Bottom:** 2015 ex ONI: Self, Bob Molloy, Geoff Metcalfe. We still occasionally meet up for lunch in South Shields, and talk over old times.

Pages 451 & 452: World Travel. A small selection from my large collection. They obviously look much better in colour.
Breakfast patio at the Bagshot House Hotel, Trinidad; A Bangkok Klong; Cook's Bay, Moorea, Tahiti; Canal Street, New Orleans, USA; Kristiansund, Norway; Blue Mosque, Istanbul, Turkey; Mount Tasman Glacier, South Island, New Zealand; Mitre Peak, Fjordland, New Zealand; Papeete, Tahiti; English Harbour, Antigua; A Thai Temple; St Georges, Grenada; Goodwood Park Hotel, Singapore; The fabulous Drakensbergs, Durban, South Africa.

452

Chapter Sixteen
WATERS OF THE CARIBBEAN

Slightly north and east of the point at which the Isthmus that is Panama tags itself onto the emerald jungle of Colombia, in the southern Caribbean, is located the city of Cartagena, one-time glittering citadel of the Spanish Main. A jewel it still is, albeit slightly tarnished by the drug trade in my day. The very fortress that had defied the likes of Edward Teach - of Blackbeard fame - Henry Morgan, and Drake (Sir Francis, that is), still stands, as do the massive cannon that once protected it, along with the old walled town gathered below. The narrow streets and 17th century Spanish architecture look to be clinging to the fort for protection - much as would a child to her mother's skirt - and so it was; or had been. All this, and more, I discovered when dispatched to the area, post haste, back in 1977. A much more gratifying option than almost anywhere else, especially in either Africa or the Middle East.

I'd arrived in that modern galleon of the skies, the Douglas DC10. Just imagine, an all expenses paid trip to the Caribbean, wi' handsome salary to boot, forsooth! Aye, but 'twas not to be all rum and pina-colada. There was o'course ye small matter o' work, blast me bollocks an' by yer leave - Oops! sorry. 'Tis the environment, d'ye see; tends to remind one of what had once been afoot hereabouts, belike, an' a curse on that. Romance and skulduggery. Captain Kidd, Sir Henry Morgan, and such. Galleons, gold, and moonlit nights, beneath which the water's of the Caribbean gleamed like silver, an'all. Could go on about the fearsome boom of cannon, the glint and clash of Toledo steel, but I think you'll be getting the picture by now. One thing's for sure, you will if you go there. History is reflected everywhere around the islands. In the buildings, along the waterfronts, in the forts high on the hillsides, and in the names scattered about like grape shot. At English Harbour, in Antigua, we find Nelson's Dockyard - originally built in 1725 as His Majesty's Antigua Naval Yard; St Thomas, in the US Virgin Islands, has its Drake's Seat, Blackbeard's Tower and Bluebeard's Castle. The British Virgins also honour Drake, naming a channel after him, and there is the oddly named island of Dead Chest. (Arr, Jim lad. Could that be where ye treasure lies buried?) Or what of Great Dog, Little Dog, George

Dog, West Dog, Cockroach, and Fallen Jerusalem. Not a lot of thought given to the naming of those islets.

*

This trip was to signal the start of my Caribbean, Central, and South American phase of operations, and fond memories there are of the area, too. So let me conjure some up, share them with you.

In Magens Bay, St Thomas, lies what is probably the prettiest, most perfect, cliche-ridden of all Caribbean beaches. An elongated, sheltered bay of crystal clear, turquoise-coloured, water. A crescent of golden sand at one end, the whole surrounded by lush tropical growth. Only one problem; in the afternoon, when the little hand hits three and the big hand, twelve, watch out. Without fail, millions of pesky no-see-ems rise from beneath the sand. A particularly aggressive form of sandfly. Like something from a Stephen King novel they set out to devour whatever tasty morsel they can latch on to, human blood apparently top of their shopping list. Talk about flying teeth! Best to be long gone before three pm.

All right then, maybe not such a perfect beach, Magens Bay. But one that certainly did tick most of the boxes as far as tropical beaches in the Caribbean went, was Grand Anse, just outside, and south of, St Georges, Capital of the Spice Island of Grenada. A magnificent two mile sweep of white sand being gently lapped by crystal clear water, the palms' trunks growing out almost horizontal to the beach before curling up towards the sky, the emerald background. All this without the sandflies. And not too far distant, on either side of the peninsula leading to Point Saline, are two contrasting beaches, one of pure white sand, the other pure black, but sparkling sand non the less.

The capital of St Thomas, US Virgin Islands, is Charlotte Amalie, in the harbour of which anchor the many cruise liners that visit the area. They are graceful, but look huge against the backdrop of the landscape. Though the day the nuclear-powered aircraft carrier USS Enterprise paid a visit, even the cruise liners were dwarfed. The carrier was anchored offshore, well outside the harbour. Too large to even entertain thoughts of entering.

Small, colourful fishing boats are tied up alongside the tree-shaded waterfront, the sea beneath them so clear they appeared to be floating on air. Tumbledown buildings in pink and blue pastel shades - their louvred shutters thrown open to the sun of the new day - nestled amongst the green and vermilion flame trees and purple bougainvillaea. Overhead, gulls and Frigate Birds wheeled about, occasionally diving into the placid waters whilst other, more colourful species called raucously as they flitted about within the emerald backdrop.

An evening drink at one of the waterfront bars here - Sparky's, or Sebastians - is served up with the kind of sunset that even Hollywood at its most imaginative couldn't dream up. Being seated there one evening with wife number one, upon completion of a job in the area, was as good as things got to be, I imagined. We sat outside, watching life pass by along the centuries-old waterfront. Just down the road was an old fort, now the police station, up a hill somewhere behind me was Bluebeard's Castle. Reputedly, once a pirate stronghold, now an hotel. Probably never had anything to do with buccaneers. There again, it could well have, for....

Buccaneers. The word conjures up all kinds of imagery, especially in this setting: water gently lapping the shoreline, a susurrus of breeze to stir the palm fronds, the moon high overhead. Was that a plunge of muted oars I heard, the faint creak of timber, a whisper of command? Or was that, too, imagined? In my mind's eye I saw silent figures flitting through the shadows, a brief glint of steel.... Bluebeard's Castle eh? We'd dine there later on that night.

Another name that springs to mind is Hotel 1829, but for what reason I have no recollection at all, though it seems good things must have happened there.

There is a local grog which goes by the name of Miss Blyden, said to have been a great favourite of the buccaneers - the grog, that is, not necessarily Miss Blyden, whoever she may have been. Rum based, the rest of the ingredients were, as far as I could gather - the exact constituents being a closely guarded secret - the spices of the islands: cloves, cinnamon, aniseed, nutmeg, etc. These are ground to a fine powder and boiled in syrup before the rum is poured over. The mixture is then strained and bottled, after another secret process. Most of the islands have a variation of their own, and although not habitually a rum drinker, in such a setting as this I felt it my duty to sample a few. You see the clash of Toledo steel, and the wiff of gunpowder in the air may well long have disappeared, not likewise the rum. Most drinks in this part of the world are rum-based, for around the Caribbean rum is even cheaper than bottled water.

*

A light pinged above my head, the fasten seatbelts warning. Across the aisle a woman did so, rather hurriedly, she then gripped the armrests tightly, as though that were an integral part of the instruction. Not a secure flyer, then. I relaxed and looked outside as Trinidad hove into view once more.

I was in an appropriately named aircraft - an Islander - returning from a short stay in Grenada. I'd taken the opportunity of visiting during an enforced lay-up in Port of Spain, Trinidad, where we were awaiting a replacement streamer. Ah yes, nearly forgot to tell you. Rather embarrassing for the client party chief, that, having to call corporate headquarters in Dallas, Texas, via satellite, in order to request a new streamer. (You remember the streamer - hydrophones, etc., one and a half to two miles a of it?)

'An extremely long silence was what greeted me,' the party chief later revealed, as he related the passing on of his report. That wasn't hard to believe, for I could well imagine management, back in Dallas, experiencing some difficulty in absorbing the news. Twenty four hundred metres of seismic streamer - worth the better part of a million dollars (back then) - required replacing? Well, it did happen that now and again the streamer would get torn up on an uncharted reef, or be severed by a passing tanker, attacked by sharks and suchlike. Even so, the majority was usually recovered and repaired. But it wasn't the loss that so astounded, it was the answer received to the inquiry: "What happened to the old one? Didn't you recover anything?"

'Oh, we recovered it all. In fact it wasn't actually lost. It was run over by a train.

Another silence. Rather prolonged this time, and at overseas rates, via satellite, quite expensive in itself.

'Err, yes. And excuse me if I sound confused, but could you explain in a little more detail. After all, it's just possible the insurance company may ask.'

And so Dave related events as they had unfolded. How they'd needed to work on the streamer when the vessel was alongside the dock, had unreeled it, laid it out on the quayside.

'I did query the railway tracks, across which it would be necessary to lay it,' he'd told them. 'Was informed they were rarely used. Suppose this must have been one of those rare occasions.'

I could well sympathize with the guy, for a similar incident once befell me when the crew were off-loading our equipment on the dockside, inadvertently placing it in the path of a crane, the operator of which seemed to have a grudge against us!

Thus it was I got to tour Barbados and Grenada, on expenses, the trip from which I was now returning. The airline was LIAT, the inter-island airline of the Caribbean - officially, "Leeward Islands Air Transport". Colloquially, this became, "Leaves Island Any Time", which tells you something about their scheduling. About as reliable as British Rail during a strike. But that was the way of life out here in the West Indies; laid back. Their airports are not counted amongst the worlds greatest, either. Little better than a grass strip and a thatched shack, in places. Hey! but who's complaining? This is the Caribbean.

No matter, before long I was at Doc Bishop's house in Port of Spain, the Trinidadian capital. Doc was our Party Chief on this job - only natural, being as he was local - and we now sat out in his back garden, in theory, discussing operations. He had no need of the greengrocer, this guy, they were all here, surrounding us: bananas, avocados, papaya and oranges. All growing within reach of where I was seated beneath a magnolia tree, sucking on a rum and something or other. The sun streamed down and humming birds fluttered about their business.

I'd been conveyed here by Doc's son, in an American car of indeterminate age. Like most American cars favoured by the locals it was more of a chrome trimmed, white-wall tyred barge, and probably handled like one, too. But on these poorly surfaced roads it just floated along, top down, Eagles - *Hotel California* - playing as we circumnavigated the race track cum cricket ground, the upside-down Hilton on the hillside to our right. Strange place, that. After checking in, you took a lift *down* to the rooms. I was familiar with it, for we'd often visit. This was where the airline crews stayed, so we'd sit around the pool, drinking, eyeing up the British Airways stewardesses. Ah, yes. Life could be hard at times on these islands where cannon were to be found everywhere. Remnants from the glory days: Nelson, Abercromby, Raleigh, Picton. Of buccaneers and the Spanish Main; Yo, ho, ho and a bottle of rum, kind of thing.

The barrels from most of those cannon are now painted black, mounted vertically in concrete, often with chains strung between them. But this leaves an adequate number of complete units *in situ*, and although no longer threatening, still directed towards a point from which a threat could once have been expected. Some are embossed with the date of their casting; 1742, was one. Others carried the arms of their patrons: Dukes, Earls, Kings, and Emperors.

*

'Hibiscus,' I said, when the plant was pointed out to me. Back in Doc Bishop's garden we were comparing names by which the various plants were known. Not unexpectedly, we seemed to use more or less the same names. Up until now!

'Choublac,' Doc said. 'You don't use that word?' He seemed surprised I called it something different.

'No. Why should I? Never heard of it.'

'I always assumed it to be the English name,' he said.

'What gave you that impression?'

'Choublac is actually the Haitian name,' he told me. 'But it comes from a word the English buccaneers used when cleaning their shoes with it.'

To give the story credence he plucked a flower and gave it to me, indicating I should rub it on my shoes, being as he wasn't wearing any! When I did, lo and behold, a purplish juice ran out of the crushed petals and dried on the leather as a shiny black varnish. Then I understood: Choublac was a corruption of shoe black. Not many people know that. Funny, the things you learn. Different things, different situations, different places, differing states of inebriation!

Then there were the steel bands. And believe me, steel bands here were different. Or maybe it was the ambience that made them sound so. These were steel bands in steel band country, and they, along with the rum, could really get you going. Even to the extent of a mass streak down a public beach! Not me, honest; a couple of the crew. But I did capture the event on my 8mm movie camera. The locals were not impressed! Almost had us chucked off the beach.

Another thing I came to understand around these parts, South America, mainly, but it could well usefully apply in the Caribbean: "Manana" doesn't actually mean "tomorrow." To be precise, it means, "not today," making it much more fitting as a get-out clause.

Prithee. 'Twas ever thus.

*

Catherine, wife number one, had flown out to join me on completion of this Caribbean "tour", and, after spending time in Antigua, and San Juan, Puerto Rico, we'd moved on again, for

458

a few glorious days in Charlotte Amalie, capital of the US Virgin Island of St Thomas, to complete a fabulous two weeks holiday in the Carribean. We'd even made a day trip to the British Virgin Island of Tortola, fortuitously, on the very day our Queen was visiting. Here I was, among maybe a couple of hundred others, suddenly confronted by my ex-boss! We'd not even been aware a Caribbean Tour was in progress, Royal or otherwise. Well, who reads newspapers when on holiday!

Now it was time for us to return to the UK, via St Croix and Antigua, a fairly tight schedule. Being as we were not offered a berth on the Royal Yacht Britannia, which was anchored offshore, we instead boarded the aircraft that would carry us on the first leg of this journey, an Avro 748 of LIAT, (remember? "Leaves Island Any Time"). All went well until we prepared to depart St Croix, when a fire warning on one engine had the crew in a bit of a panic. They immediately discharged the extinguisher into the engine, even though there was no exterior sign of fire, and we had yet to leave the dispersal. That it subsequently turned out to be a false alarm mattered not one iota, the extinguisher bottles required changing, at the very least, and none were immediately available. Scratch that flight, which left Catherine and I in something of a predicament; we were about to miss our Antigua connection. When informed of this, LIAT decided to fly us on to Antigua in the aircraft which was bringing an engineer and the replacement fire bottles, a Beechcraft Twin Bonanza. Good try, but to no avail, for BA's 747 to London lifted off even as we were still ten minutes out. Although BA had kindly delayed the take off especially for us, they couldn't stretch it any further, which left us alone and unwanted. LIAT declined all responsibility, and there was little we could do about that, for they were not signed up members of IATA, the airline cartel that sets the rules. But, not about to give up hope, we took a taxi down to Nelson's Dockyard, at English Harbour, and checked ourselves into the Admiral's Inn. The inn itself had been constructed from the stone and brick that was carried out from England as ship's ballast, the beams had once been ship's timbers. Out front was a shaded terrace that overlooked the harbour, and coloured birds flitted about. Perfect. We had visited English Harbour ten days ago, decided it was a place at which we would one day like to stay. No time like the present, for the next BA flight was yet two days in the future. The idea was that I would submit an all-expenses claim to LIAT in the hope I would one day be reimbursed - as with

IATA airlines. Ha! Some hope. They didn't even extend the courtesy of replying to my letter. But what the hell, I worked, as they say, in oil & gas. Was compensated appropriately.

(The back end of 2007 saw me taking the opportunity of once more escaping the European winter, this time to make a return to the Caribbean. It was something I looked forward to with much anticipation. I was about to sail down from New York on the Cunard liner, Queen Mary II, for their Christmas cruise around a selection of the Islands. It had sounded like the ideal way to spend Christmas, and the QMII was certainly as spectacular a vessel as the brochures portrayed it to be. But one man's meat etc, as the saying goes! I recall later describing it to friends as being the equivalent of "Butlin's at sea". I'm obviously not one for cruising. But it wasn't only the cruising - which to me had anyway been secondary - it was the Islands that disappointed. We made return visits to some of those well remembered places, but this time they wore a very different face; built up, crowded, mercenary. Not at all as I remembered them. It was as if they had somehow shed their magic. Only one place we visited impressed me: the island of Dominica. Although it was one island I had not previously visited, this was the Caribbean as I remembered it, natural and unspoilt. Only the Cruise Director chose to describe it as being undeveloped. From their point of view, perhaps - ie no money to be made here! - but the residents seemed to like it, were happy with their lot.)

*   *

....AND ON DOWN THE GRINGO TRAIL

Rio de Janeiro, one of the most glamorous cities in South America, has to be located in one of nature's most glorious settings, the geography adding greatly to its charm. Up on the mountain called Corcovado, the statue of Christ maintains a ceaseless vigil over the city. It is a city of the sea, beautiful beaches, and even more beautiful, the girls. You could go mad just looking at girls which, in this part of the world really are something else, as a visit to any one of those world famous beaches will reveal. And I do mean *reveal*. After all, Copacabana is where the string bikini originated, many of these girls appearing to have misplaced their swim suits altogether.

Vendors patrolled the sand, selling glasses of tea, and soft drinks, possibly to cool your ardour! They stroll along beating on a small drum, the drinks dispensed from a large chromed tank slung from a shoulder. Some even have elaborate back-packs from which the liquid is extracted via an over the shoulder pump handle.

Hot girls and cold drinks. Just don't allow yourself to become distracted enough to give the thieves free reign, for it's not only your inhibitions that can disappear. If you're not careful, wallets, jewellery, cameras and such will likely perform a similar feat in the blink of an eye!

Rio's nightclubs are something else as well. I recall one where girls danced on the tables. They were completely nude. They were also mostly young and pretty, with good figures. That changed in the next bar we visited. Here the performers were of both sexes. And what they were doing to one another could in no way, shape, or form, be described as dancing! The things people dream up to coax drinkers into their particular establishment.

Away from the busy harbour area in the central business district, the city spreads itself along the coastline, stretching out over a series of beaches whose names are renown the world over: Copacabana, Ipanema, Leblon, and more. Each a curving swathe of golden sand. Alongside Copacabana runs the wide Avenida Atlantica, its accompanying sidewalks made up of a wonderful mosaic, swirling patterns of black and white tiles. And all of this is overlooked by bars, restaurants and flashy hotels. Hotels in which elegant showcases line the walls. These shrines to the rich and famous displayed equally elegant offerings: items fashioned from gold, emeralds, diamonds, rubies, topaz, and the locally mined amethyst. Rolex, Omega, and Patek Phillipe were there in profusion. But these were not aimed at the locals, or even the regular tourists. The people one bumped into and mingled with here were, at least in their own opinion, gods on their way to stardom. Or those who had already reached those imagined heights. The kind of people whose telephone numbers are unlisted, and whose faces stare out from the covers of glossy international magazines.

There is of course another side to Rio, not too far removed from all this luxury, either, geographically speaking. In fact, well within sight of those fine hotels which line Copacabana, but high in the hills behind. It is up here that the city begins to crumble into ruins, for here perch the Favelas - slums and shantytowns - where the poor and wretched pick through the garbage. Thousands of peasants existing amid

461

conditions which contrasted sadly with the opulence of the hotels. And despite advice to the contrary, I would go for a look-see, as was my wont. If it was off the tourist trail, so much the better. The tourist sights you can see in a book, illustrated with a photograph taken in ideal lighting conditions. My way I got to see much more; things the tourists did not see, experienced things they did not experience.

Whereas the majority of my associates were not generally very adventurous sightseers, I was just the opposite, wandering off at will. But I'd dress the part. No jewellery or watch in sight, no flashy, ostentatious clothes, mini Pentax hidden, but ready for instant use, in my pocket. I'd keep my eyes open, remain friendly. A wave here, a smile there, perhaps a few Cruzeiros. It all helped, and as I rarely encountered problems, it either works or I've been extraordinarily lucky. But the people always seemed happy to see me. Maybe that was in part because they never expected me to be there, were pleased that I was.

Up there the scorched air was tainted with the stench of poverty. It was a sad-looking kind of place. You couldn't say run-down, as in certain areas of England - boarded-up windows, overgrown gardens, incomprehensible graffiti, the remains of cars jacked up on piles of bricks kind of thing - this whole place was run-down, had never been up. Shanties and lean-to's were constructed of cast away wood, corrugated iron, cardboard, beaten-flat tin. Anything useful or handy, a lot that was not. Still they crumbled with decay. Between them ran festering, open drains. Rubbish served only to block already inadequate gutters, giving birth to fetid pools in which children played, floating things around. Occasionally indescribable things.

After my wandering I'd descend the hill, take to sitting out in the sun at a pavement cafe, watching the world pass by, especially in the centre of Rio. The waiters were mostly young, but even in the heat they dressed as waiters. White, long-sleeved shirt, black waistcoat, trousers and shoes. Clean, smart, and cheerful. One I recall seemed determined to practice his English, which, it appeared, he was learning from a dictionary of quotations. Fair enough. The words may not have been in exactly the required sequence - to paraphrase Eric Morcame - but at least they *were* English. My Portuguese was Spanish, poor at that! 'Dua cervesa, por favor.'

'Ah!' he replied, leafing quickly through his mental file

'You can't draw beer from a stone.' Then, when I thanked him, using up my extensive repertoire of Portuguese in a one word sentence; 'Obrigada,' and waving off the few coins he offered as change, 'Every cloud has silver inside.' As he walked off he turned, "Don't change horses in the middle of a river,' he advised, getting very close.

The Brazilian long distance bus service is something else again. The central terminal in Rio is more like an airport terminal than a bus station. There are check-in and ticket booths for the various services; competing companies vying for your custom on the same route. On board you will find a stewardess service - cold beer, sandwiches, snacks, and the seating is reasonable; could say comfortable had it not been for the standard of driving. It's no surprise that Brazil has produced World Motor Racing Champions the likes of Emerson Fittipaldi, Nelson Piquet, and Ayrton Senna; their bus drivers appear to be the ones that failed to make it as far as Formula One!

I used the busses a lot. That was me, needed to see everything for myself, good and bad. Same thing went for Bogota, Colombia (kidnap capital of the world - or was, back then. Though these days it seems to have been overtaken by the middle east). No one bothered me there either, though from recent reports I don't think I'd attempt it today. Got to see rather a lot of the rest of Colombia, too, away from the cities, for some of our stations were located high in the mountains. I'm talking eight to ten thousand feet now, real mountains, the station often lost in the clouds. But it was the journey up there that could be spectacular. Dusty, one-street villages of neat little houses with pantiled roofs. Those that stretched themselves to more than one street usually also boasted a square, in which would be sited a wedding-cake like church. All around were hills and valleys, green, though fading to purple with distance. But let's face it, this was the Andes, where 2-3000 feet is barely above sea level. Some of those hills are mountains themselves, some of which seem to reach up forever. There were occasional splashes of colour, too; red, and yellow, and pink, as though some careless artist had dripped paint on his canvas. I recall looking across vistas of subtropical forest, with coffee and bananas growing in the areas cleared for them. And, who knows, maybe even coca - basis of cocaine - a major product of the area. Certainly the height was about right, between two and six thousand feet. Supposedly ideal for the cultivation of such a crop.

463

To arrive at one of these villages at the wrong time - siesta - was to find a place that looked deserted; windows and doors shuttered and closed. Like one of those Mexican towns in the Westerns, where the occupants are expecting a visit from El Baddo. Abandoned by all, with the possible exception of a flea-bitten mongrel, stretched out in the sun, even that too lethargic to scratch.

As things turned out, with the usual impeccable sense of timing, our arrival almost always seemed to coincide with an hour when it was possible to partake of the odd tepid beer or two. It would be the same movie Western though: groups of men sitting around drinking beer from the bottle, their horses hitched up outside in a line, waiting. The difference was the headgear. Here they wore battered trilbies rather than Stetsons. Further on down the Gringo Trail, say in Peru, or Ecuador, they favoured the bowler hat.

*

I was never caught up in drugs at all, dead set against them, but in Colombia you just knew they were never far away. Many of the gringos we spoke to were probably involved. Almost certainly, in fact, for the hotel at which we usually stayed when in Bogota was supposedly the place favoured by the dealers, the buyers, and the couriers - the so called mules. So the intrigue, the scheming, and the machinations of the drug trade were no doubt being enacted all around us. I'd probably even shaken hands with the odd cocaine baron or two. (Just as in Sicily I had almost certainly shaken the Mafia's hand. One had even invited me to take a ride with him. Though not the kind of ride from which one never returns. This was in a Ferrari 308 GT4. And those kind of opportunities don't occur too often. Which is how I found myself roaring around the streets of Syracuse alongside our agent's son.)

The drug syndicates were certainly operational up along the Caribbean coast, where most of our work took place: Cartagena, Barranquilla, Santa Marta, and Riohacha - on the Guajira Peninsula, with its hidden coves and disguised airstrips. Not only was the area naturally inhospitable, those who had business there made sure it remained so. Their kind of business brooked no uninvited guests, no unwanted interference. In fact, not only were strangers decidedly unwelcome, they were likely to face extreme danger, for this was an area where it would not be too difficult to put on weight in a hurry. That is to say, 44 magnum, 250 grain type weight!

We were even refused permission to install a station on the rising ground to the south of Santa Marta. Was this because the area was a known site for illegal marijuana growing, and some official was protecting his interests? After all, we did carry radios and other electronic devices - no matter how ancient and seemingly innocent-looking - so who was to say it was only a navigation station? Or maybe the authorities had no involvement whatsoever, just felt unable to offer sufficient protection in that particular area. We certainly made the odd contact offshore. One time playing our part in terminating a smuggling operation, albeit inadvertently.

We were conducting a survey off the Columbian coast, a round-the-clock operation, as is most oil related business, where time is money. Naturally, when towing a streamer, up to two miles in length, in the dark, one needs to keep a sharp eye on the radar.

'Strange, eh?' the skipper remarked. 'Lots of green blobs on the radar, nothing to be seen outside! They're close enough, too. If they were running with lights, we couldn't fail to spot them.'

'Have you tried calling on the radio? the client representative enquired.

'Sure have. But no one answers.'

'Just have to keep an eye open, then. If they look like getting too close, fire off a red.'

All we were interested in was protecting a multi million dollar legitimate business. But on this particular occasion someone's luck was "out to lunch," as was ours.

'We've got noise on the tail end,' came the call from the recording room. 'Streamer tension increasing.'

This told us all was not well.

'OK, abort the line. We'll have to pick up and check it out.'

Nothing else to be done, and as it takes hours to recover everything, it's not exactly top of the list of popular activities among those involved. This time the operation was proving even more labourious; lots of backing down, which suggested the tail end was still supported. Probably something related to the two large green blobs in that area glowing on the radar screen.

'No! Not two,' the skipper said. 'Three, four, ten. They're breeding. Anyone see anything out there?'

But in the dark nothing was visible on the flat calm

ocean.

With dawn came the mist, and after a time, out of the mist loomed our tailbuoy, in the shape of a pleasure cruiser. Another stood off, close by. The one we'd 'caught' was large - ten plus metres, twin screws - and he wasn't going anywhere. He must have crossed the end of the streamer, caught the tailbuoy rope in a propeller. Panic! Full power. Which only served to wrap the streamer itself around his propellor-shaft. And as the foundations of a streamer are three, very strong, stainless steel cables, there was no way he was about to escape without assistance. Our assistance. Not because we empathized with him in his plight; we needed to get back to work. Luckily, we carried scuba gear on board, plenty of volunteers, so over we went, in pairs, one with a hacksaw, one on shark watch; didn't fancy old Jaws sneaking up on us.

It took a long time, but we were eventually successful, even going so far as to fashion a new propeller key for him. This became a necessity when the person to whom I was handing the original, dropped the thing. Or maybe I did? No matter. Quite deep in places, the Caribbean. I watched that key sink slowly through the green depths, down to an inky blackness. Lucky not to drop the prop, too! Much heavier than imagined. Just as well we had a line attached when we removed it.

So, eventually both vessels roared off into the haze, our captain logging names and registrations; a report would need to be filed with the authorities somewhere or other. After all, those expensive hours of "Lost Time" were likely to be covered by someone's insurance.

It was then we came across the cause of our spurious radar returns: bales of hay, bobbing around in the water. Only it wasn't hay, was it! That was marijuana.

They must have dumped it in a panic, probably suspecting they'd been caught red handed.

No, we did not recover it. I kid you not.

*

I next found myself at Isla de Guanaja, Honduras. We were there to set shore stations for a short job, equipment having already arrived. It was a picturesque town, the majority of which consisted of wooden, corrugated-iron roofed shanty houses, perched over the sea on stilted walkways. It was hot and dry, had been for some time, so the conditions were ripe. Extreme caution needed to be exercised with regard to the prevention of fire. They were not.

In one house, lunch was apparently being prepared. Probably in many more than one, but in this one in particular, the frying pan and its contents were temporarily neglected, left unattended. And we all know what happens next. Most of us even know what to do about it, providing we have the presence of mind, and don't panic. Here it couldn't have been easier; just throw the pan out of the open window, into the sea. But panic did set in, the unfortunate "cook" charging off to get help!

It took but a few hours for most of the town to become a smoking ruin. Over fifty houses, the seafood packing plant - their major source of income - their only restaurant, towed out to sea to form a firebreak, and one death, being the end result.

For some reason I was wearing my solid gold Omega at the start of this project, so I gave it to the Party Chief to take ashore, rather than risking it out in the bush. His canoe capsized on the return trip, and although he was wearing it (luckily), my expensive watch became waterlogged. OK though, for the company did cover the cost of repair. This was also expensive, though no doubt covered by their insurance.

*

The location of my least memorable job was also in this area - Buenaventura, on the Pacific Coast of Colombia. A town seemingly filled with thieves.

Heaven is to sit out on the pavement in some tropical paradise, at sunset, cooling drink to hand, being serenaded by

467

the frogs and cicada, possibly watching a cabaret of monkeys. Not so in Buenaventura. To sit outside here was to encourage theft. Leave your cigarettes, or anything, on the table and they would be gone in a flash as some kid appeared as if from nowhere, grabbed them, and continued running without pause. The only response you could expect from any watching adults would be laughter. It was as if it were all a huge joke. Even when paying the waiter you needed to ensure the cash was in his hand before releasing your grip on it, otherwise, same, same! Once transferred to his hand, it became his problem.

During our whole month in the town we never did find a decent restaurant. And as for hotels.....

South American countries can be noisy, especially if your hotel has a fan and no airconditioning, as did mine. Actually, it did have aircon, only it didn't work. This gave me the choice of laying there with the window open, squeaky, out of track old fan barely stirring the air. Or of closing the window on the noise outside, and sweating cobs. A cosmetic choice really, for it was still hot with the window open, though a few degrees cooler than with it closed. So, was it to be hot and noisy - with the chance of unwanted visitors - or slightly less noisy but a degree or two hotter? On top of all this, one of the two crews allocated to me was comprised of a couple of idiots. When ashore they were continually stoned out of their minds, either drugs or drink, usually both. And when offshore they were barely capable of doing the job. If anything went wrong with the equipment, they brought the boat in for me to fix things for them. As a request for replacements would have led to at least a seven day holdup, I kept quiet and carried on.

On completion of the job, this pair then had the effrontery to suggest I recommend them for a pay raise! Once my report went in, what they got was fired.

I have no happy memories of that place, or of the job, despite the fact the person to whom we were contracted, who obviously didn't miss too much, kindly sent a letter of appreciation to my company HQ, siting my 'dedication to duty' in trying circumstances! Would likely have been awarded a medal for that in the Armed Forces. In this instance it probably didn't do any harm for my future prospects.

*

What is said of criminals and thieves seemed also to apply to dedicated aviators: Takes one to know one. Many's the time I've been invited to take the vacant right-hand seat, alongside the pilot. This usually applied to charters. But in the realms of the Spanish Main it happened on a small airline named Antilles Airboats. They operated scheduled inter-island flights, utilizing such aircraft as the Grumman Goose, and Mallard, both amphibious flying boats. Aptly named, these, for like their amphibian namesakes, they too appeared to waddle as they left the water to taxi up the slipway.

Take-off whisked me back in time, to Seletar; the spray, the lurching run to get up on the step, the dripping climb. Then it changed dramatically, the scene below, magnificent. Typical Caribbean, yet it was a view of which I would never tire. Emerald, yellow fringed islands were set in a sea that seemed constantly to change colour. Blue, green, turquoise, azure; from the blue-black of the depths, to a creamy-white where it foamed over a reef.

The flight was but a short half hour. I could happily have stayed up there all day.

*

On completion of one South American assignment - myself now between wives, as it were - the wanderlust struck again. I decided to take a vacation, so asked the company if I could route myself from Brazil back to England via the Pacific rather than the Atlantic route. At the time the Brazilian currency, the Cruzeiro, was so unstable the fast falling exchange rate was quoted daily in the local paper. This situation resulted in only a portion the company's income from Brazilian sources being allowed to be paid in US dollars. The remainder was paid in Cruzeiros, into a local account. OK for paying local operating expenses, but little else. Which left the company with a growing account of almost useless currency. So, as it was OK to purchase airline tickets originating in Brazil using local currency, the answer came back for me to go ahead. Better to spend fast devaluing Cruzeiros rather than US Dollars. Especially so if the fare could be charged to the client, for payment in the US. Thus I was invited to plan my own route, a suggestion with which I was happy to comply: Iguassu Falls - Brazil; Montevideo - Uruguay; Buenos Aries - Argentina; Santiago - Chile; Easter Island - Chile; Papeete - Tahiti; Auckland - New Zealand; across the Tasman Sea, thence Australia, and on to England. Good plan, eh. But, as with most good plans, when acted upon, errors became evident. Unfortunately, as I had entered Brasil on a Panamanian Seaman's Card - one of the tricks the company got up to so as to bypass any possible visa problems - I found I had to depart via the same gateway as that through which I entered; Rio. Scratch Iguassu Falls and Montevideo. I was then to discover I was persona non grata in Argentina. Apparently, our Prime Minister of the time (Margaret Thatcher) being somewhat in disagreement with the Argentinian President over ownership of the Falkland Islands! Scratch Buenos Aries. But the rest of the trip went quite well. The Chilean capital of Santiago was a bit like a European city; magnificent, centuries old grand buildings and palaces, pleasant green parks, all surrounded by the towering Andes. To see more of the country I took a bus trip down to the main coastal port of Valparaiso. I enjoyed Chile. Which is more than can be said of my next stop, the mysterious Easter Island - known as Isla De Pascua, or Rapa Nui to the Chileans, who administer it. Here, scores of great stone heads stare sightlessly into the distance, taciturn and mute, as if to state that the secret of their existence would never be revealed. Impressive enough. But there is really little else to see, or do, and as flights only arrive and depart twice weekly, one is obliged to remain for at least three days. Ah well, Tahiti was next on my list, then on to New Zealand.

Tahiti. The word conjures up so much, but the capital, Papeete, left me largely unimpressed; just another small town. Travel outside its boundaries and you get glimpses of the South Pacific, but they are mainly across the water. So I left Tahiti behind and crossed over to its neighbouring island of Moorea, and its tall, graceful palms, the fronds of which shimmered in the cooling breeze. After Tahiti, the pace of life here slowed dramatically, a restful peace settling itself over the area. It made you wonder why you were ever in such a hurry. The girls wore a flower behind the ear.

But if you have the time, and the money, I believe Bora Bora, to the north east - but still part of the Society Islands - is the place to go. Instead, I went on to New Zealand, as planned. I knew what awaited me there.

*   *

Chapter Seventeen
MOZAMBIQUE

'Stow those for me, please, Dave. In the boot,' the pilot added, pointing at the rear fuselage, behind the cabin. Although Portugese, his English was nigh on perfect. 'Plenty of room in there.' He handed me the various covers and tie-downs which he had just removed, then carried on with his external inspection of what was more or less about to become my own private helicopter. At least for the next few weeks.

1985, and I had returned to Africa. A different Africa. The East coast this time, as opposed to all those years up and down the West. OK, maybe not so different then. After all, this was still post colonial Africa.

When the guy in our London office phoned me at my retreat in the solitude of the Yorkshire Wolds, we were in the grip of the coldest winter in twenty years. So there was really no reason for him to ask if I was ready to travel to Southern Africa. I was mentally packed even before I replaced the phone. Not only would it be warm down there - in direct contrast to the North Sea, where I seemed to be spending so much of my time these days - but the job also promised a bit of the adventure that used to be a common feature in our work, something that was sadly lacking in the health and safety conscious environment of the North Sea. It would be good to get back to fighting the elements,... or would it?

Departure from bleak, strike-bound England had taken place in mid-February. Now, it was well into the month, a couple of minutes into sunrise. Dawn is already an hour in the past.

I've always found early mornings to be such a wonderful time of day, more's the pity that to enjoy them one needs to rise at such an ungodly hour. But my present location was far from perfect. A yellow ball struggled to free itself from the pall of haze and pollution which mantled this remote corner of the continent, with not a breath of wind to clear it. Immobile, angular, fuzzy silhouettes were visible over on the far side of the airport. They looked to be abandoned, probably were. Antonovs, Mils, Migs, and Ilyushins; remnants of yet another failed Soviet incursion into this continent. Before me on the dispersal sat an American made, South African registered, British company owned helicopter, and in front of the terminal, a member of Boeing's 737 family of twin-jets; signs of the now-favoured Western influence.

A peaceful stillness ensued, even though nature's gentle awakening had already broken the silence. Man was about to add his contribution to this start of yet another day's aerial activity.

*

A week had passed since my arrival in Mozambique. Air Zimbabwe from London to Harare, where a six hour layover had afforded me chance to reacquaint myself with the capital. The only obvious change - apart from the buildings now looking rather more scruffy than I recalled - appeared to be the name; it had been Salisbury on my last visit, with the RAF, twenty-three years previous to this. In a similar vein the country had more or less disassociated itself from the memory of Cecil Rhodes, dropping Rhodesia and reverting to the ancient name of Zimbabwe. Sad, really, but what's in a name? Quite a lot, it seemed. I learned that Rhodesia used to export the very goods

Zimbabwe now found a need to import, but no longer had the cash or means to do so. It was the usual story for recently formed African nations; Rich dictator, poor country.

I'd already been reacquainted with the bush during our approach to the airport. Well, almost. It had been the captain's last flight before retirement, and, after calling up and receiving permission to "buzz" the airfield, he had gone ahead and done so (first advising us passengers of his intentions). Made a good job of it too. It was as low as I'd been in a 707, with the undercarriage retracted. Just as well there were no stray giraffes wandering about!

From Harare I was booked on Linhas Aereas De Mocambique - the local airline - to Maputo, another capital which had suffered a change of name. Previously, when a Portugese colony, it had been Lourenco Marques.

In the hands of whoever had been running it these past years, it also had suffered a change of fortune. Once the playground of wealthy Portuguese, and South Africans, it was now extremely run down, almost derelict. Its wide, tree-lined avenues were unkempt and overgrown. The once-upon-a-time abundantly-stocked stores were now empty, closed and shuttered. Grandeur had given way to decay, that austere shabbiness which appears to be the hallmark of most third world or communist countries. With all this in mind I'd expected to fly in some Russian cast-off - such as the scruffy, oil-dripping Antonov AN24 of Lina Congo which had once conveyed me between Brazzaville and Pointe Noire, or the similarly dangerous-looking Ilyushin IL14 of China's CAAC, neither of which had been exactly relaxing experiences - so I was pleasantly surprised to find C9-BAD, when it arrived, to be one of Boeing's finest. A 737 of one series or other. But that registration did happen to be appropriate. We sat on the ground in Beira for an hour and a half, awaiting the arrival of some politician, or General. Same thing really, out here. This being the case, it should have come as no surprise to find that the country was a war zone. A group named Frelimo vs a group named Renamo, this time. Frelimo - the once upon a time Marxist Government for whom we'd basically be working - apparently controlled the cites and towns. Renamo - what would, in a democratic society, be the opposition - controlled a good deal of the countryside, the very place I needed to be to do my job - hence that helicopter.

We'd already felt the effects of this still-lingering war,

the threat of attack making it impossible to transport our equipment from Johannesburg by road, as planned. And, as LAM didn't have the capacity to carry it, we had to charter a South African aircraft to do the job for us. Not a problem, or it shouldn't have been. But despite the fact that LAM couldn't handle the job, they still insisted we pay a US$2000 fee for them not flying it in. This, after all was their territory. Typical African business practice.

Now the gear had finally arrived, we were ready to go to work. And being as road travel was beyond question, the helicopter had been chartered for me to travel around in, Antonio Gordhino, my pilot.

We were about to depart on our first sortie. All covers and locks had been removed, Antonio had completed his pre-flight walk-around, particular attention being paid to the rotor head and blades, the most important parts of a helicopter. Now he climbed aboard and strapped himself in alongside me. It felt comfortable to be back in familiar surroundings, seated up front.

The first streaks of sunlight cleared the surrounding hills, filling the cockpit with promised warmth. And as I watched from the left-hand seat, Antonio ran through the start-up checks, reading off each item from a checklist located somewhere in memory, answering himself as the appropriate action was taken.

'Master switch? On.

'Fuel? Checked. Levels, OK.

'Mixture? Set.

'Rotor brake? On.'

His hands appeared to run through their tasks automatically, as I'm sure they did - immediately assuring me of his competence - and whilst awaiting the correct response to a particular action, after first initiating it, his mouth hummed a Beatles number, thus divulging his age group. It was a triple act in which he performed all three parts.

'Battery master?' the mouth asked. At which a hand reached out to flick a switch. 'On,' came the reply, followed by a couple of bars from Yellow Submarine. There was a clunk as a heavy duty relay thumped home, a click had the instrument panel flickering into life, needles jumping attentively, recording whatever it was they were supposed to record. Lights glowed brightly and, out of sight, other things clicked and whirred.

'We have power,' he exclaimed, almost sounding surprised. The eyes and fingers were just as busy as the mouth, which itself had now switched to an atonal version of *Hey Jude, Yellow Submarine* apparently having sunk without trace somewhere between "Battery? On", and "Rotor brake? Check".

A break in the musical improvisation allowed him to pose the question, 'Clear to start?' apparently at the door, for that was to where his eyes were looking. His head swivelled, allowing him to check the immediate locality, presumably for the odd stray camelopard. Obviously there were none, his answer being in the affirmative: 'Clear to start.' More switches were snapped on. His left hand now dropped to the twist-grip throttle on the collective pitch control, wound it fully open before closing it again. He then opened it fractionally as, simultaneously, his forefinger stabbed a button recessed into the end of the lever. The engine turned over with a low, dry, whine, turbine steadily building up speed. Another switch had the igniters clicking away merrily like love-sick crickets, until, with a dull whumph, fuel ignited and the whine became the gentle roaring of hot gasses. His right forefinger now redirected his eyes to a gauge by pointing at it. Its needle rose quickly through the green segment, touching briefly into the red before dropping back into the top end of the green. This was apparently OK, as the finger was removed, a thumb raised in acceptance. EGT 760c. Exhaust gas temperature, degrees Celsius, I decoded.

Antonio had introduced himself to me during the drive out to the airport. Short, dark-haired, with a cheerful smile and a wicked sense of humour, he was to be my pilot for the duration of this project I was starting up in Mozambique. His machine, a Bell 206 Jetranger, was at my beck and call, to use as and when required. That, I liked the sound of. Antonio worked for South African based Court Helicopters.

My first task was to install unmanned navigation beacons on pre-surveyed sites along the coast. These would be used to position a seismic vessel working offshore. The beacons were battery-powered, the batteries charged by solar panels. At least that was the plan. It had sounded good the previous evening, when I and the rest of the crew had sat down and discussed it. We were in a bar at the time, lubricating our throats in traditional manner. We needed to, for this was to be subjected to some serious thought, which in turn required a drink. There again, none of us being single-drink people......

At some time during the proceedings it became obvious I was slightly drunk. No, let me correct that; completely pissed. Had to be. Slightly drunk is on a par with being slightly pregnant, or slightly dead: you either are, or you ain't. Anyway, as I have previously related, it's a well known fact that no battle plan survives being put into action, so it was hardly surprising to find this one didn't come anywhere near.

The problem was with the solar panels. They just didn't appear to be up to the job, which meant I needed to change batteries every two or three days, on each of five stations. Antonio was delighted about this, for between times we stayed aboard the vessel, and I was left with the distinct impression he wasn't at all happy with that arrangement. In fact it took very little time for this to become obvious. After only twelve hours I noticed him mooching around his aircraft, tied down on the helideck on the stern. Next morning he swept in to my cabin like a pocket rocket; a one man tornado.

'Any batteries to change, Dave?' he asked hopefully. His eyes reminded me of those of a spaniel; beseeching. We'd gone a full twenty-four hours without lifting off. He was bored. Well, so was I. And, as I could easily justify flying off, away we went, Antonio's grin a sight to behold. We were going to get along just fine. But I'd already ascertained that we would.

The sites were located on such as a convenient lighthouse or, if there wasn't one, the highest point around. Trouble was, the highest ground was usually a sand dune, very difficult to climb when carrying a twenty-four volt battery, especially in what were to be extremely high-digit temperatures; sun's rays being aided by the reflection factor off the sand. This was when I really came to appreciate Antonio. He offered an alternative, which we discussed en-route, deciding to give it a try. On arrival he eased the machine sideways, feeling his way, touching a skid gently on the sand at the top of the dune. This provided him with a reference, me with a chance to leap out, my helicopter background serving to remind me to watch my head. There was no wind, which helped, but I was relying totally on Antonio's skill. I looked up briefly from my task to observe him. He was very good. The machine remained in the hover, barely moving. It reminded me of a bumble-bee pollinating a flower. Perfect. So from then on it became standard practice. No hauling awkward bits and pieces up the insides of lighthouses, either. I assembled everything at ground level then attached it to the sling beneath the fuselage as Antonio hovered above me. I then rushed up - as fast as one does rush up hundreds of narrow, winding steps, in darkness, temperatures of ninety plus - and secured it to the balcony of the light, balancing myself on top of the safety rail, Antonio releasing the sling when I gave the word. I shudder to think of it now. One false move and it was one hundred and fifty feet to oblivion. No Health & Safety Gestapo out there, but we didn't need one. I was still relatively young, and my safety was in my own hands, just as Antonio's was in his. We were both extremely careful, never really pushing the limits, so all went well. Almost perfect, actually. It saved me hours of toil and frustration. Just as well, for the only lighthouse available not only housed a light - non-operational, it also happened to house a detachment of the local militia; sort of Mozambican Observer Corps, though these were heavily armed. The walls of their rooms were plastered with recognition photos of SAAF aircraft, for South Africa was looked upon as a likely enemy of the State. Or at least a friend of the State's enemies. And in the room where my equipment was located lay a suspicious-looking tarpaulin-covered bundle. I peeked, of course. Well, you never know, it might have been something that would affect our operations. What I found were even more suspicious-looking wooden boxes, complete with Cyrillic lettering. Well, I just had to open one of those, didn't I, for I couldn't read a word of Russian! All sounded quiet so I eased the top of one open a crack. Bugger me! Hand-held ground-to-air missiles! And why not? This was the Third World. These guys might be starving, have ragged uniforms, not get paid, but they were well equipped when it came to the tools of war. Could come in handy, those, thought I. I later warned Antonio not to get stroppy with me, or else!

I also made sure the militia had a good look at our aircraft. It may not have looked much like a Mirage or a Hercules, but it did carry South African registration. Those guys we kept happy by bringing them cartons of Marlboro "ciggies" and tins of food, both of which were freely available to us, but not to the general population. There was a government-controlled store in the capital, Maputo, name of Interfranca. A kind of duty free Tesco, access to which was by passport only - unless you happened to be a member of the government, or a friend of a friend, of course. Payment was only in South African Rand or US Dollars, for even the locals weren't interested in the local currency. No wonder, either. I'd been obliged (forced) to change twenty dollars at the airport upon entry to the country, the resulting barrow-load of Meticais good only for the purchase of postcards and stamps; the very reason everyone and his dog received a postcard from me on that trip. But even though cigarettes and electronic goods were plentiful at Interfranca, fresh food was not. I recall a few boxes of apples putting in a brief appearance one day. No, brief wasn't the word to describe it! Fleeting, maybe. Or how about "bloody swift?" Which is what you needed to be if you fancied one - apple, that is, not a boxful. Even expatriates were almost coming to blows over them. It was like watching a news clip of relief supplies arriving during yet another African famine. Well... I suppose in a way it was!

As with my butter and sugar during WW2, to the militia, pure gold was of less value than those ciggies and cans. The inference was that we would be their friends, forever. Hey! Now hang on a minute... These guys neither washed nor changed their clothes, or if they did they needed a serious rethink on their choice of washing powder. I carried a can of air freshener, sprayed it ahead of me as I ascended the stairs. Antonio stayed with the aircraft. Couldn't blame him.

It was a perfect partnership I had with Antonio, and we had some great times together. I helped him with refuelling and servicing in the field, he helped me, even taught me to fly the thing - a far cry, and decidedly easier, than the old Mk.2 Whirlwinds in Malaya.

Now living in South Africa, which is where the (British, Court Line) helicopter company was based, he'd originally been in Mozambique with the Portuguese Air Force, during that country's colonial past, still had friends scattered around the area. Handy, that, too. Many of them, out in the sticks, lacked basics such as rice and potatoes, we had access to both, if not in Maputo, then off the boat - which re-supplied in South Africa. Whenever we flew up their way we carried with us some provisions. They, in return, provided hospitality and beer whenever it was necessary for us to spend a night away from base. They also kept us supplied with things they happened to have an abundance of: crayfish, and very large prawns, freshly caught. Both were almost unobtainable in the capital, yet supplies were plentiful in the coastal waters.

Come the weekend it was a simple matter for me to suddenly discover there to be a problem on one of the stations.

Something which required my presence in the area. Naturally, it would be a station that just happened to be located on a particularly agreeable site. Near enough a nice safe stretch of beach, and whatever other facilities the area could muster. Some of those problems could take quite a time to sort out, believe me, so we always carried a picnic lunch with us. No point flying with empty seats, either, so we invited others of the crew along. You know, I had this weird idea that maybe the sea was affecting propagation of the radio waves, had to go and find out. Well, you can't be too sure can you? Lucky I thought to carry my swimming gear with me, eh?

Even on genuine sorties Antonio would often tire of the distance-induced illusion of slow motion flight at five thousand feet, so, lacking almost any kind of Air Traffic management, he'd take us down for a boredom-relieving spell of the low-level stuff.

'Look, Antonio, flamingoes,' I said, pointing ahead to a sizable flock.

'Ah, yes, the flamingoes' he replied, as though it was a sight with which we were familiar. To him it was, I soon discovered; was soon to become so to me also.

When viewed from above, against the backdrop of a lake and surrounding savanna, these huge flocks of flamingoes are an incredible sight, especially when they suddenly have an urge to become airborne *en mass,* as they tend to do when a chopper screams in low over the trees. And although a hundred and twenty knots may not be much to a racing driver, to us mere mortals, travelling five feet above the sand, or skimming the waves, it was exhilarating. Dogs and other four-legged creatures - inspired to remarkable sprints of terror - took off like they were turbo-charged. They'd disappear into the undergrowth, leaving their somewhat braver, if foolish, owners to stand tall and shake a defiant fist in the air. More or less as had that gorilla in Gabon, but presenting much less of a threat. Then the message would slowly filter through: *Steel bird at five feet, lower than dis head at six feet* (or whatever was the local equivalent). Next thing they'd be hurling themselves ingloriously flat on the beach, face down to the sand, or into the sea. Sometimes the thought processes would prove rather more lethargic than usual, it was then up to Antonio to remedy the situation; a quick jink left, right, or up.

We flew low over the Limpopo - its supposedly crocodile-infested waters the colour of milky coffee - until it abruptly turned left to begin a series of wide, looping turns, meandering this way and that, as if in an attempt to delay its arrival offshore. We followed it. A real African river this, no banks to be seen. The jungle began right at the water's edge, a dense, verdant, overhanging landscape through which the river had sliced a path. And although I never did see any crocs, I did once see a swirl of vacant, muddy water, where a second or two previous I had spied a bird of some kind, so I could well imagine it hosting them, along with other exotic beasties: snakes, hippos and such.

There were many canoes being paddled around too, their progress seeming tranquil, yet at the same time intent. In this country of poor to nonexistent roads that river was a motorway.

At the last moment Antonio hauled us up, clear of the trees, climbing high enough to make radio contact, informing distant Maputo control of our imminent landing at Xai Xai (pronounced, Shy Shy). We had the rice and potatoes, were ready for some crayfish and beer.

*

I particularly recall one flight, early on in the project, when we were still in the process of evaluating procedures. We'd removed the rear doors from the cabin so as to allow the ten-foot mast sections to be carried athwartships, across the cabin floor, projecting either side. On other projects I'd just lash them to the skids, fore and aft, but the skids on this aircraft were fitted with floatation devices. Could have gone ahead anyway, but there are limits as to how far you push the safety angle. There were extensive over-water sectors on our route - especially if we were returning to the vessel, up to forty miles plus offshore - and we only had a single engine. So we went for the cabin-floor option. It worked fine, with a full load, at fairly low speed. Not so good on the return trip, with an empty cabin, when we found the airflow threatening to rip out the rear seat cushions. Well, no problem, this was a helicopter wasn't it.

We put down in a convenient spot. A clear, open area, for we weren't about to take a chance on being captured and held hostage, either. Here I removed the offending items, stowed them in the boot. And so we went merrily on our way. For a while, that is, until the seat-backs attempted the same trick. OK, down we went again. Off came the offending items, into storage. A little later, a flapping noise drew attention the fact that it was now the turn of the sound-proofing. It was being torn loose, airstream getting beneath and popping the press-studs. Down again for another unscheduled stop. Yet more of the aircraft disappearing into the spacious boot, which was by now becoming quite crowded. Not only that, the rear cabin was looking decidedly stark.

Underway once more, I looked behind me, just checking. I then looked across at Antonio, the smile on his face breaking into uncontrollable laughter. With tears streaming he explained the reason for this outbreak of mirth. He fantasized arriving back at base flying the bare skeleton of an airframe, and when questioned, explaining to his engineer the whereabouts of the remainder: "It's in the boot." That got me going, too. It was probably one of those incidents no one else would have found funny, but it had us in stitches. Spur of the moment humour.

Referring back to the safety angle, and those floatation devices. Almost had a need to use them the time we pushed the margins to the maximum. We were heading back to the vessel, almost at the limit of our range when considering the need to retain enough fuel to make it back to shore, should that prove necessary. This time, it almost was.

All things being equal, the boat should have been no more than about twenty miles from the position in which we left it, depending on how long we'd been away. No problem. We figured we only needed to navigate ourselves to within a ten mile radius, and we should be able to spot them. Only this day it was hazy, got steadily worse as we proceeded offshore, making things extremely difficult. Especially so, when for some reason we lost radio contact. We were almost at the point of no return, then Antonio just happened to glance back over his shoulder - he later said it was one of those subconscious things. There was the boat, behind us and well off to one side, barely discernable on the very edge of our vision. We smiled at each other, as though confirming it hadn't been a problem. But in reality I'm sure we'd both been aware it had not been a good situation to get into. We'd been very lucky to get away with it. God had been riding with us that day.

We drastically revised our procedures after that, remained ashore more often. Better to get wet inside rather than out!

Then it all came to an end. The job, I mean. This side of Africa had been new to me - the east coast as opposed to the west - though I had once been fortunate enough to visit Luanda, capital of Angola, over on that west coast. It had still been a Portuguese colony at the time, and in my opinion, a city unmatched for beauty in few places on this continent, outside South Africa, that is. Maputo - when it had been Lourenco Marques - must have been similar, that was plain to see. I recall they used to hold an international sports car race through the streets of this town. Not any more. Just as Luanda is now no more.

After the boat departed for the last time, we flew out to Nelspruit, South Africa, by charter - a Cherokee 6 - and I recall the border, when viewed from on high. There was a distinct line: unkempt nature to well tended fields in the blink of an eye. No mistaking it from the air. It reminded me of a pudding-basin haircut.

Believe me, after six weeks in Maputo, Johannesburg was the best place on earth. Absolute luxury. That night I dined on surf and turf: succulent steak and lobster tails, washed down by wines from the Stellenbosch area. I also discovered a very agreeable local brandy, a ten year old KWV. On a par with any reasonable Cognac.

Next day South African Airways were good enough to upgrade me to their Diamond Class for the long haul back to the UK, which put me upstairs on their 747. And travelling almost due north meant no jet-lag to contend with upon arrival. The end of a very pleasant job.

The weather had barely changed since my departure, but by mid April, the thermometer was nudging the high 50's.

*   *

THE PLEASURES OF FLIGHT

*W*aiting around in airports is purported to be one of the most trying features of travel. So many people, so many flights, you imagine it all grinding to a halt once you leave. Surely it can't be the same every minute of every day? Where could all these people be going? Where had they all come from? But you know what, it really does go on all the time, day in, day out, even when you are not around. When you are, there's a need to accept it. You need to be prepared to queue, or to time your arrival for the last minute. But I'm a person who hates unnecessary rush, so when travelling, especially alone, I always allow plenty of time. I much prefer to sit and wait for an hour or two rather than face the hustle and bustle of a late check-in. Especially so these days, with the myriad of security procedures that have to be endured, and there is a need to partially undress! Anyway, despite all that, I find airports to be fascinating places, full of interesting events, happenings, people. You just never know who you're going to bump into. They are there, all around, just need to keep your eyes open. This was especially so in days past, long before the onset of mass tourism.

For example: Terminal Two was particularly crowded. I'd done my shopping, was having difficulty finding an acceptable seat, so, even though my flight hadn't yet been called, I decided to make my way to the gate - air side, as it's officially known - past immigration and the security checks, away from all the restaurants, bars, and the "Duty Free" - a lot of which you can buy far cheaper out on the high street! Experience had taught me the gate was a place where I could sit and read in relative peace or, alternatively, stare out of the window, look at the aircraft, soak up the atmosphere. Even the endless corridors - of which Heathrow appears to have a surfeit - are always infinitely less crowded than the departure hall. Today, in fact, I was all alone. Until *was* became the operative word, that is. For a door opened, and I suddenly found myself to be surrounded. People rushed past, turned, then I was facing a battery of cameras, a barrage of flashguns. At last. My fifteen minutes of fame. But for what reason? Had I contravened some hitherto unknown piece of Heathrow ordinance, such as proceeding to gate before my flight was declared ready for boarding? Highly unlikely. I *had* spent rather a long time in the newsagents, flicking through various upper-shelf magazines without actually making a purchase. But unless they'd passed a bill in the last hour or so ...? No, not that either. Maybe I was the millionth person to check in today, had won the holiday of a lifetime? A possibility, perhaps? So I smiled and awaited the outcome.

It soon became apparent that my fifteen minutes were to be but a ten second dream.

A straw boater drifted past on my right. There was someone beneath it. Someone wearing a familiar smile, a striped blazer and funny glasses. Someone who looked suspiciously like Elton John, his entourage being towed along behind. It was Elton. Ah well, so much for the holiday of a lifetime. Didn't need it anyway, my life, on occasion, already appeared to be one long holiday.

A similar situation occurred the time I chanced upon Richard Burton, again at Heathrow. Crowds of photographers walking backwards. Not for Christmas, as Peter Sellers would have it, but from the arrival gate towards immigration, no doubt eventually to the VIP section. What I remember most clearly about that incident was the lady who complained she shouldn't have to put up with this kind of thing; the flashguns in her face and what all. Fact was, had she joined the rest of us - walking ahead of the rich and famous, the glitterati - she wouldn't have needed to. I suspect she chose to place herself in the line of fire, no doubt hoping for a cameo appearance on the front pages of the tabloids.

We'd travelled back from Geneva together, Mr Burton and I (along with Mrs Suzie Hunt - wife of Formula One racing driver, James Hunt - soon to become the next Mrs Burton). We hadn't travelled in the same class, admitted. Whilst they were up at the sharp end - of life, as well as seating - I elected to sit back in Business. At least, my company elected on my behalf. But I did have Mr Burton's full-length fur coat on the rack above my head. The rack up front had been declared too dusty, so the steward informed me. I asked him to relay an offer from me: five quid for the coat. Never did get a reply. Strange, that.

Then there was Gregory Peck. An extremely tall person, Mr Peck. And for some reason I'd always thought him to be short. He was also, I suspect, a heavy tipper. He had his hands behind his back, fiddling with a twenty pound note as someone did his checking in for him. I'd have done it for a fiver had he asked!

Australian TV show host, Paul Hogan, I snared in the baggage hall. He was clutching a carton of Marlboro. This was long before the days of "Crocodile Dundee", and I felt the need to remind him that he advertised a different brand back home in Australia.

'Can't get 'em here,' he replied, smiling knowingly. We had both just arrived on the same flight, from Australia! Which leads nicely into that cigarette advert - for Winfield - that in those days seemed to feature everywhere "Down Under". It portrayed Mr Hogan - never one noted for his sartorial elegance, at least on TV, where he usually appeared dressed in Australian Rules Footie shirt and shorts - now suavely

486

dressed; black tie and dinner jacket, leaning casually on a wall, ankles crossed in James Bond fashion, cigarette in hand. HAVE A WINFIELD, the billboards, or Mr Hogan, invited. Eye catching all right, but nothing really sensational. No, the clever ad was to follow a couple of months later. The Australian government had meantime passed a piece of anti-smoking legislation which forbade well-known personalities from promoting tobacco products, a situation that was immediately exploited by WINFIELD, or whoever it was ran their advertising campaign. Mr Hogan duly disappeared from the billboards, as was now the law. In his place? Nothing! A glaringly blank space. Pure white. Below which was the message: HAVE A WINFIELD ANYWAY.

There had been others at odd times: Peter Sellars; Ian Carmichael; Stirling Moss, various politicians and such like.

I recalled some of these anecdotes some weeks later when out for a drink, thinking to impress my mates and the locals. I even had some autographs to substantiate them. They listened politely, then, after the briefest of pauses, someone said, 'Did tha' 'ear about Mrs Daniels? Has ti go back to t'hospital next week ti have 'er foot fixed.'

So much for assumed fame by limited association. Not that I had sought out these encounters, far from it. But back in those pre Executive Lounge days, if you kept your eyes open, anyone and everyone passed through the passenger halls, occasionally to sit and read a book. They were there to see, though not necessarily to be seen. And these *were* stars, not in the fashion of today's so-called "celebrities", the majority of which few have heard of, or would even recognise in the flesh!

I did eventually achieve my fifteen minutes of fame (or perhaps those minutes were again seconds). This happened one day whilst seated at the poolside in the grounds of the Trinidad Hilton - so at least the setting was appropriate. I noticed the waiter who had just brought my gin and tonic to be staring at me. When I looked back, questioningly, he said, "I know you. You're the fella that plays James Bond."

I neither confirmed nor denied the fact, just gave the guy a wry smile and kept quiet. Although I suspected Roger Moore - the James Bond of the time - would not have been flattered, I certainly was.

It will be noted that personalities did not necessarily hide away back then, so it *was* possible to meet and talk, or at least greet them. But personalities are rarely the most interesting of people to converse with. The real education comes from talking to everyday citizens, especially in places like the US southern states, or country folk in Australia, New Zealand and the like.

*

Few people who travel by air have any interest in the rudiments of flight. For them it is merely a means of getting from A to B, therefore they miss the essentials, the magic. From an airconditioned terminal, viewed through soundproofed glass, passengers see only something which will transport them through time and space whilst they are fed and watered, their needs pampered to. Sort of! Unless, that is, you are flying Ryanair or some such! Some passengers may recognise that aircraft outside to be a "Jumbo", but that's about as far as it goes. The fundamentals remain unseen. The beauty of the machine. From the finely rounded contours of the cockpit surrounds and drag resisting nose, to the harsh, stark, heat-discoloured metal of the jet efflux things take on a sudden reality, and hugeness. But they're more than huge. Compared to the majority of aircraft, the 747 is massive. Brutal almost. Then there is the new Airbus 380. Even more impressive! Yet at the same time they are functional and purposeful. Next time the opportunity occurs, take a look at that wing planform: the size, the profile, the surface area; the very things that enable us to fly. These are the things that usually go unnoticed, impress few. I imagine Sir George Cayley would have been suitably impressed, as would his coachman "pilot", along with Wilbur and Orville. (Maybe they all are, who knows?) There are other aspects, too. Some visible, some not. Down on the tarmac the engineer walks around beneath those wings, completing his visuals, looking for anything untoward that may have been missed by the ground engineers. The captain will be checking the on-route weather, calculating all-up weight (up to something like 400,000lbs); unstick speed; logging radio frequencies; checking Notams (Notices to Airmen), which detail any late additional en route restrictions, or possible hazards. Or he may already be in the cockpit, programming the computers to fly him wherever it is he wants to go; hopefully the same place all the passengers wish to go! The first officer - having completed *his* external checks - will also be aboard, applying his magic, whilst the cabin crew check the galleys in preparation for boarding. Until then, passenger interest will be focussed on Duty Free, the newsagent, or the bar. For some, especially the bar.

Once in the departure lounge, a certain amount of

nervousness is sure to be apparent. People stand and make their way towards the gate well before the boarding announcement. Like lemmings that have received the call, they surge forward, pushing and elbowing, this despite the fact that seats are already allocated. I, of course, am compelled join them - unless I have already preempted the call by a greater margin! But my only worry is for space in the overhead lockers. No fun with your briefcase beneath your feet for ten hours. Especially when some of that "hand baggage" should really be in the hold.

(I recall the time when one particular piece of luggage should have been in the hold but wasn't. I'd arrived at Heathrow to find it was a manual check-in, being as the computers were down. My bag was misdirected to CPH (Copenhagen) instead of SVG (Stavanger) as on my boarding pass. Not that it wouldn't have happened anyway. But if the computers had been in operation we wouldn't have been required to identify our luggage before it was placed on board the aircraft. As mine was not to be found, they instigated a search, were able to rescue it before the Copenhagen flight departed. Just!)

So, we are finally seated. Baggage stowed, seatbelts fastened, safety briefing complete, engines running, tension high. At this point, most passengers meekly surrender their option to take individual action. Until touchdown all decision making becomes the responsibility of the crew, which is exactly as it should be. I relax, others check the seat pockets for freebies, glance around, fiddle with things: unimportant things. Then there is the hesitant conversation, the forced smile, both of which are nervous reactions. Of the technicalities they neither care, nor do they wish to, which is what breeds the fear they feel, creates the tension and nervousness. Fear is brought about by ignorance. Up front are the people who understand. Up there in the cockpit. The crew, with their little codes and a language all their own: VFR, and ILS, for Visual Flight Rules and Instrument Landing System. Quebec Foxtrot Echo - QFE - the current barometric pressure at the height of the airfield (or, alternatively, Quebec November Hotel - QNH - the pressure at sea level), entered to ensure the altimeter reads the correct height. Then there is the all-important, V-one, or velocity one; the decision point on the take off run. Beyond this speed the aircraft is committed to take-off, no matter what. Given their all-up weight and the prevailing climatic conditions, there will not be enough runway remaining to enable a safe stop to be made.

Which is exactly one of the things the crew would have been calculating earlier. V-R comes next - velocity rotate - lift-off speed achieved. At which point the pilot in control will gently ease back on the control column - or sidestick controller. This brings the nosewheel off the ground, a brief pause and we are flying. Now we are in the real danger zone. A few seconds only, then comes V-two; flying safety speed. The airspeed is such we are now able to continue the climb should we have the misfortune to suffer an engine failure. We don't, so now everyone can settle back and relax. Until it comes to the approach and landing. But that is yet hours in the future.

For now, the aircraft hauls itself into the sky, slowly gathering in all those bits and pieces - landing gear, flaps, slats - which, after getting us airborne, would now restrict our speed if not neatly tucked away. From this point it would take an unlikely combination of circumstances, or failures, to endanger either the aircraft or us, which makes flying the safest way to travel. You see, it usually takes more than one failure to bring an aircraft down (missiles apart!). It takes what is often referred to as an event cascade: a problem on top of a problem on top of a problem, usually in a specific, though unlikely sequence.

Generally, though, flying is as safe as the pilot makes it. His safety is in his own hands. By the same token, so is ours. Even though the best of pilots - commercial or private - are in general unlikely to be too concerned with the safety of his (or her) passengers, they do worry for their own safety. Which more or less amounts to the same thing as them worrying about ours. The main danger down there, at the "back of the bus," it seems, often comes from your fellow passengers.

*

Check in had gone well, take-off on time, I was settled and at peace with the world, felt like talking, especially as I had a sympathetic ear available. Someone I'd never see again once we landed. An American shared my row of seats. I greeted him briefly.

Big mistake. Not only was he large, amicable and jovial-looking, he also turned out to be a gregarious type, obviously felt the need to talk himself. It was as if he had just been waiting to pounce. I'm sure you've all met them. From the moment I opened my mouth it took no time at all for him to reveal that, although he'd been christened James Jonathan, and that the family name was Haverslicker, or some such, I should refer to him as JJ, as did all his friends. I refrained from pointing out that we were yet to become friends. Was possibly prevented from such by lack of a suitable pause in his dialogue in which to do so.

`You're British?' he enquired. Or maybe he was telling me, for he certainly didn't allow me the time to answer. `I just love that limey accent. Say, can I get y'all a drink?' he asked, eyes locking onto an approaching stewardess like a heat-seeking missile onto a jetpipe. And for that I thanked him; the drink, I mean. Another mistake. Out came the wallet, and the photos. Mrs Haverslicker and a whole tribe of infant Haverslickers. I'd say this for JJ, he was a prolific talker. He went on and on, even throughout the meal. Well, I'm not a good listener in such circumstances, even if the speaker is plying me with drinks. In fact, to be more forthcoming with the truth, I'm a very *poor* listener, if not rotten. But, as luck would have it, JJ was .....well, I suppose it could be said he was a prolific drinker, too. Very much so; at least two to my one. So eventually he slept. I was saved.

Across the aisle a little grey-haired old lady, whom, I assumed - from the amount and quality of her jewellery - was not exactly short of a coin or two, was busily stuffing her handbag with left-over freebies from her lunch tray. In the row ahead, a small, bespectacled gentleman from the land of the rising economic miracle - probably having just redesigned a 128 bit processor on the back of his napkin - was attempting to separate cheese from plastic wrapping, with little success. The stewardess showed him how.

'Ah so!' said he, rather predictably.

Another flight, another American. This time, one who seemed to possess intimate knowledge of every calamity or misfortune that could possibly befall a human being. He also seemed determined that I should hear about them, in all their gory details.

'Once saw a biker run headfirst into a Mack truck. I mean dead-centre of the radiator, man! Splat!' His palms slapped together. 'Jeez, what a mess. Take some cleaning up, that lot.'

Certainly will, thought I. One hand had been about to open his carton of coffee creamer, now it was; open and empty, the contents luckily missing me. He didn't seem to notice, carried on. 'Forget about crash-hats, I mean his head was somewhere down by his ass. Shit, man.. talk about strawberries. Which reminds me, once saw a guy leap from an

491

airplane. Sport they called it. Only his chute candled on the way down. Jeez, yuh should'a seen....'

'Serves him right for jumping out of a totally serviceable aircraft,' I cut in. Couldn't stand any more, so, assuming nervousness to be the cause of this verbal diarrhoea I decided to exploit the fact. Maybe wind him up a touch.

'Different to down there, eh?' I inclined my head towards the window that overlooked the rest of the world.

'How so?' Just that. I knew then I was right.

'Let's face it, down there it's a madhouse. Up here we're free from all that lunacy. It's kind of an escape, isn't it?'

'How so?' Again, just that. Figured I had him now, hook line and sinker.

'From the pressures of life,' I answered. 'No problems, no bills, no worries, especially no inquisitive women. Look out there. Sun, blue sky, white clouds. Perfect. We could be on our way to heaven.'

'Yeah! That's what worries me.'

Ah yes! In for the kill. I'd give him the Spike Milligan treatment.

'Why should you be worried?'

'Why? Flying's why. Ain't natural. Goddamn dangerous if you ask me.'

'Nah, come on, flying's not dangerous. Safer than crossing the road.' I allowed a couple of beats. 'Crashing! Now that's something else. Crashing's dangerous.'

He'd just taken a sip of coffee. He snorted, then nearly choked as it bought on a fit of coughing.

Ended up ordering him a real drink, double brandy. I eventually coaxed a laugh out of him, though. After that he was fine.

Then, on another sector, there had been the woman. American again, of course. They almost always seem to be excessively friendly. She'd also wasted little time getting round to the photographs, as if she felt the need to explain why she was travelling without her Elmer.

'That's Elmer,' she said, 'in the middle. Taken shortly before he went, that was.'

I felt like asking "Went where?", but it was plain to see he'd obviously gone to where he couldn't take it with him. Gold, silver, and diamonds hung from everywhere jewellery could hang. At least everywhere that was visible. If I had that kind of money I certainly wouldn't have been sitting back where she was.

It was foggy when we landed and I could barely see her ahead of me, walking across the tarmac to the coach which would transport us to the terminal. I could hear her though, jangling along like an alpine cow.

These days, fog rarely shuts an airport down, especially an airport with the stature of Heathrow. They, in conjunction with the aircraft that use them, possess magical electronic systems which allow landings to be made in conditions of zero visibility, and it is landings that are all important. The main reason for fog to close an airport was because it prevented a landing. Take-off wasn't the problem, it was the possibility of a problem occurring during take-off which closed the field. A problem which could demand a speedy return to the runway.

Heathrow has possessed the capability of allowing hands-off landings since back in the sixties. That BEA Trident on which Mr Burton and I returned from Geneva did so. Fog so thick you couldn't see the wingtips, auto-throttle sounding very erratic indeed, crew relying totally on technology. Which I imagine could be very frustrating, from a pilot's point of view. Like a back seat driver who also has control. Those were early days though, and Heathrow was surrounded by wide open spaces. Not all airfields are so lucky. Take Tegucigalpa, capital of Honduras, for instance: I recall the take-off from there as being quite er... well, what shall we say? Exhilarating? Yes, that'll do nicely. Vague memories of a runway which terminated on the very lip of a drop-off. Ahead, and way below, was a valley, more of a canyon, really, for once this point was reached the aircraft became airborne no matter what. The job of engines and crew from here on in was to ensure it *remained* airborne. But it was a canyon within a canyon, if you see what I mean, the airfield itself surrounded by towering mountains, thus compelling the pilot to circle within their walls until he had the altitude to clear them. Probably nothing quite that bad, but those are the images I seem to recall.

Or how about Kai Tak, Hong Kong. Here wingtips scythe through the air perilously close to buildings either side of the flight-path. Close enough to allow a brief peek into people's living rooms, therefore their lives. Can you believe that? It was so until 1958, when they built a runway out into the bay, on reclaimed land. It was an improvement, but not by much. Still one of the most difficult and dangerous approach paths of any airport, so we are told. Today the whole show has moved well away from the city, out onto another island, a multi million pound gift of an airfield (from the British taxpayer to the incoming Chinese authorities) named Chap Lek Kok. It opened for business just one day after we relinquished control of the colony to the Chinese.

Or how about this. Apparently true.

An aircraft, cruising at thirty thousand feet, was requested by an American sector controller to climb immediately to thirty-two thousand. "For noise abatement purposes", he said.

The captain complied, then, puzzled as to the reason given, requested clarification. After all, noise abatement procedures normally relate to operations close to the ground, in populated areas, ie: during take-off.

`Did you say noise-abatement? At this height?'

"Roger," came the laconic-sounding voice. "Y'all ever heard the noise of two 747's meeting head-on?'

Such are the pleasures of flight.

*   *

Chapter Eighteen

TALES FROM THE NEW WORLD
1991

I've always welcomed the opportunity to depart for warmer climes, at least for part of the long European winter; don't really need a valid excuse, though it was always possible to conjure one up, if necessary.

At the back end of 1962 therefore, it was pure coincidence that found me revisiting an old haunt: RAAF Butterworth, in northern Malaya. It was the occasion of that Far East Tour with the Secretary of State for Air, an RAF Comet C4 the means of transport. Good place to be I'd thought at the time, what with the world seemingly poised on the very brink of nuclear annihilation, the Cuban Missile Crisis in full flow at the time. It had seemed like a comfortable, away-from-it-all kind of place in which to find oneself should the worst come to the worst. (Maybe that Secretary of State knew something we didn't, eh?)

Now, with the golden days of the European summer again long gone, here I was, almost thirty years on, another coincidence to use as an excuse. Similar feelings for a similar situation, only this time my destination was New Zealand: Aoreatoa to the Maoris - Land of the Long White Cloud - location for my next assignment. Good place to be anytime, but especially now, just when it appeared the United Nations, led by America, as per usual, were - to use an American expression - about to kick ass in Iraq. Or maybe....? No matter. All would become clear once action was initiated. What mattered to me was that I should be well separated from it. Could even sit and watch it happen this time around. Did so, in fact; chilled Steinlager to hand. Well, I saw as much as Stormin' Norman Schwarzkopf, or the Department of Defence, thought I should see. But gosh and golly weren't those laser-guided bombs something else; testimony to mankind's inventiveness and absurdity apart. Talk about impressive. I swear I must have seen fifty, every one a direct hit.

What?

Ah, yes! Well, the targets did look somewhat similar, I must admit. But doesn't one bunker or bridge look very much like another? I mean, they wouldn't cheat, would they? After all, this is the Pentagon we're talking about. Upright, to-the-point type people. There again, how far could you trust the kind of people who would lumber a simple nut (you know, that which fits onto a bolt) with the term "hexaform rotatable surface compression unit"? Which I didn't just make up, believe me. Try that down at your local ironmonger and see where it gets you. 'A 25mm HRSCU, if you please, squire.' Think the ironmonger would be the one to pose the questions then.

Okay, New Zealand may not have been as far away as it was possible for me to get, but I certainly couldn't have wished for better.

*

York. Eight am: The omens looked good. Taxi arrived ten minutes early; a frosty winter morning, yet clear and sunny. A leisurely journey; arrive Leeds/Bradford Airport (LBA) with plenty of time in hand. Too much, as it happened, a one hour delay on the incoming flight. Freezing fog at London Heathrow (LHR), we are told - one of the odd occasions when it did still affect operations. Ah, well, my onward flight isn't scheduled to depart until thirteen hundred.

Nine thirty: The delay had become an hour and a half. No problem, airborne now. Forty minutes to Heathrow, another forty for the transfer to London Gatwick (LGW). Two hours to spare, I calculated.

Light smattering of snow on the Dales, down below, remnants of the blizzard conditions which had recently swept this part of the country. Skies clear and untroubled now. 'Absolutely perfect flying conditions,' the captain informed us. 'It's possible we'll make up time.'

Make up time we did. But to no avail. We joined the stack, over Epsom. Delayed flights piled above and below like tiers on a wedding cake. One thousand feet below, mirroring our movements, a British Airways 757, resplendent in the sunlight; grey, blue, and red paintwork gleaming. Below that, green fields, fingers of fog still stretching out in the tucks and folds.

Ten thirty: LHR. Met by courier, with passport, work permit, ticket, as planned. 'You'll miss the ten forty-five bus to Gatwick, but there's another at eleven,' she advised. 'Should make that.'

Didn't. Delays with the baggage due to delays with.... etc, etc.

Eleven zero-five: Close. Nowhere near close enough.

496

'Next bus, eleven fifteen,' the ticket girl answered sharply. Sullen type, couldn't care less. Clearly, on this day, a person who hated her job, her country, the world, and everyone in it.

Twelve fifteen: Traffic delays meant late arrival at Gatwick. I wanted the North terminal. Naturally, our first port of call was to the South! My reserves of patience and time were now becoming sadly eroded. Only one person off, but we had to wait for pick-ups! Time becoming a valuable commodity.

Twelve thirty: North terminal, at last - not an area with which I was familiar. Ten precious minutes to locate and struggle to the correct desk. Late check-in means no choice of seat selection; allocated a seat well to the rear of the Air New Zealand 747, area of maximum discomfort due to torsional stresses, among other things. My preference is over the wing, in the centre section. Would actually prefer to travel First or Business class, our client apparently thought along different lines. Ah well, at least I'm on board, on my way, out of the cold and the chaos. Well clear of that sullen ticket girl.

Aircraft were lined up ahead, each awaiting its take-off slot. There is a calculated interval between departures, spacing dependant on aircraft type and size. For instance, a Jumbo jet could take off close behind a Shorts 360, say, but not vice versa. The wake turbulence generated behind a 747 is such it could easily flip anything smaller onto its back and into the ground. No such problems here, I was in the "biggie".

Airborne at last, aerodynamically clean; gear, flaps, slats, retracted. I was back in my element.

Poor service. Lousy meal. Especially to someone to whom it is the first meal of the day. Wine didn't show until almost too late, but at least that was reasonable. Postprandial brandy - as opposed to the Cognac I'd requested - more akin to something from Spain. What the hell, settle back to a good film. Oh, no! Teenage Mutant Ninja Turtles, which, very much under duress, I had taken my son to see the previous week. (Unlike today, no choice back then.)

Spent an hour or so chatting to a New Zealand film producer, outside the dunny. We weren't queuing to use it, it just happened to be close to the galley, ie, the drinks. Fancied another Muller Thurgau, ordered same. What I received was what was currently on offer: Cooper's Creek chardonnay. Well, it had legs, was spicy, with excellent clarity and a lingering aftertaste.

'Not bad at all. Give us another,' the film producer later requested.

Middle of the night: Los Angeles. A four hour layover - secure in a mini transit lounge. Not the fresh air I'd hoped for. Still, being LA, the air inside was probably purer.

For some unexplained reason there was a change of aircraft here. Same flight number, but our 747-200 traded in for the latest model, a dash 400. More comfort, no discernable improvement in service. Still, couldn't complain, at least we hadn't crashed on take-off.

With clouds, sea, and sky our only companions, the aircraft droned on through the night. We were secure at Flight Level 360 (thirty-six thousand feet) enclosed in an aluminium shell, with its associated plumbing - hydraulics and pneumatics - plus a host of electronics.

Then, almost before I realized, we were there; top of descent. Depressurization so fierce that background noise was reduced to zero. New aircraft, maybe the pilots hadn't yet got the hang of it. Did good on the approach and touchdown, though, really greased it on. Welcome to Auckland International, probably the least crowded of the world's major airports, no hustle and bustle here, one reason I like this laid back, friendly country. A twelve hour time difference, six month seasonal variation. The sun shone, and it was as warm as the welcome of the New Zealanders. On top of which, I was a long way from Iraq, where all the action was taking place.

*

The little plane was dwarfed by the majestic, snow covered peaks of the Southern Alps. Precipitous walls dropped away to the fields, pastures, and the rivers which meandered through them, five thousand feet below our flight level. Directly ahead was a crystalline peak. It towered a further two thousand feet above us, ice and snow clinging to the summit like icing on a cake; brilliant, smooth, dazzlingly white in the sunshine. This was Mount Tasman, its peak only around two thousand feet lower than Mount Cook itself, which was but a stone's throw away; highest point in the Southern Hemisphere, so the guidebook told me. But it was Tasman which now filled our windscreen, its jagged slopes seemingly close enough to reach out and touch. I say our, in relation to the windscreen, for the old magic had worked its spell once more; my being offered the otherwise vacant copilot's seat.

Almost at the last minute it seemed, the pilot banked the aircraft steeply, as if flying a terrain-hugging fighter. Then, around the corner, our destination floated into view; top end of the eighteen mile Tasman glacier - over eight thousand feet above sea level. The virgin surface sparkled in the sunlight as we made an up-hill approach. With a soft bump we touched down, skis hissing over crisp, recently fallen snow as we ran on, pilot turning the machine, bringing it to a halt, side on to the slope, before switching off. With a final hiccup the engine cut, propeller shuddering to a stop.

I scrambled out eagerly, stood transfixed, awed by the incredible stillness. The brittle metallic tick of the exhaust as it cooled and contracted bearing sole responsibility for the disruption of nature's silence. As if on request, I and the other two passengers automatically lowered our voices, so as not to disturb the magic of this enchanted place. At this altitude the sky was a brilliant blue, snow crisp and glaringly white, the air sharp and clear. So clear that when I looked into space I felt quite vulnerable, exposed - as when one's cover is stripped away.

'Absolutely fantastic.' It was all I could manage.

'Isn't it just,' the pilot agreed, materializing at my side. 'We don't get too many days like this. A pleasure to fly in these conditions.'

I was happy to fly any time, though I had to admit, this took some beating. I breathed in lungs full of the pure, invigorating, mountain air as I wandered off to stretch my legs. My footprints bore sole responsibility for disrupting the pristine surface.

A few yards on I turned and looked back at the tiny, blue and white tail-dragger Cessna, Charlie Charlie X-ray, of Mount Cook Airlines, its orange dayglow stripes standing out brilliantly against the snow. Towering imperiously above, and forming a spectacular backdrop, was the peak of Mount Cook itself. It made the aircraft look like a child's toy, discarded and forgotten on a sheepskin rug. I recalled the description I had read: Highest peak in New Zealand, Mount Cook is known as Aorangi by the Maoris, the literal translation of which is "The Cloud Piercer". Now of course it is named after Captain Cook, who never actually set eyes on it; so it told me - that same guidebook.

The surface glistened, giving the impression of handsful of diamonds, cut and polished, having been scattered in the sunshine. That same sun struck blue-black shadows in the gullies and undulations, the edges of which were smoothly contoured, the result of a recent fall of windblown snow.

All too soon the pilot indicated it was time to leave, so we somewhat reluctantly clambered back on board, the fragile little machine rocking on its spindly undercarriage as we settled ourselves, and strapped in.

The propeller kicked jerkily, once, twice, then the engine coughed, caught, and roared into life, shattering the peace. Airframe vibrating as the throttle was pushed open, the pilot turned us to face down the gradient, slipstream raising a cloud of fine white powder behind. Then we moved off. Slowly at first, speed building as we bumped over the surface, pilot making fractional corrections with the rudder to hold us straight between encroaching walls. We were schussing down the piste. Vibration lessened with the onset of speed, ceasing abruptly as the tail rose and we became airborne once more, free, floating gracefully in the still conditions, propeller describing a glistening arc as it pulled us through the sky. Retracting skis and flaps, the pilot throttled back and trimmed the aircraft for the short flight back to Mount Cook airport. It was downhill all the way. Eight thousand feet.

But I wasn't here to fly, or play, I was here to work. It just so happened that for the first month or so, working was really a bit of a misnomer, given the circumstances. Therefore, as the project experienced delays not associated with my part in it, I seemed to spend more time playing golf (to the detriment of the local course, I might add), trying my hand at fly fishing (anything under three pounds went back. OK, would have, had anything come out to begin with), and ....er... drinking a little. Still, the pay was the same.

*

Remember Brian, my old school mate? Course you do, way back there in chapter two. Met up with him again this trip. He took me fishing on Lake Taupo. Forty years and he hadn't changed a bit. No, I lie. He didn't have the beard at school, grey or otherwise.

'How come you ended up in New Zealand?' I asked.

'Emigrated after leaving the army,' says he. 'Opportunity was there so I took it. Figured I may as well be poor and warm, as poor and cold.'

That was Brian, you see, no real ambition. No pretensions, either. But whether he realized it or not, he was no longer poor. He'd done all right. His own house, family, garden, fishing most weekends - probably the best waters in the world for it - and a good group of friends. Not really my friends though, they caught all the fish! Experience, I suppose. My only experience had been gained forty years ago on the banks of the Derwent. I hadn't been too successful back then, either. Seemed obvious my technique with rod and line had not improved over time, but Brian's had. Still a Norton lad at heart though, Brian; down at the bookies most days. What a life! All that, and New Zealand.

But it was the New Zealand scenery I loved. The ever-changing countryside. Trees, lush undergrowth, open pastures, and the ubiquitous Toi-toi; an indigenous form of pampas grass. There were lush forests, pine clad hillsides, the folds of which accommodated river valleys and small-holdings. And beyond the heavily sheep-speckled fields were snow-capped mountains and turquoise lakes. On the banks of one, a little old lady, secure beneath a straw hat, perched on a stool. She was faced by an easel, brushes and paints to hand, as were her sandwiches and flask. Green was in abundance. Tree trunks, rocks, virgin ground; all upholstered in a rich, velvety moss, whilst a myriad of ferns complimented the scene. The reason? The copious amount of rain to which the area was subjected. One minute dry, next, you're looking for a boat, kind of thing.

*

Another day of waiting around, another memorable flight.

The twin-engined Islander sat poised on the grass, waiting, pilot completing his visual inspection with a well aimed kick at one of the tyres.

With some forethought I chatted him up whilst we awaited the rest of the passengers, and, as hoped, was yet again invited to occupy the right-hand seat. He was quite young, the pilot, but his familiarity with, and competence in operating the machine were immediately obvious as hands and eyes completed their checks, started the engines. His fingers flicked switches, and operated levers and buttons, whilst his eyes checked the gauges. That nonchalant tyre check had obviously been just for show.

When the brakes were released the nose bobbed up, as if in relief, then the little plane surged forward, airspeed building quickly as the ground fell away. A starboard turn had us heading back towards Te Anau and up the centre of the lake, climbing steadily. We needed to, there were mountains all around. The highest of the peaks were substantially lower than those of the Mount Cook range, a result of which was that only the tallest - to be seen ahead - still retained a dusting of snow.

On a narrow plateau I noticed a group of walkers, knapsacks on their backs, striding out along a trail which traversed the ridge.

'Milford Track,' the pilot announced over the intercom. 'Said to be the finest walk in the world. Thirty three miles. Takes about three days to complete,'

The almost sheer walls fell away a couple of thousand feet, to end on the banks of a river far below. One false move and they'd be falling forever. As we circled, the hikers looked up and waved. We then followed the track, circled again over Lake Quill, watched awestruck as it spilled over the lip, creating the one thousand nine hundred foot triple drop of the Sutherland Falls. Scattered clouds floated by as we climbed once more, before the ground suddenly dropped away beneath us to form Milford sound. Those mountainous walls continued their downward progress, a further thousand feet or so beneath the surface of the fjord; plenty deep enough for the QE2 to visit, which it occasionally had.

Down we zoomed, to within a few hundred feet of the water, following the course of the fjord out to the open sea. Bank left, around the point, and we were following the coastline. Breakers crashed against the cliffs, throwing spray and spume high into the air, the white foam contrasting starkly with the yellow sandstone and the emerald clad land behind. At Doubtful Sound we turned inland, climbing to clear high ground before again descending over Lake Manapouri, back to the flat grazing land which doubled as the airfield. Look out, sheep, here we come.

*

In New Zealand as with anywhere else, in my view, the idea is to leave the cities behind. Rather than Auckland, one needs to be on the North Shore, over the bridge known as the coat-hanger, with it's Japanese-designed outer-lane extensions, referred to locally as the Nippon Clip-on. North of Albany and the chaos begins to subside.

On the South Island things are altogether different. Down there, even in the cities, life is lived at a much reduced pace.

Our pace wasn't exactly hurried either. The job, scheduled to last six weeks, sort of overran a little. Four months later it was still ongoing. Not what you'd could call a success, from someone's point of view, but I loved it.

By now, the Pohutukawa - otherwise known as the New Zealand Christmas tree - had ceased to display their bright red flowers. They put in an appearance only during the Christmas period, hence the name, although out here Christmas was the height of summer. It was now autumn, time for me to take a short break. After visiting old friends out here for a few days, I'd move on, leaving the remainder of this job to someone else.

As I was driven over the harbour bridge for the last time, on my way to the airport out at Manukau, I looked once more at the Auckland skyline, the Westhaven Boat Harbour and St Mary's Bay jam packed with yachts. Come the weekend, most of them would be out on the Waitemata, colourful spinnakers billowing. Ashore there would be parties, and barbecues. I felt sad to be leaving my friends, Ron and Lynne Hewson. Sad to be leaving these warm and friendly islands. I recalled a Maori telling me they had a saying, a form of welcome when meeting someone for the first time: "Not a stranger. An old friend I haven't yet met."

Then I was on my way, winging across the Tasman Sea to another island. An island that was also a continent; a place known colloquially as Oz, the language, "Strine."

*

`Yuh have a prison record?'

No problem with the language there. It was the Immigration Officer at Perth airport, and he was asking, not stating a fact.

Oh! I didn't realize it was still a requirement. Didn't really say that, but felt like doing so. Though, as I could imagine it would not have scored any plus points, I kept my silence and went on my way.

'Emma necks?'

Yeah, well I was always going to have trouble with that, despite the fact that this was not my first visit to the "Lucky Country", as it was known locally.

I looked up, puzzled. Not only did I not know the answer, I didn't even understand the question.

'Emma necks? he asked again. 'For brekkie?'

Ah ha. If it was my preference for breakfast he was enquiring about, it could well translate into ham and eggs. I found out it did, so I ordered, breakfasted, paid the bill, and prepared to leave.

503

'Scona rine,' the girl said, handing me my change. Easy, this one, for she also gave me a clue, taking time out to appraise the sky and nod her head. I guessed right away it was a meteorological term, for it did indeed look like it was about to rain.

That had been my re-introduction to English, as she is spoke in "Oz".

*

Over the years many people have gone to Australia for many different reasons. The early settlers had little choice, they were said to have been "transported", though not quite in the fashion of Star Trek! Next came the prospectors and adventurers, to be followed by the immigrants - voluntary, their journey heavily subsidised by the Australian Government. Then, many years later, came the tourists. I fitted none of these categories, for I was here to work - as a non-resident. But, being as we were basically working for the good of Australia, a difficult to obtain, non-resident work permit was within reach.

This wasn't my first trip Down Under. I'd previously been here with the Royal Air Force, during which we experienced a totally different Australia, rarely venturing out into the countryside. I'd also worked the Bass Straight, out of Melbourne, and Devonport, north Tasmania. Lovely place, Tassie. Melbourne was OK too, particularly the countryside round about. I took many a coach trip into the heavily forested Dandenongs, to stop at places where all the birds gather to be fed by the tourists, and the tourists themselves are served Billy tea and Lamingtons - chocolate and coconut coated sponge cakes - by the coach driver. But Victoria's weather was too variable for my liking, and the unions there on the dockside were unbelievable. I got the impression that people who couldn't make it back home in Liverpool had come out here to stir things up.

In our business, time is money, so when we found the Aussie Dockers Union members to be slow organising themselves, insisting on a "smoko" before they would even begin to think of off-loading our equipment, taking themselves off somewhere instead, we decided to do it ourselves. We were in the usual hurry, and figured it was all part of what we were paid to do, as it usually was.

Not out here. A definite no no. But we already knew that, were therefore prepared when the expected confrontation occurred.

When they eventually did decide to turn up, they immediately asked what was going on.

'Going on? We're loading *this* equipment onto *that* vessel,' we told them whilst pointing towards each. Which is when they became extremely belligerent.

'Run that by me again. You're doing what?'

'Putting our equipment on the boat.'

'And what makes you think you have the right to do that?'

'Our Equipment. Part of our job. Always has been.'

'Not on this dock, mate, bloody oath. Yuh trying to put someone out of a job, or what?'

'No. But there was no one here, and we're in a bit of a hurry.'

'Jeez! Bit of a hurry is it you pommy bastard? Well, now it's just going to take a little longer, isn't it,' they informed us. So we stood around and watched as they went aboard, carried everything off, loaded it onto the waiting trucks. Exactly what we'd been doing, even though we'd told them otherwise. Hadn't really expected them to have been so easily fooled by what we said.

They just about shut the port down as we drove off!

So much for the south coast, now it was to be the North-West again, the part of Oz I enjoyed most. Exmouth, Dampier, Port Hedland, Broome, Derby. Virtually the whole of the West coast, from Perth - where our Australian office was located - and on up; the Pilbara, as it is known. It is a vast, scarred and ancient land. An area of contrast and colour. Natural colours, red predominant. The soil is red and its dust covers everything around. It comes from the iron ore which is mined and shipped from here. Ore of such high grade, I'd heard tell it was possible to weld fragments of the rock together.

If not the Outback, these towns are at least on the very edge of it. There may be a government in Canberra, but up here the land is ruled by nature, not people. Out here is a different country entirely to that recalled from my visits with the RAF. Gum trees on the river banks stand silvery white, and those, along with the yellow flower of the Wattle, contrast sharply with the deep blue sky. For me, such a sight, in amongst the red of the land, always generates pleasant memories of the real Australia. Far more than memories of the cities could ever conjure up.

Those river-beds are dry most of the year; a dusty

dryness. So dry in fact, they look like they have little recollection of the feel of water. The rains would come eventually ("The Wet"). Gentle at first, making a drunkard of the parched earth. Then faster and heavier, until the ground was overcome and the channels began to fill once more, thence to overflow.

Some of this I knew, some I was told about whilst standing around sucking on a tinnie, outside the Roebuck Inn, Broome. Fancy name for a not so fancy - although very popular - establishment. Safer to drink outside on the western-style boardwalk than in the pub itself though. Could get dangerous in there, we were told. At least, I assume that was the inference.

'Doesn't take much to start a bit of a ding. Bloody oath,' said our guide.

I could well imagine. I noticed the juke box was chained to the wall, as had been the case in those KL bars, all those years ago. Only difference here, no glass in the window frames, just chicken wire. I'd been to similar bars in Africa, only those contained no juke box, no chicken wire. Lucky if there was any electricity.

As we stood there, soaking up the sun, the stories, and the amber nectar, I allowed my thoughts to drift, back to another time, a previous visit to the Pilbara.

*

It was a project we were about to start in the King Sound. First there was a requirement for us to set up a navigation chain in the surrounding area, around the town of Derby. And as there wasn't much around this particular town, apart from lots of bush, scrub, saltwater, and windblown sand, we were experiencing difficulty locating the actual sites - official survey points.

We had, at some cost, obtained maps of the area from the Lands and Surveys Department, before leaving Perth. Only trouble was, those maps were quite old, related more to what had once been, rather than what now was!

Onto the scene stepped the lanky, very personable, John Hughes, here to represent the oil company's interests. Arriving from Sydney, to oversee the calibration, he was a little early, as it happened. Difficult to calibrate something you don't yet have. Still, it gave us chance to get to know one another, and a more pleasant, amiable company rep I had yet to meet, it turned out.

For a variety of reasons we'd up to now only been able to locate one of the sites, and that with some difficulty. Still, we'd definitely face few problems when returning. All it required was for us to follow the trail of destruction created by our illustrious leader's "point and stop" method of navigation, as used on that first run. What I referred to in an article for the company magazine as "Clarke 1880 - Heavalo 1980". The first being the survey datum, the year in which it had been established, and by whom, the second, a reference to our Party Chief, Don Heavelo's more recent effort.

Don had seen the high ground away in the distance, couldn't miss it really, peak protruding above the surrounding dense scrub. Had to be the place. But with no obvious trail in sight, how to reach it? No problem. Don just pointed the Land Rover in the right direction, put his foot to the floor, more or less stopped when he arrived at the base of the hill. That run took an hour and a quarter, a time that was to be considerably reduced once a trail had been blazed. On one memorable occasion I donned my Mario Andretti gloves, lowered the Jackie Stewart sunglasses into place, and, accompanied by Mike "White Knuckles" Jarvis, managed to lower the record to fifteen minutes. Figured I could have shaved the odd minute or two off that had the wheels remained in contact with *terra firma* a greater percentage of the time. And Mike hardly spilled a drop of the gin and tonic he happened to have in hand. There again, Mike being Mike, it didn't get much of a chance to spill!

As a result of these difficulties, a conference was called, in the bar of the Baobab Inn, back in Derby. Naturally, the Inn being our home away from home up here. Anyway, this being the Outback, we were feeling a little parched. The outcome was that John decided the expense of an aerial search was warranted, so the appropriate flying machine was duly chartered: a twin-boom, push-pull Cessna 337. We were then introduced to our pilot "The Crazy Kiwi". But only after taking to the air did the reason for this sobriquet become apparent.

We were en-route to Oobagooma station - Australianese for cattle ranch - where one of the sites was apparently located. I, in my customary seat, up front, explained to the pilot what we were looking for, supplied him with an approximate location. He'd need that, for stations up here covered thousands of square miles.

'That look like the place?' Crazy Kiwi asked some time later, stabbing a wingtip towards a pile of rocks on top of a hill, whilst pulling a rate four turn around it for a minute or so, the resultant G, driving me down in my seat. I clawed at a window - which, due to our attitude, was now the floor - attempting to elevate myself enough to be able peer out. John, seated behind, supposedly checking the charts, was instead wrestling with a plastic bucket. For some reason, he appeared to be shouting at it. Difficult to understand the words, but it sounded like "Hughie", "Ruth", or some such thing. Very strange.

The pilot took us down low, so as to get a closer look. Very low! Then he was fiddling with something down the side of his seat, seemingly unconcerned about what lay ahead. As if to compensate, I kept *my* eyes glued to the windscreen. Yeah, that looked like the place all right. No need to get any closer.

Sometime later, back at five thousand feet over the King Sound, peace and tranquillity having been restored, a sudden shout of "BANZAI" had nose hard down, sea rushing up to meet us.

Jesus! It didn't look at all tranquil from this attitude. I said my goodbyes and silently chanted my hellos. No recovering from this, thought I, whatever this was. Yet the pilot didn't appear to be fighting for control, seemed rather relaxed, in fact. The bugger was.

'It alleviates boredom,' he told us, once he'd recovered, somehow without tearing the wings off the thing. John and I could only agree. It did tend to have that effect. A minor coronary usually does.

His later offer of, 'Another "banzai" before we land?' was firmly declined. John, who was after all effectively paying the bill, managed, with a notable lack of subtlety, to convey the fact that he was not entirely thrilled by the offer.

After landing, we again retired to the bar at the Baobab. Not because we were parched, more medicinal, this. But we didn't stay long, transferring our allegiance after a couple of beers to the disco at the Spinifex Hotel. A much livelier option, this. Typical outback pub; rough as guts. A sign advised us of the minimum dress requirements: singlet, shorts, sandals (called thongs). Some of the clientele even exceeded this, going so far as to wear a hat. Sweat-stained and battered, but then so was the rest of their gear. There was a second sign pinned up behind the bar, I noticed. For Sale, it offered: *Encyclopaedia Britannica*. Complete set. Now married, no longer needed. F***ing wife knows everything about everything.

It was interesting country all right. During "The Wet" the roads double as quagmires, become all but impassable to anything but four-wheel drive and a lot of luck. In the dry season they are rutted and rough but can be negotiated by car, so long as you don't mind the odd piece falling off. We opted for the latter. It was a hire car anyway.

Not a good place to be during the cyclone season, either, as one party chief had discovered years before. He'd been in Darwin at the time, capital of the Northern Territories. The date, December 25th 1974; the day Tracy came to town. He'd apparently been asleep through the whole thing - unconscious would probably be more accurate, he'd have to have been! His first words upon waking were classic, eternally recorded in the doodlebuggers bible.

`Serious trouble up here last night,' he told the telephone that had eventually awoken him.

`Didn't wreck the pub again, surely?' the boat manager,

down in Perth, queried upon hearing this.

'No, the pub's OK. More or less intact, fortunately. About the only place that is though. I wake up in the hotel, in bed, looking at the bloody sky. Jesus! Must have been some party, thought I. Until I looked outside, that is.'

'And...?'

'Gone! The whole bloody town's gone. Wiped out by a cyclone.'

'Like you said, must have been some party if you slept through that.'

*

One night in Melbourne a group of us decided to push the boat out, dine in style. There was a particular place we'd heard about, quite classy, in fact very smart, for Australia. They actually had a dress code that required a jacket and tie for dinner. Anyway, we decided they should be honoured with our presence, which right away posed a bit of a problem, placing a terrible strain on the resources of our limited wardrobe, some of the crew having to really scratch around to be able to comply with the dress requirement. Well, let's face it, working off the coast of Australia, all you ever needed was a tee shirt, shorts, and thongs - those rubberised sandals with the strap that fits between your toes. Otherwise known as 'Japanese safety boots'.

There was one guy with us, Gordon, who was also well versed in wine lore, so it was only natural that he be given the task of selection. Not really a demanding task, because to most of those present the notion of a fine wine seemed to be a bottle of plonk which merely stained the teeth, as opposed to removing the enamel completely.

They didn't have a wine waiter in this establishment, they had a sommelier; the kind of guy who looks down his nose when you order a Grand Cru St-Emilion with your fish and chips. As he approached - silver tastevin hanging from his neck on a silk ribbon, looking for all the world like a decoration - he smiled condescendingly.

Not sure if he was for real, or just dressed for the part, Gordon decided to check him out. He studied the extensive wine list thoughtfully, pursing his lips and shaking his head when rejecting one wine, a nod of approval for another. The head and mouth performed for some time as he went through the list, then he'd flick back a couple of pages to re-assess a choice which had previously caught his eye. Finally he looked up, `I think a bottle of the Chateau Thivin '76. Then, as if just realizing how many of us there were, added, `better make that three bottles, squire.'

The sommelier was either quite impressed, or he played his part well. `An excellent choice sir.' he said, before gliding away.

It was difficult to be certain, but I thought I caught a look on his face which suggested he had reservations as to whether this wine was about to be wasted on the present company. Regardless, he soon returned, holding a bottle so as to display the label.

Gordon nodded his assent for it to be opened.

The sommelier now showed his true worth by producing a corkscrew, as if out of thin air, and, not appearing to pause between movements, had the twist inserted. One more smooth, unbroken move saw the cork withdrawn, and passed under his nose.

Whatever Gordon had done, he'd certainly impressed this guy. At last he'd found someone who could appreciate his talents, and he was putting on the full performance.

He laid the cork on the table in front of Gordon who, well on top of the game, picked it up and sniffed at it. Again the nod of approval.

The sommelier now poured a sample, which our man held up to the light for appraisal. Had Gordon not been in his suave mood, it would be at this point he'd fix the waiter with a stare, and offer such comment as, `Don't piss about, fill it up!' Tonight though he passed the glass under his nose, savouring the bouquet before taking a sip, which he then proceeded to roll around his mouth. His eyes closed in concentration, jaw working as though chewing, then he swallowed. A second or two later the eyes flicked open. He now wore his studious look, assessing quality, before passing comment.

`Delightful. A touch too much acidity for it to be classed a great wine, probably influenced by the tertiary Jurassic deposits of the area, but a pleasant, fruity taste, good bouquet, and body as well. That will do us very nicely I think.'

The sommelier beamed, it was a pleasure to serve gentlemen the likes of these, despite their lousy sense of dress. You could see it written across his face, as with a flourish he filled the rest of the glasses, opening all three bottles, before slipping away again.

The meal proceeded apace, talk flowing almost as

freely as did the wine from the bottles. The latter being drained exceptionally quickly. By this time the room had become busy, but Gordon managed to catch the sommelier's eye. `My good fellow, bring us another three bottles of this fine wine if you please.' he said.

This done, they were duly opened, with noticeably less flourish this time, then consumed.

By now our mood was becoming quite merry, not to say boisterous, which, considering the hour spent in the cocktail bar before the meal, was not surprising. The pace had slowed somewhat, but Gordon's glass was empty as were a couple of others, so once again the sommelier was signalled. But to no avail. He was either too busy to notice, or he was now rebuffing us. The latter more likely, so the situation, it seemed, demanded drastic action.

It was at this point that Gordon, standing, and swaying slightly, showed his true colours, for when the sommelier was a couple of tables away, Gordon called loudly: `Hey waiter, bring us another bottle of this red shit.' You could almost see the man cringe.

What happened? They brought the bill is what happened. Boy, did that sober us up!

*

There are many things I like about Australia, for it is a likeable, diverse country, as is New Zealand. In Australia, weather apart, it was birds, booze, and barbies, in NZ....? Ah, yes. Similar thing, come to think of it. Different scenery though.

*

Postscript: Three months after the King Sound job I was to work with John Hughes again, by which time we had become close friends. He'd always fancied attending a European Grand Prix, so I made reservations for us to visit Monaco the following year. But before that came to be, John was gone. He killed in the crash of a light twin during one of our scheduled crew changes. The aircraft on which he was a passenger lost an engine on take-off from Portland, west of Melbourne. With the machine way over the weight limit - it was subsequently discovered - the pilot attempted to make it back to the runway, but failed. He did manage to put it down reasonably well, but the aircraft broke apart on impact, catching fire a couple of minutes later. Everyone escaped except John. He was unconscious, trapped by his legs when the main spar broke. It had proved impossible to free him before the wreckage was

512

engulfed.

A harmless person, come to harm.

It's always traumatic to learn of the death of a friend. Far worse if you happen to be close by when it occurs.

*

I got to spend a lot of time in and around Australia over the years, enjoyed myself immensely. This was especially true when on board the vessel, MV McDermott II (version one had ended its life on a submerged reef off Liberia, West Africa. The remains are stuck fast. Apparently, the words of the senior observer the moment it happened were, `Keep shooting, we may get over it.' Obviously a company man to the last.).

On the McDermott II we spent many a pleasant month working in the Bass Straight. OK, not always, for the Bass Straight could get pretty violent at times, too! But my favourite area was the West Australian coast, north of Perth and all the way up to Cape Londonderry, thence into the Northern Territory to Darwin. I recall the evenings best of all, when I used to spend time on the bridge with the skipper, my good friend, Chris Grubba. He would have tea and a packet of Tim Tams - my favourite Aussie biscuit - sent up. We'd chat about this and that as we stood around, passing time really, awaiting sunset. Then, if conditions looked good, concentration at a peak, we'd keep an eye open for the elusive "Green Flash" - a rare phenomena that only occurs given a very specific set of data: flat calm sea, cloudless horizon, and the right atmospheric conditions. Given these prerequisites, at the very instant the sun slips into the ocean, to disappear, a brief green flash can be observed at that point on the horizon. Blink and you'll miss it. We watched numerous times, but were rewarded only once. A triumph in itself, for most only hear tell of it, never actually observe it at all.

*   *

Chapter Nineteen
MIDDLE EAST MEANDERINGS.

It can be quite a daunting experience to travel on certain Middle Eastern airlines, especially on the seemingly rare occasions when they make an announcement over the public address. You know the kind of thing; 'The flight time today will be one hour forty minutes.' The difference here being the message extension; just one word - 'Inshallah!' It is that final intonation which brings one up short. Not particularly because it tells us we are in Middle Eastern hands, more due to the meaning of the word: "If God wills, or, God willing." It's as if the captain is declining to accept responsibility for anything that may go wrong.

Then there is the safety briefing. That seems not to change no matter where it is you are you are bound for. 'In the unlikely event of the aircraft having to put down on water.....' Yeah, right! Cairo to Luxor. As unlikely as would be the "flying into a mountain in Holland" scenario. With an intended flight-path that routed us over the Western Desert, finding water of a large enough quantity on which to settle an aircraft would require a navigational error of unprecedented magnitude. I settled for a quick glance at the safety instruction card. Nothing new there, either, apart from a hiccup in translation informing me of the presence of a "live" vest beneath my seat. Ah, well, I'd longed for international travel, and Egypt certainly fit in that category.

`Allaaahu Akbar, Allaaahu Akbar.'` He drew the words out as far as they would go. The eerie undulation of the Muezzin calling the faithful to prayer echoed through the evening skies in a tinny, high-pitched wail. The sound, albeit now electronically recorded, amplified, relayed via mega decibel loudspeakers, constantly serving to remind me of where I was. The Middle East. Specifically Cairo. The city was packed to the gills, not because some once in a lifetime event was about to take place, far from it, this was normal, everyday traffic. Here the less affluent packed themselves into clapped-out busses, the even-less affluent still, clung to the exterior, risking life and limb.

*

Wandering around the desert, along the shores of the Red Sea, is a gaunt reminder as to the futility of war. Acre upon acre of sand and scrub, seemingly of little use to anyone, but which had been fought over almost continually since time began. The odd wreck bore testimony to some of the later clashes, steel skeletons of tanks and other vehicles of combat, the people who had been inside, long gone, in one sense or another. Many in some haste it would appear, for there seemed to be a lot of boots scattered about. Not the ideal footwear for running in sand!

Occasionally I chanced upon barbed wire fences, but they didn't stop me, merely slowed my progress as I clambered through to some choice stretch of beach away in the distance. It was only later, after hearing the following tale, that I decided to curtail the walking, resume the drinking.

Another station, another country, not that far removed either. Next door, in fact. Gadhafi-land, but before it became so. The remnants of another, earlier war - Dessert Rats, Panzers etc. The station operator - Alan - would wander around freely, just as I tended to do. Until the night his bearer - parting for home after bringing the daily water supply - parted from this life altogether when his camel stepped on a mine. It had apparently been uncovered by the shifting sands brought about by a passing storm.

So, Abdul was gone, Alan survived. Inshallah, as they say. Yet another of those instances where death, or serious injury, could have been but a whisker away. Those little skull and crossbones signs weren't an indication that pirates once roamed hereabouts then! Thank God for Allah, or vice versa. Certainly someone up there was on my side. If not, then I'd been spared by factors unknown: Geographic location, fate, luck, the old nine-lives syndrome, or simply the fact that my number was not yet up? Who knows? What I did know was that I didn't care. I was still alive.

Once, some way in the distance a glittering flash drew my attention. My heart raced, along with my feet, only for my hopes to be dashed. I had stumbled across a sulphur lode; yellow crystals glinting in the sun.

Always, at the back of my mind, I had visions of one day blundering into something precious, often willed it to happen. It was my favourite get-rich-quick dream. Picking up diamonds off a beach in South West Africa, for instance (not much chance of getting away with that should it happen, not the way they searched us and our equipment before being allowed to leave the area), or a nugget of gold in Australia. (Whilst there, I read in the Australian press of a case where a guy had stubbed his toe on a piece of half-buried junk. He'd kicked at it in disgust, only to discover a lump of gold that was to make him rich. The Hand of Fate, as it became known; 20 kilos of the stuff.) Then there were rubies in Burma, emeralds in Columbia, other gemstones in other countries. Alas, it never happened. There again, I never stepped on one of those Egyptian mines either. Exciting times, eh? Maybe that doesn't sound like excitement, but what you have to realize is that Egypt can be a pretty dull place. At least along the Red Sea coast. Travel inland, to Luxor, and it can be just as different again. Spectacularly so.

Working along the Red Sea coast we were afforded the chance to visit the Luxor area when the vessel, with which we were working, suffered major failures: broken propeller shaft and steering problems. The locals told of a dry dock, just up the coast, only for the boat crew, once they got there, to discover a diesel winch and a couple of Eucalyptus logs! The vessel eventually ended up in Malta, and it was to be almost a month before our services were again required. Plenty of time, you would think. But hey, this was Egypt! Working in the Western Dessert, along the Red Sea coast - with Israel just over the water - required us to carry a Military pass, so as to clear the various armed check points. Luxor was not a restricted area, but the roads leading to it from our base in Hurghadah were, and it took an unbelievable amount of time to arrange clearance. We did eventually make it, but only just. Our pass was valid for a week, and as it took a day to get there, the same coming back, left us with barely enough time. We experienced similar inefficiencies in Hurghadah: frequent water supply restrictions, electricity supply often down around the 160 volt mark as opposed to 240, which meant our radios didn't always work too well. These radios were also sealed, supposedly to ensure we couldn't change frequencies. This, we understood, was to prevent us talking to anyone in Israel - about whom the Egyptians were paranoid, perhaps naturally - but more likely so they could monitor the frequency allocated, which more or less amounted to the same thing. So one wonders about the odd times when atmospheric skip occasionally allowed us to talk to our office in, way over there in Geneva!

Being sealed also meant that, in the event of a failure, we weren't allowed to fix the radio without the military guard - whom we were obliged to employ - being present. So if the guard took himself off for the day, which they often did, just when the radio failed......! Before the job ended, I had been declared 'persona non grata' in Egypt for breaking these lead seals unsupervised! Even if only because the guard was not around when he was supposed to be.

*

Like the sea, the desert is timeless. Look at it today and it could be any period in history you wish to make it. Something similar could apply to the tombs in the Valley of Kings. Those interior paintings look as if they could have been completed only recently rather than five thousand years ago, so bright are the colours. Worth seeing, those ruins. Trouble is, they too seem endless. Tombs and temples on either side of the Nile, each that little bit different, all worthy of a look. Just one problem: given time it can become boringly repetitive. After inspecting acre after acre of ruins you find yourself approaching the next with a certain lack of enthusiasm. In fact, probably the only thing that keeps you going is the sure knowledge that, should you discuss this place with anyone else, they, for sure, will have been there. Not only that, they will end up enthusing about the one you missed out on!

For our trip to the Valley of Kings, we decided to eschew the comfort and cost of the touristy taxis, or a coach trip, opted instead for the novelty of a four legged beast of burden. More fitting, we thought, as well as being much cheaper. Certainly different. Well, the one I drew was. This beast completely redefined the meaning of the word recalcitrant. If it was actually alive it had to be a very good actor. But alive it was, for when I dug my heels into its ribs, move it did, if only to accelerate with all the enthusiasm of a three-toed sloth. I named it Muffin, although there was nothing puppet-like about it; definitely had a mind of its own, this one. So set in its ways, I suspected it of being female, though I never thought to check. In fact it must have been, for it turned out to have more sense than I did. When I attempted to turn right it went straight on, or to the left. It apparently knew the trail intimately, would brook no input from me whatsoever. I could shout, quietly coax, kick, it made no difference. Naturally, when

517

seated on the back of an animal, you can't see a lot of its face, so all I got in return for my commands was a mysterious twitching of the ears. That was the only indication I had that it had even heard me. *It* knew where we were heading, where the best views were to be had, the most economical pace at which to travel. It even knew when the track was too lose for me to ride in safety, for it just stopped, refusing to budge until I dismounted. But it was definitely worth the pain and frustration, for we were afforded views the motorized tourists would miss; quite spectacular from high in the hills. There was history to be observed all around in the form of temples, excavations, and pyramids. Away in the distance was the ribbon of the Nile, a darker brown against the surrounding sand, graceful feluccas gliding along its surface. But replicating the course of the river, probably half of a mile either side, was the green fertile area in which a large percentage of the county's fresh produce was grown, always had been. It was at times like this that you felt you were a participant in history rather than just an observer. Irrigation was by ox-driven wheel, to which clay pitchers were lashed. Wooden engineered gearing then transferred water from source, via wooden channels, to very productive fields.

We had previously "done" the Giza bit, in Cairo. Arabs and camels. The Sphinx, Pyramids - until observed up close one doesn't realize how huge and awe-inspiring these actually are. And although being allowed to climb them has long since been against the law, this was Egypt, a country in which almost anyone could be bribed into allowing anything! A marvellous view from the top, so I was informed. I was prepared to take their word for it. To pay someone to allow you to climb, seemed to me the equivalent of buying a Ferrari and paying someone to drive it for you.

I found Cairo had nowhere near the impact of Luxor. And the *son et luminère* at the Temples of Karnak was far superior to the version performed around the Sphinx. Besides, we found Giza to be *too* touristy. One guy even offered to sell me a pyramid: Cheops. Can you believe that? Well, we had a bit of a discussion about it. Not all that easy an accomplishment when my knowledge of his language was mainly confined to ordering a beer. He fared rather better in mine, even if it did appear to be limited to numbers, seemingly in multiples of ten. Anyway it was a pretty pointless exercise. He must have thought I looked gullible or something, but I wasn't going to fall for that old con. I mean, how I would get it home?

*

Travelling across the desert can present all kind of problems, even *before* we feel the need to add more to the list.

We were now back on the African west coast, Spanish Sahara (now Western Sahara) again, to be precise. I had some equipment to deliver, urgently. So, due to a lack of roads and tracks there was a need to complete our journey before darkness fell. For this I employed guides, which in itself created further problems.

By my reckoning we still had a way to go by the time evening was nigh, yet we suddenly ground to a halt, everyone apart from myself piling out. They were about to brew up. Something that occurred rather too frequently for my liking.

'Fahad, I need to get to the boat, urgently.'

'Okay,' he replied, settling himself onto a mat, patting the space beside him, an indication that I should join him. He then turned and called over his shoulder. 'Abdullah, etnayn chai.'

But I understood, if not their ways, a little of their language. 'We don't have time, I need to get there quickly. They're waiting to set sail and go to work.'

'No no no.' He shook a finger at me, but at the same time he smiled. 'Patience. First tea, then business.'

This is the way of the Middle East, and I knew whatever I said wouldn't effect a change. And maybe they're right. Relaxation should come first.

And so it was that darkness enveloped us well before we reached our destination. More tea and prayer stops the cause, but also, possibly our saving. Who knows what might have happened if they'd signed off with Mohammed early, as I frequently suggested. My thinking was that we should put in as much travel as possible during the hours of daylight, not keep stopping so as to check in with some superior being. He'd know where we were. We, on the other hand, appeared at times not to. But all turned out well. A full moon replaced the sun. The payoff, maybe?

I really did need to reach the boat before they sailed. Not for the usual reason, either, a decent meal. Not on this particular boat, this particular trip. No way. The cook was Finnish. Not exactly a gourmet experience, let me tell you. Not wholly unexpected, of course, for the Finns are not specifically renowned for their cuisine.

But hang on, maybe I'm being a teeny bit harsh on the guy. I mean, who's to say he wasn't an expert on Reindeer steaks and Mooseburgers? Maybe he was. There again, as you can imagine, Moose and Reindeer are pretty thin on the ground in the Middle East.

Talk of ships' cooks reminds me of the Nigerian on a boat that had recently had the galley modernized. Among the new fittings was a potato peeler; type of thing in which you placed the potatoes, fitted the lid, turned on the water, switched a switch, and presto. Thirty seconds and the job was done, one minute, max. This guy wanted to be sure, left them for ten minutes. Never did figure out where it was the potatoes were going. Not one to admit defeat, or seek advice, he kept on refilling it. The potatoes of course disappeared, down the drain. A whole sackful!

Now I'm not saying Nigerians have a monopoly on this kind of thing, although they do seem to be rather good at it.

*

As opposed to the rest of the Arab world, flying in to and out of Israel, in 1983, presented the traveller with few problems - unless you happened to be an Arab - although if you later needed to travel back to Egypt, and other places in the Middle East, it was usually necessary to obtain a back up passport. (Should your passport display an Israeli visa, you were likely to be refused entry to certain Arab countries. The British Embassy were usually very understanding in this respect, issuing second passports to businessmen.)

No problems with airline travel either, few Middle East airlines flew to Israel, many being restricted by one country or the other. Best to take British Airways, or El Al, the Israeli airline. Once in the country we encountered few problems. Everyone was friendly and helpful, there were no restrictions such as no-go areas, concrete barriers, etc. In fact we worked the Mediterranean coast from Acre down to Ashkelon. Towns, valleys, cities, rivers, and villages hitherto just names in the Bible, or history books. When not working, I managed to travel from Galilee, down as far as very spectacular, Masada - which is actually up, as far as altitude is concerned - way above the Dead Sea. Assent of this mountain is by way of cable car, though you can walk if you chose to do so, and have a lot of time to spare - after all, that is what the Romans did.

Once we had descended again, now to well below standard sea level! I took a mandatory dip in the Dead Sea, so as to experience the phenomenon of reading a book whilst floating.

En route, to all this, I naturally took in such as Nazareth, Jerusalem, and Bethlehem, plus many more. There is a lot to see in Israel, and only occasionally did we encounter armed police. Although whilst working offshore, we were under constant close scrutiny by Israeli patrol boats - for our protection, one assumes, being as we were working for the Israeli government. Even so, it was an enjoyable two months. And I was happy to have been afforded the chance to visit.

How much the world has changed in the past thirty odd years. Certainly not for the better either, from everyone's point of view!

*   *

RETURN FROM A FOREIGN LAND

Insipid sun; an overcast sky,
Coastline below, unseen to the eye.
Then round and round, we're in the stack,
High over Epsom; welcome back.
Thank God for that, about time too,
Fourteen hours with little to do
But sit and think, and maybe dream,
Until 14A starts to yell and scream.

We're informed of emergencies, yes indeed;
Of masks which materialize, in case of need.
Life-vest located beneath your seat;
And we'll show you a movie.' What a treat!
Not much chance of anything blue,
But.. Oh, my God, no! Mutant Turtles 2.
We're offered headsets, magazines and hot towels.
We're served "plastic" meals, which play hell with our bowels.
`And, Sir. Something to drink for you?'
`Yes, please. I'll have a gin and schw..... you know who.'

Blindly following a radio beam,
We start the descent, earth still unseen.
Down, down, down, through cotton-wool clouds,
Grey and clinging, just like shrouds.
Suddenly, it's there below,
The sparkle of a river's flow.
Green, green pastures, Elysian fields,
Pleasant memories, emotions revealed.

Buildings, modern and ancient are viewed
Through eyes which now are moisture dewed.
Anonymous houses, blocks of flats.
Vortices stream back off the slats.
Buckingham Palace, the Gardens at Kew,
And, is that...? Yes! Twickenham, too.
'Gear down, please. Flaps, one third.'
Only up front are these words heard.
For us it's, seat belts, no smoking, and,
'Remain in your seat until safe at the stand.
'Welcome to Heathrow. Have a good day.
Thank you again for flying BA.'

522

Chapter Twenty
FINALE? Well...almost

1993

Never did like the sound of it; another job in Nigeria - the place to which I had vowed never to return. But, as it would take me out of the North Sea sphere of influence, and as I would be working for the Nigerian Government - no matter who happened to be in charge of that Government at the time - I figured maybe it wouldn't be too bad. Decided to take a chance, give it a try. After all, the option was always there for me to turn around and get on the next flight home if things didn't work out to my satisfaction. Well, believe it or not, they didn't. Nor did the next flight home option! Nowhere close!

First came the problem of a visa. I was requested to attend the Nigerian High Commission, in London, to tender an application. Almost as soon as I stepped through the door, certainly by the time I entered the visa section, the bad memories came flooding back.

Posters - supposedly extolling the imagined virtues of a country that didn't really welcome tourists anyway - curled off the walls, hardening Blue-Tac equating to lost adhesion. The remaining, accessible areas of wall (plus some not so accessible, which had one wondering!), were thickly plastered with grubby finger-marks. Sullen-faced staff sat around making no attempt whatsoever even to look busy, never mind deal with the mountains of paperwork that was piled up on desks.

I took a seat, as directed, smiled at the guy, inviting him to return it. He didn't. Doubts were already forming as to the wisdom of my decision in accepting this assignment.

After a long wait - hours rather than minutes - my turn did arrive. Unfortunately, no sooner than I approached the desk, a telephone rang. The girl seated behind the desk picked it up and spoke; it answered back. She then pulled open a desk drawer, stuck the handset inside, got up, and without a word to anyone, walked out of the office, presumably to find someone. I hung around for about an hour, but as she hadn't returned by then I eventually called it a day and left. Never did get my visa. Nor would it surprise me to hear that telephone is still in that drawer!

*

So, if not Nigeria, then where?

Given a clear day, from thirty thousand feet you can almost see forever. Well, hundreds of miles. I was on my way home from job in Romania. At present Bucharest would be sliding past below, almost imperceptibly. Ahead would be Hungary. Out to port, Bulgaria, with the USSR off to starboard. Difficult to be sure about this, for there are no marked boundaries, and from up here everything looks the same. But they would be there all right. No point looking though, for this was night, not day, clear or otherwise. Out there the blackness was almost total but for the stars, suspended like globules of molten silver, the flash of a wingtip strobe, and the odd light, a rare sign of habitation far below. Very rare, for the ground over which we now passed, be it Hungarian, Bulgarian, or Romanian didn't matter, it was dark and mysterious. So dark it could well be hidden beneath a coverlet of cloud, though I knew it not to be. This was pre-democratic Eastern Europe (assuming it to be now post-democratic), and I could well imagine assorted nefarious characters flitting in and out amongst the buildings down there, darker shadows among shadows, going about whatever business it is that requires such nefarious characters to flit. Seemed it was only to be expected in the communist world. It was a world I had only visited this one time, although by now the Iron Curtain had crumbled. Still, I expect my details had long since been on file with the KGB, for I *had* visited many an African country that fell under Moscow's one time sphere of influence. Places where, upon landing, my passport disappeared into some back office for long periods, and where any expatriate seen flitting about in the background - whether Boris or Ivan - were certainly nothing to do with the Ministry of Tourism.

The Palace Hotel, in which I'd stayed whilst in Constanta, looked like it could actually have been a palace at one time. Say, about seventy years ago; probably the last time any form of restoration had been affected. Which said something for the quality of materials used in the original construction. But nothing lasts forever, and I'd found it to be decidedly tatty, if one was not to be too impolite. My room door didn't even fill the frame, all it did was offer a small possibility of keeping people out. There was a large gap at the top, and an even larger one at the bottom, neither of them parallel. When closed and locked it didn't feel at all secure. I was sure a good kick would spring it open. In fact looked as if it had been opened in such a fashion on more than one occasion; like when someone came calling in the middle of the night, maybe?

But, with the job complete, I was now well on my way. Then, just about the time you expect the lights to flicker out completely, they actually burst into life, Eastern Europe having slipped astern. In next to no time we were approaching France, and breakfast was being served. The flight was serene in the still air, but that was about to change, for far ahead, and below, nature began a pyrotechnic display of some considerable brilliance. Lightning flashed on and off, clouds lit up and went out like flashbulbs at the Academy Awards ceremony. These were obviously the wrong kind of clouds for us: Cumuli Nimbus. They revealed themselves as such, lit from within; dark, threatening silhouettes. There was danger in such clouds: thousands of gallons of water and ice, enough electrical power to light this continent for a year. Worst of all were the winds they would harbor; up-draughts and down-draughts. The turbulence they created was capable of tearing an aircraft apart - in exceptional circumstances, admitted. And they straddled our course as we began the descent. A line of battlements towering over the approaching landscape. There didn't seem to be any way to avoid them. Nature's barrier would need to be challenged once more. Or would we concede defeat, divert to an alternate haven? It didn't seem likely, at least not without giving it a try. After all, diversions cost the airlines money!

Wings flexed and flapped, the gyroscopic effect of spinning turbines causing the engines to move around alarmingly in their mountings. Lightning flashed, thunder crashed, and we dropped as the bottom fell out of the sky. Chaos reigned, for of course, when an aircraft goes down the food trays go up, as do you if you're not strapped in. But all was well. And with the aircraft kitted out with the latest in electronic aids, the crew soon had us safely down at Heathrow. (In some cases, shaken but not stirred.) Another return from another job in another place. It still goes on, you see, though less frequently now. And I still travel on the old blue and gold passport would you believe; sixth issue. See me through the millennium, that, no change there. No change either in the way I dress to fly; comfortable, but smart, just the way it used to be for everyone that flew. These days it can sometimes pay off, too. Dress well, be courteous, and you could be rated SFU at the check-in desk - "suitable for upgrade". Sometimes used on over-booked flights, though less frequently these days. If not an upgrade it could see you allocated a seat by the over-wing exit, with its extra leg-room. Or maybe that's the "takes one to know one" syndrome coming into play?

*

1994.

As in the ever-changing pattern of service life, paths cross and re-cross before finally parting, often forever; hello and goodbye. Then here we were, thirty four years on, meeting for a weekend of reminiscence: the Helicopter Operations (Malayan Emergency) Association reunion. There was George Puddy, bubbling and effervescent as ever, Taff Walker and Tom Browning, pilots with which I had flown in my crewman days. Tony Tamblyn and "Spider" Taylor hadn't changed much either. In fact none of them looked a day older to me, obviously because we'd all aged at the same rate. Tom Bennett was there, too, he of the stinkwheel bicycle, with its attached box, "for putting things in". His hair had changed, from ginger to grey. Ended up an Air Commodore, Tom, and here was I, a lowly ex-corporal, on first name terms. It didn't feel quite right at first, but I soon realized it was. Although I still respected them all, I learned to accept the fact that rank didn't count for much now, we were all civilians. The main thing was, we were friends. Service camaraderie is something that lasts forever. I don't believe there is an equivalent out there in civvy street, at least not to the same extent.

Then the hangar doors were opened once more. It happens all the time when old service pals meet up. The greetings over a pint or two, the usual qualifier, "Do you remember when....?" I attempted to dredge up the images. Rather old images. But I found them all right, as did everyone. We talked of times past. Brief mention was made of pull-off checks and blade tracking, then it was people and places, helicopters and Hondas. Long-forgotten incidents were soon to be recounted with the help of photographs in albums. We swapped yarns and talked the night away, the early hours of the new day, too. We were still capable of that.

It was good to meet them all again, to find out what they had gone on to do, what they had done, what they now did - most, of course, retired. I also learned what they would be doing next year around this time. They would be back for another reunion.

Wrong.

It was the last time I was to see George.

*

I now know many things about many places, for I'm lucky enough to have been there, to have seen them. Most remain as picture postcards in my mind, and the luck seems intact. It is something we all need a little of now and again, good luck. That some people appear to have more than their fair share is not necessarily unjust, for a certain percentage of luck is engineered. Was it coincidence that Winston Churchill just happened to be in the right place at the right time when Chamberlain resigned, for instance, or did he place himself there on the off chance? The same could be said for Senator Johnson accepting the vice-presidential nomination under John F Kennedy. It could be said that such luck is deserved; earned rather than chanced upon. In a similar vein I didn't appear to have fared too badly over the years, even though there had been times when I'd seriously dispute the fact. But on balance I'd say I came out of it all rather well, for I had taken the opportunities as they were presented, a lot of people don't do that. No point waiting for fortune to smile upon you, it rarely does, that was my reasoning. What you must do is go out and grab it, or at least make the effort. I had been determined to fly, to see the earth from a bird's eye viewpoint. I had achieved that, spending over four thousand hours of my life in the air, and I don't have any regrets. Apart from that DC3 in Nigeria, all those years ago, I can honestly declare I have never refused to board an aircraft. Mind you, there were numerous occasions when, once airborne, I wished I *had* taken the train instead. This of course includes those assorted, rivet-popping, oil-spewing Illyushin, and Antonov cast-offs of China's internal airlines. But in those instances I don't suppose even the train would have presented an acceptable alternative. And although I see pilots as a special breed, I must admit to flying with the odd one or two with whom I wouldn't wish to fly again, given the choice.

So why didn't I ever attempt to become a pilot myself, or racing driver for that matter? Well, it's the physical side of things that excite me; the design and shape of the cars and aircraft, the sounds they make, the way they move through the air, or along the ground. The way they behave, react to differing situations, the way they are controlled. Skill and ability, courage and dedication were things I could observe and appreciate, even if I didn't necessarily possess them myself. And that, I suppose, was basically the true reason: lack of confidence. I never felt I would have been capable of being up there amongst the best, and average would never have been good enough for me. As the pilot of a fast-jet I'd probably have found myself as misplaced as a stunt man on Songs of Praise. Or maybe I'm just one of life's observers, as opposed to a doer?

*

Bearing in mind the fact that I claim not to be superstitious, I must admit to there being more than a few good-luck charms over the years. First was the shark's tooth on a gold chain - not too lucky for the shark, admitted, he was dead. But possession of one of his teeth was a by-product of his death, not the cause. We happened to catch him when fishing off an oil-rig in Nigerian waters. OK, so we used a crane and a trash basket as our tackle, a pound or two of beef as bait, it was still a fair catch. Skill and timing were required in the operation of that crane. There was a need for luck to be with us, too, just as it needed to be against the shark.

Next came the New Zealand Greenstone Tiki I used to wear. Superstitious rubbish I tell myself, God is my good-luck charm. But I wore them anyway. Insurance, I suppose, should God be away on holiday or something. Or perhaps I wore them in an attempt to ward off the dreams I occasionally experienced; nightmares, really. Maybe a couple of dozen over the years, though long after leaving the Air Force. A worrying, recurring sequence: an aircraft seemingly about to crash. Sometimes I'm aboard, sometimes not, it doesn't matter, I always wake up before the crash occurs, if it ever does.

One such had me staying at a London hotel, my brother visiting. We heard the characteristic whine of a large jet passing overhead.

'DC10,' I guessed aloud. 'Sounds low.' I frowned.

'Much too...' But George's words were drowned out by a fearful noise; the heart-rending "whump" of a fuel-heavy explosion. I raced to the window, looked out. Nothing to see, nothing to hear. That was normal, too, I never actually saw the crash, or its after-affects, for I awoke in an instant, with a jolt. There was a kind of swishing and whooshing going on inside my head, the death throes of a disturbed dream. Then I was

528

wide awake, yet calm and clear-headed. The images in my mind had been vivid, unnaturally lucid, as if they'd been real. Images from a dream life, or of one yet to be? As usual, I briefly wondered about this, then dismissed the thought, cast it the way of the others. Possibly the images were brought about by subconscious visions of crashes I had witnessed: that DC3 at Dishforth, and the Valetta. Or the extremely public loss of that French Air Force Breguet Atlantic at the 1968 Farnborough Airshow. A terrible piece of asymmetric flying; turning on the dead engine. I'm no pilot, but even I'd been aware that was something you should never do. Stands to reason when you think about the mechanics and aerodynamics involved.

As for the good luck charms, I still have them, tucked away in my treasure trove box, along with my gold nuggets, Krugerrands, and that Omega watch I bought in Geneva years ago. The watch is the only thing that gets an outing occasionally. That box is my fall-back fund, for when the world really does suffer a financial crisis, which is always on the cards, given the amount of debt everyone has built up, both personal and corporate. Debts need to be paid off sometime or other.

*

So what else has changed over the years? The aircraft themselves for one. A visit to the cockpit of a modern airliner served to remind me that the contemporary cockpit was far removed from those I remembered: Sunderland, Hastings, even Comet and Britannia. Modern passenger jets, even military fighters come to that, now feature digital readouts (as opposed to analogue - a direct reading rather than an easily misinterpreted pointer), all singing and dancing, lots of colours on lots of screens: blues, yellows, greens. Red is reserved for the attention-getters: the not to be exceeded limits, and the "what-the-hell-do-you-think-you're-doing" warnings. Although the basic blind flying panel is still evident, it is no longer in a form I recognised. The "glass cockpit" as it is known. Much more accurate and responsive. And where in hell was the control column, that pole to which pilots habitually clipped their notes? Replaced by something known as a sidestick controller. OK, but what about the notes, where were they? How could a pilot fly without those scribbled reminders? Ah yes, the red and amber lights, the audio and visual reminders. Then there is

'George', mark whatever. Not only does he fly the aeroplane, he also makes the decisions, based on what the pilot programmed into him to begin with - more of those missing notes, they, too have gone digital. Which leaves the crew to get on with their real function, to keep a watchful eye on things, to be able to react instantly, if and when things do go wrong, which they occasionally do. To prevent that event cascade. It also allows them time to enjoy their meal - though never the same menu for everyone on the flight-deck! Just in case.

The above reminds me of the story told at a Guild of Aviation Artists gathering by Vice President, David Shepherd, when opening their annual exhibition held at the Mall Galleries, London, in 2004. (It was an event I had taken to attending every year, even buying or commissioning the odd painting now and again. Such as the cover of this book!) Commenting on modern technology, he recalled the time he was invited onto the flight deck of a 747 by a pilot friend (obviously pre 9/11). Noting all the digital displays, including one on the centre console, he asked, "Do you really use all this technology?"

"Absolutely," the captain replied. "All the time." With which the stewardess arrived with coffee, plonking a tin of chocolate biscuits on top of the central display, covering it completely!

He then told a story which again reminded me of how laid-back things could be in the "old days", when the sun always shone, there was no hurry, and, to him, Heathrow seemed like a village airport. Said he used to wander round with his easel, etc, select a subject, set up and start painting, and no one bothered him!

He told of how this TWA Constellation was undergoing a major inspection, so he set up shop and started painting. Working methodically, he returned over the next three days to carry on. Then a crew turned up with a tractor and tow bar, preparing to move the aircraft.

"Hey, you can't move that, I'm painting it," he complained.

"Sorry, mate, it's off to Toronto," he was told.

"But I only need another three hours," he implored. With which the engineer looked at his watch, turned to his crew, and said, "I suppose we can give him a couple of hours." With which they departed and left him to it.

That, too, is how I recall things as being in what today

are termed "The bad old days"! To my mind, such an impression can only be formed by those who were not around at the time. Back then people were honest and courteous, and there wasn't a need to lock doors, to secure each and every item, no matter how small, or to observe everything by a multitude of CCTV cameras. Days when, rather than being an everyday event, murder was something of a rarity!

*

To watch an aircraft perform - a present-day fighter, say, free in its natural element - is to observe smooth beauty. Compare the same machine in the static mode and size seems strangely exaggerated. There is a sense of balance, symmetry, power; yes, for sure. Yet it now appears chunky and angular rather than sleek and smooth. A brooding presence, crouching, patiently awaiting its time. It is dead and silent until the moment the pilot climbs aboard and straps it to his back. Confident hands now set the controls, push buttons, and flick the switches that are to bring it back to life. Pressures build, electrons flow and pulse, gyros spin, turbines whine, until the silence disappears in a storm of sound. From the moment that throttle is advanced as the machine lines up at the end of the runway, shuddering and straining like a hungry predator, nose oleo compressed, it is invested with an air of sinister intent.

A little jiggle, nose bobbing up as the brakes are released and, given a second or two, things happen very quickly indeed. The sudden build-up of speed, throttle pushed into afterburner, an explosion of flame and sound - excruciating, or music to the ears, depending on one's viewpoint - aircraft roaring past before rotating smoothly into flight. Gear up quickly, then it's away, into the wild blue yonder, climbing at an unbelievable rate. Somewhere between twenty and thirty thousand feet per minute for the latest and greatest. And you thought it was dead and silent.

Now it is the massed crowds who become silent as they stand and watch, eyeballs fused to camcorder viewfinders. The clothing they wear is that of the enthusiast. Flight jackets of leather or nylon are pleated, buttoned, zippered and pocketed. They are also badged and patched, the battle honours of previous engagements: IAT '85, Duxford '87, Farnborough, Mildenhall, etc. Clothes far removed from sartorial elegance, but not at all out of place in the macho world of aviation; one reason we are known as aviation anoraks. And in this context, it would appear that the word "macho" could also apply to the female of the species, the aviatrix. (Watch the video Reaching For The Sky, part 12, The Adventure of Flight: hear Lynn Rippelemeyer's story. Watch her at work, flying the 747, then tell me I'm wrong.)

I could have been at any of the above air shows, at any time during the eighties and nineties, but I wasn't. This was Elvington, 1995, home of the Yorkshire Air Museum. These days, you see, I have no need to fly to satiate my love of aviation, a visit to an aeronautical museum will do, even the quiet of an empty hangar can be enough to stir the memories: the different aircraft that have served to transport me on my peregrinations of the globe. The Airspeed Oxford that carried me on that first flight, the nostalgia inducing biplanes: Tiger Moth, Stearman, Waco, Pitts Special. (Wow! Was it ever. Turned me inside out, that one.) There were the tri-engines, the first flight in an aircraft whose airspeed indicator was calibrated in Mach numbers rather than knots: Comet 2 (all gone now, apart from the one used as a restaurant, one as a clubroom. Even the gate-guardian at RAF Lyneham was consigned to the scrapheap in late 2013.) Descendants of the Comet 4 are still around though, reincarnated today in the RAF as the Nimrod Maritime Patrol aircraft. (After the 2009 defence cuts, these too now retired to museum displays.) Then there are the helicopters, the seaplanes, amphibians, floatplanes, and the ski-planes - refreshingly different, those. Silent flight is a sailplane, and there are the toy-like micro-lights; as serious as anything that ever left the ground, make no mistake about that.

So how about the flights I missed out on: Concorde to Bahrain - cancelled at the last minute when, on grounds of cost, the client decided my arrival on an assignment wasn't so urgent after all! - Concorde from New York, an upgrade at my own expense, but Air Canada, with whom I was booked - and would therefore lose the fare - deliberately making the switch nigh on impossible; being catapulted into the air from the deck of the USS Forrestal; that HD31, in Gabon. There were others too, missed because the chance had never been there to begin with. Aircraft I'd loved to have flown in, but never had: Meteor T7, Vampire T11, Hunter T7, the T4 Lightning, any of the V-Bombers, and most of all, the Canberra. Still, as I said, I hadn't fared too badly: over one hundred and ninety assorted types, disregarding various marks of the same type.

Then there were the countries to which those aircraft had carried me; ninety at last count. The most well remembered? Okay, remembered but never liked was Nigeria, at least, once the Biafran episode had unfolded. Prior to that, Nigeria was sort of acceptable. But come Biafra, I lost everything I could not carry on my person, even if I did escape with my life intact. The primary objective.

As for places remembered with pleasure, there were many. I'd been and seen, as the saying went: African dawns and Caribbean sunsets. The day-lit nights of the Arctic summer, the night-time days of its long, hard winter. Periods of calm, moments of storm. I'd relished the good, suffered the bad. There had been plenty of both, naturally. That, after all, was life. There are many countries to which a return visit is always something to look forward to with pleasure, few I would wish to live in if it meant rejecting England. But my out and out favourites have to be Australia and New Zealand; countries where life is lived at a much more relaxed pace.

I have to say I'm thankful I did most of my travelling and touring when the world was still relatively benign, when it was usually safe to wander off the beaten track. That way we seemed to visit places the rest of the world had yet to discover. Places as yet unchanged by commercial pressures, and tourists. Today, I wouldn't venture near ninety per cent of those countries, even if I were still being well-paid to do so. To go there on holiday, at my own expense? Forget it. Australia, New Zealand, Singapore, Continental Europe, the Caribbean and America, OK. The rest you can keep. Far too dangerous, in my opinion. And the OK countries are fast going that way too, it appears.

*

It's a long way back to those binocular-toting days of the fifties, but I still live in Yorkshire, the City of York itself now. Those same binoculars - now battered, aged, and long since retired from horse racing - continue to give valuable service, spotting aircraft. Only now the sleek-lined, propeller-driven aircraft of the fifties and sixties have been replaced by those angular, aggressive high-tech types of the twenty-first century. They'd stand no chance in an avian beauty challenge, there again, that was never their intended role. And as for those old, mainly long-forgotten airfields; some do still remain. Elvington - second longest runway in the country - more complete than most, is

533

now a museum and test track. But don't despair that others fared not so well, for a trip to a deserted airfield is something else again, even if its runways are no longer active. No aircraft approach them now - no more Lancasters, no Halifaxes, no B17's, nor any of their associated friends, the fighter escorts - but what stories those runways could tell: tales of young men at war, and of the stirring deeds they once performed.

The men and women are gone, too. All that remains, apart from those runways - potholed, and with grass thrusting up through cracked concrete - are a few derelict buildings, metal window-frames devoid of glass, their doors broken, hanging willy-nilly from the remains of hinges. Then there are the clouds in the sky above. Ah yes, the clouds. They may look the same, but clouds are silent, tell you nothing apart from possibly the kind of weather we can expect. At times though, if you listen, concentrate, imagine, familiar sounds still seem to echo in the early morning sky: air crackling with the short sharp messages of man; the popping and banging of tired, damaged, throttled back engines; the seemingly relieved screech of rubber on tarmac; relaxed-sounding voices raised in song; bar-room ballads to the accompaniment of piano improvisation - the lads, down at the mess. Then there is the real music: a once familiar theme, this. An orchestration seemingly composed especially for the Rolls-Royce Merlin. The returning ghosts of long lost heros.

All in the past. All gone.

But I do still have my suitcase. It is much smaller now, for another thing I learned was always to travel light. So, a small suitcase, well packed, its complement of dreams now fulfilled. Well... almost. I shall continue to fly and to travel as long as I remain fit and capable, and it is safe to do so! For the good times are surely by no means over. In fact, I rather hope the best is yet to come.

*   *

534

NOTEBOOK SEVEN
DOODLEBUGGER PERSONALITIES & EVENTS

As previously mentioned, ONI base station sites in some counties could be very remote, but an advantage to this was that it did often afford us sight of much more of such countries; areas and revelations possibly denied the average tourist. There again, I have been located atop a luxury hotel, and on a Club Mediterranee site in Senegal. (I had to replace an American operator at this location as he didn't take kindly to naked young ladies "prancing around", as he put it! It takes all kinds.)

Sites also varied tremendously with regard to their environment, and the facilities available, again both good and bad. From those in Nigeria, where none could be described as good, to places like Ko Samui, 400 miles south of Bangkok, Thailand; superb tropical beaches, and now a popular holiday resort. Or how about Tobago, in the Caribbean, sister island to Trinidad, but much more picturesque. Lush, tropical green, with idyllic golden beaches. Then there were such as Bird Island, a small coral speck in the Seychelles. Just blue sea, white sand, and little else.

Then there are stations like the sandy atoll off the West Australian coast. The appropriately named Sandy Island is 600 yards long by 200 wide, at low tide. At high tide the highest point is three feet in elevation. The only building on the island is a weather station, which is raised about 40 feet above the high tide mark. On March 2nd, 1977, whilst the station was occupied, along came Cyclone Karen. She started building approximately 5 miles from Sandy. With the assistance of his camp helper, Brett, operator Harry Bridges erected 40 feet of tower against the weather station for use as a ladder, climbed to the top, and found the doors padlocked. A sledgehammer and some tools were left outside. By 1800 Karen had built winds up to 100 mph. There was torrential rain and the seas were coming over the island. An attempt was made to climb the tower, but Brett was blown over, so they decided to seek shelter in what was left of the station tents until winds decreased. By nightfall Karen was packing winds of 140 mph. What remained of their tents went seawards. At 0500, with the cyclone's eye directly overhead, Harry and Brett climbed to the weather station, broke the locks and took shelter. The winds began building again at 0800 and reached 150 mph. Unknown to Harry and Brett, when they broke in they triggered a switch that sent an alarm to the Australian weather bureau in Canberra. On receiving this signal, and knowing how secure the weather station was, rescue operations - instigated by ONI management on the mainland - were called off. It would anyway have been impossible to land anyone.

Harry and Brett spent another 36 hours there before it was possible to descend and begin cleaning up and putting the station back on the air. On March 5, at 1400, they made radio contact with shore, and soon a boat was on its way with fresh supplies.

Abandoning a station was rarely an option. Occasional discomforts, even life-threatening situations, were all part of the job.

I heard one report of an operator in East Africa getting up to switch generators in the middle of the night - they were very small, portable units, so we would 'rest' them regularly - only to find a lion asleep by it! By daylight it was gone. Needless to say, the generator missed its rest that night.

Another operator told of one location in which vibrations from the generator seemed to attract various small rodents at night, which of course attracted the snakes. Not just one or two either, literally dozens.

You eventually develop various ruses to allow yourself a degree of safety at such locations.

I suppose we were often looked upon as intruders. At times welcomed, occasionally not. But owners of the "often worthless" piece of land we occupied usually found themselves well compensated, so they were usually happy.

Then there was the other side of the coin, one being a station site in Italy. Nearby was a disused, though historic, monastery, and, unbeknown to his supervisor - myself - the operator stripped dozens of decorative tiles from the walls and floor and had them shipped back to his home in the UK. ONI only learned of it when they were presented with the shipping invoices for payment, listed as expenses! It was an expense that remained unpaid.

One site in South America was to become eponymous with it's first operator. When John Narramore got blown off his mountain location he was, naturally, re-supplied. He then had a crew of locals build a 3ft thick wall around his tents. When that particular job finished, the wall remained. To this day the Indians refer to this as "El Templo de Narramore".

*

Africa, as I knew it, the West African coast in particular, was home to an extraordinary collection of expatriates. From the Empire-building breed of Englishman who seemed to spend his life in the various colonies and ex-colonies - three months home leave per annum apart - to the American oilman. They worked for such concerns as Barclays Bank, Beechams, Blue Circle Cement, Shell, Mobil, Reckit and Coleman, the lot.

A similar situation existed in the seismic industry. Quite often you'd run into the same people time and time again. Then there were the legends, their names often used like talismans, bandied about to show how "in touch" and experienced the speaker was. Most of the legends you only heard about, the odd one you'd occasionally meet and work with. For me, Davey Dale was one such.

Davey's stories were long and well embellished, for he was truly a natural raconteur, something to behold. I'm not, so I'll just give you the basics.

"Look at that old fart," Davey commented one day. He indicated to a guy across the road, as we settled back with a drink. Naturally, we were in a bar somewhere. It happened now and again. We'd sit there, drinking in the atmosphere, along with the odd beer or two, swinging the lamp and setting the world to rights kind of thing.

"Reminds me of someone," Davey said, allowing his thoughts free reign to drift back over time. "Yeah, I remember. Rio. A hotel downtown. Boat manager was a fella by the name of Kit Carson. Anyway, he asked me to drive out and pick up a replacement captain who was due in later that day. Gave me the flight details and the car keys, so off I went. It was about ten miles to the airport, hell of a trip, that. Anyway, I got there OK, sat around and waited for the flight.

"Of course, I didn't know the skipper from Adam, and he didn't know me, but I had no trouble spotting him. An old sea-dog if ever there was one. Looked like he'd stepped right out of something by Michener: battered, peaked cap, complete with gold braid, and a blue blazer from which brass buttons appeared to be still growing. His features, those that were visible beneath the shock of white hair and matching beard, told of many years and, from the way he walked, many beers. He was absolutely rat-faced. Anyway I managed to get him sorted: immigration, luggage, customs, then out to the car. I bundled him and his luggage inside, then proceeded to head back for the city.

There was a fair amount of traffic, as usual, normal carve up. Forget Formula One, this was serious stuff. Back then everyone in Brazil figured they were on a par with their World Champion, Emerson Fittipaldi.

The old man of the sea was hanging onto the door, eyes on stalks, sobering up fast, it seemed. But next time I get chance to look across, he's fast asleep. Slept the whole trip. Still that way when I pull up in front of the hotel. A bit ominous, that, thought I. So, fairly sure what the situation was, I check him out. Not breathing. The old sod had croaked on me. Well, what could I do? Not a lot, I realized, so I leave him there, go on up.

"'Hi, Davey. That was quick," says Kit. "Where's the skipper? Yuh find him OK?"

"Yeah, no problem, Kit. But if you want the boat to sail you'd better telex Dallas and order up a new one. This one's buggered."

*

Willie Williams, was another of those legends.

'You try the shower, Willie?' I asked him during one of my first forays into Africa. We'd just arrived in the Congo, had regrouped in the bar after settling in.

'Mine doesn't appear to be working too well,' I told him. 'All I got was a dribble of brown, tepid water.'

'Yeah, it's working all right. Just lucky the sun was in the right position relative to water tank, eh, otherwise it would have been brown and cold. That dribble ensures more than one guest will enjoy the privilege of any water,' he replied. He'd know, Willie, for he was an old hand with ONI. Quite a character, too, I was to find.

"A li'l ole country boy," was how W W Williams had described himself to me, which, being as how he came from a small town in the Southern States, was true enough. But did that small town ever cause problems when he tried to cash a cheque anywhere outside his home State. Seems no one was prepared to believe the Bank of War was for real. Believe me, it's there all right; War, West Virginia. Look it up in your atlas, just to the west of Bluefield. (And while you've got the atlas handy, here's another. In Norway. East of Trondheim, close by the airport, is the one place from where it is imperative you send all your friends a postcard. Everyone does, for there is nothing else to go there for. Railway yards, post office, and that's about it. There is an hotel across the tracks, but I'm not sure if it's included. I mean, hell of a place to build an hotel, Hell. But I've stayed there, sent my share of postcards from Hell.)

Country boy he might be, but Willie was certainly a tough nut. You sure didn't want Willie for an enemy, as many found to their cost.

We were in a nightclub, Willie and I. Africa again. Gabon really. Port Gentil if you must know. Okay, Lagua Club to be a little more precise, nine o'clock in the evening. Standing at the bar if you want an exact location. Though by now you should have that figured. Well, we'd suffered the usual hard day, felt in need of a little liquid refreshment. Alright, already. *More* liquid refreshment.

Bar apart, it was typical nightclub, lighting so dim you almost needed a white stick to find your way around, dance floor apart.

Willie was giving me his views on the latest addition to his crew, who had arrived that very morning. Apparently, only just.

'Bloody useless,' he said. 'Half-blooded American Indian. Not that I hold that against him, but he calls himself a Native American, as if to infer I'm not. Seems he almost missed his connection in Paris, due to the fact he wasn't entirely of sober mind at the time. His normal state, I'm told. Apparently can't hold his liquor. One drink and he assumes the mental aptitude of a retarded delinquent. If Ron Wasserman hadn't been there to wake him up and dress him, he wouldn't be here. Wish to hell he hadn't been." With which Willie paused, glancing in the mirror as he sipped his drink. Then I saw him stiffen.

"Oh, oh, don't look round," he advised. "It's bloody Hiawatha. Out there on the dance floor."

I too checked the mirror behind the bar. The floor was deserted but for a solitary figure. A guy, prancing about, clutching a large glass of booze. And when I say prancing, I use the term loosely. Very loosely indeed. He looked barely able to stand.

Inevitably, he spotted Willie, or, more likely, a form he recognised, so he staggered over. Next thing he was poking Willie in the chest with a finger. Don't know what had gone on previously between them, but "Hiawatha" certainly didn't appear to be too enamoured with Willie. And vice versa.

"Poke me once more and......' I heard Willie say as I turned to reach for my drink. There then followed a noise which suggested the warning had gone unheeded. I looked round to find "Hiawatha" on the floor. Quick. Just like that.

`Let's get out of here,' Willie suggested, already heading for the exit. I followed.

My trusty Renault 2CV was parked right outside the entrance, so we hopped in. I fired up, pumped the gear lever into reverse and backed onto the road, ready to head for pastures anew.

I glanced round just in time to see this form come hurtling out of the club and launch itself in the direction of the car. Very stylish, perfectly horizontal, feet first. A passable impersonation of guided missile with its gyros toppled. Bloody "Hiawatha".

His selected point of impact was the front door - behind which sat Willie - and, drunk or not, Hiawatha's aim was good.... or would have been.

Problem was, his befuddled brain had computed angles, velocities and trajectories based on a static vehicle. As it happened, his timing was somewhat imperfect in that I had the car in gear and on the move. I clearly recall seeing this cartoon-like image float across the rear-view mirror, still horizontal, but fast losing altitude; something related to apples falling out of trees, I seem to recall from my science lessons. He reminded me of Sylvester the cat.

The road was just dirt and gravel, and believe me, next morning at breakfast, he looked like a survivor of Custer's last stand.

'Believe you were responsible for this, Willie,' he challenged, somewhat unnecessarily pointing to his face and arms. 'I owe you one.'

'Yeah,' Willie replied, failing to arrest a smile. 'But I wouldn't bother trying to collect, or yuh'll owe me two!'

Didn't go the distance, "Hiawatha". Last I heard he was in a Singapore jail, facing charges of knifing another doodlebugger.

*

There was a tale my friend Geoff Metcalfe told me about Willie.

Geoff, a Geordie, having just joined the company, was very young and green - as I suppose were most of us at the start. He was recounting his first assignment, somewhere in the Middle East, if I recall correctly. A station that was particularly inaccessible, not to say onerous.

Willie was the Party Chief, running the crew, and he'd had a couple of operators quit from the site, was in no mood for more of the same. So, to forewarn Geoff, who was the latest replacement, and was about to be dispatched to said site, Willie decided to put him in the picture. Set out the facts.

`But what if I really don't like it?' Geoff queried, not wishing to find himself isolated in the middle of nowhere, in some foreign land.

`No problem,' Willie advised. `As long as you give me plenty of notice, I'll come and get you. And I'll buy you a ticket home.'

`Just like that?' Geoff questioned. It sounded all too easy, and in direct contrast to the stories he'd heard.

`No, not quite just like that,' Willie replied. Then, after a brief pause, `I'll kick the crap out of you first. You can use the ticket once you get out of hospital.'

Geoff remained on the station for two months. `Hey, I'll tell you what,' he admitted to me. 'I'd have quit after that first week, but I didn't dare.'

Stayed with us for years, Geoff, and when he did leave he set himself up in business, becoming a very rich industrialist. I recall the time another long term friend - Ron Hewson - brought his New Zealand "wife to be" over to Darwin, Australia, introduced her to the crew. It was to be Lynne's introduction to the ONI lifestyle.

'Hi, Lynne,' Geoff replied upon being introduced. 'I'm Geoff. I've just been down to Fannie Bay (an area in Darwin) looking for some, but there wasn't any.'

She must have felt like I did when first meeting Jose. Wondered what she was letting herself in for. But she soon got into the swing of things, as can be judged from the following.

I think everyone in ONI must have heard of the time Ron and Lynne decided to visit the casino at St Julien's Bay, Malta.

541

'Couldn't find anyone willing to babysit, Deno,' Ron told me. 'He was only a year old, so we decided to take him along in the carrycot. Inevitably, we were stopped at the door.

'"You can't take a baby in there," the bouncer said. "Have to check him in." So we did. Left him in the cloakroom hanging on a peg. Got a ticket for him, too. Lynne was called out to change him halfway through the evening, but otherwise he was fine.'

Ron also told me this story which relates to his early days with the company - before he was married, at least, officially! He and his Ghanaian camp helper "wife" were out collecting crabs. She was catching them, handing them to Ron to hold.

'She was doing well,' he told me. 'I had both hands full when one of the little sods clamped onto a finger. Naturally, I dropped the lot, and that was it. All that hard work, and there went our lunch, scampering away across the sand. She was a bit upset about that. Especially so as she said it now meant she had to go and catch a monkey instead.'

A snippet which probably serves well as a lead in to this next, which, I suppose, could be said to concern dinner rather than lunch.

*

There's not a lot to be said for Tuktoyaktuk, an Inuit town up in the far north of the Canadian Arctic, apart from the name that is - it actually translates into 'resembling a Caribou', though I'm not exactly sure in what way!

Tuktoyaktuk was where Ron was about to go, in the days before he was promoted to Party Chief - an appropriate title, maybe, though for "party" read "crew" - but perhaps not so on this occasion!

On arrival at Inuvik airport, after a long tiring flight from wherever, he was met by fellow Kiwi, another ONI legend, name of Easterbrook. And as Ron tells it, he found himself with barely enough time to dump his bags at the Eskimo Inn, where a reservation had been made.

'"Let's go get a drink, and I'll brief you on the job," says Ian, who had been known to take the odd drink. So we went for a drink. Not just beer either. I think we sampled most of the other precious fluids with which we'd occasionally anoint ourselves.

'"Fancy something to eat?" Ian suggested, sometime

later. Which meant a change of location was indicated, a place where food as well as drink was on offer. There was such a place - restaurant, bar, band, bit of a dance floor - so that's where we ended up. Even managed to find an empty table, right next to the band. Bloody noisy, so not ideal, but it would have to do. We ate, drank some more, listened to the music, messed around on the dance floor. We then returned to our table.

'Oh God. I feel sick,' says I, holding a hand over my mouth.

'"Shit, no!" Ian replied, quickly sizing up the situation, and their particular location. "Not here."

'Too late by far. That carelessly placed hand turned defence into attack, over a much wider front, band to the fore, defenceless. Not just one, I got all five of em.

'At which point Ian seemed to develop a sudden urge to dissociate himself from both me, and that place. He hustled me outside, bundled me into a taxi and disappeared. Bare chested, soiled clothes under my arm, I arrived back at the hotel, hairs on my chest frozen bloody solid. You should have seen the looks of astonishment when I asked for my room key. I could read their thoughts: *This must be one tough dude. It's about a million degrees below, outside!'*

Ron says he soaked his clothes in the bath overnight, then packed them away in a plastic bag. Early next morning he left for his station, way up the top of some Arctic mountain. Says his clothes never thawed out for weeks.

We first met in Nigeria, Ron and I. But even before joining ONI he'd spent eighteen months at the South Pole, as a member of New Zealand's 1962 Antarctic Expedition. Each member of the party had two roles, and Ron's areas of responsibility had been surveying - he was a qualified surveyor - and the Huskies. Study a detailed map of the area and you'll see a Mount Hewson somewhere down there, plus a Hewson Glacier. There could also have been a crevasse named after him, had he not got lucky. This is the one in which he almost perished. Said he owed his life to the fact of being tied to the sled he was riding. The ground suddenly opened up, sled wedging itself across the gap, leaving Ron hanging twenty feet down on the end of a rope, nothingness beneath him! And how cool can you get? He told me he actually asked his rescuers to pass his camera down so he could take some photographs

543

before they pulled him out. True, too. I've seen the photos. (There's one on page 445.)

Anyway, to get back to Tuk, as it was known to us, I got to spend the 'summer' up there two years in a row. Interesting work, and certainly different. At least I found it so when I arrived in mid June. There was not a tree to be seen, for we were well above the tree-line, and the bay was still frozen over, ice at least six inches thick! Until the boats with their icebreaker bows started charging around like demented elephants, breaking it up. That kind of different. But once the thaw proper got underway, so the ground became a quagmire, permafrost on the surface giving way to mud six inches deep. And with the thaw came the mosquitoes. Big? You could have played badminton with these.

I was a mobile operator for these projects, meaning I rode the boat, and didn't have to live in an arctic tent, out in the wilds, like the base operators. We didn't travel offshore to the vessel by helicopter, we went by snowmobile; until the ice melted. I recall stepping over the side at midnight, walking out over the frozen Beaufort Sea to take a photograph. Summer you see, so ample light, for at that time of year the sun never actually sets. Different in winter though, when it never rises. Which is why, at these latitudes, the working season is so short. Only a few months when the area is ice free, bergs apart. And as those bergs posed a considerable threat, a spotter plane regularly plotted their movements, vessels towing them out of the way if it became necessary.

Conditions could be tough alright, but we were well looked after. Never ate better on any oil industry related establishment, or most restaurants come to that. And if you happened to be ashore on a Sunday, they put on a buffet of such gigantic proportions, once the employees had finished eating, they threw open the doors to the Inuits of the local community.

Back to West Africa. We had a German guy who could be quite the racialist when it came to Nigerians. I recall a group of us sitting in a hotel room one time, having a drink, of course. Klaus was sat with his back to the balcony door, well past caring, when the talk turned to the ability of some local helpers, which really got him wound up. The drunker he became the more worked up he got, until he appeared to be on the brink of apoplexy. `There's one behind you, Klaus. Out on the balcony, looking in,' Fred goaded. It was meant as a wind-up, a joke, but Klaus was too far gone for that. The doors leading onto the balcony were old-fashioned, as were most things in Nigeria. These were the austere architecture of fifties-style council flats back home. Probably had been, bought on the cheap when England was modernizing. A flat, iron lattice frame fitted with small, glass panes, maybe six inches square.

Klaus didn't hesitate. His arm swung round viciously, punched out, and *whack!* his fist went straight through the glass. It must have hurt, almost certainly would have had he been sober. But Klaus wasn't. He was feeling no pain.

It was so instantaneous, and fortuitous - him hitting the glass like that, dead centre, avoiding the metal completely - that it looked hilarious. We all burst out laughing. Even Klaus laughed.

`Hey, Klaus. He's there again,' Pete said, conspiratorial and unexpectedly, some time later. He didn't need to state what.

`Whack! There went another pane. More laughter.

By evening's end he'd done four more. Had to pay for them next day, by which time, he said, his hand did hurt. And for him to admit to that, it really must have!

*

Rich Longton tells a story of when he was an Operations Manager in the New Orleans office. Phil Cosgrove, an Australian, had just completed a job in the States and had posted in the report, before taking a few days off, heading for .... no one knew where! Rich needed to talk to him re some missing information in his report to the client, and after trying all the usual places, without success, recalled Phil once mentioning distant relatives in Louisville, Kentucky. He phoned the local operator, who happened to know the family and put him through to the house. A maid answered to say no one was at home, but yes, Mr Cosgrove was visiting, they were all down at the church. Rich got through to the church and, eventually, Phil, who asked how he had found him, as he hadn't revealed to anyone where he was going. He was there for a cousin's wedding, and the service was about to begin. Rich persuaded him to stay and answer a few questions, then Phil returned to the wedding.

Phil and Rich again, this time in Serena Beach, Queensland, Australia. Rich again needed to speak with him, urgently. He phoned Serena Beach exchange, which was so small the operator knew everyone. Yes, Phil was around, but he'd left on a sailing trip two days ago. "Is there any way to get in touch?" Rich asked. Not really, came the reply, they could be anywhere, and there are only two islands out there with a phone. Rich asks her to put him through to one of them. Guy at the other end replies to the effect that they haven't had any boats in there for days .... But.... hang on a minute, there's one putting in now.

"Rich Longton. How the hell did you find me this time?" asks Phil, eventually.

Geoff Metcalfe told the story of when he drove out to Phil Thompson's station in Egypt with something or other but, with a lot of vicious-looking dogs around, he refused to get out of the car. Phil says to him, "Hang on, I'll show you how I deal with them." He produces a small cap pistol, points it at the dogs and fires.

It didn't exactly go as planned!

Geoff says it was like one of those cartoons. The moment Phil fired the gun he found himself charging off down the road with a pack of dogs after him. One of them latched onto his trousers, which now had a big square rip in them. Meanwhile Geoff delivered whatever it was he'd come out to deliver and was back in the car by the time Phil returned, minus the hounds.

Ron and Lynne remain friends to this day, and I often stay with them when I visit New Zealand - perhaps *overstay* at times I feel.

*

A friend and colleague who went by the name of Fergus - a tall, bearded highlander, built like a Scottish castle, got to telling of how one day he was "caught short". You know, "Gypo tummy", "Montezuma's revenge", "Dehli belly", or in this case probably "Highland Fling". He'd been in the pub awhile: pie, peas, and a couple of pints o' heavy, time passing with undue haste, as it tends to when there are schedules to be kept. In this case, a train to catch to take him to an airport, from where he was going back to work.

Another pint drained, a check of the watch, and realization, train leaves in ten minutes. Rush out of pub, turn left, cross the road at a run, pressure suddenly building, stomach cramps and, God, too late. Disaster. But, wait a minute, what's that? Yes. Fortuitously, within sight, and on track, an Army and Navy store. Quickly inside, a rack of denim jackets and jeans. Select a pair of jeans - correct waist size, no time to worry about length. Pick up suitcase, and denim, rush to checkout. One person already being attended to, goods wrapped, but suddenly decides on extra purchases and saunters off again. 'Och, I'm in a bit of a hurry, Jimmy,' says Fergus. 'Train to catch. Can ye take for these?' Hands over goods, credit card. Goods wrapped, paperwork underway. Glance at watch, look around shop, acting nonchalantly, hoping nothing shows, no seepage. Minutes ticking away. Come on will you. At last, signs, handed receipt, bag, and he's off. Train pulls out just as he slams door shut. Phew! Enters toilet. Remove soiled items, jeans and underwear. What a mess, but thank God for denim, no external signs. Smell though, do they ever. Sod it! Items bundled, and as train is now well clear of station out of the window they go.

Twenty minutes to wash and clean up, lots of water, whole roll of tissue. Much better. Huge sigh of relief. Opens package and removes... a denim jacket.

He left the toilet wearing a pair of pyjama bottoms which had been packed in his suitcase. There would be some business to be done in the airport shops that day.

Then there was Larry Parks, who must have been further round the bend than most. He actually airfreighted bare generator frames back to the Sydney office, asking if they could fix them!

*

Some countries are prudishly sensitive, others not. The Spain of General Franco was one of the former, Australia the latter, as I experienced.

August 1971 saw us in Valencia on completion of a survey off the coast, the vessel about to depart for Nigeria. The usual pattern developed, that of seeking out the hotel bar and partaking of the offerings. Mike was tucking in his shirt after some horseplay with Don. Taking advantage of loosened belt and undone zip Don crept up behind and pulled his trousers down, leaving Mike standing in his underwear. In those days a minor incident such as this was enough to warrant their being asked to leave the hotel, if not the country! As there were no Gardia Civil present, they got away with being asked to leave the bar.

Chapter Twenty-One
NORTHERN NOTES

*P*lease God, let there be another oil boom. Next time, I promise not to piss my money up against a wall. The words stared out at me from the toilet wall; just one of the familiar pieces of graffiti to be seen during the slump in offshore activities of the late seventies. And in Scandinavia, blowing your money was not too difficult a task, given that beer could cost up to £8 a pint. There we go again, basing the cost of living on such as a pint of beer! But what I'm saying is that Scandinavia was an expensive place in which to work and live, and I spent a lot of time there towards the end of my career, Norway in particular. But the working conditions, and environment, went some way towards easing any such pain as the cost of living may bring in its wake, as did expenses in the form of a per diem living allowance, based on local rates.

The western approach to Oslo's Fornebu airport takes one over numerous pretty little bays and inlets, each filled with a myriad of sail and power boats. Their owners live in the houses which pepper the surrounding hillsides. Single storey timber-framed designs, with black, red, or green tiled roofs. The bays and coastline further north also harboured a multitude of tiny islands of varying shape and size, each, with its own jetty and collection of boats. Beautiful in the summer sun. Exposed, miserable, and isolated during the long dark days of winter, one suspects. Although many of these would be second homes, summer cottages, occupied by and large only during week-ends in the summer. Surprisingly, trees are everywhere in this grey, rocky land, which seems to be comprised of a huge block of basaltic rock. But the trees do occasionally give way to lush green meadows, along with their attendant houses and small-holdings.

Such scenes are repeated throughout the country, along its west facing coastline, which of course is where we worked. Islands also meant bridges, which were few and far between. What replaced them were ferries, lots of ferries! So many, in fact, it was necessary to plan your journey around them The only way to avert this was to drive inland. A long way inland. And as all the sites we required access to were on the coast, that was clearly not a viable alternative. But the schedules were frequent, and meticulously adhered to. Although I at times I was given cause to wonder about that. Like when the expected vessel failed to appear. But this usually turned out to be a case of my reading the schedule wrongly. Working seven days a week, often the only way I knew it to be Sunday was when I stood cursing the ferry that never showed up. A quick glance at the timetable revealed that it wasn't scheduled to. Of course not. On a Sunday!

Another thing to be aware of when travelling in Scandinavia, is that road distances are given in kilometres. This is fortunate, for a kilometre is one thousand metres no matter where in the world you are. On the other hand, a Scandinavian mile is ten kilometres. Equivalent to 6.3 statute miles. A fact worth knowing when *asking* directions - especially if walking - distances for which are almost always given in miles! Especially by the elder residents. (Just as in England today, I never use kilometres, centimetres, etc! Always miles, feet and inches.)

It was in Norway that I was first introduced to mobile phone technology, in the 1980's. OK, not *quite* as mobile as today's standards, for it probably weighed in at around ten pounds, mostly the battery pack. And for that all you got to do was to call a number and talk to someone (isn't that what telephones were designed to do!), as long as you were within range of a relay station, which were few and far between. But if I was on board a ferry, say, plonked this monstrosity on the table and proceeded to call and talk to someone, or more likely they called me, it certainly marked you out as someone of importance, which of course I wasn't really. And although I did need to have it close by at all times, I did only make use of it when really necessary. Unlike today, when people continually bombard the local environment - and their brains - with the same microwaves used to cook your lunch - albeit of much depleted wattage - just to report whereabouts it is on the street they currently are!

We must never forget, the brain also uses electrical pulses of much depleted wattage to make it function! Of course, the manufacturers etc tell you they are perfectly safe. Well, what would you expect then to say!

*

Over on the peninsular's east coast, Örland and Gotland are peaceful Swedish islands that inhabit the Baltic Sea, and I'd spent a few pleasant weeks on both during our Swedish operations.

When in Visby, Gotland's capital city, our morning ritual always included coffee in a Konditori, along with a portion - possibly a chunk, but never a mere slice or piece - of some suitably, deliciously creamy concoction at which the Swedes are unsurpassed masters in producing. Very light sponge, filled and topped with real cream, strawberries, and whatever. No more than ten thousand calories, honest.

Which brings to mind a Swedish operator, and his comments on the GPS reference station at Stokkoy, on a little island back over on the west coast of Norway.

'I could happily spend the rest of my life there,' he told me when I picked him up to take him into town for a break.

And so it came to pass.

I replaced him on the site a week later. Shortly after driving him back out there, he died of a heart attack.

I'd always thought it a good station, too, and I did spend quite a few months on that site over time. Though from then on I took care not to give voice to the thought.

I remember one night in particular on that location. I had wandered out to stretch my legs. There was a distinct chill in the air. Then, suddenly, an ethereal light, a greenish luminescence glowed around me. I looked up and there it was, hanging in the still, night sky like a glowing curtain, the filigreed strands of a celestial light show; the Aurora Borealis. To us mere mortals, the Northern Lights, to the spirits of the night,....who knows? A shimmering gossamer curtain that swirled and glimmered in the troposphere, as if disturbed by a breeze unfelt here on earth, or maybe shaken by a large, unseen hand! Silent, iridescent, but in an ever changing variety of colours; greens, blues, pinks and purples. The colours of the rainbow radiated briefly along its length, then the green glow returned to surge in intensity before finally fading. It was as if someone had turned off the power via a dimmer switch, turning it first in the wrong direction.

I continued on my way, hurrying through the, by now, inky blackness, and then ..... Sod it! I tripped over a rock and my dreams crashed down with me. Had it actually existed, I found myself wondering.

Another time, as I was walking to the nearby farm - probably to replenish my supply of eggs - when, skirting the edge of a lake, I was able to perform my good deed for that particular day. The land out there is all heather and buttercups, rocks on which snakes sunbathed, streams, and leafy trails. It is lovely when the sun shines, as it did right then, even if there was still a chill in the air. (Must have been the 'green' winter, for I'd been advised by a local that Norway rarely experienced summer, just two winters - a green one and a white one. Not really true, I discovered, for I experienced many lovely, sunny, summery days during my time in the area.)

Walking along, I saw a crow on the ground ahead of me, and as it didn't fly off I assumed it had hurt a wing, for it just flapped about. Approaching slowly, so as not to disturb it too much, I saw it was caught up in the heather. It had a fish hook in its mouth, the nylon line attached to it was wrapped round one leg and tangled in the brush. Taking care, so as not to hurt or unnecessarily frighten the bird, I duly succeeded in removing the hook, and freeing it's foot from the line. All the while, three of its mates circled overhead, cawing, until eventually it was able to fly off and join them. Then a strange thing happened, they actually circled overhead as I continued on my way, as if to ensure that I too would make it safely.

The next day, as I walked back from the farm, there they were again, flying and circling overhead, as if in welcome. Then, the day after, I noticed them sitting on the fence outside, waiting. I wasn't sure whether they were planning something or if they just liked me, but as soon as I appeared they took off, circled around a few times, cawing, and then flew off again. For days after they would suddenly appear, not always immediately. I'd set off walking, completely alone, but inevitably they would put in an appearance somewhere along the way. Then, one day, they were no longer there. They disappeared, completely and forever. I like to imagine they felt they had paid off a debt. I hadn't thought to credit crows with that much intelligence, but then I read a piece in a magazine which stated that crows in Miyagi, somewhere in Japan, had taken to placing walnuts in the paths of oncoming cars. Then they just sat around, waiting for the nuts to be run over and cracked open. That apart, there is also the rarely reported, and apparently even more rarely observed, Crow's Parliament: possibly a fallacy, based on the belief that crows attack injured or otherwise abnormal members of a flock. The general conception among country people was that the species sometimes held a "parliament", during which a "criminal" bird was condemned and pecked to death.

I also recall one morning offshore, looking out from the bridge of the vessel I was on, and seeing a seagull on our back deck, which was quite unusual. Then I noticed a second, and this looked like it was dead - in fact it was - and the other bird must have been it's partner. It stayed for quite a time, before eventually flying off, no doubt grieving.

*

I remained at that idyllic Norwegian site for a month or so before I was called home for an emergency. My father was in hospital, dying.

He had never been one hundred percent fit since returning from the war - in fact he'd returned with a disability pension - but rarely had I seen him this ill. He was too weak to sit up but seemed well in control of his faculties. He knew I was there, knew who I was. Still, I felt he wouldn't last the night. Seemed he realized it too, for his thoughts drifted; he was back in India, during the war. He started to tell me about it, as if it was something I should know about before it was too late. He was clearly recalling events and faces, tears streaming down his cheeks. Not recollections of horror and death, but of the times during which he and his buddies attempted to forget the war, to cast it aside for a few hours. The tears were continuous; he wasn't in a hospital bed, he was back there. He talked of the places he'd been, remembered his mates. Then he just closed his eyes and seemed to fade away, completely relaxed.

I gave his hand a final squeeze and left, to return to the solitude of Stokkoy.

To the amazement of everyone, particularly the doctors, he was back home in his chair within three days, seemingly wondering why everyone was so astounded. He would go when *he* was ready, not before. The time had not yet come.

I was overseas again when he did die. This time I was on a vessel offshore Norway, and as there was no way I could have made it home in time for the funeral, I didn't even attempt to. I'd already made my peace with him as it were, said my goodbyes. I think he understood that; before he went, of course.

*

It is nearly midnight and the brilliant Scandinavian sun gives no indication of being about to set. In fact, at this time of the year - summer; the green one, that is - it will barely kiss the horizon

552

before bouncing back into the sky. For at these latitudes dusk didn't arrive until around midnight, but as dawn also arrived around the same time, there was little evidence of either.

But for all the pleasantries of Scandinavia, I did not enjoy working in the health and safety conscious North Sea environment, even if the seismic vessels of my twilight years did now offer amazing amounts of comfort. Single cabins, for instance, as opposed to sharing with a up to a dozen or so other people. There was also a lot less physical work to be done too. Install the GPS, the associated computer system, set everything up, enter the relevant data (taking care that it *is* relevant!) and away you went, more or less. But, as I often found with the younger people now being employed direct from University, a degree in IT skills meant little on its own. Without previous survey experience to call upon, the younger set tended to rely completely on what the computer told them, seemingly not possessing the nous to question it. If I happened to enter some erroneous data, or inadvertently selected a wrong survey datum - easily enough done - I could spot in an instant that the output was incorrect. I more or less knew the answer I expected to see, a ball park figure, and if nothing like appeared on the screen, this led to an immediate recheck of my inputs. This thanks to of years of experience during which we computed the data physically, ie, in the head. We navigated the same way too, no computers or calculators involved. Yes, it is far easier these days, and there is a much greater degree of accuracy. But you still need to use your head; a computer will only produce results based on the data it is given. In other words, garbage in, garbage out! as the saying goes. And never was a truer word spoken.

*   *

Chapter Twenty-two
INTO THE SECOND MILLENNIUM

*F*or the good times are surely by no means over. In fact, I rather hope the best is yet to come.

Never was a truer word written. There were other dreams still to be fulfilled, and, as I said, plenty of room yet in my suitcase. But, I'd decided, they were no longer to be found in doodlebugging, at least not in the European environment.

I did return to West Africa one final time. In fact I was quite looking forward to it in a way, memories fading after being away so long. That pull of the West Coast still partially evident. And I was convinced there were sure to have been changes over the years. But I was soon to change my tune; found it to be the same old place after all; if not worse!

It was hot and humid when we landed at 10 pm local, just as I remembered it. I hadn't been to Africa for 10 - 15 years, but I knew where I was from the smell. Nothing derogatory, many countries have it, all slightly different. A unique, indeterminate aroma that immediately pinpoints which country, or perhaps continent, it is you are in. There were other pointers here as well. Like the fact of my forgetting to carry my vaccination certificates not being a problem that a fistful of cash couldn't solve. Yes, this was West Africa all right! Nothing much else had changed either, certainly little for the better. This was a short trip that helped me decide in which direction my future lay. A future I had been pondering over for some time.

Thus it was that Offshore Navigation Inc and myself parted company in March 1990, with some regrets, I must admit. I could see the writing on the wall, decided to jump ship whilst there was still a ship from which to jump. I had been with them for twenty-six years, even if I did only collect three service pins. These little tie tack type pins, set with one, two, or three rubies, then the same sequence of diamonds (pseudo stones I assume!), were awarded for every five years of service, although it seemed you only received the appropriate pin if you happened to be passing through Head Office, in Harahan, New Orleans, at the pertinent moment! hence there being no ten and twenty-five year awards in my collection. The five year award was actually sent to me wherever I happened to be at the time, but that was the last such occurrence. The fifteen, and twenty I had collected personally from Ray Landry as I happened to be passing through the office for some reason or other - though not in time for the Annual Awards Ceremony, when they were presented by our President, Bob Suggs. Ray presented mine when he invited me for lunch at Smileys, across the road from his office. It was a popular lunch-time - sometimes much longer - watering hole for ONI personnel. (There was a similar establishment down on the street below our sixth storey Singapore office, equally popular come lunch time. Or any time really! It went by the name of Ai Hou Kee Oriental Lounge, and if one of the office staff happened to be seeking anyone in particular, the Ai Hou Kee was the first place to check. Here, two particular tables were more or less reserved for ONI personnel. If you happened to be short of cash, they would open a tab for you. They would even cash our company (US dollar) pay-checks for us.

Enter any such bar in the tropics and it takes a few seconds for the eyes to become accustomed to the sudden change; bright sunlight to relative darkness. The Ai Hou Kee was so dimly lit it took minutes. But it was worth the wait. We would evaporate a beer in the meantime, then another one or two. After a couple of hours someone usually came up with the excuse that we were seeing so well inside, we figured there was a possibility of damaging our eyes if we ventured back out, so we stayed. At least until the sun went down, or our presence was required in the office - probably to pick up a ticket and fly off somewhere.)

*

Although it became patently obvious to me that ONI was about to fade from the scene in the near future, the deciding factor in my leaving, was the offer of another job, along with an almost unbelievable increase in salary. Thus it was that I transferred my allegiance from New Orleans to ... well, York actually, for I now became self-employed, as a "Consultant" (didn't everyone!), assignments arranged for me by an agency in Voorschoten, Holland.

There followed another 8-9 years in the industry. Similar work, but now using a broad spectrum of equipment, GPS, and more advanced computers to the fore. I represented the interests of various navigation companies, contracted to numerous clients. I still travelled the world, initially - my first assignment being a glorious four month spell in New Zealand -

but the North Sea was gradually claiming more and more of my time, which ultimately lead me to thoughts of retirement.

I did occasionally get to meet up with other ex-ONI personnel now and again, out in the field. Some of whom were not yet "ex", along with others who had also jumped ship, or perhaps switched allegiance once the ship sank. I recall the time I found I was about to work with one. As he was arriving from somewhere on a later flight to me, I arranged to meet him at the airport upon his arrival.

I waited for him outside the customs hall, not sure if I would even remember him after all this time. I had already searched my mind for some clue as to his features, drawn a blank. Decided I'd have to rely solely on subconscious precognition.

A paunch appeared first; one that must have cost a fortune in excise duty. It was followed by a face which I almost recognised, just as I could see he almost recognised mine. It was enough. I stood and greeted him, acting as if I'd never forgotten him, whilst he did the same to me.

My last assignment was at the end of 1998 - boring old North Sea again, now with its full complement of restrictive, fatuous, Health & Safety Executive regulations. In fact, the past couple of years had seen me shuttling back and forth between the UK and Norway, the Shetlands, Denmark, Holland etc, with but barely three weeks in China - my first trip through Hong Kong's impressive new airport at Chek Lap Kok - to break the monotony. And if - as seemed likely - the majority of my work *was* now to be North Sea orientated, I wasn't really interested. With the excitement of having to fight the elements missing, and a decided lack of global flight, it became just another job; sedentary, routine. Especially so to someone who had first become involved during the industry's formative years. Even in the early sixties we had still been pioneers. Time now for another rethink on the way my life was heading.

I called my Dutch agent and advised him of my decision to retire forthwith. Although - at his insistence - my name remained on their files as still being available.

"We'll call if anything suitable comes up", he told me.

Yeah, thought I, I'll not be holding my breath. Just as well, for I never did hear anything further. Hadn't really expected to, having already nudged past the over-sixty barrier. And even if I had heard, doubt I'd have accepted, unless the location had been somewhere particularly agreeable to me, for I could now afford to be choosy: Australia, New Zealand, Pacific or Caribbean Islands, and the like! OK. Certainly not the Middle East, nor anywhere in Africa, for I had by now - especially so given that last short job with ONI - finally shaken off the old "African West Coast syndrome": that irresistible urge to return time and time again. Anyway, Africa was now a far different place to that which I had experienced all those years ago, as was the rest of the world. Colonial style Africa was a thing of the past, and from what I hear, see on TV, or read in the press, this is more to the detriment of the African people than anyone else. Never before have the ordinary people on that continent been subjected to so many famines, coups d'etat and mass killings. Poverty and misery has been enforced upon them by their own kind. Black leaders, and their favoured few, are rich beyond their dreams, their countries never poorer. And never has the so-called United Nations been so dis-united, useless, and disinterested as to the plight of these people. Well, let's face facts: these days black leaders probably enjoy a majority when it comes to voting rights in the UN.

But retirement didn't necessarily bring an end to my travels, far from it, not now that I had the time to indulge myself. My flying log was still very much an open book, my suitcase always at the ready, along with my briefcase, complete with passport and cash, available for the quick getaway, as it always had been.

I quickly learned that not having to work was one of life's good feelings, as is the physical pleasure of not knowing, nor having to care about what tomorrow may bring.

Although I did manage to log four new aircraft types, 1999 was a particularly barren year as far as flying hours went. Out of the ninety minute total flying time, a third of those were spent on board an RAF Lyneham-based, 30 Sqn Hercules - courtesy of past RAF connections. (Handy, that. And in 2001 there was to be a flight in a 10 Sqn VC10 out of Brize Norton.) A Percival Prentice got me airborne on a short flight from Coventry airport, other flights came courtesy of friends at our local flying club, Sherburn-in-Elmet, where a group known as the Bomber Barons had been formed. These were mostly ex RAF, many of them WWII veterans. We met up every Thursday for lunch, a chat, and occasionally a flight.

So much for the flying and travel. But in the meantime

I had become an "Association" person, in that I became a member of almost any group or Association with which I'd had some kind of an affinity at one time or another. The RAF Boy Entrants Association was one of the first, in 1995, a full 43 years since I first left home, on my own. Later that February day to walk through the gates of RAF Cosford. It was a little different at the first reunion I attended, to once more step through those gates. Now, not knowing to what I had aspired since leaving the Air Force, if I came across an RAF Policeman he would likely address me with a respectful "good afternoon sir", rather than with the definitely unfriendly glare of all those years ago. Then came the real meeting and greeting, lots catching up to be done over the next couple of days, a very pleasant gala dinner, then the goodbyes and the signing off, "until next year". Next came the RAF Seletar Association; RAF Changi; RAF Butterworth; RAF Lyneham; the RAF Historic Society. Then there were groups associated with the various aircraft on which I had worked, and flown in: Indian Ocean Flying Boats; Malayan Helicopter Squadrons, Britannia, Beverley, et al. This ensured I attended lots more reunions similar to that of the Boy Entrants, and, serving on various committees, I was busier than I had ever been.

Putting the novels aside - none of which has yet been published - I set to and wrote a book detailing the history of my old Singapore base, RAF Seletar, research ensuring I learned a lot more about it than I ever knew when stationed there. In this I even became quite friendly with RAF Seletar's last Commanding Officer, Group Captain Aleksander Maisner, though he was an Air Vice Marshall when I knew him, both of us long since retired from the service. And although "Air" rank officers don't really retire, this never became an issue when making a cup of tea in his home for an ex corporal. He was a really nice chap. Very friendly, and pleased that someone was about to put the Seletar story into print. He made all his data available to me, photo albums and anything else he had, which was as well, for the RAF museum had little, all the station records being lost when the Japanese took over during the war. Unfortunately, by the time we got together Alex was suffering from Parkinson's Disease, so speech was somewhat of a problem, his daughter helping with the interpretation. We did manage to write the foreword to my book. I say "we", as I wrote the words, he gave his approval. I even signed it for him, scanning and pasting his signature for an old station newsletter. That minor piece of technological forgery really pleased him.

Crowning Glory relates to those exciting times between when the base first opened, in 1928, to when Alex finally closed it as an RAF facility in 1971.

Retirement, you see, does not mean giving up on things. Us "Oldies" keep ourselves busy in all sorts of ways. We start volunteering our services to help others in one way or another; pick up on long forgotten hobbies; discover new ones, etc. Still managing to keep busy, though now doing things in our own way, at times and levels that suit us. One vital difference: no monthly pay-cheque, which is when I became to value those post-ONI years, and the private pension I could then afford to take out. Having spent much of my life overseas, and opting out of the UK tax system, my government pension was miniscule. Fair enough. If you don't pay in you can't expect to be paid out. Although the thought did occur that maybe I should have left this country altogether, then returned as an immigrant! I imagine I'd certainly have been far better off financially!

On top of all this, in conjunction with a lady-friend with whom I had been associated for some years, I also became involved with Duxford airfield, Cambridgeshire, just down the road from where Margaret lived in St Ives. We became members of the Duxford Aviation Society, becoming volunteer aircraft stewards on their "Great British Airliner" fleet of aircraft. It basically entailed turning up now and again to inform the visiting public on the history and features of any one of the dozen or so aircraft on display. As I had flown in, or been involved with most of them during the various aviation phases of my life, I found it to be an enjoyable and therapeutic way of passing the time. We met up with many interesting people along the way. It also entitled us to free passes to Duxford's round of airshows. Either in a working capacity, or purely as a spectator.

*

December 1999. Time sliding from one century to the next. You may recall this as being that period when the biggest con of all took place. The assumption had been created (probably by software engineers) that computers would not be able to differentiate between midnight on December 31st 1999, and

00:01 on January 1st 2000. This of course opened the floodgates to "must-have" software sales, or other unnecessary fixes, which must have cost the business world millions of pounds. And I'd thought computers to be intelligent! Surely it would be much easier, and cheaper, just to switch off, then restart, changing the date manually if necessary, though I. I was no expert, but this is exactly what I did, and none of my computers turned up its nose and threw a wobbly!

So the seasons once again dissolved one into another, winter replacing autumn, telling me it was time for the shorts and lightweight trousers to go into hibernation. That didn't exactly float my boat, as the saying goes! But I was sure I knew just what would.

As well as the travel, opportunities for flight had also been drying up. But I was reasonably sure things would improve dramatically were I to renew my acquaintance with Australia and New Zealand. And so, during the opening years of the new millennium, I did so; a period I referred to as, "Topsy Turvy Downunder", in the report I wrote for the York Branch RAFA newsletter, *The Aldwark Chronicle*, which I had taken to editing and producing - along with *Searchlight*, newsletter of the RAF Seletar Association.

"To travel is to live." So wrote Hans Christian Andersen as far back as 1842, and with those words I would have to agree, even if, occasionally, the travel itself can be a little confusing. Take January 16th 2001 for instance. This was, for me, a nothing day - don't even know what happened to it. I departed home on the overcast afternoon of the 15th, heading in the general direction of London - albeit via Manchester Airport - and, 23 hours later, found myself in Auckland, New Zealand, on the evening of the 17th. Not to worry though, I knew that on my return trip, one day would be considerably longer than the twenty-four hours allocated to it; the missing chunk of my life making a magical reappearance.

Although the Auckland skies were also overcast, and the temperature still read the same as it had in the UK, the difference was that in New Zealand, 28 degrees was referenced to Celsius (Centigrade) rather than Fahrenheit. And when 28 C is converted to F, it becomes 82 . Ah yes! And the days were slow and leisurely.

I was met at the airport, and taken to stay with long time friends, Ron and Lynne Hewson, at their wonderful "bush" house in Albany, well north of the bustle and clamour that was downtown Auckland.

So quickly did I settle back into the routine of New Zealand life I was given cause to wonder if I had ever been meant to live in England at all. Sun, sea, beaches, turquoise waters and a tropical environment, these were the things that appealed to me. (In fact, previous visits had seen the beginnings of three or four undertakings to move to this part of the world - either Australia or NZ. These had developed as far as buying plots of land, even houses, but on each occasion I found the pull of England, and my connections there, to be far too strong, so it never happened. Although I did manage to make a considerable amount of cash on each of the properties bought and sold!)

But the highlight of this particular holiday had to be my visit to Ardmore, an ex RNZAF airfield to the south east of Auckland International airport.

You know how it is at airports, 300 bodies jostling to board the same aircraft. We all hate it, but have to put up with it, most of the time. But there are alternatives. Flights where this does not apply - like when there is only one passenger seat, and that often a concession. The aircraft that were to bear me aloft on a damp, warm but marginal February day were in this class entirely. Nor had I flown in any of these types previously. They crouched there on the tarmac, as if awaiting my arrival - which in fact they were. This was to be the avian equivalent of sampling a fine wine, but without the slightest possibility of disappointment. OK, the Catalina had previously been ruled out - a temporary grounding due to technical problems - but what remained on my schedule was to more than make amends, for this airfield was home to the New Zealand Warbirds Association, of which I had recently become a member - a necessity, for insurance purposes!

First in line of these propeller-driven tail-draggers was ZK1057, a North American Harvard trainer, to be flown by Frank Parker. Unfortunately, a low cloud-base ensured this to be purely a flight-seeing tour of Auckland and its environs. A significant flight nonetheless. It was another first.

Next in line - even more significant, for it was to become the 150th type in my logbook - was an aircraft that bore the registration, ZK-GAC, along with an inscription on its cockpit combing: "to the memory of Mark", Hanna, so pilot, Gavin

Trewhewy explained. This was the P40N Kittyhawk, as flown by both the USAF and the RAF during WWII. Getting better, as was the rising cloud base. Even so, "Looks like we'll be limited to a few rolls," says Gavin, but even as he completed the second he spotted a clear area and went for it. Hmm. Holy moley!

Next in line was almost as good as climbing aboard a Spitfire, probably as close as I would ever get. The P51D Mustang is just as much an historic legend, and I was awestruck. I watched the pilot carry out his external checks, noting the size of the propeller on the front of that powerful Merlin engine. I also listened intently to his briefing as I strapped on my parachute for, like most aircraft - particularly, fast, single engined fighters - if anything goes wrong, it can happen so fast you could quite easily end up dead! Needed to be on the ball.

By the time I had strapped ZK2415 to my back, the cloud base had again descended. Sod it! Well, away we went, and despite the cramped conditions - with me thinking you wouldn't want to be getting out of here in a hurry - it felt good just to be up in this old warbird. Pilot, Peter Houghton, levelled out soon after take-off, heading for nearby hills in a Tornado-like terrain following exercise, down through the valleys. But by the time we crossed the coast, bingo, the clearest skies of all. Well, a hole large enough to allow for a reasonably energetic aerobatic routine. Blue sky, white clouds, turquoise sea, green land, and like that. Again and again, this way and that. Loops, rolls off the top, barrel rolls. I spotted a vessel down below, then we were diving on it - a Jap carrier? No, just a mundane old ferry or some such. Ah well. Then it was time to return to base, and a touchdown that showed he'd done it once or twice before. Absolutely marvellous. My thanks went out to all who made the day possible.

Oh! So you want some brief impressions? Well, of course they were all more than just good. The Harvard was roomy and comfortable, having being built with the intention of carrying two people. I had my own set of controls, and an instrument panel that allowed me to keep an eye on things. But because of the weather it *was* just a sightseeing sortie. The Kittyhawk was also quite comfortable, with better than expected visibility. An exciting ride, for, owing to the restricted ceiling the pilot was forced to perform a fairly tight routine, which made things quite er.... well, I had originally toyed with the idea of taking along my video camera. Ha! At times I was barely able to lift my hands off my knees due to the amount of G we were pulling - even if the figures *were* relatively small. In comparison, the Merlin engined Mustang was much quieter than I'd envisaged, afforded even better visibility - especially when inverted - and it was oh so smooth. Aircraft? Better pilot, or purely more sky to play around in now the cloud-base had lifted? It doesn't really matter, despite the crick in my neck due to my hunched up position in the rear seat, the Mustang takes the honours, but not by much. And they were all great. Wouldn't have missed it for anything.

Two days later I was to be found across the Tasman Sea, in Geelong, Australia; there for a reunion of the Australian Branch of the RAF Boy Entrant's Association, planned to coincide with the bi-annual Australian International Airshow at Avalon, a few miles up the road towards Melbourne. Avalon is the main repair base for Qantas, but every second year it hosts the southern hemisphere's equivalent of Farnborough, a week long trade show, open to the public on the last three days. This year's show marked the 80th anniversary of the formation of the RAAF, therefore attracting participation from many foreign air forces, USAF and RAF included.

Held under high blue skies and soaring temperatures, the display itself could certainly be described as spectacular, especially the "Friday Night Alight" event, which began at sunset and continued until well after dark. This alone made the show unique.

With its four turbo-compound Wright Cyclone engines at full take-off power, the dusk departure of a Super Constellation is highly spectacular, the leading edge of the wing around the engines being enveloped in purple-pink flame. Afterburner departures also take on a new dimension in the fading light, and for the aerobatic types, wingtip flares replaced smoke generators. Warbirds ended their display by lighting up the night sky with a wall of flame half the length of the runway, and to watch Manfred Radius' graceful, flare-lit aerobatics in his Salto101 sailplane, as he danced it to the accompaniment of classical music, was a joy to behold in the now chill night air. (In daylight, his routine ends with a very low level ribbon cut, inverted! You certainly need your wits about you to pull of a stunt like that.)

The evening show closed at 22:00 hours with the spectacular dump and burn routine of an RAAF F-111C Aardvark interceptor. In this, raw fuel is dumped directly into the jet-pipe, creating spectacular bursts of flame in the sky behind. But by this time I was ready for off. Dressed for the hot, sunny, Australian summer, I was by now feeling rather chilly, the temperature of the clear night sky plummeting rapidly once the sun disappeared below the horizon.

Apart from all the above, the daylight shows also featured such as the world's only airworthy Lockheed Hudson, along with Boeing's latest F/A-18F Super Hornet. The USAF brought along the F16 and B-1B, the latter giving a full display, in contrast to Farnborough's high speed, medium level, single flyby. A second B-1B, along with a B52, graced the static display. The RAF were well represented by a Nimrod, a Tornado GR1 of 617 Sqn scooping the "Best Display of Show" award from the organizers. In true Aussie fashion, the GR1's display was adjudged to have been "a ripper." A VC10 and C130's J & K support aircraft were to be seen in the static park. Radials, RR Merlin's, propellers and nostalgia galore were also liberally scattered around, and most of these vintage types took to the skies at one time or another during the show. The only disappointment was the cancellation of the RNZAF's A-4K Skyhawk aerobatic display team. This was due to a fatal crash elsewhere in Australia during a practice session before the show week.

Each day's climax was provided by the RAAF, with a repeat of the F111C dump and burn routine, after which it was the usual, head-for-the-exits act. Not so bad if you were based in Geelong, to the south, but the northbound Melbourne crowd were said to have suffered. We were probably well tanked up and tossing steaks on the barbie in our Geelong caravan park by the time they arrived home.

A week later and, heading in the general direction of "home", I had traded Victoria for West Australia; Melbourne for Perth. Here I managed a flight in one of the Royal Perth Aero Club's Chipmunks, and with cloudless skies over Freemantle harbour, there was no holding back for this pilot. Airlines? Forget it! This was *real* flying.

Yes, when it comes to something different, there is a lot to be said for a small aerobatic aircraft, a powerful warbird, or an overseas air show. And so it was that 2003, 2005, and 2011 saw me make return visits to Avalon - same crowd, same caravan park, same after-dark ritual at the barbecue - takes some beating, that.

*   *

2003 was to prove an interesting year as far as travel and flying went. Certainly the best since I retired. Probably the best ever. The downside was the fact I was now paying for it myself! Can't win them all. Anyway, I found the cost to be well worth the experience.

Late January to Mid March found me again spending time in Australia - visiting friends, with a second visit to Avalon. Then it was on to Singapore, for a tour with the RAF Seletar Association - which I had organised - to visit our old camp, and generally have a good time. This is a trip that has since become something of a bi-annual event. Something else to keep me occupied.

After a month back home, a group of us travelled to the Arras area of France. We spent a week visiting First World War battlefields of the Somme, and their associated cemeteries. All very moving, and thought provoking.

But, it was in June of that year that my most cherished dream was finally to become reality. Shortly after, it would become an impossibility.

Over the years there have, in my opinion, been three iconic aircraft, from a passenger point of view; aviation experiences not to be missed. In the early 1930s came the Handley Page HP42, a four-engined, high wing biplane that offered safe, luxurious flight. Then came the era of the Short Brothers' magnificent Empire Flying boats; England to Africa and Australia in leisurely luxury, for those that could afford it. From the windows of these aircraft, given the heights at which they flew, passengers would seldom look out over at a flat, hazy, distant surface of the world. They would instead see the earth's features; the curves of mountains, the colours of lakes, cars snaking along roads, ocean waves crashing on shores, animals in the jungles. Cloud formations would appear as a sea of powder puffs. They had been aircraft, and times, in which I would love to have flown, but obviously couldn't.

It was with these thoughts in mind, along with two missed chances, that I decided the third iconic aviation experience would not pass me by.... Well, let the pages of the Aldwark Chronicle once again tell the tale. This I titled, "Eating

Out In Style - amongst other things."

For a change, I dined out recently. So what, you might think? Well, Burger King or such-like it certainly was not. Quite special, really: Ballontine of Salmon with crème fraîche; Grilled sea bass with caviar cream sauce, Swiss chard and wild rice; a cheeseboard which offered Stilton, Chevre, and Pont L'Eveque, and like that; true gourmet food, and the service to go with it. All this was preceded by a splash or two of champagne: 1986 Pol Roger, Cuvée Sir Winston Churchill - I now understand why the great man drank so much of it! The meal itself was accompanied by a Chassagne-Montrachet 1er Cru Les Vergers 1997 Chartron et Trebuchet, another splash of champagne - Dom Perignon this time - then a Château Pape-Clement 1994 Grand Cru Classé, Pessac-Léognan with the cheese.

OK, it's possible this may well be everyday fare to some - although no one with whom I'm closely acquainted, that is for sure! But there is one little thing I have yet to mention. This restaurant was located on the lower edge of the Stratosphere, 60000 feet up in the air (that is twelve miles), travelling at 1340 mph, en route from New York's JFK airport to London's Heathrow facility; a dining experience par excellence. I had at last revelled in Concorde flight, was euphoric.

But you certainly don't fly Concorde for the dining alone - much cheaper, and more comfortable, I imagine, to fly Virgin Atlantic's Upper Class in a Boeing 747 - for, apart from this one hundred and five seat fighter being slightly cramped (though the leather-covered seats were supremely comfortable), there was barely time to enjoy the fare. Although there was certainly no excuse for anyone ending up hungry, for the experience began with a leisurely check-in, then breakfast in the Concorde lounge before boarding. Believe me, this breakfast was also a meal only the very rich would normally partake of with any regularity. And not only did this aircraft fly faster than sound (at that height, twice as fast, in fact - ie, Mach 2), but the cabin crew also seemed to work at similar speed! Out of necessity, I may add. Fast, but unhurried; Very efficient.

Three hours and twenty minutes after our JFK departure - the captain receiving special dispensation to use the nearest runway for take-off, such is the fuel consumption of the Olympus engines, especially on the ground, and the goodwill afforded Concorde by JFK's Air Traffic control - we were disembarking at Heathrow! I could barely have made it to Spain in the time, but that is what this aircraft was all about: speed. But speed with style; although some of the glitter had by then disappeared - presumably after the disastrous events of September 11th 2001 - metal cutlery being replaced with plastic, although the glassware and crockery were genuine enough. Strange, that!

So, food and drink apart, what was it like? As far as flying goes, much like any other aeroplane as a matter of fact, apart from the kick in the back when the brakes were released! Once airborne, if it weren't for the digital readouts in the cabin, you'd have little idea of the height or speed (although the sky is a much darker blue up there). It *was* supremely smooth, there again, it could just have been a smooth day. You definitely felt it when the afterburners were cut shortly after take-off (a noise abatement requirement, which ensures you get some low level flying until clear of the land), and there was a slight nudge felt when they came back in again to take us through Mach One. But had the crew not advised us this was about to happen, it could quite easily have gone unnoticed. Nor, at cruising altitude, were those close-up views of the earth's features, relevant to past icons, visible. Rather than a mountain's curves, or the colours of lakes, we were able to discern the earth's curvature, but little else. The descent was a little different, too; slightly longer. There again, it would be, wouldn't it - lots more height and speed to bleed off - and we were fortunate enough to overfly the Red Arrows, doing their thing over somewhere in Kent; Rochester, I believe (though this wasn't a guaranteed aspect of Concorde flight. As I said, fortunate). Not a lot of difference on the approach, either, but the landing seemed silky-smooth (high angle of attack, aircraft riding on a cushion of air), and the reverse thrust braking was spectacularly fierce. But of course, this *wasn't* just any other aeroplane. You were flying *Concorde*. That alone made the difference. This hadn't just been a flight from New York to London. It had been a lifetime experience as opposed to a mere journey. I felt that at last I had reached for the stars, lived the dream. And I had flown in an aviation legend, the likes of which we are unlikely to see again. Certainly not in my lifetime, anyway. Even to see it on the ground was to know it was different. The supremely smooth lines, the aeronautically sculptured wing, those benign-looking air intakes - so technically advanced internally. Computer-controlled intake doors being one of the essential features that allowed this aircraft to fly faster than sound - the needle-point nose. Just to watch it take-off, or land, was an experience, for it *was* different, so sleek and graceful. Long ago I had made the decision that this aircraft was not to be another for which all I could say was "an aircraft in which I would love to have flown." Now I had, and it *had* been something special. A flight of a lifetime.

But it was a legend that was shortly to become redundant; due mainly to politics once again, with the French - as usual - allegedly heavily involved. The scenario was that Aérospatiale, sole producer of spares for the aircraft, no longer wished to do so and, so we are led to believe, Air France no longer wished to fly the aircraft. But, despite all the crowing about *their* supersonic fleet making money - which it was, especially once they started flying air experience flights - British Airways didn't put up much of a protest either, even after recently investing millions on upgrading their aircraft, brought about by a fluke accident to an Air France Concorde in Paris! As for the Government of the day; seems they didn't even want to know. So, despite a declared interest from Richard Branson and his Virgin Group - turned down by BA, a spokesperson for which is alleged to have said, "It's not debatable because we own them" - the aircraft were more or less vandalised: electrics and fuel systems disconnected, and were eventually consigned to museums, even though, in my view, those aircraft never did belong to British Airways for them to give away. Apart from some derisory figure, they never actually purchased them, so, theoretically, they remained the property of the British taxpayer. And our so-called representatives, the Government, did absolutely nothing whatsoever on our behalf. Nothing new there then.

The fact that almost every one of the passengers expressed a wish to visit the cockpit after landing - two at a time - meant your baggage arrived on the carousel long before you were there to collect it. But who cared? And throughout all this, the flight crew remained patiently in place, answering questions, and displaying an obvious pride in the aircraft they flew. I imagined, come October, when the aircraft were to be prematurely retired, the Boeing 747 or 777 would be a bit of an anticlimax for those pilots who chose to stay on. (Unaware of the procedure, I timed my disembarkation so as to be last, thinking I could get a look at the flight-deck. Only on disembarking did I find myself at the end of a queue of like-thinking passengers.)

Would I do it again? Tomorrow, given the chance. Jacob's Creek suddenly lost what little appeal it possessed! Concorde was an ambition achieved, and worth every penny of my money. It will be a long time, if ever, before we see another airliner so spectacular and graceful. Ever since it first took to the skies it became the one dream I definitely needed to experience, before tucking it away in my suitcase. Another iconic aircraft. And this time, one in which I did have the opportunity to fly.

Now I had.

But my New York weekend wasn't just about Concorde, or the city itself, vibrant and interesting as that may be (one of my favourite cities, in fact), for, whilst on the other side of the "pond", I took the opportunity to make a trip up to the Old Rhinebeck Aerodrome Museum, in upper New York State. This is a kind of Old Warden without our Health and Safety type interference - although, naturally, the FAA (Federal Aviation Authority) do oversee all aspects of their displays. To any aviation buffs visiting the States, June through October, these twice-weekly displays (Saturday and Sunday) are not to be missed. Pennsylvania Station; take the 09.45 Amtrak (very smooth and comfortable in comparison to rail travel in the UK, although nowhere near as fast) to Montreal, not forgetting, of course, to disembark at Rhinecliff, long before reaching the Canadian border. In fact, only a couple of stops, and less than two hours out of New York City. All that remains then is to find a taxi to take you to the airfield, set in a beautiful, back-in-the-old-days-America type area - the airfield and its hangars also reflecting this ambiance, even down to the pilots and staff wearing period costume. I just loved everything about it. They have aircraft there I bet Shuttleworth would love to get their hands on. There again, I imagine the reverse applies equally well.

So, the Big Apple and Rhinebeck in one crowded weekend, opportunities made possible mainly by the availability of going supersonic in Concorde. Well, I suppose it would be possible by conventional air travel too, only I feel it would have been that much more of a hassle.

So it was that I eventually conquered Concorde. A dream converted into a memory, filed away, ready to be extracted at will.

*   *

Chapter Twenty-three
BEYOND THE BLUE HORIZON

*I*n retrospect, I suppose, rather than just a chapter in it, this book itself could have carried the above title, for that is the direction in which I have always felt inclined to look. I feel there is still so much more to see and do, adventures to be encountered, experiences to be fulfilled, probably good and bad. Who ever said it was a boring old life!

So, with the Concorde experience now behind me, and no chance of renewing my acquaintance with that legend - museums apart - time to move on. There were plenty of other avenues left to explore, a prime example of which was to account for me, just a month later, jetting off once again.

Another long awaited dream was about to be converted into a memory, for, in July, I excitedly joined a group of "aviation anoraks" at Gatwick Airport, en route for a tour of America. The Great Lakes area was our arrival point this time, but not for the lakes themselves particularly. We were visiting various aviation museums over the "Pond". Not just in America; Canada, too.

The first full day was spent at the very well appointed, Strategic Air and Space Museum at Ashland, Omaha. The heart of what used to be Strategic Air Command, and the US nuclear capability. Then it was over the border to Mount Hope Airport, Hamilton, Ontario, and the Canadian Warplane Heritage Museum. This also was well appointed, and interesting, their exhibits not only in sparkling condition, many of them airworthy. What also made this particular visit exciting, was the offer of a chance to fly in a Lancaster. Half an hour for a very reasonable C$400 (These days it is over C$2500). But despite the give away price, this was the only place on the planet where this possibility was available to the general public. I, as did everyone else, jumped at the opportunity. Although, overnight I had actually given serious thought to declining, due to the fact that I had already flown in a Lanc. But let's face it, this was almost as good as a new type to me, for any lingering memories generated by those five hours clocked up 53 years ago had long since faded to zero.

As we flew out to Niagra Falls - that aeronautical symphony by Rolls Royce, music to my ears - I wandered around. But in a Lancaster there is not far to wander. Back end, where the four temporary seats were fitted; clamber over the main spar and up to the cockpit - an area that, naturally, became quite crowded - photographs of those Merlins pounding away out on the wings; a view out of the astrodome, and that was about it. The nose and rear turrets were restricted areas as far as passengers were concerned. But what an experience.

Next day I was back over Niagra Falls, this time in a Bell 407 helicopter, another new type for my logbook. Pure sightseeing, this, but probably one of the better ways to view the Falls and surrounding area.

A day later, we really "lucked in" during a visit to Selfridge Air Force Base. We were there for their "100 Years of Aviation Air Show", as was the Yankee Air Museum's B17 Flying Fortress, Yankee Lady. Chatting to the crew we learned there was the chance of a flight on offer here, too. Only problem was, it would have to be tomorrow, when we were already scheduled to visit the Henry Ford Museum, along with the USAF Museum in Dayton, Ohio, probably the best aviation museum in America from all reports.

So, faced with a bit of a dilemma, we got together as a group (only around a dozen of us) and discussed the situation. Although at the time we were drinking and dining in Hooters, their hot-panted waitresses tending our every need, as far as food and drink went that is, it didn't take long to reach a decision. The consensus being that the museum would be there for some time to come, the chance of a B17 flight may not.

Next morning, the result of our deliberations found us visiting the Yankee Air Museum at the historic Willow Run airport, Detroit, which was also home to Boeing B17 "Yankee Lady". But, due to some quirk of insurance, B17 passenger flights were not allowed from home base, so, after a look round this fascinating museum, we were redirected to Browne Field, Saginaw, some distance to the north.

On arrival, and after a short wait, during which we were obliged to fill in and sign various declarations - we'd have signed anything, believe me! - Yankee Lady dropped out of the sky and taxied in.

Carrying four at a time, we all got to fly around the local area for half an hour or so, and there were no restrictions on where we could wander inside this aircraft during the course of the flight. Although the rear turret more or less restricted itself. Due to our size, general lack of flexibility and suppleness, the retracted tailwheel leg effectively ruled out entry. The bomb aimer's position more than made up for this, as did the waist gun openings, behind the wing.

The finale of each flight was a run and break over the airfield, something akin to Steve McQueen's performance in the film, The War Lover. A magnificent experience all round.

But more was to come.

On completion of the last flight, the aircraft was to return to its home base at Willow Run, and as we were staying nearby, so were we. But the aircraft was returning with empty seats, so we were offered the opportunity of filling them! The problem of four free seats between twelve of us was resolved by holding a short-straw draw. A result of this was that I got to log a further 35 minutes of B17 flight time. In compensation, the rest of the crew found they could spread out a little more in our minibus. Though I don't suppose they would see that as compensation!

Back at Willow Run, the whole group, along with the rest of the aircraft crew, found themselves invited to the flight engineer's (ex RAF Britannia and Concorde) house for a barbecue. The perfect end to a brilliant day.

We returned to Willow Run the following morning. This time for the start of the main event; what this tour was really all about.

*

For many years I had harboured a dream of one day visiting a small town in Wisconsin, USA. Why? Well, for one week in July, every year, the airport serving this town - Wittman Field - becomes the most important aviation centre on the planet, for during that week, it stages the EAA (Experimental Aircraft Association) Convention. Titled, AirVenture, although generally referred to as Oshkosh - for that is the town's name - this has to be the world's greatest aviation event. At this place, you can see aviation's past, present, and future, all at the same time; most of them in the air. A real cornucopia of all things aviation

As stated, I had been promising myself this trip for well over twenty years, but always something seemed to take priority - usually something known as work. (In fact, yet another title I'd had in mind for this book had been, "A Strange Thing

Happened on the Way to Oshkosh". But as at that time, for me, Oshkosh itself *hadn't* happened, neither did the title.)

What turned the tide this time around - apart from the fact I was now retired and free to roam - was the tempter of our mode of transport. After arrival in America, this was to be via the "Mats" (for ex-USAF Military Air Transport Command) Lockheed Constellation, one of my favourite aircraft since schooldays. I recalled often sketching the aircraft, dreamed of flying in it, but it remained a type that had so far eluded an entry in my logbook. Almost did this time, too!

Our collective visions took a dive immediately on arrival Stateside, when we were advised that problems of one kind or another had seen the Constellation replaced by minibus, taxi, and everyday airline travel. Extremely disappointing, to say the least. But things perked up a little with news that the Connie *was* still available for the final leg to Wittman Field. Chalk up the Connie. And what a way to arrive at the world's largest airshow!

So, Oshkosh itself, what is it really all about, and does it deserve the acclaim afforded it? I would say most certainly, provided you are aware of what it actually is. It is a convention, not primarily an air show - though the flying displays do tend to be spectacularly impressive. And although these are scheduled for the afternoon, flying is actually non-stop throughout the day, what with arrivals and departures, display practice formations, etc, all dependent on weather, of course. A notice on the door leading to Air Traffic Control - which proclaims itself to be "The Busiest Tower in the World", at least for that one week - advised that by seventeen hundred hours on the Sunday, they had dealt with just short of eighteen thousand aircraft movements since the previous Monday, and still counting. I found this not too difficult to believe after observing five aircraft on one of the two permanent runways (at ninety degrees to one another!) at the same time! Not a show formation either. Just regular "Oshkosh week" traffic! And talking of formations, the warbird displays here would take some beating, with eighty to one hundred aircraft in the air at one time. Nor are they all travelling in the same direction. There are aircraft taking off even as others are beating up the same runway, in the opposite direction! Meanwhile, twenty to thirty ship formations are passing by overhead, few of them flying the same course, either, separation purely by height and good judgement. Very professional. It's all happening up there, but this also creates its own problem. You just never know where to look, the very reason I missed a fabulous shot of a Douglas Skyraider leapfrogging a Dakota on take-off!

No such problem with the singleton displays from such as the Beech 18 being put through its paces. This performed manoeuvres one imagines are not in the Beech 18 handbook. And what of that fantastic jet-assisted Waco - an old, piston-engined biplane with a turbine engine strapped between its undercarriage legs! Boy, did that thing move along; and with the pilot's son accompanying him - wing walking! Some of the flying at Oshkosh has to be seen to be believed. The whole thing must be a nightmare for the Air Traffic Controllers, yet all are volunteers. And year after year the lists of those applying to do the job are well oversubscribed, which means they can select the cream of the crop. And boy, do they need them! The flying itself is so spectacular, polished, and professional. And should you become bored by up to five thousand aircraft on the airfield, climb on a shuttle bus and go visit the seaplane base, just a short ride away, on the shores of Lake Winnebago. Lots more aircraft here. And a flight over the airfield in such as a Ford Tri-motor is an opportunity not to be missed. But get there early!

To a pilot, an invitation to display at AirVenture is probably the equivalent of a personality receiving an invite to appear alongside Morecambe and Wise, Parkinson, or Johnny Carson - if you haven't done it, you haven't yet made it. The biggest names in aviation history have all appeared here, as have the most famous of aircraft: Concorde, Blackbird, Spitfire, Lancaster, whatever; you name it, it's sure to have been seen in the skies over Oshkosh.

Away from the aircraft - though you are unlikely ever to be more that a few feet away from one, even if only part-built - are the seminars on this and that, demonstrations on the various skills required to put together a home-build aircraft kit. (Probably two to three thousand of the aircraft here are home-builds, for that is basically what the EAA is all about). There are forums, film shows and lectures, by... whoever! You want to see and hear the likes of Chuck Yeager, Bob Hoover, Neil Armstrong etc; make your way to Oshkosh. (Mention of Neil Armstrong brings to mind an article I recently read concerning that first moon landing.

On July 20, 1969, as Commander of Apollo 11, Neil Armstrong set foot on the moon. His first words after stepping on the surface, "That's one small step for man, one giant leap for mankind," were televised to earth and heard by millions. But just before he re-entered the lander, he made the enigmatic remark "Good luck, Mr Gorsky." NASA copied it, though it was not broadcast publicly. Many at NASA thought it a casual remark concerning a soviet cosmonaut, however, upon checking, they found no Gorsky in the Russian space program.

Over the years, many people questioned Armstrong as to what the "Good luck, Mr Gorsky" statement meant; Armstrong always just smiled, saying nothing. But in July 1995, while answering questions following a speech, a reporter brought up the 26-year-old question. This time, being as Mr Gorsky was now dead, Neil Armstrong felt he could answer.

In 1938, when Neil was playing baseball with a friend in the backyard of the Armstrong house. His friend hit a ball which landed in the neighbour's yard, beneath the open bedroom window. His neighbours were Mr and Mrs Gorsky. As he leaned down to pick up the ball, young Armstrong heard Mrs Gorsky shouting: "Oral sex! You want oral sex? You'll get oral sex when the kid next door walks on the moon!" It was to be one of those odd, stick-in-the-mind kind of things. For even with the passing of thirty-one years, Neil Armstrong's mind had retained that remark.

To return to Oshkosh: there are breakfasts and barbecues, displays of aviation art, presentations by the CAA, NASA and the like, and then there is the "Flymart", where almost anything related in any way whatsoever to aviation is on sale. AirVenture even produces its own daily newspaper, just for the week, detailing the daily schedule, along with stories of what happened here yesterday, and what is about to happen today and tomorrow. This show covers every aspect of aviation in fine detail - or did I already hint at that!

As for the aircraft themselves, nowhere in the world will the general public get this close. The Americans, particularly those who attend aviation events, appear to be far more aeronautically-minded, aware, and respectful than those of most other countries. There are few barriers, just volunteers who wander around and make sure the aircraft are not subjected to acts of carelessness. You can walk around, under, and inside; talk to the owners. You may even be lucky enough to be offered a flight. One thing, be prepared to walk your socks off. Two to three thousand aircraft take up a lot of space. When I was there, the Warbirds park alone contained over four hundred - almost more than the current Royal Air Force could muster up on a good day. (And remember, this was back in 2003!)

But of course it isn't all the land of milk and honey. As with anywhere and anything, a spanner is occasionally thrown in the works. This area, at this time off year, can be subjected to some really spectacular thunderstorms; as was the case during my visit. Not every day, and not always during the hours of daylight. Nor do they always last long, but hey, can they be dramatic. And in such instances the photographic lighting can be really spectacular, bright sunlight illuminating aircraft against a backdrop of purple/black storm clouds. I took some fantastic shots whilst sheltering from a downpour beneath the welcoming wing of a Grumman Bearcat.

Another feature of the EAA at Oshkosh is their Headquarters Building, Museum, and 1930's style Pioneer Airport; all part of the Wittman Field complex, and well worth setting aside a day to visit.

So there you have it, Oshkosh in a nutshell; even if rather a large nut! If you are aviation minded, and haven't been to Oshkosh, you haven't lived.

*

As 2003 drew to a close, I reviewed what had happened during my year. Many dreams that had been generated over time had suddenly achieved fulfilment. And yet to come, taking me through to the New Year, was another Australian tour. To visit old friends across the one continent that drew me back time and time again.

*   *

Chapter Twenty-four
SUMMING UP - THE GRUMPY OLD MAN SYNDROME?

So, with over seventy-nine years of life, travel, and flight behind me, what are the outstanding memories from it all? There are of course many. They are varied, too, one being instantly brought to mind as I watched a TV programme the other day (2012), entitled, "The World's Most Dangerous Roads". It featured a couple of "celebrities" tackling roads classed as per the programme title, naturally. To me the whole thing was boring and unreal. Fill-in television. But it did serve to bring to mind the road a group of us once chanced upon in New Zealand. It was during that time in 1991, when our project was experiencing delays, during which us contractors found ourselves waiting around, with little to do.

A group of us, having rented a car and taken off for the day, now turned our attentions the return stage of the journey. We were running late so, studying the only map we had, this minor road seemed like the shortest route to get to wherever it was we needed to be. Somewhere connecting Lake Taupo with New Plymouth, I seem to recall, and with not too many hours of daylight remaining in which to make it. As a matter of course we followed this single unpaved track through a mountainous, forested area, something similar to the TV version. Only there were differences: we were in a standard front wheel drive vehicle, as opposed to the TV crew's no doubt specialist-built four wheel drive. We were alone, no camera crew vehicles, no back-up helicopter. None visible on the TV screen, either, but I'll bet there was one somewhere around. Their route would also have been researched; ours not. This was research on the hoof!

Now came the point where the two experiences differed in reality. We came across a land slip from the cliff face to the left! No way back. There being nowhere to turn around anyway, the road barely more than our vehicle's width, with a sheer drop down to the river on the right, 300ft below. But we did need to advance, and the only way was ahead. It was time for some serious soul searching and thought. But the answer was obvious really: Yes. So we went for it, little choice in the matter. That you are reading these words points to the fact we obviously made it. We could *see* it would be a dangerous thing to attempt, so everyone except myself out of the car first. Only when I had successfully negotiated past the slip area - heart in my mouth as the rear end briefly became unstable - was I rejoined by those who had walked across. And it was at this point, past the danger area, I stopped to pick up the gang. With time to reflect, the old "What if" scenario kicked in. I'll admit to shaking so much I moved over to let someone else take on the driving. The reaction and fear, you see, comes after you realize you have got away with something. Time now for thoughts of how close you had actually been to checking out! But such thoughts were soon to be replaced with a terrific feeling of achievement; knowing you had faced danger, real danger, accepted the challenge, and won.

There was one more difference between our experience and that of the TV 'celebs'; we weren't being paid to do it. Such is life. This was just one of many close shaves I'd experienced during my fifty years of world travel. Perhaps *the* closest, although other incidents may by now have surrendered themselves to the mists of time. And I can well believe others of my ilk may have come even closer! Like the time an Indian base operator was abducted from his station in the Philippines, or Thailand? and held to ransom. Kidnapped in other words. When advised of the situation, our Eastern Area Vice President, in the Singapore office, was said to have told his deputy to "put him on off-time", ie, off the payroll. He was joking, of course. At least I think he was.

The guy was eventually returned to us, for a small fee. In fact I only ever heard of one that was not, but that involved a local employee and a family feud, or some such.

These, and other stories related to in these pages may seem unbelievable to some, but I do not lie. Life was never meant to be easy. Believe me, I have heard men tell tales that sounded even more difficult to believe. Only I *knew* them to be the truth, because I had at times witnessed the same, or similar things myself. Not all of them dangerous to life and limb either, difficult to believe non the less.

*

Out there somewhere are tropical islands and golden beaches. That thought, and the sun setting with tropical haste, made me almost happy to be here, even though far away from home and family. And of course, if I took into account the fact that I was actually being paid quite well to suffer in this way, well......!

These feelings were generated whilst standing at the rail of our vessel, working off the coast of Bali. The sensation could be multiplied four fold if one happened to be onshore, seated on the verandah of a thatched-roofed, local bar, possibly still overlooking the ocean. A few beers to fuel the thought processes and who knows what may develop. For just such occasions, rare though they may be, I carried a pad and pencil, so as to record my thoughts before they were lost forever. Unfortunately, many a time have I sat down the following day and attempted to decipher that spider-like scrawl, all to no avail. But not all the time.

When I read those notes, and think back, it often generates thoughts of the late 1800s early 1900s, when the rich and affluent took what became known as The Grand Tour, encompassing Europe, and often beyond; the Oriental Express, Ocean liners, etc. These days tourism is well within reach of the majority, some locations becoming overwhelmed. I like to think we came in between. At the lower end maybe, but we saw things the affluent on their Grand Tour, and today's mass tourists, miss out on, or didn't even care about. We also saw what they did, of course, only we saw more because we were there longer Thinking back like that I am also presented with a kaleidoscopic collection of images, some good, some bad, others bright and cheerful, forever changing. The memories are at times quite vague. A series of images, like half-forgotten dreams. Other journeys present clear cut vignettes, especially if notes are taken during the inevitable hours of sitting around waiting, such as on another of my trips to Hong Kong.

The journey started with another session of "manipulate the maverick airport trolley. Then there was the check-in. How is it that everyone with any kind of a problem is always ahead of me, in the same queue! Next there were x-rays for the baggage and a security arch for ourselves. And of course, there were delays and hold-ups. None too extensive, but enough to drive one to the bar, be it coffee or otherwise. Here I sat watching my fellow passengers.

A group of businessmen wandered by trailing talk of net asset values, price/earning ratios and stock options, as electro-mechanical indicator boards set high on the walls, chattered away, switching flights around, seemingly at will. They fixed schedules and allocated gates, discarding those which had departed or closed for boarding, scrolling up to fill the gaps, introducing later flights at the bottom, all as dictated by a computer located somewhere in the bowels of Heathrow.

If one could pick an ideal time to arrive in the Crown Colony it would have to be early evening, when dusk disguises the clutter and dirt, and the tumultuous crowds. When a dying sun inflames the sky and the heavens come alive with colour, as does the city, its streets brightly lit in rainbow hues. At this time the colony becomes a veritable fairyland, the Disney World of the Orient. It was at such a time that I arrived.

Our wingtips scythed the air, perilously close to buildings either side of the flight-path it seemed, almost allowing us a view into someone's living room.

Customs and immigration formalities being minimal, I was soon on my way to the Holiday Inn - Golden Mile, my taxi negotiating narrow streets which were a crowded confusion of noise, traffic, and people. Next morning I found it to be the same in daylight. Every bit of space not already occupied by humans was under cultivation, or being built upon, the city scrambling upwards in search of extra space. There was an unfinished look about the place. With construction going on all around, in places it resembled an obstacle course, like an airport terminal undergoing modernization.

Multitudes of overcrowded, high-rise tenement buildings reached skyward, their flat roofs a forest of television antennae, daily wash fluttering from bamboo poles which protruded from almost every window or balcony. Multicolored clothing flapping in the breeze, like warships dressed overall.

In lieu of Kowloon and the shops of the Golden Mile - displays of cameras, video recorders, computers and their accessories, in fact anything electronic; (Strange though, I thought, how this high technological corner of the world still echoed with the click of the abacus; a counting frame with horizontal rods along which beads are slid. The world's first calculator, I suppose) - I set off for Hong Kong island and Victoria Peak.

In this day and age there are many ways of crossing the harbour; there is a road tunnel through which you can drive, the Mass Transit Railway also crosses beneath the sea, and on the surface runs the old (circa 1898) Star Ferry - still, arguably, the most popular way to cross. Wallah-wallah boats, the waterway taxis, also scuttled back and forth. I chose to become one of the day's 100,000 ferry passengers and boarded the *Morning*

Star.

Apart from the service being efficient, the vessels clean and reliable, this is one of the best ways to view the harbour, and we were graced by the presence of the sun in which to do so. But even on a bad day, say in the rain or during the year-end mists it still retains a sense of rugged grandeur that is beauty in another form.

Disembarking, a scrawny individual squatted on the pavement, greeting me, his parchment-like skin stretched paper thin over a bony frame much like a tissue and balsa model aircraft. Beggars, I'd been advised, should be treated as would social security scroungers back home, but I couldn't bring myself to that. Clearly this man was poor and blind, so I gave him a few coins. Possibly more than he was accustomed to receiving, for I couldn't help but notice how, with a wry smile on his lips, he held them in his hand and scrutinized them closely! Blind my arse!

The glittering shops of Central, with their up-market displays of Dior, Pierre Cardin, Gucci, Wedgwood, Rolex and the like, contrasted sharply with the stepped, hustling tumult of alleyways that formed West End. Here the narrow streets seethed with humanity. Chinese in the main; short, wiry and looking impoverished. (I was informed by a learned friend from Bradford that they were really Hong Kongies. "They only calls 'em Chinese 'cause they're slanty-eyed like," he confided in me.) Whatever, the tourists and foreigners towered over them. These *gweilos* (white ghosts) were aptly named for they were pale skinned, and they dressed entirely differently. They wore tee-shirts and cut-offs, safari suits, and Hawaiian shirts in colours more usually associated with pop stars or anti-nuclear demonstrators. It was an area of shouting, scurrying, jostling life.

Food and drink stalls were part of the life of this area, iron cauldrons bubbling and boiling over primitive stoves. As if enacting a scene from a Shakespearean play, two old crones fussed over one of them, its contents unrecognizable and unimagined, the odours giving few clues as to either origin or histology of the offering. It smelled of ... well, to be totally truthful, it smelt foul. But, seemingly unpalatable as it was to me, it was in demand by the continuous stream of customers occupying the marble topped tables which lined the street.

Perspex containers, dewed with cold, displayed pastel

coloured drinks, only one of which was recognizable, raw cane being freshly squeezed on site, the juices offered for sale. There were also blue, green, and yellow bottles of soft drinks.

Tropical fruits there were in abundance, some peeled and sliced, ready to be devoured. Mango, papaya, pineapple, banana and the spiky, malodorous, durian. They say if you can stomach the smell they are delicious, and enough people must agree for they were piled high.

A bent and wizened Chinaman with a straggly beard rushed by at all of one hundred feet per hour - flat out. He was balanced on a pair of scrawny, matchstick-like legs, and as he passed I noticed the logo on the back of his tee-shirt: Dynapack, I read.

The memory of that leads to another, in another place. A tee-shirt caption contest myself and a friend had devised whilst sitting outside a bar in Singapore, watching the world pass by, as we were occasionally wont to do. We awarded first prize - another drink for ourselves - to a New Zealand shirt which carried the message: Pettigrew Plumbing. Purveyors of Prestigious Plumbing Paraphernalia - Otorhanga.

As I rode back across Victoria harbour, on a ferry appropriately named *Evening Star*, I watched the sun set with almost equatorial suddenness, before stepping ashore in Kowloon. The crowded streets were now their usual neon-lit hubbub of nightlife. The purpose of those bright lights, after all, is to entice the visitors to part with their cash, a job in which they succeed admirably, it seems. "The Stoned Crow", "Ned Kelly's Last Stand", and "Bottoms Up", proclaimed garish signs. The whole area was the usual, wonderful, colourful kaleidoscope of shops, bars, restaurants, clubs, hotels, and "girlie bars".

Other notes reminded me of other places, such as this brief memory of a short trip made to Kota Kinabalu, Borneo: The main street appeared to be totally composed of would-be emporia, some named after who knows what! A beguiling and often amusing use of the English language. This must have been post July 1969, as the only remaining memory is that of a store which bore the name; Man on the Moon Brassier Co Ltd. I didn't go in, because I was not in need of a brassier! Anyway, it was a store which appeared to sell almost everything *but* brassieres, and had, as far as could be ascertained, absolutely no connection whatsoever with men on the moon.

Mention of which once again brings to mind another difficult to forget experience, back in 1994; the excitement of watching a shuttle launch at Cape Canaveral (Kennedy). This entailed a one and a half hour drive in a tour bus, plus a tension-filled wait of three and a half hours. All for around two minutes of spectacle. But what a two minutes!

The only sight and sound to be seen and heard at blast off, at least from our 'privileged' position - across a lagoon, seven miles distant from the pad. The closest the general public are allowed - were the cheers of the crowd packed around us, and a few lights in the far distance. Then the appearance of a silent cloud of white smoke from beneath a minute silver speck drew our attention to the actual pad in use. That minute silver speck then grew a silent tail of fire, and that was it. Until, seconds later, that is - by which time the shuttle, and the rocket upon which it rode, had reached somewhere I'd estimate as being between ten and twenty thousand feet - when a sound like rolling thunder hit us. It built in amplitude until it was a sound you could actually feel - visceral - a hollow, echoing, crackling, fearsome roar. A display of truly awesome raw power. Awesome, yes, a somewhat overused word these days, but certainly not in this context. All that was to be seen now was a pillar of flame atop that growing column of white smoke. Then, a break as separation occurred, and the shuttle - that minute silver speck - along with its second stage, was off out of earth orbit, heading towards the moon. Even up where the package now was, the sound was still audible, but fast fading. One wonders how intense it had been for those actually on site at the time of launch.

Now, silence descended like an invisible curtain. Just a drifting white smoke trail discernable in the night sky as we turned away to board our coaches, speech curtailed by the grandeur of what we had witnessed. Another dream fulfilled and filed away.

*

There was also that first trip into the then, seemingly secretive world of the People's Republic of China, shortly after it partially opened it's borders to foreign travel, and investment, in 1979.

The first requirement to entry for the likes of us was a work permit, rather than a simple tourist visa, so an application was submitted via the PRC's representative in Hong Kong. But even though we were to be working for the Chinese, on a Chinese vessel, providing employment for Chinese workers, the issue of such a permit was seemingly no straightforward task. Various checks meant we had to hang around in Hong Kong for a number of days yet. This was the Hong Kong of wine, women, and happy times, and still a British Colony. Oh dear!

The initial means of transport was by train, from Hong Kong's crowded railway station, in Kowloon. And in amongst the crowds were Chinese and Japanese tour groups, each following their leader, each of whom who carried a coloured flag, held high. Different group, different colour. Funny thing was, the leader appeared to be the smallest person in the group, so, in that crowded atrium all one noticed were lines of bobbing heads jogging along, like moles tunnelling close to the surface. Each line travelled in a different direction, each following a seemingly unsupported runaway flag.

The journey to Guangzhow - previously known as Canton - took us across miles of agricultural land: rice paddies and fields growing vegetables - the New Territories, until we crossed the border into China proper. Even then the view remained unchanged - no mechanized help, just fields full of people, with water buffalo to do the heavy work. The workers were both men and women, whom one of our party described as being "brothers and sisters of the revolution".

Customs and immigration clearance was undertaken at Guangzhow station. We were then driven to the Tung Fang hotel for the night, a beer or two (Tsingtao), and, at one point during the evening I was introduced to a liqueur named Mou Tai. A tipple I have since heard described as, liquid-landmine. It sits rather well with that title!

Onward travel from Guangzhow to Zhangjiang was via an oil streaked museum piece of the, what could well have been named, "The Honourable Gravity-Defying Chinese Flying Machine Company." Yeah, it was that bad! In fact I *have* seen better in museums. The steward or stewardess - difficult to tell, really - was seated on a wicker chair somewhere at the rear. No, I mean that literally, 'somewhere'. It was neither fixed, nor had it any seat belts, so it and its occupant tended to wander around a little. This was one aircraft I was thankful to step down from at the end of the flight. Could have done with a shot of Mou Tai at that point.

Next came a ferry trip over to Hainan Island, and, seemingly, back a few more decades in time, especially when it came to agriculture. I noticed stalks of grain were strewn over most of the roads, people seated on the verges. They were waiting for the next vehicle to come by and do their threshing for them. Water buffalo apart, I don't recall seeing any livestock, but there were ducks by the thousand. The children here were duck herders rather than shepherds.

Few of these people had ever seen a Westerner before, so they stared, silent but interested. All seemed friendly, but no doubt word had filtered down through the chain of authority that they should be 'nice to foreigners', who, it was hoped, would bring wealth to the country. Strange thing was, there are so many dialects in China, over here even our Chinese interpreter found the occasional need for an interpreter!

China was definitely something out of the ordinary, even for such as us, who had seen and done a lot during our travels. Just goes to prove, there is always something new just around the corner.

*   *

One thought that often comes to mind as I sit around filling in time and generally enjoying myself whilst awaiting another trip - that final approach and landing - I feel fortunate that I have lived through some of the better years, for life is not lived the same way any more. No one now seems to be anywhere near as happy and content as they were when times were supposedly hard. And that is the point. You always value that which you have to work for. If it comes easily, it is usually just accepted, often demanded, rarely appreciated.

There will always be rich and poor, I had seen both ends over the years - not necessarily experienced, but seen - and although I wouldn't say no to a fortune (who would?) I have been generally happy with my lot. What I'm saying is I don't enjoy sitting in the cheap seats, but that doesn't necessarily mean I have a wish to own the theatre. And let's face it, come the end of the game, the Kings, Queens, Rooks, and the Pawns, all go back in the same box.

Over the years, certainly since the Sixties, standards have been allowed to slip dramatically; morality, ethics, discipline, respect (both personal and for the law), and, especially, patriotism. All now appear to be looked upon as "old world" Christian values.

As Winston Churchill stated in Parliament, many, many years ago: "There is a forgotten, nay, almost forbidden, word in the English language. It is a word which means more to me than any other. That word is ENGLAND." Never was a truer word said. Even more-so in this day and age. There was a time when patriotism was taken into account when applying for a job, especially with such as the Royal Mail, Police, etc. Not any more. This has become patently obvious.

Falling standards apart, today's world appears to have gone money crazy; everything now governed by hard cash. People sue at the drop of a hat. Nothing to do with the self-respect , so called "closure", or the dignity they would have you believe. Purely for how much they can make out of it. They are of course egged on in this by the lawyers and the legal profession, for, win or lose, it is they who serve to make the most out of it. You only have to look at their TV advertising, or their magnificent offices, to see that.

And talking of advertising, this seems to border on who can con whom the best. These days you need to read more *between* the lines than the actual lines themselves.

What is it with the rich that they never seem to have enough? The more they have the more they seem prepared to flout the law so as to make themselves even richer. How much does one person actually need to be able to live comfortably?

I, and most of the normal people with whom I associate - many of which have served their country - live reasonably happy, comfortable, if fairly frugal lives. We have to. We are pensioners, need to live on what we have managed to put by. We have worked years for that to which we are now entitled. Yet we have immigrants, some entering the country illegally, never having never worked here, or contributed, yet becoming immediately entitled to something like three times my annual income. How can that be right?

As for the "high flyers", they are tied in to contracts which guarantee them hundreds of thousands, if not millions, in "*bonuses*", even if they prove to be a failure in the job they are already being handsomely paid to do. Once more, how can that be right?

Oh, of course! I forgot. There is no such thing as *failure* any more, it seems, and this begins in the school classroom. When we sat exams you achieved either a pass or a fail. A fail meant you had not reached the desired standard, that you needed to "pull your socks up". A pass was around sixty per cent, if I recall correctly. These days it seems not good practice to tell a child they have failed, so they don't. Even if it is a 'C', 'D', or possibly an 'E', it is still a pass. Though not one that any sensible employer would recognise. So why bother!

School results now make National News headlines on TV; children in tears because they failed to achieve the necessary grade to make University. You can almost guarantee that next day they will be banging on about how they were cheated; how the marking system needs to be changed, etc. Why can't they face up to reality. They failed. No one to blame but themselves. Don't try and pass failure off as being someone else's fault. Even though schools may have done away with winners and losers, life certainly has not! Better to learn that fact sooner rather than later.

University! I never even made it to Grammar School. Although I did possess the necessary qualifications to try, chose instead to step out into the big wide world to start earning a living. Possibly a mistake, for in later years I did on occasion feel myself to be educationally deficient in some areas. There again, maybe not, for I did alright by starting off with the necessary basics, picking up the rest as I went along. I can even answer some of the questions on University Challenge! Those which have stumped the contestants. Probably not the ones that concern themselves with Advanced Mathematics, Quantum Physics, Chemical Elements and the like, of course, but everyday subjects such as geography and current affairs. Let's face facts, a degree in some unrelated subject to the job you do, is unlikely to be a degree of much value. OK, three years at Uni, and you must learn something about life, agreed. That doesn't mean your degree is the be all and end all. You may know about a subject, but without experience it can mean nothing.

This then is the world in which we live today, far different from the one into which I was born, and spent my working life. Even the age of majority has been lowered from twenty-one to eighteen. Fair enough, really. If you're old enough to fight for your country, you're old enough to vote. Just don't assume a right to vote automatically makes you adult. Being adult relates more to the way one conducts oneself rather than to some magical time frame.

But many things were different back then. For instance,

there was very little mention of "stress" or "pressure"; words that today find regular usage. To me, those who use such terms are really stating they are unable to handle life as it is now lived. Which brings to mind the time Michael Parkinson once asked Australian Test cricketer - and ex WWII Spitfire pilot - Keith Miller, if he ever felt pressure when going out to face England at Lords. To which Miller famously responded, "Pressure is a Messerschmitt up your arse, cricket is not."

Even though it could be argued I was born on the wrong side of the tracks - though there really didn't seem to be a "best part of town". Better, maybe, but not snobbishly so - I was, as far as I'm concerned, brought up correctly. That is, I was never led to believe the world owed me a living. From the very start I knew that everything had to be earned and paid for. There were no free lunches, and the country owed me nothing. In fact, I felt it was I that owed the country. Old fashioned, right wing ideas one might think, but they served me well, and by my reckoning they are still correct.

You won't go far wrong in not relying on others to help you out of situations you were perfectly capable of getting yourself into without the help of anyone.

My schooling, plus twelve years in the Armed Forces gave me the best start in life I could have hoped for. Both experiences taught me to stand on my own two feet, become independent by fending for myself, relying on others as little as possible, and learn to cope. Grit and self reliance it is called, along with a certain amount of willpower. A piece of paper, even if in the form of a University Degree, does not necessarily confer these values upon anyone. Then there are the basic values taught me by my parents and schoolteachers, sadly, values rarely in evidence today: honesty; respect for the elderly; kindness, courtesy.

Following such guidelines served me well, for by so doing I got to see a lot of the world, a lot of which is definitely worth seeing. I also discovered that some parts are certainly not worth the trouble! Countries that are? Well, Australia and New Zealand come top of the pile for me, closely followed by Singapore, which may be a surprise to some. But I spent many happy days there, not just in my formative years, with the RAF, but also in later years. When working for ONI, our Eastern Hemisphere office was located there. I have visited the island nation many times since retirement, thanks to my membership of the RAF Seletar Association.

As a going concern, this Association went from strength to strength, more and more people feeling the urge to wander back down "Memory Lane" - a very important place during the later years of one's life. So, in the year 2000, after the originator of the idea fell by the wayside, I took on the organisation of a Singapore tour, allowing members to really recall days of yore. This proved so successful it was to become a fairly regular event, usually bi-annually. Thus it was we were also able to keep abreast of the continuing changes occurring on the camp at which we had all been based - or had formed an affinity with - at one time or another, and particularly, all over the island. Even venturing over the causeway, "up country" into Malaysia, as it had now become. We visited ancient and historic Malacca. First settled and developed by the Portugese, it eventually became Malaya's first city and port.

Two years later, during our next Singapore tour, we made another trip across the causeway and on to the beautiful waterfalls at Kota Tinggi; absolute paradise. I'd heard tell of these falls whilst serving in Singapore, people owning cars often visiting. Though back in the fifties it had apparently been something of a trek to reach them. On this occasion we were able to drive up close, for they were now a tourist attraction, with reasonable roads, and rentable chalets nearby.

It was during one of these tours that - a birthday present, this - I was finally able to turn another dream into reality - that of staying at the world-famous Raffles Hotel - to add to my burgeoning collection. Our room was even located in the so-called Writer's Wing, onetime temporary home to the likes of Maughan, Kipling, and Hemingway, and overlooking the Palm Court. Thus I was able to experience the impeccable service, and, with a little imagination, glimpse a little of what life may have been like during the early colonial era. A truly nostalgic experience.

The last of these tours actually took place in 2015 and was probably the best of the lot.

*

Favourite cities? London, of course. Crowded, noisy, nowhere as near as friendly and hospitable as it once was - there again, where is in this so-called "better world", where money means everything?

A trip down south, even if only for the day, and the

memories start to unwind.

Railway stations in England tend to harbour that same smell: an ingrained reek of soot, despite the switch to diesel and electrification.

Even today, open country lies barely five minutes out of York station. Twenty minutes and you are in Doncaster.

Looking out of train windows always conjures up memories. In days past I recall seeing mainly green fields. The landscape would also be dotted with the scars and eruptions of coal mines. Now one could barely distinguish what pithead gear that remained, from factory. Steel wheels take on a steady rhythm, singing as we traversed the counties, melody broken only as we crossed a junction.

Then, here it was; Kings Cross. Less than two hours after departing York. Although the splendour and history of this city more than make up for its defects, one really does need to remain alert whilst wandering. (And how is that possible to achieve with some electronic device plugged in to your ears, eyes focussed on a computer disguised as a mobile phone!)

I found myself strolling along Carnaby Street, recalled visiting both here and the nearby King's Road with Janette when, in the heydays of the sixties revolution, they were the in-places, peopled by the in-crowd. The hippies had been here, along with the weirdos. Occasionally, the area also offered up brief glimpses of those on their way to stardom, if you were lucky, kept your eyes open: Beatles, Stones, Hockney, Twiggy, Terrence Stamp, and from York, John Barry - long before James Bond and Hollywood. There had been long hair and short skirts, hot pants and platform shoes, clothes that were fashionably different, colourful and smart, especially when held in comparison to the scruffy, unshaven, denim-clad, trainer-shod youth that now wandered about. Denims which, had I owned them, would long since have been consigned to the bin! 'Designer' they term them, and by so doing con gullible people into paying a fortune for them; faded, ripped, so as to look worn out, but bearing labels such as Gucci, Yves St Laurent, and suchlike. The unshaven factor is termed "designer stubble"! In my book, an excuse for being too lazy to worry over personal hygiene.

I looked around; just another shopping area now. The Carnival is over. In fact it left town years ago. And, after nine or ten hours in the capital, so did I, retracing my tracks, literally, to be precise about it.

The return journey would be made during hours of darkness, most passengers' with their faces buried in newspapers and magazines. Staring out of the glass, the first thing I would see was my reflection looking back. There would be blurred lights flashing past, but I'd see little else. I didn't need to, I knew what was out there.

*

The history and splendour bit applies itself to Paris equally well. A city of contrasts, from it's twenty-first century style airport at Roissy, Charles de Gaulle (an airport in which I always did encounter difficulty finding my way around), and the architectural aberrance of the Pompidu Centre (why are all the failures named after presidents, I wonder) to buildings dating back through the centuries. Real buildings. Like looking back through the pages of history. Which in fact you are.

And should you really wish to leaf through the pages of history, no better place than a guided tour through the Houses of Parliament. I have drank on the terrace, dined in the House of Commons, walked historic Westminster Hall, with a very knowledgeable (MP) guide. None of this is difficult to achieve. All that is needed is to chat up your local MP. If he has anything about him he can arrange it, although it will take time, and it may help to be a paid-up party member, or know someone who is. Whatever, it is all very enlightening, and much better than a public group tour, very much more intimate. Via the same contact, I have even dined many times in the presence of Sir John Major, chatted to him about cricket and the like, but rarely politics.

*

New York, too, is another city steeped in history, even if not encompassing anything like the European time-frame. I recall the Christmas period spent there whilst awaiting the start of our Cunard Caribbean Christmas tour. The Christmas tree and ice skating in Rockefeller Plaza, seasonal Macys, Columbus Circle, Central Park trees bare of leaves, more ice skating at Bryant Park. No snow as yet, but it was very cold, down to minus nine degrees! But with so much to do, and see, you wrap up and forget about the cold.

I do have many abiding memories of America, having spent so much time there in the past. From New York to LA, Seattle to Galveston. It is a vast and diverse country, full of interest. Each State is almost like being in a different country, so different can they be. Take Louisiana for example, New Orleans in particular. Though not so much the splendour here, and the history is more that of the birth of Jazz. My abiding memories of New Orleans were formed when my presence was required at Company HQ, in Harahan, out by the airport, to pick up a visa so as to travel elsewhere in the world, or to look at some new system that was being introduced. Memories of sunny days; jazz whilst cruising the Mississippi on the paddle steamer, Natchez; the annual Jazz Festival and Heritage Fair at the racetrack; Breakfast at Brennans; evenings at the piano bar of Pat O'Briens; jazz at Preservation Hall, and the like. The courtyards and filigreed balconies around the old French Quarter; outstanding restaurants; and the old plantation houses dotted round about, not too far distant. But I would say my most outstanding memories of America as a whole have to be Yosemite National Park, and topping even that, the Grand Canyon. You see I am still a country boy at heart. Prefer the wide open spaces to the towering concrete jungles of the cities.

A job in the Black Sea reacquainted me with Turkey, not just the capital, Ankara, or the mosques, minarets, museums, and markets of Istanbul - some of these I had previously visited courtesy of the Royal Air Force during that Southern Capitals tour back in 1962 - but also up the Bosphorus and along to the non-tourist Turkey of the north coast, from Samsun to the Ukranian border. Heavily forested, dirt roads frequented by logging trucks, and small towns with no hotels worthy of the name. A very scenic area, but one in which spoken English is a rarity. It was a relief to later return to Istanbul: the Golden Horn, the Blue Mosque, and the Topkapi museum.

Other countries, too, have left me with similar memories. In New Zealand, spectacular Fjordland, and Milford Sound, would be tops. But the country has so much beauty that to single out any one is perhaps unfair. Waitangi, the site where the Maori chiefs signed the treaty ceding sovereignty to Queen Victoria; lovely, picturesque Russell, in the paradise called Bay of Islands. Velvety soft, rolling green pastures, with their heavy sprinkling of thick-wooled sheep; the thermal wonderland around Rotorua, where pools of satiny smooth, grey-brown mud bubbled, boiled, and spat tear shaped globules into the air, like leaping frogs, only for them to fall back with a soft plop, creating concentric rings on the surface. Deep pools of scalding hot water overflowed to trickle, steaming, over pastel coloured terraces. The famous Pohutu geyser, erupting, shooting boiling water, and clouds of steam sixty feet into the air. Further south again, Lake Taupo, where I once caught a rainbow trout that weighed in at five pounds, a smallish catch by New Zealand standards, I was informed! The splendidly showy Pohutukawa, known as the New Zealand Christmas tree - due to it being at its most decoratively flamboyant during the month of December, the New Zealand summer - its branches massed with clusters of brilliant scarlet flowers.

In Australia it would have to be the natural ruggedness of the Pilbara and the Northwest, possibly even the remote old mining township of Marble Bar, basically just a pub and a few houses now (where, in 1923/24, the temperature topped over 100 degrees F for 160 consecutive days) - definitely not on the tourist trail!

South Africa conjures up memories of the Stellenbosch area. Its vineyards covered the rolling countryside, fields of them, stretching away towards the horizon. Then there was the Dutch architecture of their Great Houses. All this, along of course with views from the top of Table Mountain. Just a few of the easily recalled memories from some of the around ninety six countries I have visited over the years. Many more are occasionally brought to mind at various times, for various reasons, or by various events.

Some places offer very little in the way of memories. Las Palmas, in the Canary Islands, for instance, where we occasionally took a break from the rigours of working in West Africa. A pleasant enough island, but the only vivid memory I seem to have of that place is of a Piano Bar which featured - Grand Piano apart - unique seating at the bar itself. These took the form of padded swings, suspended from the ceiling on velvet ropes. Here one could sit and drink in comfort, as indeed I often did, for a while. There was a problem though, as can be imagined; or perhaps it should have been regarded as a safety feature. These swings were quite difficult to master, even when sober, and as the night wore on, nigh on impossible. But they were popular, so a visit to the loo usually resulted in the loss of your seat, and if, like me, you didn't require to pay a visit for quite some time, it could well be that you would eventually fall out of the thing anyway. What kind of memory is that!

As for Africa itself, where I spent many of my years on

the West coast. Not a lot that was good to be remembered from there. Certainly not the cities or populated areas. The vast plains and the animals were something else again, but, working along the coast, we rarely found ourselves in such areas.

During 2005 I journeyed to back to Geneva, ex home of our European HQ, controlling Europe, Africa, and the Middle East. Here I was to meet up with contemporaries whose home country this was. Walter (Beinz) met me at the airport and drove me round the city in the morning. Strangely, it felt good to be back after so long, not too many noticeable changes apparent either in the preceding twenty-two years. The lakefront looked basically unchanged. Our old haunt, the Hotel Des Alpes, was still evident. We spent many a night there and, sadly, one of our contemporaries, and a friend of mine, had been murdered there. We'd had dinner together earlier. One of the not so welcome memories.

On next to Bern, by train which, as one would expect of Swiss Railways, ran like clockwork. My host, up in the hills outside the city, was Peter Studer, with whom I had worked many times in the past. That evening, after dinner, out came the slides, and there we were, back in Africa, or wherever. Old familiar faces kept cropping up, many of which Peter and I were eventually able to name, some coming easily, others requiring the help of a little liquid lubrication: Earl Benson; Dick Maddison, Adolf Zanner, Bob Molloy and the like. I occasionally still meet up with Bob, up in North Shields, along with that other Geordie, Geoff Metcalfe - who sponsors our Website. For it was around this time, after teaching myself the basics of creating such a site, I managed to put together a rudimentary version for ex ONI employees around the globe. Nothing fancy, but it does tell a bit of the story, serves to evoke the memories. It certainly put me back in touch with of a lot of old timers. Most of our ex-employees have visited, and seem to enjoy it; photos of themselves as they once were, and the places they had been. Ah! The memories. Take a look: **www.deltatango.net**

*

The old home town is the same; so sang Tom Jones. And so it seemed in reality. More traffic, yes, more people, too, and like that. But it was a hawk circling the towers and spires of York Minster that gave the game away. However citified my surroundings now, I was but a pensioner's (freedom pass) bus-ride away from the hills, valleys, and the heather of the

Yorkshire countryside: green Dales; rolling purple, heather-strewn Moors; and the Wolds. Most of this area is National Park land.

The winds that chased through the streets of Norton, where I grew up, were much the same as those which howled o'er hill and dale, coaxing piccolo tunes from the reed patches nestling below dry-stone walls. Here, I am paraphrasing a well-remembered passage written by one of my favourite Yorkshire authors - the long deceased Keith Waterhouse (Billy Liar). And to continue in similar vein: Every city and town-born Yorkshire tyke comes into this world with an inborn, umbilical attachment to the countryside; lush valleys below brooding moorland. Nestling in the folds of this great, green and purple, rumpled quilt, are fields demarcated by dry-stone walls, or hedgerows of brier and honeysuckle. Stone, pack-horse bridges span the becks, brooks, and the streams which eventually flow into the Derwent, Foss, Ouse, then out to sea via the Humber.

The place can look so forbidding and inhospitably barren from the top of one hill, so welcoming from the next. One lonely community might be little more than a pub and a row of stone cottages, the next, roses-round-the-door picturesque. This part of Yorkshire, the countryside of my youth, does remain basically the same today.

*

Leap forward to 2014, and an aging body. When even such a simple task as climbing stairs began to intrude upon my life, thoughts turned to selling off my comfortable and very convenient town house in the City of York, for a return to that nice little bungalow I'd had the foresight to buy in back 1969. Rented out for the better part of my ownership, it now became time for me to move back in. Away from the hustle and bustle of city life, for today it doesn't really matter whereabouts it is you abide, you are never far from anywhere in the world. This thought struck me only recently, as I was Skyping with my friends, Ron and Lynne. Although they live on the other side of the globe, in New Zealand - no longer in Glenfield, or Albany, both north of Auckland, they have now moved to Turanga, on the Bay of Plenty, well to the south, and on the east coast rather than the west - we see and talk to each other regularly. This particular time Ron and I were discussing some long forgotten job in Cabinda, Congo. Someone else had recently sent me some photos of the operation for use on our Website, but he'd supplied very few details. Knowing Ron had been the Party Chief on the project, I mentioned the fact. Next thing, he was showing me the same photos, filling in the details. But he also had other pictures, ones I had not been sent. When I mentioned this, he immediately scanned and e-mailed them. A couple of minutes later I *did* have them! It made me marvel at the technology I use all the time. Amazing, when you stop and think about it! So there are some good things going on in today's world after all. Brilliant, in fact. Although you must always bear in mind that if the technology is there for the good guys to use, it is also there for the bad guys! And use it they certainly do.

The Internet - which even I have to admit, can be a very useful tool indeed - is another of the things modern youth take for granted. One imagines they would find life even more difficult without it. They don't seem to realize it wasn't always so. Nor do they seem able to grasp the fact that, being as it is available to one and all, to put on whatever takes their fancy, all you read on the Internet is not necessarily fact. Nor do they seem to realize that if you bare your soul on Twitter, Facebook, and the like, you are leaving yourself wide open to abuse, or much worse! The Internet is not known as the World Wide Web without reason. You know, WWW, that group of letters which precede any Internet address!

*

I'd been there, done that, as they say. I'd also seen the book, worn the film, read the tee-shirt. What the hell, another gin and tonic, squire, if you please.

As Bob Dylan so famously predicted back in the Sixties, "Times, They Are A'changing." Well, that they had certainly done, in a big way, too. But at what cost? Well, life is probably now lived at too fast a pace; not enough hours left to enjoy. But at least, as the above goes to show, with the Internet to hand, one could live almost anywhere and not feel cut off. There again, I feel I've been privileged, and lucky enough, to have been born before the days of Internet. At a time when the world was a much simpler, more peaceful place. When jobs were plentiful enough for me to be able to pick and choose the direction in which I wished to go, the route I wished to follow, then just go ahead and do it.

We are all free to travel the world now, but once again, at what cost? I have been fortunate enough to travel at a time when it was relatively safe to do so, and off the beaten track. Not only that, for a majority of that time, someone else had been paying for me to do so!

Other things available to us in the "bad old days" had been the freedom to walk the footpaths in safety, play out in the countryside, ride a bike on the road, all without a care in the world. And, despite the lack of a Health & Safety Executive, survive it all! Easy-peasy.

So I appear not to have fared too badly after all. I've certainly lead an interesting and adventurous life, and it appears to be ending quite well too. I recall what my father told me all those years ago: "It's not the start you have in life that matters, David, it's how you conduct yourself from that point on. And the finish. That's how you'll be judged."

*   *

COUNTRIES VISITED

1/	FRANCE	27/	NEW ZEALAND
2/	MALTA	28/	CHRISTMAS IS (UK)
3/	LIBYA	29/	GREECE
4/	EGYPT	30/	TURKEY
5/	ITALY	31/	CANADA
	+ Sicily + Sardinia	32/	UNITED STATES
6/	IRAQ	33/	SUDAN
7/	PAKISTAN	34/	BAHRAIN
8/	INDIA	35/	OMAN
	+ Andaman Islands	36	GREENLAND
9/	THAILAND	37/	NORWAY
10/	SINGAPORE	38/	ZIMBABWE
11/	HONG KONG	39/	CAMEROUN
12/	MALAYA (MALAYSIA)	40/	GABON
13/	SOUTH VIETNAM	41/	NIGERIA
14/	TAIWAN	42/	BENIN REPUBLIC
15/	JAPAN	43/	LEBANON
16/	SRI LANKA	44/	IRAN
17/	SOUTH YEMEN	45/	KUWAIT
18/	GIBRALTAR	46/	GHANA
19/	KENYA	47/	SPAIN
20/	CYPRUS	48/	FERNADO PO
21/	GERMANY		Equatorial Guinee
22/	HOLLAND	49/	CANARY ISLANDS
23/	BELGIUM	50/	MOROCCO
24/	BORNEO	51/	MONACO
25/	MALDIVE ISLANDS	52/	SWITZERLAND
26/	AUSTRALIA	53/	SPANISH SAHARA

54/	ANGOLA		74/	DOMINICA
55/	CONGO REPUBLIC		75/	ST KITTS
56/	BAHAMAS		76/	COLOMBIA
57/	SENEGAL		77/	HONDURAS
58/	DENMARK		78/	PANAMA
59/	SWEDEN		79/	EQUADOR
60/	INDONESIA		80/	VENEZUELA
61/	IVORY COAST		81/	BRAZIL
62/	QATAR		82/	P.R.CHINA
63/	U.A.E.		83/	FIJI
	Dubai/Abu Dhabi		84/	TAHITI
64/	TRINIDAD		85/	CHILE+Easter Is
65/	BARBADOS		86/	SOUTH AFRICA
66/	GRENADA		87/	ISRAEL
67/	MARTINIQUE		88/	MOZAMBIQUE
68/	ANTIQUA		89/	KOREA
69/	PUERTO RICO		90/	TUNISIA
70/	U.S. VIRGIN ISLANDS		91/	ROMANIA
71/	BRITISH VIRGIN ISLES			
72/	ST MAARTEN			
73/	CURACAO			

AIRFIELDS VISITED

(Dates refer to year of firstvisit)

UNITED KINGDOM (RAF):

Driffield	1950
Leuchars	
Waddington	
Finningley	1951
Dishforth	
Rufforth	
Cosford	1953
Millom	
Lyneham	1955
Valley	
Aldergrove	
Abingdon	1962
Benson	
Colerne	
Scampton	
Waterbeach	1963
Wyton	
Wattisham	
Leeming	1983
Linton-on-Ouse	
Brize Norton	
Fairford	
Conningsby	

UNITED KINGDOM (Civil)

Doncaster	1952

Stanstead	1957
Heathrow	1962
Manchester(Ringway)	1964
Glasgow (Prestwick)	
Luton	1968
Southend	
Gatwick	1970
Leeds/Bradford	1972
East Midlands	1982
Sutton Bank	
Inverness	1987
Aberdeen	1990
Sumburgh	
Humberside	
Bagby	
Breighton	
Edinburgh	1991
Birmingham	1996
Liverpool	
Coventry (Baginton)	
Sherburn in Elmet	
Beverley	
Kirkbride	
Old Warden	
Duxford	2003
Newquay(St Mawgan)	2004
Sleap	2005
Lissett	2012

Catfoss	2012

LIBYA

Castel Benito (Idris)	1955
El Adem	1961

EGYPT

Fayid	1955
Cairo	
1975	
Luxor	1976
Hurghadha	

FRANCE

Istres	1955
Paris (Orly)	1962
Toulouse	
Paris (Le Bourget)	1964
Paris (Charles de Gaulle)	
Nice (Cote d'zur)	1968
Marseilles	1973
Bordeaux	
Dijon	
Carpiquet	2004

MALTA

Luqa	1955

ITALY

Brindisi	1957
Rome (Ciampino)	1962
Naples (Capodichino)	
Sardinia	1963
Rome (Fiumicino)	1965
Genoa	1968
Isola de Lampedusa	1972
Crotone	
Forli	1976
Bologna	
Milan (Linate)	1977
Trapani (Sicily)	
Palermo "	
Catania "	1979

IRAQ

Baghdad	1957

PAKISTAN

Karachi (Drigh Road)	1957

INDIA

Delhi (Saftar Jung)	1957
Calcutta (Dum Dum)	
Bombay (Santa Cruz)	1975
Port Blair(Andaman)	1982

THAILAND

Bangkok (Don Muang) 1957

Haadyai   1974

SINGAPORE

Payar Lebar   1957

RAF Seletar

RAF Changi   1958

Changi International   1974

HONG KONG

Kai Tak   1958

Chek Lap Kok   1998

MALAYA/MALAYSIA

Kuala Lumpur   1958

Butterworth

Malacca   1959

Ipoh

Kuantan   1960

Penang

Labuan   1962

Kota Kinabalu   1979

Kerith   1997

Tioman Island   2004

VIET NAM

Saigon   1960

TAIWAN

Taipei   1960

KENYA

Nairobi (Eastleigh)   1961

ADEN

Khormaksar   1961

CYPRUS

Nicosia   1962

Akrotiri

MALDIVE ISLANDS

Gan   1962

CHANNEL ISLANDS

Jersey   1961

NEW ZEALAND

Wellington (Rangotai) 1962

Auckland (Whenuapai)

Christchurch   1981

Te Anau

Manapouri

Mount Cook

Auckland (Manakau)

Rotarua

Palmerston North

Queenstown   1989

Dunedin

New Plymouth

Taupo

RNZAF Wigram

Tekapo

Glentanner

Ardmore

GREECE

Larissa	1962
Athens (Hellinikon)	
Kavala	1974
Thessaloniki	
Kos	1992

TURKEY

Ankara (Esonboga)	1962
Istanbul (Yesilkoy)	
Samsun	1972

SUDAN

Khartoum(Wadi Seidna)1963

LEBANON

| Beirut | 1965 |

GHANA

| Accra (Kotoka) | 1965 |

CANADA

Gander	1962
RCAF Rivers	
Goose Bay	
Toronto	1963
Ottowa (Uplands)	
Quebec City	
Calgary	1978
Edmonton	
Yellowknife	
Inuvik	
Tuktoyaktuk	
Halifax	1979
Saglek	
Fort Chimo	
Scheferville	
Montreal (Dorval)	
Vancouver	
Hamilton(Mount Hope)	2003
Brantford	2003

FIJI

| Nadi | 1980 |

JAPAN

| Osaka | 1960 |
| Tokyo (Haneda) | |

NIGERIA

Lagos (Ikeja)	1964
Port Harcourt	1965
Kano	1966
Warri	1967
Kalabar	1970
Enugu	

IRAN

Abadan	1965
Boushehr	
Karg Island	
Tehran (Mehrabad)	1972
Isfhan	
Shiraz	

CAMEROON

Douala	1964
Victoria	1967
Yaounde	1972

GABON

Libreville	1964
Port Gentil	
Gamba	1973
Mayumba	
N'Dindi	

CONGO

Brazzaville(Maya Maya)	1973

Pointe Noire

DAHOMEY(BENIN)

Cotonu	1972

TOGO

Lome	1973

FRENCH POLYNESIA

Tahiti (Faaa)	1981
Moorea	

UNITED STATES

Sheppard AFB	1962
Elmondorf AFB	1963
Hickam AFB	
Andrews AFB	
Selfridge AFB	2003
Norfolk	
Jacksonville	
New York (Idlewild)	1964
Baltimore	
Atlanta	1964
New Orleans Int	
New Orleans Lakefront	1978
Memphis	
St Louis	
Chicago (Midaway, O'Hare)	
Seattle	

Portland	
Astoria	
San Francisco	
Los Angeles	
Orlando	1976
Tampa	
Dallas/Fort Worth	
Miami	
Washington (Dulles)	1978
Denver	
Cleveland	1979
Anchorage	1989
Minniapolis/St Paul	2003
Omaha	2003
Detroit	2003
Saginaw	2003
Willow Run (Detroit)	2003
Wittman Field (Oshkosh)	
Green Bay	2003

SWITZERLAND

Geneva (Cointrin)	1972
Zurich	

GREENLAND

Thule	1963

RHODESIA (ZIMBABWE)

Salisbury (Thorn Hill)	1963

GIBRALTAR

Gibraltar	1968

NORWAY

Bardufoss	1963
Andoya	
Bergen	1983
Haugesund	1984
Stavanger	
Oslo (Fornebu)	
Kristiansund	1985
Trondheim	
Sondnessjoen	
Alesund	
Bronnoysund	
Molde	
Bodo	1988
Rost	

SPAIN

Valencia	1966
Seville	
Madrid (Barajas)	
Barcelona	1968
Alicante	1987
Ibiza (Balerics)	1990

SPANISH SAHARA

El Aaiun	1971

Villa Cisneros   1973

CANARY ISLANDS

Las Palmas   1968

Teneriffe

MOROCCO

Casablanca   1968

Tangier

FERNANDO PO (BIOKO)

Santa Isabel   1967

LINE ISLANDS

Kiritimati(Christmas Is)1963

SWEDEN

Stockholm (Arlanda)   1974

Stockholm (Bromma)

Ronnerby

Malmo

Kalmar

Visby   1976

DENMARK

Copenhagen (Kastrup)1974

Billund   1998

GERMANY

RAF Wildenwrath   1962

Stuttgart   1968

Cologne

Frankfurt-am-Main   1972

BELGIUM

Ostend   1968

Brussels (Melsbroek) 1974

Brussels (Charleroi) 2002

HOLLAND

Amsterdam (Schipol) 1974

Den Helder   1997

AUSTRIA

Vienna (Schwechat)   1993

ROMANIA

Constanta   1993

PORTUGAL

Lisbon (Portela)   1978

INDONESIA

Medan   1974

Seunagan

Jakarta (Kemayoran) 1991

Surabya (Juanda)

Bali (Denpasar)

CHINA

Canton (Baiyun) 1979

Zhanjiang

Hai Koi

Ningbo

CEYLON (SRI LANKA)

Colombo (Ratmalana) 1982

KOREA

Seoul 1989

Pusan

Cheju

SOUTH AFRICA

Durban(Louis Botha) 1983

Jo'burg (Jan Smuts)

Port Elizabeth

Nelspruit 1985

MAURITANIA

Nouakchott 1973

SENEGAL

Dakar (Yoff) 1973

IVORY COAST

Abijan 1972

ZIARE

Kinshasa 1983

MOZAMBIQUE

Beira 1985

Maputo

Xai Xai

ISRAEL

Tel Aviv (Lod) 1972

Tel Aviv (Ben Gurion) 1983

SAUDI ARABIA

Dahran 1976

QATAR

Doha 1976

DUBAI

Dubai 1977

ABU DHABI

Abu Dhabi 1983

MUSCAT & OMAN

Masirah Island 1963

BAHRAIN ISLAND

Bahrain 1963

KUWAIT

Kuwait City 1965

BORNEO

Labuan 1962

BERMUDA

Kindley Field 1973

BAHAMAS

Nassau 1973

PUERTO RICO

San Jaun 1977

US VIRGIN ISLANDS

St Thomas (HS Truman)1977

St Croix (Alexander Hamilton)

BRITISH VIRGIN ISLANDS

Tortola (East End) 1977

ST MAARTEN

Princess Juliana 1977

ANTIGUA

Coolidge 1977

GUADELOUPE

Le Raizet 1977

MARTINIQUE

Lamentin 1977

BARBADOS

Grantley Adams 1977

GRENADA

Pearls 1977

TRINIDAD

Piarco 1977

BELIZE

Belize City 1978

HONDURAS

San Pedro Sula	1978
Tegucigalpa (Toncontin)	
La Ceiba	

PANAMA

Panama(Tocumen)	1978

AUSTRALIA

RAAF Richmond (Syd)	1962
RAAF Fairbain (Can)	
Melbourne	
RAAF Edinburgh Field (Ad)	
Woomera	
RAAF Pearce (Perth)	
Darwin	1963
Sydney (K Smith)	1980
Launceston	
Perth	
Devonport	
Flinders Island	
Bairnsdale	
Port Hedland	
Broome	
Adelaide	
Derby	
Kununurra	1981
Garden Point	

Elcho Island	
Geralton	
Carnavon	
Learmonth	
Karratha	
Warrnambool	1982
Narrogin	
Brisbane	1989
Alice Springs	1997
Mackay	
Hamilton Island	
Cairns	
Avalon	2005
Hobart	2006

ANGOLA

Luanda (Belas)	1972

EQUADOR

Quito	1978

COLOMBIA

Bogata (Eldorado)	1977
Cartegena	
Isla de San Andres	1978
Barranquilla	
Buenaventura	
Cali	1979

BRAZIL

Rio (Galeao)   1979

Brasilla

Sao Paulo (Congonhas)

Rio (Santos Dumont)   1981

Macae

CHILE

Santiago (Pudahuel)   1982

Easter Island

PERU

Lima (Jorge Chavez)   1979

VENEZUELA

Caracas (Simon Bolivar) 1978

AIRCRAFT TYPES IN WHICH FLOWN

AERO/ROCKWELL:

Commander
Shrike Commander
Commander 114

AIRBUS:
A300B
A310
A319
A320
A330
A340
A380

AIRSPEED:
Oxford
Ambassador

AEROSPATIALE:
Alouette II
Alouette III
Puma
350 Squirrel
ATR 42
Dauphin

ANTONOV:
AN24

ARMSTRONG WHITWORTH:
Argosy

AUSTER:
AOP9

AVRO:
Anson
Lancaster
748

BEECH:
18
Baron 55
Twin Bonanza

BELL:
47D
Ranger
206 Jetranger
Longranger
212
407

BENEZ-MRAZ:
Sokol M1C

BLACKBURN:
Beverley

BOEING:
Stearman
B17 Fortress
707
717
720
727

737
747
747SP
757
767
777

BRISTOL:
170 Freighter
171 Sycamore
Britannia

BRITTEN NORMAN:
Islander
Trislander

BRITISH AIRCRAFT CORP:
1-11
Concorde

BRITISH AEROSPACE:
146
748 Super
ATP

CESSNA:
152 II
172 Skyhawk 2
180
182 Skywagon
185
206
310J
337
402

411

CONVAIR:
990
240 Metropolitan

CURTIS:
P40N Kittyhawk

de HAVILLAND:
86 Tiger Moth
87B Hornet Moth
89 Dragon Rapide

90 Dragonfly
106 Comet 2
Comet 4C
114 Heron

de HAVILLAND CANADA:
Chipmunk
Twin Otter
Dash 7
Dash 8

DORNIER:
228

DOUGLAS:
DC3 Dakota
DC4
DC6B
DC7C
DC8
DC9-41
DC9-81

DC10

McDONELL DOUGLAS:

MD80
MD82
MD87
MD90

EMBRAER:

110 Bandeirante

FOCKE-WULF

FW44 Stieglitz

FOKKER:

F27 Friendship
F28 Fellowship
F50
F70
F100

FORD:

Tri-motor

GAF:

Nomad N22B

GARDAN:

Horizon GY80

GLIDER/POWER GLIDER:

Sedburgh
BlanikFalke SF25C
Falke S261F
Ask 21

GRUMMAN:

Trader
Goose G21a
Mallard G73
Gulfstream 1

HANDLEY PAGE:

Hastings
Hermes
Herald

HAWKER SIDDLEY:

Trident 1
Trident 2
Trident 3

HILLER:

UH-12E
UH-12E 4

HUGHES:

500C
500D

ILLYUSHIN:

IL14M

LOCKHEED:

Electra
C121 Constellation
1011 Tristar
Hercules Mk3

LUSCOMBE:

Silvaire 8E

MAX HOLSTE:

Broussard

MICRO LIGHTS:
Gemini
Thruster
Coyote II
Mainair
Pioneer 300

MILES:
Magister

NAMC:
YS11a

NORTH AMERICAN:
T6 Havard
P51 Mustang

PARTENAVIA:
P68B Victor

PERCIVAL:
Prentice

PIPER:
Aztec
Navajo
Chieftain
Cherokee D
Cherokee 6
Warrior II

PITTS:
S2A

ROBIN:
Regent

ROBINSON:
R44

SAAB:
340

SCOTTISH AVIATION:
Pioneer
Twin Pioneer
Jetstream 31
Jetstream 41

SHORT BROS:
Sunderland V
Skyvan
Skyliner
SD3-30
SD3-60

SOCATA:
Tampico
Tobago

SUD EST:
Caravelle

VARGA:
T2150A

VICKERS:
Wellington

Valetta
Vanguard
Viscount
VC10

WACO:
Super Waco

WESTLAND/SIKORSKY:
Whirlwind Mk2
Whirlwind Mk10
Widgeon
Wessex
S61N
S68T
S76 Spirit

YAKOVLEV:
Yak 52